Department of Trade and Industry

Reference Library
NOT FOR LOAN

Digest of United Kingdom Energy Statistics 2001

Production editor: Mari Scullion

A National Statistics publication

London: The Stationery Office

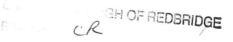

Digest of United Kingdom Energy Statistics

Enquiries about statistics in this publication should be made to the contact named at the end of the relevant chapter. Brief extracts from this publication may be reproduced provided the source is fully acknowledged. General enquiries about the publication, and proposals for reproduction of larger extracts, should be addressed to the Production Editor, Mari Scullion, at the address given in paragraph XXVI of the Introduction.

The Department of Trade and Industry reserves the right to revise or discontinue the text or any table contained in this Digest without prior notice.

About The Stationery Office's Standing Order Service

The Standing Order Service, open to all Stationery Office account holders, allows customers to automatically receive the publications they require in a specified subject area, thereby saving them the time, trouble and expense of placing individual orders, also without handling charges normally incurred when placing ad-hoc orders.

Customers may choose from over 4,000 classifications arranged in 250 sub groups under 30 major subject areas. These classifications enable customers to choose from a wide variety of subjects, those publications which are of special interest to them. This is a particularly valuable service for the specialist library or research body. All publications will be dispatched immediately after publication date. A Standing Orders Handbook describing the service in detail and a complete list of classifications may be obtained on request. Write to The Stationery Office, Standing Order Department, PO Box 29, St Crispins, Duke Street, Norwich, NR3 1GN, quoting reference 12.01.013; Alternatively telephone 0870 600 5522 and select the Standing Order Department (option 2); fax us on 0870 600 5533; or finally e-mail us at book.standing.orders@theso.co.uk.

National Statistics

National Statistics are produced to high professional standards set out in the National Statistics Code of Practice. They undergo regular quality assurance reviews to ensure that they meet customer needs. They are produced free from any political interference.

You can find a range of National Statistics on the Internet – www.statistics.gov.uk

---

Contents

		Page
Introduction		5
Contact list		8
Comparison of table numbers		9
Chapter 1	Energy	11
Chapter 2	Solid fuels and derived gases	51
Chapter 3	Petroleum	73
Chapter 4	Gas	113
Chapter 5	Electricity	129
Chapter 6	Combined heat and power	161
Chapter 7	Renewable sources of energy	181
Chapter 8	Foreign trade	201
Annex A	Energy and commodity balances, calorific values and conversion factors	219
Annex B	Energy and the environment	229
Annex C	UK oil and gas resources	231
Annex D	Glossary	249
Annex E	Major events in the energy industry	257
Annex F	Further sources	271

A list of tables

Table no.   **Page**

Chapter 1 Energy

Table no.		Page
1.1	Aggregate energy balance 2000	25
1.2	Aggregate energy balance 1999	26
1.3	Aggregate energy balance 1998	27
1.4	Value balance of traded energy in 2000	28
1.5	Value balance of traded energy in 1999	29
1.6	Value balance of traded energy in 1998	30
1.7	Sales of electricity and gas by sector	31
1.8	Final energy consumption by main industrial groups	32
1.9	Fuels consumed for electricity generation (autogeneration) by main industrial groups	34
1.10	Inland consumption of primary fuels and equivalents for energy use, 1970 to 2000	36
1.11	Availability and consumption of primary fuels and equivalents (energy supplied basis) 1970 to 2000	38
1.12	Comparison of net imports of fuel with total consumption of primary fuels and equivalents, 1970 to 2000	40
1.13	Primary energy consumption, gross domestic product and energy ratio, 1970 to 2000	41
1.14	Energy consumption by final user (energy supplied basis), 1970 to 2000	42
1.15	Expenditure on energy by final user, 1970 to 2000	47
1.16	Mean air temperatures	49
1.17	Mean air temperatures, 1970 to 2000	50

Chapter 2 Solid fuels and derived gases

Table no.		Page
2.1	Coal: Commodity balances 2000	59
2.2	Coal: Commodity balances 1999	60
2.3	Coal: Commodity balances 1998	61
2.4	Manufactured fuels: Commodity balances 2000	62
2.5	Manufactured fuels: Commodity balances 1999	63
2.6	Manufactured fuels: Commodity balances 1998	64
2.7	Supply and consumption of coal	65
2.8	Supply and consumption of coke oven coke, coke breeze and other manufactured solid fuels	66
2.9	Supply and consumption of coke oven gas, blast furnace gas, benzole and tars	67
2.10	Coal production and stocks, 1970 to 2000	68
2.11	Inland consumption of solid fuels, 1970 to 2000	69
2.12	Major deep mines in production, May 2001	70
2.13	Opencast sites in production, May 2001	71

Chapter 3 Petroleum

Table no.		Page
3.1	Primary oil: Commodity balances 2000	95
3.2	Primary oil: Commodity balances 1999	96
3.3	Primary oil: Commodity balances 1998	97
3.4	Petroleum products: Commodity balances 2000	98
3.5	Petroleum products: Commodity balances 1999	100
3.6	Petroleum products: Commodity balances 1998	102
3.7	Supply and disposal of petroleum	104
3.8	Additional information on inland deliveries of selected products	105
3.9	Inland deliveries by country	106
3.10	Stocks of crude oil and petroleum products at end of year	107
3.11	Crude oil and petroleum products: production, imports and exports, 1970 to 2000	108
3.12	Inland deliveries of petroleum, 1970 to 2000	110

Chapter 4 Gas

4.1	Commodity balances 1998 to 2000	123
4.2	Supply and consumption of natural gas and colliery methane	124
4.3	UK continental shelf and onshore natural gas production and supply	125
4.4	Natural gas and colliery methane production and consumption 1970 to 2000	126

Chapter 5 Electricity

5.1	Commodity balances 1998 to 2000	142
5.2	Electricity supply and consumption	144
5.3	Commodity balances, public distribution system and other generators, 1998 to 2000	145
5.4	Fuel used in generation	146
5.5	Electricity supply, electricity supplied (net), electricity available and electricity consumption	147
5.6	Electricity fuel use, generation and supply	148
5.7	Plant capacity	150
5.8	Capacity of other generators	151
5.9	Plant loads, demand and efficiency	151
5.10	Fuel input for electricity generation, 1970 to 2000	152
5.11	Electricity supply, availability and consumption, 1970 to 2000	153
5.12	Electricity generated and supplied, 1970 to 2000	154
5.13	Power stations in the United Kingdom, May 2001	156

Chapter 6 Combined heat and power

6.1	CHP installations by capacity and size range	170
6.2	Fuel used to generate electricity and heat in CHP plants	170
6.3	Fuel used by types of CHP installation	171
6.4	CHP - electricity generated by fuel and type of installation	172
6.5	CHP - electrical capacity by fuel and type of installation	173
6.6	CHP - heat generated by fuel and type of installation	174
6.7	CHP - heat capacity by fuel and type of installation	175
6.8	CHP capacity, output and total fuel use by sector	176
6.9	CHP - use of fuels by sector	179

Chapter 7 Renewable sources of energy

7.1	Commodity balances 2000	190
7.2	Commodity balances 1999	192
7.3	Commodity balances 1998	194
7.4	Capacity of, and electricity generated from, renewable sources	196
7.5	Renewable orders and operational capacity	197
7.6	Renewable sources used to generate electricity and heat	199

Chapter 8 Foreign trade

8.1	Imports and exports of fuels	207
8.2	Value of imports and exports of fuels, 1970 to 2000	208
8.3	Imports and exports of crude oil and petroleum products	210
8.4	Imports and exports of crude oil by country	212
8.5	Imports and exports of solid fuels	214

Annex A Energy, commodity balances, calorific values and conversion factors

	Standard conversion factors	225
A.1	Estimated average gross calorific values of fuels	226
A.2	Estimated average gross calorific values of fuels 1970 to 2000	227

3

Annex C United Kingdom oil and gas resources

C.I	UK reserves of oil and gas	**232**
C.II	Top ten UK crude oil producing fields in 2000	**235**
C.III	Gas flaring at oil fields and terminals, 1996 to 2000	**237**
C.1	Estimated oil and gas reserves on United Kingdom Continental Shelf	**239**
C.2	Offshore oil and gas fields and associated facilities	**240**
C.3	Production of oil and gas	**240**
C.4	Transportation of crude oil production	**241**
C.5	Disposals of crude oil	**241**
C.6	Production of crude oil by field	**242**
C.7	Production of methane by field	**245**
C.8	Sales and expenditure by operators and other production licensees	**248**

Introduction

I   This issue of the Digest of United Kingdom Energy Statistics continues a series which commenced with the Ministry of Fuel and Power Statistical Digest for the years 1948 and 1949, published in 1950. The Ministry of Fuel and Power Statistical Digest was previously published as a Command Paper, the first being that for the years 1938 to 1943, published in July 1944 (Cmd. 6538).

II   The current issue updates the figures given in the Department of Trade and Industry's *Digest of United Kingdom Energy Statistics 2000*, published in July 2000.

III   This issue consists of eight chapters, the first of which deals with overall energy. The other chapters cover the specific fuels, combined heat and power, renewable sources of energy and trade. The period covered in detail in the fuel chapters is 1998 to 2000, although most chapters also contain some detailed information covering 1996 to 2000 as well as data on long term trends. As in previous years, there is an annex dealing with energy and the impact of its production and consumption on the environment. However, in order to avoid duplication of data that are published elsewhere, the annex in this edition contains a summary of the main issues with references to other data sources. Other annexes cover major events in the energy industries, calorific values and conversion factors, a glossary of terms and further sources of information.

IV   The prices chapter which has appeared in previous editions of this publication has been removed. The annual information on prices is now included in the publication *Quarterly Energy Prices*. This is available together with *Energy Trends* on subscription from the DTI. Further information on these publications can be found in Annex F.

V   The series available on a long term trend basis go back to 1970 in most cases, although for some series data are not readily available for all the years. However, sufficient data have been included to provide a comprehensive view of developments in energy supply and consumption over the last thirty-one years. Long term trends data back to 1960 can be found for most tables in the 2000 edition of this publication.

VI   Where necessary, data have been converted or adjusted to provide consistent series, however, in some cases changes in methods of data collection have affected the continuity of the series. The presence of remaining discontinuities is indicated in the chapter text or in footnotes to the tables.

VII   The first chapter covers general energy statistics and includes tables showing energy consumption by final users and an analysis of energy consumption by main industrial groups. Fuel production and consumption statistics are derived mainly from the records of fuel producers and suppliers. In general the statistics have the same coverage as those in other chapters and where this is so the explanatory notes in these chapters are applicable. Statistics in the Foreign Trade chapter are derived largely from HM Customs and Excise data, published in the *Overseas Trade Statistics of the United Kingdom*. However, some of the data shown in this Digest may contain unpublished revisions and estimates of trade from additional sources.

VIII   Chapters 6 and 7 summarise the results of surveys conducted by ETSU on behalf of the Department of Trade and Industry and the Statistical Office of the European Communities. These estimate the contribution made by combined heat and power (CHP) and renewable energy sources to the United Kingdom's energy during the period from 1996 to 2000.

IX   In Chapters 2, 3, 4, 5 and 7 production and consumption of individual fuels are presented using *commodity balances*. A commodity balance shows the flows of an individual fuel through from production to final consumption, showing its use in transformation and energy industry own use. Commodity balances are presented for years 1998 to 2000. Further details of commodity balances and their use are given in the Annex A, paragraphs A.7 to A.41.

X   The individual commodity balances are combined in an *energy balance*. The energy balance differs from a commodity balance in that it shows the interactions between different fuels in addition to illustrating their consumption. The energy balance thus gives a fuller picture of the production, transformation and use of energy showing all the flows. Chapter 1, Energy, presents energy balances for years 1998 to 2000. Expenditure on energy is also presented in energy balance format in Chapter 1.

Further details of the energy balance and its use are given in Annex A, paragraphs A.42 to A.57.

Definitions

XI   The text at the beginning of each chapter explains the main features of the tables. Technical notes and definitions, given at the end of this text, provide detailed explanations of the figures in the tables and how they are derived. Explanations of the logic behind an energy balance and for commodity balances are given in Annex A.

XII   Most chapters contain some information on 'oil' or 'petroleum'; these terms are used in a general sense and vary according to usage in the field examined. In their widest sense they are used to include all mineral oil and related hydrocarbons (except methane) and any products derived therefrom.

XIII   An explanation of the terms used to describe electricity generating companies is given in Chapter 5, paragraphs 5.58 to 5.59.

XIV   Data in this issue have been prepared on the basis of the Standard Industrial Classification (SIC) 1992 as far as is practicable. For further details of classification of consumers see Chapter 1, paragraphs 1.77 to 1.81.

XV   Where appropriate, further explanations and qualifications are given in footnotes to the tables.

Geographical coverage

XVI   The geographical coverage of the statistics is indicated on each table. Almost all the tables relate to the United Kingdom; the main exceptions being the tables on temperatures (Tables 1.16 and 1.17) and the tables in Annex C on oil and gas resources (Tables C.1 to C.6) which give data for the United Kingdom Continental Shelf. Exports to the Channel Islands and the Isle of Man from the United Kingdom are not classed as exports, and supplies of solid fuel and petroleum to these islands are therefore included as part of United Kingdom inland consumption or deliveries.

Periods

XVII   Data in this Digest are for calendar years or periods of 52 weeks, depending on the reporting procedures within the fuel industry concerned. Actual periods covered are given in the notes to the individual fuel sections.

Revisions

XVIII   The tables contain revisions to some of the previously published figures, and where practicable the revised data have been indicated by an 'r'.

Energy data on the Internet

XIX   The digest is also available on the internet at www.dti.gov.uk/epa/dukes.htm. Information on DTI energy publications can also be found on the DTI Internet site at: www.dti.gov.uk/energy/index.htm. Further details of energy publications on the Internet are given in Annex F.

Other sources

XX   The Department also publishes 'UK Energy in Brief', a booklet summarising the main statistics presented in this Digest.

XXI   Short term statistics are published:

- monthly, by the DTI on the internet at www.dti.gov.uk/energy/energystats/energystats.htm

- quarterly, by the DTI in paper and on the internet in Energy Trends, and Quarterly Energy Prices.

- quarterly, by the DTI in Statistical Press Release which provides a summary of information published in Energy Trends and Quarterly Energy Prices publications.

- monthly, by the Office for National Statistics in the Monthly Digest of Statistics (The Stationery Office).

To subscribe to Energy Trends and Quarterly Energy Prices, or for free copies of the 'UK Energy in Brief' booklet please contact Gillian Purkis or Clive Sarjantson at the address given at paragraph XXVI.

Table numbering

XXII   The numbering and order of some tables in this issue differ from that in earlier issues. Page 9 contains a list showing the tables in the order in which they appear in this issue, and their corresponding numbers and pages in previous issues.

Symbols used

XXIII The following symbols are used in this Digest:-

..	not available
-	nil or negligible (less than half the final digit shown)
r	Revised since the previous edition

Rounding convention

XXIV Individual entries in the tables are rounded independently and this can result in totals which are different from the sum of their constituent items.

Acknowledgements

XXV Acknowledgement is made to the main coal producing companies, the electricity companies, the oil companies, the gas pipeline operators, the gas suppliers, Transco, the Institute of Petroleum, the Coal Authority, the United Kingdom Iron and Steel Statistics Bureau, the National Environmental Technology Centre, ETSU, the Department of the Environment, Transport and the Regions, the HM Customs & Excise, the Office for National Statistics, and other contributors to the enquiries used in producing this publication.

Contacts

XXVI For general enquiries on energy statistics contact:
Gillian Purkis on 020-7215 2697
(E-mail: Gillian.Purkis@dti.gsi.gov.uk),
or Clive Sarjantson on 020-7215 2698,
(E-mail: Clive.Sarjantson@dti.gsi.gov.uk) or:-

Gillian Purkis/Clive Sarjantson
Department of Trade and Industry
Bay 1108
1 Victoria Street
London SW1H 0ET
Fax: 020-7215 2723

Enquirers with hearing difficulties can contact the Department on the DTI Textphone: 020-7215 6740.

XXVII For enquiries concerning particular data series or chapters contact those named on page 8 or at the end of the relevant chapter.

Mari Scullion, Editor
July 2001

Contact list

The following people in the Department of Trade and Industry may be contacted for further information about the topics listed:

Chapter	Contact	Telephone	E-mail
		020-7215	
Energy	Rachael Winther	6178	Rachael.Winther@dti.gsi.gov.uk
	Chenab Mangat	2710	Chenab.Mangat@dti.gsi.gov.uk
Solid fuels and derived gases	Mike Janes	5186	Mike.Janes@dti.gsi.gov.uk
	James Achur	2717	James.Achur@dti.gsi.gov.uk
Oil and gas resources	Kevin Williamson	5184	Kevin.Williamson@dti.gsi.gov.uk
	Clive Evans	5189	Clive.Evans@dti.gsi.gov.uk
North Sea profits, operating costs and investments	Suhail Siddiqui	5262	Suhail.Siddiqui@dti.gsi.gov.uk
	Philip Beckett	5260	Philip.Beckett@dti.gsi.gov.uk
Petroleum (downstream)	Kevin Williamson	5184	Kevin.Williamson@dti.gsi.gov.uk
	Clive Evans	5189	Clive.Evans@dti.gsi.gov.uk
Gas supply (downstream)	Mike Janes	5186	Mike.Janes@dti.gsi.gov.uk
	John Castle	2718	John.Castle@dti.gsi.gov.uk
Electricity	Mike Janes	5186	Mike.Janes@dti.gsi.gov.uk
	Joe Ewins	5190	Joe.Ewins@dti.gsi.gov.uk
Combined heat and power	Mike Janes	5186	Mike.Janes@dti.gsi.gov.uk
Prices and values:	Lesley Petrie	2720	Lesley.Petrie@dti.gsi.gov.uk
Domestic prices	Sharon Young	6531	Sharon.Young@dti.gsi.gov.uk
Industrial, international and oil prices	Sara Atkins	6532	Sara.Atkins@dti.gsi.gov.uk
Foreign trade	Rachael Winther	6178	Rachael.Winther@dti.gsi.gov.uk
Renewable sources of energy	Mike Janes	5186	Mike.Janes@dti.gsi.gov.uk
Energy and the environment	Rachael Winther	6178	Rachael.Winther@dti.gsi.gov.uk
	Kevin Williamson	5184	Kevin.Williamson@dti.gsi.gov.uk
Calorific values and conversion factors	Rachael Winther	6178	Rachael.Winther@dti.gsi.gov.uk
	Kevin Williamson	5184	Kevin.Williamson@dti.gsi.gov.uk
General enquiries (energy helpdesk)	Gillian Purkis	2697	Gillian.Purkis@dti.gsi.gov.uk
	Clive Sarjantson	2698	Clive.Sarjantson@dti.gsi.gov.uk

All the above can be contacted by fax on 020-7215 2723

Tables as they appear in this issue and their corresponding numbers in the previous four issues

Section	1997	1998	1999	2000	2001	Section	1997	1998	1999	2000	2001
ENERGY	1	1	-	-		**ELECTRICITY**	-	-	5.1	5.1	5.1
	3	1.3	1.1	1.1	1.1		58	6.1	5.2	5.4	5.4
	2	1.2	1.2	1.2	1.2		-	-	5.3	5.2	5.2
	-	-	1.3	1.3	1.3		59	6.2	5.4	5.5	5.6
	4	1.4	1.4	1.4	1.4		60	6.3	-	5.3	5.3
	-	-	1.5	1.5	1.5		-	-	-	5.6	5.5
	-	-	1.6	1.6	1.6	(Note: Table A9.1 in	61	6.4	A9.1	A9.1	A9.1
	5	1.5	-	-	-	ENERGY)	62	6.5	5.5	5.7	5.7
	6	1.6	-	-	-		63	6.6	5.6	5.8	5.8
	7	1.7	-	-	-		64	6.7	5.7	5.9	5.9
	8	1.8	-	-	-		65	6.8	5.8	5.10	5.10
	9	1.9	1.7	1.7	1.8		67	6.10	5.9	5.11	5.11
	10	1.10	1.8	1.8	1.9		66	6.9	5.10	5.12	5.12
	13	1.13	1.9	1.9	1.10		-	-	-	-	5.13
	14	1.14	1.10	1.10	1.11						
	15	1.15	1.11	1.11	1.12	**COMBINED**	-	-	-	6.1	6.1
	16	1.16	1.12	1.12	1.13	**HEAT AND**	68	7.1	6.1	6.2	6.2
	17	1.17	1.13	1.13	1.14	**POWER**	69	7.2	6.2	6.3	6.3
	-	-	1.14	1.14	1.15		70	7.3	6.3	6.4	6.4
	11	1.11	1.15	1.15	1.16		71	7.4	6.4	6.5	6.5
	12	1.12	1.16	1.16	1.17		72	7.5	6.5	6.6	6.6
(Note: previously in	54/61	5.4/6.4	A9.1	A9.1	1.7		73	7.6	6.6	6.7	6.7
PRICES and VALUES)							74	7.7	6.7	6.8	6.8
							75	7.8	6.8	6.9	6.9
SOLID FUELS &	-	-	2.1	2.1	2.1						
DERIVED GASES	-	-	2.2	2.2	2.2		7.2	7B	6A	6A	6A
	-	-	2.3	2.3	2.3		-	-	6B	6B	6B
	-	-	2.4	2.4	2.4		-	-	6C	-	-
	-	-	2.5	2.5	2.5		7.1	7A	6D	6C	6C
	-	-	2.6	2.6	2.6		-	-	6E	6D	6E
	18	2.1	2.7	2.7	2.7		-	-	6F	6E	6D
	19/21	2.2-4	2.8	2.8	2.8		-	-	-	-	6F
	22	2.5	-	-	-		-	-	-	-	6G
	24	2.7	-	-	-		-	-	-	-	6H
	-	-	2.9	2.9	2.9	**RENEWABLE**	-	-	7.1	7.1	7.1
	25	2.8	2.10	2.10	2.10	**SOURCES**	-	-	7.2	7.2	7.2
	26	2.9	2.11	2.11	2.11		-	-	7.3	7.3	7.3
	-	-	-	-	2.12		96	10.2	7.4	7.4	7.4
	-	-	-	-	2.13		10.1	10A	7.5	7.5	7.5
PETROLEUM	-	-	3.1	3.1	3.1		95	10.1	7.6	7.6	7.6
	-	-	3.2	3.2	3.2						
	-	-	3.3	3.3	3.3						
	-	-	3.4	3.4	3.4						
	-	-	3.5	3.5	3.5						
	-	-	3.6	3.6	3.6	**FOREIGN**	90	9.1	8.1	8.1	8.1
	37	4.4	3.7	3.7	3.7	**TRADE**	94	9.2	8.2	8.2	8.2
	38	4.2	-	-	-		91	9.3	8.3	8.3	8.3
	39	4.3	-	-	-		92	9.4	8.4	8.4	8.4
	40	4.1	3.8	-	-		23/93	2.6/9.5	8.5	8.5	8.5
	41	4.5	-	-	-						
	42	4.6	-	-	-	**ANNEX C:**	27	3.1	A3.1	C.1	C.1
	43	4.7	-	-	-	**UK OIL AND GAS**	28	3.2	A3.2	C.2	C.2
	44	4.8	3.9	3.8	3.8	**RESOURCES**	29	3.3	A3.3	C.3	C.3
	45	4.9	-	-	-		32	3.6	A3.4	C.4	C.4
	-	-	3.10	-	-		33	3.7	A3.5	C.5	C.5
	46	4.10	3.11	-	-		31	3.5	A3.6	C.6	C.6
	47	4.11	3.12	3.9	3.9		30	3.4	A3.7	C.7	C.7
	48	4.12	3.13	3.10	3.10		-	-	A3.8	C.8	-
	49	4.13	3.14	3.11	3.11		36	3.10	A3.9	C.9	C.8
	50	4.14	3.15	3.12	3.12		34	3.8	-	-	-
NATURAL GAS	-	-	4.1	4.1	4.1		35	3.9	-	-	-
	-	-	4.2	4.2	4.2	**CALORIFIC**	B.1	B.1	B.1	A.1	A.1
	51	5.1	-	-	-	**VALUES**	-	-	-	A.2	A.2
	52	5.2	-	-	-						
	53	5.3	4.3	4.3	4.3						
	57	5.7	4.4	4.4	4.4						
(Note: Table A9.1 in	54	5.4	A9.1	A9.1	A9.1						
ENERGY)	55	5.5	-	-	-						
	56	5.6	-	-	-						

Chapter 1
Energy

Introduction

1.1 This chapter presents figures on overall energy production and consumption. Figures showing the flow of energy from production, transformation and energy industry use through to final consumption are presented in the format of an energy balance based on the individual commodity balances presented in Chapters 2 to 5 and 7.

1.2 The chapter begins with aggregate energy balances covering the last three years (Tables 1.1, 1.2 and 1.3) starting with the latest year, 2000. Energy value balances then follow this for the same years (Tables 1.4, 1.5 and 1.6) and Table 1.7 shows sales of electricity and gas by sector. Table 1.8 covers final energy consumption by the main industrial sectors over the last five years followed by Table 1.9 which shows the fuels used for electricity generation by these industrial sectors. Tables 1.10 to 1.15 present long-term trends for energy production, consumption and expenditure on energy as well as analyses such as the relationship between energy consumption and the economy of the UK. The final tables (Tables 1.16 and 1.17) present figures for average temperatures. The explanation of the principles behind the energy balance and commodity balance presentations are in Annex A.

The energy industries

1.3 The energy industries in the UK play a central role in the economy by producing, transforming and supplying energy in its various forms to all sectors. They are also major contributors to the UK's Balance of Payments through the exports of crude oil and oil products. The box below summarises the energy industries' contribution to the economy:

- 4 per cent of GDP

- 8 per cent of total investment

- 28 per cent of industrial investment

- Value added per head 6 times the industrial average

- 165 thousand people directly employed (4 per cent of industrial employment)

- Many others indirectly employed (e.g. an estimated 360,000 in support of UK Continental Shelf activities)

- Trade surplus in fuels of £6.7 billion.

Aggregate energy balance (Tables 1.1, 1.2 and 1.3)

1.4 These tables show the flows of energy in the United Kingdom from production to final consumption through conversion into secondary fuels such as coke, petroleum products and secondary electricity. The principles behind the presentation used and how this links with the figures presented in the other chapters are explained in Annex A. The figures are presented on an energy supplied basis, in tonnes of oil equivalent, see paragraphs 1.46 to 1.49.

1.5 In 2000 the primary supply of fuels was 246.7 million tonnes of oil equivalent, an increase of 1 per cent compared to 1999. However indigenous production in 2000 was 3 per cent lower than in 1999. Chart 1.1 illustrates the figures for the production and consumption of individual primary fuels in 2000. In 2000, as in the previous 7 years, overall primary fuel consumption was fully met by indigenous production, with the trade balances for petroleum and its products and gas more than offsetting net imports of coal, manufactured fuels and electricity.

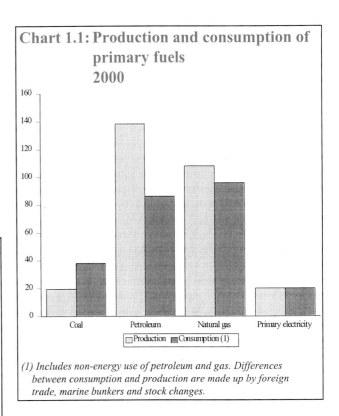

Chart 1.1: Production and consumption of primary fuels 2000

(1) Includes non-energy use of petroleum and gas. Differences between consumption and production are made up by foreign trade, marine bunkers and stock changes.

1.6 Total primary energy demand was just under ½ per cent higher in 2000 than in 1999 at 244.1 million tonnes of oil equivalent. Chart 1.2 shows the composition of primary demand in 2000.

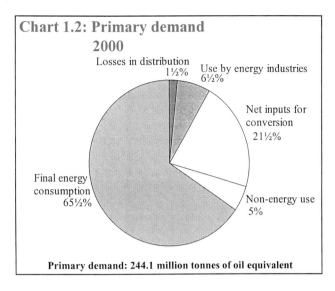

Chart 1.2: Primary demand 2000

- Losses in distribution 1½%
- Use by energy industries 6½%
- Net inputs for conversion 21½%
- Non-energy use 5%
- Final energy consumption 65½%

Primary demand: 244.1 million tonnes of oil equivalent

industry use amounted to 16,206 thousand tonnes of oil equivalent of energy, a decrease of 3½ per cent on 1999 and a 7 per cent decrease on 1998.

1.10 Losses presented in the energy balance include distribution and transmission losses in the supply of manufactured gases, natural gas, and electricity. These losses have increased between 1999 and 2000, following a fall of 3½ per cent between 1998 and 1999. The large increase between 1999 and 2000 was due to the metering differences that were used to collect information on losses for gas. From January 2001 a simplified reporting system was introduced that has improved the quality of data and reduced losses reported so far in the data reported for 2001. Further details can be found in paragraph 4.29 in Chapter 4.

1.11 Total final consumption, which includes non-energy use of fuels, in 2000 was 172,305 thousand tonnes of oil equivalent, a small increase on 1999. Final energy consumption in 2000 was mainly accounted for by the transport sector (32 per cent), the domestic sector (27 per cent), industry (21 per cent) and non-energy use (7 per cent). These figures are illustrated in Chart 1.3. Recent trends in industrial consumption are shown in Table 1.8 and discussed in paragraphs 1.20 to 1.22.

1.12 The main fuels used by final consumers in 2000 were petroleum products (45 per cent), natural gas (35 per cent) and electricity (16 per cent). Of the petroleum products consumed by final users 14 per cent was for non-energy purposes; for natural gas 2 per cent was consumed for non-energy purposes.

1.13 Non-energy use of fuels includes use as chemical feedstocks and other uses such as lubricants. Non-energy use of fuels for 2000 are shown in Table 1A. Further details of non-energy use are given in Chapter 3, paragraphs 3.77 to 3.83 and Chapter 4, paragraphs 4.16.

1.7 The transfers row in Tables 1.1, 1.2 and 1.3 should ideally sum to zero with transfers from primary oils to petroleum products amounting to a net figure of zero. Similarly the manufactured gases and natural gas transfers should sum to zero; the net difference is due to transfers of coke to breeze.

1.8 The transformation section of the energy balance shows, for each fuel, the net inputs for transformation uses. For example on Table 1.1 6,131 thousand tonnes of oil equivalent of coal feeds into the production of 5,629 thousand tonnes of oil equivalent of coke, representing a loss of 502 thousand tonnes of oil equivalent in the manufacture of coke in 2000. In 2000 energy losses during the production of electricity and other secondary fuels amounted to 51,999 thousand tonnes of oil equivalent, shown in the transformation row in Table 1.1.

1.9 The next section of the table represents use of fuels by the energy industries themselves. This section also includes consumption by those parts of the iron and steel industry which behave like an energy industry i.e. are involved in transformation processes (see paragraph A.28 of Annex A). In 2000 energy

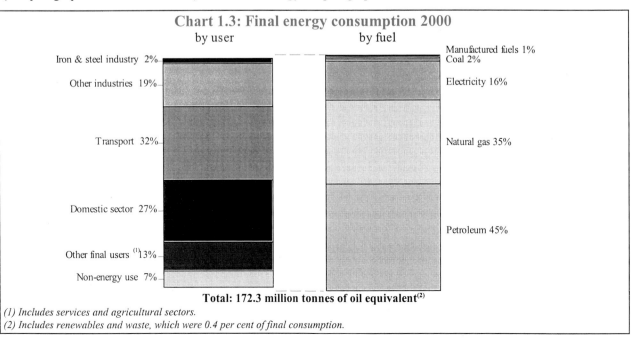

Chart 1.3: Final energy consumption 2000

by user | by fuel

- Iron & steel industry 2%
- Other industries 19%
- Transport 32%
- Domestic sector 27%
- Other final users [1] 13%
- Non-energy use 7%

- Manufactured fuels 1%
- Coal 2%
- Electricity 16%
- Natural gas 35%
- Petroleum 45%

Total: 172.3 million tonnes of oil equivalent[2]

(1) Includes services and agricultural sectors.
(2) Includes renewables and waste, which were 0.4 per cent of final consumption.

Table 1A: Non-energy use of fuels 2000

Thousand tonnes of oil equivalent

	Petroleum	Natural gas
Petrochemical feedstocks	6,755	1,118
Other	4,374	-
Total	**11,128**	**1,118**

1.14   One fuel not shown in the energy balances is the amount of heat sold. This is a growing market in the UK and it is planned to introduce heat into the energy balances for the next edition of the Digest.

Value balance of traded energy (Tables 1.4, 1.5 and 1.6)

1.15   Tables 1.4 to 1.6 provide a new presentation of the value of traded energy in a similar format to the energy balances. The balance shows how the value of inland energy supply is made up from the value of indigenous production, trade, tax and margins (profit and distribution costs). The lower half of the table then shows how this value is generated from the final expenditure on energy through transformation processes and other energy sector users as well as from the industrial and domestic sectors. The balances only contain values of energy which is traded i.e. where a transparent market price is applicable. Further technical notes are given in paragraphs 1.57 to 1.62.

1.16   Total expenditure by final consumers in 2000 is estimated at £69,900 million, (£69,630 million shown as actual final consumption and £270 million of coal consumed by the iron and steel sector in producing coke for their own consumption). Of the final consumption, 49 per cent represents the basic value of primary fuels, i.e. the value of the fuels at the pit or landing terminal. Whilst a further 36 per cent was accounted for by Duty and VAT. Distribution costs and margins accounted for the remainder.

1.17   This balance provides a guide on how the value chain works in the production and consumption of energy. For example in 2000, £17,185 million of crude oil were indigenously produced of which £12,560 million were exported and £6,875 million were imported. Allowing for stock changes this provides a total value of inland crude oil supply of £11,660 million. This fuel was then completely consumed within petroleum in the process of producing £16,985 million of petroleum products. Again some external trade and stock changes took place before arriving at a basic value of petroleum products of £15,230 million. In supplying the fuel to final consumers distribution costs were incurred and some profit was made amounting to £1,880 million whilst duty and tax meant a further £30,325 million was added to the basic price to arrive at the final market value of £47,435 million. This was the value of petroleum products purchased of which industry purchases £1,165 million, domestic consumers for heating £735 million, with the vast majority purchased within the transportation sectors, £43,185 million.

1.18   Of the total final expenditure on energy in 2000 (£69,900 million) the biggest share, 62 per cent fell to the transport sector. Of the remaining 38 per cent industry purchased around a quarter or £6,180 million with the domestic sector purchasing nearly three quarters or £14,105 million.

Sales of electricity and gas by sector (Table 1.7)

1.19   Table 1.7 shows broad estimates for the total value of electricity and gas to final consumption. Net selling values provide some indication of typical prices paid in broad sectors and can be of use to supplement more detailed and accurate information contained in the rest of this chapter.

Energy consumption by main industrial groups (Table 1.8)

1.20   This table presents final energy consumption for the main industrial sub-sectors over the last 5 years.

1.21   So far as is practicable, the user categories have been grouped on the basis of the 1992 Standard Industrial Classification (see paragraphs 1.77 to 1.81). However, some data suppliers have difficulty in classifying consumers to this level of detail and the breakdown presented in these tables must therefore be treated with caution. The groupings used are consistent with those used in Table 1.9 which shows industrial sectors' use of fuels for generation of electricity (autogeneration).

1.22   In 2000, 36.2 million tonnes of oil equivalent were consumed by the main industrial groups. The largest consuming groups were chemicals (21 per cent), iron and steel and non-ferrous metals (14½ per

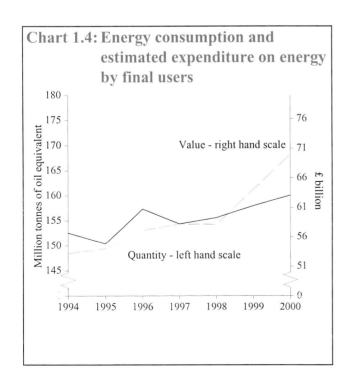

Chart 1.4: Energy consumption and estimated expenditure on energy by final users

cent), metal products, machinery and equipment (12½ per cent), food, beverages and tobacco (12 per cent), and paper, printing and publishing (7½ per cent). The remaining groups accounted for 33 per cent of total final energy consumption by industry. The figures are illustrated in Chart 1.5.

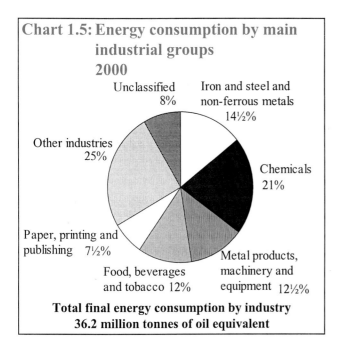

Chart 1.5: Energy consumption by main industrial groups 2000

Unclassified 8%

Iron and steel and non-ferrous metals 14½%

Other industries 25%

Chemicals 21%

Paper, printing and publishing 7½%

Metal products, machinery and equipment 12½%

Food, beverages and tobacco 12%

Total final energy consumption by industry 36.2 million tonnes of oil equivalent

Fuels consumed for electricity generation by main industrial groups (autogeneration) (Table 1.9)

1.23 This table gives details of the amount of each fuel consumed by industries in order to generate electricity for their own use. Fuel consumption is consistent with the figures given for "other generators" in Table 5.4 of Chapter 5. The term autogeneration is explained further in paragraphs 1.53 and 1.54. Electricity produced via autogeneration is included within the figures for electricity consumed by industrial sectors in Table 1.8. Table 1.9 has been produced using the information currently available and shows the same sector detail as Table 1.8, data cannot be given in as much detail as in the individual commodity balances and the energy balance because it could disclose information about individual companies. Table 1.9 allows users to allocate the fuel used for autogeneration to individual industry groups in place of the electricity consumed. Further information on the way Table 1.9 links with the other tables is given in paragraph 1.54.

Long term trends

Inland consumption of primary fuels (Table 1.10)

1.24 The trends for inland consumption of primary fuels for energy use are illustrated in Chart 1.6. Overall consumption for energy use increased steadily up to 1973, when the oil price rise following the Arab-Israeli war of that year led to a major change in patterns of fuel consumption. Having reached a level of over 220 million tonnes of oil equivalent in 1973, energy use fell, but by 1979 had returned to a similar level to that in 1973. After the outbreak of another Middle East war, consumption fell back to less than 200 million tonnes of oil equivalent in the years 1981 to 1984. It has since grown again, and by 1996 had exceeded the peak levels of 1973 and 1979. Overall consumption increased by 1 per cent between 1999 and 2000 to a new record high of 232.5 million tonnes of oil equivalent.

1.25 The changing trend in overall energy consumption was affected by petroleum consumption, which had continued to grow in the period 1970 to 1973 despite the strong growth in consumption of natural gas and primary electricity, mainly nuclear. After 1973 petroleum consumption declined for ten years, following much the same pattern as coal use. Over the last ten years petroleum consumption has risen again, although it fell back in 1995 and again in 1997, 1999 and 2000. Over the same period the decline in coal consumption has continued at an increasing rate except for 2000 when there was increased demand for coal at power stations. Consumption of natural gas has continued to grow and accounted for 41 per cent of all fuels consumed in 2000. Consumption of energy from renewables and waste has been increasing in recent years and has been separately identified in Table 1.10 for the first time.

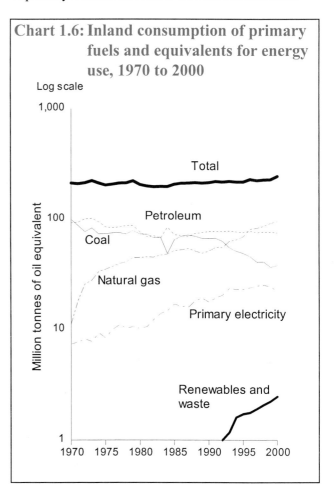

Chart 1.6: Inland consumption of primary fuels and equivalents for energy use, 1970 to 2000

Log scale

1,000

Total

Petroleum

Coal

Natural gas

Primary electricity

Renewables and waste

Million tonnes of oil equivalent

100

10

1

1970 1975 1980 1985 1990 1995 2000

Availability and consumption of primary fuels and equivalents (Table 1.11)

1.26 An overall view of energy presented in the form of energy balances is given in Table 1.11. It is based on Tables 1.1 to 1.3 with the time series extended back to 1970. Supplies and uses of energy are expressed on an energy-supplied basis in tonnes of oil equivalent, and are balanced by fuel and for total energy. More details on the derivation of these balances and on the calculation of energy contents are given in paragraphs 1.48 to 1.49. Calorific values of fuels are shown in Annex A.

1.27 Trends in the production of primary fuels in the United Kingdom are illustrated in Chart 1.7.

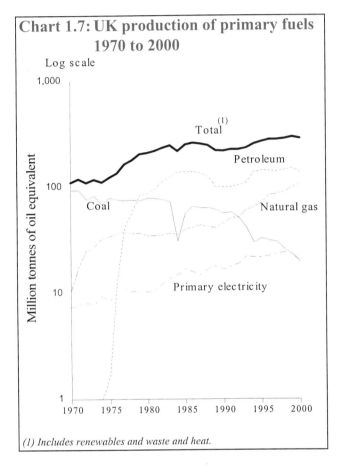

Chart 1.7: UK production of primary fuels 1970 to 2000

(1) Includes renewables and waste and heat.

1.28 In 1970 total energy production was around 110 million tonnes of oil equivalent with coal accounting for some 84 per cent. Natural gas from the North Sea started to be produced in substantial quantities from the early 1970s, accounting for 9½ per cent of total production in 1970. From 1975, petroleum production also grew rapidly to peak at over 139 million tonnes of oil equivalent in 1985 when it accounted for 55 per cent of total energy production at 252.5 million tonnes of oil equivalent. By 1991, temporary production problems had reduced petroleum production to less than 100 million tonnes of oil equivalent. Since then petroleum production has steadily recovered, reaching a record level of 150.2 million tonnes of oil equivalent in 1999. In 2000, production of petroleum fell by 8 per cent on 1999 levels and represented 48 per cent of total energy production. Gas production was at a record level of 108.3 million tonnes of oil equivalent

in 2000, 38 per cent of total energy production. At the same time, coal accounted for 7 per cent of energy production and nuclear and hydro electricity together 7 per cent.

Comparison of net imports of fuel with total consumption of primary fuels and equivalents (Table 1.12)

1.29 In Table 1.12 gross consumption in the United Kingdom, including non-energy use and international marine bunkers, is compared with net imports of fuel to show net import dependency or net export ratio.

1.30 A comparison of the overall trends in energy production (from Table 1.11) and total consumption (from Table 1.12) is given in Chart 1.8.

1.31 Chart 1.8 shows United Kingdom primary energy production and consumption and illustrates the degree to which the United Kingdom was dependent on energy imports prior to North Sea oil and gas becoming available. In the early 1970s energy imports accounted for over 50 per cent of United Kingdom consumption, but in 1983 the United Kingdom was a net exporter at a level equivalent to 18 per cent of inland consumption. After 1986 net exports declined. Following temporary production losses in the North Sea, the United Kingdom became a small net importer of energy between 1989 and 1992. Since then North Sea production has recovered and the United Kingdom has become a net exporter again. Net exports represented 16 per cent of inland consumption in 1997, 16 per cent in 1998, 21 per cent in 1999 and 17 per cent in 2000.

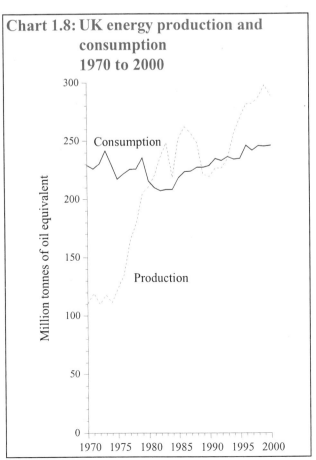

Chart 1.8: UK energy production and consumption 1970 to 2000

Energy ratio (Table 1.13)

1.32 The relationship between energy consumption and economic activity at the aggregate level can be gauged by comparing a country's temperature corrected inland primary energy consumption with its gross domestic product (GDP). This approach is simple and comprehensive but it has a number of drawbacks which were discussed in articles in the August 1976, May 1981 and May 1989 issues of *Economic Trends* (The Stationery Office).

1.33 The columns in Table 1.13 show the United Kingdom's temperature corrected inland primary energy consumption and GDP at constant prices since 1970, both expressed in absolute units (millions of tonnes of oil equivalent and billions of 1995 pounds sterling respectively). Dividing energy consumption by GDP yields the energy ratio, which is expressed in column C of the table as energy consumed per million pound of GDP and in column D as an index number based on 1995=100. For GDP at constant prices the published measure of GDP at market prices at 1995 prices has been used. The GDP figures used are now on the European System of Accounts (ESA 95) basis, consistent with the UK national accounts.

1.34 Energy consumption, GDP and the energy ratio over the period 1970 to 2000 (indexed to 1970 = 100) are illustrated in Chart 1.9.

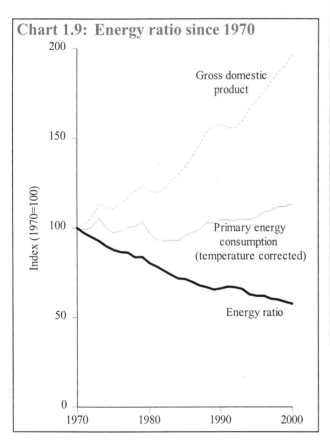

Chart 1.9: Energy ratio since 1970

1.35 Chart 1.9 shows that the energy ratio fell to 80 per cent of its 1970 level by 1980 and to 58 per cent by 2000, an average decrease of nearly 2 per cent per annum. It rose slightly during the early 1990s, but started falling again in 1991. The strong downward trend since 1970 is explained by at least four factors:

improvements in energy efficiency; saturation in the ownership levels of the main domestic appliances; the unresponsiveness of certain industrial uses, like space heating, to long run output growth; and a structural shift away from energy intensive activities (such as steel making) towards low energy industries (such as services).

Energy consumption by final user (Table 1.14)

1.36 Figures for consumption of fuel for energy uses by category of final user are given in Table 1.14. This table excludes non-energy use. Final users' consumption is net of the fuel industries' own use and conversion, transmission and distribution losses, but it includes conversion losses by final users. The user categories are industry (including iron and steel), transport (including coastal shipping), domestic and other final users (public administration, agriculture, commerce and other sectors), see paragraphs 1.77 to 1.81.

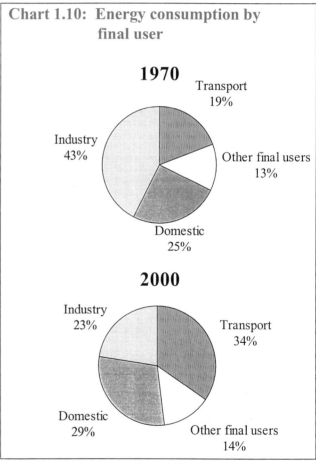

Chart 1.10: Energy consumption by final user

1970

Transport 19%
Industry 43%
Other final users 13%
Domestic 25%

2000

Industry 23%
Transport 34%
Domestic 29%
Other final users 14%

1.37 Up to 1986 data for final consumption of electricity include acquisitions from public supply, output of industrial nuclear stations, and amounts produced by transport undertakings and industrial hydropower for final consumption. From 1987 onwards, all consumption of electricity, whether produced by major power producers or by other generators is included. There is a corresponding change in treatment, between 1986 and 1987, for other fuels used in electricity generation (see paragraph 1.56).

1.38 Overall consumption by final users followed the same pattern as overall primary energy consumption since 1970, accounting for around 70 per cent of the total consumption throughout the period.

1.39 In 1970 industry (including iron and steel) was the sector with the greatest level of consumption, with 43 per cent of total final consumption. However, since 1970 this sector has steadily reduced its consumption so that it now stands at 23 per cent of total final consumption for energy use. This share is now less than that of the domestic sector which, at 29 per cent, has retained around the same share since 1985. Greatest growth has been in the transport sector; this had a share of 19 per cent in 1970, which has risen to 34 per cent in 2000.

1.40 A comparison of energy consumption for energy purposes by final users in 1970 and 2000 is shown in Chart 1.10.

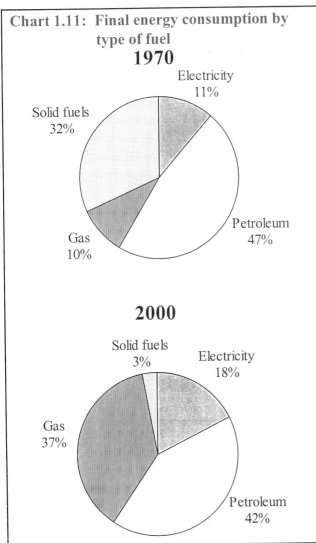

Chart 1.11: Final energy consumption by type of fuel

1970

Electricity 11%
Solid fuels 32%
Gas 10%
Petroleum 47%

2000

Solid fuels 3%
Electricity 18%
Gas 37%
Petroleum 42%

1.41 Table 1.14 also shows trends in final energy consumption for individual fuels. In 1970, consumption of coal and other solid fuels accounted for 32 per cent of final energy consumption, but this share has declined steadily, as the level of natural gas usage increased at the expense of both solid fuel and petroleum consumption. Electricity consumption has

made steady progress over the last thirty years, rising from 11 per cent of the total in 1970 to 18 per cent in 2000. A comparison of final energy consumption for individual fuels in 1970 and 2000 is shown in Chart 1.11.

Expenditure on energy by final user (Table 1.15)

1.42 Total expenditure on fuels is presented in Table 1.15 from 1970; and figures for recent years are illustrated in Chart 1.4. Data for the latest years are taken from the value balances (Tables 1.4 to 1.6) whilst earlier years are taken from their forerunner tables of estimated values of energy purchases by sector. The total fuels series is simply the sum of fuels presented in the table and so is slightly different from the value presented in the value balances as other fuel (which accounted for around 0.1 per cent of total final expenditure in 2000) is excluded but coal purchased by the iron and steel sector is included as a final purchase of coal.

1.43 Overall final expenditure on energy rose by around £5,840 million (about 9 per cent) in 2000 compared to 1999. The level of £69,865 million represents a 30 per cent rise on 1995 and 51 per cent more than in 1990. The final expenditure fell for all fuels in 2000 with the exception of gas and petroleum where expenditure rose by 7 and 15 per cent, partly reflecting increases in the prices of these fuels in 2000.

1.44 The make up of total expenditure has changed through time reflecting structural or long term changes in fuel and shorter term price and consumption effects. In 1970, expenditure on coal and coke accounted for around 15 per cent of total final expenditure but was down to 1½ per cent in 1999. By contrast, the general increase in the consumer price of petroleum (where duty is a major component) has meant petroleum has risen from 45 per cent of all expenditure in 1970 to 65 per cent in 2000. Electricity, despite seeing over a 70 per cent increase in volume consumed since 1970, still accounts for roughly the same share of total expenditure, 30 per cent in 1970, 23 per cent in 2000, as prices have seen significant real term falls.

Mean air temperatures (Tables 1.16 and 1.17)

1.45 These tables give the average air temperatures in Great Britain between 1961 and 1990 by year, part year and month. Deviations from these means are presented for January 1996 to May 2001. Average monthly temperatures back to 1970 are also given in Table 1.17. These temperature deviations are used to provide the temperature corrected consumption series in Table 1.13. The average temperature in 2000 was just over 1 degree Celsius higher than the long term mean, similar to the averages in 1997, 1998 and 1999.

Technical notes and definitions

I Units and measurement of energy

Units of measurement

1.46 The original units of measurement appropriate to each fuel are used in the individual fuel chapters. A common unit of measurement, the tonne of oil equivalent (toe), which enables different fuels to be compared and aggregated, is used in Chapter 1. For consistency with the International Energy Agency and with the Statistical Office of the European Communities, the tonne of oil equivalent is defined as follows:

1 tonne of oil equivalent $= 10^7$ kilocalories
$= 396.83$ therms
$= 41.868$ Gigajoules (GJ)
$= 11,630$ kWh

1.47 This unit should be regarded as a measure of energy content rather than a physical quantity. There is no intention to represent an actual physical tonne of oil, and indeed actual tonnes of oil will normally have measurements in tonnes of oil equivalent which differ from unity.

Thermal content - energy supplied basis of measurement

1.48 Tables 1.1, 1.2, 1.3, 1.8, and 1.10 to 1.14 are compiled on an energy-supplied basis. Detailed data for individual fuels are converted from original units to tonnes of oil equivalent using gross calorific values and conversion factors appropriate to each category of fuel. The results are then aggregated according to the categories used in the tables. Gross calorific values represent the total energy content of the fuel, including the energy needed to evaporate the water present in the fuel (see also paragraph 1.75).

1.49 Estimated gross calorific values for 2000 are given on page 226. Calorific values are reviewed each year in collaboration with the fuel industries, and figures for earlier years can be found in Table A.2 on page 227. To construct energy balances on an energy supplied basis; calorific values are required for production, trade, and stocks, as follows:

Coal The weighted average gross calorific value of all indigenous coal consumed is used to derive the thermal content of coal production and undistributed stocks. Thermal contents of imports and exports allow for the quality of coal. Thermal contents of changes in coal stocks at secondary fuel producers are the average calorific values of indigenous coal consumed.

Petroleum Work was carried out in 1997 to revise calorific values for petroleum products. It has not been possible to find any recent work on the subject. In the absence of such work, the gross calorific values, included in Annex A, and used in the construction of these energy balances from 1990 onwards have been calculated using a formula derived by the US Bureau of Standards. This formula estimates the gross calorific value of products according to their density. This formula is as follows:

$$Gj = 51.83 - 8.78 \times d^2$$

where d is the density of the product in terms of kilograms per litre.

For crude petroleum and refinery losses, the weighted average calorific value for all petroleum products from UK refineries is used. A notional figure of 43.3 GJ per tonne is used for non-energy petroleum products (industrial and white spirits, lubricants, bitumen, petroleum coke, waxes and miscellaneous products).

Gases Although the original unit for gases is the cubic metre, figures for gases are generally presented in the fuel sections of this Digest in gigawatt hours (GWh), having been converted from cubic metres using gross calorific values provided by the industries concerned. Conversion factors between units of energy are given on the flap inside the back cover.

Electricity Unlike the other fuels, the original unit used to measure electricity - GWh - is a measure of energy. The figures for electricity can therefore be converted directly to toe using the conversion factors on the flap inside the back cover.

Primary electricity Hydro electricity and net imports of electricity are presented in terms of the energy content of the electricity produced (the energy supplied basis). This is consistent with international practice. Primary inputs for nuclear electricity assume the thermal efficiencies at nuclear stations given in Chapter 5, Table 5.9 (37.3 per cent in 2000). (See Chapter 5, paragraphs 5.27, 5.42 and 5.66.)

Temperature corrected primary fuel consumption (Tables 1.13)

1.50 The temperature corrected series of total inland fuel consumption given in Table 1.13 indicates what annual consumption might have been if the average temperature during the year had been the same as the average for the years 1961 to 1990. This average is given, with annual deviations, in Table 1.16 whilst Table 1.17 shows average temperatures for each month from 1970. The corrections used to increase demand per degree Celsius above average are:

Coal	2.1 per cent
Petroleum	0.7 per cent (June - August)
	1.8 per cent (September - May)

1.51 Figures for natural gas are corrected using a method developed by British Gas Transco. Prior to 1990, the annual temperature adjustment applied by the DTI differed from that applied by British Gas due to the effect of seasonal adjustment of the monthly data. From 1990 onwards, the DTI's annual adjustment to the gas figures for temperature is the same as that applied by BG Transco. Nuclear, hydro and net imports of electricity are not corrected for temperature.

Non-energy uses of fuel

1.52 Energy use of fuel mainly comprises use for lighting, heating, motive power and power for appliances. Non-energy use includes for example use as chemical feedstocks, solvents, lubricants, and road making material. The non-energy use of natural gas as a chemical feedstock was separately identified for the first time in the 1994 edition of the Digest. It should be noted that the estimated amounts of non-energy gas included in the Digest are very approximate. Non-energy uses of petroleum and gas are now included in the figures for final energy consumption following the move over to the presentation of energy data in the format of commodity and energy balances in this edition. Further discussion of non-energy uses of lubricating oils and petroleum coke appears in Chapter 3, paragraphs 3.77 to 3.83.

Autogeneration of electricity

1.53 Autogeneration is defined as the generation of electricity by companies whose main business is not electricity generation, the electricity being produced mainly for that company's own use. Estimated amounts of fuel used for thermal generation of electricity by such companies, the output of electricity and the thermal losses incurred in generation are included within the Transformation sector in the energy balances shown in Tables 1.1, 1.2 and 1.3. Electricity used within the power generation process by autogenerators is shown within the Energy industry use sector. Electricity consumed by industry and commerce from its own generation is included as part of Final consumption. This treatment is in line with the practice in international energy statistics.

1.54 Figures for the total amount of fuel used and electricity generated by autogenerators along with the amount of electricity they consume themselves are shown in Tables 1.9, 5.1, 5.3, 5.4 and 5.6. Table 1.9 summarises the figures according to broad industrial sector. Much of the power generated is from combined heat and power (CHP) plants and data from Chapter 6 are included within Table 1.9. Differences will occur where CHP plants are classified to major power producers, and this mainly affects the chemicals sector. The method of allocating fuel used in CHP plants between electricity production and heat production is described in paragraph 6.31 of Chapter 6. This method conforms with international practice although countries adopt different percentages for the assumed efficiencies of heat-only boilers. However it can give rise to high implied conversion efficiencies in some sectors, most notably in the iron and steel sector. A large number of revised figures appear for autogeneration this year reflecting further work undertaken to improve the quality of CHP data as set out in Chapter 6.

Final consumption, deliveries, stock changes

1.55 Figures for final consumption relate to deliveries, if fuels can be stored by users and data on actual consumption are not available. Final consumption of petroleum and solid fuel is on a deliveries basis throughout, except for the use of solid fuel by the iron and steel industry. Figures for domestic use of coal are based on deliveries to merchants. Figures for stock changes in Tables 1.1 to 1.3 cover stocks held by primary and secondary fuel producers, major distributors of petroleum products, and stocks of coke and breeze held by the iron and steel industry. Figures for stock changes in natural gas represent the net amount put into storage by gas companies operating pipelines.

1.56 Figures for final consumption of electricity include sales by the public distribution system and consumption of electricity produced by generators other than the major electricity producing companies. Thus electricity consumption includes that produced by industry and figures for deliveries of other fuels to industry exclude amounts used to generate electricity (except for years prior to 1987 - see paragraph 1.37).

Valuation of energy purchases (Tables 1.4, 1.5, 1.6, 1.15)

1.57 In common with the rest of the chapter, these tables covering energy expenditure now follow a balance format. Whilst a user may derive data on a similar basis as that previously published, the balance table allows for more varied use and interpretation of traded energy value data. That said the table continues to only show values for energy that has to be purchased and therefore does not include estimated values of a sectors internal consumption, such as coal used in the process of coal extraction.

The balance

1.58 The table balances around **market value of inland consumption** with the lower half of the table showing the total value of consumption by end users, sub divided into energy sector users and final users both for energy and non energy use. The top half of the table shows the supply components that go to make up the final market value of inland consumption, namely upstream cost of production, imports, taxes and the margins and costs of delivering and packaging the fuel for the final consumer. The total final consumers value of energy consumption is represented by the lines 'total non energy sector use' and iron and steel sectors purchases of coal for use in solid fuel manufacture.

Fuel definitions in value balances

1.59 **Crude oil** includes NGLs and refinery feedstocks. **Natural gas** does not include colliery methane. **Electricity** only includes electricity delivered via the public distribution system and therefore does not value electricity produced and consumed by autogenerators, but the input fuels are included in transformation. **Manufactured solid fuels** includes coke, breeze and other solid manufactured fuels, mainly products from patent fuel and carbonisation plants. **Other fuels** includes all other fuels not listed, where they can be clearly considered as traded and some reasonable valuation can be made. Fuels mainly contributing to this year's values are wood, coke oven and colliery methane gases sold on to other industrial users and some use of waste products such as tyres.

Valuation

1.60   All figures are estimates and have been rounded to the nearest £5 million.

Energy end use

1.61   Values represent the cost to the final user including transportation of the fuel. They are derived, except where actual values are available, from the traded element of the volumes presented in aggregate energy balance and end user prices collected from information supplied by users or energy suppliers. The **energy sector** consists of those industries engaged in the production and sale of energy products, but values are not given for consumption of self generated fuels e.g. coke oven gas used by coke producers. Many of the processes in the **iron and steel** industry are considered to be part of the energy sector in the energy balances, but for the purposes of this economic balance their genuine purchases are treated as those of final consumers, except for purchases of coal directly used in coke manufacture, which is shown separately as part of manufacture of solid fuel. Coal used directly in or to heat blast furnaces is shown as iron and steel final use. **Transformation** are those fuels used directly in producing other fuels e.g. crude oil in petroleum products. **Electricity generators** keep and use significant stocks of coal and the stocks used in consumption each year are shown separately. The value and margins for these being assumed to be the same as other coal purchased in the year. **Road transport** includes all motor spirit and DERV use. **Commercial and other users** includes public administration and miscellaneous uses not classified to the industrial sector.

Supply

1.62   The supply side money chain is derived using various methods. **Indigenous production** represents the estimated basic value of in year sales by the upstream producers. This value is gross of any taxes or cost they must meet. The valuation problems in attributing network losses in gas and electricity between upstream and downstream within this value chain, means any costs borne are included in the production value. **Imports and exports** are valued in accordance with Chapter 8. However crude oil is treated differently where the value is formed from price data taken from a census survey of refiners and volume data taken from Tables 3.1 to 3.3. These values are considered to reflect the complete money chain more accurately than Tables 8.1 to 8.4. **Stock changes** are those for undistributed stocks except for coal where coke oven and generators stocks are included. A stock increase takes money out of the money chain and is therefore represented as a negative. **Distribution costs** are arrived at by removing an estimate of producers value along with any taxes from the end user values shown. For most fuel the estimate of producer value is derived from the consumption used for end use and the producer price taken from survey of producers. For electricity the Pool Purchase Price is used to value public distribution supply. No sector breakdown is given for gas and electricity margins because it is not possible to accurately measure delivery costs for each sector. **Taxes** include VAT where not refundable and duties paid on downstream sales. Excluded are the gas and fossil fuel levies, petroleum revenue tax and production royalties and licence fees. The proceeds from the fossil fuel levy are redistributed across the electricity industry, whilst the rest are treated as part of the production costs.

Sales of electricity and gas by sector (Table 1.7)

1.63   This table provides data previously contained in the prices chapter on the total value of gas and electricity sold to final consumers. The data are collected from the energy supply companies. The data are useful in indicating relative total expenditure between sectors, but the quality of data provided in terms of industrial classification has been worsening in recent years.

II Energy balances (Tables 1.1,1.2 and 1.3)

1.64   Tables 1.1, 1.2 and 1.3 show the energy flows as the primary fuels are processed (or used) and as the consequent secondary fuels are used. The net inputs to transformation are shown in the transformation rows and hence outputs from transformation processes into which primary fuels are input (such as electricity generation or petroleum refining) appear as positive figures in the transformation rows under the secondary product's heading in the tables. Similarly the net inputs are shown as negative figures under the primary fuel headings.

1.64   Readers should note that following the consultation on the 1998 edition of this publication, and the responses received from that, that the energy balance presentation changed from the 1999 edition, as has the presentation of individual fuel figures throughout this publication. Annex A explains in detail the principles behind the presentation.

1.65   It is planned that heat sold will be separately identified in the energy balances next year to reflect the growing demand for heat within the UK. There are two main sources of heat in the UK, from CHP plants and from district heating.

III Measurement of energy consumption

Primary fuel input basis

1.67 Energy consumption is usually measured in one of three different ways. The first, known as the primary fuel input basis, assesses the total input of primary fuels and their equivalents. This measure includes energy used or lost in the conversion of primary fuels to secondary fuels (for example in power stations and oil refineries), energy lost in the distribution of fuels (for example in transmission lines) and energy conversion losses by final users. Primary demands as in Table 1.1, 1.2 and 1.3 is on this basis.

Final consumption - energy supplied basis

1.68 The second method, known as the energy supplied basis, measures the energy content of the fuels, both primary and secondary, supplied to final users. Thus it is net of fuel industry own use and conversion, transmission and distribution losses, but it includes conversion losses by final users. The final consumption figures are presented on this basis throughout Chapter 1.

1.69 Although this is the usual and most direct way to measure final energy consumption, it is also possible to present final consumption on a primary fuel input basis. This can be done by allocating the conversion losses, distribution losses and energy industry use to final users. This approach can be used to compare the total primary fuel use for which each sector of the economy is responsible. Table 1C presents shares of final consumption on this basis.

Final consumption - useful energy basis

1.70 Thirdly, final consumption may be expressed in the form of useful energy available after deduction of the losses incurred when final users convert energy supplied into space or process heat, motive power or light. Such losses depend on the type and quality of fuel and the equipment used and on the purpose, conditions, duration and intensity of use. Statistics on useful energy are not sufficiently reliable to be given in this Digest; there is a lack of data on utilisation efficiencies and on the purposes for which fuels are used.

Shares of each fuel in energy supply and demand

1.71 The relative importance of the energy consumption of each sector of the economy depends on the method used to measure consumption. Shares of final consumption on an energy supplied basis (that is in terms of the primary and secondary fuels directly consumed) in 2000 are presented in Table 1B. For comparison, Table 1C presents shares of final consumption on a primary fuel input basis.

Table 1B: Primary and secondary fuels consumed by final users in 2000 - energy supplied basis

| | Percentage of each fuel | | | | |
	Industry	Transport	Domestic	Others	Total
Solid fuels	53	-	42	5	100
Petroleum	10	82	5	4	100
Gas	29	-	53	18	100
Secondary electricity	35	3	34	29	100
All fuels	23	34	29	14	100

| | Percentage of each sector | | | | |
	Solid fuels	Petroleum	Gas	Secondary electricity	Total
Industry	7	18	48	27	100
Transport	-	99	-	1	100
Domestic	4	7	68	21	100
Others	1	11	50	37	100
All users	3	42	37	18	100

Table 1C: Total primary fuel consumption by final users in 2000 - primary input basis

| | Percentage of each fuel | | | | |
	Industry	Transport	Domestic	Others	Total
Coal	37	2	35	25	100
Petroleum	10	80	6	4	100
Gas	31	1	47	22	100
Primary electricity	35	3	34	29	100
All fuels	25	27	30	17	100

| | Percentage of each sector | | | | |
	Coal	Petroleum	Gas	Primary electricity	Total
Industry	23	13	50	13	100
Transport	1	96	1	1	100
Domestic	18	6	65	11	100
Others	23	8	52	16	100
All users	16	32	42	10	100

1.72 In 2000, every 1 toe of secondary electricity consumed by final users required, on average, 1.0 toe of coal, 1.0 toe of natural gas, 0.7 toe of primary electricity (nuclear, natural flow hydro and imports) and 0.2 toe of oil and renewables combined. The extent of this primary consumption is hidden in Table 1B, which presents final consumption only in terms of the fuels directly consumed. When all such primary consumption is allocated to final users, as in Table 1C, the relative importance of fuels and sectors changes; the transport sector, which uses very little electricity, declines in importance, whilst the true cost of final consumption in terms of coal use can now be seen.

1.73 Another view comes from shares of users' expenditure on each fuel (Table 1D based on Table 1.4). In this case the importance of fuels which require most handling by the user (solids and liquid fuels) is slightly understated, and the importance of uses taxed at higher rates (transport) is overstated in the All users line.

Table 1D: Value of fuels purchased by final users in 2000

	Solid fuels	Petroleum	Gas	Secondary electricity	Total
				percentage of each sector	
Industry	7	19	18	56	100
Transport	-	99	-	1	100
Domestic	3	5	39	52	100
Others	-	8	16	76	100
All users	-	65	11	23	100

Systems of measurement - international statistics

1.74 The systems of energy measurement used in various international statistics differ from the methods of this Digest as follows.

Net calorific values

1.75 Calorific values (thermal contents) used internationally are net rather than gross. The difference between the net and gross thermal content is the amount of energy necessary to evaporate the water present in the fuel or formed during the combustion process. The differences between gross and net values are taken to be 5 per cent for liquid and solid fuels (except for coke and coke breeze where there is no difference), 10 per cent for gases (except for blast furnace gas, 1 per cent), 15 per cent for straw, and 16 per cent for poultry litter. The calorific value of wood is highly dependent on its moisture content. In Annex A the gross calorific value is given as 10 GJ per tonne at 50 per cent moisture content and this rises to 14.5 GJ at 25 per cent moisture content and 19 GJ for dry wood (equivalent to a net calorific value).

IV Definitions of fuels

1.76 The following paragraphs explain what is covered under the terms "primary" and "secondary" fuels.

Primary fuels

Coal - Production comprises all grades of coal, including slurry.

Primary oils - This includes crude oil, natural gas liquids (NGLs) and feedstock.

Natural gas liquids - Natural gas liquids (NGLs) consist of condensates (C_5 or heavier) and petroleum gases other than methane C_1, that is ethane C_2, propane C_3 and butane C_4, obtained from the onshore processing of associated and non-associated gas. These are treated as primary fuels when looking at primary supply but in the consumption data presented in this chapter these fuels are treated as secondary fuels, being transferred from the primary oils column in Tables 1.1, 1.2 and 1.3.

Natural gas - Production relates to associated or non-associated methane C_1 from land and the United Kingdom sector of the Continental Shelf. It includes that used for drilling production and pumping operations, but excludes gas flared or re-injected. It also includes colliery methane piped to the surface and consumed by collieries or others.

Nuclear electricity - Electricity generated by nuclear power stations belonging to the major power producers. See paragraphs 5.58 to 5.59.

Natural flow hydro-electricity - Electricity generated by public supply and industrial natural flow hydroelectric power stations. Pumped storage stations are not included (see under secondary electricity below).

Renewable energy sources - In this chapter figure are presented for renewables and waste in total. Further details, including a detailed breakdown of the commodities covered are in Chapter 7.

Secondary fuels

Manufactured fuel - This heading includes manufactured solid fuels such as coke and breeze, other manufactured solid fuels, liquids such as benzole and tars and gases such as coke oven gas and blast furnace gas. Further details are given in Chapter 2, Tables 2.4, 2.5 and 2.6.

Coke and breeze - Coke oven coke and hard coke breeze (Tables 2.4, 2.5 and 2.6).

Other manufactured solid fuels –

Manufactured solid fuels produced at low temperature carbonisation plants and other manufactured fuel and briquetting plants (Tables 2.4, 2.5 and 2.6).

Coke oven gas - Gas produced at coke ovens, excluding low temperature carbonisation plants. Gas bled or burnt to waste is included in production and losses (Tables 2.4, 2.5 and 2.6).

Blast furnace gas - Blast furnace gas is mainly produced and consumed within the iron and steel industry (Tables 2.4, 2.5 and 2.6).

Petroleum products - Petroleum products produced mainly at refineries, together with inland deliveries of natural gas liquids.

Secondary electricity - Secondary electricity is that generated by the combustion of another fuel, usually coal, natural gas or oil. The figure for outputs from transformation in the electricity column of Tables 1.1, 1.2 and 1.3 is the total of primary and secondary electricity, and the subsequent analysis of consumption is based on this total.

V Classification of consumers

1.77 This issue of the Digest has been prepared, as far as is practicable, on the basis of the *Standard Industrial Classification (SIC) 1992* (The Stationery Office 1991). However, not all consumption/disposals data are on this basis, and where they are, there are sometimes constraints on the detail available.

Between 1986 and 1994 data in the Digest were prepared on the basis of the previous classification, SIC 1980. The exceptions are Tables, 2.8, and 3.11 in this Digest and the corresponding tables in previous editions which have been prepared largely on the basis of SIC 1968. The main differences between the 1968 SIC (which was used as the basis for most data published for years prior to 1984) and the 1980 SIC were described in the 1986 and 1987 issues of the Digest. The differences between SIC 1980 and SIC 1992 are relatively minor. At the time of the change from the 1980 SIC to the 1992 SIC the main difference was that under the former showrooms belonging to the fuel supply industries were classified to the energy sector, whilst in the latter they are in the commercial sector. Since privatisation few gas, coal and electricity companies have retained showrooms and the difference is therefore minimal.

1.78   Table 1E shows the categories of consumer together with their codes in SIC 1992. The coverage varies between tables (e.g. in some instances the 'other' category is split into major constituents, whereas elsewhere it may include transport). This is because the coverage is dictated by what data suppliers can provide. The table also shows the disaggregation available within industry. This disaggregation forms the basis of virtually all the tables that show a disaggregated industrial breakdown. There are a few notable exceptions that are detailed in paragraph 1.77.

Table 1E: SIC 1992 classifications

Fuel producers	10-12, 23, 40

Final consumers:

Industrial

Unclassified	See text below
Iron and steel	27, *excluding* 27.4, 27.53, 27.54
Non-ferrous metals	27.4, 27.53, 27.54
Mineral products	14, 26
Chemicals	24
Mechanical engineering and metal products	28, 29
Electrical and instrument engineering	30-33
Vehicles	34, 35
Food, beverages & tobacco	15, 16
Textiles, clothing, leather, & footwear	17-19
Paper, printing & publishing	21, 22
Other industries	13, 20, 25, 36, 37, 41
Construction	45
Transport	60-63

Other final users

Domestic	Not covered by SIC 1992.
Public administration	75, 80, 85
Commercial	50-52, 55, 64-67, 70-74
Agriculture	01, 02, 05
Miscellaneous	90-93, 99

1.79   There is also an 'unclassified' category in the industry sector (see Table 1E). Wherever the data supplier is unable to allocate an amount between categories, but the Department of Trade and Industry has additional information, not readily available to readers, with which to allocate between categories, then this has been done. Where such additional information is not available the data are included in the 'unclassified' category, enabling the reader to decide whether to accept a residual, pro-rate, or otherwise adjust the figures. The 'miscellaneous' category also contains some unallocated figures for the services sector.

1.80   In Tables 6.7 and 6.8 of Chapter 6 the following abbreviated grouping of industries, based on SIC 1992, is used in order to prevent disclosure of information about individual companies:

Table 1F: Abbreviated grouping of Industry

Iron and steel and non-ferrous metal	27
Chemicals	24
Oil refineries	23.2
Paper, printing & publishing	21, 22
Food, beverages & tobacco	15, 16
Metal products, machinery and equipment	28, 29, 30, 31, 32, 34, 35
Extraction, mining and agglomeration of solid fuels	10, 11
Other industrial branches	12, 13, 14, 17, 18, 19, 20, 23.1, 23.3, 25, 26, 33, 36, 37, 40.1, 40.2, 45
Transport, commerce, and administration	1, 2, 5, 50 to 99 (except 90 and 92)
Other	40.3, 90, 92

1.81   In Tables 1.8 and 1.9 the list above is further condensed and includes only manufacturing industry and construction as follows:

Table 1G: Abbreviated grouping of Industry for Tables 1.7 and 1.8

Iron and steel and non-ferrous metals	27
Chemicals	24
Paper, printing & publishing	21, 22
Food, beverages & tobacco	15, 16
Metal products, machinery and equipment	28, 29, 30, 31, 32, 34, 35
Other (including construction)	12, 13, 14, 17, 18, 19, 20, 23.1, 23.3, 25, 26, 33, 36, 37, 45

VI Monthly and quarterly data

1.82   Monthly and quarterly data on energy production and consumption (including on a seasonally adjusted and temperature corrected basis) split by fuel type are provided on the DTI website at www.dti.gov.uk/energy/energystats/energystats.htm. Quarterly figures are also published in the DTI's quarterly statistical bulletin *Energy Trends*. See Annex F for more information about *Energy Trends*.

Contact: Rachael Winther (Statistician) 020 7215 6178
Chenab Mangat, 020 7215 2710

1.1 Aggregate energy balance 2000

Thousand tonnes of oil equivalent

	Coal	Manufactured fuel (1)	Primary oils	Petroleum products	Natural gas (2)	Renewable & waste (3)	Primary electricity	Electricity	Total
Supply									
Indigenous production	19,553	-	138,282	-	108,258	2,476	20,155	-	288,725
Imports	15,731	348	59,342	15,529	2,238	-	-	1,230	94,419
Exports	-498	-315	-101,585	-22,383	-12,583	-	-	-12	-137,377
Marine bunkers	-	-	-	-2,207	-	-	-	-	-2,207
Stock change (4)	+3,336	-233	+1,196	-386	-809	-	-	-	+3,105
Primary supply	**38,122**	**-200**	**97,234**	**-9,447**	**97,105**	**2,476**	**20,155**	**1,219**	**246,664**
Statistical difference (5)	**+58**	**-195**	**+541**	**+963**	**+1,118**	**-**	**-**	**+99**	**+2,585**
Primary demand	**38,064**	**-5**	**96,693**	**-10,410**	**95,987**	**2,476**	**20,155**	**1,120**	**244,079**
									-
Transfers	-	127	-195	307	-37	-	-521	521	202
Transformation	**-35,441**	**3,121**	**-96,141**	**93,211**	**-26,887**	**-1,711**	**-19,634**	**31,483**	**-51,999**
Electricity generation	-28,587	-911	-	-1,072	-26,887	-1,711	-19,634	31,483	-47,320
Major power producers	-27,748	-	-	-427	-24,401	-219	-19,634	28,784	-43,645
Autogenerators	-839	-911	-	-645	-2,486	-1,492	-	2,699	-3,674
Petroleum refineries	-	-	-96,141	94,483	-	-	-	-	-1,658
Coke manufacture	-6,131	5,629	-	-	-	-	-	-	-502
Blast furnaces	-340	-1,992	-	-200	-	-	-	-	-2,532
Patent fuel manufacture	-383	395	-	-	-	-	-	-	13
Other	-	-	-	-	-	-	-	-	-
Energy industry use	**8**	**1,129**	**357**	**5,502**	**6,917**	**-**	**-**	**2,293**	**16,206**
Electricity generation	-	-	-	-	-	-	-	1,398	1,398
Oil and gas extraction	-	-	357	-	5,641	-	-	45	6,043
Petroleum refineries	-	-	-	5,337	456	-	-	435	6,228
Coal extraction	8	-	-	-	19	-	-	111	139
Coke manufacture	-	568	-	-	1	-	-	-	569
Blast furnaces	-	526	-	118	61	-	-	77	783
Patent fuel manufacture	-	35	-	-	-	-	-	-	35
Pumped storage	-	-	-	-	-	-	-	69	69
Other	-	-	-	47	739	-	-	157	942
Losses	**-**	**158**	**-**	**-**	**1,065**	**-**	**-**	**2,549**	**3,772**
Final consumption	**2,615**	**1,957**	**-**	**77,606**	**61,081**	**765**	**-**	**28,282**	**172,305**
Industry	**941**	**1,488**	**-**	**6,373**	**17,254**	**364**	**-**	**9,759**	**36,178**
Unclassified	-	260	-	2,318	10	364	-	-	2,952
Iron and steel	1	1,114	-	136	1,834	-	-	849	3,935
Non-ferrous metals	71	114	-	42	497	-	-	508	1,232
Mineral products	184	-	-	261	1,305	-	-	637	2,386
Chemicals	292	-	-	384	4,915	-	-	1,961	7,552
Mechanical engineering etc.	9	-	-	224	930	-	-	780	1,944
Electrical engineering etc.	2	-	-	51	365	-	-	525	944
Vehicles	42	-	-	147	963	-	-	489	1,640
Food, beverages, etc.	137	-	-	310	2,755	-	-	1,071	4,272
Textiles, leather, etc.	36	-	-	149	641	-	-	336	1,162
Paper, printing etc.	75	-	-	75	1,511	-	-	970	2,631
Other industries	93	-	-	1,808	1,346	-	-	1,496	4,744
Construction	-	-	-	467	180	-	-	136	784
Transport	**-**	**-**	**-**	**54,446**	**-**	**-**	**-**	**758**	**55,204**
Air	-	-	-	11,859	-	-	-	-	11,859
Rail	-	-	-	481	-	-	-	-	481
Road	-	-	-	41,071	-	-	-	-	41,071
National navigation	-	-	-	1,036	-	-	-	-	1,036
Pipelines	-	-	-	-	-	-	-	-	-
Other	**1,674**	**468**	**-**	**5,659**	**42,709**	**401**	**-**	**17,765**	**68,676**
Domestic	1,466	468	-	3,239	31,807	236	-	9,617	46,833
Public administration	197	-	-	1,145	4,680	81	-	1,948	8,052
Commercial	-	-	-	495	3,744	-	-	5,875	10,114
Agriculture	5	-	-	633	127	72	-	325	1,162
Miscellaneous	6	-	-	147	2,350	12	-	-	2,514
Non energy use	**-**	**-**	**-**	**11,128**	**1,118**	**-**	**-**	**-**	**12,246**

(1) Includes all manufactured solid fuels, benzole, tars, coke oven gas and blast furnace gas.
(2) Includes colliery methane.
(3) Includes geothermal and solar heat.
(4) Stock fall (+), stock rise (-).
(5) Primary supply minus primary demand.

1.2 Aggregate energy balance 1999

Thousand tonnes of oil equivalent

	Coal	Manufactured fuel (1)	Primary oils	Petroleum products	Natural gas (2)	Renewable & waste (3)	Primary electricity	Electricity	Total
Supply									
Indigenous production	23,219r	-	150,160r	-	99,109r	2,236r	22,944r	-	297,669r
Imports	13,734r	305r	48,964r	15,178r	1,106	-	-	1,247	80,534r
Exports	-578r	-195r	-100,396r	-23,580r	-7,260	-	-	-23	-132,033r
Marine bunkers	-	-	-	-2,469	-	-	-	-	-2,469
Stock change (4)	-686r	222r	-214	636	670r	-	-	-	+627r
Primary supply	**35,688r**	**332r**	**98,514r**	**-10,236r**	**93,625r**	**2,236r**	**22,944r**	**1,225**	**244,328r**
Statistical difference (5)	-415r	-224r	+68r	+404r	+1,142r	-	-	128r	+1,103r
Primary demand	**36,103r**	**556r**	**98,446r**	**-10,639r**	**92,483r**	**2,236r**	**22,944r**	**1,097r**	**243,224r**
Transfers	-	-20r	-1,650r	1,694r	-44	-	-534r	534r	-19r
Transformation	**-32,203r**	**2,854r**	**-96,406r**	**93,608r**	**-26,476r**	**-1,434**	**-22,410r**	**30,890r**	**-51,575r**
Electricity generation	-25,408r	-914r	-	-1,097r	-26,476r	-1,434	-22,410r	30,890r	-46,848r
Major power producers	-24,502r	-	-	-386r	-24,247r	-1,434	-22,410r	28,302r	-43,436r
Autogenerators	-906r	-914r	-	-710r	-2,229r	-1,241	-	2,588r	-3,412r
Petroleum refineries	-	-	-96,406r	94,984r	-	-	-	-	-1,422r
Coke manufacture	-5,964r	5,401r	-	-	-	-	-	-	-563r
Blast furnaces	-372r	-2,101r	-	-279	-	-	-	-	-2,752r
Patent fuel manufacture.	-460r	469r	-	-	-	-	-	-	9r
Other	-	-	-	-	-	-	-	-	-
Energy industry use	**7**	**1,120r**	**391**	**6,278r**	**6,672r**	**-**	**-**	**2,334r**	**16,802r**
Electricity generation	-	-	-	-	-	-	-	1,435r	1,435r
Oil & gas extraction	-	-	391	-	5,558r	-	-	35	5,983r
Petroleum refineries	-	-	-	6,077r	411r	-	-	429r	6,916r
Coal extraction	7	-	-	-	22r	-	-	117	145r
Coke manufacture	-	547r	-	-	1	-	-	-	548r
Blast furnaces	-	548r	-	141r	55	-	-	82	826r
Patent fuel manufacture	-	24	-	-	-	-	-	-	24
Pumped storage	-	-	-	-	-	-	-	75	75
Other	-	-	-	60r	626	-	-	162r	848r
Losses	**-**	**163r**	**-**	**-**	**539r**	**-**	**-**	**2,433**	**3,135r**
Final consumption	**3,893r**	**2,107r**	**-**	**78,385r**	**58,753r**	**802r**	**-**	**27,753r**	**171,693r**
Industry	**1,762r**	**1,611r**	**-**	**6,455r**	**16,539r**	**397r**	**-**	**9,532r**	**36,297r**
Unclassified	-	256r	-	2,347r	13	397r	-	-	3,014r
Iron and steel	12r	1,253r	-	97r	1,878r	-	-	841r	4,082r
Non-ferrous metals	212r	102	-	40r	479r	-	-	507	1,340r
Mineral products	425r	-	-	228r	1,257r	-	-	625r	2,535r
Chemicals	546r	-	-	327r	4,696r	-	-	1,836r	7,404r
Mechanical engineering etc.	22r	-	-	226r	880r	-	-	757r	1,886r
Electrical engineering etc.	6	-	-	48r	339	-	-	516	910r
Vehicles	68	-	-	145r	916r	-	-	483	1,611r
Food, beverages, etc.	202r	-	-	390r	2,543r	-	-	1,085r	4,220r
Textiles, leather, etc.	49r	-	-	124r	599	-	-	323	1,095r
Paper, printing etc.	118r	-	-	104r	1,445r	-	-	952r	2,619r
Other industries	102r	-	-	1,868r	1,310r	-	-	1,477r	4,756r
Construction	-	-	-	511r	184r	-	-	131r	826r
Transport	**-**	**-**	**-**	**53,987r**	**-**	**-**	**-**	**736r**	**54,723r**
Air	-	-	-	11,017r	-	-	-	-	11,017r
Rail	-	-	-	504r	-	-	-	-	504r
Road	-	-	-	41,399r	-	-	-	-	41,399r
National navigation	-	-	-	1,067r	-	-	-	-	1,067r
Pipelines	-	-	-	-	-	-	-	-	-
Other	**2,131r**	**496r**	**-**	**6,036r**	**41,095r**	**405**	**-**	**17,486**	**67,649r**
Domestic	1,914r	496r	-	3,162r	30,788r	231	-	9,485r	46,076r
Public admin	193r	-	-	1,401r	4,459r	95	-	1,931r	8,080r
Commercial	-	-	-	561r	3,536	-	-	5,739r	9,836r
Agriculture	5	-	-	752r	128	72	-	330	1,286r
Miscellaneous	19r	-	-	160	2,184r	7	-	-	2,371r
Non energy use	**-**	**-**	**-**	**11,907r**	**1,118r**	**-**	**-**	**-**	**13,025r**

(1) Includes all manufactured solid fuels, benzole, tars, coke oven gas and blast furnace gas.
(2) Includes colliery methane.
(3) Includes geothermal and solar heat.
(4) Stock fall (+), stock rise (-).
(5) Primary supply minus primary demand.

1.3 Aggregate energy balance 1998

Thousand tonnes of oil equivalent

	Coal	Manufactured fuel (1)	Primary oils	Petroleum products	Natural gas (2)	Renewable & waste (3)	Primary electricity	Electricity	Total
Supply									
Indigenous production	25,758r	-	145,263r	-	90,181r	2,077r	23,950r	-	287,229r
Imports	14,782r	590	52,352r	12,423r	910	-	-	1,083r	82,139r
Exports	-706r	-225r	-92,516r	-26,454r	-2,717	-	-	-11r	-122,629r
Marine bunkers	-	-	-	-3,256r	-	-	-	-	-3,256r
Stock change (4)	+907r	-99r	-649r	-96	-32	-	-	-	+31r
Primary supply	**40,740r**	**266r**	**104,450r**	**-17,383r**	**88,341r**	**2,077r**	**23,950r**	**1,072**	**243,514r**
Statistical difference (5)	+123r	-76r	-1,147r	+437r	+1,163r	-	-	+147r	+648r
Primary demand	**40,617r**	**342r**	**105,597r**	**-17,820r**	**87,178r**	**2,077r**	**23,950r**	**925r**	**242,865r**
Transfers	-	-129	-2,729r	2,706r	-52	-	-515r	515r	-205r
Transformation	**-36,853r**	**3,373r**	**-102,442r**	**99,719r**	**-22,412r**	**-1,212**	**-23,435r**	**30,532r**	**-52,731r**
Electricity generation	-29,865r	-911r	-	-1,482r	-22,417r	-1,212	-23,435r	30,532r	-48,785r
Major power producers	-28,713r	-	-	-784r	-20,317r	-147	-23,435r	28,188r	-45,208r
Autogenerators	-1,152r	-911r	-	-698r	-2,095r	-1,065	-	2,344r	-3,577r
Petroleum refineries	-	-	-102,442r	101,478r	-	-	-	-	-965r
Coke manufacture	-6,112r	5,737	-	-	-	-	-	-	-375r
Blast furnaces	-418r	-1,904	-	-277	-	-	-	-	-2,599r
Patent fuel manufacture	-459r	452	-	-	-	-	-	-	-7r
Other	-	-	-	-	-	-	-	-	-
Energy industry use	**4r**	**1,185**	**426**	**6,850r**	**6,582r**	**-**	**-**	**2,408r**	**17,455r**
Electricity generation	-	-	-	-	-	-	-	1,493r	1,493r
Oil and gas extraction	-	-	426	-	5,632r	-	-	46	6,103r
Petroleum refineries	-	-	-	6,655r	371r	-	-	442r	7,468r
Coal extraction	4r	-	-	-	28	-	-	115	147r
Coke manufacture	-	583	-	-	1	-	-	-	583
Blast furnaces	-	572r	-	141r	45	-	-	82r	840r
Patent fuel manufacture	-	30r	-	-	-	-	-	-	30r
Pumped storage	-	-	-	-	-	-	-	83	83
Other	-	-	-	55	505	-	-	148r	708r
Losses	**-**	**156**	**-**	**-**	**689**	**-**	**-**	**2,404r**	**3,249r**
Final consumption	**3,760r**	**2,246r**	**-**	**77,754r**	**57,442**	**865**	**-**	**27,160r**	**169,226r**
Industry	**1,650r**	**1,721r**	**-**	**6,328r**	**15,647r**	**461r**	**-**	**9,220r**	**35,027r**
Unclassified	-	292r	-	1,929r	15r	461r	-	-	2,697r
Iron and steel	7	1,334r	-	89r	1,732r	-	-	823r	3,983r
Non-ferrous metals	110r	95	-	41	477r	-	-	490	1,214r
Mineral products	504r	-	-	241	1,273r	-	-	614r	2,632r
Chemicals	468r	-	-	605r	4,254r	-	-	1,804r	7,131r
Mechanical engineering etc.	20	-	-	215r	862r	-	-	732r	1,828r
Electrical engineering etc.	2	-	-	92	302r	-	-	516	912r
Vehicles	32r	-	-	134	886r	-	-	480r	1,533r
Food, beverages, etc.	215r	-	-	418r	2,408r	-	-	1,022r	4,063r
Textiles, leather, etc.	50	-	-	100	625r	-	-	315	1,090r
Paper, printing etc.	76r	-	-	125r	1,331r	-	-	923r	2,454r
Other industries	166r	-	-	1,787r	1,295r	-	-	1,369r	4,618r
Construction	-	-	-	551r	189r	-	-	132	871r
Transport	**-**	**-**	**-**	**52,955r**	**-**	**-**	**-**	**728r**	**53,683r**
Air	-	-	-	10,237r	-	-	-	-	10,237r
Rail	-	-	-	522r	-	-	-	-	522r
Road	-	-	-	41,020r	-	-	-	-	41,020r
National navigation	-	-	-	1,175r	-	-	-	-	1,175r
Pipelines	-	-	-	-	-	-	-	-	-
Other	**2,109r**	**525r**	**-**	**6,687r**	**40,765r**	**404**	**-**	**17,211r**	**67,702r**
Domestic	1,819r	525r	-	3,543r	30,600	230	-	9,407r	46,124r
Public administration	220r	-	-	1,501r	4,509r	96	-	1,887r	8,212r
Commercial	-	-	-	605r	3,501	-	-	5,585r	9,691r
Agriculture	6	-	-	851r	116	72	-	333	1,377
Miscellaneous	65r	-	-	187r	2,039	6	-	-	2,298r
Non energy use	**-**	**-**	**-**	**11,784r**	**1,030r**	**-**	**-**	**-**	**12,814r**

(1) Includes all manufactured solid fuels, benzole, tars, coke oven gas and blast furnace gas.
(2) Includes colliery methane.
(3) Includes geothermal and solar heat.
(4) Stock fall (+), stock rise (-).
(5) Primary supply minus primary demand.

1.4 Value balance of traded energy in 2000[1]

£ million

	Coal	Manufactured solid fuels	Crude oil	Petroleum products	Natural gas	Electricity	Other fuels	Total
Supply								
Indigenous production	965	200	17,185	16,985	5,840	7,480	70	49,090
Imports	665	25	6,875	3,430	135	375	-	11,500
Exports	-30	-30	-12,560	-4,870	-575	-	-	-18,070
Marine bunkers	-	-	-	-285	-	-	-	-285
Stock change	+110	+5	+165	-35	+5	-	-	+255
Basic value of inland consumption	1,710	205	11,660	15,230	5,400	8,215	70	42,490
Tax and margins								
Distribution costs and margins	**300**	**35**	**-**	**1,880**	**4,090**	**7,375**	**-**	**13,680**
Electricity generation	20	-	-	10	-	-	-	30
Solid fuel manufacture	40	-	-	-	-	-	-	40
of which iron & steel sector	35	-	-	-	-	-	-	35
Iron & steel final use	-	5	-	5	-	-	-	10
Other industry	10	15	-	125	-	-	-	150
Air transport	-	-	-	210	-	-	-	210
Rail and national navigation	-	-	-	25	-	-	-	25
Road transport	-	-	-	965	-	-	-	965
Domestic	225	15	-	130	-	-	-	365
Agriculture	-	-	-	25	-	-	-	25
Commercial and other services	5	-	-	60	-	-	-	65
Non energy use	-	-	-	330	95	-	-	425
VAT and duties	**15**	**5**	**-**	**30,325**	**265**	**350**	**-**	**30,965**
Electricity generation	-	-	-	30	-	-	-	30
Iron & steel final use	-	-	-	15	-	-	-	15
Other industry	-	-	-	125	-	-	-	125
Air transport	-	-	-	20	-	-	-	20
Rail and national navigation	-	-	-	50	-	-	-	50
Road transport	-	-	-	29,970	-	-	-	29,.970
Domestic	15	5	-	40	265	350	-	680
Agriculture	-	-	-	20	-	-	-	20
Commercial and other services	-	-	-	60	--	-	-	**60**
Total tax and margins	**320**	**40**	**-**	**322,205**	**4,350**	**7,730**	**-**	**44,645**
Market value of inland consumption	**2,025**	**245**	**11,660**	**47,435**	**9,755**	**15,940**	**70**	**87,135**
Energy end use								
Total energy sector	**1,625**	**-**	**11,660**	**210**	**2,065**	**165**	**10**	**15,740**
Transformation	1,625	-	11,660	200	1,975	-	10	15,480
Electricity generation	1,320	-	-	200	1,975	-	10	3,510
of which from stocks	25	-	-	-	-	-	-	25
Petroleum refineries	-	-	11,660	-	-	-	-	11,660
Solid fuel manufacture	305	-	-	-	-	-	-	305
of which iron & steel sector	270	-	-	-	-	-	-	270
Other energy sector use	**-**	**-**	**-**	**10**	**90**	**165**	**-**	**265**
Oil & gas extraction	-	-	-	-	-	15	-	15
Petroleum refineries	-	-	-	-	40	105	-	140
Coal extraction	-	-	-	-	-	50	-	50
Other energy sector	-	-	-	10	50	-	-	60
Total non energy sector use	**400**	**245**	**-**	**45,560**	**7,620**	**15,775**	**60**	**69,665**
Industry	**55**	**120**	**-**	**1,165**	**1,140**	**3,430**	**30**	**5,940**
Iron & steel final use	15	75	-	65	130	135	-	425
Other industry	40	45	-	1,095	1,010	3,295	30	5,520
Transport	**-**	**-**	**-**	**43,185**	**-**	**285**	**-**	**43,470**
Air	-	-	-	2,460	-	-	-	2,460
Rail and national navigation	-	-	-	280	-	285	-	565
Road	-	-	-	40,445	-	-	-	40,445
Other final users	**345**	**125**	**-**	**1,215**	**6,480**	**12,055**	**30**	**20,255**
Domestic	330	125	-	735	5,525	7,390	30	14,145
Agriculture	-	-	-	130	15	230	-	370
Commercial and other services	10	-	-	350	940	4,435	-	5,740
Total value of energy end use	**2,025**	**245**	**11,660**	**45,770**	**9,690**	**15,940**	**70**	**85,405**
Value of non energy end use	**-**	**-**	**-**	**1,660**	**65**	**-**	**-**	**1,725**
Market value of inland consumption	**2,025**	**245**	**11,660**	**47,435**	**9,755**	**15,940**	**70**	**87,135**

(1) For further information see paragraphs 1.57 to 1.62.

1.5 Value balance of traded energy in 1999[1]

£ million

	Coal	Manufactured solid fuels	Crude oil	Petroleum products	Natural gas	Electricity	Other fuels	Total
Supply								
Indigenous production	1,160r	215r	10,910	11,105r	4,830	7,620	75r	35,915r
Imports	565	20	3,280	1,960	25	395	-	6,250r
Exports	-40	-20	-7,155	-2,855	-225	-	-	-10,295
Marine bunkers	-	-	-	-190	-	-	-	-190
Stock change	-40r	-	-30	+60	-5	-	-	-10r
Basic value of inland consumption	1,645	215r	7,005	10,085r	4,630	8,015	75r	31,670r
Tax and margins								
Distribution costs and margins	305r	30	-	1,255	4,250	7,935	-	13,780r
Electricity generation	25r	-	-	5	-	-	-	25r
Solid fuel manufacture	10	-	-	-	-	-	-	10
of which iron & steel sector	5	-	-	-	-	-	-	5
Iron & steel final use	-	5	-	-	-	-	-	5
Other industry	25	15	-	35r	-	-	-	75r
Air transport	-	-	-	40r	-	-	-	40r
Rail and national navigation	-	-	-	-	-	-	-	-
Road transport	-	-	-	765r	-	-	-	765r
Domestic	240r	15	-	85r	-	-	-	340r
Agriculture	-	-	-	10	-	-	-	10
Commercial and other services	5	-	-	30	-	-	-	40r
Non energy use	-	-	-	285r	70r	-	-	355r
VAT and duties	20	5	-	29,975r	245	355	-	30,605r
Electricity generation	-	-	-	20r	-	-	-	20r
Iron & steel final use	-	-	-	15	-	-	-	15
Other industry	-	-	-	120	-	-	-	120
Air transport	-	-	-	15	-	-	-	15
Rail and national navigation	-	-	-	50	-	-	-	50
Road transport	-	-	-	29,640r	-	-	-	29,640r
Domestic	20	5	-	30r	245	355	-	655
Agriculture	-	-	-	25	-	-	-	25
Commercial and other services	-	-	-	65r	-	-	-	65r
Total tax and margins	325r	40r	-	31,235r	4,500r	8,290	-	44,385r
Market value of inland consumption	1,970r	250	7,005	41,315r	9,130r	16,305	75r	76,055r
Energy end use								
Total energy sector	1,440r	-	7,005	105r	1,960r	140	15	10,665r
Transformation	1,440r	-	7,005	100r	1,885r	-	15	10,445r
Electricity generation	1,170r	-	-	100r	1,885r	-	15	3,170r
of which from stocks	30	-	-	-	-	-	-	30
Petroleum refineries	-	-	7,005	-	-	-	-	7,005
Solid fuel manufacture	270r	-	-	-	-	-	-	270r
of which iron & steel sector	225	-	-	-	-	-	-	225
Other energy sector use	-	-	-	5	75r	140	-	220r
Oil & gas extraction	-	-	-	-	-	15	-	15
Petroleum refineries	-	-	-	-	30r	80	-	110r
Coal extraction	-	-	-	-	-	45	-	45r
Other energy sector	-	-	-	5	45	-	-	50
Total non energy sector use	530r	250	-	39,710r	7,105r	16,165	65r	63,825r
Industry	110r	120r	-	785r	1,055r	3,705	35r	5,805r
Iron & steel final use	15	75	-	50	115	230	-	485r
Other industry	95r	45r	-	735r	935r	3,475	35r	5,320r
Transport	-	-	-	38,080r	-	305	-	38,385r
Air	-	-	-	1,210r	-	-	-	1,210r
Rail and national navigation	-	-	-	190r	-	305	-	500
Road	-	-	-	36,680r	-	-	-	36,680r
Other final users	425r	135	-	840r	6,050r	12,155	30	19,630r
Domestic	405r	135	-	465r	5,175	7,450	30	13,660r
Agriculture	-	-	-	100	15	220	-	335
Commercial and other services	15	-	-	275r	865r	4,480	-	5,635r
Total value of energy end use	1,970r	250	7,005	39,815r	9,065r	16,305	75r	74,490r
Value of non energy end use	-	-	-	1,500r	65	-	-	1,565r
Market value of inland consumption	1,970r	250	7,005	41,315r	9,130r	16,305	75r	76,055r

(1) For further information see paragraphs 1.57 to 1.62.

1.6 Value balance of traded energy in 1998[1]

£ million

	Coal	Manufactured solid fuels	Crude oil	Petroleum products	Natural gas	Electricity	Other fuels	Total
Supply								
Indigenous production	1,315r	160r	8,080r	8,880r	5,250r	7,640	75r	31,405r
Imports	640	45	2,275	1,410	45	375	-	4,785
Exports	-45	-25	-5,085r	-2,300	-80	-	-	-7,530r
Marine bunkers	-	-	-	-230	-	-	-	-230
Stock change	40r	5	-35	-5	-	-	-	-r
Basic value of inland consumption	1,950	190r	5,235r	7,755r	5,215r	8,015	75r	28,435r
Tax and margins								
Distribution costs and margins	330r	80	-	1,875r	4,265r	8,310	-	14,860r
Electricity generation	35	-	-	-	-	-	-	35r
Solid fuel manufacture	35	-	-	-	-	-	-	35
of which iron & steel sector	35	-	-	-	-	-	-	35
Iron & steel final use	-	10	-	-	-	-	-	10
Other industry	15	20	-	60	-	-	-	100r
Air transport	-	-	-	85	-	-	-	85
Rail and national navigation	-	-	-	15	-	-	-	15
Road transport	-	-	-	1,355	-	-	-	1,355
Domestic	225	50	-	120	-	-	-	395
Agriculture	-	-	-	25	-	-	-	30
Commercial and other services	10	-	-	70	-	-	-	80
Non energy use	-	-	-	145r	65r	-	-	215r
VAT and duties	20	5	-	24,460r	285	365	-	25,140r
Electricity generation	-	-	-	25	-	-	-	25r
Iron & steel final use	-	-	-	10	-	-	-	10
Other industry	-	-	-	120r	-	-	-	120r
Air transport	-	-	-	10	-	-	-	10
Rail and national navigation	-	-	-	50	-	-	-	50
Road transport	-	-	-	24,130	-	-	-	24,130
Domestic	20	5	-	30	285	365	-	710
Agriculture	-	-	-	25	-	-	-	25
Commercial and other services	-	-	-	65	-	-	-	65
Total tax and margins	345	85	-	26,335r	4,555r	8,675	-	40,000r
Market value of inland consumption	2,300r	275r	5,235r	34,090r	9,770r	16,690	75r	68,435r
Energy end use								
Total energy sector	1,780	-	5,235r	125r	1,775r	180	10	9,105r
Transformation	1,780	-	5,235r	115r	1,710r	-	10	8,855r
Electricity generation	1,440	-	-	115r	1,710r	-	10	3,275r
of which from stocks	35	-	-	-	-	-	-	35
Petroleum refineries	-	-	5,235r	-	-	-	-	5,235r
Solid fuel manufacture	340	-	-	-	-	-	-	340
of which iron & steel sector	305	-	-	-	-	-	-	305
Other energy sector use	-	-	-	5	65	180	-	255r
Oil & gas extraction	-	-	-	-	-	15r	-	15r
Petroleum refineries	-	-	-	-	30r	115	-	145r
Coal extraction	-	-	-	-	-	50r	-	50
Other energy sector	-	-	-	5	40	-	-	45
Total non energy sector use	515	275r	-	32,555r	7,925r	16,515	70r	57,855r
Industry	110	135r	-	715r	1020r	3,535	40r	5,555r
Iron & steel final use	20	80	-	45	110r	230r	-	485
Other industry	85r	55r	-	670r	910r	3,305r	40r	5,070r
Transport	-	-	-	30,965	-	300	-	31,265
Air	-	-	-	965	-	-	-	965
Rail and national navigation	-	-	-	190r	-	300	-	495
Road	-	-	-	29,810	-	-	-	29,810
Other final users	410r	140	-	875	6,905	12,675	30	21,030r
Domestic	385	140	-	465	6,015	7,700	30	14,730
Agriculture	-	-	-	115	10	220	-	345
Commercial and other services	25r	-	-	295	875	4,755	-	5,955r
Total value of energy end use	2,300r	275r	5,235r	32,680r	9,705r	16,690	75r	66,960r
Value of non energy end use	-	-	-	1,410r	65	-	-	1,475r
Market value of inland consumption	2,300r	275r	5,235r	34,090r	9,770r	16,690	75r	68,435r

(1) For further information see paragraphs 1.56 to 1.61.

1.7 Sales of electricity and gas by sector

United Kingdom

	1996	1997	1998	1999	2000
Total selling value (£ million) (1)					
Electricity generation - Gas	1,198	1,619	1,749	1,921	1,860
Industrial - Gas	891	920	1,053	1,120	1,290
- Electricity	4,075	3,805	3,698	3,844	3,598
of which:					
Fuel industries	221	179	162	141	166
Industrial sector	3,854	3,626	3,536	3,703	3,432
Domestic sector - Gas	6,067	5,725	5,290	4,928	5,264
- Electricity	7,759	7,443	7,335	7,096	7,040
Other - Gas	998	894	910	915	1,021
- Electricity	5,632	5,422	5,275	5,010	4,951
of which:					
Agricultural sector	260	246	219	222	228
Commercial sector	3,702	3,689	3,577	3,363	3,374
Transport sector	309	297	301	306	287
Public lighting	145	146	122	100	99
Public admin. and other services	1,216	1,044	1,056	1,019	963
Total, all consumers	**26,620**	**25,828**	**25,310**	**24,834**	**25,024**
of which gas	**9,154**	**9,158**	**9,002**	**8,884**	**9,435**
of which electricity	**17,466**	**16,670**	**16,308**	**15,950**	**15,589**
Average net selling value per kWh sold (pence) (1)					
Electricity generation - Gas	0.628	0.647	0.656	0.613	0.595
Industrial - Gas	0.472	0.516	0.565	0.548	0.582
- Electricity	4.159	3.860	3.795	3.900	3.529
of which:					
Fuel industries	4.013	3.530	3.585	3.436	3.524
Industrial sector	4.167	3.878	3.806	3.920	3.530
Domestic sector - Gas	1.700	1.657	1.468	1.399	1.423
- Electricity	7.172	6.984	6.583	6.495	6.295
Other - Gas	0.816	0.749	0.770	0.757	0.805
- Electricity	6.032	5.519	5.377	5.052	4.912
of which:					
Agricultural sector	6.803	6.463	5.711	5.736	6.033
Commercial sector	6.138	5.565	5.399	5.061	4.938
Transport sector	4.615	4.316	4.430	4.459	4.018
Public lighting	5.625	5.450	5.563	5.097	4.985
Public admin. and other services	6.091	5.616	5.549	5.090	4.921
Average, all consumers	**2.298**	**2.158**	**2.044**	**1.913**	**1.860**
of which gas	**1.066**	**1.025**	**0.966**	**0.897**	**0.915**
of which electricity	**5.831**	**5.495**	**5.313**	**5.196**	**4.955**

(1) Excludes VAT where payable - see paragraph 1.63 for a definition of average net selling value.

			Thousand tonnes of oil equivalent		
	1996	1997	1998	1999	2000
Iron and steel and non-ferrous metals					
Coal	78r	90	117r	224r	72
Manufactured solid fuels (2)	936	833	764	791r	752
Blast furnace gas	702	754r	289r	224r	129
Coke oven gas	536	560r	375r	342r	348
Natural gas	2,236	2,167r	2,209r	2,357r	2,332
Petroleum	142r	165r	130r	137r	178
Electricity	1,250r	1,282	1,313r	1,348r	1,357
Total iron and steel and non-ferrous metals	**5,879r**	**5,850r**	**5,198r**	**5,422r**	**5,167**
Chemicals					
Coal	395r	425r	468r	546r	292
Natural gas	3,135	3,971	4,254r	4,696r	4,915
Petroleum	754r	558	605r	327r	384
Electricity	1,635r	1,667	1,804r	1,836r	1,961
Total chemicals	**5,920r**	**6,620**	**7,131r**	**7,404r**	**7,552**
Metal products, machinery and equipment					
Coal	97r	86r	54r	96r	53
Natural gas	1,920	1,872	2,050r	2,136r	2,258
Petroleum	622r	515	441r	419r	422
Electricity	1,704r	1,727	1,728r	1,757r	1,795
Total metal products, machinery and equipment	**4,343r**	**4,201r**	**4,273r**	**4,407r**	**4,528**
Food, beverages and tobacco					
Coal	250r	252	215r	202r	137
Natural gas	2,333	2,295	2,408r	2,543r	2,755
Petroleum	621r	480	418r	390r	310
Electricity	974r	995	1,022r	1,085r	1,071
Total food, beverages and tobacco	**4,178r**	**4,022**	**4,063r**	**4,220r**	**4,272**

(1) Industrial categories used are described in Table 1G.
(2) Includes tars, benzole, coke and breeze and other manufactured solid fuel.

1.8 Final energy consumption by main industrial groups[1] (continued)

					Thousand tonnes of oil equivalent
	1996	1997	1998	1999	2000
Paper, printing and publishing					
Coal	171r	152	76r	118r	75
Natural gas	1,289	1,189	1,331r	1,445r	1,511
Petroleum	172r	126	125r	104r	75
Electricity	821r	927	923r	952r	970
Total paper, printing and publishing	**2,452r**	**2,394**	**2,454r**	**2,619r**	**2,631**
Other industries					
Coal	980r	942r	720r	576r	313
Natural gas	3,069	3,179	3,381r	3,350r	3,472
Petroleum	2,755r	2,557r	2,679r	2,731r	2,685
Electricity	2,381r	2,423	2,430r	2,555r	2,606
Total other industries	**9,186r**	**9,101r**	**9,211r**	**9,212r**	**9,075**
Unclassified					
Manufactured solid fuels (2)	152r	203r	282r	244r	231
Coke oven gas	18	19	10	11	29
Natural gas	17	13	15	13	10
Petroleum	1,992r	1,914	1,929r	2,347r	2,318
Renewables & waste	533	532	461r	397r	364
Total unclassified	**2,711r**	**2,680**	**2,697r**	**3,012r**	**2,952**
Total					
Coal	1,971r	1,948r	1,650r	1,762r	941
Manufactured solid fuels (2)	1,088	1,035	1,046r	1,035r	982
Blast furnace gas	702	754r	289r	224r	129
Coke oven gas	554	579r	385r	353r	377
Natural gas	14,000r	14,685	15,647r	16,539r	17,254
Petroleum	7,058r	6,315r	6,328r	6,455r	6,373
Renewables & waste	533	532	461r	397r	364
Electricity	8,764r	9,020	9,220r	9,532r	9,759
Total	**34,670r**	**34,868r**	**35,027r**	**36,297r**	**36,178**

1.9 Fuels consumed for electricity generation (autogeneration) by main industrial groups[1]

Thousand tonnes of oil equivalent
(except where shown otherwise)

	1996	1997	1998	1999	2000
Iron and steel and non-ferrous metals					
Coal	789	788	851r	714r	693
Blast furnace gas	694	693	719r	723r	722
Coke oven gas	140	136	158r	158r	158
Natural gas	31	32	48r	44r	44
Petroleum	62	59	59r	56r	56
Other (including renewables) (2)	62	64	89r	80r	80
Total fuel input (3)	**1,778**	**1,772**	**1,924r**	**1,775r**	**1,753**
Electricity generated by iron and steel and non-ferrous metals (4)	**532** 6,187 GWh	**553** 6,428 GWh	**536r** 6,231 GWh	**545r** 6,338 GWh	**459** 5,338 GWh
Electricity consumed by iron and steel and non-ferrous metals from own generation (5)	**366** 4,257 GWh	**382** 4,444 GWh	**387r** 4,505 GWh	**400r** 4,657 GWh	**369** 4,292 GWh
Chemicals					
Coal	311	279	171r	73r	54
Natural gas	813	926	709r	577r	795
Petroleum	146	131	71r	74r	40
Other (including renewables) (2)	78	78	391r	365r	386
Total fuel input (3)	**1,348**	**1,414**	**1,342r**	**1,089r**	**1,275**
Electricity generated by chemicals (4)	**456** 5,303 GWh	**476** 5,538 GWh	**674r** 7,841 GWh	**702r** 8,160 GWh	**857** 9,962 GWh
Electricity consumed by chemicals from own generation (5)	**379** 4,408 GWh	**397** 4,613 GWh	**556r** 6,469 GWh	**557r** 6,474 GWh	**675** 7,852 GWh
Metal products, machinery and equipment					
Coal	4	2	-r	-	-
Natural gas	24	29	18r	20r	38
Petroleum	-	-	7	7	7
Other (including renewables) (2)	-	-	-	-	-
Total fuel input (3)	**28**	**31**	**24r**	**27r**	**45**
Electricity generated by metal products, machinery and equipment (4)	**13** 145 GWh	**14** 166 GWh	**12r** 143 GWh	**14r** 160 GWh	**24** 283 GWh
Electricity consumed by metal products, machinery and equipment from own generation (5)	**12** 139 GWh	**14** 159 GWh	**12r** 137 GWh	**13r** 153 GWh	**10** 110 GWh
Food, beverages and tobacco					
Coal	30	33	24r	20r	13
Natural gas	126	150	173r	310r	285
Petroleum	26	18	11r	9r	1
Other (including renewables) (2)	-	-	-	-	-
Total fuel input (3)	**182**	**201**	**208r**	**338r**	**299**
Electricity generated by food, beverages and tobacco (4)	**77** 896 GWh	**85** 991 GWh	**123r** 1,432 GWh	**199r** 2,313 GWh	**216** 2,509 GWh
Electricity consumed by food, beverages and tobacco from own generation (5)	**64** 749 GWh	**72** 838 GWh	**106r** 1,236 GWh	**180r** 2,098 GWh	**130** 1,517 GWh

(1) Industrial categories used are described in Table 1G.
(2) Includes hydro electricity, solid and gaseous renewables and waste.
(3) Total fuels used for generation of electricity. Consistent with figures for fuels used by other generators in Table 5.4.

1.9 Fuels consumed for electricity generation (autogeneration) by main industrial groups[1] (continued)

Thousand tonnes of oil equivalent
(except where shown otherwise)

	1996	1997	1998	1999	2000
Paper, printing and publishing					
Coal	76	56	62r	55r	37
Natural gas	294	417	323r	388r	385
Petroleum	11	12	7r	11r	9
Other (including renewables) (2)	-	-	-r	-	-
Total fuel input (3)	**381**	**485**	**393r**	**455r**	**430**
Electricity generated by paper, printing and publishing (4)	**168** 1,953 GWh	**222** 2,580 GWh	**233r** 2,705 GWh	**274r** 3,182 GWh	**297** 3,458 GWh
Electricity consumed by paper, printing and publishing from own generation (5)	**156** 1,808 GWh	**207** 2,407 GWh	**215r** 2,503 GWh	**245r** 2,854 GWh	**252** 2,927 GWh
Other industries					
Coal	-	-	22r	22r	22
Coke oven gas	20	20	4r	5r	6
Natural gas	35	30	62r	55r	81
Petroleum	6	8	21r	13r	8
Other (including renewables) (2)	367	435	515r	838r	838
Total fuel input (3)	**428**	**493**	**625r**	**933r**	**955**
Electricity generated by other industries (4)	**88** 1,023 GWh	**86** 1,001 GWh	**92r** 1,072 GWh	**96r** 1,118 GWh	**116** 1,353 GWh
Electricity consumed by other industries from own generation (5)	**27** 311 GWh	**20** 238 GWh	**60r** 692 GWh	**68r** 794 GWh	**75** 867 GWh
Total					
Coal	1,210	1,158	1,131r	884r	819
Blast furnace gas	694	693	719r	723r	722
Coke oven gas	160	156	162r	163r	164
Natural gas	1,323	1,584	1,332r	1,393r	1,628
Petroleum	251	228	176r	169r	121
Other (including renewables) (2)	507	577	995r	1,283r	1,304
Total fuel input (3)	**4,145**	**4,396**	**4,514r**	**4,616r**	**4,758**
Electricity generated (4)	**1,333** 15,507 GWh	**1,436** 16,704 GWh	**1,670r** 19,424 GWh	**1,829r** 21,270 GWh	**1,969** 22,903 GWh
Electricity consumed from own generation (5)	**1,004** 11,672 GWh	**1,092** 12,699 GWh	**1,336r** 15,542 GWh	**1,464r** 17,028 GWh	**1,510** 17,564 GWh

(4) Combined heat and power (CHP) generation (i.e. electrical output from Table 6.8) plus non-chp generation, so that the total electricity generated is consistent with the "other generators" figures in Table 5.6.

(5) This is the electricity consumed by the industrial sector from its own generation and is consistent with the other generators finalisers figures used within the electricity balances (Tables 5.1 and 5.2). These figures are less than the total generated because some of the electricity is sold to the public distribution system and other users.

(6) The figures presented here are consistent with other figures presented elsewhere in this publication as detailed at (3), (4), and (5) above but are further disaggregated. Overall totals covering all autogenerators can be derived by adding in figures for transport, services and the fuel industries. These can be summarised as follows:

Fuel input	1996	1997	1998	1999	2000
			Thousand tonnes of oil equivalent		
All industry	4,145	4,396	4,514	4,616	4,758
Fuel industries	1,087	1,239	950	838	486
Transport	373	385	385	388	366
Services	412	498	660	929	964
Total fuel input	6,017	6,518	6,510	6,770	6,574
Electricity generated	1,952	2,105	2,495	2,741	2,847
Electricity consumed	1,446	1,543	1,907	2,072	2,065
					GWh
Electricity generated	22,704	24,478	29,019	31,879	33,115
Electricity consumed	16,823	17,945	22,180	24,098	24,012

1.10 Inland consumption of primary fuels and equivalents for energy use, 1970 to 2000

		1970	1971	1972	1973	1974	1975	1976	1977
In original units of measurement									
	Unit								
Coal *(1)*	M.tonnes	156.9	139.3	122.4	133.0	117.9	120.0	122.0	122.7
Petroleum *(2)*	"	87.0	88.0	94.2	95.3	88.5	79.4	77.8	79.3
Natural gas *(3)*	GWh	131,472	212,037	300,808	325,455	389,286	407,750	432,661	459,858
Nuclear electricity *(4)*	"	26,039	27,418	29,275	27,757	33,377	30,215	35,570	39,575
Hydro electricity *(4)(5)*	"	4,539	3,397	3,429	3,874	4,095	3,789	4,552	3,919
Million tonnes of oil equivalent									
Coal *(1)*		99.0	87.7	76.8	83.2	73.3	73.7	75.0	75.3
Petroleum *(2)*		92.4	93.5	100.2	101.5	94.3	85.0	83.5	85.1
Natural gas *(3)*		11.3	18.2	25.9	28.0	33.5	35.1r	37.2	39.5
Nuclear electricity		7.0	7.4	7.9	7.5	9.0	8.1	9.6	10.6
Hydro electricity *(5)*		0.4	0.3	0.3	0.3	0.4	0.3	0.4	0.3
Total		210.1	207.1	211.0	220.5	210.4	202.2	205.6	210.9
Percentage shares (energy supplied basis)									
Coal		47.1	42.3	36.4	37.7	34.8	36.5	36.5	35.7
Petroleum		44.0	45.2	47.5	46.0	44.8	42.0	40.6	40.4
Natural gas		5.4	8.8	12.3	12.7	15.9	17.3	18.1	18.7
Nuclear electricity		3.3	3.6	3.7	3.4	4.3	4.0	4.6	5.0
Hydro electricity		0.2	0.1	0.1	0.2	0.2	0.2	0.2	0.2

		1978	1979	1980	1981	1982	1983	1984	1985
In original units of measurement									
	Unit								
Coal *(1)*	M.tonnes	119.9	129.6	120.8	118.2	110.7	111.5	79.0	105.3
Petroleum *(2)*	"	81.2	81.6	70.5	64.2	65.2	61.7	78.6	66.5
Natural gas *(3)*	GWh	477,002	521,197	521,051	528,114	525,476	547,750	560,410	602,701
Nuclear electricity *(4)*	"	37,065	38,062	36,870	37,897	44,212	50,138	53,957	61,391
Hydro electricity *(4)(5)*	"	4,038	4,289	3,934	4,383	4,558	4,563	4,005	4,093
Net electricity imports									
Million tonnes of oil equivalent									
Coal *(1)*		73.3	78.8	73.3	72.9	68.0	68.6	48.7	64.8
Petroleum *(2)*		87.2	87.7	76.2	69.5	70.7	67.2	84.7	72.2
Natural gas *(3)*		41.0	44.8r	44.8	45.4	45.2	47.1	48.2	51.8
Nuclear electricity		10.0	10.2	9.9	10.2	11.9	13.5	14.5	16.5
Hydro electricity *(5)*		0.3	0.4	0.3	0.4	0.4	0.4	0.3	0.4
Total		211.8	221.9	204.5	198.4	196.1	196.8	196.4	205.7
Percentage shares (energy supplied basis)									
Coal		34.6	35.5	35.8	36.7	34.7	34.9	24.8	31.5
Petroleum		41.2	39.5	37.3	35.0	36.0	34.2	43.1	35.1
Natural gas		19.4	20.2	21.9	22.9	23.0	23.9	24.5	25.2
Nuclear electricity		4.7	4.6	4.8	5.1	6.1	6.8	7.4	8.0
Hydro electricity		0.2	0.2	0.2	0.2	0.2	0.2	0.2	0.2

(1) Includes other solid fuels.
(2) Excludes petroleum for non-energy use and marine bunkers. The petroleum figures from 1970 to 1995 have been revised since the last edition to be on a consistent basis with the balances fomat; this will in turn affect the totals and percentage shares. For details see paragraph 3.44 in Chapter 3.
(3) Includes colliery methane, non-energy use of natural gas up to 1988. Following the introduction of the presentation of energy data in the format of an energy balance it has been possible to separately identify the losses from the statistical difference for gas, bringing gas onto the same basis as other fuels. This has resulted in downwards revisions of the consumption figures for gas from 1994 onwards.
(4) Electricity generated i.e. including own use.
(5) Excludes pumped storage. Includes generation at wind stations from 1988.

1.10 Inland consumption of primary fuels and equivalents for energy use, 1970 to 2000 (continued)

	Unit	1986	1987	1988	1989	1990	1991	1992	1993
In original units of measurement									
Coal (1)	M.tonnes	113.5	116.2	112.0	108.1	108.4	107.6	101.1	87.4
Petroleum (2)	"	65.3	63.5	67.8	69.0	70.6	70.6	70.9	71.5
Natural gas (3)	GWh	612,724	629,311	597,220	571,187	595,131	643,863	640,459	732,090
Nuclear electricity (4)	"	59,079	55,238	63,456	71,734	65,749	70,543	76,807	76,807
Hydro electricity (4)(5)	"	4,780	4,198	4,919	4,758	5,216	4,635	5,465	5,465
Net electricity imports	"	4,255	11,635	12,830	12,631	11,943	16,408	16,694	16,716
Million tonnes of oil equivalent									
Coal (1)		70.0	71.7	70.0	67.0	66.9	67.1	63.0	55.0
Petroleum (2)		71.1	69.4	74.0	75.4	77.2	77.1	77.5	78.1
Natural gas (3)		52.7	54.1	51.4r	49.1r	51.2	55.4r	55.1	62.9r
Nuclear electricity		15.4	14.4	16.6	17.7	16.3	17.4	18.5	21.6
Hydro electricity (5)		0.4	0.4	0.4	0.4	0.4	0.4	0.5	0.5r
Net electricity imports		0.4	1.0	1.1	1.1	1.0	1.4	1.4	1.4
Renewables & waste					0.7	0.7	0.7	0.8	1.2
Total (6)		210.0	211.0	213.5	211.4	213.6	219.5	216.7	220.7
Percentage shares (energy supplied basis)									
Coal		33.3	34.0	32.8	31.7	31.3	30.6	29.1	24.9
Petroleum		33.9	32.9	34.7	35.7	36.1	35.1	35.8	35.4
Natural gas		25.1	25.6	24.1	23.2	24.0	25.2	25.4	28.5
Nuclear electricity		7.4	6.8	7.8	8.4	7.6	7.9	8.5	9.8
Hydro electricity		0.2	0.2	0.2	0.2	0.2	0.2	0.2	0.2
Net electricity imports		0.2	0.5	0.5	0.5	0.5	0.6	0.7	0.7
Renewables & waste					0.3	0.3	0.3	0.4	0.5

	Unit	1994	1995	1996	1997	1998	1999	2000
In original units of measurement								
Coal (1)	M.tonnes	82.1	77.2	72.1r	63.5r	63.6r	56.5r	58.9
Petroleum (2)	"	70.0	68.9	71.3	68.7	69.1r	69.1r	68.4
Natural gas (3)	GWh	754,284	805,058	940,372	961,968	1,001,954r	1,062,560r	1,103,312
Nuclear electricity (4)	"	89,353	88,282	94,671	98,146	99,486r	95,133r	85,063
Hydro electricity (4)(5)	"	4,521	5,438	3,847	4,836	5,994r	6,212r	6,057
Net electricity imports	"	16,887	16,313	16,677	16,574r	12,468	14,244	14,174
Million tonnes of oil equivalent								
Coal (1)		51.3	48.9	45.7r	40.8r	41.0r	36.7r	38.1
Petroleum (2)		76.7	75.4	77.8r	75.4	76.0r	75.9r	75.2
Natural gas (3)		64.9r	69.2	80.9	82.7	86.2r	91.4r	94.9
Nuclear electricity		21.2	21.3r	22.1	23.0	23.4r	22.2r	19.6
Hydro electricity (5)		0.4r	0.5	0.3	0.4	0.5	0.5	0.5
Net electricity imports		1.5	1.4	1.4	1.4	1.1	1.2	1.2
Renewables & waste		1.6	1.7	1.8	1.9	2.1	2.2	2.5
Total (6)		217.5	218.4	230.3	226.1r	230.7r	230.7r	232.5
Percentage shares (energy supplied basis)								
Coal		23.6	22.4	19.9r	18.0r	17.8r	15.9r	16.4
Petroleum		35.3	34.5	33.8	33.4r	32.9r	32.9r	32.3
Natural gas		29.8	31.7r	35.1r	36.6	37.3r	39.6r	40.8
Nuclear electricity		9.7	9.7r	9.6	10.2	10.2r	9.6r	8.4
Hydro electricity		0.2	0.2	0.1	0.2	0.2	0.2	0.2
Net electricity imports		0.7	0.6	0.6	0.6	0.5	0.5	0.5
Renewables & waste		0.7	0.8	0.8	0.8	0.9	1.0	1.1

(6) Following the introduction of the energy balance presentation it has been possible to separately identify the losses from the statistical difference for electricity, bringing electricity onto the same basis as other fuels. This has been accounted for in the total from 1994 onwards.

1.11 Availability and consumption of primary fuels and equivalents (energy supplied basis) 1970 to 2000

Thousand tonnes of oil equivalent

	Available supply												
	Production					Imports					Exports		
	Coal	Petroleum	Natural gas	Primary electricity	Total	Coal	Petroleum	Natural gas	Elec-tricity	Total	Coal	Petroleum	Total
		(1)	(2)	(3)	(4)	(5)	(6)				(5)	(6)	(7)
1970	92,792	166	10,461	7,388	110,807	81	131,142	839	48	132,109	2,620	19,762	22,381
1971	94,178	227	17,384	7,661	119,450	2,887	136,359	836	10	140,092	2,048	20,024	22,071
1972	76,484	358	25,084	8,163	110,089	3,408	138,253	771	40	142,472	1,433	21,160	22,593
1973	82,636	400	27,235	7,793	118,064	1,214	144,117	738	5	146,074	2,131	22,026	24,157
1974	68,630	438	32,847	9,322	111,237	2,317	136,472	612	5	139,407	2,149	17,283	19,432
1975	79,172	1,675	34,203	8,446	123,496	3,209	111,703	844	8	115,763	1,975	16,517	18,492
1976	75,988	13,114	36,221	9,951	135,274	2,010	108,818	967	-	111,796	1,506	21,671	23,177
1977	74,769	41,186	37,845	10,973	164,773	1,761	90,004	1,680	-	93,445	1,753	33,112	34,865
1978	75,479	58,184	36,241	10,308	180,212	1,736	85,815	4,758	-	92,309	2,164	41,289	43,460
1979	74,028	83,966	36,596	10,598	205,188	3,169	77,903	8,323	-	89,394	2,025	57,607	59,632
1980	78,502	86,911	34,790	10,247	210,450	5,030	60,385	9,995	-	75,411	3,320	58,385	61,705
1981	78,008	96,941	34,712	10,562	220,223	3,192	50,040	10,681	-	63,912	6,884	69,615	76,500
1982	76,069	112,519	35,281	12,274	236,143	3,360	49,944	9,885	-	63,189	5,693	80,595	86,288
1983	72,696	125,482	36,379	13,866	248,423	3,713	43,543	10,701	-	57,957	4,844	90,608	95,452
1984	30,719	137,646	35,563	14,845	218,773	7,980	59,146	12,606	-	79,731	1,668	101,289	102,957
1985	56,572	139,404	39,679	16,851	252,506	9,482	52,577	12,645	-	74,703	2,441	106,602	109,043
1986	65,592	139,084	41,717	15,839	262,232	7,794	57,610	11,784	366	77,553	2,615	112,166	114,796
1987	63,189	135,071	43,674	14,797	256,731	7,363	54,305	11,079	1,000	73,746	1,872	107,108	108,980
1988	63,303	125,469	42,059	16,990	248,469	9,270	58,254	9,922	1,103	78,550	1,595	97,266	98,861
1989	60,882	100,373	41,188	18,150	221,320	8,840	64,153	9,784	1,163	83,941	1,738	74,434	76,249
1990	56,443	100,104	45,480	16,706	219,446	10,271	69,217	6,866	1,031	87,385	1,880	80,408	82,293
1991	57,555	99,890	50,638	17,830	226,669	13,493	72,942	6,193	1,412	94,040	1,526	81,105	82,632
1992	51,514	103,734	51,494	18,924	226,547	13,955	74,025	5,268	1,438	94,686	854	85,245	86,155
1993	41,588	109,613	60,542	21,969	234,882	13,103	77,612	4,173	1,438	96,326	954	95,312	96,854
1994	29,704	138,937	64,636	21,670	256,559	10,840	68,680	2,843	1,452	83,815	1,098	114,083	116,003
1995	32,751	142,746	70,807	21,735	269,738	11,615	63,341	1,673	1,405	78,034	889	116,001	117,859
1996	31,135r	142,079r	84,176	22,390	281,567r	13,141r	64,347r	1,703	1,444r	80,635r	896r	114,909r	117,115r
1997	30,303r	140,443r	85,883	23,409	281,952r	14,400r	63,900r	1,209	1,429	80,938r	1,062r	115,863r	118,791r
1998	25,758r	145,263r	90,181r	23,950r	287,229r	15,371r	64,775r	910	1,083r	82,139r	931r	118,970r	122,629r
1999	23,219r	150,160r	99,109r	22,944r	297,669r	14,039r	64,142r	1,106	1,247	80,534r	774r	123,977r	132,033r
2000	19,553	138,282	108,258	20,155	288,725	16,079	74,871	2,238	1,230	94,419	813	123,969	137,377

(1) Crude oil plus all condensates and petroleum gases extracted at gas separation plants.
(2) Includes colliery methane.
(3) Nuclear and natural flow hydro electricty excluding generation of pumped storage stations. From 1988 includes generation at wind stations.
(4) Includes solar and geothermal heat, solid renewable sources (wood, waste, etc), and gaseous renewable sources (landfill gas, sewage gas) from 1988.
(5) Includes other solid fuels.
(6) Crude and process oils and petroleum products.
(7) Includes exports of natural gas and electricity.

1.11 Availability and consumption of primary fuels and equivalents (energy supplied basis) 1970 to 2000 (continued)

Thousand tonnes of oil equivalent

	Marine Bunkers Petroleum	Stock changes (8) Coal (5)	Stock changes (8) Petroleum (6)	Stock changes (8) Natural gas	Statistical Difference (9) Coal (5)	Statistical Difference (9) Petroleum (6)	Total (13)	Gross inland consumption (14)	Non-energy use (10)	Inland Coal (5)	Inland Petroleum (6)(15)	Inland Natural gas (2)(11)	Primary Electricity (3)(12)	Total (4)
1970	5,721	+8,542	-680		+199	+466	+665	**223,341**	10,859	98,994	92,366	11,300	7,435	**210,095**
1971	5,874	-7,046	-3,489		-239	-652	-891	**220,170**	10,839	87,732	93,543	18,220	7,672	**207,167**
1972	5,265	-1,370	+2,904		-242	-887	-1,129	**225,109**	11,474	76,847	100,212	25,855	8,203	**211,117**
1973	5,769	+1,456	+458		+60	-340	-280	**235,847**	12,635	83,235	101,501	27,974	7,797	**220,507**
1974	4,922	+4,839	-5,139		-360	-514	-874	**225,116**	12,865	73,278	94,327	33,460	9,326	**210,391**
1975	3,572	-6,489	+3,660		-202	-395	-597	**213,769**	10,255	73,716	84,963	35,060r	8,453	**202,192**
1976	3,698	-1,597	-348		+121	-254	-133	**218,116**	10,925	75,016	83,480	37,188	9,951	**205,635**
1977	2,942	+600	+2,466		-113	-557	-670	**222,806**	10,517	75,263	85,110	39,526	10,973	**210,872**
1978	2,733	-1,368	-814		-363	-569	-932	**223,214**	10,245	73,321	87,177	40,999	10,301	**211,798**
1979	2,789	+3,600	-2,229		+43	-806	-763	**232,768**	10,232	78,814	87,681	44,919	10,597	**222,011**
1980	2,562	-6,789	+40		-171	-1,567	-1,738	**213,118**	7,464	73,263	76,197	44,785	10,247	**204,492**
1981	2,156	-2,013	+3,882		+562	-154	+408	**207,756**	8,111	72,865	69,539	45,392	10,564	**198,360**
1982	2,715	-5,660	+2,305		-118	-2,315	-2,433	**204,540**	8,134	67,958	70,671	45,166	12,274	**196,069**
1983	2,118	-3,209	+1,010		+234	-544	-310	**206,290**	8,625	68,590	67,228	47,080	13,866	**196,764**
1984	2,370	+11,842	+922		-136	+247	+111	**206,052**	8,847	48,738	84,651	48,168	14,845	**196,402**
1985	2,239	+1,461	+297	-521	-249	-731	-980	**216,184**	9,230	64,824	72,179	51,803	16,851	**205,657**
1986	2,212	-1,889	+338	-836	+1,126	-83	+1,043	**221,432**	10,247	70,008	71,148	52,665	16,189	**210,010**
1987	1,756	+3,396	+338	-662	-355	-146	-501	**222,311**	10,290	71,721	69,431	54,090	15,796	**211,038**
1988	1,932	-1,547	+1,272	-637	+189	-111	+78	**225,392**	10,970	69,621	74,042	51,352r	18,083	**213,098**
1989	2,525	-1,787	-628	-281	+817	+159	+976	**224,767**	12,039	67,014	75,399	49,113r	19,236	**210,762**
1990	2,666	+891	+1,049	+108	+1,229	+990	+2,219	**226,139**	11,252	66,954	77,159	51,187	17,733	**213,033**
1991	2,618	-3,402	-851	-273	+947	+448	+1,395	**232,330**	12,184	67,067	77,137	55,362r	19,240	**218,807**
1992	2,688	-2,439	+709	-348	+884	-647	+237	**230,549**	12,890	63,060	77,492	55,080	20,359	**215,991**
1993	2,618	+766	-631	+84	+411	+1,597	+2,008	**233,964**	13,012	54,913	78,126	62,948r	23,406	**219,394**
1994	2,451	+11,055	+454	+233	+772	-1,668	-87	**231,956**	13,521	51,272	76,668	64,857r	23,087	**215,883**
1995	2,602	+5,088	+1,122	+820	+820	-426	+1,752	**232,458**	13,735	48,924	75,421	69,236	23,116	**216,697**
1996	2,813r	+2,521r	-315	-236	+156r	-1,814r	+742r	**243,502r**	13,664r	45,746r	77,819r	80,857r	23,824	**230,018r**
1997	3,121	-2,578r	+324r	-354	+265r	-1,785r	-559r	**238,928r**	13,093r	40,799r	75,430r	82,714r	24,831r	**225,687r**
1998	3,256r	+808r	-745r	-32	+47r	-710r	+648r	**242,865r**	12,814r	40,959r	75,993r	86,153r	25,027r	**230,208r**
1999	2,469	-464r	+422	+670r	-639r	+472r	+1,103r	**243,224r**	13,025r	36,659r	75,900r	91,364r	23,979r	**230,137r**
2000	2,207	+3,103	+810	-809	-137	+1,504	+2,585	**244,079**	12,246	38,059	75,155	94,868	21,380	**231,937**

(8) Stock fall (+), stock rise (-).

(9) Recorded demand minus supply.

(10) Petroleum products for feedstock for petrochemical plants, industrial and white spirits, lubricants bitumen and wax. Also includes from 1968 miscellaneous petroleum products mainly for inland consumption but excludes small quantities derived from coal. From 1989 also includes estimated quantities of natural gas used for non-energy purposes. Data for non-energy use of natural gas from 1994 can be found in Tables 1.1-1.3 and 4.1 and 4.2.

(11) Includes non-energy use of natural gas up to 1988. (See footnote 11).

(12) Includes net imports of electricity.

(13) As of 1994 this total includes the statistical differences for electricity and natural gas.

(14) Equivalent to primary demand as in Tables 1.1 , 1.2 and 1.3.

(15) The petroleum figures from 1970 to 1995 have been revised since the last edition to be on a consistent basis with the balances format. For details see paragraph 3.44 in Chapter 3.

1.12 Comparison of net imports of fuel with total consumption of primary fuels and equivalents 1970 to 2000

	Gross inland consumption of primary fuels (1) plus marine bunkers (A)	Net imports (+) /net exports (-) of fuels (B)	Import dependency (2) (C)	Export ratio (3) (D)
	Million tonnes of oil equivalent		Per cent	
1970	229.1	109.7	47.9	-
1971	226.0	118.0	52.2	-
1972	230.4	119.9	52.0	-
1973	241.6	121.9	50.5	-
1974	230.0	120.0	52.2	-
1975	217.3	97.3	44.8	-
1976	221.8	88.6	40.0	-
1977	225.7	58.6	25.9	-
1978	225.9	48.8	21.6	-
1979	235.6	29.8	12.6	-
1980	215.7	13.7	6.4	-
1981	209.9	-12.6	-	6.0
1982	207.3	-23.1	-	11.1
1983	208.4	-37.5	-	18.0
1984	208.4	-23.2	-	11.1
1985	218.4	-34.3	-	15.7
1986	223.6	-37.2	-	16.7
1987	224.1	-35.2	-	15.7
1988	227.3	-20.3	-	8.9
1989	227.3	7.7	3.4	-
1990	228.8	5.1	2.2	-
1991	234.9	11.4	4.9	-
1992	233.2	8.5	3.7	-
1993	236.6	-0.5	-	0.2
1994	234.4	-32.2	-	13.7
1995	235.1	-39.8	-	16.9
1996	246.3r	-36.5	-	14.8
1997	242.0r	-37.9	-	15.6r
1998	246.1r	-40.5r	-	16.5r
1999	245.7r	-51.5r	-	21.0r
2000	246.3	-43.0	-	17.4

(1) Includes non-energy use. Equivalent to primary demand plus marine bunkers.

(2) Import dependency (C) = $\dfrac{\text{Net imports (B)}}{\text{(A)}} \times 100$

(3) Export ratio (D) = $\dfrac{\text{Net exports (B)}}{\text{(A)}} \times 100$

1.13 Primary energy consumption, gross domestic product and the energy ratio[1], 1970 to 2000

	Total inland consumption of primary energy (temperature corrected) (2)	Gross domestic product at market prices (1995 prices)(3)	Energy ratio (4)	
	Million tonnes of oil equivalent (A)	£ billion (B)	Tonnes of oil equivalent per £1 million GDP (C)	Index 1995 = 100 (D)
1970	211.9	417.4	508	161.3
1971	209.7	425.8	493	156.5
1972	212.6	441.2	482	153.1
1973	223.1	473.5	471	149.7
1974	212.4	465.5	456	145.0
1975	206.0	462.4	446	141.6
1976	208.9	475.3	439	139.6
1977	213.1	486.6	438	139.2
1978	213.7	503.1	425	135.0
1979	220.0	517.0	426	135.2
1980	206.2	505.7	408	129.6
1981	198.7	499.3	398	126.5
1982	196.3	508.2	386	122.7
1983	197.5	527.3	375	119.0
1984	196.7	540.2	364	115.7
1985	203.1	560.6	362	115.1
1986	206.8	584.2	354	112.5
1987	210.0	610.1	344	109.4
1988	217.7	641.6	339	107.8
1989	217.8	655.2	332	105.6
1990	221.6	659.5	336	106.8
1991	221.4	649.8	341	108.3
1992	220.6	650.3	339	107.8
1993	222.5	665.4	334	106.2
1994	221.5	694.6	319	101.3
1995	224.7r	714.0	315	100.0
1996	230.6r	732.2	315	100.1
1997	232.5r	757.9	307	97.5
1998	236.8r	777.9	304	96.7
1999	237.3r	795.7	298	94.8
2000	240.1	819.9	293	93.0

(1) See paragraphs 1.31 to 34
(2) The methodology used to temperature correct gas consumption as been modified from 1990 onwards. See paragraph 1.51.
(3) GDP revised to be on ESA95 basis.
(4) Energy ratio (C) = $\frac{(A)}{(B)}$

1.14 Energy consumption by final user (energy supplied basis)[(1)] 1970 to 2000

Thousand tonnes of oil equivalent

Industry (2)

	Coal	Coke and Breeze (3)	Other solid Fuels(4)	Coke oven gas	Town gas	Natural gas (5)	Electricity	Renewables	Petroleum	Total(3)
1970	12,681	9,655	209	1,164	1,778	1,788	6,275	-	28,397	**62,333**
1971	10,232	8,298	176	1,118	1,038	5,194	6,313	-	28,130	**60,746**
1972	7,675	7,832	252	1,111	1,154	8,136	6,292	-	28,674	**61,307**
1973	7,950	8,340	226	1,290	788	10,791	6,884	-	28,691	**65,149**
1974	7,290	7,167	201	975	494	12,320	6,517	-	24,968	**60,058**
1975	6,373	6,338	199	1,038	222	12,555	6,479	-	22,145	**55,444**
1976	5,902	7,129	131	1,091	68	14,237	6,950	-	21,966	**57,584**
1977	5,947	6,368	158	1,010	30	14,940	7,053	-	21,978	**57,574**
1978	5,627	5,932	179	899	15	15,149	7,222	-	21,570	**56,673**
1979	6,081	6,512	148	977	18	15,663	7,527	-	21,590	**58,564**
1980	5,083	3,335	133	642	13	15,258	6,854	-	16,938	**48,291**
1981	4,534	4,564	116	665	13	14,489	6,622	-	14,761	**45,776**
1982	4,668	4,083	144	605	8	14,588	6,353	-	13,530	**44,007**
1983	4,708	4,307	126	635	5	14,021	6,376	-	11,988	**42,191**
1984	3,796	4,408	68	537	5	14,686	6,758	-	10,859	**41,138**
1985	4,708	4,655	151	768	3	14,865	6,837	-	9,701	**41,702**
1986(11)	5,242	4,144	98	778	3	13,542	6,884	-	10,240	**40,931**
1987	4,048	4,660	80	821	3	14,137	8,005		8,456	**40,211**
1988	4,166	5,041	55	771	-	12,883	8,350	100	9,441	**40,807r**
1989	4,489	4,286	30	613	-	12,515	8,550	102	8,820	**39,405r**
					-					
1990	4,172	3,951	42	602	-	12,889	8,655	107	8,242	**38,660r**
1991	4,270	3,691	14	570	-	12,311	8,563	109	8,729	**38,257**
1992	4,375	3,601	14	534	-	11,380	8,194	279	8,334	**36,711r**
1993	3,553	3,613	7	560	-	11,521	8,328	266	8,592	**36,440**
1994	3,402	3,818r	194	590r	-	12,885	8,082	487	8,253	**37,711r**
1995	2,840	3,750r	184	576	-	12,696	8,654	526	7,066	**36,292r**
1996	1,971r	855	232r	554	-	14,000r	8,764r	533	7,058r	**34,670r**
1997	1,948r	787	248r	579r	-	14,685	9,020	532	6,315r	**34,868r**
1998	1,650r	803r	243	385r	-	15,647r	9,220r	461	6,328r	**35,027r**
1999	1,762r	820r	215r	353r	-	16,539r	9,532r	397	6,455r	**36,297r**
2000	941	757	225	377	-	17,254	9,759	364	6,373	**36,178**

(1) Excluding non-energy use of fuels.

(2) Includes the iron and steel industry, but from 1994 onwards excludes Iron and Steel use of fuels for transformation and energy industry own use purposes.

(3) Blast furnace gas is included in coke and breeze up to 1995 and covers electricity transformation, use by coke ovens and losses. From 1996 onwards, blast furnace gas is included in the total and covers just coke ovens and losses, which is consistent with the methodology used for compiling the energy balances.

(4) Includes, from 1994, manufactured liquid fuels.

(5) Includes colliery methane. Up to 1988 also includes non-energy use of natural gas.

1.14 Energy consumption by final user (energy supplied basis)[1] 1970 to 2000 (continued)

Thousand tonnes of oil equivalent

		Transport									
			Rail			Road		Water		Air	
		Coke					Coal				
		and breeze	Electricity		Electricity		derived				**Total**
	Coal		(6)	Petroleum		Petroleum	fuel	Coal	Petroleum	Petroleum	(7)
1970	88	35	234	1,254	3	21,406	15	88	1,184	3,869	**28,174**
1971	68	13	237	1,186	-	22,412	-	63	1,081	4,247	**29,306**
1972	53	5	229	1,121	-	23,535	-	23	962	4,514	**30,442**
1973	58	-	224	1,123	-	25,125	-	10	1,088	4,806	**32,435**
1974	50	-	234	1,048	-	24,465	-	10	1,239	4,219	**31,266**
1975	40	-	249	1,000	-	23,948	-	8	1,300	4,340	**30,885**
1976	43	3	247	945	-	24,994	-	8	1,317	4,476	**32,032**
1977	40	3	252	950	-	25,633	-	8	1,312	4,678	**32,875**
1978	45	3	254	967	-	26,946	-	5	1,300	5,051	**34,571**
1979	43	3	254	947	-	27,520	-	5	1,363	5,224	**35,359**
1980	38	3	262	919	-	27,815	-	5	1,257	5,242	**35,541**
1981	38	-	259	877	-	27,009	-	-	1,101	5,020	**34,304**
1982	35	-	229	793	-	27,797	-	3	1,186	4,993	**35,037**
1983	15	-	247	849	-	28,646	-	3	1,207	5,093	**36,059**
1984	3	-	247	816	-	30,006	-	-	1,328	5,383	**37,782**
1985	3	-	254	821	-	30,586	-	-	1,254	5,582	**38,500**
1986(11)	3	-	259	809	-	32,606	-	-	1,151	6,126	**40,954**
1987	3	-	264	761	-	34,062	-	-	1,103	6,479	**42,672**
1988	-	-	282	766	-	36,233	-	-	1,159	6,905	**45,345**
1989	3	-	272	702	-	37,801	-	-	1,355	7,308	**47,442**
1990	2	-	455	668	-	38,816	-	-	1,363	7,332	**48,635**
1991	-	-	454	685	-	38,535	-	-	1,424	6,872	**47,973**
1992	-	-	461	715	-	39,363	-	-	1,377	7,435	**49,355**
1993	-	-	641	665	-	39,502	-	-	1,341	7,871	**50,024**
1994	-	-	599	651	-	39,690	-	-	1,239	8,070	**50,253**
1995	-	-	636	654	-	39,268	-	-	1,193	8,485	**50,238**
1996	-	-	638	629r	-	40,772r	-	-	1,294r	8,917r	**52,250r**
1997	-	-	723	516r	-	41,259r	-	-	1,256r	9,322r	**53,076r**
1998	-	-	728r	522r	-	41,020r	-	-	1,175r	10,237r	**53,683r**
1999	-	-	736r	504r	-	41,399r	-	-	1,067r	11,017r	**54,723r**
2000	-	-	758	481	-	41,071	-	-	1,036	11,859	**55,204**

(6) Includes, from 1990, electricity used at transport premises (see footnote 8). See Chapter 5, paragraph 5.15.
(7) Includes small amounts of natural gas for road transport.

1.14 Energy consumption by final user (energy supplied basis)[1] 1970 to 2000 (continued)

Thousand tonnes of oil equivalent

		Coke and breeze	Other solid fuels	Natural gas (8)	Electricity	Renewables	Petroleum	Total (4)
	Coal							
	Domestic							
1970	14,242	1,761	1,975	8,922	6,622	-	3,363	**36,884**
1971	12,164	1,136	2,156	9,900	6,937	-	3,328	**35,621**
1972	10,602	849	2,144	11,359	7,471	-	3,836	**36,261**
1973	10,565	778	2,053	12,129	7,849	-	4,202	**37,576**
1974	9,968	821	1,955	13,562	7,963	-	3,733	**38,002**
1975	8,517	645	1,778	14,840	7,670	-	3,612	**37,062**
1976	7,910	549	1,640	15,602	7,318	-	3,615	**36,634**
1977	8,136	534	1,589	16,600	7,386	-	3,653	**37,898**
1978	7,476	471	1,464	18,291	7,378	-	3,610	**38,689**
1979	7,688	479	1,431	20,718	7,711	-	3,539	**41,566**
1980	6,575	401	1,370	21,258	7,403	-	2,834	**39,841**
1981	6,214	368	1,202	22,076	7,260	-	2,554	**39,674**
1982	6,242	365	1,146	21,963	7,116	-	2,385	**39,218**
1983	5,796	335	1,141	22,346	7,129	-	2,267	**39,014**
1984	4,733	335	728	22,502	7,212	-	2,385	**37,896**
1985	6,290	385	957	24,394	7,582	-	2,454	**42,062**
1986(11)	6,121	335	965	25,797	7,892	-	2,590	**43,700**
1987	5,189	315	1,018	26,450	8,015	-	2,474	**43,460**
1988	4,741	300	907	25,833	7,940	205	2,441	**42,367r**
1989	3,719	239	815	24,988	7,935	207	2,355	**40,258r**
1990	3,153	254	762	25,835	8,066	206	2,480	**40,756r**
1991	3,582	210	785	28,721	8,436	209	2,825	**44,768r**
1992	3,105	176	709	28,389	8,555	243	2,889	**44,066r**
1993	3,498	147	751	29,254	8,639	241	3,019	**45,549**
1994	2,957	67	601	28,355	8,721	242	3,004	**43,947**
1995	2,077	78	470	28,037	8,790	242	2,997	**42,691r**
1996	2,084r	129	588r	32,315	9,244	241	3,518	**48,118**
1997	1,992r	59	419	29,709	8,981	225	3,389	**44,773r**
1998	1,819r	85r	439r	30,600	9,407r	230	3,543r	**46,124r**
1999	1,914r	86r	410r	30,788r	9,485r	231	3,162r	**46,076r**
2000	1,466	103	365	31,807	9,617	236	3,239	**46,833**

(8) Includes town gas prior to 1989. (Separate figures maybe found in previous editions of this Digest).

1.14 Energy consumption by final user (energy supplied basis)$^{(1)}$ 1970 to 2000 (continued)

Thousand tonnes of oil equivalent

		Other final users (9)					
	Coal	Coke and breeze	Natural gas (8)	Electricity	Renewables	Petroleum	Total (4)
1970	2,723	1,499	1,919	3,408	-	9,038	18,586
1971	2,328	688	2,181	3,534	-	9,184	17,915
1972	2,013	537	2,509	3,650	-	9,487	18,195
1973	1,731	602	2,728	3,940	-	9,585	18,586
1974	1,685	567	3,197	3,642	-	8,401	17,492
1975	1,234	408	3,393	3,894	-	8,431	17,360
1976	1,300	335	3,831	4,023	-	8,668	18,157
1977	1,370	315	3,998	4,257	-	9,157	19,097
1978	1,300	275	4,393	4,481	-	8,764	19,213
1979	1,307	285	4,955	4,731	-	8,754	20,031
1980	1,154	237	5,194	4,733	-	7,403	18,721
1981	1,174	204	5,315	4,804	-	7,096	18,592
1982	1,222	212	5,486	4,867	-	6,678	18,464
1983	1,166	257	5,915	5,106	-	6,403	18,847
1984	1,141	252	6,101	5,063	-	6,381	18,938
1985	1,123	297	6,718	5,446	-	6,018	19,603
1986(11)	982	390	7,308	5,731	-	5,723	20,135
1987	935	368	7,534	5,965	-	4,988	19,790
1988	831	264	7,569	6,240	138	5,008	20,050r
1989	698	119	7,278	6,497	138	4,345	19,075r
1990	795	127	7,329	6,426	139	4,402	19,218r
1991	753	105	8,640	6,717	149	4,456	20,820r
1992	622	88	8,585	6,996	150	4,518	20,959
1993	566	74	8,504	6,999	146	4,446	20,735r
1994	496	34	8,695	6,951	172	4,289	20,637r
1995	362	39	9,374	7,199	189	4,016	21,179r
1996	424r	-	10,260	7,531r	181	3,909r	22,306r
1997	448r	-	9,773r	7,891	174	3,362r	21,648r
1998	291r	-	10,165r	7,804r	174	3,144r	21,578r
1999	217r	-	10,307r	8,001r	174	2,874r	21,573r
2000	208	-	10,902	8,148	165	2,420	21,843

(9) Mainly agriculture, public administration and commerce. Prior to 1990, including electricity used at transport premises (see footnote 6).

1.14 Energy consumption by final user (energy supplied basis)[1] 1970 to 2000 (continued)

Thousand tonnes of oil equivalent

	Coal	Coke and breeze	Other solid fuels (4)	Coke oven gas	Town gas	Natural gas (4)	Electri-city	Renewables	Petroleum	Total (3)(10)
					All final users					
1970	29,822	12,950	2,184	1,164	10,746	3,662	16,542	-	68,511	**145,977**
1971	24,855	10,134	2,333	1,118	8,882	9,431	17,021	-	69,568	**143,589**
1972	20,366	9,222	2,396	1,111	8,094	15,063	17,643	-	72,129	**146,205**
1973	20,313	9,721	2,280	1,290	5,852	20,584	18,898	-	74,620	**153,744**
1974	19,003	8,555	2,156	975	3,836	25,736	18,356	-	68,072	**146,818**
1975	16,172	7,391	1,977	1,038	1,796	29,212	18,293	-	64,776	**140,751**
1976	15,162	8,016	1,771	1,091	534	33,204	18,537	-	65,981	**144,407**
1977	15,502	7,220	1,748	1,010	174	35,393	18,948	-	67,361	**147,444**
1978	14,454	6,681	1,642	899	81	37,766	19,336	-	68,208	**149,146**
1979	15,124	7,279	1,579	977	91	42,262	20,223	-	68,937	**155,521**
1980	12,854	3,975	1,504	642	76	41,647	19,252	-	62,408	**142,394**
1981	11,960	5,136	1,317	665	65	41,828	18,945	-	58,420	**138,346**
1982	12,169	4,660	1,290	605	55	41,990	18,567	-	57,360	**136,726**
1983	11,688	4,899	1,267	635	45	42,242	18,856	-	56,453	**136,111**
1984	9,673	4,995	796	537	43	43,251	19,280	-	57,158	**135,753**
1985	12,124	5,338	1,108	768	40	45,940	20,118	-	56,416	**141,867**
1986(11)	12,348	4,869	1,063	778	28	46,622	20,763	-	59,245	**145,719**
1987	10,174	5,343	1,098	821	28	48,096	22,252	-	58,325	**146,132**
1988	9,738	5,605	962r	771	8	46,277r	22,811	443	61,952	**148,569r**
1989	8,909	4,645	845r	613	-	44,780	23,254	447	62,685	**146,180r**
1990	8,122	4,333	804r	602	-	46,052	23,601	451	63,302	**147,268**
1991	8,605	4,006	799	570	-	49,676	24,170	467	63,525	**151,818**
1992	8,101	3,866	723	534	-	48,357	24,206	672	64,632	**151,091r**
1993	7,617	3,833	758	560	-	49,282	24,607	652	65,437	**152,747r**
1994	6,855	3,919r	795r	590r	-	49,935r	24,353	901	65,196	**152,548r**
1995	5,279r	3,867r	654r	576r	-	50,107r	25,279r	956	63,679r	**150,399r**
1996	4,480r	984	820	554r	-	56,576r	26,177	954	66,096r	**157,344r**
1997	4,389r	846	667	579r	-	54,167r	26,616r	930	65,418r	**154,366r**
1998	3,760r	889r	682r	385r	-	56,412	27,160r	865	65,969r	**156,412r**
1999	3,893r	906r	625r	353r	-	57,634r	27,753r	802	66,479r	**158,668r**
2000	2,615	861	590	377	-	59,962	28,282	765	66,478	**160,059**

(10) Before 1971 includes the use for transport of liquid fuel made from coal.
(11) See paragraph 1.37 about changed treatment of electricity produced, and fuel used by, companies other than major power producers.

1.15 Expenditure on energy by final user, 1970 to 2000[1]

United Kingdom

£ million

	Industry					Domestic				
	Coal and solid fuels (3)	Natural gas (4)	Electricity	Petroleum products (5)	Total (6)	Coal and solid fuels (3)	Natural gas (4)	Electricity	Petroleum products (5)	Total (6)
1970	285	70	475	300	**1,130**	395	385	645	85	**1,510**
1971	285	85	530	350	**1,250**	385	430	730	90	**1,635**
1972	280	120	540	345	**1,285**	360	505	830	110	**1,805**
1973	320	150	595	390	**1,455**	370	535	885	140	**1,930**
1974	410	195	775	880	**2,260**	405	605	1,070	200	**2,280**
1975	545	240	1,015	920	**2,720**	440	760	1,495	235	**2,930**
1976	720	380	1,260	1,065	**3,425**	500	1,000	1,825	295	**3,620**
1977	780	535	1,470	1,305	**4,090**	595	1,205	2,135	360	**4,295**
1978	800	695	1,670	1,255	**4,420**	620	1,365	2,380	370	**4,735**
1979	1,010	820	1,925	1,570	**5,325**	770	1,575	2,675	475	**5,495**
1980	675	1,060	2,185	1,815	**5,735**	920	1,875	3,310	510	**6,615**
1981	850	1,215	2,420	1,890	**6,375**	960	2,460	3,905	560	**7,885**
1982	860	1,335	2,560	1,870	**6,625**	995	3,070	4,200	610	**8,875**
1983	900	1,375	2,655	1,800	**6,730**	1,015	3,520	4,300	645	**9,480**
1984	845	1,555	2,695	1,810	**6,905**	830	3,655	4,495	640	**9,620**
1985	990	1,735	2,750	1,740	**7,215**	1,120	4,090	4,840	665	**10,715**
1986	1,000	1,350	2,765	1,065	**6,180**	1,135	4,385	5,105	460	**11,085**
1987	865	1,375	3,285	865	**6,390**	990	4,465	5,140	410	**11,005**
1988	880	1,225	3,590	785	**6,480**	830	4,385	5,340	365	**10,920**
1989	905	1,210	3,965	845	**6,925**	730	4,455	5,800	390	**11,375**
1990	930	1,260	3,985	900	**7,075**	700	4,865	6,255	485	**12,305**
1991	910	1,115	4,120	905	**7,050**	795	5,775	7,105	460	**14,135**
1992	775	970	4,180	790	**6,715**	710	5,685	7,460	460	**14,315**
1993	740	915	3,940	895	**6,490**	780	5,705	7,590	465	**14,540**
1994	650	1,010	3,855	865	**6,380**	685	6,020	7,870	455	**15,030**
1995	605	1,015	3,970	830	**6,420**	615	6,010	8,060	470	**15,155**
1996	590	755	3,900	965	**6,210**	640	6,510	8,380	630	**16,165**
1997	565	870	3,625	890	**5,950**	560	6,125	7,965	560	**15,210**
1998	550r	1020r	3,535	715r	**5,820r**	525r	6,015	7,700	465	**14,705**
1999	455	1,055r	3,705	785r	**6,000r**	540r	5,175	7,450	465r	**13,630r**
2000	445	1,140	3,430	1,165	**6,180**	455	5,525	7,390	735	**14,105**

(1) All data is to the nearest £5 million. VAT is only included where not refundable. Methodology used to calculate the series has changed over the years, as such the data provides a guide to changing patterns of expenditure on energy, but not too much significance should be drawn from small changes.

(2) Includes commercial, public administration, agriculture and all fuels used for transport purposes.

(3) Includes coal, coke, breeze and other manufactured solid fuel. Prior to 1996 an estimate of the value of coke produced in coke ovens owned by the iron and steel industry was included, this has now been replaced by an estimate of the value of coal purchased for such ovens, which is the actual monetary trade.

(4) Includes town gas.

(5) Includes heating oils, LPG etc. Excludes motor transport fuels.

(6) Excludes other fuels not listed e.g. crude oil, coke oven gas etc.

United Kingdom

£ mil▸

	Other final users (2)						All final users				
	Coal and solid fuels (3)	Natural gas (4)	Electricity	Petroleum products	Of which road transport	Total (6)	Coal and solid fuels (3)	Natural gas (4)	Electricity	Petroleum	To▸
1970	60	70	390	1,910	1,720	**2,430**	740	525	1,510	2,295	5,0
1971	45	80	435	2,105	1,885	**2,665**	715	595	1,695	2,545	5,5
1972	45	80	480	2,305	2,070	**2,910**	685	705	1,850	2760	6,0
1973	45	90	515	2,580	2,305	**3,230**	735	775	1,995	3,110	6,6
1974	60	105	590	3,885	3,150	**4,640**	875	905	2,435	4,965	9,1
1975	70	140	835	4,685	3,845	**5,730**	1,05	1,140	3,345	5,840	11,3
1976	90	200	1,030	5,305	4,325	**6,625**	1,310	1,580	4,115	6,665	13,6
1977	115	255	1,200	6,030	4,835	**7,600**	1,490	1,995	4,805	7,695	15,9
1978	115	310	1,375	6,075	4,890	**7,875**	1,535	2,370	5,425	7,700	17,0
1979	130	385	1,655	8,265	6,660	**10,435**	1,910	2,780	6,255	10,310	21,2
1980	115	520	1,985	10,735	8,650	**13,355**	1,710	3,455	7,480	13,060	25,7
1981	110	585	2,460	12,345	10,060	**15,500**	1,920	4,260	8,785	14,795	29,7
1982	135	655	2,690	13,470	10,950	**16,950**	1,990	5,060	9,450	15,950	32,4
1983	135	745	2,855	14,965	12,240	**18,700**	2,050	5,640	9,810	17,410	34,9
1984	135	795	2,980	16,140	13,250	**20,050**	1,810	6,005	10,170	18,590	36,5
1985	155	920	3,265	17,640	14,615	**21,980**	2,265	6,745	10,855	20,045	39,9
1986	140	1,045	3,485	15,845	13,745	**20,515**	2,275	6,780	11,355	17,370	37,7
1987	125	1,035	3,490	16,630	14,525	**21,280**	1,980	6,870	11,915	17,905	38,6
1988	95	1,025	3,810	16,855	14,960	**21,785**	1,805	6,635	12,740	18,005	39,1
1989	95	1,015	4,185	18,755	16,690	**24,050**	1,730	6,680	13,950	19,980	42,3
1990	105	1,085	4,465	21,120	19,020	**26,775**	1,735	7,210	14,705	22,505	46,1
1991	85	1,310	4,960	21,900	19,995	**28,255**	1,790	8,200	16,185	23,265	49,4
1992	95	1,245	5,495	22,455	20,825	**29,290**	1,580	7,900	17,135	23,705	50,3
1993	70	1,155	5,555	24,365	22,540	**31,145**	1,590	7,775	17,115	25,725	52,2
1994	50	1,125	5,380	25,190	23,515	**31,745**	1,385	8,155	17,140	26,510	53,1
1995	35	1,110	5,300	25,895	24,140	**32,340**	1,255	8,135	17,330	27,195	53,9
1996	30	975	5,405	28,240	26,145	**34,650**	1,260	8,240	17,685	29,835	57,0
1997	35	855	5,420	30,645	28,685	**36,955**	1,165	7,850	17,010	32,095	58,1
1998	25r	885r	5,275	31,375	29,810	**37,560r**	1,100r	7,920r	16,510	32,555r	58,0
1999	15	880r	5,050r	38,455r	36,680r	**44,400r**	1,010r	7,110r	16,205r	39,705r	64,0
2000	10	955	4,950	43,665	40,445	**49,580**	910	7,620	15,770	45,565	69,8

1.16 Mean air temperatures[1][2]

Great Britain

Degrees Celsius

	Average	Deviations from normal (average 1961-90)				
	1961-90	1996	1997	1998	1999	2000
Calendar year	9.5	-0.1	+1.2	+1.0	+1.2r	+1.1
First half year	7.7	-0.2	+1.1	+1.7	+1.4	+1.3
Second half year (3)	11.1	+0.3r	+1.5	+0.6r	+1.2r	+0.8
First quarter (3)	4.5	-0.3	+1.5r	+2.6	+1.8	+2.0
Second quarter (3)	10.9	-0.1	+0.6r	+0.7r	+1.1	+0.6
Third quarter	15.0	+0.6	+1.7	+0.4	+1.5	+0.9
Fourth quarter	7.3	-0.1	+1.2	+0.6	+0.7r	+0.5
Summer (4)	12.9	+0.3	+1.2	+0.6	+1.4r	+0.9
Winter (4)	5.9	+0.7r	+1.9r	+1.2r	+1.4r	+0.4
January	3.9	+0.9	-1.0	+1.6	+1.9	+1.6
February	3.9	-0.8	+3.0	+3.8	+1.7	+2.5
March	5.7	-1.1	+2.7	+2.3	+1.7	+1.8
April	7.8	+0.9	+1.3	-	+1.6	+0.1
May	10.9	-1.6	+0.6	+2.0	+1.9	+1.2
June	13.9	+0.5	+0.1	+0.2	-0.2	+0.8
July	15.8	+0.6	+1.1	-0.3	+1.7	-0.6
August	15.6	+1.1	+3.0	+0.3	+0.7	+1.1
September	13.5	+0.2	+1.0	+1.3	+2.2	+2.4
October	10.6	+1.2	-0.1	-	+0.4	-0.1
November	6.6	-0.4	+2.3	+0.7	+1.5	+0.5
December	4.7	-1.2	+1.4	+1.2	+0.3r	+1.1

(1) See Energy Trends on the internet for the latest monthly figures – See paragraph 1.82 of Chapter 1.
(2) Based on data provided by the Meteorological Office. The figures are averages of the monthly mean temperatures as recorded at 16 meteorological stations selected as representative of fuel consumption in Great Britain - 2 in Scotland, 2 in Wales and 12 in England, four of which are counted twice. (Prior to September 1990, recordings were from 15 stations - 2 in Scotland, 2 in Wales and 11 in England, five of which were counted twice.)
(3) A more refined method has been used in this edition to calculate the aggregate figures which has resulted in some revisions to years where the monthly data have remained unchanged between the 2000 and 2001 editions of the digest.
(4) The summer period is from April to September inclusive, and the winter period is the six months beginning in October and ending with March of the following year.

1.17 Mean air temperatures[1][2], 1970 to 2000

Great Britain

Degrees Celsius

	January	February	March	April	May	June	July	August	September	October	November	December
1970	4.0	3.2	4.0	6.8	12.7	16.1	15.4	16.1	14.5	10.9	7.9	4.5
1971	4.7	5.0	5.4	7.8	11.5	12.5	16.9	15.6	14.3	11.6	6.4	7.1
1972	4.2	4.6	6.5	8.6	10.6	11.9	15.5	15.2	11.9	10.7	6.4	5.8
1973	4.7	4.7	6.5	7.2	11.3	14.9	15.7	16.5	14.3	9.4	6.2	5.1
1974	6.1	5.8	5.8	8.0	10.9	13.7	15.1	15.2	12.1	7.9	6.7	8.0
1975	6.7	4.7	5.0	8.3	9.7	14.5	17.2	18.2	13.4	10.2	6.3	5.3
1976	5.9	4.8	5.0	8.0	11.8	16.7	18.3	17.3	13.4	10.7	6.2	2.2
1977	3.0	5.1	7.0	7.3	10.4	12.4	15.9	15.3	13.1	11.7	6.4	6.2
1978	3.4	3.6	6.8	6.4	11.3	13.6	14.7	14.9	14.0	11.9	8.6	4.3
1979	0.5	1.4	4.8	7.6	9.7	14.1	16.2	14.9	13.2	11.2	7.0	5.5
1980	2.4	6.0	4.9	8.7	11.0	13.8	14.5	15.7	14.6	9.0	6.6	5.8
1981	4.8	3.3	6.6	7.8	10.5	13.3	15.6	16.2	14.6	7.6	7.7	0.8
1982	2.8	4.8	5.8	8.2	11.1	11.2	16.2	15.4	13.8	9.8	7.4	4.1
1983	6.2	1.9	6.1	6.3	9.6	13.6	18.4	16.8	13.2	10.0	7.3	5.5
1984	3.3	3.5	4.5	7.7	9.5	13.9	16.2	17.0	13.2	10.7	7.7	5.0
1985	1.0	2.5	4.4	8.0	10.4	12.2	15.6	14.2	14.1	10.7	4.0	6.1
1986	3.2	-0.5	4.9	5.4	10.6	14.1	15.4	13.2	11.0	10.6	7.3	5.8
1987	1.1	3.7	4.1	9.4	9.7	12.2	15.5	15.2	13.3	9.3	6.4	4.7
1988	4.9	4.5	5.8	7.8	11.2	14.0	14.4	14.9	13.2	9.4	5.3	7.1
1989	6.1	5.8	7.0	6.1	12.5	14.0	17.4	16.1	14.1	11.5	6.4	4.5
1990	6.3	7.0	8.0	7.7	12.1	13.3	16.3	17.6	13.1	12.0	7.2	5.1
1991	3.7	2.4	7.8	8.0	11.0	12.2	17.1	17.0	14.7	10.3	7.0	5.0
1992	4.0	5.9	7.4	8.6	13.1	15.5	16.1	15.3	13.2	7.8	7.5	4.1
1993	6.0	5.4	6.6	9.3	11.2	14.4	15.1	14.4	12.5	8.5	5.0	5.3
1994	5.2	3.5	7.6	8.1	10.4	14.3	17.6	15.9	12.7	10.2	10.1	6.4
1995	4.9	6.7	5.6	8.9	11.6	14.0	18.4	18.9	13.8	13.2	8.1	2.8
1996	4.8	3.1	4.6	8.7	9.3	14.4	16.4	16.7	13.7	11.8	6.2	3.5
1997	2.9	6.9	8.4	9.1	11.5	14.0	16.9	18.6	14.5	10.5	8.9	6.1
1998	5.5	7.7	8.0	7.8	12.9	14.1	15.5	15.9	14.8	10.6	7.3	5.9
1999	5.8	5.6	7.4	9.4	12.8	13.7	17.5	16.3	15.7	11.0	8.1	5.0r
2000	5.5	6.4	7.5	7.9	12.1	14.7	15.2	16.7	15.9	10.5	7.1	5.8

(1) See Energy Trends on the internet for the latest monthly figures – See paragraph 1.82 of Chapter 1.

(2) Average mean air temperatures calculated from the maximum and minimum daily temperature as recorded at 16 meteorological stations (17 up to 1976, 15 between 1977 and August 1990), selected as representative of fuel consumption in Great Britain - 2 in Scotland, 2 in Wales and 12 in England, 4 of which are counted twice (13 in England up to 1976, 7 of which were counted twice, and between 1977 and 1990 11 in England, 5 of which were counted twice). Data on temperatures recorded are provided by the Meteorological Office.

Chapter 2
Solid fuels and derived gases

Introduction

2.1   This chapter presents figures on the supply and demand for coal and solid fuels derived from coal, and on the production and consumption of gases derived from the processing of solid fuels.

2.2   The structure of this chapter is largely unchanged this year.   Balances for coal and for manufactured fuels covering each of the last three years form the first six tables (Tables 2.1 to 2.6). These are followed by a 5 year table showing the supply and consumption of coal as a time series (Table 2.7). Comparable 5 year tables bring together data for coke oven coke, coke breeze and manufactured solid fuels (Table 2.8) and coke oven gas, blast furnace gas, benzole and tars (Table 2.9).   The long term trends tables on coal production and stocks (Table 2.10) and on coal consumption (Table 2.11) follow.   Two new tables that previously appeared in "The Energy Report" complete the chapter.   These are tables showing deep mines in production (Table 2.12) and opencast sites in production (Table 2.13).

2.3   Imports and exports of solid fuels are given in Chapter 8, and solid renewables are covered in Chapter 7.

2.4   Figures for actual consumption of coal are available for all fuel producers and for final use by the iron and steel industry. For the remaining final users consumption figures are based on information on disposals by producers and on imports. For further details see the technical notes and definitions section which begins at paragraph 2.36 of this chapter.

Structure of the coal industry

2.5   Following the privatisation of the coal industry at the end of 1994 the four main coal producers were RJB Mining, Mining Scotland, Celtic Energy and Coal Investments.   The last mentioned went into receivership in June 1996 and only two of their mines remained as going concerns under the company name of Midlands Mining. One of these two mines closed at the end of 1998 and the other at the beginning of 2000. The other four collieries reverted to the Coal Authority and were subsequently closed.

2.6   There are also a number of independent deep mines which are listed in Table 2.12.   Independent opencast coal producers, are similarly listed in Table 2.13. Some further coal and slurry are supplied from recovery operations.

Commodity balances for coal (Tables 2.1, 2.2 and 2.3).

2.7   These balance tables separately identify the three main types of coal, steam coal, coking coal, and anthracite and show the variation both in the sources of supply and where the various types of coal are mainly used.

2.8   In 2000, 80 per cent of coal demand was for steam coal, 15 per cent was for coking coal and 5 per cent was for anthracite.   Electricity generation accounted for 95 per cent of demand for steam coal and 46½ per cent of demand for anthracite. Coking coal was nearly all used in coke ovens (95 per cent), but 5 per cent was directly injected into blast furnaces.

2.9   Only 6 per cent of the total demand for coal was for final consumption, where it was used for steam raising, space or hot water heating or heat for processing. Steam coal accounted for 71 per cent of this final consumption with just under half of final consumption being steam coal for industry where mineral products (eg cement, glass and bricks) and chemicals were the largest users. The domestic sector accounted for 53 per cent of the final demand for coal with just over half of this demand being for steam coal and just under half for anthracite.

2.10   Chart 2.1, below, compares the sources of coal supplies in the UK in 2000, along with a breakdown of consumption by user and serves to illustrate some of the features brought out below.

2.11   In 2000, 29 per cent of the total supply figure in Table 2.1 was met from deep-mined production, 23 per cent from opencast operations, 38½ per cent from net imports and 1 per cent from other sources such as slurry.   Supply from all these sources was not sufficient to meet demand and so 5.1 million tonnes (equivalent to 8½ per cent of total supply) was drawn down from coal stocks.

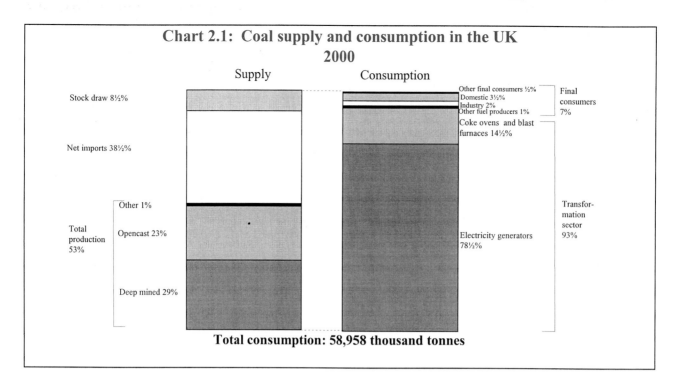

Chart 2.1: Coal supply and consumption in the UK 2000

Supply | Consumption

Stock draw 8½%

Net imports 38½%

Total production 53%

Other 1%

Opencast 23%

Deep mined 29%

Other final consumers ½%
Domestic 3½%
Industry 2%
Other fuel producers 1%

Coke ovens and blast furnaces 14½%

Electricity generators 78½%

Final consumers 7%

Transformation sector 93%

Total consumption: 58,958 thousand tonnes

2.12   Recent trends in coal production and consumption are described in paragraphs 2.20 to 2.26.

Commodity balances for manufactured fuels (Table 2.4, 2.5 and 2.6).

2.13   The balance tables for manufactured fuels cover fuels manufactured from coal, and gases produced when coal is used in coke ovens and blast furnaces. Definitions of terms associated with coke, breeze and other manufactured solid fuels are to be found in paragraphs 2.48 to 2.51.

2.14   The majority of **coke oven coke**, is home produced with imports amounting to only 7 per cent of the home produced volume. About 4 per cent of home production was exported in 2000. The amount screened out by producers as breeze and fines, amounted to about 14 per cent of production plus imports in 2000, and this 0.9 million tonnes appears in the coke breeze column of the balance. Transfers out are not equal to transfers in because of differences in the timing and location of measurements. In 2000, nearly 90 per cent of the demand for coke was at blast furnaces (part of the transformation sector) with the remainder going into final consumption in either the non-ferrous metals sector (eg foundry coke) or the domestic sector.

2.15   Most of the supply of **coke breeze** is from re-screened coke oven coke, with exports more than matching the small quantities that are produced directly or imported. Some breeze is re-used in coke manufacture or in blast furnaces, but the majority is boiler fuel.

2.16   Patent fuels are manufactured smokeless fuels produced mainly for the domestic market, as the balances show. A small amount of these fuels (only 3 per cent of total supply in 2000) is imported, but exports generally exceed imports. Imports and exports of manufactured fuels can contain small quantities of non-smokeless fuels.

2.17   Chart 2.3 shows the sources of coke, breeze and other manufactured solid fuels and a breakdown of their consumption.

2.18   The carbonisation and gasification of solid fuels at coke ovens produces **coke oven gas** as a by-product. Some of this (over 40 per cent in 2000) is used to fuel the coke ovens themselves while at steel works some is piped to blast furnaces and used in the production of steel (9 per cent in 2000). Elsewhere at steel works, the gas is used for electricity generation (15 per cent) or for heat production for other iron and steel making processes (30 per cent).

2.19   **Blast furnace gas** is a by-product of iron making in a blast furnace. A similar product is obtained when steel is made in basic oxygen steel converters, and "BOS" gas is included in this category. Most of this gas is used in other parts of integrated steel works, with 48 per cent being used for electricity generation in 2000, 34 per cent being used in coke ovens and blast furnaces themselves, and 9 per cent being used for general heat production. The remaining 9 per cent is lost or burned as waste.

Supply and consumption of coal (Table 2.7).

2.20 **Production** - Figures for 2000 show that coal production (including slurry) fell by 16 per cent compared to production in 1999. Deep-mined production fell by 17½ per cent compared to 1999 while opencast production fell by 12 per cent. In contrast, overall demand for coal was up 6 per cent on 1999. To meet this demand there was a rise in net imports of 16½ per cent (see paragraph 2.23, below) and 5.1 million tonnes was withdrawn from stocks. One major deep mine (Annesley-Bentinck) closed in January 2000. Longer term trends in production are illustrated in Chart 2.4.

2.21 Table 2A shows how production of coal is divided between England, Wales and Scotland. In 2000/2001 68 per cent of the coal output was in England, 25 per cent in Scotland, and 7 per cent in Wales.

Table 2A: Output from UK coal mines [1]

Million tonnes

	April 1998 to March 1999	April 1999 to March 2000	April 2000 to March 2001
Deep-mined			
England	21.4	17.9	15.9
Scotland	1.6	1.0	0.7
Wales	0.7	0.6	0.7
Total	23.7	19.5	17.3
Opencast			
England	7.0	6.2	4.8
Scotland	6.4	7.2	7.1
Wales	1.5	1.5	1.4
Total	14.9	14.9	13.3
Total			
England	28.4	24.1	20.7
Scotland	8.0	8.2	7.8
Wales	2.2	2.1	2.1
Total	38.6	34.4	30.6

Source: The Coal Authority

(1) Output is the tonnage declared by operators to the Coal Authority, including estimated tonnages. It excludes estimates of slurry recovered from dumps, ponds, rivers, etc.

2.22 Table 2B shows how numbers employed in the production of coal have changed over the last three years. During 2000/2001 employment including contractors rose by 2 per cent. At 31 March 2001, 73 per cent of the 11,430 people employed in UK coal mining worked in England, while 18 per cent were in Scotland and 9 per cent in Wales.

2.23 **Foreign trade -** Imports of coal in 2000 were 15½ per cent higher than in 1999 and at a new record level of 23.4 million tonnes, 10½ per cent above the previous record set in 1998. Within this imports of steam coal rose by 23½ per cent. The trends in coal

Table 2B: Employment in UK coal mines [1]

	end March 1999	end March 2000	end March 2001
Deep-mined			
England	9,016	7,064	7,316
Scotland	802	643	771
Wales	664	536	552
Total	10,482	8,243	8,639
Opencast			
England	1,882	1,300	1,068
Scotland	1,301	1,252	1,267
Wales	550	433	456
Total	3,733	2,985	2,791
Total			
England	10,898	8,364	8,384
Scotland	2,103	1,895	2,038
Wales	1,214	969	1,008
Total	14,215	11,228	11,430

Source: The Coal Authority

(1) Employment includes contractors and is as declared by licensees to the Coal Authority at 31 March each year.

imports and exports are discussed in greater detail in Chapter 8, paragraphs 8.19 to 8.22.

2.24 **Transformation** - The 6 per cent rise in coal consumption during 2000 mainly results from a 14 per cent rise in consumption by major power producers. This 5.1 million tonnes increase in coal consumption at power stations resulted from coal being used to make up for reduced levels of nuclear and (during the summer) gas fired generation arising from outages for maintenance and repair. In November and December 2000 coal fired generation was able to outbid gas fired generation because of higher gas prices.

2.25 **Consumption** - Consumption by final consumers showed a 36 per cent fall compared with 1999, but this overstates the current trend rate of decline. Consumption in 1999 was higher than in 1998 partly because consumers appeared to have replenished stocks during 1999. Domestic sector consumption in 2000 was 24 per cent down, and fell below 2 million tonnes for the first time having been around 2.5 million tonnes in each of the previous 5 years. Industrial consumption was down more sharply, by almost 50 per cent, at 1.4 million tonnes.

2.26 Long term trends in the consumption of coal in the UK since 1970 onwards are presented in Table 2.11.

2.27 **Stocks** – Production and net imports together in 2000 were 4½ per cent lower than in 1999, while demand for coal rose by 6 per cent. This led to stocks of coal falling by 5.1 million tonnes (27½ per cent). In contrast, 1.1 million tonnes were added to stocks in 1999. Total stocks at the end of 2000 were therefore equivalent to 22½ per cent of the year's coal consumption having fallen from over 33 per cent in 1999. At the previous low point in 1996 stock levels were only 21 per cent of the year's consumption. Stocks held at collieries and opencast sites at the end of 2000 were 3.5 million tonnes lower than a year earlier while stocks held by the major power producers were 1.4 million tonnes lower. The recent changes in coal stocks are illustrated in Chart 2.2.

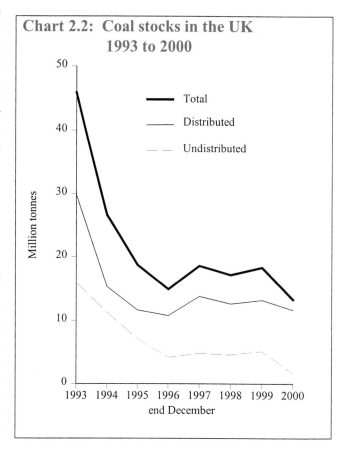

Chart 2.2: Coal stocks in the UK 1993 to 2000

Supply and consumption of coke oven coke, coke breeze and other manufactured fuels (Table 2.8)

2.28   This table presents figures for the most recent five years on the same basis as the balance tables. Figures for stocks are also included. Coal used to produce these manufactured fuels is shown in Table 2.7. For **coke oven coke**, 2000 saw a decrease in demand of 5½ per cent. However, production was 4 per cent higher. Imports were 10½ per cent higher, but exports rose to a greater extent so net imports were 40 per cent lower, although already small in volume compared with production. As a result stocks of coke rose.

2.29   In 2000, the demand for **coke breeze** fell by 8 per cent, but re-screenings were also down so there was a fall in stocks. There was a 9 per cent decline in the demand for **other manufactured solid fuels**, mainly because of a 10½ per cent fall in domestic sector demand. UK production was down 15½ per cent on 1999 levels.

Supply and consumption of coke oven gas, blast furnace gas, benzole and tars (Table 2.9)

2.30   This table presents figures for the most recent five years on the same basis as the balance tables. Demand for **coke oven gas** rose by 4½ per cent in 2000, but demand has remained close to 13,000 GWh

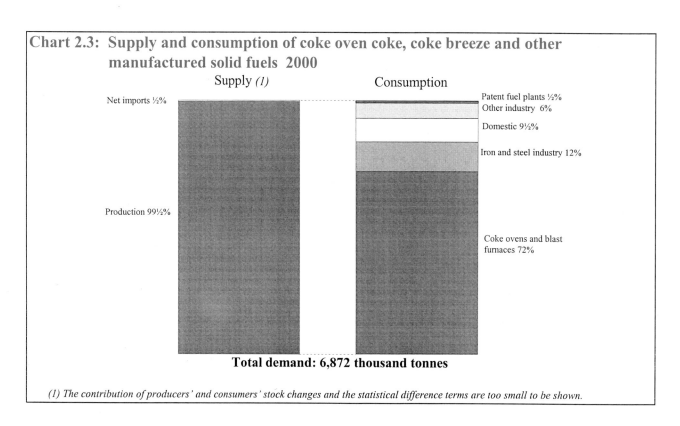

Chart 2.3: Supply and consumption of coke oven coke, coke breeze and other manufactured solid fuels 2000

(1) The contribution of producers' and consumers' stock changes and the statistical difference terms are too small to be shown.

in each of the last 5 years. Use in electricity generation and in blast furnaces fell, but use in coke ovens and for general heating purposes in the iron and steel industry both rose. Both production and demand for **blast furnace gas** were lower in 2000 than in 1999 by around 7½ per cent. This decline cut across all areas of use.

Long term trends

Coal production and stocks (Table 2.10)

2.31 Figures for coal production, imports, overseas shipments and stocks are given in Table 2.10 which is in turn based on Table 2.7 with the series extended back to 1970.

2.32 Table 2.10 shows a decline in deep-mined production of more than 87 per cent since the highest level shown in this table in 1970. Opencast production in 2000 was the lowest since 1979. Table 2.10 also shows that imports, initially of coal types in short supply in this country, started in 1970. By 2000 imports had grown to be ¾ of the level of UK production. Both these trends are illustrated in Chart 2.4. Stock levels in the early '90s were relatively high reaching a peak of 53 per cent of annual inland coal consumption in 1993. After this electricity generators began to run down their stocks sharply so that at the end of 1996 stocks were only 21 per cent of annual consumption, but between 1997 and 1999 they rose again in proportionate terms to 33½ per cent of annual consumption before falling back to 22½ per cent in 2000 (see paragraph 2.27, above, and Chart 2.2).

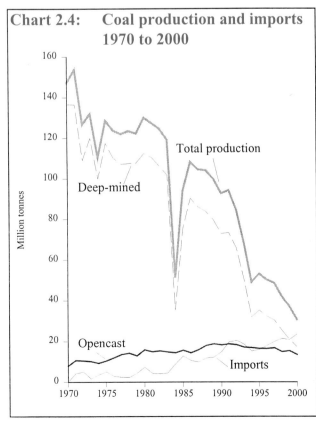

Chart 2.4: Coal production and imports 1970 to 2000

Inland consumption of solid fuels (Table 2.11)

2.33 Figures for inland consumption of coal by fuel producers and final users are given in Table 2.11, which is in turn based on Table 2.7. The table also shows final consumption figures for coke and breeze and other solid fuels based on Table 2.8 These products are mainly supplied from the conversion of coal, supplemented by a small amount of foreign trade. Where possible the series have been extended back to 1970.

2.34 Trends in inland consumption of coal, in total and by power stations, coke ovens, and final consumers, are illustrated in Chart 2.5 below.

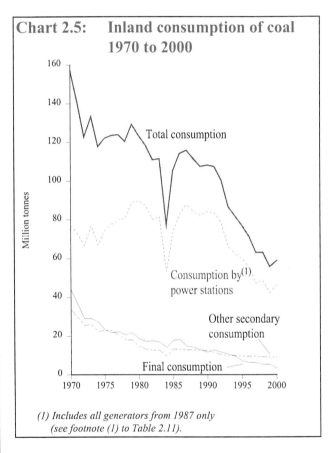

Chart 2.5: Inland consumption of coal 1970 to 2000

(1) Includes all generators from 1987 only (see footnote (1) to Table 2.11).

2.35 Total inland consumption of coal fell by 62 per cent from 157 million tonnes in 1970 to 59 million tonnes in 2000. Consumption by the electricity generators increased from 77 million tonnes in 1970 to a peak of 90 million tonnes in 1980 and continued in the 80-90 million tonnes range until 1991 with the exception of the miners' strike years. With the increased use of nuclear power and natural gas, the consumption of coal by the generators fell steadily after 1991. However, there was a pause in this trend in 1998 when coal fired generation was called upon to make up for the temporary reduction in imported electricity from France and again in 2000 when nuclear generation suffered a large number of outages for repair and maintenance. At the end of 2000 the rise in gas prices enabled coal to bid into the pool to generate in place of some gas fired stations. The proportion of electricity supplied from coal in the early

1990s was around 70 per cent, falling to 28 per cent in 1999, but increasing to 31 per cent in 2000 (see Chapter 5). At 46 million tonnes in 2000, use of coal at power stations represents 79 per cent of total coal consumption, compared with only 49 per cent in 1970.

Technical notes and definitions

2.36   These notes and definitions are in addition to the technical notes and definitions covering all fuels and energy as a whole in Chapter 1, paragraphs 1.46 to 1.81. For notes on the commodity balances and definitions of the terms used in the row headings see the Annex A, paragraphs A.7 to A.41.

Steam coal, coking coal, and anthracite

2.37   **Steam coal** is coal classified as such by UK coal producers and by importers of coal. It tends to be coal having lower calorific values.

2.38   **Coking coal** is coal sold by producers for use in coke ovens and similar carbonising processes. The definition is not therefore determined by the calorific value or caking qualities of each batch of coal sold, although calorific values tend to be higher than for steam coal.

2.39   **Anthracite** is coal classified as such by UK coal producers and importers of coal. Typically it has a high heat content making it particularly suitable for certain industrial processes and for use as a domestic fuel. Some UK anthracite producers have found a market for their lower calorific value output at power stations.

Coal production

2.40   **Deep-mined** - The statistics cover saleable output from deep mines including coal obtained from working on both revenue and capital accounts. All licensed collieries (and British Coal collieries prior to 1995) are included, even where coal is only a subsidiary product.

2.41   **Opencast** - The figures cover saleable output and include the output of sites worked by operators under agency agreements and licences, as well as the output of sites licensed for the production of coal as a subsidiary to the production of other minerals.

2.42   **Other** - Estimates of slurry etc. recovered and disposed of from dumps, ponds, rivers, etc.

Imports and exports of coal and other solid fuels

2.43   Figures are derived from returns made to HM Customs and Excise and are broken down in greater detail in Chapter 8, Table 8.5.

2.44   However, in Tables 2.4, 2.5, 2.6 and 2.8, the export figures used for hard coke, coke breeze and other manufactured solid fuels for the years before 1998 are quantities of fuel exported as reported to DTI by the companies concerned, rather than quantities recorded by HM Customs and Excise in their Trade Statistics.

Allocation of imported coal

2.45   Although data are available on consumption of home produced coal, and also on consumption of imported coal by secondary fuel producers there is only very limited direct information on consumption of imported coal by final users. Following surveys conducted in 1992 and 1995, 75 per cent of steam coal imports, excluding those used by electricity generators, was allocated to industry each year and 25 per cent to the domestic sector. A further survey in 1998 showed that it was more appropriate to allocate 15 per cent of steam coal imports to the public administration sector in 1998, 1997 and 1996, 10 per cent in 1995 and 5 per cent in 1994 because of coal consumption in schools and hospitals. Correspondingly the allocation to industry has been reduced by the same percentages (ie to 60 per cent in 1996 to 1998). The 1998 proportions have been retained for 1999 and 2000. In addition, 10 per cent of anthracite imports, excluding cleaned smalls, are allocated to industry, with 90 per cent to the domestic sector in all years shown in the tables. All imports of coking coal and cleaned anthracite smalls are allocated to coke and other solid fuel producers.

Stocks of coal

2.46   Undistributed stocks are those held at collieries and opencast sites. It is not possible to distinguish these two locations separately in the stock figures. Distributed stocks are those held at power stations and stocking grounds of the major power producing companies (as defined in Chapter 5, paragraph 5.58), coke ovens and low temperature carbonisation plants, and patent fuel plants.

Transformation, energy industry use and consumption of solid fuels

2.47   Annex A of this Digest outlines the principles of energy and commodity balances and defines the activities that fall within these parts of the balances. However, the following additional notes relevant to solid fuels are given below:

Transformation: Blast furnaces - Coking coal injected into blast furnaces is shown separately within the balance tables.

Transformation: Low temperature carbonisation plants and patent fuel plants - Coal used at these plants for the manufacture of domestic coke such as Coalite and of briquetted fuels such as Phurnacite and Homefire.

Consumption: Industry - The statistics comprise sales of coal by the eight main coal producers to the iron and steel industry (excluding that used at coke ovens and blast furnaces) and to other industrial sectors and estimated proportions of anthracite and steam coal imports. The figures exclude coal used for industries' own generation of electricity which appears separately under transformation.

Consumption: Domestic - Coal supplied free of charge or at reduced prices to current and retired miners, officials, etc in the coalfields. The concessionary fuel provided to miners in 2000 is estimated at 290 thousand tonnes. This estimate is included in the domestic steam coal and domestic anthracite figures.

Consumption of coke and other manufactured solid fuels - These are disposals from coke ovens to merchants. The figures also include estimated proportions of coke imports.

Coke oven coke (hard coke) and hard coke breeze

2.48   The statistics cover coke produced at coke ovens owned by Corus plc (formerly British Steel), Coal Products Ltd and other producers. Low temperature carbonisation plants are not included (see paragraph 2.51, below). Breeze (as defined in paragraph 2.49) is excluded from the figures for coke oven coke.

2.49   Breeze can generally be described as coke screened below 19 mm (¾ inch) with no fines removed, but the screen size may vary in different areas and to meet the requirements of particular markets. Coke that has been transported from one location to another is usually re-screened before use to remove smaller sizes, giving rise to further breeze.

2.50   In 1998, an assessment using industry data showed that on average over the last five years 91 per cent of imports have been coke and 9 per cent breeze and it is these proportions that have been used for 1998, 1999 and 2000 in Tables 2.4, 2.5, 2.6 and 2.8.

2.51   Other manufactured solid fuels are mainly solid smokeless fuels for the domestic market for use in both open fires and in boilers. A smaller quantity is exported (although exports are largely offset by similar quantities of imports in most years). Manufacture takes place in patented fuel plants and low temperature carbonisation plants. The brand names used for these fuels include Homefire, Phurnacite, Ancit and Coalite.

Blast furnace gas, coke oven gas, benzole and tars

2.52   The following definitions are used in the tables that include these fuels:

Blast furnace gas - includes basic oxygen steel furnace (BOS) gas. Blast furnace gas is the gas produced during iron ore smelting when hot air passes over coke within the blast ovens. It contains carbon monoxide, carbon dioxide, hydrogen and nitrogen. In a basic oxygen steel furnace the aim is not to introduce nitrogen or hydrogen into the steel making process, so pure oxygen gas and suitable fluxes are used to remove the carbon and phosphorous from the molten pig iron and steel scrap. A similar fuel gas is thus produced.

Coke oven gas - is a gas produced during the carbonisation of coal to form coke at coke ovens.

Synthetic coke oven gas - is mainly natural gas which is mixed with smaller amounts of blast furnace and BOS gas to produce a gas with almost the same quantities as coke oven gas. The transfers row of Tables 2.4, 2.5 and 2.6 shows the quantities of blast furnace gas used for this purpose and the total input of gases to the synthetic coke oven gas process. There is a corresponding outward transfer from natural gas in Chapter 4, Table 4.1.

Benzole - a colourless, liquid, flammable, aromatic hydrocarbon by-product of the iron and steel making process. It is used as a solvent in the manufacture of styrenes and phenols but can also be used as a motor fuel.

Tars - viscous materials usually derived from the destructive distillation of coal which are by-products of the coke and iron making processes.

Periods covered

2.53   Figures in this chapter generally relate to periods of 52 weeks or 53 weeks as follows:

Year	53 weeks ended
1996	28 December 1996
	52 weeks ended
1997	27 December 1997
1998	26 December 1998
1999	25 December 1999
	53 weeks ended
2000	30 December 2000

The 53 week data for 1996 have been adjusted to 52 week equivalents by taking 13/14ths of the 14 week first quarter of 1996. The 53 week data for 2000 have been adjusted by omitting data for an average week based on information provided by the largest companies for the first week in April 2000.

2.54   Data for coal used for electricity generation by major power producers follow the electricity industry calendar (see Chapter 5, paragraph 5.67) and coal use by other generators is for the 12 months ended 31 December each year. HM Customs and Excise data on imports and exports are also for the 12 months ended 31 December each year. Data for coal and coke use in the iron and steel industry, and for gases, benzole and tars produced by the iron and steel industry follow the iron and steel industry calendar (see Chapter 5, paragraph 5.68).

Data collection

2.55   Since 1995 aggregate data on coal production have been obtained from the Coal Authority. In addition the largest producers (Betws Anthracite, Celtic Energy, Coal Contractors Ltd, Goitre Tower Anthracite, Hatfield Coal Company, H J Banks, Midlands Mining, Miller Group Ltd, Mining Scotland, Monktonhall Colliery and RJB Mining)[1] have provided data in response to an annual DTI inquiry covering production (deep-mined and opencast), trade, stocks, and disposals. The Iron and Steel Statistics Bureau (ISSB) provides DTI with an annual statement of coke and breeze production and use of coal, coke and breeze within that industry. The ISSB is also the source of data on gases produced by the iron and steel industry (coke oven gas, blast furnace gas and basic oxygen steel furnace gas). DTI directly surveys producers of manufactured fuels other than coke or breeze.

2.56   Trade in solid fuels is also covered by using data from HM Customs and Excise as described in Chapter 8 paragraphs 8.23 to 8.30. Consumption of coal for electricity generation is covered by data collected by DTI from electricity generators described in Chapter 5, paragraphs 5.70 to 5.72.

Monthly and quarterly data

2.57   Monthly data on coal production, foreign trade, consumption and stocks are available on DTI's Energy Statistics web site (www.dti.gov.uk/energy/energystats/energystats.htm) in Tables 2.4, 2.5, and 2.6. Three quarterly commodity balances for coal; coke oven coke, coke breeze and other manufactured solid fuels; and coke oven gas, blast furnace gas, benzole and tars are published in DTI's quarterly statistical bulletin *Energy Trends* and also available on DTI's Energy Statistics web site Tables 2.1, 2.2 and 2.3. See Annex F for more information about *Energy Trends*.

Statistical differences

2.58   Tables 2.1 to 2.9 each contain a statistical difference term covering the difference between recorded supply and recorded demand. These statistical differences arise for a number of reasons. Firstly the data within each table are taken from varied sources, as described above, such as producers, intermediate consumers (such as electricity generators), final consumers (such as the iron and steel industry), and H M Customs and Excise. Secondly some of these industries work to different statistical calendars (see paragraphs 2.53 and 2.54, above), and thirdly some of the figures are estimated either because data in the required detail are not readily available within the industry or because the methods of collecting the data do not cover the smallest members of the industry.

Contact: *Mike Janes (Statistician)*
mike.janes@dti.gsi.gov.uk
020-7215 5186

James Achur
james.achur@dti.gsi.gov.uk
020-7215 2717

---

[1] Midlands Mining succeeded Coal Investments during 1996 but ceased to produce coal in January 2000 and ceased to sell coal after June 2000. Monktonhall colliery ceased production in 1997. RJB Mining became UK Coal in May 2001.

2.1 Commodity balances 2000

Coal

Thousand tonnes

	Steam coal	Coking coal	Anthracite	Total
Supply				
Production	..	255	..	30,600
Other sources	..	-	..	598
Imports	14,425	8,462	558	23,445
Exports	-351	-4	-306	-661
Marine bunkers	-	-	-	-
Stock change *(1)*	..	+140	..	+5,056
Transfers	-	-	-	-
Total supply	..	8,853	..	59,038
Statistical difference *(2)*	..	+168	..	+84
Total demand	47,317	8,685	2,952	58,954
Transformation	44,762	8,685	1,913	55,360
Electricity generation	44,762	-	1,373	46,135
Major power producers	43,389	-	1,373	44,762
Autogenerators	1,373	-	-	1,373
Petroleum refineries	-	-	-	-
Coke manufacture	-	8,229	-	8,229
Blast furnaces	-	456	-	456
Patent fuel manufacture and low temperature carbonisation	-	-	540	540
Energy industry use	..	-	..	12
Electricity generation	-	-	-	-
Oil and gas extraction	-	-	-	-
Petroleum refineries	-	-	-	-
Coal extraction	..	-	..	12
Coke manufacture	-	-	-	-
Blast furnaces	-	-	-	-
Patent fuel manufacture	-	-	-	-
Pumped storage	-	-	-	-
Other	-	-	-	-
Losses	-	-	-	-
Final consumption	2,546	-	1,036	3,582
Industry	1,258	-	119	1,377
Unclassified	-	-	-	-
Iron and steel	2	-	-	2
Non-ferrous metals	..	-	..	118
Mineral products	..	-	..	270
Chemicals	..	-	..	426
Mechanical engineering etc	..	-	..	12
Electrical engineering etc	..	-	..	3
Vehicles	..	-	..	61
Food, beverages etc	..	-	..	194
Textiles, leather, etc	..	-	..	49
Paper, printing etc	..	-	..	109
Other industries	..	-	..	133
Construction	-	-	-	-
Transport	-	-	-	-
Air	-	-	-	-
Rail	-	-	-	-
Road	-	-	-	-
National navigation	-	-	-	-
Pipelines	-	-	-	-
Other	..	-	..	2,205
Domestic	990	-	917	1,907
Public administration	..	-	..	276
Commercial	-	-	-	7
Agriculture	..	-	..	7
Miscellaneous	..	-	..	8
Non energy use	-	-	-	-

(1) Stock fall (+), stock rise (-).
(2) Total supply minus total demand.

2.2 Commodity balances 1999

Coal

Thousand tonnes

	Steam coal	Coking coal	Anthracite	Total
Supply				
Production	..	263r	..	36,163
Other sources	..	-	..	914
Imports	11,675r	8,020	598r	20,293r
Exports	-434	-	-327r	-761r
Marine bunkers	-	-	-	-
Stock change *(1)*	..	+258	..	-1,164r
Transfers	-	-	-	-
Total supply	..	8,541r	..	55,445r
Statistical difference *(2)*	..	+128r	..	-275r
Total demand	44,837r	8,413r	2,470r	55,720r
Transformation	40,268r	8,413r	1,446r	50,127r
Electricity generation	40,268r	-	800r	41,068r
Major power producers	38,783r	-	800r	39,583r
Autogenerators	1,485r	-	-	1,485r
Petroleum refineries	-	-	-	-
Coke manufacture	-	7,919r	-	7,919r
Blast furnaces	-	494	-	494
Patent fuel manufacture and low temperature carbonisation	-	-	646r	646r
Energy industry use	..	-	..	10
Electricity generation	-	-	-	-
Oil and gas extraction	-	-	-	-
Petroleum refineries	-	-	-	-
Coal extraction	..	-	..	10
Coke manufacture	-	-	-	-
Blast furnaces	-	-	-	-
Patent fuel manufacture	-	-	-	-
Pumped storage	-	-	-	-
Other	-	-	-	-
Losses	-	-	-	-
Final consumption	4,560r	-	1,023r	5,583r
Industry	2,581r	-	123r	2,704r
Unclassified	-	-	-	-
Iron and steel	16r	-	-	16r
Non-ferrous metals	..	-	..	354r
Mineral products	..	-	..	667r
Chemicals	..	-	..	841r
Mechanical engineering etc	..	-	..	31r
Electrical engineering etc	..	-	..	9r
Vehicles	..	-	..	98r
Food, beverages etc	..	-	..	290r
Textiles, leather, etc	..	-	..	73r
Paper, printing etc	..	-	..	179r
Other industries	..	-	..	146r
Construction	-	-	-	-
Transport	-	-	-	-
Air	-	-	-	-
Rail	-	-	-	-
Road	-	-	-	-
National navigation	-	-	-	-
Pipelines	-	-	-	-
Other	..	-	..	2,879r
Domestic	1,619r	-	898r	2,517r
Public administration	..	-	..	320r
Commercial	-	-	-	4
Agriculture	..	-	..	7
Miscellaneous	..	-	..	31r
Non energy use	-	-	-	-

(1) Stock fall (+), stock rise (-).
(2) Total supply minus total demand.

2.3 Commodity balances 1998

Coal

Thousand tonnes

	Steam coal	Coking coal	Anthracite	Total
Supply				
Production	..	542r	..	40,046
Other sources	..	-	..	1,131
Imports	12,079	8,646	519	21,244
Exports	-689	-	-282	-971
Marine bunkers	-	-	-	-
Stock change *(1)*	..	-184	..	+1,421r
Transfers	-	-	-	-
Total supply	..	9,004r	..	62,871r
Statistical difference *(2)*	..	+276r	..	-281r
Total demand	51,997r	8,728	2,427r	63,152r
Transformation	47,785r	8,728	1,376r	57,889r
Electricity generation	47,785r	-	741r	48,526r
Major power producers	45,886r	-	741r	46,627
Autogenerators	1,899r	-	-	1,899r
Petroleum refineries	-	-	-	-
Coke manufacture	-	8,169	-	8,169
Blast furnaces	-	559	-	559
Patent fuel manufacture and low temperature carbonisation	-	-	635	635
Energy industry use	..	-	..	5r
Electricity generation	-	-	-	-
Oil and gas extraction	-	-	-	-
Petroleum refineries	-	-	-	-
Coal extraction	..	-	..	5r
Coke manufacture	-	-	-	-
Blast furnaces	-	-	-	-
Patent fuel manufacture	-	-	-	-
Pumped storage	-	-	-	-
Other	-	-	-	-
Losses	-	-	-	-
Final consumption	4,208r	-	1,050r	5,258r
Industry	2,391r	-	85r	2,476r
Unclassified	-	-	-	-
Iron and steel	9	-	-	9
Non-ferrous metals	..	-	..	189r
Mineral products	..	-	..	793r
Chemicals	..	-	..	677r
Mechanical engineering etc	..	-	..	28
Electrical engineering etc	..	-	..	3
Vehicles	..	-	..	47r
Food, beverages etc	..	-	..	303r
Textiles, leather, etc	..	-	..	69
Paper, printing etc	..	-	..	110r
Other industries	..	-	..	248r
Construction	-	-	-	-
Transport	-	-	-	-
Air	-	-	-	-
Rail	-	-	-	-
Road	-	-	-	-
National navigation	-	-	-	-
Pipelines	-	-	-	-
Other	..	-	..	2,782r
Domestic	1,413r	-	953r	2,366r
Public administration	..	-	..	312r
Commercial	-	-	-	4
Agriculture	..	-	..	9
Miscellaneous	..	-	..	91r
Non energy use	-	-	-	-

(1) Stock fall (+), stock rise (-).
(2) Total supply minus total demand.

2.4　Commodity balances 2000

Manufactured fuels

	Thousand tonnes				GWh		
	Coke oven coke	Coke breeze	Other manuf. solid fuel	Total manuf. solid fuel	Benzole and tars (4)	Coke oven gas	Blast furnace gas
Supply							
Production	6,058	37	537	6,632	2,393	12,678	17,564
Other sources	-	-	-	-	-	-	-
Imports	430	53	14	497	-	-	-
Exports	-243	-138	-79	-460	-	-	-
Marine bunkers	-	-	-	-	-	-	-
Stock change (1)	-405	+46	+38	-321	-	-	-
Transfers (3)	-641	+923	-	+282	-	+443	-17
Total supply	**5,199**	**921**	**510**	**6,630**	**2,393**	**13,121**	**17,547**
Statistical difference (2)	-117	-102	-22	-241	-	-265	-104
Total demand	**5,316**	**1,023**	**532**	**6,871**	**2,393**	**13,386**	**17,651**
Transformation	**4,764**	**189**	**-**	**4,953**	**-**	**1,996**	**8,601**
Electricity generation	-	-	-	-	-	1,996	8,601
Major power producers	-	-	-	-	-	-	-
Autogenerators	-	-	-	-	-	1,996	8,601
Petroleum refineries	-	-	-	-	-	-	-
Coke manufacture	-	1	-	1	-	-	-
Blast furnaces	4,764	188	-	4,952	-	-	-
Patent fuel manufacture	-	-	-	-	-	-	-
Low temperature carbonisation	-	-	-	-	-	-	-
Energy industry use	**37**	**-**	**11**	**48**	**-**	**6,748**	**5,974**
Electricity generation	-	-	-	-	-	-	-
Oil and gas extraction	-	-	-	-	-	-	-
Petroleum refineries	-	-	-	-	-	-	-
Coal extraction	-	-	-	-	-	-	-
Coke manufacture	-	-	-	-	-	5,555	1,046
Blast furnaces	-	-	-	-	-	1,193	4,928
Patent fuel manufacture	37	-	11	48	-	-	-
Pumped storage	-	-	-	-	-	-	-
Other	-	-	-	-	-	-	-
Losses	**-**	**-**	**-**	**-**	**-**	**257**	**1,576**
Final consumption	**515**	**834**	**521**	**1,870**	**2,393**	**4,385**	**1,500**
Industry	**370**	**834**	**25**	**1,229**	**2,393**	**4,385**	**1,500**
Unclassified	191	41	25	257	597	341	-
Iron and steel	19	793	-	812	1,796	4,044	1,500
Non-ferrous metals	160	-	-	160	-	-	-
Mineral products	-	-	-	-	-	-	-
Chemicals	-	-	-	-	-	-	-
Mechanical engineering etc	-	-	-	-	-	-	-
Electrical engineering etc	-	-	-	-	-	-	-
Vehicles	-	-	-	-	-	-	-
Food, beverages etc	-	-	-	-	-	-	-
Textiles, leather, etc	-	-	-	-	-	-	-
Paper, printing etc	-	-	-	-	-	-	-
Other industries	-	-	-	-	-	-	-
Construction	-	-	-	-	-	-	-
Transport	-	-	-	-	-	-	-
Air	-	-	-	-	-	-	-
Rail	-	-	-	-	-	-	-
Road	-	-	-	-	-	-	-
National navigation	-	-	-	-	-	-	-
Pipelines	-	-	-	-	-	-	-
Other	**145**	**-**	**496**	**641**	-	-	-
Domestic	145	-	496	641	-	-	-
Public administration	-	-	-	-	-	-	-
Commercial	-	-	-	-	-	-	-
Agriculture	-	-	-	-	-	-	-
Miscellaneous	-	-	-	-	-	-	-
Non energy use	-	-	-	-	-	-	-

(1) Stock fall (+), stock rise (-).
(2) Total supply minus total demand.
(3) Coke oven gas and blast furnace gas transfers are for synthetic coke oven gas, see paragraph 2.52.

(4) Because of the small number of benzole suppliers, figures for benzole and tars cannot be given separately.

2.5 Commodity balances 1999

Manufactured fuels

| | Thousand tonnes | | | | | GWh | |
	Coke oven coke	Coke breeze	Other manuf. solid fuel	Total manuf. solid fuel	Benzole and tars (4)	Coke oven gas	Blast furnace gas
Supply							
Production	5,837	33	635	6,505r	2,343r	12,090r	19,023r
Other sources	-	-	-	-	-	-	-
Imports	389	40	6	435r	-	-	-
Exports	-79	-165	-54	-298r	-	-	-
Marine bunkers	-	-	-	-	-	-	-
Stock change (1)	+353	-40r	-7	+306r	-	-	-
Transfers (3)	-951	+1,035	-	+84r	-	+528	-22
Total supply	**5,549**	**903r**	**580**	**7,032r**	**2,343r**	**12,618r**	**19,001r**
Statistical difference (2)	-91r	-206r	-5	-302r	-	-209r	-142r
Total demand	**5,640r**	**1,109r**	**585**	**7,334r**	**2,343r**	**12,827r**	**19,143r**
Transformation	**5,113r**	**189r**	**-**	**5,302r**	**-**	**2,030r**	**8,601r**
Electricity generation	-	-	-	-	-	2,030r	8,601r
Major power producers	-	-	-	-	-	-	-
Autogenerators	-	-	-	-	-	2,030r	8,601r
Petroleum refineries	-	-	-	-	-	-	-
Coke manufacture	-	24r	-	24r	-	-	-
Blast furnaces	5,113r	165r	-	5,278r	-	-	-
Patent fuel manufacture	-	-	-	-	-	-	-
Low temperature carbonisation	-	-	-	-	-	-	-
Energy industry use	**20**	**-**	**13**	**33**	**-**	**6,522**	**6,219r**
Electricity generation	-	-	-	-	-	-	-
Oil and gas extraction	-	-	-	-	-	-	-
Petroleum refineries	-	-	-	-	-	-	-
Coal extraction	-	-	-	-	-	-	-
Coke manufacture	-	-	-	-	-	5,283	1,083r
Blast furnaces	-	-	-	-	-	1,239	5,136r
Patent fuel manufacture	20	-	13	33	-	-	-
Pumped storage	-	-	-	-	-	-	-
Other	-	-	-	-	-	173r	1,723r
Losses	**-**	**-**	**-**	**-**	**-**	**173r**	**1,723r**
Final consumption	**507r**	**920r**	**572**	**1,999r**	**2,343r**	**4,102r**	**2,600r**
Industry	**386r**	**920r**	**18**	**1,324r**	**2,343r**	**4,102r**	**2,600r**
Unclassified	226r	33r	18	277r	580r	124	-
Iron and steel	17r	887r	-	904r	1,763	3,978r	2,600r
Non-ferrous metals	143	-	-	143	-	-	-
Mineral products	-	-	-	-	-	-	-
Chemicals	-	-	-	-	-	-	-
Mechanical engineering etc	-	-	-	-	-	-	-
Electrical engineering etc	-	-	-	-	-	-	-
Vehicles	-	-	-	-	-	-	-
Food, beverages etc	-	-	-	-	-	-	-
Textiles, leather, etc	-	-	-	-	-	-	-
Paper, printing etc	-	-	-	-	-	-	-
Other industries	-	-	-	-	-	-	-
Construction	-	-	-	-	-	-	-
Transport	**-**	**-**	**-**	**-**	**-**	**-**	**-**
Air	-	-	-	-	-	-	-
Rail	-	-	-	-	-	-	-
Road	-	-	-	-	-	-	-
National navigation	-	-	-	-	-	-	-
Pipelines	-	-	-	-	-	-	-
Other	**121r**	**-**	**554**	**675r**	**-**	**-**	**-**
Domestic	121r	-	554	675r	-	-	-
Public administration	-	-	-	-	-	-	-
Commercial	-	-	-	-	-	-	-
Agriculture	-	-	-	-	-	-	-
Miscellaneous	-	-	-	-	-	-	-
Non energy use	**-**	**-**	**-**	**-**	**-**	**-**	**-**

(1) Stock fall (+), stock rise (-).
(2) Total supply minus total demand.
(3) Coke oven gas and blast furnace gas transfers are for synthetic coke oven gas, see paragraph 2.52.

(4) Because of the small number of benzole suppliers, figures for benzole and tars cannot be given separately.

2.6 Commodity balances 1998

Manufactured fuels

	Thousand tonnes				GWh	
	Coke oven coke	Coke breeze	Other manuf. solid fuel	Total manuf. solid fuel	Benzole and tars (4)	Coke oven gas	Blast furnace gas
Supply							
Production	6,178	37	616	6,831	2,542	13,126	20,114r
Other sources	-	-	-	-	-	-	-
Imports	753	78	10	841	-	-	-
Exports	- 93	- 196	- 56	- 345	-	-	-
Marine bunkers	-	-	-	-	-	-	-
Stock change (1)	-264	+42	+87r	-135r	-	-	-
Transfers (3)	-1,223	+1,163	-	-60	-	+630	-22
Total supply	**5,351**	**1,124**	**657r**	**7,132r**	**2,542**	**13,756**	**20,092r**
Statistical difference (2)	-81r	-66r	+13r	-134r	-	+127r	+33r
Total demand	**5,432r**	**1,190r**	**644r**	**7,266r**	**2,542**	**13,629r**	**20,059r**
Transformation	**4,908**	**287**	**-**	**5,195**	**-**	**1,957r**	**8,641r**
Electricity generation	-	-	-	-	-	1,957r	8,641r
Major power producers	-	-	-	-	-	-	-
Autogenerators	-	-	-	-	-	1,957r	8,641r
Petroleum refineries	-	-	-	-	-	-	-
Coke manufacture	-	50	-	50	-	-	-
Blast furnaces	4,908	237	-	5,145	-	-	-
Patent fuel manufacture	-	-	-	-	-	-	-
Low temperature carbonisation	-	-	-	-	-	-	-
Energy industry use	**27**	**-**	**14**	**41**	**-**	**6,855**	**6,578r**
Electricity generation	-	-	-	-	-	-	-
Oil and gas extraction	-	-	-	-	-	-	-
Petroleum refineries	-	-	-	-	-	-	-
Coal extraction	-	-	-	-	-	-	-
Coke manufacture	-	-	-	-	-	5,690	1,085
Blast furnaces	-	-	-	-	-	1,165	5,493r
Patent fuel manufacture	27	-	14	41	-	-	-
Pumped storage	-	-	-	-	-	-	-
Other	-	-	-	-	-	-	-
Losses	**-**	**-**	**-**	**-**	**-**	**335**	**1,474**
Final consumption	**497r**	**903r**	**630r**	**2,030r**	**2,542**	**4,482r**	**3,366r**
Industry	**377r**	**903r**	**32**	**1,312r**	**2,542**	**4,482r**	**3,366r**
Unclassified	220r	81r	32	333r	617	116	-
Iron and steel	23	822	-	845	1,925	4,366r	3,366r
Non-ferrous metals	134	-	-	134	-	-	-
Mineral products	-	-	-	-	-	-	-
Chemicals	-	-	-	-	-	-	-
Mechanical engineering etc	-	-	-	-	-	-	-
Electrical engineering etc	-	-	-	-	-	-	-
Vehicles	-	-	-	-	-	-	-
Food, beverages etc	-	-	-	-	-	-	-
Textiles, leather, etc	-	-	-	-	-	-	-
Paper, printing etc	-	-	-	-	-	-	-
Other industries	-	-	-	-	-	-	-
Construction	-	-	-	-	-	-	-
Transport	**-**	**-**	**-**	**-**	**-**	**-**	**-**
Air	-	-	-	-	-	-	-
Rail	-	-	-	-	-	-	-
Road	-	-	-	-	-	-	-
National navigation	-	-	-	-	-	-	-
Pipelines	-	-	-	-	-	-	-
Other	**120r**	**-**	**598r**	**718r**	**-**	**-**	**-**
Domestic	120r	-	598r	718r	-	-	-
Public administration	-	-	-	-	-	-	-
Commercial	-	-	-	-	-	-	-
Agriculture	-	-	-	-	-	-	-
Miscellaneous	-	-	-	-	-	-	-
Non energy use	**-**	**-**	**-**	**-**	**-**	**-**	**-**

(1) Stock fall (+), stock rise (-).
(2) Total supply minus total demand.
(3) Coke oven gas and blast furnace gas transfers are for synthetic coke oven gas, see paragraph 2.52.
(4) Because of the small number of benzole suppliers, figures for benzole and tars cannot be given separately.

2.7   Supply and consumption of coal

Thousand tonnes

	1996	1997	1998	1999	2000
Supply					
Production	48,538	46,981	40,046	36,163	30,600
Deep-mined	32,223	30,281	25,507r	20,888	17,188
Opencast	16,315	16,700	14,539r	15,275	13,412
Other sources *(3)*	1,659	1,514	1,131	914	598
Imports	17,799	19,757r	21,244	20,293r	23,445
Exports	-988	-1,146	-971	-761r	-661
Stock change *(1)*	+3,825	-3,683r	+1,421r	-1,164r	+5,056
Total supply	**70,833**	**63,423r**	**62,871r**	**55,445r**	**59,038**
Statistical difference *(2)*	-567	+343r	-281r	-275r	+84
Total demand	**71,400**	**63,080**	**63,152r**	**55,720r**	**58,954**
Transformation	**64,471r**	**56,864**	**57,889r**	**50,127r**	**55,360**
Electricity generation	54,893r	47,250	48,526r	41,068r	46,135
Major power producers	53,423	45,323	46,627	39,583r	44,762
Autogenerators	1,470r	1,927	1,899r	1,485r	1,373
Coke manufacture	8,049	8,143	8,169	7,919r	8,229
Blast furnaces	583	607	559	494	456
Patent fuel manufacture and low temperature carbonisation	946	864	635	646r	540
Energy industry use	**8**	**8**	**5r**	**10**	**12**
Coal extraction	8	8	5r	10	12
Final consumption	**6,921r**	**6,208**	**5,258r**	**5,583r**	**3,582**
Industry	**3,639r**	**2,970**	**2,476r**	**2,704r**	**1,377**
Unclassified	-	-	-	-	-
Iron and steel	3	1	9	16r	2
Non-ferrous metals	282r	149	189r	354r	118
Mineral products	1,025r	926	793r	667r	270
Chemicals	891r	650	677r	841r	426
Mechanical engineering etc	29	22	28	31r	12
Electrical engineering etc	-	-	3	9r	3
Vehicles	119	102	47r	98r	61
Food, beverages etc	384	368	303r	290r	194
Textiles, clothing, leather, etc	126	68	69	73r	49
Pulp, paper, printing etc	267	233	110r	179r	109
Other industries	513r	451	248r	146r	133
Construction	-	-	-	-	-
Transport	**-**	**-**	**-**	**-**	**-**
Other	**3,282**	**3,238**	**2,782r**	**2,879r**	**2,205**
Domestic	2,705	2,587	2,366r	2,517r	1,907
Public administration	388	455	312r	320r	276
Commercial	-	-	4	4	7
Agriculture	13	7	9	7	7
Miscellaneous	176	189	91r	31r	8
Non energy use	**-**	**-**	**-**	**-**	**-**
Stocks at end of year *(4)*					
Distributed stocks	10,752	13,785r	12,602r	13,174r	11,629
Of which:					
Major power producers	9,495	12,619r	11,270r	12,097r	10,687
Coke ovens	1,228	1,128	1,312	1,054	914
Undistributed stocks	4,153	4,803r	4,565r	5,157r	1,646
Total stocks	**14,905**	**18,588r**	**17,167r**	**18,331r**	**13,275**

(1) Stock fall (+), stock rise (-).
(2) Total supply minus total demand.
(3) Estimates of slurry etc. recovered from ponds, dumps, rivers etc.
(4) Excludes distributed stocks held in merchants' yards, etc., mainly for the domestic market, and stocks held by the industrial sector.

2.8 Supply and consumption of coke oven coke, coke breeze and other manufactured solid fuels

Thousand tonnes

	1996	1997	1998	1999	2000
Coke oven coke					
Supply					
Production	6,178	6,192	6,178	5,837	6,058
Imports	668	749r	753	389	430
Exports	-88	-61	-93	-79	-243
Stock change (1)	+167	-72	-264	+353	-405
Transfers	-1,209	-1,257	-1,223	-951	-641
Total supply	**5,716**	**5,551r**	**5,351**	**5,549**	**5,199**
Statistical difference (2)	-102	-94r	-81r	-91r	-117
Total demand	**5,818**	**5,645**	**5,432r**	**5,640r**	**5,316**
Transformation	**5,180**	**5,196**	**4,908**	**5,113r**	**4,764**
Blast furnaces	5,180	5,196	4,908	5,113r	4,764
Energy industry use	-	**18**	**27**	**20**	**37**
Final consumption	**638**	**431**	**497r**	**507r**	**515**
Industry	**457**	**348**	**377r**	**386r**	**370**
Unclassified	78	127	220r	226r	191
Iron and steel	25	40	23	17r	19
Non-ferrous metals	354	181	134	143	160
Other	**181**	**83**	**120r**	**121r**	**145**
Domestic	181	83	120r	121r	145
Stocks at end of year (3)	**237**	**309**	**573**	**220**	**625**
Coke breeze					
Supply					
Production	44	41	37	33	37
Imports	100	112	78	40	53
Exports	-123	-201	-196	-165	-138
Stock change (1)	-110	+64	+42	-40r	+46
Transfers	+1,281	+1,336	+1,163	+1,035	+923
Total supply	**1,192**	**1,352r**	**1,124**	**903r**	**921**
Statistical difference (2)	+17	+131	-66r	-206r	-102
Total demand	**1,175**	**1,221**	**1,190r**	**1,109r**	**1,023**
Transformation	**280**	**310**	**287**	**189r**	**189**
Coke manufacture	68	64	50	24r	1
Blast furnaces	212	246	237	165r	188
Energy industry use	-	-	-	-	-
Final consumption	**895**	**911**	**903r**	**920r**	**834**
Industry	**895**	**911**	**903r**	**920r**	**834**
Unclassified	54	55	81r	33r	41
Iron and steel	841	856	822	887r	793
Stocks at end of year (3)	**295**	**231**	**189**	**229r**	**183**
Other manufactured solid fuels					
Supply					
Production	862	741	616	635	537
Imports	50	24	10	6	14
Exports	-90	-83	-56	-54	-79
Stock change (1)	71r	-42r	87r	-7	+38
Total supply	**893r**	**640r**	**657r**	**580**	**510**
Statistical difference (2)	+25r	-5r	+13r	-5	-22
Total demand	**868**	**645**	**644r**	**585**	**532**
Transformation	-	-	-	-	-
Energy industry use	**33**	**29**	**14**	**13**	**11**
Patent fuel manufacture	33	29	14	13	11
Final consumption	**835**	**616**	**630r**	**572**	**521**
Industry	**20**	**38**	**32**	**18**	**25**
Unclassified	20	38	32	18	25
Other	**815**	**578**	**598r**	**554**	**496**
Domestic	815	578	598r	554	496
Stocks at end of year (3)	**180r**	**222**	**134**	**141r**	**103**

(1) Stock fall (+), stock rise (-).
(2) Total supply minus total demand.

(3) Producers stocks and distributed stocks.

2.9 Supply and consumption of coke oven gas, blast furnace gas, benzole and tars

GWh

	1996	1997	1998	1999	2000
Coke oven gas					
Supply					
Production	13,246	13,282	13,126	12,090r	12,678
Imports	-	-	-	-	-
Exports	-	-	-	-	-
Transfers *(1)*	+286	+559	+630	+528	+443
Total supply	**13,532**	**13,841**	**13,756**	**12,618r**	**13,121**
Statistical difference *(2)*	+239	+346	+127r	-209r	-265
Total demand	**13,293**	**13,495**	**13,629r**	**12,827r**	**13,386**
Transformation	**529r**	**549r**	**1,957r**	**2,030r**	**1,996**
Electricity generation	529r	549r	1,957r	2,030r	1,996
Other	-	-	-	-	-
Energy industry use	**6,030**	**6,013**	**6,855**	**6,522**	**6,748**
Coke manufacture	4,983	4,909	5,690	5,283	5,555
Blast furnaces	1,047	1,104	1,165	1,239	1,193
Other	-	-	-	-	-
Losses	**296**	**202**	**335**	**173r**	**257**
Final consumption	**6,438r**	**6,731r**	**4,482r**	**4,102r**	**4,385**
Industry	**6,438r**	**6,731r**	**4,482r**	**4,102r**	**4,385**
Unclassified	208	220	116	124	341
Iron and steel	6,230r	6,511r	4,366r	3,978r	4,044
Blast furnace gas					
Supply					
Production	20,109	20,762	20,114r	19,023r	17,564
Imports	-	-	-	-	-
Exports	-	-	-	-	-
Transfers *(1)*	-16	-63	-22	-22	-17
Total supply	**20,093**	**20,699**	**20,092r**	**19,001r**	**17,547**
Statistical difference *(2)*	-166	-207r	+33r	-142r	-104
Total demand	**20,259**	**20,906r**	**20,059r**	**19,143r**	**17,651**
Transformation	**3,487r**	**3,604r**	**8,641r**	**8,601r**	**8,601**
Electricity generation	3,487r	3,604r	8,641r	8,601r	8,601
Other	-	-	-	-	-
Energy industry use	**6,754**	**6,939**	**6,578r**	**6,219r**	**5,974**
Coke manufacture	1,122	1,137	1,085	1,083r	1,046
Blast furnaces	5,632	5,802	5,493r	5,136r	4,928
Other	-	-	-	-	-
Losses	**1,850**	**1,597**	**1,474**	**1,723r**	**1,576**
Final consumption	**8,168r**	**8,766r**	**3,366r**	**2,600r**	**1,500**
Industry	**8,168r**	**8,766r**	**3,366r**	**2,600r**	**1,500**
Unclassified	-	-	-	-	-
Iron and steel	8,168r	8,766r	3,366r	2,600r	1,500
Benzole and tars *(3)*					
Supply					
Production	2,534	2,567	2,542	2,343r	2,393
Final consumption	**2,534**	**2,567**	**2,542**	**2,343r**	**2,393**
Unclassified	582	606	617	580r	597
Iron and steel	1,952	1,961	1,925	1,763r	1,796

(1) To and from synthetic coke oven gas, see paragraph 2.52.
(2) Total supply minus total demand.
(3) Because of the small number of benzole suppliers, figures for benzole and tars cannot be given separately.

2.10 Coal production and stocks, 1970 to 2000

Thousand tonnes

	Coal production			Imports (3)	Exports (4)	Coal stocks (at year end) (1)		
	Total (2)	Deep-mined	Opencast			Total	Distributed	Undistributed
1970	**147,195**	136,686	7,885	79	3,191	**20,630**	13,414	7,216
1971	**153,683**	136,478	10,666	4,241	2,667	**28,664**	18,271	10,393
1972	**126,834**	109,086	10,438	4,998	1,796	**30,460**	19,351	11,110
1973	**131,984**	120,030	10,123	1,675	2,693	**27,886**	17,035	10,850
1974	**110,452**	99,993	9,231	3,547	1,865	**21,807**	15,827	5,979
1975	**128,683**	117,412	10,414	5,083	2,182	**31,159**	20,541	10,618
1976	**123,801**	110,265	11,944	2,837	1,436	**33,115**	22,457	10,658
1977	**122,150**	107,123	13,551	2,439	1,835	**31,444**	21,704	9,740
1978	**123,577**	107,528	14,167	2,352	2,253	**34,475**	22,038	12,437
1979	**122,369**	107,775	12,862	4,375	2,175	**27,908**	18,339	9,569
1980	**130,097**	112,430	15,779	7,334	3,809	**37,687**	20,370	17,317
1981	**127,469**	110,473	14,828	4,290	9,113	**42,253**	20,136	22,117
1982	**124,711**	106,161	15,266	4,063	7,447	**52,377**	30,422	21,955
1983	**119,254**	101,742	14,706	4,456	6,561	**57,960**	33,964	23,996
1984	**51,182**	35,243	14,306	8,894	2,293	**36,548**	15,794	20,753
1985	**94,111**	75,289	15,569	12,732	2,432	**34,979**	25,752	9,228
1986	**108,099**	90,366	14,275	10,554	2,677	**38,481**	29,776	8,704
1987	**104,533**	85,957	15,786	9,781	2,353	**33,246**	27,104	6,142
1988	**104,066**	83,762	17,899	11,685	1,822	**36,166**	28,834	7,332
1989	**99,820**	79,628	18,657	12,137	2,049	**39,244**	29,191	10,053
1990	**92,762**	72,899	18,134	14,783	2,307	**37,760**	28,747	9,013
1991	**94,202**	73,357	18,636	19,611	1,824	**43,321**	32,343	10,977
1992	**84,493**	65,800	18,187	20,339	973	**47,207**	33,493	13,714
1993	**68,199**	50,457	17,006	18,400	1,114	**45,860**	29,872	15,989
1994	**49,785**	31,854	16,804	15,088	1,236	**26,572r**	15,301r	11,271
1995	**53,037**	35,150	16,369	15,896	859	**18,730**	11,626	7,104
1996	**50,197**	32,223	16,315	17,799	988	**14,905**	10,752	4,153
1997	**48,495**	30,281	16,700	19,757r	1,146	**18,588r**	13,785r	4,803r
1998	**41,177**	25,507r	14,539r	21,244	971	**17,167r**	12,602r	4,565r
1999	**37,077**	20,888	15,275	20,293r	761r	**18,331r**	13,174r	5,157r
2000	**31,198**	17,188	13,412	23,445	661	**13,275**	11,629	1,646

(1) Excludes distributed stocks held in merchants' yards etc mainly for the domestic market and stocks held by the industrial sector.
(2) Includes estimates for slurry etc recovered from dumps, ponds, rivers etc.
(3) The 1993 import figure includes an additional estimate for unrecorded trade.
(4) From 1990 based on HM Custom and Excise data; before 1990 based on British Coal's shipments.

2.11 Inland consumption of solid fuels, 1970 to 2000

Thousand tonnes

	Total inland consumption of coal	Coal consumption by fuel producers						Final consumption				Coke and breeze (3)	Other solid fuel (4)
		Primary	Secondary					Coal (1)					
		Collieries	Power stations(1)	Coke ovens (2)	Other solid fuel plants (3)	Gas works	Total	Industry	Domestic	Other	Total		
1970	156,886	1,916	77,237	25,340	4,150	4,280	111,006	19,613	20,190	4,159	43,962	18,090	3,203
1971	140,932	1,581	72,847	23,554	4,477	1,855	102,733	16,105	17,185	3,327	36,617	15,100	3,456
1972	122,884	1,405	66,664	20,476	4,547	575	92,261	11,663	14,554	2,999	29,216	14,090	3,514
1973	133,370	1,381	76,838	21,888	3,607	512	102,845	12,062	14,502	2,581	29,145	15,000	3,375
1974	117,888	1,256	67,026	18,461	3,788	107	89,382	11,077	13,667	2,505	27,249	13,220	3,184
1975	122,217	1,238	74,569	19,085	4,063	9	97,725	9,685	11,616	1,948	23,253	11,640	2,919
1976	123,604	1,132	77,819	19,402	3,405	8	100,632	8,970	10,823	2,045	21,838	12,460	2,647
1977	123,978	1,124	79,956	17,406	3,173	-	100,536	9,033	11,136	2,149	22,318	11,310	2,609
1978	120,477	1,010	80,643	14,946	3,070	-	98,659	8,550	10,217	2,041	20,808	10,484	2,453
1979	129,378	834	88,790	15,081	2,883	-	106,753	9,232	10,508	2,051	21,791	11,361	2,364
1980	123,460	663	89,569	11,610	3,022	-	104,201	7,898	8,946	1,752	18,596	6,221	2,252
1981	118,386	616	87,226	10,805	2,458	-	100,489	7,046	8,454	1,781	17,281	7,952	1,975
1982	110,998	534	80,228	10,406	2,326	-	92,960	7,175	8,474	1,855	17,504	7,248	1,921
1983	111,475	486	81,565	10,448	2,114	-	94,127	7,218	7,872	1,772	16,862	7,600	1,889
1984	77,309	209	53,411	8,246	1,300	-	62,957	7,006	5,406	1,731	14,143	7,653	1,186
1985	105,386	332	73,940	11,122	2,176	-	87,237	8,313	7,799	1,704	17,817	8,230	1,658
1986	114,234	306	82,652	11,122	1,959	-	95,732	9,278	7,421	1,496	18,196	7,558	1,601
1987	115,894	235	87,960	10,859	2,052	-	100,871	6,827	6,536	1,425	14,789	8,233	1,652
1988	111,498	196	84,258	10,902	2,006	-	97,166	7,131	5,741	1,265	14,135	8,591	1,443
1989	107,581	146	82,053	10,792	1,717	-	94,562	6,763	5,048	1,062	12,873	8,159	1,253
1990	108,256	117	84,014	10,852	1,544	-	96,409	6,280	4,239	1,211	11,730	7,637	1,214
1991	107,513	112	83,542	10,011	1,501	-	95,054	6,426	4,778	1,144	12,348	7,136	1,200
1992	100,580	79	78,469	9,031	1,319	-	88,819	6,581	4,156	945	11,682	6,887	1,089
1993	86,757	48	66,136	8,479	1,329	-	75,944	5,300	4,638	826	10,765	6,638	1,138
1994	81,767r	22	62,406	8,581r	1,190	-	72,177r	4,946r	3,901	721	9,568r	6,578	949
1995	76,942r	8	59,588r	8,657r	982	-	69,227r	4,494r	2,690	523	7,707r	6,541	742
1996	71,400	8	54,893r	8,632	946	-	64,471r	3,639r	2,705	577	6,921r	6,925	835
1997	63,080	8	47,250	8,750	864	-	56,864	2,970	2,587	651	6,208	6,784	616
1998	63,152r	5r	48,526r	8,728	635	-	57,889r	2,476r	2,366r	416r	5,258r	6,545r	630r
1999	55,720r	10	41,068r	8,413r	646r	-	50,127r	2,704r	2,517r	362r	5,583r	6,705r	572
2000	58,954	12	46,135	8,685	540	-	55,360	1,377	1,907	298	3,582	6,301	521

(1) Up to 1986 power stations include those in the public electricity supply, railways and transport industries. Consumption by other generators is included in final coal consumption. From 1987, coal consumption at power stations also includes other generators' consumption, which is therefore excluded from final coal consumption (see also Table 2.7).

(2) Includes blast furnaces.

(3) This series comprises final consumption and consumption at blast furnaces which can now be separated following production of energy balances in Tables 2.4 to 2.6. Pure final consumption figures for coke and breeze in 1998, 1999, and 2000 were 1,400, 1,427, and 1,349 thousand tonnes respectively.

(4) Low temperature carbonisation and patent fuel plants and their products.

2.12 Major deep mines in production at 16 May 2001[1]

Licensee	Site	Location
Betws Anthracite Ltd	Betws Colliery	Carmarthenshire
Blenkinsopp Collieries Ltd	Castle Drift Mine	Northumberland
J Flack & Sons Ltd	Hay Royds Colliery	Kirklees
Goitre Tower Anthracite Ltd	Tower Colliery	Rhondda, Cynon, Taff
Hatfield Coal Company	Hatfield Colliery	Doncaster
RJB Mining (UK) Ltd [2]	Clipstone Colliery	Nottinghamshire
	Daw Mill Colliery	Warwickshire
	Ellington Colliery	Northumberland
	Harworth Colliery	Doncaster
	Kellingley Colliery	North Yorkshire
	Maltby Colliery	Yorkshire
	Prince of Wales	Yorkshire
	Riccall/Whitemoor	North Yorkshire
	Rossington Colliery	Doncaster
	Stillingfleet Combine	North Yorkshire
	Thoresby Colliery	Nottinghamshire
	Welbeck Colliery	Nottinghamshire
	Wistow Mine	North Yorkshire
The Scottish Coal Company Ltd	Longannet	Clackmannanshire

(1) In addition there were 14 smaller collieries in production at 16 May 2001.
(2) On 25 May 2001 RJB Mining changed its name to UK Coal.

Source: The Coal Authority

2.13 Opencast sites in production at 16 May 2001[1]

Licensee	Site Name	Location
Aardvark TMC Ltd (trading as ATH Resources)	Skares Road, Nr Cumnock	East Ayrshire
C Rees & Sons Plant Hire Ltd	Lletty'r Crudd	Neath & Port Talbot
Celtic Energy Ltd	Brynhenllys Revised	Powys
	East Pit Extension	Neath & Port Talbot
	Park Slip West	Bridgend
	Selar	Neath & Port Talbot
Coal Contractors Ltd	Broomhill	East Ayrshire
	Randolph Colliery Bing Remediation	Fife
Cumberland Coal Ltd	Keekle Head	Cumbria
Faldane Ltd	Monteith Houses	Midlothian
	Oxenfoord West	Midlothian
Fitzwise Ltd	Hall Lane Waste Site	Derbyshire
G M Mining Ltd	Drumshangie	North Lanarkshire
	Heatherywood Extension	Fife
George Raeburn	Edge Farm Extension	South Lanarkshire
H J Banks & Company Ltd	Carrington Farm	Derbyshire
	Midland (Stonebroom)	Derbyshire
	Pegswood Moor Farm	Northumberland
	Watsonhead	North Lanarkshire
Henlan Coal Ltd	Nant-y-Cafn Colliery Restoration Site	Neath & Port Talbot
I & H Brown Ltd	Colton Remainder	Fife
J Fenton & Sons (Contractors) Ltd	Meadowhill Farm Gartknowie Extension	Clackmannanshire
Law Mining Ltd	Garleffan Site	East Ayrshire
LEM Resources Ltd	Crock Hey Site	St Helens
Lothian Mining (Scotland) Ltd	Mossband Farm	North Lanarkshire
Parnell Contract Hire Ltd	Nant-y-Glo Opencast Site	Neath Port Talbot
RJB Mining (UK) Ltd (2)	Arkwright Colliery Reclamation	Derbyshire
	Ashby Woulds (Hicks Lodge)	Leicestershire
	Eldon Deep Site	Durham
	Maiden's Hall	Northumberland
	Orgreave Reclamation	Rotherham
	St Aidan's Remainder	Leeds
	Stobswood	Northumberland
The Scottish Coal Company Ltd	Chalmerston	East Ayrshire
	Dalquhandy	South Lanarkshire
	Dalquhandy Extension	South Lanarkshire
	Darnside	North Lanarkshire
	Greenbank	Fife
	House of Water	East Ayrshire
	Pennyvenie	East Ayrshire
	Powharnal	East Ayrshire
Walters Mining Ltd	Fforch-y-Garn/Tyn-y-Wern	Neath Port Talbot
Ward Brothers Mining Ltd	Darrell Extension	Neath & Port Talbot
	Elwyn Complex	Neath & Port Talbot
Ward Brothers Plant Hire Ltd	Prestwick Pit	Northumberland

(1) There were 45 opencast sites in production as at 16 May 2001. In addition, one site was under development.
(2) On 25 May 2001 RJB Mining changed its name to UK Coal.
Source: The Coal Authority

Chapter 3
Petroleum

Introduction

3.1 This chapter contains commodity balances covering the supply and disposal of primary oils (crude oil and natural gas liquids), feedstocks (including partly processed oils) and petroleum products in the UK in the period 1998 to 2000. These balances are given in Tables 3.1 to 3.6. Additional data has been included in supplementary tables on areas not covered by the format of the balances. This extra information includes details on refinery capacities and aggregates for refinery operations, and extra detail on deliveries into consumption, including breakdowns by country, sector and industry. Long term series for selected headings covering the period 1970 to 2000 are presented in Tables 3.11 and 3.12.

3.2 Statistics of imports and exports of crude oil, other refinery feedstocks and petroleum products, refinery receipts, refinery throughput and output and deliveries of petroleum products are obtained from the United Kingdom Petroleum Industry Association, and the Department of Trade and Industry's Petroleum Production Reporting System.

3.3 The annual figures relate to calendar years or the ends of calendar years. In the majority of tables the data cover the United Kingdom.

3.4 Also included at the end of the Digest is an annex on the oil and gas resources of the UK (Annex C). This information is included to provide a more complete picture of the UK oil and gas production sector.

Commodity balances for primary oil (Tables 3.1, 3.2 and 3.3)

3.5 These tables show details of the production, supply and disposals of primary oils (crude oil and natural gas liquids (NGLs)) and feedstocks in 2000, 1999 and 1998. The upper half of the table (Supply) equates to the upstream oil industry, covering the supply chain from the production of oil and NGLs recorded by individual fields to the disposal of oil and NGLs to export or to UK refineries. The lower half of the table covers the uses made of these primary oils, including the amounts recorded as used as a fuel during the extraction process (i.e. burned to provide power for drilling and pumping operations) and as inputs into refineries, as recorded by refineries. The statistical difference in the tables thus represents the differences between data reported by these different sources and the sites of production and consumption.

3.6 Gross production of crude oil and NGLs in 2000 was 126 million tonnes, a decline of 8 per cent on the record level of production seen in 1999 which, at 137 million tonnes, was the highest annual production since oil was first produced from the North Sea in 1975. Three-quarters of the United Kingdom's primary oil production in 2000 was exported, and imported crude oil accounted for 61 per cent of UK requirements. Feedstocks (including partly processed oils) made up about one-tenth of total imports of oil in 2000. Total oil imports in 2000 were more than 20 per cent higher than in 1999. Exports of primary oils and feedstocks exceeded imports by 76 per cent in 1998 and in 1999 exports were more than double the level of imports. While the level of net exports reduced in 2000, exports were still 70 per cent higher than imports, making a significant contribution to the UK economy (see Chapter 8). While exports in 2000 continued at around the same level as in 1999, refiners needed to import increased volumes of crude oil to make up for the reduction in indigenous production. Chart 3.1 illustrates recent trends in production, imports and exports of crude oil, NGLs and feedstocks.

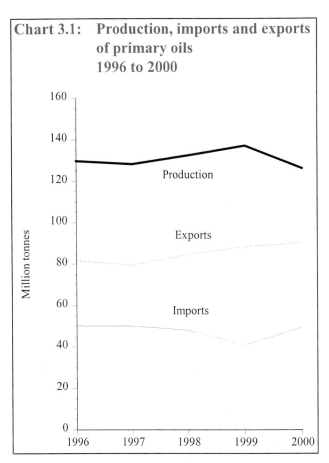

Chart 3.1: Production, imports and exports of primary oils 1996 to 2000

3.7 The UK produces more than enough crude oil to meet its own needs, but imports still take place. As it generally contains lower levels of contaminants such as sulphur (which can make the crude oil difficult to refine), UK crude oil can command a higher price than other crude oils on the international market. It also contains a higher proportion of the lighter hydrocarbon molecules, resulting in higher yields of products such as motor spirit and other transport fuels. These two factors together make it financially attractive to export the crude oil rather than use it in the UK, with imports being brought in to make up the difference. In addition, some crude oils are specifically imported for the heavier hydrocarbons they contain which are needed for the manufacture of various petroleum products, such as bitumen and lubricating oils.

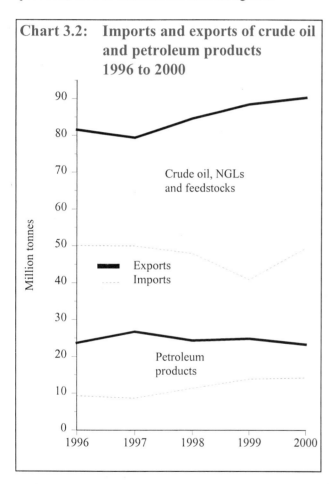

Chart 3.2: Imports and exports of crude oil and petroleum products 1996 to 2000

3.8 Chart 3.2 compares the level of imports and exports of crude oil, NGLs and feedstocks with those for petroleum products over the period 1996 to 2000. Imports of crude oil, which increased between 1992 and 1993, were lower between 1996 and 2000 due to the increased levels of output from the United Kingdom Continental Shelf during this period. Imports of petroleum products during the period continued to decline between 1995 and 1997 while exports of products increased fuelled by increased production by UK refineries. In 1998 a reversal of these trends occurred due to the closure of the Gulf Oil refinery in Milford Haven in December 1997. The impact of this reduction in refinery processing capacity in the UK carried through into 1999, and there was a continued reduction in processing in the

UK in 2000 due to the closure of Shell's Shell Haven refinery in Essex at the end of November 1999. The reduction in capacity has led to reductions in both the levels of exports of petroleum products along with a corresponding increase in the level of imports of products to ensure UK demand for the products continues to be met. At the same time there has been a reduction in imports of crude oil and feedstocks, with imports in 2000 being 35 per cent lower than in 1998. Additional analysis of the exports and imports of oil products is given in paragraphs 3.11 to 3.19 and 3.91 to 3.98 and additional explanations for the decline in exports of crude oil in 1997 are given in Annex C, paragraphs C.32 to C.34.

3.9 It will be seen from the balances in Tables 3.1 to 3.3 that while the overall statistical difference in the primary oil balance for 2000 is +613 thousand tonnes. That is, the total quantities of crude oil and NGLs reported as being produced by the individual production fields in the UK are 613 thousand tonnes greater than the totals reported by UK oil companies as being received by refineries or going for export. This is discussed later in paragraphs 3.35 to 3.44.

Commodity balances - Petroleum products (Tables 3.4 to 3.6)

3.10 These tables show details of the production, supply and disposals of petroleum products into the UK market in 2000, 1999 and 1998. The upper half of the table (Supply) covers details of the overall availability of these products in the UK as calculated by observing production at refineries, and adding in the impact of trade (imports and exports), stock changes, product transfers and deliveries to international marine bunkers. The lower half of the table covers the uses made of these products, including the uses made within refineries as fuels in the refining process, and details of the amounts reported by oil companies within the UK as delivered for final consumption.

Supply of petroleum products

3.11 Looking at refinery operations first, total output from UK refineries in 2000, at 86½ million tonnes of products, was virtually the same as in 1999 (½ per cent lower), but 7 per cent lower than the level in 1998. The first half of 1999 saw depressed international markets for crude oil and oil products, resulting in decreased profit margins for refining companies, and this led to a general slowdown in refinery activity during the early part of 1999. This was countered in the second half of the year by increased prices for crude oil and products due to increased demand and a reduction in world supplies. This is explained in more detail in Annex C, paragraphs C.30 to C.34. Prices on international markets for key oil products remained high during 2000, which led to the level of refinery activity in the UK staying at the same level as in 1999. This was achieved despite the effects of the closure of Shell's Shell Haven refinery in December 1999 on the UK's overall refinery capacity. The remaining UK refineries looked to take advantage of the high prices for products on international markets by increasing both their processing capacity and their level of utilisation to take advantage of the more profitable market conditions.

3.12 In terms of output of individual products, output of aviation turbine fuel and motor spirit both decreased in 2000 compared to 1999 (by 10½ and 7 per cent respectively), while output of gas oil/diesel oil increased by 9 per cent. This increased production was partly to make up demand for Ultra Low Sulphur DERV fuel (ULSD) in the UK following the introduction of a 3 pence per litre duty differential in favour of ULSD. This duty differential is also the reasons for the decrease in imports of gas diesel oil in 2000, as UK refinery production of low sulphur fuels replaced imports of these fuels from Germany and Sweden. More information on the introduction of ULSD into the UK is given in paragraphs 3.59 to 3.61. The recovery of international prices in late 1999 and through 2000 also gave an increased incentive to UK refiners to produce and export gas diesel oil for use as heating oil and also as a refinery and petrochemical feedstock.

3.13 The decrease in production of aviation turbine fuel is partly due to the fact that this product and gas diesel oil are extracted from the same fraction of crude oil, the middle distillates, but to different quality criteria. As such, by increasing production of gas diesel oil, less of this fraction of the crude oil processed at refineries was available for production of aviation turbine fuel. In addition, the Shell Haven refineries, which closed at the end of 1999, was predominantly a producer of aviation turbine fuel and motor spirit, with these two fuels making up over 50 per cent of its total production. As such, the closure of the Shell Haven refinery has had a significant effect on reducing the output of these two fuels in 2000. More information on refinery capacity in the UK and refinery capacity utilisation is given in paragraphs 3.45 and 3.46.

3.14 Every year since 1974, with the exception of 1984 due to the effects of the industrial action in the coal-mining sector, the UK has been a net exporter of oil products. In 2000, exports of petroleum products were 21 million tonnes, 5 per cent lower than exports in 1999 and 15 per cent lower than in 1998. The decrease in exports is mainly due to the closure of the Gulf Oil and Shell Haven refineries mentioned above. Related to these closures, the 14 million tonnes of oil products imported into the UK in 2000 were 8 per cent higher than in 1999 and 24 per cent higher than in 1998. However, despite these increased imports the

UK remained very much a net exporter of products in 2000 at 6.5 million tonnes, but lower than the level seen in 1999 of 7.8 million tonnes.

3.15 The US remains one of the key markets for UK exports of oil products, with 3 million tonnes being exported there from the UK in 2000. These exports made up 14 per cent of total UK exports of oil products in 2000, with the main other countries receiving UK exports of petroleum products being Ireland, Italy, France, the Netherlands, Germany and Spain. The main sources of the UK's imports of petroleum products in 2000 were France, the Netherlands and Norway.

3.16 Chart 3.3 shows how the UK has penetrated selected overseas markets for its petroleum products. UK products supplied 5 per cent of the total volume of US imports of petroleum products in 2000 (mostly in the form of motor spirit) and 12, 4 and 6 per cent of total imports of petroleum products into France, Germany and the Netherlands (mostly as gas oil for heating, motor spirit and fuel oil). The UK regularly supplies the vast majority of total oil products imported into Ireland (mostly motor spirit and DERV fuel for transport and gas diesel oil and burning oil for heating).

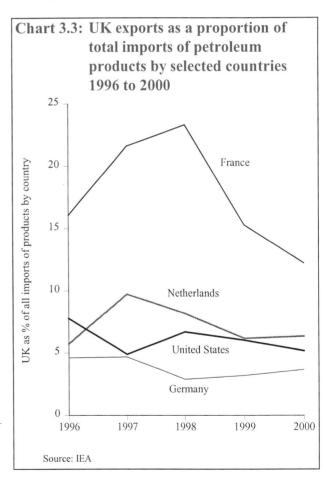

Chart 3.3: UK exports as a proportion of total imports of petroleum products by selected countries 1996 to 2000

Source: IEA

3.17 It may be asked why the UK imports petroleum products at all if it has such a surplus of them available for export. This can be explained if you look at the difference in the product detail. Exports in 2000 were mainly made up of motor spirit (5 million tonnes), gas oil/diesel oil (6½ million tonnes) and fuel oil (5 million tonnes). Imports were made up of aviation turbine fuel (4½ million tonnes), motor spirit (2½ million tonnes) and gas oil/diesel oil (4 million tonnes). The make up of refinery structure in the UK is such that it contains a surplus of motor spirit capacity, leading to a surplus availability within the UK, which is exported. The imports of motor spirit were of grades of products that UK refineries could not manufacture. For example, this includes Ultra Low Sulphur versions of motor spirit and DERV fuel. The imports also take place to cover specific periods of heavy demand within the UK, such as around the time of the Budget in March or during the summer.

3.18 Similarly for gas oil/diesel oil, the exports from the UK tend to be of lower grades of gas oil/diesel oil for use as heating fuels, while the imports tend to be of higher grade gas oil/diesel oil with a low sulphur content. For example, the imports cover products such as Ultra Low Sulphur Diesel (ULSD). With the introduction of low sulphur DERV fuel and motor spirit into the UK market (see paragraphs 3.59 to 3.64 below) and the related increased production capacity at UK refineries for these fuels, UK imports of these products will reduce in 2001 and 2002. Aviation turbine fuel is imported simply because the UK cannot make enough of it to meet demand. It is derived from the same sort of hydrocarbons as gas oil/diesel oil, and as such there is a physical limit to how much can be made from the amount of oil processed in the UK.

3.19 More information on the structure of refineries in the UK and trends in imports and exports of crude oil and oil products is given in the section discussing Table 3.11 (paragraphs 3.91 to 3.98).

3.20 In 2000, 8 per cent of UK production of fuel oil and 4 per cent of gas oil/diesel oil production went into international marine bunkers, totalling 2 million tonnes of products, 2.4 per cent of total UK refinery production in the year. These are sales of fuels that are destined for consumption on ocean going vessels. As such the products cannot be classified as being consumed within the UK, and these quantities are thus treated in a similar way to exports in the commodity balances. It should be noted that these quantities do not include deliveries of fuels for use in UK coastal waters. These deliveries are counted as UK consumption and the figures given in the transport section of the commodity balances.

3.21 Details are given in the balances of stocks of products held within the UK either at refineries or oil distribution centres such as coastal oil terminals (undistributed stocks). In addition, some information is available on stocks of oil products held by major electricity generators (distributed stocks). However, these figures do not include any details of stocks held by distributors of fuels or stocks held at retail sites, such as petrol stations. The figures for stocks in the

balances also solely relate to those stocks currently present in the UK. As such they do not include details of any stocks that might be held by UK oil companies in other countries under bilateral agreements.

3.22 In order for the UK to be prepared for any oil emergency, the UK Government places an obligation on companies supplying oil products into final consumption in the UK to maintain a certain level of stocks of oil products used as fuels. As part of this, oil companies are allowed to hold stocks abroad under official governmental bilateral agreements that can count towards their stocking obligations. As such, to give a true picture of the amount of stocks available to the UK, i.e. that are owned by UK companies, the stocks figures in Table 3.10 take account of these bilateral stocks (see paragraphs 3.86 to 3.89).

Consumption of petroleum products

3.23 To help users gain the maximum information from the commodity balances, this section of the text will go through the data given on the consumption of oil products in the period 1998 to 2000. The main sectors of consumers will be looked at first (going down the tables) and then the data for individual products will be looked at (going across the tables).

3.24 Table 3.4 shows how overall deliveries of petroleum products into consumption in the UK in 2000, including those used by the UK refining industry as fuels within the refining process and all other uses, totalled 76½ million tonnes. This was 2 per cent lower than in 1999 and 2½ per cent lower than in 1998. As such, deliveries are following the trend of a decline seen since 1990, barring the slight increase in 1996.

3.25 As can be seen from the tables, one of the most significant changes in deliveries of products in recent years has been the decline in use for electricity generation. In 2000 only 0.8 million tonnes of oil products were used for electricity generation by major power producers and autogenerators of electricity, compared with 1.4 million tonnes in 1998 and much higher levels in earlier years (see Table 3.12). This change is primarily a result of the move by major electricity producers away from oil based fuels towards using natural gas as their fuel for electricity generation. This trend is reflected in the fact that the level of usage by auto-producers of electricity has been fairly constant over the period, despite the growth in auto-generation of electricity by industry as a whole. The data for fuels used in autogeneration of electricity in 1998 and 1999 have been revised in the light of new information that has become available.

3.26 The data included against the blast furnaces heading in the Transformation sector represents fuel oil used in the manufacture of iron and steel which is directly injected into blast furnaces, as opposed to being used as a fuel to heat the blast furnaces. The fuel used for the latter (mostly gas oil/diesel oil) is included against the blast furnaces heading in the Energy Industry Use sector.

3.27 The other figures in the Energy Industry Use sector relate to uses within the UK refining industry in the manufacture of oil products. These are products either used as fuels during refining processes or products used by the refineries themselves as opposed to being sold to other consumers, but excluding any fuels used for the generation of electricity. These amounts are included in the Transformation sector totals. Given that there is a degree of interest in the total amounts of fuels used within refineries, Table 3.7 includes data on total refinery fuel usage (i.e. including that used in the generation of electricity) over the period 1996 to 2000. The data under the other headings of the Energy Industry Use sector represent fuels used by the gas supply industry.

3.28 Final consumption of oil products in 2000, i.e. excluding any uses by the energy industries themselves or for transformation purposes, amounted to 70¼ million tonnes, 1 per cent lower than in 1999 but only slightly lower than in 1998. Chart 3.4 shows the breakdown of consumption for energy uses by each sector in 2000.

3.29 The total amount of oil products used by industry has remained fairly stable over the three-year period after a decline in the middle-1990s due to industry as a whole generally moving away from the use of oil products as an energy source. Industrial usage in 2000 totalled some 5.8 million tonnes, the same as in 1998.

3.30 Transport sector consumption in 2000 was 1½ per cent higher than in 1999 (3 per cent higher than in 1998). Increased usage for air transport in 2000 compared to 1999 (up 7½ per cent) was offset by slightly lower consumption of motor spirit (down 1¾ per cent) with only a slight increase in use of DERV fuel (up ¾ per cent). In 2000, transport usage totalled 49 million tonnes, and thus accounted for nearly three-quarters of total final consumption of oil products in 2000. Consumption by other sectors decreased by 6 per cent in 2000 compared with 1999.

3.31 The 1998 edition of the Digest included estimates for the use of gas for road vehicles for the first time. These estimates were based on information on the amounts of duty received by HM Government from the tax on gas used as a road fuel. It has been possible to repeat this exercise, and it is estimated that some 22 thousand tonnes of gas (mostly butane or propane) was used in road vehicles in the UK in 2000. While a very small use when compared to overall consumption of these fuels and the consumption of fuels for road transport as a whole, the consumption of these gases in road transport in 2000 has nearly tripled since 1999. The DTI is currently working with the member companies of the Liquid Petroleum Gas Association to further improve the estimates of the amounts of these fuels being used for transport purposes in the UK.

3.32 Consumption of non-energy products decreased slightly in 2000, by 6 per cent compared to 1999. In 2000, non-energy products made up 14 per cent of final consumption of oil products, compared with 15 per cent in 1999 and 1998. More detail on the non-energy uses of oil products, by product and by type of use where such information is available, is given in Table 3.D and paragraphs 3.77 to 3.83 later in this text.

3.33 Looking at the final consumption of individual products, three quarters of total final consumption in 2000 was made up of consumption of just three products; aviation turbine fuel, motor spirit and gas oil/diesel oil, i.e. transport products. Consumption of aviation turbine fuel increased by 7½ per cent in 2000 to 10¾ million tonnes, continuing the pattern seen in the 1990s of annual increases in the level of consumption. For motor spirit, consumption decreased by 1¾ per cent in 2000. Total consumption of gas oil/diesel oil was virtually unchanged in 2000, but that part of the total consumed as road fuel (i.e. as DERV) increased slightly (by ¾ per cent.). More detailed information on consumption of motor spirit and gas oil/diesel oil over the period 1996 to 2000 is given in Table 3.8 and discussed in paragraphs 3.47 to 3.73. Similarly, the increased consumption of aviation spirit in 2000 is also discussed.

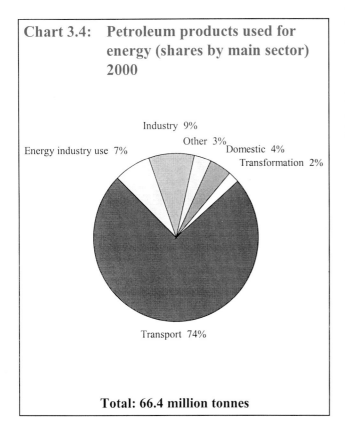

Chart 3.4: Petroleum products used for energy (shares by main sector) 2000

Industry 9%
Other 3%
Energy industry use 7%
Domestic 4%
Transformation 2%
Transport 74%

Total: 66.4 million tonnes

3.34 As mentioned above, consumption of fuel oil in the UK has declined in recent years. In 2000 final consumption was down to 1¼ million tonnes, 30 per cent down on its level in 1998. This is due to decreased use by industry (down 17 per cent) and decreased use by domestic and other premises for heating purposes and by other sectors (down by 51 per cent). Detail on the consumption of fuel oil broken down by grade is given in Table 3.8.

Supply and disposal of products (Table 3.7)

3.35 This table brings together the commodity balances for primary oils and for petroleum products into a single overall balance table. As such, whilst it follows the same general format as previously used for such balances (e.g. as used in Table 4.4 in the 1997 edition of the Digest), the headings have been revised so that the format of the commodity balances is followed.

3.36 The statistical difference for primary oils in the table is accounted for by own use in onshore terminals and gas separation plants, losses, platform and other field stock changes. Also a factor is the time lag that can exist between production and loading onto tankers being reported at an offshore field and the arrival of these tankers at onshore refineries and oil terminals. This gap is usually minimal and works such that any effect of this at the start of a month is balanced by a similar counterpart effect at the end of a month. However, there can be instances where the length of this interval can be significant and, if it happens at the end of a year, significant effects on the statistical differences seen for the years involved can result.

3.37 As well as the known possible causes of error, such as clerical errors being made in the reporting of data at terminals and errors due to non-standard conditions being used to meter the flow of oil, there are several other technical factors that could cause errors in recording.

3.38 There are issues related to the accuracy of the metering process, in that meters are only required to be accurate to within a certain percentage range. There is also a technical issue related to the recording of quantities at the producing field (which is the input for the production data) and at oil terminals and refineries, since they are in effect measuring different types of oil. Terminals and refineries are able to measure a standardised, stabilised crude oil, i.e. with its water content and content of NGLs at a standard level and with the amounts being measured at standard conditions. However, at the producing field they are dealing with a "live" crude oil that can have a varying level of water and NGLs within it. Producing companies are asked to make adjustments so that production is recorded in terms of stabilised crude oil, but it is known that this estimation is very difficult to carry out. As such the quantities reported by a terminal for its receipts from any individual field will differ from the data reported by the field itself.

3.39 Part of the overall statistical difference may also be due to problems with the reporting of individual NGLs correctly at the production site and at terminals and refineries. It is known that there is some mixing of condensate and other NGLs in with what might otherwise be stabilised crude oil before it enters the pipeline. This mixing happens for several reasons. It saves having to have separate pipeline systems for transporting the NGLs. It also allows the viscosity of the oil passing down the pipeline to be varied as necessary. As said above, the quantity figures recorded by terminals are in terms of stabilised crude oil, with the NGL component removed, but there may be situations where what is being reported does not comply with this requirement.

3.40 It is known that there are some quantities of condensate extracted at gas terminals from the stream of gas extracted from some gas fields on the UKCS. Whilst of small quantity, these amounts will be recorded by terminals and refineries as UK indigenous receipts but will not be recorded as UK production.

3.41 From July 2000 a simplified reporting system for the production of crude oil, NGLs and natural gas in the UK was introduced. It is hoped that by simplifying the reporting system the quality of data being reported under it will improve. Certainly, the process of introducing the system has involved extensive contacts between the DTI and oil and gas production companies during the implementation process. This has resulted in a better understanding by all concerned of the operations of the companies and the needs of the DTI for data. With effect from January 2001, the new system was fully implemented, although some companies are still in the process of converting their systems to produce data on the new basis. Later in 2001 a review of the impact of the introduction of the new system on the quality of data being reported to the DTI will be carried out, the results of which will be published when available.

3.42 Refinery data is collated from details of individual shipments received and made by each refinery and terminal operating company. There are thousands of such shipments each year, and it is an immense task to cross-reference each shipment, which may be reported separately by two or three different companies involved in the movement. Whilst intensive work is carried out to check these returns, it is possible that some double counting of receipts might be occurring.

3.43 With the downstream sector, the statistical differences can similarly be used to assess the validity and consistency of the data. As can be seen in the tables, these differences are generally a very small proportion of the totals involved. However, analysis of data for 1998 and 1999 showed the size of these differences to be increasing, with calculated deliveries to final consumption being some 1-1½ per cent higher than observed deliveries. More information on the reasons why these differences exist is given in paragraphs 3.107 to 3.115.

Table 3A: UK refinery processing capacity as at end 2000 (1)

(symbols relates to Map 3.A)	Million tonnes per annum		
	Distillation	Reforming	Cracking & Conversion
Shell UK Ltd			
❶ Stanlow	11.5	1.4	3.8
Shell Haven (2)	-	-	-
Total (Shell)	11.5	1.4	3.8
Esso Petroleum Co. Ltd			
❷ Fawley	15.6	2.8	4.5
BP Amoco Ltd			
❸ Coryton (3)	9.6	1.7	3.6
❹ Grangemouth	10.1	1.9	3.2
Total (BP Amoco)	19.7	3.6	6.8
TotalFinaElf Ltd.			
❺ Lindsey Oil Refinery Ltd South Killingholme	10.0	1.4	4.1
Texaco Refining Co. Ltd			
❻ Pembroke (4)	10.1	1.5	6.1
Conoco Ltd			
❼ Killingholme	9.4	2.1	9.0
Gulf Oil Refining Ltd			
Milford Haven (4)	-	-	-
Elf Oil Ltd / Murco Pet. Ltd			
❽ Milford Haven	5.3	0.2	1.7
Petroplus International Ltd			
❾ North Tees	5.0	0.0	0.0
Carless Solvents Ltd			
① Harwich	0.6	0.0	0.0
Eastham Refinery Ltd			
② Eastham	1.0	0.0	0.0
Nynas UK AB			
③ Dundee (Camperdown)	0.7	0.0	0.0
Total all refineries	88.8	12.9	36.0

(1) Rated design capacity per day on stream multiplied by the average number of days on stream.
(2) Shell Haven closed in December 1999.
(3) Prior to 1996 owned by Mobil.
(4) Gulf Oil's refinery at Milford Haven closed in November 1995. The cracking facilities jointly owned by Gulf and Texaco as the Pembroke Cracking Company are now wholly owned by Texaco.

3.44 A full review of the system for reporting the data on the downstream sector was started in 2000, and while this review is still on-going, analysis of the detailed refinery throughput and production data and checking of data reporting methods with the oil companies has identified some discrepancies in the reporting of refinery production data. It appears that what are potentially losses within the refining system have been incorrectly reported elsewhere within the reporting system. Although this investigative work is still on going and will be intensified during the second half of 2001, given the impact of these factors on the statistical differences reported in the balances it was decided to incorporate corrections for the balances data for those years that appear to be affected, i.e.

1998, 1999 and 2000. These can be seen in the "Losses in refining process" line in Table 3.7.

Refinery capacity

3.45 Editions of the Digest pre-1999 included a table showing distillation capacity (total, and by refinery); reforming and cracking/conversion capacity (totals). The data for refinery capacity as at the end of 2000 is presented in Table 3.A, with the location of these refineries illustrated in Map 3.A. These figures are collected annually by the Department of Trade and Industry from individual oil companies. Capacity per annum for each refinery is derived by applying the rated capacity of the plant per day when on-stream by the number of days the plant was on stream during the year. Fluctuations in the number of days the refinery is active is usually the main reason for annual changes in the level of capacity. Reforming capacity covers catalytic reforming, and Cracking/Conversion capacity covers processes for upgrading residual oils to lighter products, e.g. catalytic, thermal or hydro-cracking, visbreaking and coking.

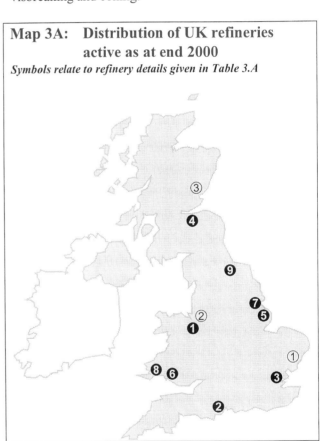

Map 3A: Distribution of UK refineries active as at end 2000
Symbols relate to refinery details given in Table 3.A

3.46 At the end of 2000 the UK had 9 major refineries operating, with three minor refineries in existence. Distillation capacity in the UK at the end of 2000 was 89 million tonnes, only slightly higher than at the end of 1999. Similarly, total UK reforming capacity at the end of 2000 was 13 million tonnes, and cracking and conversion capacity was 36 million tonnes, both virtually the same levels as at the end of 1999.

Additional information on inland deliveries of selected products (Table 3.8)

3.47 This table gives details for consumption of motor spirit, gas oil/diesel oil and fuel oils given in the main commodity balance tables for the period 1996 to 2000. This includes information on retail and commercial deliveries of motor spirit and DERV fuel that cannot be accommodated within the structure of the commodity balances, but which are of interest. Also included in the table are details of the quantities of motor spirit and DERV fuel sold collectively by hypermarket and supermarket companies in the UK.

3.48 Motor spirit deliveries in 2000 were 1¾ per cent down compared to 1999, and 4½ per cent lower than in 1996. Deliveries of DERV fuel were only slightly higher (by ¾ per cent) in 2000 compared to 1999, but they were 9 per cent higher than in 1996.

3.49 Several factors are behind the differing trends seen for motor spirit and DERV fuel. There has been an increase in the number of diesel-engined vehicles in use in the UK. Improved technology has resulted in the development of vehicles with performance and characteristics that are more acceptable to the motorist. While diesel vehicles have also been priced at levels comparable with their petrol equivalents, they deliver more miles per gallon. In the National Travel Survey for 1995 to 1998 carried out by the Department for Transport, Local Government and Regions, diesel-engined cars averaged 51 miles per gallon of fuel, compared with 33 miles per gallon for petrol-engined cars.

3.50 In addition, during the early 1990s there was a significant differential in prices between DERV fuel and motor spirit prices that worked in favour of using DERV fuel. For example, in 1990, a typical retail price for a litre of 4-star petrol would have been 44.87 pence, compared with 40.48 pence for a litre of DERV fuel, representing a 10 per cent saving. This difference was seen at a time when fuel prices were rising as the Gulf crisis had an adverse effect on world markets, increasing the attraction that the efficiency gains of diesel vehicles had for the customer. In December 2000, average retail prices for a litre of the most common grade of motor spirit purchased (premium unleaded), and DERV fuel were 79.83 and 84.56 pence per litre respectively. It is thought that the removal of the favourable differential, and government policy to increase the level of taxation on DERV fuel for environmental reasons, has had a significant effect on slowing down in recent years the numbers of persons switching from petrol to diesel engined vehicles.

3.51 Chart 3.5 shows how the share of total motor spirit deliveries accounted for by unleaded fuel has increased from 68 per cent in 1996 to effectively 100 per cent in 2000. It should be remembered that, with effect from 1st January 2000, retails sales of leaded petrol ceased as a result of the implementation of a European strategy to reduce pollution from road traffic (known as the Auto-Oil Directive). This is discussed in more detail in paragraphs 3.53 to 3.57 below. As such, in 2000 effectively all petrol sold was unleaded petrol. Super premium unleaded reached a 3 per cent share of total motor spirit deliveries in 1996, but this has since fallen to 2 per cent in 2000. The current high level of duty applied to this fuel compared to the other grades of motor spirit has done much to reduce demand.

3.52 Since 1990 there has been an overall trend of a reduction in the consumption of motor spirit in the UK. Consumption in 2000 was 12 per cent lower than the peak of 24 million tonnes of motor spirit consumed in 1990. There are several reasons for this. Firstly, as Chart 3.5 shows, there has been a drop in the level of consumption of leaded fuel in particular. However, this is not the cause of the overall drop in total consumption of motor spirit as the main reason for this decrease is motorists switching to using unleaded petrol in their vehicles.

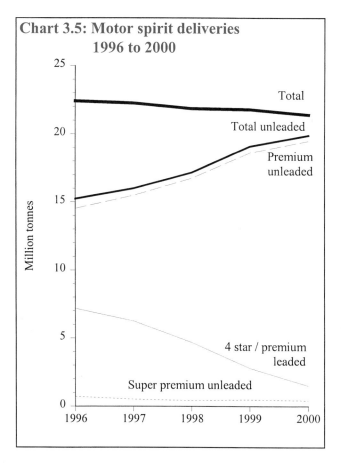

Chart 3.5: Motor spirit deliveries 1996 to 2000

3.53   As mentioned above (paragraph 3.50) and as illustrated in Chart 3.6, there is a large differential between the price of a litre of leaded and unleaded motor spirit.   This factor has helped encourage motorists to switch from leaded to unleaded petrol. In addition, as part of a European strategy to reduce pollution from road traffic (known as the Auto-Oil Directive), leaded petrol (4-star) was banned from general sale from 1st January 2000, which gave an additional push, particularly during the second half of 1999, towards motorists switching to unleaded fuels.

3.54   Although some vehicles originally designed to use leaded fuel could use unleaded fuel, quite frequently the desire on the part of motorists to change to using unleaded fuel has provided an impetus for people to change their vehicles to either new ones or one of more recent manufacture. As a result, studies have shown that the percentage of the UK car fleet that can run on unleaded fuel increased from 45 per cent in 1990 to 75 per cent in 1997, with its share increasing by around 4 per cent each year in more recent years.

3.55   With regards to the phase-out of sales of leaded petrol, some vehicles that were using leaded petrol could safely switch to using unleaded petrol in their cars with no adjustments being necessary.   Other vehicles could switch to unleaded petrol, but required some adjustment to the ignition timing in order to use Premium grade unleaded fuel.   Some older cars do need the lead in petrol to protect their engines from premature wear, and for these a variety of solutions were introduced to allow their continued use.

3.56   Lead in petrol does two things. It increases the fuel's octane rating making it less prone to 'knock' or 'pinking' caused by the fuel in the engine burning in an uncontrolled manner, potentially causing damage to the engine. Secondly, it protects the engine's exhaust valve seats from wear. Cars designed to run on unleaded fuel have very hard valve seats that resist wear. Vehicles that require leaded petrol for its high octane rating can use Super Unleaded petrol where it is available or LRP (Lead Replacement Petrol), which contains an AWA. An AWA (Anti-Wear Additive) is an alternative to lead to protect the engine's exhaust valve seats from excessive wear. Vehicles needing the protection from wear that leaded petrol provides can use LRP or buy an AWA for mixing with unleaded fuel of the correct octane rating or can have the engine modified to run on unleaded fuel.

3.57   LRP began to be widely available as a direct substitute for leaded petrol from the autumn of 1999. Where petrol stations offer LRP, it replaced 4 star at leaded petrol pumps. Pumps dispensing the new fuel are clearly labelled and have a wide nozzle that does not fit the fuel filler of cars equipped with catalytic converters. It is also possible to buy, as an alternative to LRP, an AWA for mixing with unleaded petrol. These additives are available in bottles or syringe-like

injection applicators.   However, very few such additives are on the market, and in most cases LRP is used. It is expected that there will continue to be a decline in sales of LRP over the next few years. It is thus likely that its sale may cease from some petrol stations.   If this happens it is possible that bottled additives may start to be more widely available. For further information on this subject, a free leaflet is available from the Department for Transport, Local Government and Regions free publications service (tel. 0870-1226-236), which can be viewed on the DTLR Internet site at:

www.environment.dtlr.gov.uk/unleaded

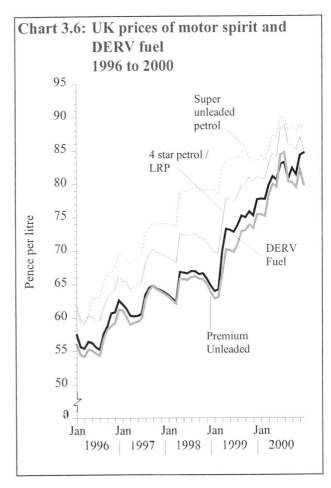

Chart 3.6: UK prices of motor spirit and DERV fuel 1996 to 2000

3.58   Chart 3.6 also illustrates the large differential that has existed for some time between the price of 4-star leaded petrol and DERV fuel, with the latter being priced at similar levels to premium grade unleaded petrol. As with the differential between leaded and unleaded petrol, this price differential also worked to encourage motorists to convert to diesel-engined vehicles. Chart 3.7 contains details of vehicle licence registrations for private cars during each year for the period 1990 to 1999, the latest year for which data is available, broken down by type of engine. Whilst the number of petrol engined vehicles licensed only grew by 4 per cent, the number of diesel-engined vehicles licensed has increased more than four-fold in the same period.

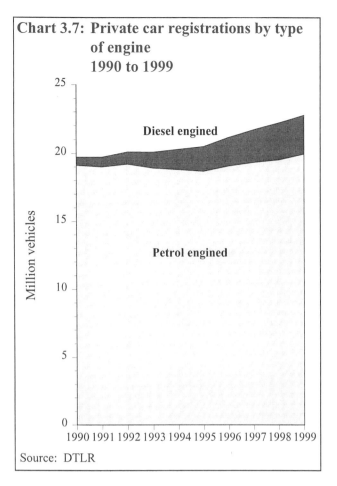

Chart 3.7: Private car registrations by type of engine 1990 to 1999

Source: DTLR

3.59 In 1997, a differential rate of duty was introduced for Ultra Low Sulphur Diesel fuel (ULSD). Initially set at 1 pence per litre, this differential was increased in the March 1999 Budget to 2 pence per litre, and up to 3 pence per litre in the March 2000 Budget. This extra differential has mostly been used to allow producers to cover the additional costs of providing the ULSD, either through funding changes in refinery processes or through covering the extra cost of importing these low sulphur products. The introduction of this duty differential has had a significant effect on moving consumers over to what is regarded as a more environmentally friendly fuel. As such, HM Customs & Excise estimate that, as at the end of 2000, all sales of DERV fuel are now of ULSD.

3.60 ULSD has a maximum sulphur content of 50 parts per million by weight (0.005 per cent). This compares with the previous limit of 500 parts per million (0.05 per cent) in the UK, and the limit of 350 parts per million (0.035 per cent) which came into place from 1/1/2000 as part of the European strategy to reduce pollution from road traffic mentioned in paragraph 3.51. More information on the Auto-Oil Directive can be obtained from the European Commission at www.europa.eu.int.

3.61 The European strategy calls for a further reduction is sulphur levels in road fuels in 2005. This will require a reduction in the level of sulphur in motor spirit from the 150 parts per million in place from 1 January 2000 to 50 parts per million. However, a duty differentials in favour of ULSP of 1 pence per litre

was introduced in the March 2000 Budget, and came into force from 1st October 2000. This differential was increased in March 2001 to 3 pence per litre, and as such was increased to encourage both production and use in the UK of ULSP in advance of the 2005 deadline. As such, part of the differential was expected to be effectively "kept" by refiners to cover the increased cost of manufacture of the low sulphur fuel. For example, there is the cost of investing in refineries in the UK to convert them to produce the fuel, and also the possible higher costs of importing the low sulphur fuel, if UK refinery production is not enough to meet demand. The rest of the differential was expected to be passed on to consumers in order to give an incentive for consumers to switch to the new, cleaner fuel. As such, the idea was to build on the substantial success of the duty incentive for ultra low sulphur diesel that has meant that this cleaner fuel is now 100 per cent of the UK diesel market, 5 years ahead of the EC deadline.

3.62 There are several significant environmental benefits from switching from ordinary unleaded petrol to ULSP. The Department of the Environment, Transport and the Regions has carried out research into these potential benefits of ULSP. ULSP can lead to reductions in emissions of nitrogen oxides of up to 6 per cent, carbon monoxide of between 6 and 18 per cent and reductions in hydrocarbon emissions of up to 15 per cent. There are also substantial reductions in emissions of non-regulated pollutants such as benzene, 1,3 butadiene, acetaldehyde and formaldehyde. The wider availability of ULSP will also allow the introduction of new engine technologies such as gasoline direct injection (GDI) that can improve fuel efficiency by up to 20 per cent. The reduction in fuel consumed would clearly lead to a reduction in carbon dioxide emissions.

3.63 Although not specifically covered by the statistics included in this Digest, the rollout of ULSP across the UK petrol retail network has taken place very quickly. The 3 pence per litre duty differential has provided the incentives needed for the widespread introduction of this fuel in the UK. As at 1st June 2001, over 90 per cent of refinery capacity in the UK for the production of premium grade unleaded petrol (the grade replaced by ULSP) has been converted over to produce ULSP. This means that UK refineries have sufficient capacity to meet the increased levels of demand for ULSP in the UK, although some increased imports of ULSP were needed earlier in the year while refineries were converting over to the new fuel, and will be needed later in 2001 to cover periods of peak demand.

3.64 It is estimated that, as at 1st June 2001, 98 per cent of the total of 13,000 retail sites that exist in the UK will have converted to selling ULSP instead of ordinary premium grade unleaded petrol. The major retailers such as the oil companies and super/hypermarket companies were very quick to switch over to the new fuel. Due to their high volumes of sales, the volumes of ULSP sold increased very quickly during 2001, such that by 1st June 2001 over 99 per cent of sales of unleaded petrol were ULSP. This represents a significant achievement by the UK oil industry.

3.65 Sales by super/hypermarkets have taken an increasing share of retail deliveries (i.e. deliveries to dealers) of motor spirit and DERV fuel in recent years as Table 3.B shows. These figures have been derived from a survey of super/hypermarket companies to collect details of their sales of motor spirit and DERV fuel. The share of total deliveries (i.e. including deliveries direct to commercial consumers) is shown in brackets.

Table 3B: Super/hypermarkets share of retail deliveries

per cent

	Motor spirit		DERV fuel	
1996	21.8	(21.3)	15.4	(6.0)
1997	22.7	(22.3)	16.7	(6.8)
1998	24.0	(22.6)	17.5	(7.6)
1999	25.4	(24.9)	18.3	(8.4)
2000	26.9	(26.2)	18.9	(9.0)

3.66 The flattening of the upwards trend in super/hypermarkets share of retail deliveries in 1996 reflects increased action from other retailers to preserve their market shares (for example, the *Pricewatch* campaign operated by ESSO). The increases seen in subsequent years represent some slight increase in sales by super/hypermarket companies, but the percentage shares are also affected by the decline in the overall deliveries of motor spirit in the UK seen in these years as mentioned earlier.

3.67 The share of unleaded in total motor spirit deliveries by super/hypermarkets, 94 per cent in 2000, continues to be slightly higher than for other types of retail outlet (93 per cent in 2000).

Fuel protests in 2000

3.68 In September 2000 supply disruptions were seen in the UK due to widespread protests occurring at fuel refineries and distribution terminals in reaction to high fuel prices, with these protests having widespread public support. The protestors were mostly from the road haulage and farming industries, both of whom had been significantly affected by the rises in fuel prices that resulted from the recovery in crude oil prices from their low levels in 1998 to 1999. For the haulage industry, fuel represents a major component of their costs, and as such the increased directly affected their profitability. For the farming industry, coming as they did on top of other factors affecting the industry, the increases in fuel prices were a significant adverse factor. Farmers are able to make use of "red diesel",

which is taxed at a much lower rate than normal DERV fuel and as such is to be used solely in off-road agricultural vehicles. However, due to its lower tax rate, the impact of any increase in prices for these fuels is magnified.

3.69 To illustrate this, in December 1998, the costs of crude oil acquired by UK refineries was down to 55% of the average cost in 1995. By September 2000 it had nearly quadrupled in costs up to 203 per cent of the average cost in 1995. Ordinary road users saw the price of DERV fuel increase from 64.8 in December 1998 to 82.3 pence per litre in September 2000, an increase of 27 per cent. However, the price excluding duty and VAT, which is akin to the price that farmers would be paying for their "red diesel" more than doubled from 10.13 in December 1998 to 21.23 pence per litre in September 2000.

3.70 These protests, along with the associated heavy demand from the public for the key road fuels, led to severe shortages of oil products occurring very rapidly. They showed how quickly such widespread problems with the oil supply chain could result in significant adverse effects for the UK, both in economic and social terms.

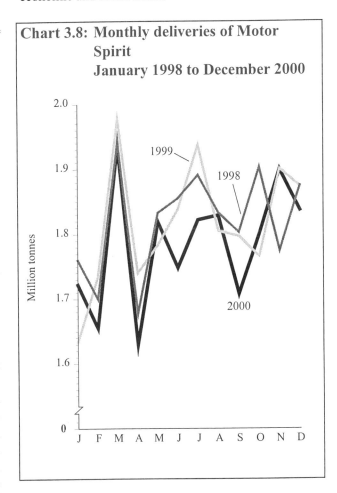

Chart 3.8: Monthly deliveries of Motor Spirit January 1998 to December 2000

3.71 Even though the protests had a significant impact on supplies moving to final consumers, and there were widespread shortages of road fuels at retail sites across the UK, as Chart 3.8 illustrates, there was a slight, but not significant impact on total deliveries of motor spirit in the month of September 2000 as a whole. Similarly Chart 3.9 shows how there does not appear to have been any overall impact on DERV fuel deliveries during September 2000.

3.72 There are several reasons why the overall impact on deliveries in the month for either fuel was not greater, and also why there was apparently no impact on DERV deliveries at all. Taking motor spirit first, while demand for motor spirit was very high during the periods of the protests, it was followed by a period of lower demand. This was due to consumers already having filled their petrol tanks. There was also a reduction in road traffic seen during the period as consumers worked to conserve their fuel, which further reduced demand. As such, this period of lower demand more than offset the period of high demand to produce the slight decline in deliveries in September 2000 visible in Chart 3.8

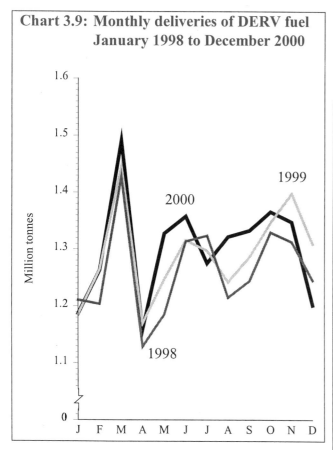

Chart 3.9: Monthly deliveries of DERV fuel January 1998 to December 2000

3.73 With DERV fuel, as well as the pattern of increased and then reduced demand at retail sites in September, there was additionally increased demand seen from the commercial sector. While deliveries of motor spirit are virtually all to retail sites, deliveries of DERV fuel are split fairly equally between deliveries to retail and to commercial sites. This increased demand included sites such as refuelling depots for freight companies, emergency services, etc. as well as demand from individual sites such as hospitals. Many of these sites have been operating under minimal stockholding arrangements in recent years (i.e. "just in time" stocking) to keep their operating costs to a minimum, After the protests in mid-September, many of these sites sought to significantly increase their level of stock holding up from the minimal levels they

had previously been operating to protect themselves form the impact of any future disruptions. This led to an extended period of higher than normal demand, as shown in Chart 3.9. It is interesting to note that deliveries of DERV fuel in November and December 2000 were slightly below normal levels. This was due to there being a corresponding period of lower demand once the apparent risk of any future supply disruptions was over, and companies started to return to their lower levels of operating stocks.

Aviation fuel

3.74 Data is given in Tables 3.4 to 3.7 and in table 3.12 on the increasing amounts of aviation turbine fuel kerosene being consumed in the UK. Chart 3.14 illustrates the trend seen since 1970 in the use of ATF kerosene in the UK. Deliveries in the UK in 2000 were 9 per cent higher than in 1999. Whilst this partly reflects the trend seen during the 1980s and 1990s for increased air transport both of people and of freight, there were special circumstances in 2000 which led to a greater than expected increase in demand for this fuel in the UK.

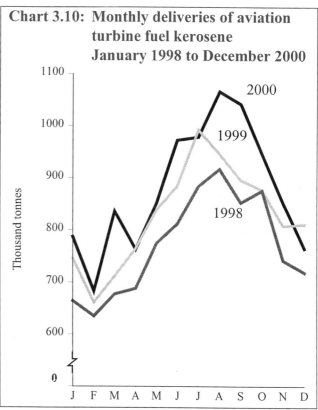

Chart 3.10: Monthly deliveries of aviation turbine fuel kerosene January 1998 to December 2000

3.75 Chart 3.10 shows monthly deliveries of ATF Kerosene in the UK during 1998, 1999 and 2000. The seasonal peak in deliveries in the summer months is clearly evident. In 2000 the deliveries in the summer months were much higher than expected. This was due to the impact of the problem with the rail industry following the various accidents that occurred in 2000. These resulted in widespread disruptions to the rail service in the UK which in turn prompted a significant increase in the level of domestic passenger movements in the UK, as travellers turned to air travel as an alternative to rail travel.

3.76 Transport statistics from the DETR for 2000 on aircraft kilometres flown, passenger movements, mail services and seat kilometres used (a measure of the total distances passengers flew) have all increased on previous levels. Chart 3.11 illustrates this with details of passenger numbers on domestic flights operated by UK airlines in 2000 compared with figures for 1998 and 1999.

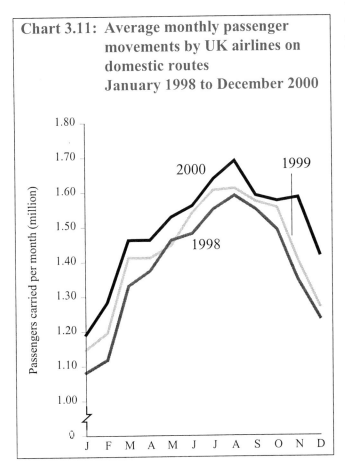

Chart 3.11: Average monthly passenger movements by UK airlines on domestic routes January 1998 to December 2000

Additional information on inland deliveries for non-energy uses

3.77 Table 3.C below summarises additional data on the uses made of the total deliveries of oil products for non-energy uses included as the bottom line in the commodity balances in Tables 3.4 to 3.6. In it, extra information on the uses of lubricating oils and greases by use, and details of products used as petro-chemical feedstocks are given.

3.78 All inland deliveries of lubricating oils and petroleum coke have been classified as going for non-energy uses only. However, a certain part of each does go for energy uses, but it is difficult to estimate figures for energy use for these products with a great degree of accuracy, hence no estimates for energy use appear in the commodity balance tables.

3.79 For lubricating oils, work done by the International Energy Agency suggests that some 50 per cent of inland deliveries each year are re-used as a fuel, through either being burnt whilst being used as lubricants or by being recycled by being re-refined into fuel oils which are then burnt. The available data

for the UK suggest a slightly lower figure of 40 per cent (equal to around 290 to 330 thousand tonnes per year).

3.80 For petroleum coke, more information is available which has allowed more accurate estimates to be made. It has been possible to analyse the data available for the imports of petroleum coke to identify which type of company is importing the product. This work has shown that a significant proportion of petroleum coke imports each year are made by energy companies, such as power generators or fuels merchants, with a significant proportion also being imported by cement manufacturers. Whilst it cannot be certain that these imports are being used as a fuel, information on the use of petroleum coke in cement manufacture does suggest that it is being used as a fuel.

Table 3C: Additional information on inland deliveries for non-energy uses 1998 to 2000

			Thousand tonnes
	1998	1999	2000
Feedstock for petroleum chemical plants:			
Propane	794	642	670
Butane	383	415	259
Other gases	1,465	1,755	1,626
Total gases	2,642	2,812	2,555
Naphtha (L.D.F.)	2,882	3,100	2,344
Middle Distillate Feedstock (M.D.F.)	760	844	945
Other products	-	-	-
Total feedstock	6,284	6,756	5,844
Lubricating oils and grease:			
Aviation	2	2	2
Industrial	502	470	519
Marine	40	38	33
Motors	254	265	239
Agricultural	15	15	11
Fuel oil sold as lubricant	-	-	-
Total lubricating oils & grease	813	790	804
Other non-energy products:			
Industrial spirit	83	77	83
White spirit	96	97	87
Bitumen	1,967	1,928	1,975
Petroleum wax	18	37	32
Petroleum coke	887	660	776
Miscellaneous products	538	388	463
Total non-energy use	10,686	10,733	10,062

3.81 Using the data available for imports, estimates have been constructed for 1998, 1999 and 2000 which show that possibly up to 50 per cent of inland deliveries in some recent years (equal to around 550 thousand tonnes) of petroleum coke are imported by these companies for energy uses. In 1999 there was a reduction in the level of imports, such that only around 280 thousand tonnes of petroleum coke is estimated to have gone for energy uses. Of this, approximately 20 per cent was for electricity generation, with 30 per cent for use as a fuel in the manufacture of cement, and the remainder being imported for sale as a solid fuel or to be used as an input into the manufacture of other solid fuels. In 2000, these proportions remained the same, and the overall level for energy use was around 340 thousand tonnes or 44 per cent of total supplies.

3.82 Data on the prices paid by industry for petroleum coke on a basis comparable with the other price data in Chapter 9 of the Digest are not available. However, analysis of the data on the quantity and value of imports of petroleum coke into the UK from HM Customs & Excise provides some estimates for the cost of imports and gives some indication of the prices being paid. These are only indicative of the prices being paid in the port of importation, and do not include the extra transport costs from the port to the final destination that would be part of more rigorous price estimate. Details of these estimates are included in Chapter 8 on trade in fuels, as part of Table 8.3. A breakdown has been made by grade of petroleum coke and type of use for imports into the UK, which is given in Table 3.D below. Calcined petroleum coke is virtually pure carbon, and as such is more valuable than non-calcined (otherwise known as "green") petroleum coke, as shown by the higher £ per tonne it commands and the fact that it is not used simply as a fuel.

3.83 Petroleum coke is a relatively low energy content fuel, having a calorific value of 39.5 GJ per tonne, compared with an average for petroleum products of 45.2 GJ per tonne, and 43.2 GJ per tonne for fuel oil. It is however higher than coal (27.3 GJ per tonne) and in certain areas is competing with coal as a fuel. It has the advantage of being a very cheap fuel, since it is often regarded as a waste product rather than a specific output from the refining process. Compared to imports of coal, prices per GJ are about 25 per cent lower.

Table 3D: Estimated £ per tonne for imports of petroleum coke into the UK

| | Non-calcined ("green") petroleum coke | | | Calcined petroleum coke |
	Energy	Non-energy	Total	Non-energy
1998	26.7	61.1	37.4	142.5
1999	20.0	31.7	25.3	117.1
2000	21.8	33.4	26.2	146.1

Inland deliveries of gas oil/diesel fuel and fuel oils for energy use

3.84 In the 2000 edition of the Digest, it was reported that, after a review, the table showing inland deliveries of these fuels, with a detailed breakdown by final user, last included as Table 3.11 in the 1999 edition of the Digest, was dropped. Most of the industrial breakdown previously given in this table is included in the main commodity balances (Tables 3.4 to 3.6). The additional information that was given in this table under each industry heading was of limited quality. Oil companies have reported as accurately as possible their deliveries to the detailed industries. However, due to the fact that a certain percentage of their deliveries into the UK market of these fuels are sold to distributors for onward sale rather than being sold direct to the consuming company, the very detailed figures in this table are of limited accuracy. As such it was decided to discontinue this table in the Digest. However, users may still obtain a copy of the table direct from the contact details listed after paragraph 3.124.

Inland deliveries by country (Table 3.9)

3.85 This table shows deliveries in England and Wales, Scotland, and Northern Ireland. The figures for deliveries for energy use between 1998 and 2000 show a fall in use for Scotland and Northern Ireland but an increase in use in England and Wales. The increase in use in England and Wales is primarily due to increased deliveries of ATF kerosene (due to the growth of air traffic in the UK mainly being seen at airports in England) and DERV fuel - up by 17 and 5 per cent respectively. These increases more than offset the fall in use of fuel oil in England and Wales over the period (down by 36 per cent). Similar falls in the use of fuel oils were seen in Scotland and Northern Ireland over the period (down 35 and 50 per cent respectively, the latter reflecting the switch in fuel use at the Ballylumford power station in 1997 from fuel oil to gas). Feedstocks for use in petrochemical plants in Scotland decreased in 2000 compared to 1999 (down by 14 per cent), related to problems at BP's Grangemouth refinery and petro-chemical plant during 2000. The decrease in deliveries of motor spirit and DERV fuel in Northern Ireland (down by 27 and 42 per cent respectively) is due to cross-border movements of fuels from the Republic of Ireland replacing sales in Northern Ireland. Some of these movements are legitimate cross-border shopping for petrol and derv, i.e. private motorists filling up in the Republic to take advantage of the lower fuel duty rates in the Republic of Ireland and advantageous exchange rates. However, there is a significant amount of cross-border smuggling thought to be taking place of low-price fuel from the Republic of Ireland being moved into Northern Ireland. HM Customs and Excise are actively investigating and taking action against this illegal trade.

Stocks of oil (Table 3.10)

3.86 This table shows stocks of crude oil, feedstocks (including partly processed oils) and products (in detail) at the end of each year. Stocks of crude oil and feedstocks decreased in 2000, with decreases in stocks held at refineries and at offshore facilities offsetting a slight increase in stocks held at oil terminals. The increase in stocks held at terminals is related to increased throughput as a result of the increased level of output from UK production installations. Offshore stocks have decreased due to the increased price of crude oil on international markets resulting is faster throughput of oil from these fields being seen. The decrease in refinery stocks reflects to some extent refinery closures and also companies working to reduce cost levels as much as possible.

3.87 As stated in paragraphs 3.21 and 3.22, the details of stocks of petroleum products (and crude and process oils) included in Table 3.10 are all stocks that are owned by UK companies, and thus include details of any stocks owned but held abroad, e.g. in Rotterdam, under bilateral government agreements. As such, the level of stocks in this table represents the full availability of stocks to the UK in case of any oil emergency occurring from a disruption to international supplies.

3.88 Stocks of petroleum products at the end of 2000 were 11 per cent lower than a year earlier. From July 1999 the UK Government implemented a revised EU Directive (EU Directive 93/98) setting obligations on EU member states to hold stocks of oil for emergency situations. Part of the changes was a reduction in the level of stocking obligation placed on the UK due to it being a producer of oil. The benefits of this reduction in obligation were passed on to oil companies in the UK as soon as possible, and so a reduction in the level of oil stocks held by UK companies, both in terms of products and also crude oil held at refineries, was seen during the middle part of 1999, and during 2000 companies continued to reduce their level of stock-holding, primarily through reducing the amounts of stocks held abroad under bilateral stocking agreements. The total stocks of crude oil and products held by UK companies at the end of 2000 would be sufficient to meet the UK's needs for approximately 68 days.

3.89 More information on these changes was provided in an article published in the September 2000 edition of *Energy Trends*, a copy of which can be obtained from the contact persons listed at the end of this chapter.

Long term trends

3.90 Tables 3.11 and 3.12 present extended time series of selected more aggregated data from the preceding tables, with a view to giving additional background on the historic development of the crude oil and petroleum sectors.

Crude oil and petroleum products: production, imports and exports (Table 3.11)

3.91 Table 3.11 shows data from 1970 to 2000 for production, imports and exports of crude oil (including natural gas liquids and feedstocks) and oil products. It also shows United Kingdom refinery throughput of crude oil, and the inland deliveries of oil products. Indigenous production of crude oil is shown in total with landward production shown separately.

3.92 The second (right-hand) part of the table consists of time series showing key aggregates, net exports figures, shares, etc. It should be noted that exports of crude oil include some imports that have been re-exported. In years of significant indigenous production these have little effect on exports as a proportion of indigenous production, but in the earlier years (approximately pre-1975) the re-exports exceeded indigenous production and thus the ratio of exports to indigenous production was over 1.

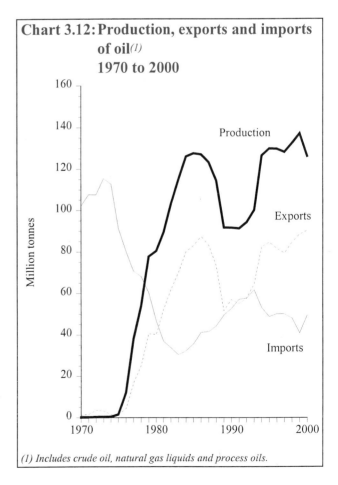

Chart 3.12: Production, exports and imports of oil[1] **1970 to 2000**

(1) Includes crude oil, natural gas liquids and process oils.

3.93 Chart 3.12 illustrates the trends in the production, exports and imports of crude oil. It shows that indigenous production of crude oil, etc. was negligible up to 1974 and then increased rapidly as North Sea production came on stream. Imports peaked in 1973, immediately prior to the first OPEC price 'hike'. The chart shows the rapid decline of net imports thereafter as imports fell and indigenous production rose, until 1981 when the surplus turned from net imports to net exports. Net exports peaked in 1984, one year before the peak for North Sea production in 1985.

3.94 The large fall in production in 1988 and particularly 1989 reflects the effects of the Piper Alpha accident and subsequent incidents, and the continued 'low' production in 1990 and 1991 reflects the consequent safety work. Production increased in 1992 and again in 1993 topping 100 million tonnes for the first time since 1988. In 1996 production at 127 million tonnes returned to previous peak levels, and in 1999 set a new record at 137 million tonnes. However, production declined in 2000 to be 8 per cent lower than in 1999. More information on the reasons behind this reduction can be found in Annex C, paragraph C.20

3.95 Table 3.11 shows that the imports share of refinery throughput of crude oil fell from around 100 per cent, before North Sea oil production started, to a low of 39 per cent in 1983 (the lowest year for imports), before rising to 64 per cent in 1993. Since then, with the significant increase in indigenous production, the imports share fell back to 46 per cent in 1999, the year of record UK production of crude oil, but rose to 56 per cent in 2000 due to the lower level of production mentioned above. These developments are mirrored by the changes in the ratio of indigenous production to refinery throughput. Ignoring pre-1976 figures, the proportion of indigenous production exported increased from 35 per cent to around two-thirds towards the end of the 1980s. Although the decreases in production in the late 1980s (paragraph 3.94) did lead to some reduction in the level of exports, the proportion of production exported has continued at roughly this level during the 1990s.

3.96 Net exports of oil products increased during the early 1990s to a record high in 1993. The increases in net exports of products in the 1990s reflects the increased throughput from refineries mainly feeding through to increased exports of product rather than increases in deliveries to the domestic market. With the closure of the Gulf Oil refinery from December 1997, net exports of products decreased in both 1998 and 1999, with the closure of Shell's Shell Haven refinery being the main reason for the decline seen in net exports of products in 2000. Imports of crude oil in 1991 (and marginally again in 1992) exceeded exports for the first time since 1980. Net exports of crude oil resumed in 1993, and have continued to rise since that time. In 1999, at 47½ million tonnes, net exports of crude oil were the highest since 1984 and overall net exports of crude oil and products at 58½

million tonnes were at a new record level. However, the decreased level of crude oil production in 2000 saw the overall level of net exports of crude and products decrease to 50 million tonnes.

3.97 Refinery throughput peaked in 1973, and subsequently both this and refinery output (the difference is refinery use of fuel and gains/losses) fell to pre-1970 levels. Since the low point of 1983, both refinery throughput and output have increased by over 25 per cent. However, both fell in 1994 and again in 1996, partly as a result of the fire mentioned above. Refinery throughput and output in 1998 were both the largest seen since 1979, but with the closure of the Gulf Oil refinery in December 1997, refinery output fell by 3½ per cent in 1998 and then by another 6 per cent in 1999 to the lowest level seen since 1989. However, as mentioned previously, the remaining refineries in the UK have worked to increase their capacity and utilisation rates and have to a large extent offset both the closure of Gulf's refinery and the closure of Shell's Shell Haven refinery as well. A sign of this is that despite the Shell Haven closure from December 1999, refinery output in 2000 is slightly higher than in 1999.

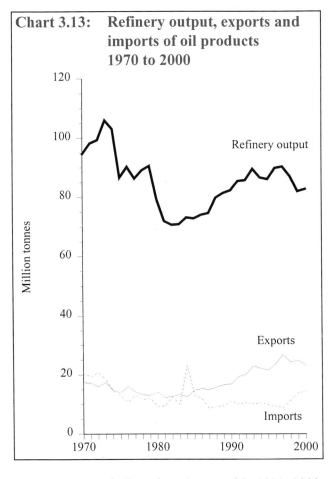

Chart 3.13: Refinery output, exports and imports of oil products 1970 to 2000

3.98 Exports of oil products increased in 1991, 1992 and 1993, comfortably exceeding the earlier peak at the beginning of the 1970s, but fell in 1994 and 1995. In 1997 at 26.8 million tonnes they were the highest ever recorded. Imports of oil products were at their highest in 1967 and, apart from a 'blip' in 1984 as a result of the miners' strike, have been less than half this peak in recent years. As a result, 1984 apart, exports of oil products have exceeded imports in every year since 1974. In 2000, imports made up 20 per cent of inland deliveries compared with over 30 per cent in the early to mid-1960s. Chart 3.13 summarises the trend in refinery output, exports and imports of oil products over the period.

Inland deliveries of petroleum products (Table 3.12)

3.99 Table 3.12 shows data from 1970 to 2000 of deliveries of petroleum products split between non-energy uses in total and the major products delivered for energy use. The data in this table have been slightly revised from earlier versions to put the data presented on the same basis as the energy balances tables used for more recent years. This has involved the adding in of those volumes of fuels used within refineries as a refinery fuel into the data previously presented in the right-hand half of the table. This data shows trends over the period in petroleum products delivered to the main energy industries and to different categories of final user. It should be noted that whilst data for deliveries are considered to be a good proxy for consumption, differences can occur mainly because in the former no account is taken of the effect of stock changes at points further along the chain of consumption. The total of deliveries for energy use shown in the first (left-hand) half of the table thus includes 'own use' by refineries shown in the right-hand part of the table, whereas it used to exclude it.

3.100 Deliveries of petroleum products, in common with many other aggregate figures, (see Table 3.11) peaked in 1973. The 'blip' in 1984 reflects the increased deliveries of fuel oil, in particular, during the miners' strike. Fuel oil deliveries are now about 10 per cent of, and gas oil (other than DERV fuel) about half of the levels reached in the early 1970s. In contrast, deliveries of motor spirit and aviation turbine fuel have grown virtually continuously throughout the period. After limited growth during the 1970s and early 1980s, deliveries of DERV fuel resumed the high growth rates apparent in the 1960s, and have nearly doubled over the last 10 years. The upward surge of deliveries of transport fuels slowed in 1990 and ceased in 1991 with the twin impacts of the Gulf crisis and recession, with some recovery being seen in 1992.

3.101 Since 1990, deliveries of motor spirit have been decreasing each year, with the exception of 1996 which is 2 per cent higher than 1995, but is still 8 per cent lower than the level seen in 1990, and deliveries in 1995 were at their lowest level since 1986. 2000 has seen a 1¾ per cent reduction over 1999. These changes reflect the switch to diesel-engined cars during the late 1980s and early 1990s, although this switch has lessened in recent years. As such, they are mirrored by the consistent pattern of increases in deliveries of DERV fuel each year since 1990,

although this rate of increase has been slowing in recent years. Deliveries of aviation turbine fuel have also consistently increased each year since 1990. In 2000, deliveries of DERV fuel were 47 per cent higher than in 1990, and deliveries of aviation turbine fuel had increased by 62 per cent over the same period. Chart 3.14 shows the trends in transport fuels from 1970 to 2000.

3.102 By the end of the 1980s and so far in the 1990s deliveries for non-energy uses were not far off their peak of the early to mid-1970s, in contrast to energy uses, which, despite the growth for transport, remains at around three-quarters of their peak levels.

3.103 The right-hand half of the table illustrates the growth in transport use - this includes the use of the fuels as given in the left hand side of the table plus other energy uses of petroleum products. In this the figures for use by the Iron & Steel industry have been reduced by the inclusion of the fuels used in blast furnaces in the "other energy industry uses" column, which has been inserted. Total uses by the transport industry are now nearly double the amount delivered in 1970. Deliveries to every other major sector are below 1973 levels - well below for electricity generators, gas works, iron and steel and 'other industries', and other final users (mainly agriculture, public administration and commerce).

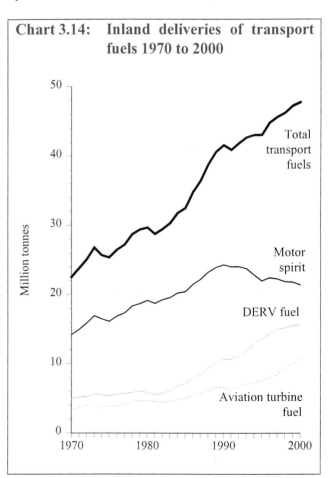

Chart 3.14: Inland deliveries of transport fuels 1970 to 2000

Technical notes and definitions

Indigenous production

3.104 The term indigenous is used throughout this section and includes oil from the UK Continental Shelf both offshore and onshore.

Deliveries

3.105 These are deliveries into consumption, as opposed to being estimates of actual consumption or use. They are split between inland deliveries and deliveries to marine bunkers. Inland deliveries will not necessarily be consumed in the United Kingdom (e.g. aviation fuels).

Sources of data

3.106 The majority of the data included in the text and tables of this chapter are derived from the UK Petroleum Industry Association (UKPIA) data collection system. In this, UKPIA collect data relating to the inland operations of the UK oil industry (i.e. information on the supply, refining and distribution of oil in the UK). The format and coverage of the data is such that it meets most of the needs of both government and the industry itself. As such, it operates by each member of UKPIA providing returns on its refining activities and deliveries of various products to the internal UK market. This information is supplemented whenever necessary to allow for complete coverage within the statistics, with separate exercises carried out on special topics (for example, the work on super/hypermarkets referred to in paragraph 3.65).

Statistical differences

3.107 In Tables 3.1 to 3.7, there are headings titled "statistical differences". These are differences that are seen between the separately observed figures for production and deliver of crude oil and products during the path of their movement from the point of production to the point of consumption.

3.108 These headings listed in the primary oil commodity balances (Tables 3.1 to 3.3) are differences that are seen between the separately observed and reported figures for production from onshore or offshore fields and supply to the UK market that cannot be accounted for by any specific factors. As such, they are primarily the result of the various inaccuracies in the meters at various points along offshore pipelines. These meters vary slightly in their accuracy within accepted tolerances, giving rises to both losses and gains when the volumes of oil flowing are measured. Temperature, pressure and natural leakage also contribute to the statistical differences as well. In addition, where data are shown on an energy basis, small discrepancies can occur between the estimated calorific values used at the field and the more accurately measured calorific value at the onshore terminal. There are also factors such as errors due to rounding or unrecorded losses, such as leakage.

3.109 Other contributory factors in these balances are inaccuracies in the recording of the amounts of these substances reported as being disposed of to the various activities listed, including differences between the amounts reported as going to refineries and the actual amounts that pass through refineries.

3.110 Similar to this, the data under these headings in Tables 3.4 to 3.6 are the differences between the deliveries of petroleum products to the inland UK market reported by the supplying companies and estimates for such deliveries. These estimates are calculated by taking the output of products reported by refineries and then adjusting it by the relevant factors (such as imports and exports of the products, changes in the levels of stocks etc.).

3.111 As the data underlying both the observed deliveries into the UK market and the individual components of the estimates (i.e. production, imports, exports, stocks) comes from the same source (the oil companies), it may be thought that such differences should not exist. While it is true that each oil company provides data on its own activities in each area, there are separate areas of operation within the companies that report their own part of the overall data. The table below illustrates this.

Table 3E: Sources of data within oil companies

Area covered	Source
Refinery production	Refinery
Imports & Exports	Refinery, logistics departments, oil traders
Stocks	Refinery, crude & product terminals, major storage and distribution sites
Final deliveries	Sales, marketing & accounts depts.

3.112 Each individual reporting source will have a direct interest in the data it is reporting. Refineries will be clear on what they produce and how much leaves the refinery gate as part of routine monitoring of the refinery operations. Sales to final consumers represent a company's main source of income, and so they will similarly be monitored closely, as will imports and exports. Companies will ensure that each component set of data reported is as accurate as possible, but in some cases the systems used are not integrated, which means that internal consistency checks to ensure consistency across all of the data reported cannot be made. Each part of a company may also work to different timings as well, which may further add to the degree of differences seen, but the main area where there is known to be a problem is with the "Transfers" heading in the commodity balances.

3.113 The data reported under this heading has two components. Firstly there is an allowance for reclassification of products within the refining process. For example, butane is added to motor spirit to improve the octane rating, aviation turbine fuel could be reclassified as gas diesel oil if its quality deteriorates, and much of the fuel oil imported into the UK is further refined into other petroleum products. In addition to these inter-product transfers the data also includes an allowance to cover the receipt of backflows of products from petrochemical plants. Such plants are often very closely integrated with refineries (for example, BP's refinery at Grangemouth is right next to the petrochemical plant). A deduction for these backflows thus needs to be included under the "Transfers" heading so that calculated estimates reflect net output and are thus more comparable with the basis of the observed deliveries data.

3.114 However, there is scope for error in the recording of these two components. With inter-product transfers, the data is recorded within the refinery during the refining and blending processes. However, during these processes the usual units used to record the changes are volume rather than masses. As shown by the conversion factors given in Annex A, different factors apply for each product when converting from a volume to mass basis. What might be a balanced transfer in volume terms is thus not when converted to a mass basis. This is thought to be the main source of error within the individual product balances.

3.115 With the backflows data, as the observed data for deliveries derived from sales data are on a "net" basis they will exclude the element of backflows. However, it is thought that there is significant scope for error in the recording of the backflows when they are received at a refinery. For example, these could be seen simply as an input of fuel oils to be used as a feedstock, and thus recorded as an input without their precise nature being recorded – in effect a form of double-counting. It is this relationship between the petrochemical sector and refineries that is thought to be the main source of error in the overall oil commodity balances, and one which is being looked at during the review of the reporting system mentioned in paragraph 3.44.

Imports and exports

3.116 The information given under the headings "imports" and "exports" in this chapter are the figures recorded by importers and exporters of oil. They thus differ in some cases from the import and export figures provided by HM Customs and Excise that are given in Chapter 8 of this Digest. These differences may arise since whilst the trader's figures are a record of actual movements in the period, for non-EU trade, HM Customs and Excise figures show the trade as declared by exporters on documents received during the period stated. The Customs figures also include re-exports. These are products that may have originally entered the UK as imports from another country and been stored in the UK prior to being exported back out of the UK, as opposed to having been actually produced in the UK.

3.117 In previous versions of the Digest, these imports and exports were called "arrivals" and "shipments" in an attempt to highlight their difference from the other sources of trade data. However, their name has now been changed to more clearly represent what the movements actually are; movements in and out of the United Kingdom.

Marine bunkers

3.118 This covers deliveries to ocean going and coastal vessels under international bunker contracts. Other deliveries to fishing, coastal and inland vessels are excluded.

Crude and process oils

3.119 These are all feedstocks, other than distillation benzene, for refining at refinery plants. Gasoline feedstock is any process oil whether clean or dirty which is used as a refinery feedstock for the manufacture of gasoline or naphtha. Other refinery feedstock is any process oil used for the manufacture of any other petroleum products.

Refineries

3.120 Refineries distilling crude and process oils to obtain petroleum products. This excludes petrochemical plants, plants only engaged in re-distilling products to obtain better grades, crude oil stabilisation plants and gas separation plants.

Products used as fuel (energy use)

3.121 The following paragraphs define the product headings used in the text and tables of this chapter, which are used for energy in some way, either directly as a fuel or as an input into electricity generation.

Refinery fuel - Petroleum products used as fuel at refineries.

Ethane - An ethane (C_2H_6) rich gas in natural gas and refinery gas streams. Primarily used, or intended to be used, as a chemical feedstock.

Propane - Hydrocarbon containing three carbon atoms, gaseous at normal temperature but generally stored and transported under pressure as a liquid.

Used mainly for industrial purposes and some domestic heating and cooking.

Butane - Hydrocarbon containing four carbon atoms, otherwise as for propane. Additional uses - as a constituent of motor spirit to increase vapour pressure and as a chemical feedstock.

Other gases for gasworks - Ethane and other refinery gases resulting from the processing of crude petroleum.

Naphtha (Light distillate feedstock) - Petroleum distillate boiling predominantly below $200^{\circ}C$.

Aviation spirit - All light hydrocarbon oils intended for use in aviation piston-engine power units, whether in the air, on land, or on water, including bench testing of aircraft engines.

Motor spirit - Blended light petroleum components used as fuel for spark-ignition internal-combustion engines other than aircraft engines:

(i)   4 star grade - all finished motor spirit with an octane number (research method) not less than 97, conforming to British Standard 4040. This can include leaded petrol or unleaded petrol containing an alternative to lead as an anti-wear additive (lead replacement petrol – LRP).

(ii)   Premium unleaded grade - all finished motor spirit, with an octane number (research method) not less than 95, conforming to British Standard 7070.

(iii) Ultra Low Sulphur Petrol - this is finished motor spirit with a specification similar to that for Premium unleaded grade, but with a sulphur content of less that 50 parts per million.

(iv)   Super premium unleaded grade - all finished motor spirit, with an octane number (research method) not less than 97, conforming to British Standard 7800.

Aviation turbine fuel - All other turbine fuel intended for use in aviation gas-turbine power units, whether in the air, on land or on water, including bench testing of aircraft engines.

Burning oil (kerosene) - Refined petroleum fuel, intermediate in volatility between motor spirit and gas oil, used for lighting and heating. White spirit and kerosene used for lubricant blends are excluded.

Gas oil/automotive diesel - Petroleum fuel having a distillation range immediately between kerosene and light-lubricating oil.

(i)   **DERV (Diesel Engined Road Vehicle) fuel** - automotive diesel fuel for use in high speed, compression ignition engines in vehicles subject to Vehicle Excise Duty.

(ii)   **Ultra Los Sulphur Diesel** – A grade of DERV fuel with less than 50 ppm sulphur (below 0.005 per cent).

(iii) **Gas oil** - used as a burner fuel in heating installations, for industrial gas turbines and as for DERV (but in vehicles not subject to Vehicle Excise Duty e.g. Agriculture vehicles, fishing vessels, construction equipment).

(iv)   **Marine diesel oil** - heavier type of gas oil suitable for heavy industrial and marine compression-ignition engines.

Fuel oil - Heavy petroleum residue blends used in atomising burners and for heavy duty marine diesel engines (marine bunkers, etc.) normally requiring pre-heating before combustion, but excluding fuel oil for grease making or lubricating oil and fuel oil sold as such for road making.

Orimulsion - An emulsion of bitumen in water used as a fuel primarily in power stations. In the tables Orimulsion is normally excluded from fuel oil, but where it is not shown separately it will be designated as part of fuel oils. From May 1996 Orimulsion has been classified as a type of bitumen for overseas trade purposes (see below). It was last imported in February 1998. Since that time the sole power station in the UK that was using it as a fuel has changed to alternative sources of energy.

Products not used as fuel (non-energy use)

3.122 The following paragraphs define the product headings used in the text and tables of this chapter, which are used for non-energy purposes.

Feedstock for petroleum chemical plants - All petroleum products intended for use in the manufacture of petroleum chemicals. This includes middle distillate feedstock of which there are several grades depending on viscosity. The boiling point ranges between $200^{\circ}C$ and $400^{\circ}C$. (A deduction has been made from these figures equal to the quantity of feedstock used in making the conventional petroleum products that are produced during the processing of the feedstock. The output and deliveries of these conventional petroleum products are included elsewhere as appropriate.)

White spirit - A highly refined distillate with a boiling range of about $150^{\circ}C$ to $200^{\circ}C$ used as a paint solvent and for dry cleaning purposes etc.

Industrial spirit - Refined petroleum fractions with boiling ranges up to $200^{\circ}C$ dependent on the use to which they are put - e.g. seed extraction, rubber solvents, perfume etc.

Lubricating oils (and grease) - Refined heavy distillates obtained from the vacuum distillation of petroleum residues. Includes liquid and solid hydrocarbons sold by the lubricating oil trade, either alone or blended with fixed oils, metallic soaps and other organic and/or inorganic bodies. A certain percentage of inland deliveries are re-used as a fuel (see paragraphs 3.77 to 3.83).

Bitumen - The residue left after the production of lubricating oil distillates and vacuum gas oil for upgrading plant feedstock. Used mainly for road making and building construction purposes. Includes other petroleum products, creosote and tar mixed with bitumen for these purposes and fuel oil sold as such for road making. In May 1996 harmonisation of EU trade categories, resulted in Orimulsion being reclassified as a bitumen, but for this chapter Orimulsion is still included under products used as fuel (energy use).

Petroleum wax - Includes paraffin wax, which is a white crystalline hydrocarbon material of low oil content normally obtained during the refining of lubricating oil distillate, paraffin scale, slack wax, microcrystalline wax and wax emulsions. Used for candle manufacture, polishes, food containers, wrappings etc.

Petroleum cokes - Carbonaceous material derived from hydrocarbon oils, uses for which include metallurgical electrode manufacture. Quantities of imports of this product are used as a fuel, primarily in the manufacture of cement (see paragraphs 3.77 to 3.83).

Miscellaneous products - Includes aromatic extracts, defoament solvents and other minor miscellaneous products.

Main classes of consumer

3.123 The following are definitions of the main groupings of users of petroleum products used in the text and tables of this chapter.

Gas works - Deliveries of petroleum products to establishments producing gas for public supply.

Electricity generators - Petroleum products delivered for use by major power producers and other companies for electricity generation including those deliveries to the other industries listed below which are used for autogeneration of electricity (Tables 3.4 to 3.6). This includes petroleum products used to generate electricity at oil refineries and is recorded in the Transformation sector, as opposed to other uses of refinery fuels which are recorded in the Energy Industry Use sector.

Agriculture - Deliveries of fuel oil and gas oil/diesel oil for use in agricultural power units, dryers and heaters. Burning oil for farm use.

Iron and steel - Deliveries of petroleum products to steel works and iron foundries.

Other industries - The industries covered correspond to the industrial groups shown in Table 1.E excluding Iron and Steel of Chapter 1.

Marine - Fuel oil and gas oil/diesel oil delivered, other than under international bunker contracts, for fishing vessels, UK oil and gas exploration and production, coastal and inland shipping and for use in ports and harbours.

Railways - Deliveries of fuel oil, gas oil/diesel oil and burning oil to railways, excluding deliveries to railway power stations.

Air transport - Total inland deliveries of aviation turbine fuel and aviation spirit. The figures cover deliveries of aviation fuels in the United Kingdom to international and other airlines, British and foreign governments (including armed services) and for private flying.

Road transport - Deliveries of motor spirit and DERV fuel for use in road vehicles of all kinds. Petroleum industry estimates for the consumption of road transport fuels by different vehicle classes, formerly provided in this Digest, are no longer available to the Department. The Department of the Environment, Transport and the Regions has provided alternative estimates. These are based on details of average vehicle mileages and assumed miles per gallon. The methodology behind these analyses and the estimates themselves are currently in the process of being updated. As such listed below is an indicative breakdown of road fuel consumption. More up-to-date information should be available from the DETR later in the year.

Table 3F: Estimated consumption of road transport fuels by vehicle class

Motor spirit:	
Cars and taxis	95%
Goods vehicles, mainly light vans	4%
Remainder, mainly motor cycles,	
Mopeds, etc.	1%
DERV:	
Goods vehicles	68%
Buses and coaches	7%
Remainder, mainly diesel-engined cars	
And taxis.	25%

Source: DTLR

Domestic - Fuel oil and gas oil/diesel oil delivered for central heating of private houses and other dwellings and deliveries of kerosene (burning oil) and liquefied petroleum gases for domestic purposes (see Tables 3.4 to 3.6).

Public services - Deliveries to national and local government premises (including educational, medical and welfare establishments and British and foreign armed forces) of fuel oil and gas oil/diesel oil for central heating and of kerosene (burning oil).

Miscellaneous - Deliveries of fuel oil and gas oil/diesel oil for central heating in premises other than those classified as domestic or public.

Monthly and quarterly data

3.124 Monthly or quarterly aggregate data for certain series presented in this chapter are available. This information can be obtained free of charge by following the links given at the Energy Statistics section of the DTI web-site, at:
www.dti.gov.uk/energy/energystats/energystats.htm

Contact: Kevin Williamson (Statistician)
020 7215 5184
Clive Evans
020 7215 5189
Ian Corrie
020 7215 2714

3.1 Commodity balances 2000[(1)]

Primary oil

Thousand tonnes

	Crude oil	Ethane	Propane	Butane	Condensate	Total NGL	Feedstock	Total primary oil
Supply								
Production	117,882	1,884	2,725	1,783	1,971	8,363	-	126,245
Other sources	-	-	-	-	-	-	-	-
Imports	48,868	-	-	-	-	-	5,519	54,387
Exports	-86,533	-18	-1,810	-942	-779	-3,549	-2,836	-92,918
Marine bunkers	-	-	-	-	-	-	-	-
Stock change (2)	+1,171	..	..	..	..	-17	-56	+1,098
Transfers	-	-1,411	-977	-995	-	-3,383	+3,493	+110
Total supply	**81,388**	..	..	..	..	**1,414**	**6,120**	**88,922**
Statistical difference (3)(4)	+697	..	..	..	..	-564	+480	+613
Total demand (4)	**80,691**	..	..	..	..	**1,978**	**5,640**	**88,309**
Transformation(4)	**80,691**	..	..	..	..	**1,683**	**5,640**	**88,014**
Electricity generation	-	-	-	-	-	-	-	-
Major power producers	-	-	-	-	-	-	-	-
Autogenerators	-	-	-	-	-	-	-	-
Petroleum refineries	80,691	..	..	..	..	1,683	5,640	88,014
Coke manufacture	-	-	-	-	-	-	-	-
Blast furnaces	-	-	-	-	-	-	-	-
Patent fuel manufacture	-	-	-	-	-	-	-	-
Other	-	-	-	-	-	-	-	-
Energy industry use	-	**294**	**1**	-	-	**295**	-	**295**
Electricity generation	-	-	-	-	-	-	-	-
Oil & gas extraction(4)	-	294	1	-	-	295	-	295
Petroleum refineries	-	-	-	-	-	-	-	-
Coal extraction	-	-	-	-	-	-	-	-
Coke manufacture	-	-	-	-	-	-	-	-
Blast furnaces	-	-	-	-	-	-	-	-
Patent fuel manufacture	-	-	-	-	-	-	-	-
Pumped storage	-	-	-	-	-	-	-	-
Other	-	-	-	-	-	-	-	-
Losses	-	-	-	-	-	-	-	-

(1) As there is no use made of primary oils and feedstocks by industries other than the oil and gas extraction and petroleum refining industries, other industry headings have not been included in this table. As such, this table is a summary of the activity of what is known as the Upstream oil industry.

(2) Stock fall (+), stock rise (-).

(3) Total supply minus total demand.

(4) Figures for total demand for the individual NGLs (and thus for the statistical differences as well) are not available. While separate data are available on the use of individual NGLs in the extraction of oil and gas, details of inputs into refineries of NGLs are only available at aggregate level for total NGLs, resulting in accurate estimates for the total demand for each NGL not being possible. As they are available, details of the use of individual NGLs in the extraction of oil and gas are included in this table.

3.2 Commodity balances 1999[1]

Primary oil

Thousand tonnes

	Crude oil	Ethane	Propane	Butane	Condensate	Total NGL	Feedstock	Total primary oil
Supply								
Production	128,262	2,022	2,853	2,005	1,957	8,837	-	137,099
Other sources	-	-	-	-	-	-	-	-
Imports	39,321	-	-	-	-	-	5,548r	44,869r
Exports	-85,052	-36	-1,980	-1,154	-700	-3,870	-2,875	-91,797
Marine bunkers	-	-	-	-	-	-	-	-
Stock change (2)	-347	..	..	..	..	+17	+132	-198
Transfers	-	-1,527	-865	-931	-	-3,323	+2,105	-1,218
Total supply	**82,184**	..	..	..	..	**1,661**	**4,910r**	**88,755r**
Statistical difference (3)(4)	+636	..	..	..	..	+42	-532r	+146r
Total demand (4)	**81,548**	..	..	..	..	**1,619**	**5,442**	**88,609**
Transformation(4)	**81,548**	..	..	..	..	**1,296**	**5,442**	**88,286**
Electricity generation	-	-	-	-	-	-	-	-
Major power producers	-	-	-	-	-	-	-	-
Autogenerators	-	-	-	-	-	-	-	-
Petroleum refineries	81,548	..	..	..	..	1,296	5,442	88,286
Coke manufacture	-	-	-	-	-	-	-	-
Blast furnaces	-	-	-	-	-	-	-	-
Patent fuel manufacture	-	-	-	-	-	-	-	-
Other	-	-	-	-	-	-	-	-
Energy industry use	**-**	**316**	**7**	**-**	**-**	**323**	**-**	**323**
Electricity generation	-	-	-	-	-	-	-	-
Oil & gas extraction(4)	-	316	7	-	-	323	-	323
Petroleum refineries	-	-	-	-	-	-	-	-
Coal extraction	-	-	-	-	-	-	-	-
Coke manufacture	-	-	-	-	-	-	-	-
Blast furnaces	-	-	-	-	-	-	-	-
Patent fuel manufacture	-	-	-	-	-	-	-	-
Pumped storage	-	-	-	-	-	-	-	-
Other	-	-	-	-	-	-	-	-
Losses	**-**	**-**	**-**	**-**	**-**	**-**	**-**	**-**

(1) As there is no use made of primary oils and feedstocks by industries other than the oil and gas extraction and petroleum refining industries, other industry headings have not been included in this table. As such, this table is a summary of the activity of what is known as the Upstream oil industry.

(2) Stock fall (+), stock rise (-).

(3) Total supply minus total demand.

(4) Figures for total demand for the individual NGLs (and thus for the statistical differences as well) are not available. While separate data are available on the use of individual NGLs in the extraction of oil and gas, details of inputs into refineries of NGLs are only available at aggregate level for total NGLs, resulting in accurate estimates for the total demand for each NGL not being possible. As they are available, details of the use of individual NGLs in the extraction of oil and gas are included in this table.

3.3 Commodity balances 1998[1]

Primary oil

Thousand tonnes

	Crude oil	Ethane	Propane	Butane	Condensate	Total NGL	Feedstock	Total primary oil
Supply								
Production	124,222	1,646r	3,031	2,000r	1,734	8,411r	-	132,633r
Other sources	-	-	-	-	-	-	-	-
Imports	39,460r	-	-	-	-	-	8,498r	47,958r
Exports	-79,651	-40	-1,842	-856	-640r	-3,378r	-1,581	-84,610r
Marine bunkers	-	-	-	-	-	-	-	-
Stock change (2)	-622	..	..	..	..	-29	+58	-593
Transfers	-	-1,215	-1,071	-1,171	-	-3,457	1,255	-2,202
Total supply	**83,409r**	..	..	..	..	**1,547r**	**8,230r**	**93,186r**
Statistical difference (3)(4)	-1,101r	..	..	..	..	-163r	+300r	-964r
Total demand (4)	**84,510**	..	..	..	..	**1,710**	**7,930**	**94,150**
Transformation(4)	**84,510**	..	..	..	..	**1,357**	**7,930**	**93,797**
Electricity generation	-	-	-	-	-	-	-	-
Major power producers	-	-	-	-	-	-	-	-
Autogenerators	-	-	-	-	-	-	-	-
Petroleum refineries	84,510	..	..	..	..	1,357	7,930	93,797
Coke manufacture	-	-	-	-	-	-	-	-
Blast furnaces	-	-	-	-	-	-	-	-
Patent fuel manufacture	-	-	-	-	-	-	-	-
Other	-	-	-	-	-	-	-	-
Energy industry use	**-**	**301r**	**39r**	**13**	**-**	**353**	**-**	**353**
Electricity generation	-	-	-	-	-	-	-	-
Oil & gas extraction(4)	-	301r	39r	13	-	353	-	353
Petroleum refineries	-	-	-	-	-	-	-	-
Coal extraction	-	-	-	-	-	-	-	-
Coke manufacture	-	-	-	-	-	-	-	-
Blast furnaces	-	-	-	-	-	-	-	-
Patent fuel manufacture	-	-	-	-	-	-	-	-
Pumped storage	-	-	-	-	-	-	-	-
Other	-	-	-	-	-	-	-	-
Losses	**-**	**-**	**-**	**-**	**-**	**-**	**-**	**-**

(1) As there is no use made of primary oils and feedstocks by industries other than the oil and gas extraction and petroleum refining industries, other industry headings have not been included in this table. As such, this table is a summary of the activity of what is known as the Upstream oil industry.

(2) Stock fall (+), stock rise (-).

(3) Total supply minus total demand.

(4) Figures for total demand for the individual NGLs (and thus for the statistical differences as well) are not available. While separate data are available on the use of individual NGLs in the extraction of oil and gas, details of inputs into refineries of NGLs are only available at aggregate level for total NGLs, resulting in accurate estimates for the total demand for each NGL not being possible. As they are available, details of the use of individual NGLs in the extraction of oil and gas are included in this table.

3.4 Commodity balances 2000

Petroleum products

	Ethane	Propane	Butane	Other gases	Naptha	Aviation spirit	Motor spirit	Industrial spirit	White spirit	Aviation turbine fuel	Burning oil
Supply											
Production	52	1,406	576	2,818	3,099	30	23,440	6	116	6,485	3,077
Other sources	1,411	977	995	-	-	-	-	-	-	-	-
Imports	-	78	253	-	348	16	2,443	34	3	4,675	86
Exports	-	-560	-150	-	-973	-	-4,708	-3	-6	-487	-199
Marine bunkers	-	-	-	-	-	-	-	-	-	-	-
Stock change (1)	-1	-18	-	+3	-58	+2	+260	-	-	-25	-70
Transfers	-60	-222	-438	-37	-568	-11	+625	-	-	+429	+587
Total supply	**1,403**	**1,662**	**1,237**	**2,783**	**1,848**	**37**	**22,061**	**38**	**112**	**11,077**	**3,480**
Statistical difference(2)	-188	+30	+797	-93	-515	-16	+658	-45	+25	+378	-267
Total demand	**1,590**	**1,631**	**440**	**2,876**	**2,363**	**52**	**21,403**	**83**	**87**	**10,698**	**3,748**
Transformation	-	37	-	205	-	-	-	-	-	-	-
Electricity generation	-	37	-	205	-	-	-	-	-	-	-
Major power producers	-	-	-	-	-	-	-	-	-	-	-
Autogenerators	-	37	-	205	-	-	-	-	-	-	-
Petroleum refineries	-	-	-	-	-	-	-	-	-	-	-
Coke manufacture	-	-	-	-	-	-	-	-	-	-	-
Blast furnaces	-	-	-	-	-	-	-	-	-	-	-
Patent fuel manufacture	-	-	-	-	-	-	-	-	-	-	-
Other	-	-	-	-	-	-	-	-	-	-	-
Energy industry use	**50**	**16**	**26**	**2,505**	**19**	-	-	-	-	-	-
Electricity generation	-	-	-	-	-	-	-	-	-	-	-
Oil & gas extraction	-	-	-	-	-	-	-	-	-	-	-
Petroleum refineries	50	2	-	2,505	19	-	-	-	-	-	-
Coal extraction	-	-	-	-	-	-	-	-	-	-	-
Coke manufacture	-	-	-	-	-	-	-	-	-	-	-
Blast furnaces	-	-	-	-	-	-	-	-	-	-	-
Patent fuel manufacture	-	-	-	-	-	-	-	-	-	-	-
Pumped storage	-	-	-	-	-	-	-	-	-	-	-
Other	-	14	26	-	-	-	-	-	-	-	-
Losses	-	-	-	-	-	-	-	-	-	-	-
Final consumption	**1,540**	**1,579**	**414**	**166**	**2,344**	**52**	**21,403**	**83**	**87**	**10,698**	**3,748**
Industry	**80**	**762**	-	-	-	-	-	-	-	-	**1,221**
Unclassified	80	738	-	-	-	-	-	-	-	-	1,221
Iron & steel	-	24	-	-	-	-	-	-	-	-	-
Non-ferrous metals	-	-	-	-	-	-	-	-	-	-	-
Mineral products	-	-	-	-	-	-	-	-	-	-	-
Chemicals	-	-	-	-	-	-	-	-	-	-	-
Mechanical engineering etc	-	-	-	-	-	-	-	-	-	-	-
Electrical engineering etc	-	-	-	-	-	-	-	-	-	-	-
Vehicles	-	-	-	-	-	-	-	-	-	-	-
Food, beverages etc	-	-	-	-	-	-	-	-	-	-	-
Textiles, leather, etc	-	-	-	-	-	-	-	-	-	-	-
Paper, printing etc	-	-	-	-	-	-	-	-	-	-	-
Other industries	-	-	-	-	-	-	-	-	-	-	-
Construction	-	-	-	-	-	-	-	-	-	-	-
Transport	-	-	**22**	-	-	**52**	**21,403**	-	-	**10,698**	**12**
Air	-	-	-	-	-	52	-	-	-	10,698	-
Rail	-	-	-	-	-	-	-	-	-	-	12
Road	-	-	22	-	-	-	21,403	-	-	-	-
National navigation	-	-	-	-	-	-	-	-	-	-	-
Pipelines	-	-	-	-	-	-	-	-	-	-	-
Other	-	**147**	**133**	-	-	-	-	-	-	-	**2,514**
Domestic	-	147	133	-	-	-	-	-	-	-	2,490
Public administration	-	-	-	-	-	-	-	-	-	-	12
Commercial	-	-	-	-	-	-	-	-	-	-	-
Agriculture	-	-	-	-	-	-	-	-	-	-	12
Miscellaneous	-	-	-	-	-	-	-	-	-	-	-
Non energy use	**1,460**	**670**	**259**	**166**	**2,344**	-	-	**83**	**87**	-	-

(1) Stock fall (+), stock rise (-).
(2) Total supply minus total demand.

3.4 Commodity balances 2000 (continued)

Petroleum products

Gas oil	Marine diesel oil	Fuel oils	Lubri-cants	Bitu-men	Petroleum wax	Petroleum coke	Orimul-sion	Misc. products	Total Products	
										Supply
28,292	6	11,621	703	1,438	436	1,796	-	943	86,341	Production
-	-	-	-	-	-	-	-	-	3,383	Other sources
3,815	-	596	211	255	23	657	-	718	14,212	Imports
-6,416	-	-5,360	-636	-283	-51	-502	-	-342	-20,677	Exports
-1,080	-61	-938	-	-	-	-	-	-	-2,079	Marine bunkers
-54	+1	+266	-26	+25	+35	+36	-	-707	-332	Stock change (1)
-794	+11	-2,773	+249	+319	-360	+1	-	-451	-3,493	Transfers
23,762	-43	3,411	501	1,754	83	1,989	-	161	77,357	**Total supply**
+636	-84	+113	-300	-221	+51	+236	-	-317	+879	**Statistical difference (2)**
23,127	41	3,298	801	1,975	32	1,753	-	478	76,477	**Total demand**
172	-	**778**	-	-	-	-	-	-	**1,192**	**Transformation**
172	-	583	-	-	-	-	-	-	997	Electricity generation
135	-	272	-	-	-	-	-	-	407	Major power producers
37	-	311	-	-	-	-	-	-	590	Autogenerators
-	-	-	-	-	-	-	-	-	-	Petroleum refineries
-	-	-	-	-	-	-	-	-	-	Coke manufacture
-	-	195	-	-	-	-	-	-	195	Blast furnaces
-	-	-	-	-	-	-	-	-	-	Patent fuel manufacture
-	-	-	-	-	-	-	-	-	-	Other
173	-	**1,270**	-	-	-	**977**	-	**15**	**5,050**	**Energy industry use**
-	-	-	-	-	-	-	-	-	-	Electricity generation
-	-	-	-	-	-	-	-	-	-	Oil & gas extraction
64	-	1,270	-	-	-	977	-	15	4,902	Petroleum refineries
-	-	-	-	-	-	-	-	-	-	Coal extraction
-	-	-	-	-	-	-	-	-	-	Coke manufacture
109	-	-	-	-	-	-	-	-	109	Blast furnaces
-	-	-	-	-	-	-	-	-	-	Patent fuel manufacture
-	-	-	-	-	-	-	-	-	-	Pumped storage
-	-	-	-	-	-	-	-	-	40	Other
-	-	-	-	-	-	-	-	-	-	**Losses**
22,782	41	1,250	801	1,975	32	776	-	463	70,235	**Final Consumption**
2,785	-	**965**	-	-	-	-	-	-	**5,815**	**Industry**
-	-	-	-	-	-	-	-	-	2,040	Unclassified
69	-	31	-	-	-	-	-	-	125	Iron & steel
29	-	10	-	-	-	-	-	-	39	Non-ferrous metals
195	-	47	-	-	-	-	-	-	242	Mineral products
130	-	236	-	-	-	-	-	-	366	Chemicals
169	-	39	-	-	-	-	-	-	208	Mechanical engineering etc
22	-	26	-	-	-	-	-	-	48	Electrical engineering etc
116	-	20	-	-	-	-	-	-	136	Vehicles
139	-	154	-	-	-	-	-	-	293	Food, beverages etc
53	-	89	-	-	-	-	-	-	142	Textiles, leather, etc
22	-	50	-	-	-	-	-	-	72	Paper, printing etc
1,414	-	261	-	-	-	-	-	-	1,675	Other industries
427	-	2	-	-	-	-	-	-	429	Construction
19,932	**43**	**42**	-	-	-	-	-	-	**49,203**	**Transport**
-	-	-	-	-	-	-	-	-	10,751	Air
429	-	-	-	-	-	-	-	-	441	Rail
15,632	-	-	-	-	-	-	-	-	37,057	Road
871	43	42	-	-	-	-	-	-	954	National navigation
-	-	-	-	-	-	-	-	-	-	Pipelines
2,119	-	**243**	-	-	-	-	-	-	**5,156**	**Other**
147	-	3	-	-	-	-	-	-	2,920	Domestic
879	-	170	-	-	-	-	-	-	1,061	Public administration
403	-	55	-	-	-	-	-	-	458	Commercial
560	-	10	-	-	-	-	-	-	582	Agriculture
130	-	5	-	-	-	-	-	-	135	Miscellaneous
945	-	-	801	1,975	32	776	-	463	10,062	**Non energy use**

3.5 Commodity balances 1999

Petroleum products

Thousand tonnes

	Ethane	Propane	Butane	Other gases	Naptha	Aviation spirit	Motor spirit	Industrial spirit	White spirit	Aviation turbine fuel	Burning oil
Supply											
Production	33	1,505r	471r	2,815r	2,451r	16	25,230r	20	109r	7,249r	3,553r
Other sources	1,527	865	931	-	-	-	-	-	-	-	-
Imports	-	101r	264r	-	608r	15r	2,492r	58r	4r	2,945r	212r
Exports	-15r	-316	-169	-	-605	-1	-6,332	-13	-2	-739	-253
Marine bunkers	-	-	-	-	-	-	-	-	-	-	-
Stock change (1)	+1	-24	+3	+1	+113	+7	+125	+10	-1	+173	-82
Transfers	-28	-110	-557	-33	+181	+28	+143	+12	-	+274	+44
Total supply	1,518r	2,021r	944r	2,783r	2,748r	64r	21,657r	87r	109	9,903r	3,474r
Statistical difference (2)	-136r	+378r	+337r	-91r	-373r	+19	-130r	+12	+14r	-36r	-159r
Total demand	1,654	1,643r	607r	2,874r	3,121r	45r	21,787r	77r	97r	9,939r	3,633r
Transformation	-	37r	-	212r	-	-	-	-	-	-	-
Electricity generation	-	37r	-	212r	-	-	-	-	-	-	-
Major power producers	-	-	-	-	-	-	-	-	-	-	-
Autogenerators	-	37r	-	212r	-	-	-	-	-	-	-
Petroleum refineries	-	-	-	-	-	-	-	-	-	-	-
Coke manufacture	-	-	-	-	-	-	-	-	-	-	-
Blast furnaces	-	-	-	-	-	-	-	-	-	-	-
Patent fuel manufacture	-	-	-	-	-	-	-	-	-	-	-
Other	-	-	-	-	-	-	-	-	-	-	-
Energy industry use	33	25	25	2,454r	21	-	-	-	-	-	-
Electricity generation	-	-	-	-	-	-	-	-	-	-	-
Oil & gas extraction	-	-	-	-	-	-	-	-	-	-	-
Petroleum refineries	33	1	-	2,454r	21	-	-	-	-	-	-
Coal extraction	-	-	-	-	-	-	-	-	-	-	-
Coke manufacture	-	-	-	-	-	-	-	-	-	-	-
Blast furnaces	-	3	-	-	-	-	-	-	-	-	-
Patent fuel manufacture	-	-	-	-	-	-	-	-	-	-	-
Pumped storage	-	-	-	-	-	-	-	-	-	-	-
Other	-	21	25	-	-	-	-	-	-	-	-
Losses	-	-	-	-	-	-	-	-	-	-	-
Final consumption	1,621	1,581r	582r	208	3,100r	45r	21,787r	77r	97r	9,939r	3,633r
Industry	74	800r	-	-	-	-	-	-	-	-	1,211r
Unclassified	74	779r	-	-	-	-	-	-	-	-	1,211r
Iron & steel	-	21	-	-	-	-	-	-	-	-	-
Non-ferrous metals	-	-	-	-	-	-	-	-	-	-	-
Mineral products	-	-	-	-	-	-	-	-	-	-	-
Chemicals	-	-	-	-	-	-	-	-	-	-	-
Mechanical engineering etc	-	-	-	-	-	-	-	-	-	-	-
Electrical engineering etc	-	-	-	-	-	-	-	-	-	-	-
Vehicles	-	-	-	-	-	-	-	-	-	-	-
Food, beverages etc	-	-	-	-	-	-	-	-	-	-	-
Textiles, leather, etc	-	-	-	-	-	-	-	-	-	-	-
Paper, printing etc	-	-	-	-	-	-	-	-	-	-	-
Other industries	-	-	-	-	-	-	-	-	-	-	-
Construction	-	-	-	-	-	-	-	-	-	-	-
Transport	-	-	8	-	-	45r	21,787r	-	-	9,939r	12
Air	-	-	-	-	-	45r	-	-	-	9,939r	-
Rail	-	-	-	-	-	-	-	-	-	-	12
Road	-	-	8	-	-	-	21,787r	-	-	-	-
National navigation	-	-	-	-	-	-	-	-	-	-	-
Pipelines	-	-	-	-	-	-	-	-	-	-	-
Other	-	139r	159r	-	-	-	-	-	-	-	2,410r
Domestic	-	139r	159r	-	-	-	-	-	-	-	2,386r
Public administration	-	-	-	-	-	-	-	-	-	-	12
Commercial	-	-	-	-	-	-	-	-	-	-	-
Agriculture	-	-	-	-	-	-	-	-	-	-	12
Miscellaneous	-	-	-	-	-	-	-	-	-	-	-
Non energy use	1,547	642r	415	208	3,100r	-	-	77r	97r	-	-

(1) Stock fall (+), stock rise (-).
(2) Total supply minus total demand.

3.5 Commodity balances 1999 (continued)

Petroleum products

Thousand tonnes

Gas oil	Marine diesel oil	Fuel oils	Lubri-cants	Bitu-men	Petroleum wax	Petroleum coke	Orimul-sion	Misc. products	Total products	
										Supply
25,865r	5	12,195r	907r	1,644r	261r	1,813r	-	593r	86,733r	Production
-	-	-	-	-	-	-	-	-	3,323	Other sources
5,425r	-	657r	182r	259r	18	643r	-	13r	13,896r	Imports
-6,667	-	-4,929	-673	-271	-17	-642r	-	-86r	-21,656r	Exports
-1,061	-90	-1,179	-	-	-	-	-	-	-2,329	Marine bunkers
+232	-1	+65	+123	+4	-32	-40	-	-102	+575	Stock change (1)
-702	+12	-1,683	+110	+380	-228	-6	-	+58	-2,105	Transfers
23,092r	-73r	5,126r	649r	2,016r	1r	1,768r	-	476r	78,363r	**Total supply**
+29r	-90r	+676r	-141r	+88r	-36r	-57	-	+88r	+388r	**Statistical difference** (2)
23,064r	17r	4,450r	790	1,928r	37r	1,825r	-	388r	77,976r	**Total demand**
93r	-	950r	-	-	-	-	-	-	1,292r	**Transformation**
93r	-	676r	-	-	-	-	-	-	1,022r	Electricity generation
58r	-	313r	-	-	-	-	-	-	371r	Major power producers
35r	-	367r	-	-	-	-	-	-	651r	Autogenerators
-	-	-	-	-	-	-	-	-	-	Petroleum refineries
-	-	-	-	-	-	-	-	-	-	Coke manufacture
-	-	270	-	-	-	-	-	-	270	Blast furnaces
-	-	-	-	-	-	-	-	-	-	Patent fuel manufacture
-	-	-	-	-	-	-	-	-	-	Other
242r	-	1,843r	-	-	-	1,165r	-	-	5,810r	**Energy industry use**
-	-	-	-	-	-	-	-	-	-	Electricity generation
-	-	-	-	-	-	-	-	-	-	Oil & gas extraction
115r	2r	1,838r	-	-	-	1,165r	-	-	5,629r	Petroleum refineries
-	-	-	-	-	-	-	-	-	-	Coal extraction
-	-	-	-	-	-	-	-	-	-	Coke manufacture
126r	-	-	-	-	-	-	-	-	129r	Blast furnaces
-	-	-	-	-	-	-	-	-	-	Patent fuel manufacture
-	-	-	-	-	-	-	-	-	-	Pumped storage
1	-	5r	-	-	-	-	-	-	52r	Other
-	-	-	-	-	-	-	-	-	-	**Losses**
22,728r	15	1,657r	790	1,928r	37r	660r	-	388r	70,873r	**Final Consumption**
2,760r	-	1,044r	-	-	-	-	-	-	5,859r	**Industry**
-	-	-	-	-	-	-	-	-	2,064r	Unclassified
13	-	56r	-	-	-	-	-	-	90r	Iron & steel
22r	-	16r	-	-	-	-	-	-	38r	Non-ferrous metals
155r	-	57r	-	-	-	-	-	-	212r	Mineral products
122r	-	188r	-	-	-	-	-	-	310r	Chemicals
145r	-	66r	-	-	-	-	-	-	211r	Mechanical engineering etc
23r	-	22r	-	-	-	-	-	-	45r	Electrical engineering etc
98r	-	37r	-	-	-	-	-	-	135r	Vehicles
130r	-	241r	-	-	-	-	-	-	371r	Food, beverages etc
39r	-	79r	-	-	-	-	-	-	118r	Textiles, leather, etc
25r	-	74r	-	-	-	-	-	-	99r	Paper, printing etc
1,522r	-	204r	-	-	-	-	-	-	1,726r	Other industries
466r	-	4	-	-	-	-	-	-	470r	Construction
16,856r	15	72r	-	-	-	-	-	-	48,734r	**Transport**
-	-	-	-	-	-	-	-	-	9,984r	Air
451r	-	-	-	-	-	-	-	-	463r	Rail
15,508r	-	-	-	-	-	-	-	-	37,303r	Road
897r	15	72r	-	-	-	-	-	-	984r	National navigation
-	-	-	-	-	-	-	-	-	-	Pipelines
2,268r	-	541r	-	-	-	-	-	-	5,517r	**Other**
161r	-	5r	-	-	-	-	-	-	2,850r	Domestic
935r	-	358r	-	-	-	-	-	-	1,305r	Public administration
446r	-	73r	-	-	-	-	-	-	519r	Commercial
590r	-	93r	-	-	-	-	-	-	695r	Agriculture
136r	-	12r	-	-	-	-	-	-	148r	Miscellaneous
844	-	-	790	1,928r	37r	660r	-	388r	10,733r	**Non energy use**

3.6 Commodity balances 1998

Petroleum products

	Ethane	Propane	Butane	Other gases	Naptha	Aviation spirit	Motor spirit	Industrial spirit	White spirit	Aviation turbine fuel	Burning oil
Supply											
Production	36	1,538r	424r	2,924r	2,333r	-	27,166r	2	133r	7,876r	3,442r
Other sources	1,215	1,071	1,171	-	-	-	-	-	-	-	-
Imports	-	82	158	-	855	32	1,986	49	2	2,660	131
Exports	13r	-727	-155r	-	-520	-1	-7,986r	-23	-9	-828	-267
Marine bunkers	-	-	-	-	-	-	-	-	-	-	-
Stock change (1)	+1	+38	+1	-1	-117	-6	+244	-3	-5	-60	+31
Transfers	-17	-19	-1,351	-44	-153	-3	+1,103	+89	-8	-131	+166
Total supply	**1,222r**	**1,983r**	**248r**	**2.879r**	**2,398r**	**22**	**22,513r**	**114**	**113r**	**9,515r**	**3,503r**
Statistical difference (2)	-174r	+178	-317r	-43r	-501r	-14	+665r	+31	+17r	+276r	-71r
Total demand	**1,396**	**1,805**	**565**	**2,922**	**2,899**	**36**	**21,848**	**83**	**96**	**9,241**	**3,574**
Transformation	-	**37r**	-	**218r**	-	-	-	-	-	-	-
Electricity generation	-	37r	-	218r	-	-	-	-	-	-	-
Major power producers	-	-	-	-	-	-	-	-	-	-	-
Autogenerators	-	37r	-	218r	-	-	-	-	-	-	-
Petroleum refineries	-	-	-	-	-	-	-	-	-	-	-
Coke manufacture	-	-	-	-	-	-	-	-	-	-	-
Blast furnaces	-	-	-	-	-	-	-	-	-	-	-
Patent fuel manufacture	-	-	-	-	-	-	-	-	-	-	-
Other	-	-	-	-	-	-	-	-	-	-	-
Energy industry use	**36**	**28**	**22**	**2,530r**	**17**	-	-	-	-	-	-
Electricity generation	-	-	-	-	-	-	-	-	-	-	-
Oil & gas extraction	-	-	-	-	-	-	-	-	-	-	-
Petroleum refineries	36	1	-	2,530r	17	-	-	-	-	-	-
Coal extraction	-	-	-	-	-	-	-	-	-	-	-
Coke manufacture	-	-	-	-	-	-	-	-	-	-	-
Blast furnaces	-	3	-	-	-	-	-	-	-	-	-
Patent fuel manufacture	-	-	-	-	-	-	-	-	-	-	-
Pumped storage	-	-	-	-	-	-	-	-	-	-	-
Other	-	24	22	-	-	-	-	-	-	-	-
Losses	-	-	-	-	-	-	-	-	-	-	-
Final consumption	**1,360**	**1,740r**	**543**	**174**	**2,882**	**36**	**21,848**	**83**	**96**	**9,241**	**3,574**
Industry	**69**	**797**	-	-	-	-	-	-	-	-	**840**
Unclassified	69	776	-	-	-	-	-	-	-	-	840
Iron & steel	-	21	-	-	-	-	-	-	-	-	-
Non-ferrous metals	-	-	-	-	-	-	-	-	-	-	-
Mineral products	-	-	-	-	-	-	-	-	-	-	-
Chemicals	-	-	-	-	-	-	-	-	-	-	-
Mechanical engineering etc	-	-	-	-	-	-	-	-	-	-	-
Electrical engineering etc	-	-	-	-	-	-	-	-	-	-	-
Vehicles	-	-	-	-	-	-	-	-	-	-	-
Food, beverages etc	-	-	-	-	-	-	-	-	-	-	-
Textiles, leather, etc	-	-	-	-	-	-	-	-	-	-	-
Paper, printing etc	-	-	-	-	-	-	-	-	-	-	-
Other industries	-	-	-	-	-	-	-	-	-	-	-
Construction	-	-	-	-	-	-	-	-	-	-	-
Transport	-	-	**4**	-	-	**36**	**21,848**	-	-	**9,241**	**12**
Air	-	-	-	-	-	36	-	-	-	9,241	-
Rail	-	-	-	-	-	-	-	-	-	-	12
Road	-	-	4	-	-	-	21,848	-	-	-	-
National navigation	-	-	-	-	-	-	-	-	-	-	-
Pipelines	-	-	-	-	-	-	-	-	-	-	-
Other	-	**149**	**156**	-	-	-	-	-	-	-	**2,722**
Domestic	-	149	156	-	-	-	-	-	-	-	2,698
Public administration	-	-	-	-	-	-	-	-	-	-	12
Commercial	-	-	-	-	-	-	-	-	-	-	-
Agriculture	-	-	-	-	-	-	-	-	-	-	12
Miscellaneous	-	-	-	-	-	-	-	-	-	-	-
Non energy use	**1,291**	**794r**	**383**	**174**	**2,882**	-	-	**83**	**96**	-	-

(1) Stock fall (+), stock rise (-).
(2) Total supply minus total demand.

3.6   Commodity balances 1998 (continued)

Petroleum products

Thousand tonnes

Gas oil	Marine diesel oil	Fuel oils	Lubri-cants	Bitu-men	Petroleum wax	Petroleum coke	Orimul-sion	Misc. products	Total products	
										Supply
27,694r	10	13,365r	1,125r	2,172r	59	1,869r	-	625r	92,792r	Production
-	-	-	-	-	-	-	-	-	3,457	Other sources
3,468	-	791	198	76	-	883r	-	47r	11,418r	Imports
-6,201	-	-5,834	-632	-334	-14	-831r	-	-	-24,375r	Exports
-1,204	-192	-1,684	-	-	-	-	-	-	-3,080	Marine bunkers
-215	-	+84	-5	+20	+5	-42	-	-63r	-93r	Stock change (1)
-103	+40	-949	+71	+57	-28	+8	-	+17	-1,255	Transfers
23,439r	**-142**	**5,773r**	**757r**	**1,991r**	**22**	**1,887r**	**-**	**626r**	**78,864r**	**Total supply**
+226r	-143	+428r	-56r	+24r	+4	-191r	-	+88r	+426r	**Statistical difference** (2)
23,213	1	5,345	813	1,967	18	2,078	-	538	78,438	**Total demand**
76r	**-**	**1,332r**	**-**	**-**	**-**	**-**	**-**	**-**	**1,663r**	**Transformation**
76r	-	1,064r	-	-	-	-	-	-	1,395r	Electricity generation
56	-	700	-	-	-	-	-	-	756	Major power producers
20r	-	364r	-	-	-	-	-	-	639r	Autogenerators
-	-	-	-	-	-	-	-	-	-	Petroleum refineries
-	-	-	-	-	-	-	-	-	-	Coke manufacture
-	-	268	-	-	-	-	-	-	268	Blast furnaces
-	-	-	-	-	-	-	-	-	-	Patent fuel manufacture
-	-	-	-	-	-	-	-	-	-	Other
289r	**-**	**2,240r**	**-**	**-**	**-**	**1,191**	**-**	**-**	**6,353r**	**Energy industry use**
-	-	-	-	-	-	-	-	-	-	Electricity generation
-	-	-	-	-	-	-	-	-	-	Oil & gas extraction
162r	-	2,240r	-	-	-	1,191	-	-	6,177r	Petroleum refineries
-	-	-	-	-	-	-	-	-	-	Coal extraction
-	-	-	-	-	-	-	-	-	-	Coke manufacture
126	-	-	-	-	-	-	-	-	129	Blast furnaces
-	-	-	-	-	-	-	-	-	-	Patent fuel manufacture
-	-	-	-	-	-	-	-	-	-	Pumped storage
1	-	-	-	-	-	-	-	-	47	Other
-	-	-	-	-	-	-	-	-	-	**Losses**
22,848r	**1**	**1,773r**	**813**	**1,967**	**18**	**887**	**-**	**538**	**70,422r**	**Final Consumption**
2,912r	**-**	**1,169r**	**-**	**-**	**-**	**-**	**-**	**-**	**5,787r**	**Industry**
-	-	-	-	-	-	-	-	-	1,685	Unclassified
31	-	29r	-	-	-	-	-	-	81r	Iron & steel
22	-	17	-	-	-	-	-	-	39	Non-ferrous metals
176	-	48	-	-	-	-	-	-	224	Mineral products
153r	-	425r	-	-	-	-	-	-	578r	Chemicals
165	-	34r	-	-	-	-	-	-	199r	Mechanical engineering etc
27	-	61	-	-	-	-	-	-	88r	Electrical engineering etc
93	-	32	-	-	-	-	-	-	125	Vehicles
151	-	246r	-	-	-	-	-	-	397r	Food, beverages etc
38	-	57	-	-	-	-	-	-	95	Textiles, leather, etc
35r	-	84r	-	-	-	-	-	-	119r	Paper, printing etc
1,526r	-	124r	-	-	-	-	-	-	1,650r	Other industries
495	-	12	-	-	-	-	-	-	507	Construction
16,592r	**1**	**104r**	**-**	**-**	**-**	**-**	**-**	**-**	**47,838r**	**Transport**
-	-	-	-	-	-	-	-	-	9,277	Air
468r	-	-	-	-	-	-	-	-	479r	Rail
15,143	-	-	-	-	-	-	-	-	36,995	Road
981	1	104r	-	-	-	-	-	-	1,086	National navigation
-	-	-	-	-	-	-	-	-	-	Pipelines
2,584r	**-**	**500r**	**-**	**-**	**-**	**-**	**-**	**-**	**6,111r**	**Other**
191	-	1	-	-	-	-	-	-	3,195	Domestic
1,022r	-	364r	-	-	-	-	-	-	1,398r	Public administration
512r	-	47r	-	-	-	-	-	-	559r	Commercial
698	-	76	-	-	-	-	-	-	786	Agriculture
161	-	12	-	-	-	-	-	-	173r	Miscellaneous
760	**-**	**-**	**813**	**1,967**	**18**	**887**	**-**	**538**	**10,686r**	**Non energy use**

3.7 Supply and disposal of petroleum [1]

Thousand tonnes

	1996	1997	1998	1999	2000
Primary oils (Crude oil, NGLs and feedstocks)					
Indigenous production [2]	129,742	128,234	132,363r	137,099	126,245
Imports	50,099	49,994	47,958r	44,869r	54,387
Exports [3]	-81,563	-79,400	-84,610r	-91,797	-92,918
Transfers - Transfers to products [4]	-3,267	-3,416	-3,457	-3,323	-3,383
Product rebrands [5]	+997	+794	+1,255	+2,105	+3,493
Stock change [6] - Offshore	-2	-200	-127	-83	+550
Oil terminals	-354	-8	-466	-115	+548
Use during production [7]	-401	-350	-353	-323	-295
Calculated refinery throughput [8]	95,251	95,648	92,563r	88,432r	88,627
Overall statistical difference [9] [10]	-1,409	-1,375	-1,234r	+146r	+613
Actual refinery throughput	**96,660**	**97,023**	**93,797**	**88,286**	**88,014**
Petroleum products					
Losses in refining process [11]	152	86	1,005r	1,554r	1,672
Refinery gross production [11] [12]	96,508	96,937	92,792r	86,733r	86,341
Transfers - Transfers to products [4]	+3,267	+3,416	+3,457	+3,323	+3,383
Product rebrands [5]	-997	-794	-1,255	-2,105	-3,493
Imports	9,315	8,706	11,418r	13,896r	14,212
Exports [13]	-23,681	-26,755	-24,375r	-21,730r	-20,677
Marine bunkers	-2,665	-2,962	-3,080	-2,329r	-2,079
Stock changes [6] - Refineries	-76	+417	-65r	+399	-425
Power generators	+168	+106	-28	+176	+94
Calculated total supply	81,839	79,071	78,864r	78,363r	77,357
Statistical difference [9]	-176	-178	+426r	+388r	+879
Total demand [4]	**82,015**	**79,249**	**78,438r**	**77,975**	**76,477**
Of which:					
Energy use	70,702	68,297	67,752r	67,242	66,415
Of which, for electricity generation [14]	4,028	2,241	1,395r	1,022r	997
total refinery fuels [14]	6,623	6,572	6,468	5,969r	5,245
Non-energy use	11,293	10,952	10,686r	10,733r	10,062

(1) *Aggregate monthly data on oil production, trade, refinery throughput and inland deliveries are available - see paragraph 3.aa and Annex F.*
(2) *Crude oil plus condensates and petroleum gases derived at onshore treatment plants.*
(3) *Includes NGLs, process oils and re-exports.*
(4) *Disposals of NGLs by direct sale (excluding exports) or for blending.*
(5) *Product rebrands (inter-product blends or transfers) represent petroleum products received at refineries/ plants as process oils for refinery or cracking unit operations.*
(6) *Impact of stock changes on supplies. A stock fall is shown as (+) as it increases supplies, and vice-versa for a stock rise (-).*
(7) *Own use in onshore terminals and gas separation plants.*
(8) *Equivalent to the total supplies reported against the upstream transformation sector in Tables 3.1 to 3.3.*
(9) *Supply greater than (+) or less than (-) recorded throughput or disposals.*
(10) *This total includes differences between the figures for indigenous production as recorded by individual fields and indigenous receipts, which is accounted for by own use in onshore terminals and gas separation plants, losses, platform and other field stock changes and the time lag between production on offshore loaders and tankers arrival at refineries. The size of this component of the overall statistical difference was previously given separately, and is given in the table below for information. See Chapter 3, paragraphs 3.33 to 3.41 for information on the large 1995 and 1996 differences.*

	1996	**1997**	**1998**	**1999**	**2000**
Indigenous receipts	130,792	129,037	133,125	137,220r	126,116
Statistical difference - upstream production sector	*-1,453*	*-1,353*	*-972r*	*-527*	*+384*

(11) *Data for 1998, 1999 and 2000 incorporate an extra adjustment for what are thought to be losses within the refining system following the initial results of investigations into the detailed reporting of refinery activity in the UK which were initiated due to the increasing size of the statistical difference for petroleum products in recent years. This work is still on going, and is being expanded during the second half of 2001. When completed, the results of this investigation will be published in the DTI publication Energy Trends - see paragraph 3.aa and Annex F.*
(12) *Includes refinery fuels.*
(13) *Excludes NGLs.*
(14) *Figures cover petroleum used to generate electricity by all major power producers and by all other generators, including petroleum used to generate electricity at refineries. These quantities are also included in the totals reported as used as refinery fuel, so there is thus some overlap in these figures.*

3.8 Additional information on inland deliveries of selected products[1][2][3]

Thousand tonnes

	1996	1997	1998	1999	2000
Motor spirit					
Retail deliveries *(4)*					
Hypermarkets*(5)*					
Leaded premium / Lead Replacement Petrol *(6)*	1,451	1,253	1,001	641	339
Super premium unleaded	55	24	18	13	9
Premium unleaded	3,278	3,680	4,130	4,775	5,261
Total hypermarkets	4,784	4,957	5,149	5,429	5,609
Refiners/other traders					
Leaded premium / Lead Replacement Petrol *(6)*	5,592	4,885	3,594	2,087r	1,123
Super premium unleaded	643	482	391	460r	394
Premium unleaded	10,950	11,508	12,302	13,532r	13,747
Total Refiners/other traders	17,185	16,875	16,287	15,981r	15,264
Total retail deliveries					
Leaded premium / Lead Replacement Petrol *(6)*	7,043	6,138	4,595	2,728r	1,462
Super premium unleaded	698	506	409	473r	403
Premium unleaded	14,228	15,188	16,432	18,307r	19,008
Total retail deliveries	21,969	21,832	21,436	21,410r	20,873
Commercial consumers *(7)*					
Leaded premium / Lead Replacement Petrol *(6)*	135	112	91	61r	44
Super premium unleaded	11	9	4	6r	6
Premium unleaded	294	298	318r	311r	480
Total commercial consumers	440	419	413r	378r	530
Total motor spirit	**22,409**	**22,251**	**21,849r**	**21,789r**	**21,403**
Unleaded as % of Total motor spirit	68.0	71.9	78.6	87.6r	93.0
Gas oil/diesel oil					
DERV fuel:					
Retail deliveries *(4)*:					
Hypermarkets *(5)*	855	1,023	1,153	1,306	1,411
Refiners/other traders	4,682	5,104	5,449	5,831r	6,052
Total retail deliveries	5,537	6,127	6,602	7,137r	7,463
Commercial consumers *(7)*	8,828	8,849	8,541	8,371r	8,168
Total DERV fuel	14,365	14,976	15,143	15,508r	15,631
Gas oil	7,631	7,325	7,244	6,667r	6,542
Marine diesel oil	-	1	1	15	41
Total Gas oil/diesel oil	**21,996**	**22,302**	**22,388**	**22,190r**	**22,214**
Fuel oils *(8)*					
Light	108	135	76	74	44
Medium	484	381	259	419r	390
Heavy	5,390	3,238	2,600	1,922r	1,399
Orimulsion *(9)*	872	182	-	-	-
Total fuel oils	**6,854**	**3,936**	**2,935**	**2,415r**	**1,833**

(1) Aggregate monthly data for inland deliveries of oil products are available - see paragraph 3.124 and Annex F.
(2) The end use section analyses are based partly on recorded figures and on estimates made by the Institute of Petroleum and the Department of Trade and Industry and are intended to be for general guidance only. See also the notes in the main text of this chapter.
(3) For a full breakdown of the end-uses of all oil products, see Commodity Balances in Tables 3.4 to 3.6.
(4) Retail deliveries - deliveries to garages, etc. mainly for resale to final consumers.
(5) Data for sales by super and hypermarket companies are collected via a separate reporting system, but are consistent with the main data collected from UKPIA member companies - see paragraph 3.106.
(6) Sales of Leaded Petrol ceased on 31 December 1999 - see paragraphs 3.53 to 3.57.
(7) Commercial consumers - direct deliveries for use in consumer's business.
(8) Inland deliveries excluding that used as a fuel in refineries, but including that used for electricity generation by major electricity producers and other industries.
(9) Deliveries of Orimulsion ceased in February 1997.

3.9 Inland deliveries by country[1]

Thousand tonnes

	England and Wales [2]			Scotland			Northern Ireland		
	1998	1999	2000	1998	1999	2000	1998	1999	2000
Energy use									
Gases for gasworks and other uses									
Butane and propane	974	1,001r	995	146	124r	79	34	30	30
Other gases	-	-	-	69	74	80	-	-	-
Aviation spirit	32	36	45	3	5	4	1	3	4
Motor spirit:									
Dealers	19,662	19,733r	19,441	1,373	1,364	1,145	401	313r	287
Commercial consumers	368	338r	484	29	30	30	16	10r	16
Total motor spirit	20,030	20,071r	19,925	1,402	1,394	1,175	417	323	303
Kerosenes									
Aviation turbine fuel	8,742	9,389r	10,216	429	479	411	70	72	71
Burning oil	2,665	2,681r	2,889	221	247	230	688	704r	629
Gas oil/diesel oil									
DERV fuel	13,680	14,121r	14,382	1,189	1,175r	1,089	274	212	160
Other [3]	5,554	5,121r	5,213	1,301	1,137r	1,004	390	424r	366
Fuel oils	2,292	1,846r	1,464	333r	304	215	310	265	154
Total products used as energy	**53,969**	**54,266r**	**55,129**	**5,093**	**4,939r**	**4,287**	**2,184**	**2,033r**	**1,717**
Non-energy use									
Feedstock for petroleum chemical plants	3,871	4,122r	3580	2,452	2,671r	2302	-	-	-
Industrial spirit	82	76r	83	2	2	-	-	-	-
White spirit	96	97r	87	-	-	-	-	-	-
Lubricating oils	770	749	765	36	33	31	7	8	6
Bitumen	1,634	1,611r	1,710	242	205	193	90	111r	72
Petroleum wax	12	30r	31	6	7	1	-	-	-
Total products used as non-energy [4]	**7,884**	**7,731r**	**7,489**	**2,742**	**2,921r**	**2,531**	**97**	**119r**	**78**
Total all products	**61,853**	**61,997r**	**62,618**	**7,835**	**7,860r**	**6,818**	**2,281**	**2,152r**	**1,795**

(1) Excludes products used as a fuel within refineries that are included in Tables 3.4 to 3.6.
(2) Includes the Channel Islands and the Isle of Man.
(3) Includes deliveries of marine diesel oil.
(4) Includes deliveries of miscellaneous products and petroleum coke.

3.10 Stocks of crude oil and petroleum products at end of year[1]

					Thousand tonnes
	1996	1997	1998	1999	2000
Crude and process oils					
Refineries (2)	4,971	4,977	5,074	4,560	3,917
Terminals (3)	1,461	1,463	1,832	2,461	2,556
Offshore (4)	590r	790	917	1,000	450
Total crude and process oils (5)	**7,065r**	**7,390**	**7,883**	**8,080**	**6,992**
Petroleum products					
Ethane	8	7	6	6	6
Propane	120	157	120	144	162
Butane	61	92	92	89	88
Other petroleum gases	4	2	3	3	-
Naphtha	379	344	461	349	407
Aviation spirit	7	6	12	5	4
Motor spirit	2,502	2,218	1,984	1,425	1,078
Industrial spirit	11	15	17	7	7
White spirit	15	10	14	15	15
Aviation turbine fuel	573	573	637	461	486
Burning oil	284	288	257	339	409
Gas oil (6) (7)	1,678	1,639	3,703	2,984	1,910
Marine diesel oil	-	-	-	1	-
Fuel oils (7)	2,963	2,880	1,466	1,401	1,120
Lubricating oils	289	287	292	169	195
Bitumen	189	214	194	189	164
Petroleum wax	9	8	3	36	1
Petroleum coke	289	245	287	327	291
Miscellaneous products	66	154	217	320	1,027
Total all products	**9,447**	**9,139**	**9,765**	**8,269**	**7,370**
Of which : net bilateral stocks (8)	1,484	1,698	2,228	1,307	77

(1) Aggregate monthly data on the level of stocks of crude oil and oil products are available - see paragraph 3.124 and Annex F.
(2) Stocks of crude oil, NGLs and process oils at UK refineries.
(3) Stocks of crude oil and NGLs at UKCS pipeline terminals.
(4) Stocks of crude oil in tanks and partially loaded tankers at offshore fields.
(5) Includes process oils held abroad for UK use approved by bilateral agreements.
(6) Includes middle distillate feedstock.
(7) The increase in gas oil stocks and the decrease in fuel oil stocks can be attributed to the change in patterns of stocks held abroad, under bilateral agreements, by UK companies as part of their national stocking obligation.
(8) The difference between stocks held abroad for UK use under approved bilateral agreements and the equivalent stocks held in the UK for foreign use.

3.11 Crude oil and petroleum products: production, imports and exports[1][2], 1970 to 2000

Thousand tonnes

	Crude oil [3]					Oil products			
	Imports	Indigenous production		Exports	Refinery throughput	Refinery Output [4]	Exports	Imports	Inland Deliveries [4]
		Total	Landward						
1970	102,155	156	83	1,182	101,911	94,696	17,424	20,428	91,151
1971	107,736	212	85	1,569	105,342	98,245	17,166	19,369	91,991
1972	107,706	333	85	3,558	106,980	99,368	15,979	20,827	98,469
1973	115,472	372	88	3,235	114,338	105,954	17,404	18,300	99,786
1974	112,822	410	107	1,404	111,217	103,060	14,631	14,537	93,409
1975	91,366	1,564	99	1,524	93,597	86,647	13,924	12,786	82,824
1976	80,466	12,169	99	4,285	97,784	90,284	15,988	10,709	81,579
1977	70,697	38,265	99	16,793	93,615	86,338	14,160	13,050	82,759
1978	68,144	54,006	88	25,200	96,390	89,156	13,194	11,586	84,141
1979	60,380	77,748	121	40,569	97,806	90,583	12,988	12,035	84,554
1980	46,717	80,467	237	40,180	86,341	79,227	14,110	9,245	71,177
1981	36,855	89,454	232	52,206	78,287	72,006	12,256	9,402	66,256
1982	33,754	103,211	253	61,670	77,130	70,747	12,637	12,524	67,246
1983	30,324	114,960	316	69,923	76,876	70,927	13,331	9,907	64,464
1984	32,272	126,065	345	80,143	79,117	73,187	12,478	23,082	81,435
1985	35,576	127,611	380	82,980	78,431	72,904	14,828	13,101	69,781
1986	41,209	127,068	504	87,437	80,155	74,089	15,283	11,767	69,227
1987	41,541	123,351	578	83,220	80,449	74,656	14,980	8,570	67,701
1988	44,272	114,459	761	73,330	85,662	79,837	15,802	9,219	72,317
1989	49,500	91,710	722	51,664	87,669	81,392	16,683	9,479	73,028
1990	52,710	91,604	1,758	56,999	88,692	82,286	16,899	11,005	73,943
1991	57,084	91,261	3,703	55,131	92,001	85,476	19,351	10,140	74,506
1992	57,683	94,251	3,962	57,627	92,334	85,783	20,250	10,567	75,470
1993	61,701	100,189	3,737	64,415	96,273	89,584	23,031	10,064	75,790
1994	53,096	126,542	4,649	82,393	93,161	86,644	22,156	10,441	74,957
1995	48,749	129,894	5,051	84,577	92,743	86,133	21,614	9,878	73,694
1996	50,099	129,742	5,251	81,563	96,660	89,885	23,681	9,315	75,390
1997	49,994	128,234	4,981	79,400	97,023	90,366	26,755	8,706	72,501
1998	47,957	132,491r	5,161	84,612	93,797	87,096	24,333	11,371	71,969
1999	40,891r	137,125r	4,285	88,419r	88,285r	81,987	24,826r	13,853r	72,009r
2000	49,386	126,245	3,247	90,231	88,013	82,739	23,265	14,212	71,233

(1) Aggregate monthly data on crude oil production and trade in oil and oil products are available - see paragraph 3.124 and Annex F.
(2) See paragraphs 3.91 to 3.98.
(3) Includes natural gas liquids and feedstocks.
(4) Excludes products used as fuels within refinery processes.

3.11 Crude oil and petroleum products: production, imports and exports[1][2], 1970 to 2000 (continued)

	Net exports			Crude oil			Oil products
	Crude oil (5)	Oil products (5)	Total (5)	Ratio of imports to ref. throughput	Ratio of indigenous production to ref. throughput	Ratio of exports to indigenous production	Imports: Share of inland deliveries
		Thousand tonnes			Ratio		Percentage
1970	(100,973)	(3,004)	(103,977)	1.002	0.001	7.577	22.4
1971	(106,167)	(2,203)	(108,370)	1.023	0.001	7.401	21.1
1972	(104,148)	(4,848)	(108,996)	1.007	0.002	10.685	21.2
1973	(112,237)	(896)	(113,133)	1.010	0.002	8.696	18.3
1974	(111,418)	94	(111,324)	1.014	0.002	3.424	15.6
1975	(89,842)	1,138	(88,704)	0.976	0.012	0.974	15.4
1976	(86,181)	5,279	(80,902)	0.925	0.118	0.352	13.1
1977	(53,904)	1,110	(52,794)	0.755	0.409	0.439	15.8
1978	(42,944)	1,608	(41,336)	0.707	0.560	0.467	13.8
1979	(19,811)	953	(18,858)	0.617	0.796	0.522	14.2
1980	(6,537)	4,865	(1,672)	0.541	0.932	0.499	13.0
1981	15,351	2,854	18,205	0.471	1.143	0.583	14.2
1982	27,916	113	28,029	0.438	1.338	0.597	18.6
1983	39,599	3,424	43,023	0.394	1.497	0.608	15.4
1984	48,141	(10,604)	37,537	0.408	1.593	0.638	28.3
1985	47,404	1,727	49,131	0.454	1.627	0.650	18.8
1986	46,228	3,516	49,744	0.514	1.585	0.688	17.0
1987	41,679	6,410	48,089	0.516	1.533	0.675	12.7
1988	29,057	6,583	35,640	0.517	1.336	0.641	12.7
1989	2,164	7,204	9,368	0.565	1.046	0.563	13.0
1990	4,289	5,894	10,183	0.594	1.033	0.622	14.9
1991	(1,953)	9,211	7,258	0.620	0.992	0.604	13.6
1992	(56)	9,683	9,627	0.625	1.021	0.611	14.0
1993	2,714	12,967	15,681	0.641	1.041	0.643	13.3
1994	29,297	11,715	41,012	0.570	1.359	0.651	13.9
1995	35,828	11,736	47,564	0.526	1.401	0.651	13.4
1996	31,464	14,366	45,830	0.518	1.342	0.629	12.1
1997	29,406	18,037	47,443	0.515	1.322	0.619	12.0
1998	36,655	12,962	49,617	0.511	1.413r	0.639r	15.7
1999	47,528r	10,973r	58,501r	0.463r	1.553	0.645r	19.2r
2000	40,845	9,053	49,898	0.561	1.434	0.715	20.0

(5) Figures in brackets signify that in that particular year imports were greater than exports, producing a negative net exports figure.

3.12 Inland deliveries of petroleum, 1970 to 2000[1] [2]

Million tonnes

	Total	Deliveries for energy uses								Deliveries for non-energy uses
		Motor spirit	DERV fuel	Aviation turbine fuel	Burning oil	Gas oil (3)	Fuel oils (4)	Petroleum gases	Total for energy uses (5)	
1970	97.18	14.24	5.04	3.25	2.48	11.56	42.12	3.54	87.05	10.13
1971	98.17	14.96	5.19	3.67	2.57	12.13	42.74	3.84	88.04	10.13
1972	104.89	15.90	5.25	3.93	2.93	14.56	44.85	4.08	94.21	10.68
1973	106.84	16.93	5.66	4.20	3.18	14.60	43.40	4.43	95.25	11.59
1974	100.39	16.48	5.52	3.69	2.78	13.12	40.71	3.80	88.53	11.86
1975	88.85	16.13	5.41	3.83	2.63	12.61	33.81	3.51	79.41	9.44
1976	87.92	16.88	5.59	3.99	2.62	12.53	30.90	3.85	77.81	10.11
1977	89.00	17.34	5.71	4.17	2.62	13.38	30.74	3.88	79.28	9.72
1978	90.56	18.35	5.88	4.51	2.65	13.19	31.50	3.84	81.16	9.40
1979	91.09	18.69	6.06	4.67	2.70	13.49	30.95	3.88	81.56	9.53
1980	77.50	19.15	5.85	4.69	2.10	11.62	22.69	3.52	70.50	7.00
1981	71.70	18.72	5.55	4.50	1.91	10.93	18.64	3.15	64.15	7.55
1982	72.79	19.25	5.73	4.47	1.75	10.50	19.16	3.45	65.19	7.60
1983	69.77	19.57	6.18	4.57	1.66	9.88	15.03	3.84	61.75	8.02
1984	86.79	20.23	6.76	4.83	1.71	9.92	30.26	3.79	78.61	8.18
1985	74.96	20.40	7.11	5.01	1.87	9.71	18.19	3.15	66.48	8.48
1986	74.62	21.47	7.87	5.50	2.02	9.22	14.64	3.46	65.26	9.36
1987	72.92	22.18	8.47	5.82	2.03	8.51	11.90	3.45	63.52	9.40
1988	77.80	23.25	9.37	6.20	1.99	8.39	13.83	3.62	67.80	10.00
1989	78.85	23.92	10.12	6.56	1.94	8.26	13.14	3.88	68.97	9.88
1990	79.78	24.31	10.65	6.59	2.06	8.03	14.02	3.88	70.61	9.17
1991	80.56	24.02	10.69	6.18	2.38	8.02	14.17	4.00	70.61	9.95
1992	81.55	24.04	11.13	6.67	2.47	7.86	13.74	3.84	70.92	10.63
1993	82.18	23.77	11.81	7.11	2.63	7.78	13.13	4.05	71.45	10.73
1994	81.22	22.84	12.91	7.28	2.66	7.51	11.73	4.06	70.04	11.18
1995	80.17	21.95	13.46	7.66	2.77	7.25	10.30	4.26	68.85	11.32
1996	82.01	22.41	14.37	8.05	3.34	7.65	9.15	4.55	70.72	11.29
1997	79.25	22.25	14.98	8.41	3.34	7.38	6.25	4.22	68.30	10.95
1998	78.44	21.85	15.14	9.24	3.57	7.32	5.35	4.00	67.75	10.69
1999	77.98	21.79	15.51	9.94	3.63	6.69	4.50	3.91	67.24	10.73
2000	76.48	21.40	15.63	10.70	3.75	6.58	3.39	4.01	66.42	10.06

(1) *Aggregate monthly and quarterly data on inland deliveries of oil products are available - see paragraph 3.124 and Annex F.*

(2) *This table has been revised from previous editions to be fully compliant with the commodity balances format used in Tables 3.4 to 3.6. This has involved adding in the refinery fuel elements into the above product totals, and an adjustment to the data for fuels used by the iron and steel industry as detailed in footnote (6) on the facing page*

(3) *Other than DERV fuel*

(4) *Includes Orimulsion from 1989. Imports / deliveries of orimulsion ceased in February 1997.*

(5) *Includes aviation spirit, naphtha (LDF) for gasworks, marine diesel oil and wide cut gasoline.*

3.12 Inland deliveries of petroleum, 1970 to 2000[1] [2] (continued)

Million tonnes

	Energy industry use				Final users				
	Electricity generators	Gas works	Refineries	Other energy industry uses (6)	Iron & steel	Other industries	Transport	Domestic	Other final users (7)
1970	12.60	4.56	6.03	4.25	1.42	21.55	25.00	3.05	8.59
1971	14.68	2.59	6.18	3.97	1.32	21.55	26.07	3.01	8.67
1972	18.87	2.21	6.42	3.78	1.26	22.14	27.14	3.48	8.91
1973	16.95	2.32	7.05	3.74	1.25	22.18	28.96	3.80	9.00
1974	17.21	1.28	6.95	3.02	1.01	19.82	27.92	3.38	7.95
1975	12.82	0.59	6.03	2.48	0.83	17.89	27.57	3.27	7.93
1976	10.18	0.25	6.34	2.48	0.83	18.06	28.60	3.27	7.80
1977	10.60	0.16	6.24	2.21	0.74	18.06	29.37	3.31	8.60
1978	11.64	0.35	6.42	2.12	0.71	17.55	30.87	3.26	8.24
1979	11.12	0.42	6.49	2.14	0.71	17.62	31.58	3.21	8.27
1980	6.52	0.31	6.27	1.19	0.40	14.51	31.74	2.55	7.01
1981	4.86	0.25	5.45	1.00	0.33	12.67	30.63	2.31	6.65
1982	6.87	0.21	5.55	0.89	0.30	11.64	31.31	2.15	6.28
1983	4.65	0.16	5.30	0.77	0.26	10.23	32.25	2.14	6.00
1984	20.91	0.16	5.35	0.63	0.21	9.39	33.82	2.14	6.00
1985	9.72	0.15	5.18	0.52	0.17	8.43	34.46	2.20	5.65
1986	5.66	0.17	5.40	0.50	0.17	9.02	36.66	2.32	5.36
1987	5.36	0.09	5.05	0.42	0.14	7.36	38.22	2.21	4.67
1988	6.07	0.06	5.29	0.55	0.18	8.23	40.62	2.13	4.67
1989	6.17	0.05	5.62	0.56	0.19	7.52	42.54	2.11	4.21
1990	7.98	0.05	5.07	0.53	0.18	7.03	43.45	2.22	4.11
1991	7.56	0.05	5.26	0.53	0.18	7.49	42.86	2.52	4.17
1992	8.32	0.04	4.16	0.51	0.17	7.13	43.79	2.58	4.22
1993	6.02	0.04	5.89	0.64	0.21	7.17	44.56	2.71	4.21
1994	4.04	0.05	6.04	0.67	0.22	7.47	44.82	2.70	4.03
1995	4.37	0.05	5.99	0.62	0.21	6.41	44.81	2.70	3.69
1996	3.57	0.05	6.50	0.65	0.09	6.41	46.64	3.17	3.65
1997	2.24	0.05	6.16	0.57	0.11	5.68	47.32	3.06	3.12
1998	1.40	0.05	6.18	0.40	0.08	5.71	47.84	3.20	2.88
1999	1.02	0.05	5.63	0.40	0.09	5.80	48.73	2.85	2.67
2000	1.00	0.04	4.92	0.34	0.13	5.69	49.20	2.92	2.24

(6) *Mainly use of gas diesel oil and fuel oil in the Iron and steel industry in blast furnaces.*
(7) *Mainly agriculture, public administration, commerce and other services.*

Chapter 4
Natural gas

Introduction

4.1   This chapter presents figures on the production, transmission and consumption of natural gas and colliery methane. One change to the structure of this chapter this year is a map showing the gas transmission system in Great Britain (page 122). As previously, four tables are presented. The commodity balances for natural gas and colliery methane form the first table (Table 4.1). This is followed by a 5 year table showing the supply, transmission and consumption of these gases as a time series (Table 4.2). A more detailed examination of the various stages of natural gas from gross production through to consumption is given in Table 4.3. Table 4.4 is a long term trends table of production and consumption of gas back to 1970.

4.2   Petroleum gases are covered in Chapter 3. Gases manufactured in the coke making and iron and steel making processes (coke oven gas and blast furnace gas) appear in Chapter 2. Biogases (landfill gas and sewage gas) are part of Chapter 7. Details of net selling values of gas for the domestic sector are to be found in Chapter 1.

The gas supply industry
Great Britain

4.3   When British Gas was privatised in 1986, it was given a statutory monopoly over supplies of natural gas (methane) to premises taking less than 732,000 kWh (25,000 therms) a year. Under the Oil and Gas (Enterprise) Act 1982, contract customers taking more than this were able to buy their gas from other suppliers but no other suppliers entered the market until 1990.

4.4   In 1991, the Office of Fair Trading (OFT) followed up an examination of the contract market by the Monopolies and Mergers Commission (MMC) that had taken place in 1988. It reviewed progress towards a competitive market and found that the steps taken in 1988 had been ineffective in encouraging self-sustaining competition. British Gas undertook in March 1992 to allow competitors to take by 1995 at least 60 per cent of the contract market above 732,000 kWh (25,000 therms) a year (subsequently redefined as 45 per cent of the market above 73,200 kWh (2,500 therms)); to release to competitors the gas necessary to achieve this; and to establish a separate transport and storage unit with regulated charges. At the same time, the Government took powers in the 1992 Competition and Service (Utilities) Act to reduce or remove the tariff monopoly, and in July 1992 it lowered the tariff threshold from 732,000 kWh (25,000 therms) to 73,200 kWh (2,500 therms).

4.5   Difficulties in implementing the March 1992 undertakings led to further references to the MMC. As

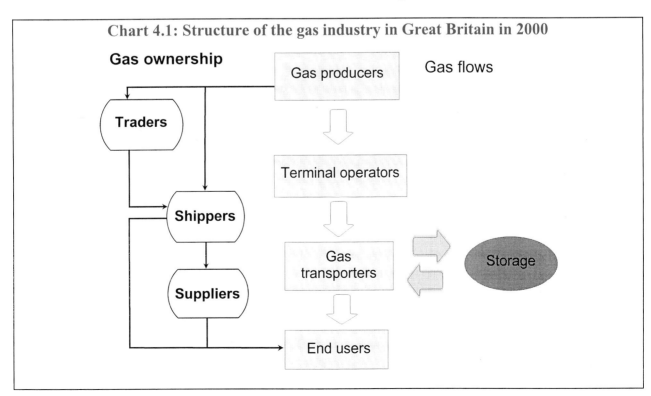

Chart 4.1: Structure of the gas industry in Great Britain in 2000

a result of the new recommendations made by the MMC in 1993, the President of the Board of Trade decided in December 1993 to require full internal separation of British Gas's supply and transportation activities, but not divestment, and to accelerate removal of the tariff monopoly to April 1996, with a phased opening of the domestic market by the regulator over the following two years.

4.6　In November 1995 the Gas Bill received Royal Assent, clearing the way for the extension of competition into the domestic gas supply market on a phased basis between 1996 and 1998. This was carried out in stages between April 1996 and May 1998. By December 2000 over 5½ million gas consumers (29½ per cent) were no longer supplied by British Gas Trading. Table 4A gives market penetration in more detail, by local distribution zone (LDZ). For standard credit customers it is in the market in Wales that new suppliers have had most success, while for direct debit customers it is the Northern region that has been the most successful for new suppliers. At the end of Q4 2000 British Gas Trading had lost around 28 per cent of the credit and 33 per cent of the direct debit market compared to 13 per cent of the pre-payment market, although it should be noted that British Gas's pre-payment prices are below the average of new suppliers. At the end of 2000, 28 suppliers were licensed to supply gas to domestic customers.

Table 4A: Domestic gas market penetration (in terms of percentage of customers supplied) by local distribution zone and payment type, fourth quarter of 2000

Region	British Gas Trading			Non-British Gas		
	Credit	Direct Debit	Prepay-ment	Credit	Direct Debit	Prepay-ment
Wales	63	70	76	37	30	24
East Midlands	71	64	85	29	36	15
Eastern	71	66	88	29	34	12
North East	71	66	84	29	34	16
North Thames	71	74	90	29	26	10
North West	72	71	85	28	29	15
South East	72	63	88	28	37	12
Northern	74	60	87	26	40	13
Scotland	74	61	94	26	39	6
West Midlands	75	74	87	25	26	13
Southern	76	61	89	24	39	11
South West	78	68	87	22	32	13
Great Britain	72	67	87	28	33	13

4.7　Following the 1995 Act, the business of British Gas was fully separated into two corporate entities. The supply and shipping businesses were devolved to a subsidiary, British Gas Trading Limited, while the transportation business (Transco) remained within British Gas plc. In February 1997, Centrica plc was demerged from British Gas plc (which was itself renamed as BG plc) completing the division of the business into two independent entities. Centrica is now the holding company for British Gas Trading, British Gas Services, the Retail Energy Centres and the company producing gas from the North and South Morecambe fields. BG plc comprised the gas transportation and storage business of Transco, along with British Gas's exploration and production, international downstream, research and technology and property activities. In October 2000 BG plc demerged into two separately listed companies, of which Lattice Group plc is the holding company for Transco, while BG Group plc includes the international and gas storage businesses.

4.8　The introduction of effective competition into the contract market has taken both time and heavy regulatory intervention. Since 1990 a number of independent gas suppliers have started to supply natural gas to non-tariff customers and, where applicable, these supplies are included in the totals. The new supply companies nearly all use the pipeline system owned by Transco to supply gas to their customers. Terms for the use of the pipeline network are set out in Transco's "Network Code". In some areas low pressure spur networks are being developed by new transporters competing with Transco to bring gas supplies to new customers (mainly domestic). By the end of May 2001 spur networks to nearly 5,000 housing developments were either operated or due to be operated (when completed) by such new competing transporters. Some very large loads (above 60 GWh) are serviced by pipelines operated independently, some by North Sea producers.

4.9　By the end of 1994, competitors had exceeded the target 45 per cent of the market above 73,200 kWh (2,500 therms), but virtually all of this was in the firm gas market. From 1995 British Gas's competitors made inroads into the interruptible market and in 2000 Centrica's share of the industrial and commercial market had fallen to around 14 per cent. At the end of 2000, 58 suppliers were active in the contract market. The structure of the gas industry in Great Britain as it stood at the end of 2000 is shown in Chart 4.1.

Regional analysis

4.10　Table 4B gives the number of consumers with a gas demand below 73,200 kWh per year in 2000. It covers both domestic and small business customers receiving gas from the national transmission system. It is this section of the market that was progressively opened up to competition between April 1996 and May 1998. The regions shown are Transco's 13 local distribution zones (LDZs). Table 4C gives the corresponding information for all consumers of gas.

Table 4B: Consumption by customers below 73,200 kWh (2,500 therms) annual demand 2000

Local distribution zones	Number of consumers (thousands)	Gas sales 2000 (GWh)
North Western	2,592	52,820
South Eastern	2,344	47,469
North Thames	2,214	44,383
East Midlands	2,094	41,735
West Midlands	1,884	37,474
Eastern	1,626	33,000
Scotland	1,606	33,080
Southern	1,464	29,460
North Eastern	1,279	24,943
South Western	1,281	23,862
Northern	1,116	23,405
Wales South	765	15.388
Wales North	211	3,977
Great Britain	20,487	410,997

Source: Transco

Table 4C: Consumption by all customers 2000

Local distribution zones	Number of consumers (thousands)	Gas sales 2000 (GWh)
North Western	2,640	93,472
South Eastern	2,399	70,110
North Thames	2,266	76,329
East Midlands	2,129	77,756
West Midlands	1,919	66,476
Eastern	1,655	52,424
Scotland	1,637	64,168
Southern	1,492	45,638
North Eastern	1,304	46,165
South Western	1,303	35,933
Northern	1,133	40,811
Wales South	777	28,221
Wales North	215	7,808
Great Britain	20,866	708,909

Source: Transco

Northern Ireland

4.11 Before 1997, Northern Ireland did not have a public natural gas supply. The construction of a natural gas pipeline from Portpatrick in Scotland to Northern Ireland was completed in 1996 and provided the means of establishing such a system. The primary market is Ballylumford power station, which was purchased by British Gas in 1992 and converted from oil to gas firing (with a heavy fuel oil back up). The onshore line has been extended to serve wider industrial, commercial and domestic markets and this extension is continuing. In 2000, 91 per cent of all gas supplies in Northern Ireland were used to generate electricity.

Competition

4.12 Paragraphs 4.3 to 4.11 above referred to the developments in recent years in opening up the non-domestic market to competition. About three-quarters of this market (by volume) in the United Kingdom was opened to competition at the end of 1982, and the remainder in August 1992 (with the reduction in the tariff threshold). As mentioned above, however, no other suppliers entered the market until 1990. After 1990 there was a rapid increase in the number of independent companies supplying gas, although in 1999 there were signs of some consolidation. Chart 4.2 shows how in the mid 1990s sales of gas became less concentrated in the hands of the largest companies. However, for industrial sales between 1997 and 1999, the largest companies increased their share of the market. This was brought about through larger companies absorbing smaller suppliers and through an expansion of industrial sales by Centrica. In 2000 there was a movement towards less concentration once again. The three largest suppliers now jointly account for 44 per cent of sales to industry compared with 40 per cent in 1996. For the purpose of this chart industrial sales include sales of gas to autogenerators in the industrial sector, an area that has continued to expand more rapidly than industrial sales for heating and processing. For commercial sector sales, in 1999 the second to tenth largest firms all gained market share at the expense of the largest and smallest suppliers, but here too more competition was evident in 2000. Sales of gas for electricity generation grew rapidly in the late 1990s and the number of firms selling to generators expanded, but with the slower growth in 2000 sales became slightly more concentrated in the hands of the larger suppliers.

Commodity balances for gas (Table 4.1)

4.13 For the last three years production of natural gas has been greater than supply because exports have been larger than imports. However, net exports of natural gas, although growing rapidly, were not large in absolute terms, amounting to only 9½ per cent of total production in 2000. Imports and exports of natural gas are described in greater detail below (paragraph 4.18).

4.14 Demand for natural gas is traditionally less than supply because of the various measurement differences described in paragraphs 4.46 to 4.49.

4.15 In 2000, 28 per cent of natural gas demand was for electricity generation (transformation sector), the same proportion as in 1999. A further 7½ per cent was consumed for heating purposes within the energy industries. One per cent was accounted for by distribution losses within the gas network. (For an explanation of the items included under losses, see paragraphs 4.46 to 4.49.) Of the remaining 63½ per cent, 18 per cent was accounted for by the industrial sector with the chemicals industry (excluding natural

Chart 4.2: Competition in natural gas supplies - 1996 to 2000

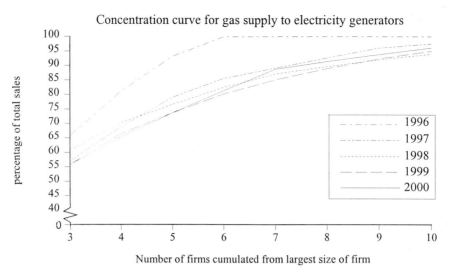

Concentration curve for gas supply to electricity generators

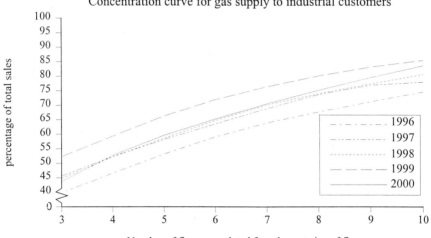

Concentration curve for gas supply to industrial customers

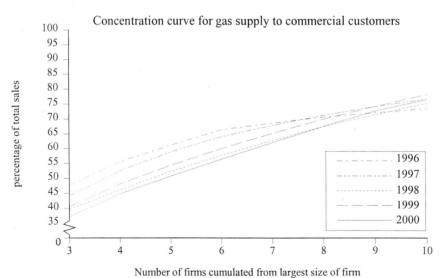

Concentration curve for gas supply to commercial customers

Illustrating increasing competition using concentration curves:

Concentration curves can be used to show the increase (or decrease) in competition within an industry. The sets of curves for the three sectors shown in Chart 4.2 are all constructed in the same way. In any particular year, in a particular sector, the proportion (expressed as a percentage) of total sales of gas (by volume) accounted for by the three firms with the largest sales is calculated. This calculation is repeated for the largest four firms, the largest five firms and so on up to the largest 10 firms. These percentages of total sales are plotted. If each of 10 firms had an equal share of gas sales the plot would form a straight diagonal line from the origin to 100 per cent at the 10 firm point. For a monopoly the curve lies on the vertical axis. When an industry is concentrated in the hands of a few firms, the curve is well above and to the left of the diagonal line and moves towards the diagonal as competition increases. In 1996 the three largest firms in terms of sales to the commercial sector accounted for 48 per cent of sales, the six largest 66 per cent, and the ten largest 72 per cent. By 2000 the curve had moved downwards to the right indicating more competition since the largest three firms accounted for only 36 per cent of total sales to industry and the largest six firms 56 per cent, although the proportion for the largest ten had grown to 75 per cent.

116

gas for petrochemical feedstocks), iron and steel and the food industry being the largest consumers. The chemicals sector accounted for over a quarter of the industrial consumption of natural gas.

4.16   Sales of gas to households (domestic sector) produced 33 per cent of gas demand, while public administration consumed 5 per cent of total demand. Public administration consumes almost as much gas as the chemicals sector. The commercial, agriculture and miscellaneous sectors together took up 6½ per cent. Non energy use of gas accounted for the remaining 1 per cent. Non-energy use of natural gas was lower in 1997 than in other recent years (see Table 4.2) because of re-fitting work at one petrochemical plant. As Table 4D, below, shows, non-energy use of gas is small relative to total use (see the technical notes section, paragraph 4.39 for more details on non-energy use of gas).

Table 4D: Non-energy use: share of natural gas demand

	Continental shelf and onshore natural gas
1996	1.5%
1997	1.3%
1998	1.2%
1999	1.2%
2000	1.2%

4.17   Care should be exercised in interpreting the figures for individual industries in these commodity balance tables. As more companies have entered the gas supply market, it has not been possible to ensure consistent classification between and within industry sectors and across years. The breakdown of final consumption includes a substantial amount of estimated data. For about 11 per cent of consumption the allocation to consuming sector is wholly estimated and for a further 6 per cent of consumption the sector figures are partially estimated.

4.18   Imports of natural gas from the Norwegian sector of the North Sea began to decline in the late 1980s as output from the Frigg field tailed off. In 1999, and again in 2000, there was an increase in imports brought about by inflows through the Bacton-Zeebrugge interconnector (although the UK was a net exporter through this interconnector in both 1999 and 2000). Imports added only about 2 per cent to UK production. Exports to mainland Europe from the United Kingdom's share of the Markham field began in 1992 with Windermere's output being added in 1997. Exports to the Republic of Ireland began in 1995. The interconnector linking the UK's transmission network with Belgium via a Bacton to Zeebrugge pipeline began to operate in October 1998. Since then the interconnector has facilitated both imports and exports of natural gas. Exports accounted

for 11½ per cent of production in 2000. Exports of natural gas exceeded imports for the first time in 1997 but grew rapidly (by 46 per cent in 1998, then by over 2½ times in 1999, and by 73 per cent in 2000). The volume of exports was 5½ times the volume of gas imports in 2000.

4.19   Chart 4.3 shows the increase in indigenous production and consumption of natural gas over the past five years and how net exports have grown.

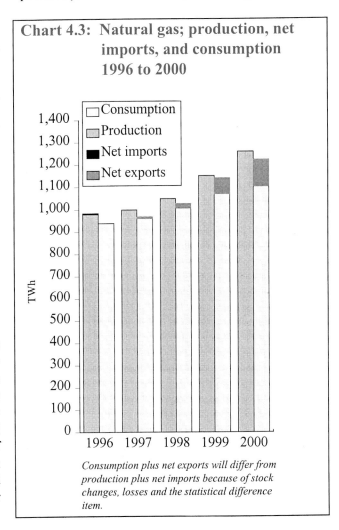

Chart 4.3: Natural gas; production, net imports, and consumption 1996 to 2000

Consumption plus net exports will differ from production plus net imports because of stock changes, losses and the statistical difference item.

Supply and consumption of natural gas and colliery methane (Table 4.2)

4.20   This table summarises the production and consumption of gas from these sources in the United Kingdom over the last 5 years.

4.21   As Chart 4.4 shows, the growth in consumption for electricity generation has dominated the growth in natural gas consumption over the last 10 years. Most of this gas was used in Combined Cycle Gas Turbine (CCGT) stations, although the use of gas in dual fired conventional steam stations was a growth area in 1997 and 1998. However, growth rates for electricity generation over the last four years first declined from 25 per cent in 1997 to 4 per cent in 1998, but then grew again in 1999 to 18 per cent. The growth rate fell back to 1½ per cent in 2000 in part because of strong competition from coal at the end of the year when high gas prices pushed some gas fired stations down the merit order. In 2000 the transformation sector accounted for 28 per cent of gas demand compared with only 21 per cent in 1996.

	GWh
Total UK consumption (Table 4.3)	1,030,714
plus Producers own use	65,605
plus Operators own use	6,701
equals	
"Consumption of natural gas" (see paragraph 4.31)	1,103,020
plus Other losses and metering differences (upstream)	10,286
plus Metering differences (transmission)	2,098
equals	
Total demand (Tables 4.1 and 4.2)	1,115,404

4.22   Over the four years since 1996, industrial use of gas has grown by 23 per cent, use by the public administration sector by 4½ per cent, use by the commercial sector by 19 per cent, and use in the energy industries other than electricity generation by 22 per cent.

4.23   Gas use in the domestic sector is particularly dependent on winter temperatures and mild winters in each of the previous three years accounted for domestic consumption being lower than in the particularly cold year (by recent standards) of 1996. 2000 was a cooler year and domestic demand was 3½ per cent up on 1999, still 1½ per cent below 1996's peak. Although demand from the domestic sector increased by 7 per cent between 1997 and 2000, its share of total demand fell from 35½ per cent to 33 per cent.

4.24   Maximum daily demand for natural gas through the National Transmission System in winter 2000/01 was 4,540 GWh on 16 January 2001. On that day natural gas demand in Northern Ireland was 7.6 GWh. This total maximum daily demand was 8 per cent higher than the previous record daily level recorded during the colder winter of 1996 (February).

4.25   It is estimated that sales of gas supplied on an interruptible basis accounted for around 26 per cent of total gas sales in 2000, a small increase on the proportion to 1999.

UK continental shelf and onshore natural gas (Table 4.3)

4.26   This table shows the flows for natural gas from production through transmission to consumption. The footnotes to the table give more information about each table row. This table departs from the standard balance methodology and definitions in order to maintain the link with past data and with monthly data given at DTI's energy statistics web site (see paragraph 4.45. The relationship between total UK gas consumption shown in this table and total demand for gas given in the balance tables (4.1 and 4.2) is illustrated for 2000 in the table below.

4.27   Gross production increased by 28½ per cent between 1996 and 2000. In 2000, the increase was 9

per cent, compared with 10 per cent and 5 per cent respectively in 1999 and 1998. Gas available at UK terminals has increased by a lesser amount (15 per cent) over this four year period mainly because of the increase in exports and decrease in imports described in paragraph 4.18. Producers' and operators' own use of gas have tended to grow in proportion to the volumes of gas produced and transmitted. Output from the transmission system also increased by 15 per cent between 1996 and 2000, while total UK consumption of natural gas increased by 17½ per cent. Consumption increased by more than the output from the transmission system because distribution losses and metering differences have been reduced as a proportion of consumption over these four years.

4.28   For a discussion of the various losses and statistical differences terms in this table, see paragraphs 4.46 to 4.49 in the technical notes and definitions section. Changes to accounting practices within the industry resulted in substantial reductions in the sizes of two of the statistical difference terms since 1997. It is not possible to separate "losses" and "statistical differences" in a completely satisfactory manner. Losses in the distribution system are not separately identifiable and are included under statistical differences. The convention used is set out in paragraph 4.49.

4.29   Losses and metering differences attributable to the information provided on the upstream gas industry increased in 2000 to 10.3 TWh from 5.6 TWh in 1999. This is primarily due to discrepancies seen within the production data reported for three major offshore production systems. These systems each contain several separate production facilities which are linked together via pipeline systems before the gas is transported by pipeline to on-shore terminals, and as such are more prone than other less complex systems to the impact of the metering differences discussed in paragraphs 4.46 to 4.49. From 1st January 2001, a simplified reporting system for the production of crude oil, NGLs and natural gas in the UK was implemented (See Chapter 3, paragraph 3.41). This simplification of the reporting system has improved the quality of data on gas production being reported, with these losses and metering differences being reduced so far in the data reported in 2001.

Long term trends

Natural gas and colliery methane production and consumption
(Table 4.4)

4.30   Table 4.4 shows data for production, imports, exports, and the consumption of natural gas and colliery methane by major sector in each year from 1970 to 2000   Separate figures are shown for consumption of town gas and methane.

4.31   Total consumption in Table 4.4 is defined to match the definition of gas consumption used in the gas tables before the 1999 Digest. This enables a consistent long term series to be presented. Total consumption of natural gas and colliery methane in this table is related to total UK consumption of natural gas in Table 4.3 as follows:

	GWh
Total consumption (Table 4.4)	1,103,508
less Colliery methane	- 488
equals	
Total consumption of natural gas	1,103,020
less Producers' own use	- 65,605
less Operators' own use	- 6,701
equals	
Total UK consumption (Table 4.3)	1,030,714

Paragraph 4.26 shows how natural gas consumption in Table 4.3 relates to total demand in the balances Tables 4.1 and 4.2.

4.32   Chart 4.4 illustrates the data in Table 4.4. It shows how the supply of natural gas became established during the first part of the 1970s and the decline of town gas to zero by the middle of that decade.   Thereafter, the supply of natural gas continued to grow less rapidly, with indigenous production bolstered from 1977 by increasing imports from the Norwegian sector of the North Sea. In 1998 imports fell to only 7 per cent of their peak in the mid-1980s, but rose in 1999 and 2000, because of inflows through the Bacton-Zeebrugge interconnector.   In 2000 imports added only 2 per cent to indigenous production compared with about one-third in the mid-1980s. This is largely because of the depletion of the (mainly Norwegian) Frigg field, but also due to the resurgence of UK production which has achieved a new record each year since 1989. Production of gas in 2000 was nearly 2½ times that of 10 years earlier. 1992 saw the first exports of natural gas from the United Kingdom's share of the Markham gas field. In 1995 these were supplemented by the first exports to the Republic of Ireland, followed by the start of gas exports from the Windermere field via the Markham field during 1997, and exports by the UK-Belgium interconnector during 1998. By 2000 exports were 5½ times the volume of imports.

4.33   Table 4.4 also shows that the bulk of the rapid growth in the 1970s in consumption of natural gas was in the domestic and industrial sectors. In the 1980s and early 1990s there was a fall in industrial use, but gas consumption by industry has been on an upward trend since 1992 and by 2000 it exceeded the previous peak of 1985 by 24 per cent. Since 1980 there has been a doubling of gas consumption by the service sector (which for this table is defined as including public administration, commercial activities and agriculture) while domestic sector consumption has increased by 50 per cent over the same period. The increase in total consumption accelerated in the early 1990s because of the large increase in consumption by electricity generators.   Even if consumption by electricity generators is excluded, consumption in 2000 was 57 per cent up on its level in 1980.

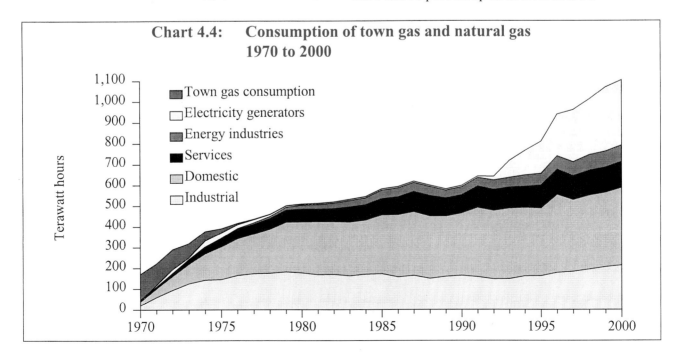

Chart 4.4:   Consumption of town gas and natural gas 1970 to 2000

Technical notes and definitions

4.34
These notes and definitions are in addition to the technical notes and definitions covering all fuels and energy as a whole in Chapter 1, paragraphs 1.46 to 1.81. For notes on the commodity balances and definitions of the terms used in the row headings see the Annex A, paragraphs A.7 to A.41.

Definitions used for production and consumption

4.35 Natural gas production in Tables 4.1 and 4.2 relates to the output of indigenous methane at land terminals and gas separation plants (includes producers' and processors' own use). For further explanation, see the Annex C, paragraph C.18 under 'Production of oil and gas'. Output of the Norwegian share of the Frigg and Murchison fields is included under imports. A small quantity of onshore produced methane (other than colliery methane) is also included.

4.36 Table 4.3 shows production, transmission and consumption figures for UK continental shelf and onshore natural gas. Production includes waste and own use for drilling, production and pumping operations, but excludes gas flared. Gas available in the United Kingdom excludes waste, own use for drilling etc, stock change, and includes imports net of exports. Gas transmitted (input into inland transmission systems) is after stock change, own use, and losses at inland terminals. The amount consumed in the United Kingdom differs from the total gas transmitted by the gas supply industry, because of losses in transmission, differences in temperature and pressure between the points at which the gas is measured, delays in reading meters and consumption in the works, offices, shops, etc of the undertakings. The figures include an adjustment to the quantities billed to consumers to allow for the estimated consumption remaining unread at the end of the year.

4.37 Colliery methane production is colliery methane piped to the surface and consumed at collieries or transmitted by pipeline to consumers. As the output of deep-mined coal declines so does the production of colliery methane, unless a use can be found for gas that was previously vented. The supply of methane from coal measures that are no longer being worked or from drilling into coal measures is licensed under the same legislation as used for offshore gas production. Production data, when it becomes available, will be reported as natural gas in the balances. If possible, separate production details will be included in future versions of Annex C.

4.38 Transfers of natural gas include natural gas use within the iron and steel industry for mixing with blast furnace gas to form a synthetic coke oven gas. For further details see paragraph 2.52 in Chapter 2.

4.39 Non-energy gas: Non-energy use is gas used as feedstock for petrochemical plants in the chemical industry as raw material for the production of ammonia (an essential intermediate chemical in the production of nitrogen fertilisers) and methanol. The contribution of liquefied petroleum gases (propane and butane) and other petroleum gases are shown in Tables 3.4 to 3.6 of Chapter 3. Firm data for natural gas are not available, but estimates for 1996 to 2000 are shown in Table 4.2. and estimates for 1998 to 2000 in Table 4.1 Estimates for 1996 to 1999 have been obtained from the National Atmospheric Emissions Inventory (NAEI); 2000 data are DTI extrapolations.

Sectors used for sales/consumption

4.40 For definitions of the various sectors used for sales and consumption analyses see the Chapter 1 paragraphs 1.74 to 1.78 and Annex A paragraphs A.30 to A.41. However, **miscellaneous** has a wider coverage than in the commodity balances of other fuels. This is because some gas supply companies are currently unable to provide a full breakdown of the services sector and the gas they supply to consumers is allocated to miscellaneous when there is no reliable basis for allocating it elsewhere.

Data collection

4.41 Production figures are generally obtained from returns made under the Department of Trade and Industry's Petroleum Production Reporting System and from other sources. DTI obtain data on the transmission of natural gas from BG Transco (who operate the National Transmission System) and from other pipeline operators. Data on consumption are based on returns from gas suppliers and UKCS producers who supply gas directly to customers.

4.42 The production data are for the United Kingdom (including natural gas from the UKCS - offshore and onshore). The restoration of a public gas supply to parts of Northern Ireland in 1997 (see paragraph 4.11 means that all tables in this chapter (except 4B and 4C) cover the United Kingdom.

4.43 DTI carry out an annual survey of gas suppliers to obtain details of gas sales to the various categories of consumer. Estimates are included for the suppliers with the smallest market share since the DTI inquiry covers only the largest suppliers (i.e. those with more than about a ½ per cent share of the UK market up to 1997 and those known to supply more than 1,750 GWh per year for 1998 onwards).

Period covered

4.44 Figures generally relate to years ended 31 December. However, data for natural gas for electricity generation relate to periods of 52 weeks as set out in Chapter 5, paragraphs 5.67 and 5.68.

Monthly and quarterly data

4.45 Monthly data on natural gas production and supply, are available from the DTI's Energy Statistics web site www.dti.gov.uk/energy/energystats/energystats.htm in Table 4.2. A quarterly commodity balance for natural gas (which includes consumption data) is published in DTI's quarterly statistical bulletin *Energy Trends* and is also available from DTI's Energy Statistics web site Table 4.1. See Annex F for more information about *Energy Trends*.

Statistical and metering differences

4.46 In Table 4.3 there are several headings that refer to statistical or metering differences. These arise because measurement of gas flows, in volume and energy terms, takes place at several points along the supply chain. The main sub-headings in the table represent the instances in the supply chain where accurate reports are made of the gas flows at that particular key point in the supply process. It is possible to derive alternative estimates of the flow of gas at any particular point by taking the estimate for the previous point in the supply chain and then applying the known losses and gains in the subsequent part of the supply chain. The differences seen when the actual reported flow of gas at any point and the derived estimate are compared are separately identified in the table wherever possible, under the headings statistical or metering differences.

4.47 The differences arise from several factors:-

- Limitations in the accuracy of meters used at various points of the supply chain. While standards are in place on the accuracy of meters, there is a degree of error allowed which, when large flows of gas are being recorded, can become significant.

- Differences in the methods used to calculate the flow of gas in energy terms. For example, at the production end, rougher estimates of the calorific value of the gas produced are used which may only be revised periodically, rather than the more accurate and more frequent analyses carried out further down the supply chain. At the supply end, although the calorific value of gas shows day-to-day variations, for the purposes of recording the gas supplied to customers a single calorific value is used. Until 1997 this was the lowest of the range of calorific values for the actual gas being supplied within each LDZ, resulting in a "loss" of gas in energy terms. In 1997 there was a change to a "capped flow-weighted average" algorithm for calculating calorific values resulting in a reduction in the losses shown in the penultimate row of Table 4.3. This change in algorithm, along with improved meter validation and auditing procedures, has also reduced the level of "metering differences" row within the downstream part of Table 4.3.

- Differences in temperature and pressure between the various points at which gas is measured. Until February 1997 British Gas used "uncorrected therms" on their billing system for tariff customers when converting from a volume measure of the gas used to an energy measure. This made their supply figure too small by a factor of 2.2 per cent, equivalent to about 1 per cent of the wholesale market.

- Differences in the timing of reading meters. While National Transmission System meters are read daily, customers' meters are read less frequently (perhaps only annually for some domestic customers) and profiling is used to estimate consumption. Profiling will tend to under estimate consumption in a strongly rising market.

- Other losses from the system, for example, leakage from offshore gas pipelines, leakage from the local distribution systems, theft through meter tampering.

4.48 The headings in Table 4.3 show where, in the various stages of the supply process, it has been possible to identify these metering differences as having an effect. Usually they are aggregated with other net losses as the two factors cannot be separated. Whilst the factors listed above can give rise to either losses or gains, losses are more common.

4.49 The box below shows how in 2000 the wastage, losses and metering differences figures in Table 4.3 are related to the losses row in the balance Tables 4.1 and 4.2:

Table 4.3	GWh
Upstream gas industry:	
Other losses and metering differences	10,286
Downstream gas industry:	
Transmission system metering differences	2,098
Tables 4.1 and 4.2	
Losses	12,384

Similarly the statistical difference row in Tables 4.1 and 4.2 is made up of the following components in 2000:

Table 4.3	GWh
Statistical difference between gas available from upstream and gas input to downstream	+ 234
plus Downstream gas industry:	
Distribution losses, metering differences and transfers	13,197
less Transfers (Tables 4.1 and 4.2)	-426
Tables 4.1 and 4.2	
Statistical difference	13,005

Contact: Mike Janes (Statistician)
mike.janes@dti.gsi.gov.uk
020-7215 5186

John Castle
john.castle@dti.gsi.gov.uk
020-7215 2718

The National gas transmission system, 2000

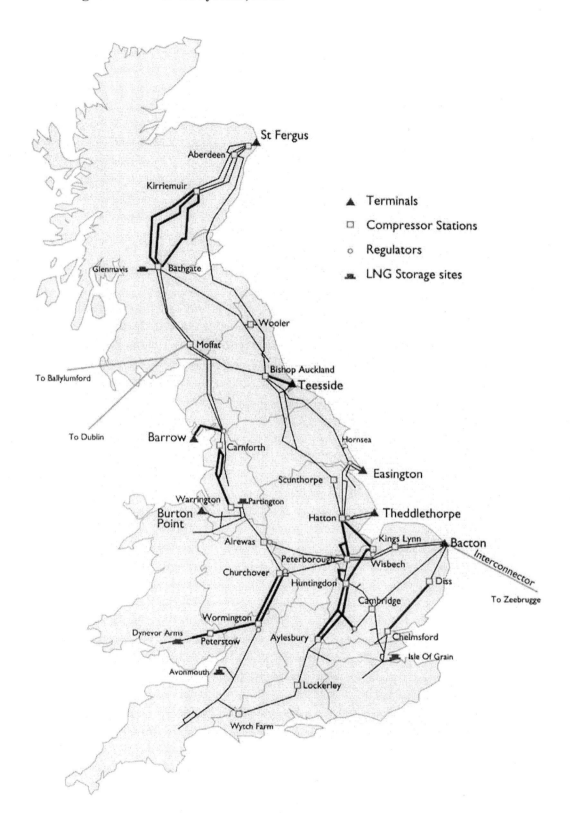

Legend:
- ▲ Terminals
- □ Compressor Stations
- ○ Regulators
- ▬ LNG Storage sites

Map labels: St Fergus, Aberdeen, Kirriemuir, Glenmavis, Bathgate, Wooler, Moffat, To Ballylumford, Bishop Auckland, Teesside, To Dublin, Barrow, Carnforth, Hornsea, Scunthorpe, Easington, Warrington, Partington, Burton Point, Hatton, Theddlethorpe, Alrewas, Kings Lynn, Bacton, Interconnector, Peterborough, Wisbech, Churchover, Huntingdon, Diss, Cambridge, To Zeebrugge, Wormington, Dynevor Arms, Peterstow, Aylesbury, Chelmsford, Isle Of Grain, Avonmouth, Lockerley, Wytch Farm

Source: Transco

4.1 Commodity balances 1998 to 2000

Natural gas

GWh

	1998			1999			2000		
	Natural gas	Colliery methane	Total natural gas	Natural gas	Colliery methane	Total natural gas	Natural gas	Colliery methane	Total natural gas
Supply									
Production	1,048,385r	474	1,048,859r	1,152,154r	481	1,152,635r	1,258,549	488	1,259,037
Other sources	-	-	-	-	-	-	-	-	-
Imports	10,582	-	10,582	12,862	-	12,862	26,032	-	26,032
Exports	-31,604	-	-31,604	-84,433	-	-84,433	-146,342	-	-146,342
Marine bunkers	-	-	-	-	-	-	-	-	-
Stock change (1)	-374	-	-374	+7,787r	-	+7,787r	-9,404	-	-9,404
Transfers (3)	-608	-	-608	-506	-	-506	-426	-	-426
Total supply	1,026,381r	474	1,027,603r	1,087,864r	481	1,088,345r	1,128,409	488	1,128,897
Statistical difference (2)	+13,532r	-	+13,532r	+13,285r	-	+13,285r	+13,005	-	+13,005
Total demand	1,012,849r	474	1,013,323r	1,074,579r	481	1,075,060r	1,115,404	488	1,115,892
Transformation	260,631r	30	260,661r	307,818r	93	307,911r	312,545	150	312,695
Electricity generation	260,631r	30	260,661r	307,818r	93	307,911r	312,545	150	312,695
Major power producers	236,300r	-	236,300r	281,988r	-	281,988r	283,784	-	283,784
Autogenerators	24,331r	30	24,361r	25,830r	93	25,923r	28,761	150	28,911
Petroleum refineries	-	-	-	-	-	-	-	-	-
Coke manufacture	-	-	-	-	-	-	-	-	-
Blast furnaces	-	-	-	-	-	-	-	-	-
Patent fuel manufacture	-	-	-	-	-	-	-	-	-
Other	-	-	-	-	-	-	-	-	-
Energy industry use	76,294r	264	76,558r	77,355r	238	77,593r	80,232	218	80,450
Electricity generation	-	-	-	-	-	-	-	-	-
Oil and gas extraction	65,500r		65,500r	64,634r	-	64,634r	65,605	-	65,605
Petroleum refineries	4,318r	-	4,318r	4,775r	-	4,775r	5,300	-	5,300
Coal extraction	67	264	331	14r	238	252r	6	218	224
Coke manufacture	7	-	7	13	-	13	17	-	17
Blast furnaces	527	-	527	643	-	643	712	-	712
Patent fuel manufacture	-	-	-	-	-	-	-	-	-
Pumped storage	-	-	-	-	-	-	-	-	-
Other	5,875	-	5,875	7,276	-	7,276	8,592	-	8,592
Losses (4)	8,017r	-	8,017r	6,267r	-	6,267r	12,384	-	12,384
Final consumption	667,907r	180	668,087r	683,139r	150	683,289r	710,243	120	710,363
Industry	181,808r	180	181,988r	192,197r	150	192,347r	200,539	120	200,659
Unclassified	-	180	180	-	150	150	-	120	120
Iron and steel	20,139r	-	20,139r	21,838r	-	21,838r	21,331	-	21,331
Non-ferrous metals	5,548r	-	5,548r	5,574r	-	5,574r	5,785	-	5,785
Mineral products	14,800r	-	14,800r	14,620r	-	14,620r	15,174	-	15,174
Chemicals	49,475r	-	49,475r	54,612r	-	54,612r	57,159	-	57,159
Mechanical Engineering etc	10,022r	-	10,022r	10,238r	-	10,238r	10,821	-	10,821
Electrical engineering etc	3,508r	-	3,508r	3,948r	-	3,948r	4,250	-	4,250
Vehicles	10,307r	-	10,307r	10,650r	-	10,650r	11,195	-	11,195
Food, beverages etc	28,011r	-	28,011r	29,576r	-	29,576r	32,046	-	32,046
Textiles, leather, etc	7,265r	-	7,265r	6,969r	-	6,969r	7,451	-	7,451
Paper, printing etc	15,477r	-	15,477r	16,806r	-	16,806r	17,572	-	17,572
Other industries	15,060r	-	15,060r	15,231r	-	15,231r	15,656	-	15,656
Construction	2,196r	-	2,196r	2,135r	-	2,135r	2,099	-	2,099
Transport	-	-	-	-	-	-	-	-	-
Air	-	-	-	-	-	-	-	-	-
Rail	-	-	-	-	-	-	-	-	-
Road (5)	-	-	-	-	-	-	-	-	-
National navigation	-	-	-	-	-	-	-	-	-
Pipelines	-	-	-	-	-	-	-	-	-
Other	474,122r	-	474,122r	477,936r	-	477,936r	496,698	-	496,698
Domestic	355,895	-	355,895	358,066r	-	358,066r	369,909	-	369,909
Public administration	52,441r	-	52,441r	51,861r	-	51,861r	54,432	-	54,432
Commercial	40,722	-	40,722	41,122	-	41,122	43,546	-	43,546
Agriculture	1,344	-	1,344	1,486	-	1,486	1,475	-	1,475
Miscellaneous	23,720r	-	23,720r	25,401r	-	25,401r	27,336	-	27,336
Non energy use	11,977r	-	11,977r	13,006r	-	13,006r	13,006	-	13,006

(1) Stock fall (+), stock rise (-).
(2) Total supply minus total demand.
(3) Natural gas used in the manufacture of synthetic coke oven gas.
(4) See paragraph 4.49.
(5) See footnote 5 to Table 4.2.

4.2 Supply and consumption of natural gas and colliery methane[1]

GWh

	1996	1997	1998	1999	2000
Supply					
Production	979,019	998,871	1,048,859r	1,152,635r	1,259,037
Imports	19,804	14,062	10,582	12,862	26,032
Exports	-15,203	-21,666	-31,604	-84,433	-146,342
Stock change (2)	-2,749	-4,119	-374	+7,787r	-9,404
Transfers	-270	-496	-608	-506	-426
Total supply	**980,601**	**986,652**	**1,026,855r**	**1,088,345r**	**1,128,897**
Statistical difference (3)	+25,611	+12,947	+13,532r	+13,285r	+13,005
Total demand	**954,990**	**973,705**	**1,013,323r**	**1,075,060r**	**1,115,892**
Transformation	**199,932**	**250,190**	**260,661r**	**307,911r**	**312,695**
Electricity generation	199,932	250,190	260,661r	307,911r	312,695
Major power producers	176,702	223,691	236,300r	281,988r	283,784
Autogenerators	23,230	26,499	24,361r	25,923r	28,911
Other	-	-	-	-	-
Energy industry use	**65,905**	**67,722**	**76,558r**	**77,593r**	**80,450**
Electricity generation	-	-	-	-	-
Oil and gas extraction	55,871	58,281	65,500r	64,634r	65,605
Petroleum refineries	2,975	3,122	4,318r	4,775r	5,300
Coal extraction	670	486	331	252r	224
Coke manufacture	23	15	7	13	17
Blast furnaces	478	342	527	643	712
Other	5,888	5,476	5,875	7,276	8,592
Losses (4)	**16,256**	**13,462**	**8,017r**	**6,267r**	**12,384**
Final consumption	**672,897**	**642,331**	**668,087r**	**683,289r**	**710,363**
Industry	**162,832**	**170,851**	**181,988r**	**192,347r**	**200,659**
Unclassified	200	200	180	150	120
Iron and steel	21,159	20,577	20,139r	21,838r	21,331
Non-ferrous metals	4,848	4,622	5,548r	5,574r	5,785
Mineral products	14,567	14,618	14,800r	14,620r	15,174
Chemicals	36,465	46,185	49,475r	54,612r	57,159
Mechanical engineering etc	9,943	9,621	10,022r	10,238r	10,821
Electrical engineering etc	2,955	2,916	3,508r	3,948r	4,250
Vehicles	9,437	9,240	10,307r	10,650r	11,195
Food, beverages etc	27,135	26,690	28,011r	29,576r	32,046
Textiles, leather, etc	6,897	6,746	7,265r	6,969r	7,451
Paper, printing etc	14,991	13,828	15,477r	16,806r	17,572
Other industries	12,449	13,888	15,060r	15,231r	15,656
Construction	1,786	1,720	2,196r	2,135r	2,099
Transport	**-**	**-**	**-**	**-**	**-**
Road (5)	-	-	-	-	-
Other	**495,177**	**459,200**	**474,122r**	**477,936r**	**496,698**
Domestic	375,841	345,532	355,895	358,066r	369,909
Public administration	51,411	53,203	52,441r	51,861r	54,432
Commercial	39,156	36,373	40,722	41,122	43,546
Agriculture	1,420	1,443	1,344	1,486	1,475
Miscellaneous	27,348	22,649	23,720r	25,401r	27,336
Non energy use	**14,888**	**12,280**	**11,977r**	**13,006r**	**13,006**

(1) Colliery methane figures included within these totals are as follows:

	1996	1997	1998	1999	2000
Total production	**566**	**528**	**474**	**481**	**488**
Electricity generation	40	35	30	93	150
Coal extraction	326	293	264	238	218
Other industries	200	200	180	150	120
Total consumption	**566**	**528**	**474**	**481**	**488**

(2) Stock fall (+), stock rise (-).
(3) Total supply minus total demand.
(4) For an explanation of what is included under losses, see paragraphs 4.49.

(5) A small amount of natural gas is consumed by road transport, but gas use in this sector is predominantly of petroleum gases, hence road use of gas is reported in the petroleum products balances in Chapter 3.

4.3 UK continental shelf and onshore natural gas production and supply[1]

GWh

	1996	1997	1998	1999	2000
Upstream gas industry:					
Gross production (2)	978,453	998,343	1,048,385r	1,152,154r	1,258,549
Minus Producers' own use (3)	55,871	58,281	65,500r	64,634r	65,605
Exports	15,203	21,666	31,604	84,433	146,342
Stock change (pipelines) (4)	-883	-2,220	-1,721	-842r	161
Waste (5)	114	94	89	-	-
Other losses and metering differences (6)(7)	5,623	6,794	7,419	5,634r	10,286
Plus Imports of gas	19,804	14,062	10,582	12,862	26,032
Gas available at terminals (8)	922,329	927,790	956,076	1,011,157r	1,062,187
Minus Statistical difference (7)	-1,469	-1,081	+734	-127	+234
Downstream gas industry:					
Gas input into the national transmission system (9)	923,798	928,871	955,342	1,011,284	1,061,953
Minus Operators' own use (10)	4,576	4,066	4,337	5,626	6,701
Stock change (storage sites) (11)	+3,632	+6,339	+2,095	-6,945	9,243
Metering differences (7)	10,519	6,668	509	633	2,098
Gas output from the national transmission system (12)	905,071	911,798	948,401	1,011,970	1,043,911
Minus Distribution losses, metering differences and transfers (7)(13)	27,350	14,430	13,406r	13,918r	13,197
Total UK consumption (14)	**877,721**	**897,368**	**934,995r**	**998,052r**	**1,030,714**

(1) For details of where to find monthly updates of natural gas production and supply see paragraph 4.45.

(2) Includes waste and producers' own use, but excludes gas flared.

(3) Gas used for drilling, production and pumping operations.

(4) Gas held within the UKCS pipeline system. As sections are opened and closed between fields, gas moves in and out of the system, hence it is regarded as a change in stocks.

(5) Gas vented from oil and gas platforms as part of the production process. With effect from 1999 gas vented is deducted from the Gross Production figure.

(6) Losses due to pipeline leakage.

(7) Measurement of gas flows, in volume and energy terms, occurs at several points along the supply chain. As such, differences are seen between the actual recorded flow through any one point and estimates calculated for the flow of gas at that point. More detail on the reasons for these differences is given in the technical notes and definitions section of this chapter, paragraphs 4.46 to 4.49.

(8) The volume of gas available at terminals for consumption in the UK as recorded by the terminal operators. The percentage of gas available for consumption in the UK from indigenous sources in 2000 was 97.6 per cent, compared with 98.7 per cent in 1999.

(9) Gas received as reported by the pipeline operators. The pipeline operators include Transco, who run the national pipeline network, and other pipelines that take North Sea gas supplies direct to consumers.

(10) Gas consumed by pipeline operators in pumping operations and on their own sites, office, etc.

(11) Stocks of gas held in specific storage sites, either as liquefied natural gas, pumped into salt cavities or stored by pumping the gas back into an offshore field. Stock rise (+), stock fall (-).

(12) Including public gas supply, direct supplies by North Sea producers, third party supplies and stock changes.

(13) Includes losses due to leakage through the local distribution system, theft or the effect of accounting procedures (estimated as roughly 1 per cent of demand). Changes to accounting procedures in 1997 led to a substantial reduction in this element in 1997 which has been maintained in subsequent years. Transfers are the use within the iron and steel industry for use in the manufacture of synthetic coke oven gas.

(14) See paragraph 4.27 for an explanation of the relationship between these "Total UK consumption" figures and "Total demand" shown within the balance tables.

4.4 Natural gas and colliery methane production and consumption 1970 to 2000

	Production		Imports	Exports	Total for consumption			Domestic	
	Town gas *(1)*	Methane *(2)*	Methane *(3)*	Methane	**Total**	Town gas	Methane *(2)*	Town gas	Methane
1970	49,617	121,712	9,759	-	**171,564**	125,933	45,631	85,430	18,376
1971	24,882	201,721	9,730	-	**222,616**	104,245	118,371	73,502	41,675
1972	17,848	291,078	8,968	-	**290,287**	95,834	194,453	64,974	67,172
1973	21,336	317,132	8,587	-	**319,917**	68,286	251,631	46,598	94,515
1974	12,221	382,253	7,122	-	**377,388**	44,840	332,548	30,450	127,339
1975	5,393	397,932	9,818	-	**391,250**	21,013	370,237	14,507	158,141
1976	1,700	421,700	11,254	-	**417,655**	6,535	411,120	4,250	177,279
1977	762	440,544	19,548	-	**436,793**	2,051	434,742	1,290	191,844
1978	615	422,257	55,361	-	**460,297**	938	459,359	557	212,242
1979	674	425,832	95,424	-	**502,382**	1,055	501,327	586	240,465
1980	586	404,760	116,291	-	**508,684**	909	507,775	557	246,766
1981	557	401,742	124,262	-	**512,112**	791	511,321	469	256,379
1982	557	405,815	115,001	-	**518,149**	674	517,475	410	255,118
1983	586	416,454	124,497	-	**528,642**	528	528,114	322	259,661
1984	557	414,314	147,415	-	**544,584**	498	544,086	293	261,507
1985	498	461,851	147,122	-	**581,717**	469	581,248	293	283,517
1986	440	483,040	137,099	-	**588,691**	410	588,281	234	299,929
1987 *(4)*	322	508,126	128,893	-	**614,247**	322	613,925	147	307,578
1988	88	489,133	115,441	-	**594,766**	88	594,678	29	300,515
1989	-	478,931	113,770	-	**580,522**	-	580,522	-	290,557
1990	-	528,843	79,833	-	**597,046**	-	597,046	-	300,410
1991	-	588,822	72,007	-	**641,763**	-	641,763	-	333,963
1992	-	598,761	61,255	620	**640,818**	-	640,818	-	330,101
1993	-	703,971	48,528	6,824	**717,357**	-	717,357	-	340,162
1994	-	751,588	33,053	9,557	**764,667**	-	764,667	-	329,710
1995	-	823,336	19,457	11,232	**808,786**	-	808,786	-	326,010
1996	-	979,019	19,804	15,203	**938,734**	-	938,734	-	375,841
1997	-	998,871	14,062	21,666	**960,243**	-	960,243	-	345,532
1998	-	1,048,859r	10,582	31,604	**1,005,306r**	-	1,005,306r	-	355,895
1999	-	1,152,635r	12,862	84,433	**1,068,793r**	-	1,068,793r	-	358,066
2000	-	1,259,037	26,032	146,342	**1,103,508**	-	1,103,508	-	369,909

(1) In most years production of town gas is less than consumption because of transfers into town gas of north sea and imported methane.
(2) Includes colliery methane.
(3) Before 1977 imports were of liquefied natural gas. These imports continued until the early 1980s.
(4) From 1987 data for industrial use of gas exclude gas used for electricity generation within industry (see paragraph 1.53).

4.4 Natural gas and colliery methane production and consumption 1970 to 2000 (continued)

GWh

Industrial (5)		Electricity generators	Other energy industries (6)		Services (7)		
Town gas	Methane (2)	Methane (2)	Town gas (8)	Methane (2)	Town gas	Methane	
20,691	20,808	1,858	-	1,160	19,812	3,428	1970
12,075	60,431	7,808	-	926	18,669	7,531	1971
13,423	94,662	18,563	-	633	17,438	13,423	1972
9,173	125,552	8,453	-	2,743	12,514	20,369	1973
5,744	143,341	28,967	-	3,094	8,646	29,806	1974
2,579	146,067	25,245	-	3,241	3,898	37,542	1975
791	165,644	19,501	-	3,563	1,231	45,132	1976
352	173,820	15,310	-	7,637	410	46,131	1977
176	176,253	10,006	-	9,952	205	50,906	1978
205	182,232	7,104	-	14,143	264	57,382	1979
147	177,513	4,027	-	19,096	205	60,373	1980
147	168,574	4,174	-	22,320	176	59,874	1981
88	169,717	3,793	-	26,657	176	62,190	1982
59	163,123	2,357	-	30,819	147	72,154	1983
59	170,831	5,317	-	33,193	147	73,238	1984
29	172,941	5,873	-	41,135	147	77,781	1985
29	157,496	2,269	-	43,421	147	85,166	1986
29	164,442	2,415	-	43,743	147	95,746	1987 (4)
-	149,935	2,407	-	44,109	59	97,712	1988
-	159,701	6,210	-	37,850	-	86,204	1989
-	164,595	6,513	-	39,159	-	86,369	1990
-	157,932	6,650	-	41,472	-	101,746	1991
-	147,218	17,969	-	45,660	-	99,871	1992
-	148,522	81,848	-	47,006	-	99,819	1993
-	161,815	117,606	-	54,700	-	100,836	1994
-	162,797	154,393	-	56,565	-	109,020	1995
-	178,221	199,932	-	65,404	-	119,336	1996
-	183,488	250,190	-	67,365	-	113,668	1997
-	194,499r	260,661r	-	76,024r	-	118,227r	1998
-	206,009r	307,911r	-	76,937r	-	119,870r	1999
-	214,394	312,695	-	79,721	-	126,789	2000

(5) Industrial consumption in Tables 4.1 and 4.2 plus use in coke manufacture and blast furnaces and non energy gas use.
(6) Energy industry use in Tables 4.1 and 4.2 less use in coke manufacture and blast furnaces.
(7) Public administration, commercial, agriculture and miscellaneous in Tables 4.1 and 4.2.
(8) Town gas consumption by the energy industries is included with the industrial sector.

Chapter 5
Electricity

Introduction

5.1   This Chapter presents statistics on electricity from generation through to sales. Also shown are data for the capacity of plant, for fuel use and for load factors and efficiencies. This year a map showing the transmission system in Great Britain and the location of the main power stations is also included (page 138).

5.2   The structure of this chapter is largely unchanged this year. Commodity balances for electricity for each of the last three years form the introductory table (Table 5.1). The supply and consumption elements of the electricity balance are presented as 5-year time series in Table 5.2. Table 5.3 separates out the public distribution system for electricity from electricity generated and consumed by autogenerators and uses a commodity balance format. Fuels used to generate electricity in the United Kingdom in each of the last five years are covered in Table 5.4. Table 5.5 shows the relationship between the commodity balance definitions and traditional Digest definitions for electricity so that the most recent data can be linked to the long term trends data presented in Tables 5.11 and 5.12. Table 5.6 shows the relationship between fuels used, generation and supply in each of the latest five years (expanded from the 3 year format given in the previous Digest). As in previous years, tables on plant capacity (Tables 5.7 and 5.8) and on plant loads and efficiency (Table 5.9) have been included, as has a long term trends table on fuel use (Table 5.10). A new table that previously appeared in "The Energy Report" completes the chapter. This table lists individual power stations in operation (Table 5.13).

Structure of the industry

5.3   On 27 March 2001 the structure of the electricity industry changed with the introduction in England and Wales of the New Electricity Trading Arrangements (NETA). The new arrangements are based on bi-lateral trading between generators, suppliers, traders and customers and are designed to be more efficient and provide greater choice for market participants whilst maintaining the operation of a secure and reliable electricity system. The system includes forwards and futures markets, a balancing mechanism to enable the National Grid Company, as systems operator, to balance the system, and a settlement process.

5.4   The previous structure of the electricity industry in Great Britain in 2000 is illustrated in Chart 5.1. This is the structure that was in place at the time of the latest statistics presented in this Chapter. Under that structure, generators and suppliers in England and Wales traded electricity through the Electricity Pool. The Pool was regulated by its members and operated by the National Grid Company which also owns the transmission network. Commercial contracts between generators and suppliers were used to hedge against the uncertainty of future prices in the Pool. Électricité de France (EdF), together with the generation businesses of Scottish Power and Scottish and Southern Energy, were external members of the England and Wales Pool. Each of these had a number of commercially negotiated contracts to sell electricity through the interconnectors to suppliers in England and Wales.

5.5   In addition to their distribution activities the Regional Electricity Companies (RECs) have an obligation to supply electricity to customers in their own areas in competition with other suppliers. In turn they may also supply customers in the competitive market nation-wide.

5.6   A number of the major generators also operate as suppliers in the competitive market. In recent years there has been a move towards vertical integration with some generators acquiring supply businesses, and some REC owners acquiring generation businesses.

5.7   In Scotland, the two main companies, Scottish Power and Scottish and Southern Energy, cover the full range of electricity provision. They operate generation, transmission, distribution and supply businesses. Like the RECs in England and Wales, they retain the obligation to supply customers in their own areas in competition with other suppliers. The entire output of the two nuclear power stations in Scotland, which are owned by British Energy plc, is sold to these two Public Electricity Suppliers (PESs) under long-term contracts. In addition, there are about 25 small independent hydro stations and some independent generators operating fossil-fuelled stations which sell their output to the PESs.

5.8   The electricity supply industry in Northern Ireland is also in private hands. Northern Ireland

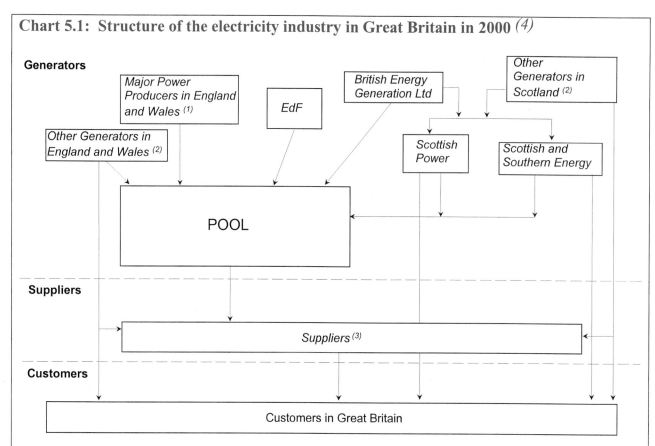

Chart 5.1: Structure of the electricity industry in Great Britain in 2000 [4]

Generators

Major Power Producers in England and Wales [1]

EdF

British Energy Generation Ltd

Other Generators in Scotland [2]

Other Generators in England and Wales [2]

Scottish Power

Scottish and Southern Energy

POOL

Suppliers

Suppliers [3]

Customers

Customers in Great Britain

(1) See paragraph 5.59 for the list of major power producers at the end of 2000.

(2) Generators other than major power producers, some of which, as licence exempt suppliers, meet their own electricity needs and sell electricity directly to other local customers.

(3) Main suppliers in England and Wales are: East Midlands Electricity (part of PowerGen), NORWEB (now owned by TXU Europe), Eastern Electricity (part of TXU Europe), SEEBOARD, London Electricity (part of EdF), SWALEC (owned by Scottish and Southern Energy), MANWEB (part of Scottish Power), SWEB (owned by London Electricity), Midlands Electricity (now Npower, part of Innogy), Southern Electric (part of Scottish and Southern Energy), Yorkshire Electricity (owned by Innogy), Northern Electric.) Often different companies own and operate the distribution network within an authorised area. Distributors are therefore not necessarily the same companies as those listed in note 3. The distribution businesses of SWALEC and SWEB for example are owned by Western Power Distribution while that of Midlands is owned by GPU Distribution.

(4) Note that in 2001 under the New Electricity Trading Arrangements the structure of the electricity industry changed, see paragraph 5.3.

Electricity plc (NIE) (part of the Viridian Group) is responsible for power procurement, transmission, distribution and supply in the Province. Generation is in the hands of three private sector companies who own the four major power stations. There is a link (re-established in 1996) between the Northern Ireland grid and that of the Irish Republic along which electricity is both imported and exported.

5.9 In Great Britain competition in generation and supply has developed as follows:

(a) From 1 April 1990, customers with peak loads of more than 1 MW (about 45 per cent of the non-domestic market) were able to choose their supplier. The Office of Gas and Electricity Markets (OFGEM) estimated that whereas in 1990/91 customers accounting for 43 per cent of the output in the 1 MW market in England and Wales chose to take their supply from a company other than their local REC, by 1999/2000 this had increased to 80 per cent.

(b) From 1 April 1994 customers with peak loads of more than 100 kW were able to choose their supplier. OFGEM estimates that in 1999/2000 customers accounting for 67 per cent of the output in the 100 kW to 1 MW market in England and Wales chose to take their supply from a company other than their local REC.

(c) Between September 1998 and May 1999 the remaining part of the electricity market (i.e. below 100 kW peak load) was opened up to competition. Paragraph 5.10 and Table 5A give more details of the opening up of the domestic gas and electricity markets to competition.

(d) Since vesting, a number of new companies have entered the generation market. In 2000 these companies produced 40 per cent of the electricity generated by major power producers in the United Kingdom.

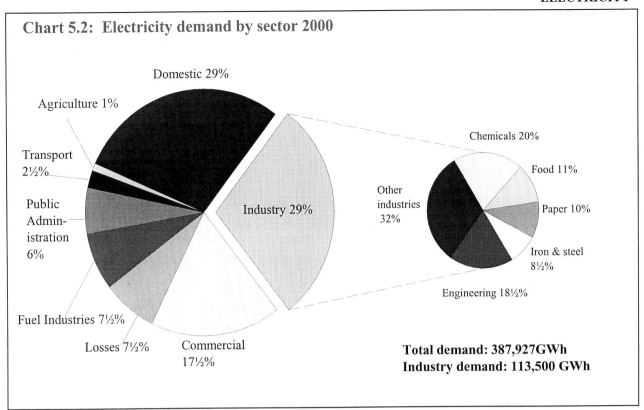

Chart 5.2: Electricity demand by sector 2000

Domestic 29%
Agriculture 1%
Transport 2½%
Public Administration 6%
Fuel Industries 7½%
Losses 7½%
Commercial 17½%
Industry 29%

Chemicals 20%
Food 11%
Paper 10%
Iron & steel 8½%
Engineering 18½%
Other industries 32%

Total demand: 387,927GWh
Industry demand: 113,500 GWh

5.10 By December 2000 just over 5½ million electricity consumers (23½ per cent) were no longer with their home supplier. Table 5A gives market penetration in the fourth quarter of 2000. For quarterly credit customers it is in the markets in North Wales and Merseyside, and the East and West Midlands that new suppliers had the most success. At the end of 2000, the regional electricity companies had lost around 22 per cent of the credit and 30 per cent of the direct debit market compared to 12 per cent of the pre-payment market.

Table 5A: Domestic electricity market penetration (in terms of percentage of customers supplied) by Public Electricity Supply area and payment type, fourth quarter of 2000

Region	Home Supplier			Non-Home Supplier		
	Credit	Direct Debit	Prepay-ment	Credit	Direct Debit	Prepay-Ment
Merseyside and North Wales	67	68	89	33	32	11
East Midlands	72	69	80	28	31	20
West Midlands	75	71	89	25	29	11
North East	76	65	85	24	35	15
Eastern	78	68	85	22	32	15
London	78	71	86	22	29	14
South Wales	78	71	94	22	29	6
North West	79	69	90	21	31	10
South East	79	74	89	21	26	11
South	79	72	92	21	28	8
Yorkshire	79	72	88	21	28	12
South Scotland	80	61	86	20	39	14
South West	85	72	97	15	28	3
North Scotland	87	78	94	13	22	6
Great Britain	78	70	88	22	30	12

Commodity balances for electricity (Table 5.1)

5.11 The first page of this balance table shows that 96½ per cent of UK electricity supply in 2000 was home produced and 3½ per cent was from imports. Of the 372 TWh produced (excluding pumped storage production) 91 per cent was from major power producers and 9 per cent from autoproducers, 24½ per cent was from primary sources and 75½ per cent from secondary sources.

5.12 Electricity generated by each type of fuel is shown on the second page of the commodity balance table. The link between electricity generated and electricity supplied is made in Table 5.6 and electricity supplied by each type of fuel is illustrated in Chart 5.3. Paragraph 5.28 examines further the ways of presenting each fuel's contribution to electricity production.

5.13 Demand for electricity is predominantly from final consumers who accounted for 85 per cent in 2000. The remaining 15 per cent is split 7½ per cent to energy industries' use and 7½ per cent to losses. 55 per cent of the energy industries' use of electricity is by the electricity industry itself, with petroleum refineries being the next most significant consumer. The losses item has three components. Firstly transmissions losses from the high voltage transmission system represented about 19 per cent of the figure in 2000. Secondly distribution losses which occur between the gateways to the public supply system's network and the customers meters accounted for about 75 per cent of losses. Thirdly a small amount was lost through theft or meter fraud (6 per cent) (see also paragraphs 5.75 to 5.76).

5.14 Industrial consumption was 34½ per cent of final consumption in 2000, slightly more than the consumption by households (34 per cent), with transport and the services sector accounting for the remaining 31½ per cent. Within the industrial sector the four largest consuming industries are chemicals, food, paper and iron and steel, which together account for 50 per cent of industrial consumption. The iron and steel sector excludes blast furnace and coke oven uses of electricity which are included under energy industry uses. This is because electricity is used by coke ovens and blast furnaces in the transformation of solid fuels into coke, coke oven gas and blast furnace gas. Taken together the engineering industries accounted for a further 18 per cent. A note on the estimates included within these figures is to be found at paragraph 5.76. Chart 5.2 shows diagrammatically the demand for electricity in 2000.

5.15 The transport sector covers electricity consumed by companies involved in transport, storage and communications. Within the overall total of 8,800 GWh it is known that national railways consume about 2,700 GWh each year for traction purposes, and this figure has been shown separately in the balances.

Supply and consumption of electricity (Table 5.2)

5.16 There was a 1¾ per cent increase in the supply of electricity in 2000. Production (including pumped storage production) also increased by 1¾ per cent because the change in net imports of electricity was very small (less than ½ per cent decrease). The volume of imports from France in both 1999 and 2000, was over 10 per cent lower than the average annual volume recorded in the mid 1990s. Exports of electricity in 2000 fell because of a decrease in the use of the interconnector between the Irish Republic and Northern Ireland.

5.17 Energy industry use of electricity as a proportion of electricity demand (7½ per cent) fell slightly in 2000, while losses as a proportion of total demand were also 7½ per cent, the same as in 1999. Industrial consumption of electricity grew by 2½ per cent in 2000, reflecting a continuing recovery in industrial output, while consumption in the services sector rose by 1¾ per cent. Consumption by transport, storage and communications grew by 3 per cent. Domestic sector sales increased by 1½ per cent in 2000, and were 4 per cent higher than the previous peak for this sector in 1996. The actual level in any one year is influenced by temperatures in the winter

months, as customers adjust heating levels in their homes. On average, temperatures in the winter months were lower in 1996, 1999 and 2000 than in the milder years of 1997 and 1998.

Regional electricity data

5.18 The restructuring of the electricity industry in 1990 and the privatisation of the electricity companies meant that it was no longer possible for this Digest to present regional data on the supply of electricity, as it would disclose information about individual businesses which were in competition with each other. However, distribution, the physical delivery of electricity, is a monopoly activity for each public electricity supplier inside its own geographic area. These areas vary in terms of square kilometres covered, number of customers and electricity distributed within the area as Table 5B shows.

Table 5B: Electricity distributed by public electricity suppliers, 2000[1][2]

	Area (sq. km)	Number of customers (thousand)	Customer density (No per sq. km)	Electricity distributed (GWh)
Eastern	20,300	3,394	167	33,749
South	16,900	2,827	167	31,539
East Midlands	16,000	2,459	154	27,301
Midlands	13,300	2,383	179	26,555
London	665	2,305	3,467	24,267
North West	12,500	2,300	184	24,095
Yorkshire	10,700	2,169	203	23,368
South East	8,200	2,136	261	20,563
South Scotland	22,950	2,075	90	19,407
North East	14,400	1,548	108	16,297
South West	14,400	1,454	101	14,847
Merseyside and North Wales	12,200	1,443	118	17,209
South Wales	11,800	1,053	89	12,535
North Scotland	54,390	830	15	9,064
Northern Ireland	13,506	692	51	7,536
Total	242,211	29,068	120	308,332

1. The figures for the area and number of customers were provided by OFGEM and Northern Ireland Electricity. Number of customers figures are number of meter points. Electricity distributed is taken from returns made to DTI for 2000.
2. The figures for electricity distributed exclude electricity sold directly to customers over high voltage lines.

5.19 The difference between total electricity distributed, shown in this table and total consumption is accounted for by electricity, sold directly to large users by generators via the high voltage grid without passing through the distribution network of the regional companies, electricity consumed by the company generating the electricity (autogeneration plus electricity industry own use), and transmission losses.

Table 5C: Number of sites by sector and size band, 1999, adjusted for double counting of customers changing supplier in mid-year

	Industry	Transport storage and communications	Commercial, agriculture, public lighting, public administration and other services	Domestic	Total
Less than 9 GWh	187,671	24,913	2,197,159	26,555,281	28,965,024
9 GWh but less than 20 GWh	879	58	717	-	1,654
20 GWh but less than 40 GWh	352	35	99	-	486
40 GWh or more	266	25	57	-	347
Total	189,168	25,031	2,198,032	26,555,281	28,967,512

Numbers of consumers and consumption bands

5.20   An estimate of the total number of consumers of electricity in terms of sites supplied is also available from information provided to DTI by the electricity companies. This information can be broken down into broad sectors and into consumption bands as Table 5C shows. The figures in this table relate to 1999 and have been adjusted within DTI to remove the double counting of sites that changed supplier during the year. For these reasons the numbers are not directly comparable with the customer numbers in Table 5B.

Commodity balances for the public distribution system and for other generators (Table 5.3)

5.21   Table 5.3 expands on the commodity balance format to show consumption divided between electricity distributed over the public distribution system and electricity provided by other generators (autogeneration). Autogeneration is the generation of electricity wholly or partly for a company's own use as an activity which supplements the primary activity. In addition the domestic sector is expanded to show consumption by payment type and the commercial sector is expanded to show detailed data beyond that presented in Tables 5.1 and 5.2.

5.22   The proportion of electricity supplied by generators other than major power producers continues to increase, growing from 7¾ per cent in 1998, to 8¼ per cent in 1999, and 8½ per cent in 2000. Over these three years the proportion of this electricity transferred to the public distribution system has increased from 19 per cent to 23½ per cent. Other generators' data has been revised this year in line with improved data from combined heat and power (CHP) schemes (see Chapter 6).

5.23   In 2000, nearly 6 per cent of final consumption of electricity was by other generators and did not pass over the public distribution system. This was the same proportion as in 1999 but half a percentage point up on 1998. A greater proportion of electricity is self generated in the energy industries with the proportion over 20 per cent in all three years shown in the table. At petroleum refineries the proportion is even higher

and in 2000 nearly 70 per cent of electricity was self generated.

5.24   About 14 per cent of the industrial demand for electricity was met by autogeneration. There was also a lesser proportion (about 2½ per cent) from autogeneration within the commercial and transport sectors. Table 1.9 in Chapter 1 shows the fuels used by autogenerators to generate this electricity within each major sector and also the quantities of electricity generated and consumed.

5.25   Within the domestic sector, about a third of the electricity consumed was purchased under some form of off-peak pricing structure (the same as in the previous two years). About 16 per cent of consumption was through prepayment systems showing a slight increasing trend over the three years shown.

Fuel used in generation (Table 5.4)

5.26   In this table fuel used by electricity generators is measured in both original units and for comparative purposes, in the common unit of million tonnes of oil equivalent. In Table 5.6 figures are quoted in a third unit, namely GWh, in order to show the link between fuel use and electricity generated.

5.27   The energy supplied basis defines the primary input (in million tonnes of oil equivalent) needed to produce 1 TWh of hydro, wind, or imported electricity as:

Electricity generated (TWh) × 0.085985 .

The primary input needed to produce 1 TWh of nuclear electricity is similarly

$$\frac{\text{Electricity generated (TWh)} \times 0.085985}{\text{Thermal efficiency of nuclear stations}}$$

In the United Kingdom the thermal efficiency of nuclear stations has risen in stages from 32 per cent in 1982 to 37¼ per cent in 2000 (see Table 5.9 and paragraph 5.66 for the definition)[1]. The factor of

---

[1] *Note that the International Energy Agency uses 0.33 in its calculations, which is the European average thermal efficiency of nuclear stations in 1989, measured in net terms rather than the UK's gross terms.*

0.085985 is the energy content of one TWh divided by the energy content of one million tonnes of oil equivalent (see page 225 and inside back cover flap).

5.28 Figures on fuel use for electricity generation can be compared in two ways. Table 5.4 illustrates one way by using the volumes of **fuel input** to power stations (after conversion of inputs to an oil equivalent basis), but this takes no account of how efficiently that fuel is converted into electricity. The fuel input basis is the most appropriate to use for analysis of the quantities of particular fuels used in electricity generation (eg to determine the amount of coal at risk from displacement by gas or other fuels). A second way uses the amount of electricity generated and supplied by each fuel. This **output** basis is appropriate for comparing how much, and what percentage, of electricity generation comes from a particular fuel. It is the most appropriate method to use to examine the dominance of any fuel, and for diversity issues. Percentage shares based on fuel outputs reduce the contribution of coal and nuclear, and increase the contribution of gas (by about 6 percentage points in 2000) compared with the fuel input basis, because of the higher conversion efficiency of the latter. This output basis is used in Chart 5.3, taking electricity supplied (gross) figures from Table 5.6. Trends in fuel used on this electricity supplied basis are described in the section on Table 5.6, in paragraphs 5.31 to 5.34, below.

5.29 Table 5.10 gives an historical series of fuel used in generation on a consistent, energy supplied, fuel input basis.

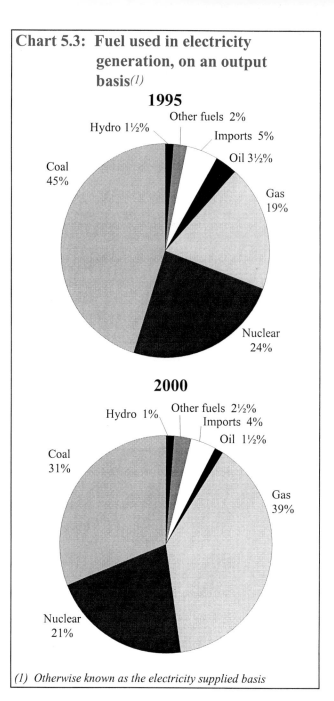

Chart 5.3: Fuel used in electricity generation, on an output basis(1)

(1) Otherwise known as the electricity supplied basis

Relating measurements of supply, consumption and availability (Table 5.5)

5.30 The balance methodology uses terms that cannot be readily employed for earlier years' data because statistics were not available in sufficient detail. Table 5.5 shows the relationship between these terms for the latest five years. For the full definitions of the terms used in the commodity balances see the Annex A, paragraphs A.7 to A.41.

Electricity generated, and supplied (Table 5.6)

5.31 Until 1995 data on electricity generation and supply were collected by type of station. From 1996 onwards data on generation and supply have been collected by fuel, and figures in Table 5.6 are presented on this basis. The table links back to the earlier basis by including figures for generation from conventional steam stations and from combined cycle gas turbine stations.

5.32 Total electricity generated in the United Kingdom in 2000 exceeded generation in 1999 by 1¾ per cent. This rate of growth was about the same as the average rate of growth over the previous four years. Major power producers (as defined in paragraph 5.59) accounted for 91 per cent of electricity generation in 2000. Generation by other generators was 1 per cent higher than a year earlier.

5.33 The mix of plant used to generate the electricity within the UK continued to evolve in capacity terms, but there was a break in the trend of the generation pattern in 2000. Generation from coal fired stations rose by 13 per cent having fallen at an average rate of 9½ per cent per year over the previous 4 years. Generation from gas rose by only 2½ per cent having recorded average growth of 22 per cent a year over the previous four years. This low rate of growth was despite four new CCGT stations (and one second stage) coming on stream during the year. Generation from nuclear sources fell by 10½ per cent having grown at 2 per cent a year over the previous four years. The main cause of this turn around was that increased outages for repairs, maintenance and safety case work reduced nuclear output; coal fired stations were called upon to make up for this. Later in the year rising gas prices meant that coal fired stations were able to outbid some of the gas fired stations to supply the electricity pool.

5.34   Table 5.6 also shows electricity supplied data. These data take into account the fact that some stations use relatively more electricity in the generation process itself. In total, electricity supplied (gross) was 4½ per cent less than the volume generated in 2000, but for nuclear stations it was 8 per cent less while for gas fired stations it was only 2 per cent less. Chart 5.3 shows how shares of the generation market in terms of electricity output have changed over the last five years. Despite the reversals described in paragraph 5.33, gas' share of electricity supplied (net) plus imports has moved up sharply from 19 per cent in 1995 to 39 per cent in 2000, while coal's share has fallen from 45 per cent to 31 per cent. Nuclear's share rose to a peak in 1997 but then fell back, and in 2000 recorded a share of 21 per cent, 3 percentage points lower than in 1995. Oil's share has fallen by 2 percentage points over the five years shown.

Plant capacity (Tables 5.7 and 5.8)

5.35   Table 5.7 shows capacity, i.e. the maximum power available at any one time, for major power producers and other generators by type of plant.

5.36   In 2000 there was an increase of over 2,400 MW (3½ per cent) in the capacity of major power producers. Over 3,200 MW of new CCGT capacity is included in 2000 with new stations coming on stream at Enfield, Saltend, Damhead Creek, and Shoreham and additional capacity at Seabank.   Coal fired capacity fell by 750 MW but this was the combination of the closure of over 1,100 MW of capacity and the opening of the new 350 MW station at Fifoots Point. One nuclear station (470 MW) closed. Nearly 700 MW of oil fired capacity was re-instated.   In December 2000 major power producers accounted for 92 per cent of the total generating capacity, which is a slightly lower proportion than at the end of 1999 because of the 19 per cent increase in the capacity of other generators.   Over 600 MWe of good quality CHP capacity was added during 2000 (see Chapter 6) and 150 MW of renewables capacity (see Chapter 7).

5.37   A breakdown of the capacity of the major power producers' plant at the end of March each year from 1993 to 1996 and at the end of December for 1996 to 2000 is shown in Chart 5.4.

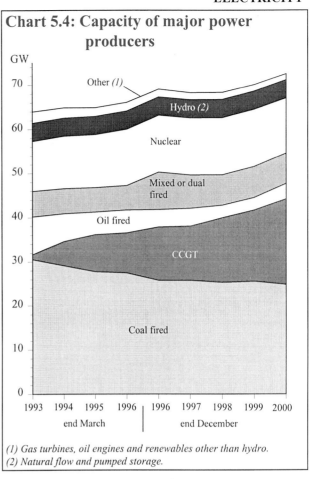

Chart 5.4: Capacity of major power producers

(1) Gas turbines, oil engines and renewables other than hydro.
(2) Natural flow and pumped storage.

5.38   In Table 5.8 data for the generating capacity of industrial, commercial and transport undertakings are shown according to the industrial classification of the generator.   A quarter of the capacity is in the chemicals sector.   Petroleum refineries have 16 per cent of capacity, engineering and other metal trades, and paper, printing and publishing each have a 9 per cent share.

Plant loads, demand and efficiency (Table 5.9)

5.39   Table 5.9 shows the maximum load met each year, load factors (by type of plant and for the system in total) and indicators of thermal efficiency. Maximum demand figures cover the winter period ending the following March.

5.40   Maximum demand during the winter of 2000/2001 occurred in January 2001. This was 1.0 per cent above the previous maximum achieved in December 1999.   Maximum demand in 2000/2001 was only 81 per cent of the capacity of major power producers (Table 5.7) as measured at the end of December 2000, compared with 82½ in 1999/2000 and just under 82½ per cent in 1998/99.

5.41   Plant load factors measure how intensively each type of plant has been used. The recent trend has been conventional thermal plant to be used less intensively and CCGT stations more intensively. However, in 2000 increased maintenance and repair at nuclear stations and at CCGT stations, coupled with high gas prices at the end of the year, led to a departure from this trend. The use of coal-fired stations to make up for the nuclear shortfall and in competition with gas (see paragraph 5.32) is reflected in the increased load factor for conventional thermal stations and the reduced load factors for both CCGTs and nuclear stations. Rainfall in the catchment areas for hydro was not as plentiful as in 1999 and so both hydro and pumped storage were used less in 2000 than in 1999.

5.42 Thermal efficiency measures the efficiency with which the heat energy in fuel is converted into electrical energy. The efficiency of coal fired stations had been on a downward trend as coal became the marginal fuel for generation, but its increased role in 2000 saw an increase in the thermal efficiency of coal fired generation. Although during the start up phase new CCGT stations operate at much lower efficiencies, new CCGT stations have a much smaller influence now that the CCGT stock is already substantial. CCGT efficiency in 2000 reached just under 50 per cent for the first time. The efficiency of nuclear stations rose in 2000 because stations most affected by maintenance and safety case work were the less efficient Magnox stations. The efficiencies presented in this table are calculated using **gross** calorific values to obtain the energy content of the fuel inputs. If **net** calorific values are used efficiencies are higher, for example CCGT efficiencies rise by about 5 percentage points.

Long term trends

Fuel input for electricity generation (Table 5.10)

5.43 This table extends the series shown in Table 5.4 back to 1970. For the period up to 1987, only fuel inputs for electricity generation at stations owned by the major power producers, transport undertakings, and industrial hydro-electric and nuclear power stations are given; data for conventional thermal electricity generated by industrial producers are not available for this period. From 1987 onwards the table covers **all** generating companies.

5.44 The unit of measurement used in this table is the tonne of oil equivalent. An outline of the method used for converting both fossil and non-fossil fuel energy sources to this unit is given in paragraph 5.27, above.

5.45 Trends in fuel input for electricity generation are shown in Chart 5.5.

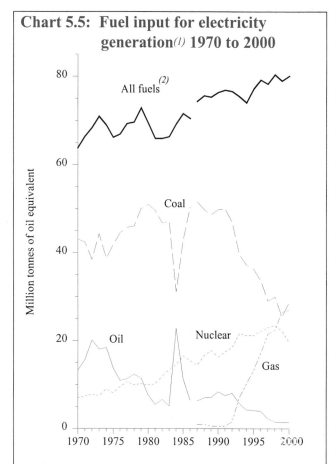

Chart 5.5: Fuel input for electricity generation(1) 1970 to 2000

(1) Prior to 1987 major power producers, transport undertakings and industrial hydro and nuclear stations only.
  From 1987 all generators are covered, hence there is a break in the series for all fuels other than nuclear.
(2) Including hydro, other renewables, coke and other fuels, but excluding electricity imports.

5.46 In 1970, coal provided over two thirds of the fuel input for electricity generation, with oil making up two thirds of the rest. Oil use reached a peak in 1972 when it accounted for 29 per cent of fuel input, but after the oil supply crisis in the following year, its use declined, apart from a temporary increase during the 1984/85 miners' dispute. By 2000, the use of oil for electricity generation had fallen to 2 per cent. Nuclear generation has grown steadily from 11 per cent in 1970 until in 1998 it reached a peak when its oil equivalent input amounted to 29 per cent of total fuel input. Between 1975 and 1990 a European Community directive limited the use of natural gas in public supply power stations. Since 1991 the role of gas in electricity generation has grown rapidly, its share rising from 2 per cent in 1992 to 13½ per cent in 1994, 21½ per cent in 1996, and 28 per cent in 1998. Then in 1999 its share exceeded that of both coal and nuclear and reached 33½ per cent. However in 2000 its share remained at 33½ per cent. Coal still provided a substantial input, but by 1999 its share had fallen to 32 per cent, having been 50 per cent as recently as 5 years earlier, and 65 per cent 10 years earlier. In 2000, because coal was called upon to make up for unavailable nuclear and gas fired stations and as a substitute for high priced gas, its share re-bounded a little to 36 per cent.

Electricity supply, availability and consumption (Table 5.11)

5.47 Figures for the supply, availability and consumption of electricity are given in Table 5.11, This table retains the nomenclature of electricity chapters in the 1999 and earlier Digests, whereas the balance methodology has introduced new nomenclature (see paragraph 5.30, above and Table 5.5). The series are extended back to 1970.

5.48 For the period up to 1986 the data for electricity supplied cover major power producers, transport undertakings and industrial hydro and nuclear stations only. Purchases from other electricity producers are also included, along with net imports, to give electricity available. Losses are deducted from electricity available to give consumption, which is shown by type of consumer. Availability and consumption before 1986 exclude electricity consumed or sold by other generators without passing through the public distribution system.

5.49 The table shows that virtually all electricity available came from home supply until 1986 when the interconnector between France and England commenced operations. In 2000, net imports from France, combined with net imports into Northern Ireland from the Irish Republic over the interconnector re-instated in 1996, amounted to 4 per cent of total electricity available, although this was less than the peak contribution of imports of 5½ per cent in 1994.

5.50 Consumption of electricity by industry accounted of 37 per cent of total consumption in 1970 but despite increased mechanisation which brought about a 57 per cent increase in electricity consumption by industry, this proportion fell to 34 per cent in 2000.

The domestic sector's share of total consumption has fallen from 39 per cent in 1970 to 33 per cent in 2000 despite a 45 per cent increase in electricity consumed. The biggest growth has been in the services sector where in 2000 electricity consumption was nearly 2½ times its level in 1970, and the share of consumption has risen from 21 per cent in 1970 to 31 per cent in 2000.

Electricity generated and supplied (Table 5.12)

5.51 Figures for the generation and supply of electricity are given in Table 5.12. This table retains the nomenclature of electricity chapters in the 1999 Digest and earlier, whereas the balance methodology has introduced new nomenclature (see paragraph 5.30, above and Table 5.5). Data are given for major power producers, for other generators and for all generators in total, with separate series for the different types of power station.

5.52 Over the whole period 1970 to 2000 total gross electricity supplied by all generating companies has increased at an average annual rate of 1½ per cent. However, within these thirty years there was growth at over 2½ per cent a year in the early 1970s, 2 per cent a year in the late 1970s, a decline of 1 per cent a year on average during the early 1980s, 2 per cent growth again in the late 1980s, 1 per cent growth in the early 1990s and most recently growth of 2½ per cent a year on average since 1995.

5.53 In the period between 1970 and 1994 electricity output by generators other than the major producers fluctuated between 11,000 and 18,000 GWh, but moved up to over 20,000 GWh in 1995. Subsequently it has increased every year to reach 31,800 GWh in

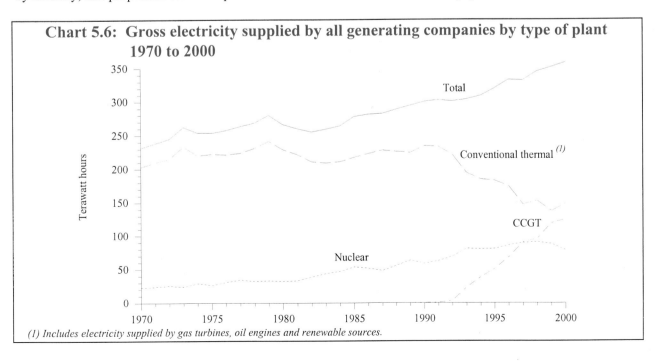

Chart 5.6: Gross electricity supplied by all generating companies by type of plant 1970 to 2000

(1) Includes electricity supplied by gas turbines, oil engines and renewable sources.

2000, mainly as a result of the greater capacity of combined heat and power schemes now in use (see Chapter 6). The contribution of other generators to total supply was under 7 per cent in 1970 and fell to under 5½ per cent in 1990, but it has since increased again to reach 9 per cent in 2000. Trends in electricity supplied by all generators by type of plant are illustrated in Chart 5.6.

5.54 In 1970, conventional thermal power stations produced 88 per cent of the gross electricity supplied. Output from these stations rose, peaking in 1990 before falling back because of the development of new generating technologies. Firstly there was the development of nuclear generation, which supplied only 11 per cent of electricity supplied in 1970 but by 1997 accounted for 27 per cent of the electricity supplied in the United Kingdom. Nuclear sources have since fallen back to a 22 per cent share in 2000. Secondly there was the growth of combined cycle gas turbine stations (CCGTs) which overtook nuclear in 1997 and in 2000 supplied 35 per cent. Despite the small recovery in 2000, gross supply from non-CCGT thermal stations has fallen by 38 per cent from the 1990 peak and by 2000 such stations accounted for 41 per cent of electricity supplied.

The Electricity Supply System in Great Britain in 2000

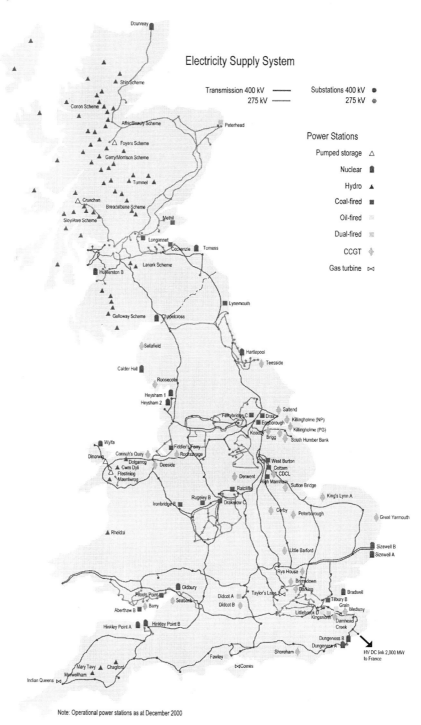

Note: Operational power stations as at December 2000

Technical notes and definitions

5.55 These notes and definitions are in addition to the technical notes and definitions covering all fuels and energy as a whole in Chapter 1, paragraphs 1.46 to 1.81. For notes on the commodity balances and definitions of the terms used in the row headings see the Annex A, paragraphs A.7 to A.41.

Electricity generation from renewable sources

5.56 Figures on electricity generation from renewable energy sources are included in the tables in this section. Further detailed information on the use of renewable energy sources and, in particular, the capacity, fuel use and the amount of electricity generated from such sources are included in Chapter 7.

Combined heat and power

5.57 Electricity generated from combined heat and power (CHP) schemes and CHP generating capacities and fuel used for electricity generation are included in the tables in this chapter. However, more detailed analyses of CHP schemes are set out in Chapter 6.

Generating companies

5.58 Following the restructuring of the electricity supply industry in 1990, the term "Major generating companies" was introduced into the electricity tables to describe the activities of the former nationalised industries and distinguish them from those of autogenerators and new independent companies set up to generate electricity. The activities of the autogenerators and the independent companies were classified under the heading "Other generating companies". In the 1994 Digest a new terminology was adopted to encompass the new independent producers who were then beginning to make a significant contribution to electricity supply. Under this terminology, all companies whose prime purpose is the generation of electricity are included under the heading "Major power producers" (or MPPs). The term "Other generators" ("Autogenerators" in the balance tables) is restricted to companies who produce electricity as part of their manufacturing or other commercial activities, but whose main business is not electricity generation. "Other generators" also covers generation by energy services companies at power stations on an industrial or commercial site where the main purpose is the supply of electricity to that site, even if the energy service company is a subsidiary of a major power producer.

5.59 **Major power producers at the end of 2000 were:-**
AES Electric Ltd, Anglian Power Generation, Barking Power Ltd, BNFL Magnox, British Energy plc,

Coolkeeragh Power Ltd, Corby Power Ltd, Deeside Power, Derwent Co-generation Ltd, Edison Mission Energy Ltd, Enfield Energy Centre, Entergy Power Group Ltd, Fellside Heat and Power Ltd, Fibrogen Ltd, Fibropower Ltd, Fibrothetford Ltd, Fife Power Ltd, Humber Power Ltd, Innogy plc, International Power, plc, Killingholme Power Ltd, Lakeland Power Ltd, Medway Power Ltd, NIGEN, Peterborough Power Ltd, PowerGen plc, Premier Power Ltd, Regional Power Generators Ltd, Rocksavage Power Company Ltd, Sita Tyre Recycling Ltd, Scottish Power plc, Scottish and Southern Energy plc, Seabank Power Ltd, SELCHP Ltd, South Coast Power Ltd, South Western Electricity, Sutton Bridge Power Ltd, Teesside Power Ltd, TXU Europe Power Ltd.

Types of station

5.60 The various types of station identified in the tables of this chapter are as follows:

Conventional steam stations are stations which generate electricity by burning fossil fuels to convert water into steam, which then powers steam turbines.

Nuclear stations are also steam stations but the heat needed to produce the steam comes from nuclear fission.

Gas turbines use pressurised combustion gases from fuel burned in one or more combustion chambers to turn a series of bladed fan wheels and rotate the shaft on which they are mounted. This then drives the generator. The fuel burnt is usually natural gas or gas oil.

Combined cycle gas turbine (CCGT) stations combine in the same plant gas turbines and steam turbines connected to one or more electrical generators. This enables electricity to be produced at higher efficiencies than is otherwise possible when either gas or steam turbines are used in isolation. The gas turbine (usually fuelled by natural gas or oil) produces mechanical power (to drive the generator) and waste heat. The hot exhaust gases (waste heat) are fed to a boiler, where steam is raised at pressure to drive a conventional steam turbine which is also connected to an electrical generator.

Natural flow hydro-electric stations use natural water flows to turn turbines.

Pumped storage hydro-electric stations use electricity to pump water into a high level reservoir. This water is then released to generate electricity at peak times. Where the reservoir is open, some natural flow electricity is also generated by the stations; this is included with natural flow generation. As electricity is used in the pumping process, pumped storage stations are net consumers of electricity.

Other stations include wind turbines and stations burning fuels such as landfill gas, sewage sludge and waste.

Public distribution system

5.61 This comprises the grids in England and Wales, Scotland and Northern Ireland.

Sectors used for sales/consumption

5.62 The various sectors used for sales and consumption analyses are standardised across all chapters of the 2001 Digest. For definitions of the sectors see the Chapter 1 paragraphs 1.77 to 1.81 and Annex A paragraphs A.30 to A.41.

Declared net capability and declared net capacity

5.63 Declared net capability is the maximum power available for export from a power station on a continuous basis minus any power imported by the station from the network to run its own plant. It represents the nominal maximum capability of a generating set to supply electricity to consumers. The registered capacity of a generating set differs from declared net capability in that, for registered capacity, not all power consumed by the plant is subtracted from the normal full load capacity, only the MW consumed by the generating set through its transformer when generating at its normal full load capacity.

5.64 Declared net capacity is used to measure the maximum power available from generating stations that use renewable resources. For wind and tidal power a factor is applied to declared net capability to take account of the intermittent nature of the energy source (eg 0.43 for wind and 0.33 for tidal).

Load factors

5.65 The following definitions are used in Table 5.9:

Maximum load - Twice the largest number of units supplied in any consecutive thirty minutes commencing or terminating at the hour.

Simultaneous maximum load met - The maximum load on the grid at any one time. It is measured by the sum of the maximum load met in England and Wales and the loads met at the same time by companies in other parts of the United Kingdom.

Plant load factor - The average hourly quantity of electricity supplied during the year, expressed as a percentage of the average output capability at the beginning and the end of year.

System load factor - The average hourly quantity of electricity available during the year expressed as a percentage of the maximum demand nearest the end of the year or early the following year.

Thermal efficiency

5.66 Thermal efficiency is the efficiency with which heat energy contained in fuel is converted into electrical energy. It is calculated for fossil fuel burning stations by expressing electricity generated as a percentage of the total energy content of the fuel consumed (based on average gross calorific values). For nuclear stations it is calculated using the quantity of heat released as a result of fission of the nuclear fuel inside the reactor. The efficiency of CHP systems is discussed separately in Chapter 6, paragraph 6.31 and Table 6E. Efficiencies based on gross calorific value of the fuel (sometimes referred to as higher heating values or HHV) are lower than the efficiencies based on net calorific value (or lower heating value LHV). The difference between HHV and LHV is due to the energy associated with the latent heat of the evaporation of water products from the steam cycle which cannot be recovered and put to economic use.

Period covered

5.67 Figures for the major power producers relate to periods of 52 weeks as follows:-

Year	52 weeks ended
1995	31 December 1995
1996	29 December 1996
1997	28 December 1997
	53 weeks ended
1998	3 January 1999
	52 weeks ended
1999	2 January 2000
2000	31 December 2000

Some data provided by electricity supply companies relate to calendar months.

5.68 Figures for industrial and transport undertakings relate to years ended 31 December, except for the iron and steel industry where figures relate to the following 52 week periods:-

Year	52 weeks ended
1995	30 December 1995
1996	28 December 1996
1997	27 December 1997
	53 weeks ended
1998	2 January 1999
	52 weeks ended
1999	1 January 2000
2000	30 December 2000

5.69 Statistical years that contain 53 weeks are adjusted to 52 week equivalents by taking 5/6ths of the 6-week December period values.

Monthly and quarterly data

5.70 Monthly and quarterly data on fuel use, electricity generation and supply and electricity availability and consumption are available on DTI's Energy Statistics web site (www.dti.gov.uk/energy/ energystats/energystats.htm). Monthly data on fuel used in electricity generation by major power producers are given in Table 5.3 and monthly data on supplies by type of plant and type of fuel are given in Table 5.4, while monthly data on availability and consumption of electricity by the main sectors of the economy are given in Table 5.5. A quarterly commodity balance for electricity is published in DTI's quarterly statistical bulletin *Energy Trends* (Table 5.2) along with a quarterly table of fuel use for generation by all generators and electricity supplied by major power producers (Table 5.1). Both these quarterly tables are also available from DTI's Energy Statistics web site. See Annex F for more information about *Energy Trends*.

Data collection

5.71 For Major Power Producers, as defined in paragraph 5.59 the data in these tables are obtained from the results of an annual DTI inquiry sent to each company covering generating capacity, fuel use, generation, sales and distribution of electricity.

5.72 Another annual inquiry is sent to regional electricity companies, to Northern Ireland Electricity and to other licensed suppliers of electricity to establish electricity sales and electricity distributed by these companies.

5.73 Companies that generate electricity mainly for their own use (known as autogenerators or autoproducers - see paragraph 5.58, above) are covered by an annual inquiry commissioned by DTI but carried out by the Office for National Statistics (ONS) from their Newport offices. Where autogenerators operate a combined heat and power (CHP) plant, this survey is now supplemented by information from the CHP Quality Assessment scheme (for autogenerators have registered under the scheme - see Chapter 6 on CHP). The ONS inquiry covers only generators with capacities greater than 250 kWe and DTI estimates fuel use and electricity generation for smaller companies or includes estimates made by

ETSU for CHP electricity, described in Chapter 6. There are two areas of autogeneration that are covered by direct data collection by DTI, mainly because the return contains additional energy information needed by the Department. These are the Iron and Steel industry, and generation on behalf of London Underground.

Losses and statistical differences

5.74 Statistical differences are included in Tables 5.1, 5.2 and 5.3. These arise because data collected on production and supply do not match exactly with data collected on sales or consumption. One of the reasons for this is that some of the data are based on different calendars as described in paragraphs 5.67 and 5.68, above. Sales data based on calendar years will always include more electricity consumption than the slightly shorter statistical year of exactly 52 weeks.

5.75 Of the losses shown in the commodity balance for electricity of 29,600 GWh in 2000, it is estimated that about 5,600 GWh (1½ per cent of electricity available) were lost from the high voltage transmission system of the National Grid and 22,200 GWh (6 per cent) between the grid supply points (the gateways to the public supply system's distribution network) and customers' meters. The balance (less than ½ per cent of electricity available) is accounted for by theft and meter fraud, accounting differences and calendar differences (as described in paragraph 5.74, above).

5.76 Care should be exercised in interpreting the figures for individual industries in the commodity balance tables. As new suppliers have entered the market and companies have moved between suppliers, it has not been possible to ensure consistent classification between and within industry sectors and across years. The breakdown of final consumption includes some estimated data. For about 6 per cent of consumption of electricity supplied by the public distribution system the sector figures are partially estimated.

Contact: *Mike Janes (Statistician)*
mike.janes@dti.gsi.gov.uk
020-7215 5186

Joe Ewins
joe ewins@dti.gsi.gov.uk
020-7215 5190

5.1 Commodity balances 1998 to 2000

Electricity

	1998	1999	GWh 2000
Total electricity			
Supply			
Production	361,096r	365,462r	372,206
Other sources *(1)*	1,624	2,902	2,694
Imports	12,599r	14,507	14,308
Exports	-131r	-263	-134
Marine bunkers	-	-	-
Stock change *(2)*	-	-	-
Transfers	-	-	-
Total supply	**375,188r**	**382,608r**	**389,074**
Statistical difference *(3)*	**+1,715r**	**+1,491r**	**+1,148**
Total demand	**373,473r**	**381,117r**	**387,926**
Transformation	**-**	**-**	**-**
Electricity generation	-	-	-
Major power producers	-	-	-
Autogenerators	-	-	-
Petroleum refineries	-	-	-
Coke manufacture	-	-	-
Blast furnaces	-	-	-
Patent fuel manufacture	-	-	-
Other	-	-	-
Energy industry use	**29,633r**	**30,049r**	**29,359**
Electricity generation	17,362r	16,693r	16,260
Oil and gas extraction	537	408	527
Petroleum refineries	5,141r	4,986r	5,063
Coal extraction	-	-	-
Coke manufacture	1,334r	1,358	1,289
Blast furnaces	948r	948	900
Patent fuel manufacture	-	-	-
Pumped storage	2,594	3,774	3,499
Other	1,717r	1,882r	1,821
Losses	**27,957r**	**28,298**	**29,648**
Final consumption	**315,883r**	**322,770r**	**328,919**
Industry	**107,237r**	**110,856r**	**113,500**
Unclassified	-	-	-
Iron and steel	9,572r	9,779r	9,870
Non-ferrous metals	5,698	5,895	5,910
Mineral products	7,142r	7,265r	7,408
Chemicals	20,983r	21,348r	22,811
Mechanical engineering etc	8,514r	8,807r	9,077
Electrical engineering etc	5,996	6,006	6,109
Vehicles	5,586r	5,616	5,684
Food, beverages etc	11,888r	12,617r	12,451
Textiles, leather, etc	3,666	3,751	3,909
Paper, printing etc	10,733r	11,068r	11,286
Other industries	15,925r	17,176r	17,399
Construction	1,534r	1,528r	1,586
Transport	**8,469r**	**8,558r**	**8,816**
Air	-	-	-
Rail *(4)*	2,700	2,700	2,700
Road	-	-	-
National navigation	-	-	-
Pipelines	-	-	-
Other	**200,177r**	**203,356r**	**206,603**
Domestic	109,410r	110,308r	111,842
Public administration	21,943r	22,463r	22,659
Commercial	64,952r	66,748r	68,321
Agriculture	3,872	3,837	3,781
Miscellaneous	-	-	-
Non energy use	**-**	**-**	**-**

5.1 Commodity balances 1998 to 2000 (continued)

Electricity

GWh

	1998	1999	2000
Electricity production			
Total production *(5)*	**361,096r**	**365,462r**	**372,206**
Primary electricity			
Major power producers	**103,723r**	**99,564r**	**89,394**
Nuclear	99,486r	95,133r	85,063
Large scale hydro *(5)*	4,237r	4,431r	4,331
Small scale hydro	-	-	-
Wind	-	-	-
Autogenerators	**1,757**	**1,781r**	**1,726**
Nuclear	-	-	-
Large scale hydro	674	698	540
Small scale hydro	206	232	239
Wind	877	851r	947
Secondary electricity			
Major power producers	**228,355r**	**234,020r**	**249,697**
Coal	118,595	102,074r	117,025
Oil	3,442r	2,943r	2,414
Gas	105,804r	128,365r	129,558
Renewables	514r	638r	700
Other	-	-	-
Autogenerators	**27,261r**	**30,097r**	**31,389**
Coal	4,358r	4,038r	2,935
Oil	2,918r	2,742r	3,183
Gas	12,054r	14,687r	17,249
Renewables	2,592	3,341	3,658
Other	5,339r	5,289r	4,364
Primary and secondary production *(6)*			
Nuclear	99,486r	95,133r	85,063
Hydro	5,117r	5,361r	5,110
Wind	877	851r	947
Coal	122,953r	106,112r	119,960
Oil	6,360r	5,685r	5,597
Gas	117,858r	143,052r	146,807
Other renewables	3,106r	3,979r	4,358
Other	5,339r	5,289r	4,364
Total production	**361,096r**	**365,462r**	**372,206**

(1) Pumped storage production.

(2) Stock fall (+), stock rise (-).

(3) Total supply minus total demand.

(4) See paragraph 5.15.

(5) Excludes pumped storage production.

(6) These figures are the same as the electricity generated figures in Table 5.6 except that they exclude pumped storage production. Table 5.6 shows that electricity used on works is deducted to obtain electricity supplied. It is electricity supplied that is used to produce Chart 5.3 showing each fuel's share of electricity output (see paragraph 5.28).

5.2 Electricity supply and consumption

GWh

	1996	1997	1998	1999	2000
Supply					
Production	348,991	346,965	361,096r	365,462r	372,206
Other sources *(1)*	1,556	1,486	1,624	2,902	2,694
Imports	16,792	16,615	12,599r	14,507	14,308
Exports	-37	-41	-131	-263	-134
Total supply	**367,302**	**365,025**	**375,188r**	**382,608r**	**389,074**
Statistical difference *(2)*	+3,794	-1,721	+1,715r	+1,491r	+1,148
Total demand	**365,508**	**366,746**	**373,473r**	**381,117r**	**387,926**
Transformation	-	-	-	-	-
Energy industry use	**30,185**	**28,519**	**29,633r**	**30,049r**	**29,359**
Electricity generation	17,704	16,503	17,362r	16,693r	16,260
Oil and gas extraction	772	674	537	408	527
Petroleum refineries	5,237	5,284	5,141r	4,986r	5,063
Coal and coke	1,793	1,528	1,334r	1,358	1,289
Blast furnaces	864	904	948r	948	900
Pumped storage	2,430	2,477	2,594	3,774	3,499
Other	1,385	1,149	1,717r	1,882r	1,821
Losses	**27,501**	**28,670**	**27,957r**	**28,298**	**29,648**
Final consumption	**305,822**	**309,557**	**315,883r**	**322,770r**	**328,919**
Industry	**103,115**	**104,914**	**107,237r**	**110,856r**	**113,500**
Unclassified	-	-	-	-	-
Iron and steel	10,214	9,649	9,572r	9,779r	9,870
Non-ferrous metals	5,581	5,261	5,698	5,895	5,910
Mineral products	7,292	7,097	7,142r	7,265r	7,408
Chemicals	19,329	19,384	20,983r	21,348r	22,811
Mechanical engineering etc	7,804	8,333	8,514r	8,807r	9,077
Electrical engineering etc	5,574	6,113	5,996	6,006	6,109
Vehicles	6,549	5,642	5,586r	5,616	5,684
Food, beverages etc	11,276	11,568	11,888r	12,617r	12,451
Textiles, leather, etc	3,151	3,736	3,666	3,751	3,909
Paper, printing etc	9,516	10,781	10,733r	11,068r	11,286
Other industries	14,985	15,803	15,925r	17,176r	17,399
Construction	1,844	1,547	1,534r	1,528r	1,586
Transport	**8,118**	**8,406**	**8,469r**	**8,558r**	**8,816**
Other	**194,589**	**196,237**	**200,177r**	**203,356r**	**206,603**
Domestic	107,513	104,455	109,410r	110,308r	111,842
Public administration	22,939	21,688	21,943r	22,463r	22,659
Commercial	60,315	66,286	64,952r	66,748r	68,321
Agriculture	3,822	3,808	3,872	3,837	3,781
Miscellaneous	-	-	-	-	-
Non energy use	-	-	-	-	-

(1) Pumped storage production.
(2) Total supply minus total demand.

5.3 Commodity balances 1998 to 2000

Public distribution system and other generators

GWh

	1998			1999			2000		
	Public distribution system	Other generators	Total	Public distribution system	Other generators	Total	Public distribution system	Other generators	Total
Supply									
Major power producers	332,078r	-	332,078r	333,584r	-	333,584r	339,091	-	339,091
Other generators	-	29,018r	29,018r	-	31,878r	31,878r	-	33,115	33,115
Other sources (1)	1,624	-	1,624	2,902	-	2,902	2,694	-	2,694
Imports	12,599r	-	12,599r	14,507	-	14,507	14,308	-	14,308
Exports	-131r	-	-131	-263	-	-263	-134	-	-134
Transfers	+5,566r	-5,566r	-	+6,440r	-6,440r	-	+7,812	-7,812	-
Total supply	**351,736r**	**23,452r**	**375,188r**	**357,170r**	**25,438r**	**382,608r**	**363,771**	**25,303**	**389,074**
Statistical difference (2)	+1,726r	-11r	+1,715r	+1,505r	-14r	+1,491r	+1,164	-16	+1,148
Total demand	**350,010r**	**23,463r**	**373,473r**	**355,665r**	**25,452r**	**381,117r**	**362,607**	**25,319**	**387,926**
Transformation	-	-	-	-	-	-	-	-	-
Energy industry use	**23,195r**	**6,438r**	**29,633r**	**23,215r**	**6,834r**	**30,049r**	**23,162**	**6,197**	**29,359**
Electricity generation	16,078r	1,284r	17,362r	15,338r	1,355r	16,693r	14,954	1,306	16,260
Oil and gas extraction	537	-	537	408	-	408	527	-	527
Petroleum refineries	1,646	3,495r	5,141r	1,214	3,772r	4,986r	1,665	3,398	5,063
Coke manufacture	1,150	184r	1,334r	1,174	184	1,358	1,097	192	1,289
Blast furnaces	-	948r	948r	-	948	948	-	900	900
Pumped storage	2,594	-	2,594	3,774	-	3,774	3,499	-	3,499
Other fuel industries	1,190	527r	1,717r	1,307	575r	1,882r	1,420	401	1,821
Losses	**27,854**	**103r**	**27,957r**	**28,195**	**103**	**28,298**	**29,568**	**80**	**29,648**
Final consumption	**298,961r**	**16,922r**	**315,883r**	**304,255r**	**18,515r**	**322,770r**	**309,877**	**19,042**	**328,919**
Industry	**92,941**	**14,296r**	**107,237r**	**95,121r**	**15,735r**	**110,856r**	**97,236**	**16,264**	**113,500**
Iron and steel	8,282	1,290r	9,572r	8,486	1,293r	9,779r	8,538	1,332	9,870
Non-ferrous metals	3,718	1,980	5,698	3,767	2,128	5,895	4,122	1,788	5,910
Mineral products	6,996	146r	7,142r	7,159	106r	7,265r	7,176	232	7,408
Chemicals	14,514	6,469r	20,983r	14,874	6,474r	21,348r	14,959	7,852	22,811
Mechanical engineering etc	8,479	35r	8,514r	8,772	35r	8,807r	9,006	71	9,077
Electrical engineering etc	5,994	2	5,996	5,992	14	6,006	6,086	23	6,109
Vehicles	5,487	99r	5,586r	5,512	104	5,616	5,668	16	5,684
Food, beverages etc	10,652	1,236r	11,888r	10,519	2,098r	12,617r	10,934	1,517	12,451
Textiles, leather, etc	3,653	13	3,666	3,749	2	3,751	3,907	2	3,909
Paper, printing etc	8,230	2,503r	10,733r	8,215	2,853r	11,068r	8,359	2,927	11,286
Other industries	15,422	503r	15,925r	16,568	608r	17,176r	16,910	489	17,399
Construction	1,514	20r	1,534r	1,508	20	1,528r	1,571	15	1,586
Transport	**6,790**	**1,679r**	**8,469r**	**6,862**	**1,696r**	**8,558r**	**7,142**	**1,674**	**8,816**
Of which National Rail (3)	2,700	-	2,700	2,700	-	2,700	2,700	-	2,700
Other	**199,230r**	**947r**	**200,177r**	**202,272r**	**1,084r**	**203,356r**	**205,499**	**1,104**	**206,603**
Domestic	109,410r	-	109,410r	110,308r	-	110,308r	111,842	-	111,842
Standard	60,541r	-	60,541r	60,708r	-	60,708r	61,543	-	61,543
Economy 7 and other off-peak	32,570	-	32,570	32,445r	-	32,445r	32,880	-	32,880
Prepayment (standard)	11,314	-	11,314	11,779	-	11,779	12,109	-	12,109
Prepayment (off-peak)	4,447	-	4,447	4,860r	-	4,860r	5,007	-	5,007
Sales under any other arrangement	538	-	538	516r	-	516r	303	-	303
Public administration	20,998r	945r	21,943r	21,381r	1,082r	22,463r	21,557	1,102	22,659
Public lighting (4)	2,182	-	2,182	2,162r	-	2,162r	1,986	-	1,986
Other public sector	18,816r	945r	19,761r	19,219r	1,082r	20,301r	19,571	1,102	20,673
Commercial	64,952r	-	64,952r	66,748r	-	66,748r	68,321	-	68,321
Shops	29,612	-	29,612	30,826r	-	30,826r	31,906	-	31,906
Offices	18,451	-	18,451	18,720	-	18,720	19,111	-	19,111
Hotels	7,361r	-	7,361r	7,623	-	7,623	8,000	-	8,000
Combined domestic/ commercial premises	1,669	-	1,669	1,671	-	1,671	1,711	-	1,711
Post and telecommunications	5,049	-	5,049	5,184r	-	5,184r	5,393	-	5,393
Unclassified	2,810r	-	2,810r	2,724r	-	2,724r	2,200	-	2,200
Agriculture	3,870	2	3,872	3,835	2	3,837	3,779	2	3,781

(1) Pumped storage production.
(2) Total supply minus total demand.
(3) See paragraph 5.15.
(4) Sales for public lighting purposes are increasingly covered by wider contracts that cannot distinguish the public lighting element.

5.4   Fuel used in generation[1]

	Unit	1996	1997	1998	1999	2000
		Original units of measurement				
Major power producers (2)						
Coal	M tonnes	53.42	45.34	46.63	39.58r	44.76
Oil (3)	"	3.18	1.38	0.82r	0.79	0.75
Gas	GWh	176,702	223,691	236,300r	281,988r	283,784
Other generators (2)						
Transport undertakings:						
Gas	GWh	2,722	2,595	2,555	2,496	2,194
Undertakings in industrial and commercial sectors:						
Coal (4)	M tonnes	2.03	1.93	1.93r	1.51r	1.40
Oil (5)	"	0.90	0.85	0.58r	0.61r	0.56
Gas (6)	GWh	20,508	23,904	21,806r	23,427r	26.717
		Million tonnes of oil equivalent				
Major power producers (2)						
Coal		32.400	27.713	28.722r	24.506r	27.765
Oil (3)		3.018	1.377	0.845r	0.817	0.772
Gas		15.194	19.233	20.318r	24.247r	24.401
Nuclear		22.180	22.993	23.443r	22.216r	19.635
Hydro (natural flow) (7)		0.241r	0.287	0.364r	0.381r	0.372
Other renewables (7)		0.131	0.139	0.201r	0.219r	0.219
Net imports		1.441	1.425	1.072r	1.225	1.219
Total major power producers (2)		**74.605r**	**73.167**	**74.965r**	**73.611r**	**74.383**
Of which: conventional thermal and other stations (9)		38.112	31.874	32.775r	28.622r	32.775
combined cycle gas turbine stations		12.496	16.536	17.311	21.167	20.382
Other generators (2)						
Transport undertakings:						
Gas		0.234	0.223	0.220	0.215	0.189
Undertakings in industrial and commercial sectors:						
Coal (4)		1.230	1.318	1.174r	0.926r	0.861
Oil (5)		0.980	0.923	0.659r	0.665r	0.644
Gas (6)		1.763	2.055	1.875r	2.014r	2.297
Hydro (natural flow) (7)		0.051r	0.072	0.076	0.080	0.067
Other renewables (7)		0.735	0.901	1.096r	1.288r	1.574
Other fuels (8)		1.032	1.026	1.471r	1.421r	1.270
Total other generators (2)		**6.025r**	**6.518**	**6.571r**	**6.609r**	**6.902**
All generating companies						
Coal (4)		33.630	29.031	29.896r	25.432r	28.626
Oil (3)(5)		3.998	2.300	1.504r	1.482r	1.416
Gas (6)		17.191	21.511	22.413r	26.476r	26.887
Nuclear		22.180	22.993	23.443r	22.216r	19.635
Hydro (natural flow) (7)		0.292r	0.359	0.440r	0.461r	0.439
Other renewables (7)		0.866	1.040	1.297r	1.507r	1.793
Other fuels (8)		1.032	1.026	1.471r	1.421r	1.270
Net imports		1.441	1.425	1.072r	1.225	1.219
Total all generating companies		**80.630r**	**79.685**	**81.536r**	**80.220r**	**81.285**

(1) For details of where to find monthly updates of fuel used in electricity generation by major power producers and quarterly updates of fuel used in electricity generation by all generating companies see paragraph 5.70.
(2) See paragraphs 5.58 and 5.59 for information on companies covered.
(3) Includes Orimulsion, oil used in gas turbine and diesel plant, and oil used for lighting up coal fired boilers.
(4) Includes coke oven coke
(5) Includes refinery gas.
(6) Includes colliery methane.
(7) Renewable sources which are included under hydro and other renewables in this table are shown separately in Table 7.6 of Chapter 7.
(8) Main fuels included are coke oven gas, blast furnace gas, and waste products from chemical processes.
(9) Includes gas turbines and oil engines and plants producing electricity from renewable sources other than hydro.

5.5 Electricity supply, electricity supplied (net), electricity available and electricity consumption

					GWh
	1996	1997	1998	1999	2000
Total supply					
(as given in Tables 5.1 and 5.2)	367,302	365,025	375,188r	382,608r	389,074
less imports of electricity	-16,792	-16,615	-12,599r	-14,507	-14,308
plus exports of electricity	+37	+41	+131r	+263	+134
less electricity used in pumped storage	-2,430	-2,477	-2,594	-3,774	-3,499
less electricity used on works	-17,704	-16,503	-17,362r	-16,693r	-16,260
Equals					
Electricity supplied (net)	330,413	329,471	342,764r	347,897r	355,141
(as given in Tables, 5.6, 5.11 and 5.12)					
Total supply					
(as given in Tables 5.1 and 5.2)	367,302	365,025	375,188r	382,608r	389,074
less electricity used in pumped storage	-2,430	-2,477	-2,594	-3,774	-3,499
less electricity used on works	-17,704	-16,503	-17,362r	-16,693r	-16,260
equals					
Electricity available	347,168	346,045	355,232r	362,141r	369,315
(as given in Tables 5.11)					
Final consumption					
(as given in Tables 5.2 and 5.3)	305,822	309,557	315,883r	322,770r	328,919
plus Iron and steel consumption counted as Energy industry use	+1,202	+1,245	+1,266	+1,272	+1,174
equals					
Final users	307,024	310,802	317,149r	324,042r	330,093
(as given in Tables 5.11)					

5.6 Electricity fuel use, generation and supply

| | Thermal sources | | | | | | | Non-thermal sources | | | Total |
	Coal	Oil	Gas	Nuclear	Renew -ables (1)	Other (3)	Total	Hydro- natural flow	Hydro- pumped storage	Other (4)	All sources
1996											
Major power producers *(2)*											
Fuel used	376,812	35,099	176,702	257,953	1,524	-	848,090	2,801	1,556	-	852,447
Generation	141,943	11,132	75,301	94,671	439	-	323,486	2,801	1,556	-	327,843
Used on works	5,949	800	937	8,851	50	-	16,587	38	49	-	16,674
Supplied (gross)	135,994	10,332	74,364	85,820	389	-	306,899	2,763	1,507	-	311,169
Used in pumping											2,430
Supplied (net)											308,739
Other generators *(2)*											
Fuel used	14,305	11,397	23,230	-	8,060	12,002	68,994	592	-	488	70,074
Generation	4,913	2,545	7,658	-	1,781	4,727	21,623	592	-	488	22,703
Used on works	249	188	259	-	125	201	1,022	7	-	-	1,029
Supplied	4,664	2,357	7,399	-	1,656	4,526	20,601	585	-	488	21,674
All generating companies											
Fuel used	391,117	46,496	199,932	257,953	9,584	12,002	917,084	3,393	1,556	488	922,521
Generation	146,856	13,677	82,959	94,671	2,221	4,727	345,110	3,393	1,556	488	350,547
Used on works	6,198	988	1,196	8,851	175	201	17,610	45	49	-	17,704
Supplied (gross)	140,658	12,689	81,763	85,820	2,045	4,526	327,500	3,348	1,507	488	332,843
Used in pumping											2,430
Supplied (net)											330,413
1997											
Major power producers *(2)*											
Fuel used	322,302	16,015	223,691	267,428	1,617	-	831,053	3,337	1,486	-	835,876
Generation	114,968	5,267	100,330	98,146	439	-	319,150	3,337	1,486	-	323,973
Used on works	4,909	378	1,177	8,805	50	-	15,319	38	47	-	15,404
Supplied (gross)	110,059r	4,889	99,153	89,341	389	-	303,831	3,299	1,439	-	308,569
Used in pumping											2,477
Supplied (net)											306,092
Other generators *(2)*											
Fuel used	15,328	10,734	26,499	-	9,816	11,937	74,314	832	-	667	75,813
Generation	4,659	2,587	9,185	-	2,153	4,395	22,979	832	-	667	24,478
Used on works	237	191	306	-	153	203	1,090	9	-	-	1,099
Supplied	4,422r	2,396	8,879	-	2,000	4,192	21,889	823	-	667	23,379
All generating companies											
Fuel used	337,630	26,749	250,190	267,428	11,433	11,937	905,367	4,169	1,486	667	911,689
Generation	119,627	7,854	109,515	98,146	2,592	4,395	342,129	4,169	1,486	667	348,451
Used on works	5,146	569	1,483	8,805	203	203	16,409	47	47	-	16,503
Supplied (gross)	114,481	7,285	108,032	89,341	2,389	4,192	325,720	4,122	1,439	667	331,948
Used in pumping											2,477
Supplied (net)											329,471
1998											
Major power producers *(2)*											
Fuel used	334,037r	9,827r	236,298r	272,642r	2,338r	-	855,142r	4,237r	1,624	-	861,003r
Generation	118,595	3,442r	105,804r	99,486r	514r	-	327,841r	4,237r	1,624	-	333,702r
Used on works	5,701r	231	1,116r	8,896r	67r	-	16,011r	12r	55	-	16,078r
Supplied (gross)	112,894r	3,211r	104,688	90,590r	447r	-	311,830r	4,225r	1,569	-	317,624r
Used in pumping											2,594
Supplied (net)											315,030r
Other generators *(2)*											
Fuel used	13,659r	7,664r	24,362r	-	11,868r	17,113r	74,666r	880	-	877	76,423r
Generation	4,358r	2,918r	12,054r	-	2,592	5,339r	27,261r	880	-	877	29,018r
Used on works	234r	208r	394r	-	191	246r	1,273r	11r	-	-	1,284r
Supplied	4,124r	2,710r	11,660r	-	2,401	5,093r	25,988r	869r	-	877	27,734r
All generating companies											
Fuel used	347,696r	17,491r	260,660r	272,642r	14,206r	17,113r	929,808r	5,117r	1,624	877	937,426r
Generation	122,953r	6,360r	117,858r	99,486r	3,106r	5,339r	355,102r	5,117r	1,624	877	362,720r
Used on works	5,935r	439r	1,510r	8,896r	258r	246r	17,284r	23r	55	-	17,362r
Supplied (gross)	117,018r	5,921r	116,348r	90,590r	2,848r	5,093r	337,818r	5,094r	1,569	877	345,358r
Used in pumping											2,594
Supplied (net)											342,764r

5.6 Electricity fuel use, generation and supply (continued)

GWh

	Thermal sources							Non-thermal sources			Total
	Coal	Oil	Gas	Nuclear	Renew-ables (1)	Other (3)	Total	Hydro-natural flow	Hydro-pumped storage	Other (4)	All sources
1999											
Major power producers (2)											
Fuel used	285,005r	9,502r	281,986r	258,372r	2,547r	-	837,412r	4,431r	2,902	-	844,744r
Generation	102,074r	2,943r	128,365r	95,133r	638r	-	329,153r	4,431r	2,902	-	336,486r
Used on works	4,725r	210r	2,759r	7,461r	64r	-	15,219r	21r	98	-	15,338r
Supplied (gross)	97,349r	2,733r	125,606	87,672	574	-	313,934r	4,410r	2,804	-	321,148r
Used in pumping											3,774
Supplied (net)											317,374r
Other generators (2)											
Fuel used	10,772r	7,731r	25,923r	-	14,127r	16,530r	75,083r	930	-	851r	76,864r
Generation	4,038r	2,742r	14,687r	-	3,341	5,289r	30,097r	930	-	851r	31,878r
Used on works	194r	203r	475r	-	227r	243r	1,342r	13	-	-	1,355r
Supplied	3,844r	2,539r	14,212r	-	3,114r	5,046r	28,755r	917	-	851r	30,523
All generating companies											
Fuel used	295,777r	17,233r	307,909r	258,372r	16,674r	16,530r	912,495r	5,361r	2,902	851r	921,608r
Generation	106,112r	5,685r	143,052r	95,133r	3,979r	5,289r	359,250r	5,361r	2,902	851r	368,364r
Used on works	4,919r	413r	3,234r	7,461r	291r	243r	16,561	34r	98	-	16,693r
Supplied (gross)	101,193r	5,272r	139,818r	87,672	3,688r	5,046r	342,689r	5,327r	2,804	851r	351,671r
Used in pumping											3,774
Supplied (net)											347,897r
2000											
Major power producers (2)											
Fuel used	322,907	8,978	283,781	228,355	2,547	-	846,568	4,331	2,694	-	853,593
Generation	117,025	2,414	129,558	85,063	700	-	334,760	4,331	2,694	-	341,785
Used on works	5,175	291	2,592	6,729	60	-	14,847	15	91	-	14,953
Supplied (gross)	111,850	2,123	126,966	78,334	640	-	319,913	4,316	2,603	-	326,832
Used in pumping											3,499
Supplied (net)											323,333
Other generators (2)											
Fuel used	10,018	7,485	28,911	-	17,353	14,775	78,542	779	-	947	80,268
Generation	2,935	3,183	17,249	-	3,658	4,364	31,389	779	-	947	33,115
Used on works	141	236	552	-	164	201	1,294	13	-	-	1,307
Supplied	2,794	2,947	16,697	-	3,494	4,163	30,095	766	-	947	31,808
All generating companies											
Fuel used	332,925	16,463	312,692	228,355	19,900	14,775	925,110	5,110	2,694	947	933,861
Generation	119,960	5,597	146,807	85,063	4,358	4,364	366,149	5,110	2,694	947	374,900
Used on works	5,316	527	3,144	6,729	224	201	16,141	28	91	-	16,260
Supplied (gross)	114,644	5,070	143,663	78,334	4,134	4,163	350,008	5,082	2,603	947	358,640
Used in pumping											3,499
Supplied (net)											355,141

	1996		1997		1998		1999		2000	
	Conv-entional thermal (5)	CCGT	Conv-entional thermal (5)	CCGT	Conv-entional thermal (5)	CCGT	Conv-entional thermal (5)	CCGT	Conv-entional thermal (5)	CCGT
Major power producers (2)										
Generated	160,565	65,880	133,132	86,974	134,314	93,832	118,762	114,620	130,515	117,965
Supplied (gross)	155,475	65,604	127,808	86,682	128,235	93,005	113,494	112,768	125,469	116,110
Other generators										
Generated	20,879	1,232	22,146	1,500	25,290	2,848	24,415	6,533	23,643	8,693
Supplied (gross)	19,909	1,180	21,131	1,425	24,159	2,706	23,399	6,207	22,618	8,424
All generating companies										
Generated	181,444	67,112	155,278	88,474	159,604	96,680	143,177	121,153	154,158	126,658
Supplied (gross)	175,384	66,784	148,939	88,107	152,394	95,711	136,893	118,975	148,087	124,534

(1) Thermal renewable sources are those included under biofuels in Chapter 7.
(2) See paragraphs 5.58 and 5.59 on companies covered.
(3) Other thermal sources include coke oven gas, blast furnace gas, and waste products from chemical processes.
(4) Other non-thermal sources include wind, and solar photovoltaics.
(5) Includes gas turbines and oil engines and plants producing electricity from renewable sources other than hydro.

5.7 Plant capacity

MW

	end-Dec 1996	end-Dec 1997	end-Dec 1998	end-Dec 1999	end-Dec 2000
Major power producers (1)					
Total declared net capability	**69,090**	**68,288**	**68,390**	**70,057r**	**72,531**
Of which:					
Conventional steam stations:	38,230	37,395	35,081	35,427	35,221
Coal fired	25,796	25,796	25,324	25,581	24,835
Oil fired	3,989	4,069	2,829	2,829	3,514
Mixed or dual fired (2)	8,445	7,530	6,928	7,017	6,872
Combined cycle gas turbine stations	12,052	12,252	14,638	16,110r	19,349
Nuclear stations	12,916	12,946	12,956	12,956	12,486
Gas turbines and oil engines	1,721	1,526	1,492	1,333	1,243
Hydro-electric stations:					
Natural flow	1,313	1,311	1,327	1,327	1,327
Pumped storage	2,788	2,788	2,788	2,788	2,788
Renewables other than hydro	70	70	108	117	117
Other generators (1)					
Total capacity of own generating plant	**4,181**	**4,577r**	**4,943r**	**5,349r**	**6,360**
Of which:					
Conventional steam stations (3)	3,192	3,485r	3,496r	3,571r	3,616
Combined cycle gas turbine stations	410	464r	710r	948r	1,742
Hydro-electric stations (natural flow)	142	145	148	150	158
Renewables other than hydro	437	483r	589	680r	844
All generating companies					
Total capacity	**73,271**	**72,865r**	**73,333r**	**75,406r**	**78,891**
Of which:					
Conventional steam stations (3)	41,422	40,880r	38,577r	38,998r	38,837
Combined cycle gas turbine stations	12,462	12,716r	15,348r	17,058r	21,091
Nuclear stations	12,916	12,946r	12,956	12,956	12,486
Gas turbines and oil engines	1,721	1,526r	1,492	1,333	1,243
Hydro-electric stations:					
Natural flow	1,455	1,456r	1,475	1,477	1,485
Pumped storage	2,788	2,788	2,788	2,788	2,788
Renewables other than hydro	507	553r	697	797r	961

(1) See paragraphs 5.58 and 5.59 for information on companies covered.
(2) Includes gas fired stations that are not Combined Cycle Gas Turbines.
(3) For other generators, conventional steam stations include combined heat and power plants (electrical capacity only), but exclude combined cycle gas turbine plants and hydro-electric stations and plants using renewable sources.

5.8 Capacity of other generators

MW

	end-December				
	1996	1997	1998	1999	2000
Capacity of own generating plant (1)					
Undertakings in industrial and commercial sector:					
Petroleum refineries	648	773r	757r	887r	1,003
Iron and steel	359	359	355	355	373
Chemicals	927	1,228r	1,292r	1,304r	1,585
Engineering and other metal trades	506	504r	502r	514r	565
Food, drink and tobacco	207	236r	340r	434r	474
Paper, printing and publishing	369	440r	491r	498r	554
Other (2)	859	755r	923r	1,075r	1,524
Total industrial and commercial sector	3,875	4,294r	4,660r	5,066r	6,077
Undertakings in transport sector	306	283	283	283	283
Total other generators	**4,181**	**4,577r**	**4,943r**	**5,349r**	**6,360**

(1) For combined heat and power plants the electrical capacity only is included. Further CHP capacity is included under major power producers in Table 5.7. A detailed analysis of CHP capacity is given in the tables of Chapter 6.
(2) Includes companies in the commercial sector.

5.9 Plant loads, demand and efficiency

Major power producers (1)

	Unit	1996	1997	1998	1999	2000
Simultaneous maximum load met (2)	MW	56,815	56,965	56,312	57,849	58,452
Plant load factor						
Combined cycle gas turbine stations	Per cent	71.2r	81.7r	79.2r	84.0r	75.0
Nuclear stations	"	76.5r	79.1r	80.1r	77.2	70.5
Hydro-electric stations:						
Natural flow	"	24.1r	28.8r	36.7r	38.0r	37.2
Pumped storage	"	6.2	5.9	6.4	11.5	10.7
Conventional thermal and other stations (3)	"	43.7r	36.8r	38.6r	35.1r	38.7
All plant	"	**52.7r**	**51.4r**	**53.2r**	**53.1r**	**52.5**
System load factor	"	**66.3r**	**65.7r**	**67.4r**	**66.7r**	**67.4r**
Thermal efficiency **(gross calorific value basis)**						
Combined cycle gas turbine stations	"	45.3	45.2	46.6	46.6r	49.8
Coal fired stations (4)	"	37.2	.35.7	35.5	35.8	36.2
Nuclear stations	"	36.9	36.7	36.5	36.8	37.3

(1) See paragraphs 5.58 and 5.59 for information on companies covered.
(2) Data for 1996 to 2000 cover the years ending March 1997 to March 2001, respectively.
(3) Conventional steam plants, gas turbines and oil engines and plants producing electricity from renewable sources other than hydro.
(4) Data for coal fired stations are now given in place of all conventional steam stations data shown in previous Digests.

5.10 Fuel input for electricity generation[1]
1970 to 2000

Million tonnes of oil equivalent

	Total all fuels	Coal	Oil (2)	Natural gas (3)	Electricity Nuclear	Natural flow hydro	Coke and breeze	Other fuels (4)
1970	**63.84**	43.07	13.27	0.11	7.00	0.39	-	
1971	**66.46**	42.42	15.63	0.64	7.37	0.29	0.11	
1972	**68.37**	38.47	20.13	1.61	7.87	0.29	-	
1973	**70.93**	44.30	18.09	0.64	7.46	0.33	0.11	
1974	**69.01**	38.71	18.41	2.46	8.97	0.35	0.11	
1975	**66.25**	41.85	13.70	2.14	8.12	0.33	0.11	
1976	**66.97**	44.49	10.92	1.61	9.56	0.39	-	
1977	**69.32**	45.71	11.35	1.28	10.64	0.34	-	
1978	**69.64**	46.05	12.31	0.86	9.96	0.35	0.11	
1979	**72.80**	50.10	11.45	0.54	10.23	0.37	0.11	
1980	**69.46**	51.01	7.67	0.42	9.91	0.34	0.11	
1981	**65.98**	49.64	5.46	0.21	10.18	0.38	0.11	
1982	**65.98**	46.75	6.64	0.21	11.88	0.39	0.11	
1983	**66.37**	47.16	5.14	0.21	13.47	0.39	-	
1984	**69.18**	31.07	22.80	0.42	14.50	0.39	-	
1985	**71.54**	42.81	11.35	0.54	16.50	0.34	-	
1986	**70.46**	47.91	6.51	0.18	15.44	0.41	-	
1987 (5)	**70.50**	50.37	5.14	0.19	14.44	0.36	-	
1987 (5)	**74.31**	51.58	6.30	0.91	14.44	0.36	-	0.72
1988	**75.57**	49.83	7.01	0.97	16.57	0.42	-	0.77
1989	**75.27**	48.59	7.11	0.54	17.74	0.41	-	0.88
1990	**76.34**	49.84	8.40	0.56	16.26	0.44	-	0.84
1991	**76.87**	49.98	7.56	0.57	17.43	0.39	-	0.94
1992	**76.57**	46.94	8.07	1.54	18.45	0.46	-	1.09
1993	**75.40**	39.61	5.78	7.04	21.58	0.37	-	1.02
1994	**74.01**	37.10	4.11	10.10	21.20	0.44	-	1.06
1995	**77.15**	36.29	4.15	13.27	21.25	0.40	-	1.79
1996	**79.19r**	33.63	4.00	17.19	22.18	0.30	-	1.90
1997	**78.26**	29.03	2.30	21.51	22.99	0.36	-	2.07
1998	**80.46r**	29.90r	1.50r	22.41r	23.44r	0.44r	-	2.77r
1999	**79.00r**	25.43r	1.48r	26.48r	22.22r	0.46	-	2.93r
2000	**80.07**	28.63	1.42	26.89	19.64	0.44	-	3.06

(1) Fuel inputs have been calculated on an energy supplied basis - see explanatory notes at paragraph 5.28.
(2) Includes oil used in gas turbine and diesel plant or for lighting up coal fired boilers, Orimulsion, and (from 1987) refinery gas.
(3) Includes colliery methane from 1987 onwards.
(4) Main fuels included are coke oven gas, blast furnace gas, waste products from chemical processes, refuse derived fuels and other renewable sources including wind.
(5) Data for all generating companies are only available from 1987 onwards, and the figures for 1987 to 1989 include a high degree of estimation. Before 1987 the data are for major power producers, transport undertakings and industrial hydro and nuclear stations only.

5.11 Electricity supply, availability and consumption, 1970 to 2000

TWh

	Electricity supplied (net)	Purchases from other producers	Net imports (1)	Electricity available	Losses in transmission etc (2)	Total	Fuel industries	Industrial	Domestic	Other (3)	Total
									Final users		
1970	215.76	0.19	0.55	216.50	17.50	199.00	6.59	72.99	77.04	42.38	192.41
1971	222.92	0.53	0.12	223.57	19.01	204.56	6.60	73.43	80.67	43.86	197.96
1972	229.45	0.53	0.48	230.46	18.91	211.55	6.37	73.16	86.89	45.13	205.18
1973	245.42	0.59	0.06	246.07	19.59	226.48	6.67	80.07	91.30	48.44	219.81
1974	237.21	0.60	0.05	237.86	18.22	219.64	6.12	75.81	92.63	45.08	213.52
1975	237.76	0.70	0.08	238.54	19.47	219.07	6.29	75.36	89.21	48.21	212.78
1976	240.22	0.61	-0.10	240.73	18.73	222.00	6.39	80.84	85.12	49.65	215.61
1977	246.82	0.74	-	247.56	20.76	226.80	6.41	82.06	85.90	52.43	220.39
1978	252.65	0.66	-0.08	253.23	21.81	231.42	6.52	84.00	85.80	55.10	224.90
1979	264.34	0.63	-	264.97	22.97	242.00	6.78	87.55	89.67	58.00	235.22
1980	252.02	0.61	-	252.63	21.53	231.11	6.86	79.73	86.11	58.41	224.25
1981	246.60	0.74	-	247.34	20.13	227.21	6.86	77.03	84.44	58.88	220.35
1982	242.48	0.82	-	243.30	20.48	222.82	6.81	73.91	82.79	59.31	216.01
1983	246.15	1.15	-	247.30	21.21	226.09	6.69	74.17	82.95	62.28	219.40
1984	251.47	0.55	-	252.02	21.06	230.96	6.64	78.64	83.90	61.78	224.32
1985	263.56	0.92	-	264.48	22.63	241.85	7.76	79.53	88.23	66.33	234.09
1986(4)	266.81	1.10	4.26	272.17	22.83	249.34	7.68	80.15	91.83	69.68	241.66
1986(4)	278.48	-	4.26	282.73	22.91	259.82	9.51	88.80	91.83	69.68	250.31
1987	279.71	-	11.64	291.34	22.96	268.38	9.49	93.14	93.25	72.50	258.89
1988	285.71	-	12.14	297.85	23.35	274.50	9.16	97.14	92.36	75.84	265.34
1989	291.75	-	12.63	304.38	24.98	279.40	9.00	99.42	92.27	78.71	270.40
1990	297.50	-	11.91	309.41	24.99	284.42	9.99	100.64	93.79	80.00	274.43
1991	300.65	-	16.41	317.06	26.22	290.84	9.79	99.57	98.10	83.38	281.05
1992	298.55	-	16.69	315.24	23.79	291.45	9.98	95.28	99.48	86.71	281.47
1993	301.87	-	16.72	318.59	22.84	295.75	9.62	96.84	100.46	88.83	286.13
1994	306.94	-	16.89	323.83	31.00	292.83	7.52	96.12	101.41	87.78	285.31
1995	317.63	-	16.61	334.24	30.32	303.92	8.07	101.78	102.21	91.86	295.85
1996	330.41	-	16.76	347.17	31.30	315.87	8.85	104.32	107.51	95.19	307.02
1997	329.47	-	16.57	346.05	26.95	319.10	8.29	106.16	104.46	100.19	310.80
1998	342.76r	-	12.47	355.23r	29.67r	325.56r	8.41r	108.50r	109.41r	99.24r	317.15r
1999	347.90r	-	14.24	362.14r	29.79r	332.35r	8.31r	112.13r	110.31r	101.61r	324.04r
2000	355.14	-	14.17	369.32	30.80	338.52	8.43	114.67	111.84	103.58	330.09

(1) Net transfers between the Irish Republic and Northern Ireland (ceased in 1981 and recommenced in 1996) and between France and England (from 1986).

(2) Losses on the public distribution system (grid system and local networks) and other differences between data collected on sales and data collected on availability.

(3) Public administration, transport, agricultural and commercial sectors.

(4) Data for all generating companies are only available from 1986 onwards. Before 1986 the data are for major power producers, transport undertakings and industrial hydro and nuclear stations only.

5.12 Electricity generated and supplied 1970 to 2000

GWh

| | Electricity generated | Electricity used on works | Electricity supplied (gross) (1) | | | | | | Electricity used in pumping at pumped storage stations | Electricity Supplied (net) (3) |
			Total	Conventional thermal and other (2)	CCGT	Nuclear	Hydro Natural flow	Hydro Pumped storage		
1970	232,378	16,429	215,949	188,175	-	22,805	3,846	1,123	1,487	214,462
1971	240,080	17,143	222,937	195,181	-	24,013	2,835	908	1,209	221,728
1972	246,843	17,439	229,404	200,048	-	25,639	2,847	870	1,184	228,220
1973	263,140	18,157	244,983	216,796	-	24,310	3,214	663	882	244,101
1974	254,688	17,763	236,925	203,478	-	29,232	3,520	695	896	236,029
1975	255,084	17,136	237,948	207,159	-	26,463	3,186	1,140	1,430	236,518
1976	258,656	17,962	240,694	205,048	-	31,153	3,128	1,365	1,729	238,965
1977	265,649	18,468	247,181	207,904	-	34,660	3,320	1,297	1,608	245,573
1978	270,677	17,907	252,770	215,761	-	32,462	3,378	1,169	1,429	251,341
1979	283,186	18,744	264,442	226,329	-	33,335	3,617	1,161	1,424	263,018
1980	269,945	17,765	252,180	215,418	-	32,291	3,298	1,173	1,453	250,727
1981	263,658	16,983	246,675	208,589	-	33,191	3,906	989	1,196	245,479
1982	259,410	16,940	242,470	198,822	-	38,721	3,873	1,054	1,272	241,198
1983	264,589	17,380	247,209	197,600	-	43,911	3,882	1,816	2,337	244,872
1984	270,471	17,643	252,828	200,240	-	47,256	3,358	1,974	2,613	250,215
1985	284,712	18,903	265,809	205,906	-	53,767	3,435	2,701	3,494	262,315
1986	287,330	18,819	268,511	210,452	-	51,843	4,087	2,129	2,993	265,518
1987	287,701	18,740	268,961	215,290	-	48,205	3,460	2,006	2,804	266,157
1988	293,100	19,341	273,759	211,932	-	55,642	4,160	2,025	2,888	270,871
1989	297,890	19,315	278,575	209,169	-	63,602	3,992	1,812	2,572	276,003
1990	302,936	18,632	284,304	219,364	-	58,664	4,384	1,892	2,626	281,678
1991	305,704	19,142	286,562	218,260	309	62,761	3,767	1,465	2,109	284,453
1992	303,715	19,157	284,558	206,245	2,964	69,135	4,579	1,635	2,257	282,301
1993	305,433	18,170	287,264	178,773	22,611	80,979	3,513	1,388	1,948	285,316
1994	307,476	16,696	290,780	168,321	36,815	79,962	4,265	1,417	2,051	288,729
1995	315,510	16,510	299,000	164,324	48,525	80,598	4,051	1,502	2,282	296,718
1996	327,843	16,674	311,169	155,475	65,604	85,820	2,763	1,507	2,430	308,739
1997	323,973	15,404	308,569	127,808	86,682	89,341	3,299	1,439	2,477	306,092
1998	333,702r	16,078r	317,624r	128,235r	93,005	90,590r	4,225r	1,569	2,594	315,030r
1999	336,486r	15,338r	321,148r	113,494r	112,768r	87,672	4,410r	2,804	3,774	317,374r
2000	341,785	14,953	326,832	125,469	116,110	78,334	4,316	2,603	3,499	323,333

(1) Electricity generated less electricity used on works.
(2) Includes electricity supplied by gas turbines and oil engines. From 1988 also includes electricity produced by plants using renewable sources.

5.12 Electricity generated and supplied 1970 to 2000 (continued)

GWh

Other generators				All generating companies						
Electricity supplied (gross) (1)				Electricity supplied (gross)						
Total	Conventional thermal and other (2)	CCGT	Hydro natural flow	Total	Conventional thermal and other (2)	CCGT	Nuclear	Hydro	Electricity supplied (net) (3)	
15,674	14,996	-	678	231,623	203,171	-	22,805	5,647	230,136	1970
15,388	14,837	-	551	238,325	210,018	-	24,013	4,294	237,116	1971
15,746	15,175	-	571	245,150	215,223	-	25,639	4,288	243,966	1972
17,655	17,008	-	647	262,638	233,804	-	24,310	4,524	261,756	1973
17,222	16,660	-	562	254,147	220,138	-	29,232	4,777	253,251	1974
15,766	15,175	-	591	253,714	222,334	-	26,463	4,917	252,284	1975
17,013	16,414	-	599	257,707	221,462	-	31,153	5,092	255,978	1976
16,434	15,848	-	586	263,615	223,752	-	34,660	5,203	262,007	1977
16,034	15,387	-	647	268,804	231,148	-	32,462	5,194	267,375	1978
15,720	15,062	-	658	280,162	241,391	-	33,335	5,436	278,738	1979
14,132	13,509	-	623	266,312	228,927	-	32,291	5,094	264,859	1980
13,264	12,801	-	463	259,939	221,390	-	33,191	5,358	258,743	1981
12,613	11,943	-	670	255,083	210,765	-	38,721	5,597	253,811	1982
12,152	11,486	-	666	259,361	209,086	-	43,911	6,364	257,024	1983
11,319	10,685	-	634	264,148	210,925	-	47,256	5,966	261,535	1984
12,112	11,467	-	645	277,922	217,373	-	53,767	6,781	274,427	1985
12,957	12,278	-	679	281,469	222,730	-	51,843	6,895	278,476	1986
13,551	12,831	-	720	282,512	228,121	-	48,205	6,186	279,708	1987
14,840	14,085	-	755	288,599	226,018	-	55,642	6,939	285,711	1988
15,747	15,007	-	740	294,322	224,176	-	63,602	6,544	291,751	1989
15,824	14,738	280	806	300,128	234,101	280	58,664	7,082	297,502	1990
16,202	15,065	298	839	302,764	233,325	607	62,761	6,071	300,654	1991
16,246	15,020	394	832	300,804	221,265	3,358	69,135	7,046	298,547	1992
16,552	15,196	584	772	303,816	193,969	23,195	80,979	5,673	301,868	1993
18,207	16,700r	738r	769	308,987	185,021r	37,553r	79,962	6,451	306,936	1994
20,909	19,243r	933r	733	319,909	183,567r	49,458r	80,598	6,286	317,627	1995
21,674	19,909r	1,180r	585	332,843	175,384r	66,784r	85,820	4,855	330,413	1996
23,379	21,131r	1,425r	823	331,948	148,939r	88,107r	89,341	5,561	329,471	1997
27,734r	24,159r	2,706r	869r	345,358r	152,394r	95,711r	90,590r	6,663r	342,764r	1998
30,523r	23,399r	6,207	917	351,671r	136,893r	118,975r	87,672	8,131r	347,897r	1999
31,808	22,618	8,424	766	358,640	148,087	124,534	78,334	7,685	355,141	2000

(3) Electricity supplied (gross) less electricity used in pumping at pumped storage station.

5.13 Power Stations in the United Kingdom
(operational at the end of May 2001)[1]

Company Name	Station Name	Fuel	Installed Capacity (MW)	Year of Commission or year generation began
AES	Drax	coal	3,870	1974
	Drax GT	gas oil	75	1971
	Fifoots Point	coal	393	2000
	Belfast West	coal	120	1954
	Kilroot	coal/oil	520	1981
	Barry	CCGT	250	1998
	Indian Queens	oil	140	1996
Alcan	Lynemouth	coal	248	1995
Barking Power	Barking	CCGT	1,000	1994
British Energy	Dungeness B	nuclear	1,110	1985
	Hartlepool	nuclear	1,210	1989
	Heysham1	nuclear	1,150	1989
	Heysham 2	nuclear	1,250	1989
	Hinkley Point B	nuclear	1,220	1976
	Sizewell B	nuclear	1,188	1995
	Hunterston B	nuclear	1,190	1976
	Torness	nuclear	1,250	1988
	Eggborough	coal	1,960	1968
BNFL Magnox	Calder Hall	nuclear	194	1956
	Chapelcross	nuclear	196	1959
	Bradwell	nuclear	246	1962
	Dungeness A	nuclear	450	1965
	Oldbury	nuclear	434	1967
	Sizewell A	nuclear	420	1966
	Wylfa	nuclear	980	1971
	Maentwrog	hydro	30	1928
Citigen Ltd	Charterhouse St., London	gas	32	1995
Coolkeeragh Power	Coolkeeragh	oil	293	1959
Corby Power	Corby	CCGT	401	1993
Coryton Energy Company Ltd	Coryton	CCGT	750	2001
Deeside Power	Deeside	CCGT	500	1994
Derwent Cogeneration	Derwent	CHP	236	1994
Edison Mission Energy	Dinorwig	pumped storage	1,728	1983
	Ffestiniog	pumped storage	360	1961
	Ferrybridge C	coal	1,955	1966
	Fiddler's Ferry	coal	1,961	1971
	Ferrybridge GT	gas oil	34	1966
	Fiddler's Ferry GT	gas oil	34	1969
Enfield Energy Centre Ltd	Brimsdown	CCGT	396	1999
Entergy	Saltend	CCGT	1200	2000
	Damhead Creek	CCGT	805	2000
Fellside Heat and Power	Fellside	CHP	168	1993
Fibrogen	Glanford	meat & bone meal	13	1993
Fibropower Ltd	Eye, Suffolk	poultry litter	13	1992
Fibrothetford	Thetford	poultry litter	39	1998

5.13 Power Stations in the United Kingdom
(operational at the end of May 2001)[1] (continued)

Company Name	Station Name	Fuel	Installed Capacity (MW)	Year of Commission or year generation began
Fife Power	Westfield Development Centre	CCGT	75	1998
Humber Power	South Humber Bank 1	CCGT	785	1996
	South Humber Bank 2	CCGT	527	1998
Innogy Plc	Aberthaw B	coal	1,489	1971
	Tilbury B	coal/oil	714	1968
	Didcot A	coal/gas	2,020	1972
	Cowes	gas oil	140	1982
	Fawley	oil	518	1969
	Littlebrook D	oil	755	1982
	Didcot B	CCGT	1,370	1998
	Little Barford	CCGT	680	1995
	Cwm Dyli	hydro	10	1989[2]
	Dolgarrog	hydro	35	1924
Intergen	Rocksavage	CCGT	750	1997
Lakeland Power	Roosecote	CCGT	229	1991
London Electricity	Sutton Bridge	CCGT	803	1999
	Cottam	coal	2,008	1969
Medway Power	Medway	CCGT	688	1995
National Grid	Kielder	hydro	5.5	1984
NRG Energy	Killingholme	CCGT	650	1994
PowerGen	Kingsnorth	coal/oil	1,455	1970
	Ratcliffe	coal	2,000	1968
	Grain	oil	1,350	1979
	Grain GT	gas oil	55	1978
	Kingsnorth GT	gas oil	34	1967
	Ratcliffe GT	gas oil	34	1966
	Taylor's Lane GT	gas oil	132	1979
	Connahs Quay	CCGT	1,420	1996
	Killingholme	CCGT	900	1992
	Cottam Development Centre	CCGT	400	1999
	Rheidol	hydro	56	1961
Premier Power	Ballylumford	oil/gas	1,080	1968
Regional Power Generators Ltd	Brigg	CCGT	240	1993
Scottish & Southern Energy plc **Schemes:**				
Affric/Beauly	Mullardoch Tunnel	hydro	2.4	1955
	Fasnakyle	hydro	69	1951
	Deanie	hydro	38	1963
	Culligran	hydro	24	1962
	Aigas	hydro	20	1962
	Kilmorack	hydro	20	1962
Breadalbane	Lubreoch	hydro	4	1958
	Cashlie	hydro	11	1959
	Lochay	hydro	47	1958
	Finlarig	hydro	30	1955
	Lednock	hydro	3	1961
	St. Fillans	hydro	21	1957
	Dalchonzie	hydro	4	1958

5.13 Power Stations in the United Kingdom
(operational at the end of May 2001)[1] (continued)

Company Name	Station Name	Fuel	Installed Capacity (MW)	Year of Commission or year generation began
Conon	Achanalt	hydro	3	1956
	Grudie Bridge	hydro	24	1950
	Mossford	hydro	24	1957
	Luichart	hydro	34	1954
	Orrin	hydro	18	1959
	Torr Achilty	hydro	15	1954
Foyers	Foyers	hydro/pumped storage	300	1974
Great Glen	Foyers Falls	hydro	5.2	1968
	Mucomir	hydro	2	1962
	Ceannacroc	hydro	20	1956
	Livishie	hydro	15	1962
	Glenmoriston	hydro	37	1957
	Quoich	hydro	22	1955
	Ivergarry	hydro	20	1956
Shin	Cassley	hydro	10	1959
	Lairg	hydro	3.5	1959
	Shin	hydro	24	1958
Sloy/Awe	Sloy	hydro	160	1950
	Sron Mor	hydro	5	1957
	Clachan	hydro	40	1955
	Alt-na-Lairgie	hydro	6	1956
	Nant	hydro	15	1963
	Inverawe	hydro	25	1963
	Kilmelfort	hydro	2	1956
	Loch Gair	hydro	6	1961
	Lussa	hydro	2.4	1952
	Striven	hydro	8	1951
Tummel	Gaur	hydro	6.4	1953
	Cuaich	hydro	2.5	1959
	Loch Ericht	hydro	2.2	1962
	Rannoch	hydro	42	1930
	Tummel	hydro	34	1933
	Errochty	hydro	75	1955
	Clunie	hydro	61.2	1950
	Pitlochry	hydro	15	1950
Small Hydros	Chliostair	hydro	1.1	1960
	Kerry Falls	hydro	1.3	1951
	Loch Dubh	hydro	1.2	1954
	Nostie Bridge	hydro	1.3	1950
	Storr Lochs	hydro	2.4	1952
Thermal	Peterhead	oil/gas	1,550	1980
	Lerwick	diesel/gas	66	1953
	Keadby	CCGT	720	1994
	Chickerell	gas	45	1998
	Burghfield	gas	45	1998
	Thatcham	diesel	9.6	1994
	Five Oaks	diesel	11.5	1995
Scottish Power	Cockenzie	coal	1,152	1967
	Longannet	coal	2,304	1970
	Methil	coal slurry	57	1965
	Galloway (6 stations)	hydro	106	1935
	Lanark (2 stations)	hydro	17	1927
	Cruachan	pumped storage	399	1966
	Knapton	gas oil	40	1994
	Rye House	CCGT	715	1993

5.13 Power Stations in the United Kingdom

(operational at the end of May 2001)[1] (continued)

Company Name	Station Name	Fuel	Installed Capacity (MW)	Year of Commission or year generation began
Seabank Power Limited	Seabank 1	CCGT	812	1998
	Seabank 2	CCGT	410	2000
Sita Tyre Recycling Ltd	Wolverhampton	waste	20	1994
South Coast Power	Shoreham	CCGT	400	2000
South East London Combined Heat & Power Ltd	Landmann Way, London	waste	32	1994
Western Power Generation	St Marys	gas oil	6	1958
	Princetown	kerosene	3	1959
	Lynton	gas oil	2	1961
	Roseland	kerosene	5	1963
Teesside Power Ltd	Greystones	CCGT	1,875	1992
TXU Europe Power Ltd (formally Eastern Group)	Drakelow	coal	976	1965
	High Marnham	coal	945	1959
	Ironbridge	coal	970	1970
	Rugeley	coal	976	1972
	West Burton	coal	1,932	1967
	Kings Lynn	CCGT	350	1996
	Peterborough	CCGT	380	1993
	West Burton GT	gas oil	34	1966
	Rugley GT	Gas oil	50	1972
Total			**74,220**	

(1) This list covers stations of more than 1 MW capacity, but excludes some renewables stations of over 1 MW which are included in the section below.

(2) Recommissioning date.

Other power stations[3]

Station type	Fuel	Capacity (MW)
Renewable sources and combustible wastes	wind	404
	landfill gas	383
	sewage gas	85
	hydro	158
	waste	152
	other	48
CHP schemes other than major power producers and renewables	mainly gas	3,950
Other autogenerators	various fuels	1,128

(3) As at end December 2000.

Chapter 6
Combined heat and power

Introduction

6.1   This chapter sets out the contribution made by Combined Heat and Power (CHP) to the United Kingdom's energy requirements. Data have been considerably improved this year through use of information provided for the Government's new CHP Quality Assurance programme (CHPQA). A section of this chapter (paragraphs 6.10 and 6.11) sets out the changes that have resulted from the use of this new source of information.

6.2   CHP is the simultaneous generation of usable heat and power (usually electricity) in a single process. Useful outputs can be more varied: increasingly, heat is being used to drive absorption chilling, and in some cases power can be mechanical power eg to drive a compressor. The term CHP is synonymous with cogeneration and total energy, which are terms often used in other Member States of the European Community and the United States. CHP uses a variety of fuels and technologies across a wide range of sites, and scheme sizes. The basic elements of a CHP plant comprise one or more prime movers (a reciprocating engine, gas turbine, or steam turbine) driving electrical generators, where the steam or hot water generated in the process is utilised via suitable heat recovery equipment for use either in industrial processes, or in community heating and space heating.

6.3   Whereas an electricity-only plant is typically large, and connected at very high voltage to the grid transmission system, a CHP plant is typically much smaller, sized to make use of the available heat, and connected to the lower voltage distribution system (i.e. embedded). Not only is CHP more efficient through utilisation of heat, it also avoids significant transmission and distribution losses, and can provide important network services such as black start, improvements to power quality, and the ability to operate in island mode if the grid goes down.

6.4   CHP usually displaces boiler plant and electricity-only plant using a range of fuels and technologies. CHP typically achieves a 25 to 35 per cent reduction in primary energy usage compared with electricity-only generation and heat-only boilers. This can allow the host organisation to make substantial savings in costs and emissions where there is a suitable heat load.

6.5   There are four principal types of CHP system, steam turbine, gas turbine, combined cycle systems and reciprocating engines. Each of these is defined in paragraph 6.30 below.

Government policy towards CHP

6.6   The UK previously had a target of 5,000 MWe of installed CHP capacity by the end of the year 2000. Chart 6.1 shows the increases in capacity by year in relation to this target. At the end of the year 2000, installed Good Quality CHP capacity was 4,632 MWe. However, given the schemes currently under construction, 5,000 MWe of capacity should be in place during the course of the year 2001.

6.7   A detailed study of the CHP potential in industry, commerce and the public sector has been carried out for the Department for the Environment, Food and Rural Affairs (DEFRA) by ETSU (a division of AEA Technology) and is in the course of being updated. The results will inform the forthcoming CHP Strategy but the economic potential is likely to be in the range 12,000 to 20,000 MWe, depending on the range of assumptions made about future energy prices, rates of return on capital expected in industry, and other factors.

6.8   The Government has confirmed a new target of at least 10,000 MWe of CHP by 2010 as part of its Climate Change Programme. DEFRA will shortly be consulting on the Government's strategy to achieve this target.

6.9   There are a number of important issues which affect the planning framework, or the cost effectiveness of CHP:

I.   The quality of CHP is assessed by the Governments new CHPQA programme Guidelines and application forms are available from the CHPQA web site (www.chpqa.com). Certification under CHPQA is the passport to a variety of fiscal benefits.

II.   The Climate Change Levy (CCL) was introduced from April 2001, with an exemption for fuel use, and electricity generated that qualifies as Good Quality CHP where electricity is used on-site or exported to a direct customer (see CHPQA Guidance Note 41).

III. Many industrial sectors have negotiated an agreement with the Government on a reduced levy rate, subject to achieving energy efficiency targets[1]. CHP accounts for up to half the cost-effective savings in these sectors, and will benefit from such agreements.

IV. Businesses are able to claim Enhanced Capital Allowances on investment in Good Quality CHP Capacity, as determined under CHPQA (see www.eca.gov.uk). Where an investment is made by an Energy Services Company on behalf of a site, the Energy Services Company will be able to claim the allowance.

V. Plant and machinery for power generation in CHP schemes has been made exempt from business rates. This gives CHP schemes in conventional rating assessment equivalent treatment to that already given to power generators in prescribed assessment (see CHPQA Guidance Note 43).

VI. On 23 March 2001, the Government introduced new Guidelines for Power Station Developers seeking consent under Section 36 of the Electricity Act of 1989 or Section 14 of the Energy Act of 1976. New projects have to demonstrate that they have explored opportunities for supplying heat as well as generating electricity. (see www.dti.gov.uk/energy/consents.htm).

VII. New Electricity Trading Arrangements (NETA) went live on 27 March 2001. By increasing competition in the wholesale market, NETA is designed to put downward pressure on prices, as well as to level the playing field amongst generators. However, in the light of considerable concern amongst smaller generators, the Minister of State for Energy asked the Office for Gas and Electricity Markets (OFGEM) to undertake a Review of the impact of NETA on smaller generators. OFGEM are due to publish their findings by August 2001.

VIII. Under the Utilities Act, energy suppliers must fulfil Energy Efficiency Commitments (EECs). The first tranche will run for a three year period, 2002 to 2005. CHP will be one option to help meet these obligations.

IX. On 26 April 2001, The Deputy Prime Minister announced a new Community Energy programme with £50 million support for investment in CHP/Community Heating, for example for homes, hospitals and universities (see www.press.detr.gov.uk/0104/0237.htm).

X. Advice and support for those wanting to invest in or improve their CHP scheme is available from the CHPClub (www.chpclub.com).

Further issues will be discussed in the forthcoming CHP strategy.

Use of CHPQA in producing CHP statistics

6.10 The use of CHPQA as a source for CHP statistics has resulted in the following changes.

- The boundary of a CHP scheme (what is regarded as part of the CHP installation and what is not) have previously been determined by scheme operators. Now, through CHPQA, scheme operators have been given guidance on how to determine scheme boundaries. A scheme can include multiple CHP prime movers, along with supplementary boilers and generating plant, subject to appropriate metering installed to support the CHP scheme boundaries proposed, and subject to appropriate threshold criteria (see CHPQA Guidance Note 11). Metering arrangements also have prescribed tolerances (see CHPQA Guidance Notes 13-23).

- The output of a scheme is based on gross power output, ignoring parasitic loads (ie ignoring power used in pumps, fans, etc within the scheme itself). Parasitic loads vary from around 7.6 per cent for back pressure steam turbines, down to 1.8 per cent for combined cycle gas turbines (CCGT). The capacity weighted average is 2.1 per cent of both capacity and output (see Table 6E). In practice, most parasitic loads exist because of the existence of the heat network rather than because of the generation of electricity.

- The main purpose of a number of CHP schemes is the generation of electricity including export to others. Such schemes may not be sized to use all of the available heat in on-site or nearby activities. The total capacity and output of these schemes have been scaled back using the methodologies outlined in CHPQA. (The CHP Qualifying Power Capacity or CHP_{QPC}, and CHP Qualifying Power Output or CHP_{QPO}, see CHPQA Guidance Notes 26 and 27). Only the portion of the capacity, fuel use and output that qualifies as Good Quality is counted in this chapter. This much more rigorous methodology than that used previously has led to a reduction (revised across all years) of around 200-300 MWe of capacity counted as Good Quality CHP. All electricity capacity and generation, not just that which qualifies as Good Quality CHP (CHP Total Power Capacity CHP_{TPC} and CHP Total Power Output CHP_{TPO}) is included in the Electricity Chapter (Chapter 5) of this Digest. For further details of CHP_{QPC} and CHP_{QPO} see the Technical Notes and definitions section at paragraph 6.33.

---

[1] See Guidance Notes on Negotiated Agreements, and in particular NA(99)23 on CHP. Downloadable from www.etsu.com/ccltexts

162

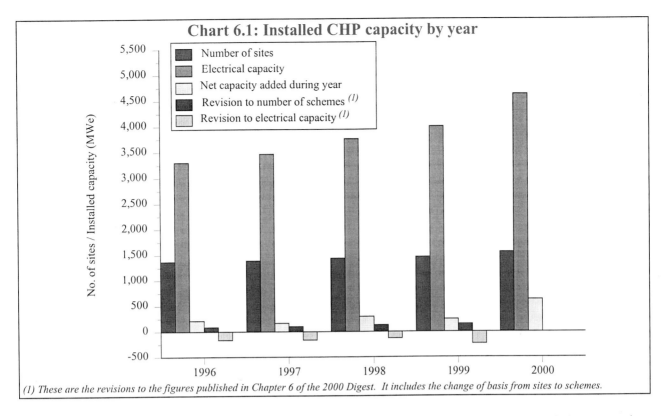

Chart 6.1: Installed CHP capacity by year

Legend:
- Number of sites
- Electrical capacity
- Net capacity added during year
- Revision to number of schemes [1]
- Revision to electrical capacity [1]

(1) These are the revisions to the figures published in Chapter 6 of the 2000 Digest. It includes the change of basis from sites to schemes.

- A number of schemes which were not previously known and therefore not previously included in the statistics, have applied for certification under CHPQA, in order to claim Climate Change Levy (CCL) exemption. There are around 100 small (20-300 kWe) schemes in this category. There are also a number of small schemes which have not yet applied to CHPQA. Many of these are supplying domestic customers excluded from CCL, or are on sewage sites and burning fuel which is exempt from CCL, and as yet these sites see little benefit in applying. However it may be that around 100 sites accounting for only a few MWe have ceased to generate, but these remain in the statistics until they have been investigated.

- Statistics on CHP_{QPC} and CHP_{QPO} include mechanical power (eg the direct drive of compressors and fans). Twelve schemes are known to include mechanical power (see paragraph 6.23 for more detail).

6.11   In the light of both better data and changed methodology, historical data have been re-evaluated, and changes in previous years' data have been made where necessary. The time-series presented in Tables 6.1 to 6.8 are on a consistent basis, and show the trends in capacity and output over the last five years.

Progress towards the Government's targets

6.12   Chart 6.1 shows the change in installed CHP capacity over the last five years. Installed capacity at the end of 2000 stood at 4,632 MWe. Over the last decade, capacity has more than doubled, representing an average growth rate over the period of 8 per cent per annum. Growth over the last year has been 16 per cent, or 628 MWe, as shown in Table 6A.

New and retired capacity in 2000

6.13   Growth in any one year depends on the rate of retirement of old plant as well as the rate at which new plant is built. Additional capacity in 2000 came from 116 new and 15 upgraded schemes, less retirements of around 20 schemes. There are a number of important and dynamic trends in new installations:

- The growth in CHP installed under energy services arrangements continues. Around two-thirds of the CHP capacity installed over the last decade (worth around £1.1 billion) has been installed under an energy services arrangement. However this proportion is rising, and around 90 per cent of capacity commissioned in the next few years will be operated under an energy services arrangement.

- Increasingly, with market liberalisation, there has been a stronger incentive to design schemes to maximise electricity generation on a given heat load, and to export electricity to adjacent customers or to the local public electricity supplier (PES). Exports now account for about a third of electricity generated in CHP (see Table 6F in the technical notes section).

- Much of the new capacity was in traditional applications such as refineries and fuel processing, and chemicals. Horticulture continues to be a market sector where growth is strong.

Table 6A: A summary of the recent development of CHP

	Unit	1996	1997	1998	1999	2000
Number of schemes		1,370	1,388	1,435	1,460	1,556
Net number of schemes added during year			18	47	25	96
Electrical capacity (CHP$_{QPC}$)	MWe	3,301	3,466	3,759	4,004	4,632
Net capacity added during year			165	293	245	628
Capacity added in percentage terms	Per cent		5	8	7	16
Heat capacity	MWth	16,079	15,294	15,398	14,972	11,956
Heat to power ratio *(1)*		3.96	3.64	3.33	2.99	2.63
Fuel input	GWh	112,539	112,512	115,212	115,421	119,163
Electricity generation (CHP$_{QPO}$)	GWh	16,079	16,949	18,836	20,477	23,295
Heat generation (CHP$_{QHO}$)	GWh	63,635	61,775	62,802	61,203	61,513
Overall efficiency *(2)*	Per cent	70.8	70.1	70.9	70.8	71.2
Load factor	Per cent	55.6	55.8	57.2	58.4	57.4

(1) Heat to power ratios are calculated from the qualifying heat output (QHO) and the qualifying power output (QPO).
(2) These are calculated using gross calorific values; overall net efficiencies are some 5 percentage points higher.

6.14 Around 65 per cent of capacity is now gas turbine based, with around three quarters of this in combined cycle mode. Continued growth in combined cycle gas turbine installations came predominantly from the upgrading of existing steam turbine based CHP schemes. In addition, there were a number of new smaller schemes employing simple cycle gas turbines and reciprocating engines. Over the last five years heat output has remained broadly stable, whilst electricity generated has increased by 45 per cent. The load factor has increased marginally over the period, and is equivalent to an average of 5,051 hours of full load operation per annum. This figure could be deceptive –many industrial schemes operate in excess of 8,000 hours a year, but not necessarily at full load. In addition, it hides a range from schemes which were only commissioned towards the end of 2000, and only ran for a few months, to schemes which ran for all but a few hours of the year.

Schemes under development in 2000

6.15 A large amount of potential new capacity has received consent under Section 36 of the Electricity Act 1989, and clearance under Section 14 of the Energy Act 1976, but is not yet in commercial operation (Table 6B). In total 2,719 MWe (TPC) has been consented but is not yet in operation. It may take 2-4 years from consent to commissioning a scheme, even if work begins immediately after consent is received. However, not all of these schemes will be additional, and may replace some existing (steam turbine) capacity. Of these:

- Schemes totalling around 400 MWe are under construction and expected to be commissioned during 2001.

- It is understood that a large portion of consented capacity is not likely to proceed at the present time, or may be built, but will be much smaller than the consented capacity. The economics of CHP are driven by the relationship between fuel prices (especially gas) and electricity prices, and the efficiency of conversion from fuel to

Table 6B: CHP schemes under development

	MWe*(1)*
Consented in 1998 (not yet in operation)	
Shotton Paper	215
Hickson & Welch CHP & PowerGen CHP	55
Total	**270**
Consented in 1999	
Rolls Royce Ansty, Coventry	49
British Sugar, York	70
Baglan Bay, Port Talbot	500
Michelin Tyres	58
Sappi Mill, Blackburn, (Scottish Power)	60
British Sugar, Cantley	70
EniChem, Southampton,	46
Kimberly Clark, Barrow-in-Furness	13
Total	**866**
Consented in 2000	
ICI Chemicals and Polymers	250
Conoco Refinery, South Killingholme	475
Cargill, Mersey Docks (PowerGen)	31
Pfizer	13
Scottish Courage	60
Sevalco Avonmouth (Northern Electric)	180
Tullis Russell, Markinch, Fife (Scottish Power)	49
Alcan Chemicals	13
Huntsman Tioxide	24
SmithKline Beecham, Ayrshire (Scottish Power)	45
Total	**1,140**
Consented in 2001 (to date)	
Conoco Refinery, South Killingholme (Stage 2)	225
Jaguar, Halewood (BP Energy)	70
Kellogs, Trafford Park	65
Nursling Generation	49
Zeneca, Huddersfield (Dalkia)	20
Astra Zeneca, Macclesfield (Dalkia)	13
Total	**442**
Total consented	**2,719**
Applications for consent under consideration	494
Total	**3,213**

(1) Consented capacity (CHPTPC)
Note: This table only includes schemes which need consent from the Secretary of State, ie schemes over 10 MWe. Up to 40 schemes below 10 MWe may be commissioned during 2001, but these are predominantly schemes of a few hundred kWe in size and will not affect projected capacity significantly.

electricity. Given the recent large increase in gas prices, and falling electricity prices, many schemes which have been consented are not seen as economic

Table 6C: CHP schemes by capacity size ranges in 2000

Electrical capacity size range	Number of schemes	Share of total (per cent)	Total electricity capacity (MWe)	Share of total (per cent)
Less than 100 kWe	724	46.5	41.3	0.9
100 kWe - 999 kWe	559	35.9	137.9	3.0
1 MWe - 9.9 MWe	196	12.6	814.9	17.6
Greater than 10 MWe	77	4.9	3,683.2	78.5
Total	**1,556**	**100.0**	**4,632.3**	**100.0**

under current market conditions. These decisions may be reviewed when market conditions change, but while there was a healthy growth in capacity in 2000, which is likely to be repeated in 2001, prospects for capacity growth over the following three years are more limited.

- At 31 May 2001 applications for another 494 MWe of CHP_{TPC} capacity were with the Department of Trade and Industry for consideration. Even if all these schemes were built, they are unlikely to be commissioned before 2005.

Installed capacity in 2000

6.16 The current installed capacity displays the following characteristics:

- CHP installations are dominated by schemes with an installed electrical capacity of less 1 MWe (82.4 per cent) as shown in Table 6C. However, schemes larger than 10 MWe represent 78.5 per cent of the total electrical capacity.

- In terms of heat capacity steam turbines continue to predominate with 38 per cent of total heat supplied. Table 6.5 provides data on electrical capacity and Table 6.7 provides data on heat capacity for each type of CHP installation. Table 6.4 provides data on electricity generated and Table 6.6 provides data on heat generated for each type of CHP installation.

6.17 Table 6A gives a summary of the overall CHP market. The electricity generated by CHP schemes (CHP_{QPO}) was 23,295 GWh. This represents about 6 per cent of the total electricity generated in the UK in 2000. Across all industry (including the fuel industries other than electricity generation) CHP's electrical output accounted for 16 per cent of electricity consumption, 3 percentage points more than in 1996. In the commercial and public sectors together, CHP supplied 2 per cent of electricity consumption in 2000. CHP schemes in total supplied 61,513 GWh of heat (CHP_{QHO}).

Fuel used by types of CHP installation

6.18 Table 6.1 shows the fuel used to generate electricity and heat in CHP schemes, (see paragraphs 6.31 and 6.32, below for an explanation of the convention for dividing fuel between electricity and heat production). Table 6.3 gives the overall fuel used by types of CHP installation (which are explained in paragraph 6.30). Total fuel use is summarised in Chart 6.2. In 2000 natural gas dominates with 62 per cent of total fuel use, and this is set to increase as most new CHP schemes are fired by natural gas. CHP schemes accounted for 7 per cent of UK gas consumption in 2000 (see Table 4.3). Fuel oil use fluctuates annually, and depends on the extent of interruptions to gas supplies (which in turn depends on weather, overall gas demand, and the extent to which individual gas contracts allow for interruptions in order to cope with peak demand).

6.19 Non-conventional fuels (gases, liquids or solids which are by-products or waste products from industrial processes, or are renewable fuels) account for a quarter of fuel used in CHP. These are fuels which are not commonly used the mainstream electricity generating industry, and some would otherwise be flared or disposed of by some means. These fuels (with the exception of some waste gases) will always be burnt in external combustion engines, such as boilers feeding steam turbines. In almost all cases, the technical nature of the combustion process (lower calorific value of the fuel, high moisture content of the fuel, the need to maintain certain combustion conditions to ensure complete disposal etc) will always imply a lower efficiency. However, given that the use of such fuels avoids the use of fossil fuels, and since they would have to have been disposed of in some way in any case, the use of these fuels for the generation of power and heat is, in environmental terms, at very low cost.

CHP capacity, output and fuel use by sector

6.20 Table 6.8 gives data on all operational schemes by economic sector. A definition of the sectors used in this table can be found in Chapter 1, paragraph 1.77 and Table 1E.

- 326 schemes (88½ per cent of capacity) are in the industrial sector and 1,230 schemes (11½ per cent of capacity) are in the commercial, public and residential sectors.

- Four industrial sectors account for three quarters of the CHP electrical capacity - chemicals (34 per

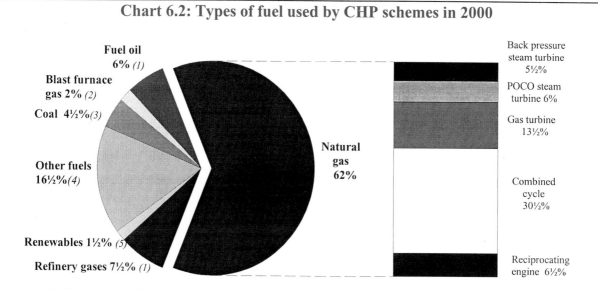

Chart 6.2: Types of fuel used by CHP schemes in 2000

Fuel oil 6% *(1)*

Blast furnace gas 2% *(2)*

Coal 4½% *(3)*

Other fuels 16½% *(4)*

Renewables 1½% *(5)*

Refinery gases 7½% *(1)*

Natural gas 62%

Back pressure steam turbine 5½%

POCO steam turbine 6%

Gas turbine 13½%

Combined cycle 30½%

Reciprocating engine 6½%

(1) Combined cycle accounts for 70 per cent of fuel oil use and over three quarters of refinery gas use.
(2) POCO steam turbines account for all blast furnace gas use.
(3) Coal use is equally divided between back pressure steam turbines and POCO steam turbines
(4) Other fuels include coke oven gas, gas oil, and process by-products.
(5) Reciprocating engines account for 70 per cent of renewable fuel use

cent of capacity), oil refineries (21½ per cent), paper, publishing and printing (11½ per cent) and food beverages and tobacco (10 per cent) as Chart 6.3 shows.

Table 6D gives a summary of the 1,136 schemes installed in the commercial, public sector and residential buildings. The vast majority of these schemes (98 per cent) are based on spark ignition reciprocating engines fuelled with natural gas, though the larger schemes use compression ignition reciprocating engines or gas turbines. The schemes in Table 6D form a major part of the "Transport, commerce and administration" and "Other" sectors in Tables 6.8 and 6.9. Table 6.9 gives details of the quantities of fuels used in each sector.

CHP schemes which export and schemes with mechanical power output

6.21 For 2000, 57 CHP schemes have provided information on the amount of electricity they export. It is estimated that this accounts for almost all the

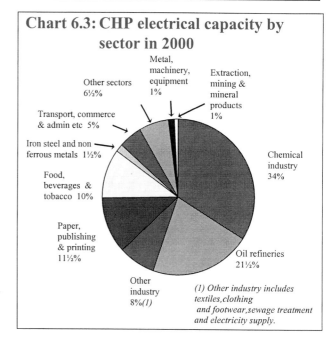

Chart 6.3: CHP electrical capacity by sector in 2000

Metal, machinery, equipment 1%

Other sectors 6½%

Extraction, mining & mineral products 1%

Transport, commerce & admin etc 5%

Iron steel and non ferrous metals 1½%

Chemical industry 34%

Food, beverages & tobacco 10%

Paper, publishing & printing 11½%

Oil refineries 21½%

Other industry 8% *(1)*

(1) Other industry includes textiles, clothing and footwear, sewage treatment and electricity supply.

electricity exported from schemes in 2000. Together these schemes account for 54 per cent of installed CHP capacity. 80 per cent of the exports

Table 6D: Number and capacity of CHP schemes installed in buildings by sector in 2000 *(1)*

	Number of schemes	Electrical capacity (MWe)	Heat capacity (MWth)
Leisure	410	36.53	64.75
Hotels	307	33.47	58.44
Health	226	103.37	207.43
Residential Group Heating	57	45.75	75.55
Offices	45	20.71	26.29
Education	31	4.85	6.07
Universities	25	25.00	61.80
Government Estate	16	13.32	22.39
Retail	6	5.57	4.23
Other *(2)*	13	26.83	58.37
Total	1,136	315.4	585.32

(1) These figures take account of a number of schemes previously unknown which have applied to CHPQA. On an equivalent basis there were 1,060 such schemes in 1999.

(2) Other includes: agriculture; airports; domestic buildings.

Table 6E: A summary of scheme performance in 2000

	Typical operating hours per annum (Full load equivalent)	Average electrical efficiency (% GCV)	Average heat efficiency (% GCV)	Average overall efficiency (% GCV)	Average heat to power ratio	Average parasitic losses (% of electrical output)
Main prime mover in CHP plant						
Back pressure steam turbine	3,863	10.0	58.9	69.0	5.88	7.6
Pass out condensing steam turbine	5,100	13.2	58.2	71.5	4.40	4.6
Gas turbine	5,715	22.4	45.1	67.4	2.02	2.9
Combined cycle	4,985	22.4	51.4	73.8	2.29	1.8
Reciprocating engine	4,983	29.6	38.6	68.2	1.30	2.5
All schemes	**5,051**	**19.5**	**51.6**	**71.2**	**2.63**	**2.1**

come from schemes where the whole scheme is certified as Good Quality. Where a scheme which exports is Good Quality for only a portion of its capacity and output, the exports have been scaled back in the same way as power output has been scaled back (see paragraph 6.33, below). Table 6F shows further details of these exports.

Table 6F: Electrical exports from CHP

	GWh
To part of same qualifying group *(1)*	681
To a firm NOT part of same qualifying group	1,627
To an electricity supplier	4,716
Destination not recorded	629
Total	**7,656**

(1) A qualifying group is a group of two or more corporate consumers which are connected or related to each other for example as a subsidiary, or via a parent or holding company, or in terms of share capital.

6.22   Around 20 large schemes supply heat to more than one customer. They have a cumulative CHP capacity of 570 MWe (12 per cent of total electrical capacity). A number of these are on mixed industrial sites. A handful are in city centres and supply heat and power to a mix of commercial and sometimes residential customers. Together they supply 7,188 GWh of heat.

6.23   There are an estimated 12 schemes with mechanical power output, accounting for 7 per cent of the power output of UK CHP schemes (CHP_{QPC}) (Table 6G). These schemes are predominantly on petro-chemicals or steel sites, using by-product fuels in boilers to drive steam turbines. The steam turbine is used to provide mechanical rather than electrical power, driving compressors, blowers or fans, rather than an alternator.

6.24   Whereas the common assumption is that CHP produces electricity and heat for on-site use, a third of power produced is electricity for export (with a third of that going directly to final customers) and 7 per cent is mechanical power rather than electrical power. Thus only 60 per cent of power produced is electricity used on-site. In addition about 12 per cent of all heat

provided from CHP in 2000 was supplied to third party customers. These figures exclude electricity and heat supplied by Energy Service Companies to a host site.

Table 6G: CHP schemes with mechanical power output

Number of schemes	12
Total Power Capacity of these schemes (CHP_{TPC})	985 MWe
Qualifying Power Capacity of these schemes (CHP_{QPC})	751 MWe
Mechanical power capacity of these schemes	327 MWe
Mechanical power as a percentage of total UK CHP power capacity (CHP_{QPC})	7 per cent

Emissions savings

6.25   The calculation of emissions savings from CHP is important, given the substantial contribution of CHP to the Climate Change Programme, but complex given that CHP displaces a variety of fuels, technologies and sizes of plant. Using the methodology and assumptions outlined in Energy Trends (http://www.dti.gov.uk/epa/bpoct2000.pdf, central assumptions) CHP saved 4.48 MtC in 2000 compared to equivalent electricity-only and heat-only generation. This is equivalent to 0.97 MtC per 1000 MWe This is an increase on the figure of 0.78 MtC per 1000 MWe for 1999 given in the Energy Trends article. This increase is due to a continued switch to gas-fired CCGT CHP schemes, and to the more strict scaling-back methodology in CHPQA.

Technical notes and definitions

6.26 These notes and definitions are in addition to the technical notes and definitions covering all fuels and energy as a whole in Chapter 1, paragraphs 1.46 to 1.81.

Data for 2000

6.27 The data are summarised from the results of a long term project being undertaken by ETSU (part of AEA Technology (AEAT) Environment) on behalf of the Department of Trade and Industry and the Statistical Office of the European Communities (Eurostat). Data are included for CHP schemes installed in all sectors of the UK economy.

6.28 The project continues to be overseen by a Steering Group that comprises officials from the Department of Trade and Industry, the Department for the Environment, Food and Rural Affairs (DEFRA), the Office of Gas and Electricity Markets (OFGEM) and the Combined Heat and Power Association (CHPA), all of whom have an interest in either the collection of information on CHP schemes or the promotion of the wider use of CHP throughout the UK economy.

6.29 Data for 2000 were based largely on data supplied to the CHPQA programme, supplemented by a survey carried out by the Office for National Statistics (ONS) between December 2000 and March 2001 of companies (other than major power producers) who generate their own electricity, either in CHP schemes or in electricity-only schemes. Information on the CHP plant included in the major power producers category comes from surveys conducted by DTI as part of the electricity statistics system. DTI also collects directly fuel use relating to the iron and steel industry. Over half of CHP schemes and around 80 per cent of capacity are based on returns under CHPQA, while around 5 per cent of schemes and 10 per cent of CHP capacity are based on data from ONS. Data for schemes not applying for CHPQA and not included in the ONS survey (eg because they were below the cut off capacity for the survey) were interpolated from historical data.

Definitions of schemes

6.30 There are four principal types of CHP system. These are:

Steam turbine, where steam at high pressure is generated in a boiler. In **back pressure steam turbine systems**, the steam is wholly or partly used in a turbine before being exhausted from the turbine at the required pressure for the site. In **pass-out condensing steam turbine systems**, a proportion of the steam used by the turbine is extracted at an intermediate pressure from the turbine with the remainder being fully condensed before it is exhausted

at the exit. (Condensing steam turbines without passout and which do not utilise steam are not included in these statistics as they are not CHP). The boilers used in such schemes can burn a wide variety of fuels including coal, gas, oil, and waste-derived fuels. With the exception of waste-fired schemes, steam turbine plant has often been in service for several decades. Steam turbine schemes capable of supplying useful steam have electrical efficiencies of between 10 and 20 per cent, depending on size, and thus between 70 per cent and 30 per cent of the fuel input is available as useful heat. Steam turbines used in CHP applications typically range in size from a few MWe to over 100 MWe.

Gas turbine systems, often aero-engine derivatives, where fuel (gas, or gas-oil) is combusted in the gas turbine and the exhaust gases are normally used in a waste heat boiler to produce usable steam, though the exhaust gases may be used directly in some process applications. Gas turbines range from 30kWe upwards, achieving electrical efficiency of 23 to 30 per cent (depending on size) and with the potential to recover up to 50 per cent of the fuel input as useful heat. They have been common in CHP since the mid 1980s. The waste heat boiler can include supplementary or auxiliary firing using a wide range of fuels, and thus the heat to power ratio of the scheme can vary.

Combined cycle systems, where the plant comprises more than one prime mover. These are usually gas turbines where the exhaust gases are utilised in a steam generator, the steam from which is passed wholly or in part into one or more steam turbines. In rare cases reciprocating engines may be linked with steam turbines. Combined cycle is suited to larger installations of 7 MWe and over. They achieve higher electrical efficiency and a lower heat to power ratio than steam turbines or gas turbines. Recently installed combined cycle gas turbine (CCGT) schemes have achieved an electrical efficiency approaching 50 per cent, with 20 per cent heat recovery, and a heat to power ratio of less than 1:1.

Reciprocating engine systems range from less than 100 kWe up to around 5 MWe, and are found in applications where production of hot water (rather than steam) is the main requirement, for example, on smaller industrial sites as well as in buildings. They are based on auto engine or marine engine derivatives converted to run on gas. Both compression ignition and spark ignition firing is used. Reciprocating engines operate at around 28 to 33 per cent electrical efficiency with around 50 per cent to 33 per cent of the fuel input available as useful heat. Reciprocating engines produce two grades of waste heat: high grade heat from the engine exhaust and low grade heat from the engine cooling circuits.

Determining fuel consumption for heat and electricity

6.31   In order to provide a comprehensive picture of electricity generation in the United Kingdom and the fuels used to generate that electricity, the energy input to CHP schemes has to be allocated between heat and electricity production. This allocation is notional and is not determinate. The present convention is that the CHP plant displaces heat-only-boiler plant with an overall efficiency of 75 per cent. The fuel that would be consumed in the heat-only-boiler plant to produce the same amount of heat that each CHP scheme produces is subtracted from the scheme's fuel consumption. The balance is the amount of fuel assumed to be used for electricity generation.

6.32   The iron and steel sector presents special problems because of the interaction of various heat sources, boilers and generators within the integrated steel works. The method used for other sectors can give negative fuel inputs for electricity generation or inputs that are less than the energy produced. Therefore an additional assumption has been made for iron and steel that fuel input for electricity was equivalent to that required to generate the electricity at an efficiency of 85 per cent.

The effects on the statistics of using CHPQA

6.33   Paragraph 6.10 described how schemes were scaled back so that only CHP_{QPC} and CHP_{QPO} were included in the CHP statistics. This is illustrated in Table 6H. In the 2000 Digest, Chapter 6, for 1999 13 schemes were scaled back with a CHP_{TPC} of 5,748 MW, and a CHP_{QPC} of 1,087 MW. The 1999 data have been amended this year and 50 schemes are now scaled back and revised to a CHP_{TPC} of 5,852 MW, and a CHP_{QPC} of 759 MW – a reduction of 328 MWe. The equivalent capacity and output data for 2000 are shown in table 6H.

Table 6H: CHP capacity, output and fuel use which has been scaled back

Number of schemes requiring scaling back	57
Total Power Capacity of these schemes (CHP_{TPC})	7,076 MWe
Qualifying Power Capacity of these schemes (CHP_{QPC})	1,045 MWe
Total power output of these schemes (CHP_{TPO})	28,329 GWh
Qualifying Power Output of these schemes (CHP_{QPO})	4,672 GWh
Electricity regarded as "Power only" not from CHP ($CHP_{TPO} - CHP_{QPO}$)	23,656 GWh
Total Fuel Input of these schemes (CHP_{TFI})	84,570 GWh
Fuel input regarded as being for "Power only" use ie not for CHP	66,493 GWh

Summary

6.34   2000 was an important year for CHP. The target of 5,000 MWe will be met during 2001, and significant new policy measures have been put in place. These include:

- the confirmation of the new target of at least 10,000 MWe by 2010,
- introduction of CHPQA as a passport to benefits such as exemption from Climate Change Levy, Enhanced Capital Allowances, and Exemption from Business Rates, as well as improvements to UK CHP statistics.

6.35   2000 has also been an extremely tough year for operators of CHP schemes with increasing gas prices and falling electricity prices. Whilst 2000 was one of the best years for growth in CHP capacity and output, it is unlikely to be matched in the coming few years.

6.36   2001 will see the new CHP strategy and further initiatives to encourage the take up of CHP, such as the development of the new Community Energy Programme.

Contacts: *Dr Mark Hinnells, ETSU*
        mark.hinnells@aeat.co.uk
        01235 433725

        Mike Janes (Statistician), DTI
        mike.janes@dti.gsi.gov.uk
        020 7215 5186

6.1 CHP installations by capacity and size range

	1996	1997	1998	1999	2000
Number of schemes (1)	**1,370r**	**1,388r**	**1,435r**	**1,460r**	**1,556**
Less than 100 kWe	707r	713r	696r	694r	724
100 kWe to 999 kWe	446r	451r	491r	514r	559
1 MWe to 9.9 MWe	153r	158r	175r	177r	196
10.0 MWe and above	64r	66r	73r	75r	77
					MWe
Total capacity	**3,301r**	**3,466r**	**3,759r**	**4,004r**	**4,632**
Less than 100 kWe	39r	40r	39r	39r	41
100 kWe to 999 kWe	108r	110r	121r	129r	138
1 MWe to 9.9 MWe	652r	666r	734r	757r	815
10.0 MWe and above	2,502r	2,650r	2,865r	3,079r	3,638

(1) A site may contain more than one CHP scheme. In previous years this table was drawn up in terms of sites.

6.2 Fuel used to generate electricity and heat in CHP plants

GWh

	1996	1997	1998	1999	2000
Fuel used to generate electricity (1)					
Coal	4,689r	4,354r	2,739r	1,527r	1,020
Fuel oil	2,658r	3,239r	3,338r	3,358r	2,091
Natural gas	10,745r	13,235r	15,749r	19,392r	24,345
Renewable fuels (2)	991r	988r	1,055r	1,104r	973
Other fuels (3)	8,610r	8,330r	8,596r	8,441r	8,719
Total all fuels	**27,693r**	**30,146r**	**31,477r**	**33,822r**	**37,148**
Fuel used to generate heat					
Coal	12,996r	11,584r	10,221r	7,531r	4,507
Fuel oil	13,154r	11,224r	10,779r	10,655r	5,111
Natural gas	32,316r	35,657r	39,271r	40,132r	49,505
Renewable fuels (2)	1,199r	1,190r	1,186r	1,115r	1,029
Other fuels (3)	25,182r	22,712r	22,279r	22,165r	21,863
Total all fuels	**84,846r**	**82,366r**	**83,735r**	**81,599r**	**82,015**
Overall fuel use					
Coal	17,685r	15,937r	12,960r	9,058r	5,527
Fuel oil	15,812r	14,463r	14,117r	14,013r	7,202
Natural gas	43,061r	48,892r	55,020r	59,523r	73,850
Renewable fuels (2)	2,190r	2,178r	2,241r	2,219r	2,002
Other fuels (3)	33,792r	31,042r	30,875r	30,606r	30,582
Total all fuels	**112,539r**	**112,512r**	**115,212r**	**115,421r**	**119,163**

(1) The allocation of fuel use between heat generation and electricity generation is largely notional. See paragraphs 6.31 and 6.32 for an explanation of the method used.
(2) Renewable fuels include: sewage gas; other biogases; clinical waste; municipal waste.
(3) Other fuels include: process by-products, coke oven gas, blast furnace gas, gas oil and uranium.

6.3 Fuel used by types of CHP installation

	1996	1997	1998	1999	2000
Coal					
Back pressure steam turbine	10,494	9,073	7,975r	3,983r	2,491
Gas turbine	162r	31r	31r	31r	30
Combined cycle	261r	303r	498r	271r	347
Reciprocating engine	-	-	-	-r	-
Pass out condensing steam turbine	6,767r	6,531r	4,456r	4,774r	2,659
Total coal	**17,685r**	**15,937r**	**12,960r**	**9,058r**	**5,527**
Fuel oil					
Back pressure steam turbine	5,539r	3,264r	2,763r	2,336r	551
Gas turbine	61r	273r	410r	503r	651
Combined cycle	3,779r	5,023r	4,756r	4,798r	5,091
Reciprocating engine	321r	299r	371r	387r	243
Pass out condensing steam turbine	6,112r	5,605r	5,817r	5,989r	666
Total fuel oil	**15,812r**	**14,463r**	**14,117r**	**14,013r**	**7,202**
Natural gas					
Back pressure steam turbine	11,141r	11,726r	9,662r	7,941r	6,502
Gas turbine	9,602r	11,490r	12,954r	13,522r	15,953
Combined cycle	12,698r	16,352r	20,332r	25,229r	36,169
Reciprocating engine	3,412r	3,476r	5,024r	5,700r	8,074
Pass out condensing steam turbine	6,208r	5,849r	7,048r	7,132r	7,154
Total natural gas	**43,061r**	**48,892r**	**55,020r**	**59,523r**	**73,850**
Renewable fuels *(1)*					
Back pressure steam turbine	282r	284r	289r	119r	119
Gas turbine	-	-	-	-	-
Combined cycle	-	-	-	-	-
Reciprocating engine	1,707r	1,692r	1,651r	1,635r	1,417
Pass out condensing steam turbine	202r	202r	301r	466r	466
Total renewable fuels	**2,190r**	**2,178r**	**2,241r**	**2,219r**	**2,002**
Other fuels *(2)*					
Back pressure steam turbine	6,696r	6,056r	5,845r	5,865r	5,175
Gas turbine	2,812r	2,549r	2,229r	2,244r	3,200
Combined cycle	6,845r	7,491r	7,673r	7,534r	8,072
Reciprocating engine	318r	305r	290r	257r	288
Pass out condensing steam turbine	17,121r	14,642r	14,838r	14,706r	13,848
Total other fuels	**33,792r**	**31,042r**	**30,875r**	**30,606r**	**30,582**
Total - all fuels					
Back pressure steam turbine	34,152r	30,402r	26,534r	20,239r	14,837
Gas turbine	12,637r	14,342r	15,623r	16,299r	19,834
Combined cycle	23,583r	29,169r	33,259r	37,832r	49,678
Reciprocating engine	5,758r	5,772r	7,336r	7,984r	10,021
Pass out condensing steam turbine	35,451r	31,855r	31,491r	32,069r	24,792
Total all fuels	**112,539r**	**112,512r**	**115,212r**	**115,421r**	**119,163**

(1) Renewable fuels include: sewage gas; other biogases; clinical waste; municipal waste.
(2) Other fuels include: process by-products, coke oven gas, blast furnace gas, gas oil and uranium.

6.4 CHP - electricity generated by fuel and type of installation

GWh

	1996	1997	1998	1999	2000
Coal					
Back pressure steam turbine	766r	666r	598r	269r	201
Gas turbine	40r	4r	4r	5r	6
Combined cycle	51r	59r	83r	44r	45
Reciprocating engine	-	-	-	-	-
Pass out condensing steam turbine	1,019r	918r	649r	661r	396
Total coal	**1,876r**	**1,647r**	**1,334r**	**978r**	**648**
Fuel oil					
Back pressure steam turbine	433r	267r	228r	199r	53
Gas turbine	12r	52r	68r	81r	116
Combined cycle	474r	603r	639r	625r	805
Reciprocating engine	67r	82r	112r	119r	73
Pass out condensing steam turbine	726r	752r	825r	862r	109
Total fuel oil	**1,712r**	**1,755r**	**1,871r**	**1,885r**	**1,158**
Natural gas					
Back pressure steam turbine	922	946r	717r	593r	557
Gas turbine	2,161r	2,724r	3,050r	3,256r	3,775
Combined cycle	3,144r	3,920r	4,815r	6,765r	9,086
Reciprocating engine	919r	970r	1,480r	1,682r	2,433
Pass out condensing steam turbine	669r	737r	956r	961r	1,076
Total natural gas	**7,814r**	**9,297r**	**11,017r**	**13,256r**	**16,927**
Renewable fuels (1)					
Back pressure steam turbine	32r	31r	31r	18r	17
Gas turbine	-	-	-	-	-
Combined cycle	-	-	-	-	-
Reciprocating engine	414r	411r	410r	409r	369
Pass out condensing steam turbine	37r	37r	49r	48r	37
Total renewable fuels	**482r**	**479r**	**490r**	**474r**	**424**
Other fuels (2)					
Back pressure steam turbine	826r	792r	768r	770r	659
Gas turbine	494r	352r	327r	336r	538
Combined cycle	833r	785r	1,178r	980r	1,192
Reciprocating engine	105r	119r	92r	80r	89
Pass out condensing steam turbine	1,937r	1,723r	1,758r	1,719r	1,661
Total other fuels	**4,195r**	**3,771r**	**4,123r**	**3,883r**	**4,139**
Total - all fuels					
Back pressure steam turbine	2,978r	2,702r	2,342r	1,848r	1,487
Gas turbine	2,707r	3,133r	3,449r	3,677r	4,435
Combined cycle	4,502r	5,365r	6,715r	8,413r	11,128
Reciprocating engine	1,505r	1,581r	2,093r	2,289r	2,965
Pass out condensing steam turbine	4,387r	4,167r	4,237r	4,250r	3,280
Total all fuels	**16,079r**	**16,949r**	**18,835r**	**20,477r**	**23,295**

(1) Renewable fuels include: sewage gas; other biogases; clinical waste; municipal waste.
(2) Other fuels include: process by-products, coke oven gas, blast furnace gas, gas oil and uranium.

6.5 CHP - electrical capacity by fuel and type of installation

MWe

	1996	1997	1998	1999	2000
Coal					
Back pressure steam turbine	192	161	155	78r	66
Gas turbine	5r	1r	1r	1r	1
Combined cycle	10	11	15	8r	8
Reciprocating engine	-	-	-	-r	-
Pass out condensing steam turbine	231r	230r	152r	192r	93
Total coal	**438r**	**403r**	**323r**	**279r**	**168**
Fuel oil					
Back pressure steam turbine	115r	74r	68r	49r	16
Gas turbine	3r	12r	21r	25r	31
Combined cycle	93r	124r	118r	116r	207
Reciprocating engine	19r	183r	28r	27r	21
Pass out condensing steam turbine	159r	22r	192r	202r	24
Total fuel oil	**390r**	**416r**	**427r**	**418r**	**299**
Natural gas					
Back pressure steam turbine	221r	225r	191r	181r	167
Gas turbine	346r	436r	461r	492r	615
Combined cycle	642r	728r	964r	1,238r	1,731
Reciprocating engine	203r	216r	294r	339r	463
Pass out condensing steam turbine	135r	147r	194r	186r	231
Total natural gas	**1,546r**	**1,752r**	**2,104r**	**2,435r**	**3,207**
Renewable fuels (1)					
Back pressure steam turbine	16r	16	16	13r	18
Gas turbine	-	-	-	-	-
Combined cycle	-	-	-	-	-
Reciprocating engine	88r	87	91r	92r	86
Pass out condensing steam turbine	13r	13r	17r	18r	18
Total renewable fuels	**117r**	**117r**	**124r**	**123r**	**122**
Other fuels (2)					
Back pressure steam turbine	148r	141r	141r	142r	119
Gas turbine	128r	114r	101r	107r	129
Combined cycle	156r	187r	199r	171r	286
Reciprocating engine	29r	31	25r	23r	26
Pass out condensing steam turbine	350r	306r	315r	306r	278
Total other fuels	**811r**	**779r**	**782r**	**749r**	**837**
Total - all fuels					
Back pressure steam turbine	691r	617r	572r	462r	385
Gas turbine	482r	564r	584r	624r	776
Combined cycle	901r	1,049r	1,295r	1,533r	2,232
Reciprocating engine	339r	517r	438r	481r	595
Pass out condensing steam turbine	888r	718r	871r	904r	643
Total all fuels	**3,301r**	**3,466r**	**3,759r**	**4,004r**	**4,632**

(1) Renewable fuels include: sewage gas; other biogases; clinical waste; municipal waste.
(2) Other fuels include: process by-products and uranium.

6.6 CHP - heat generated by fuel and type of installation

GWh

	1996	1997	1998	1999	2000
Coal					
Back pressure steam turbine	5,608r	4,637r	4,693r	2,673r	1,586
Gas turbine	57r	19r	19r	19r	17
Combined cycle	177r	200r	342r	191r	179
Reciprocating engine	-	-	-	-r	-
Pass out condensing steam turbine	3,904r	3,831r	2,612r	2,765r	1,546
Total coal	**9,747r**	**8,687r**	**7,666r**	**5,648r**	**3,328**
Fuel oil					
Back pressure steam turbine	3,793r	2,110r	1,823r	1,557r	396
Gas turbine	25r	114r	162r	194r	274
Combined cycle	2,208r	2,767r	2,549r	2,593r	2,725
Reciprocating engine	153r	107r	119r	120r	63
Pass out condensing steam turbine	3,686r	3,320r	3,431r	3,529r	376
Total fuel oil	**9,865r**	**8,418r**	**8,084r**	**7,992r**	**3,833**
Natural gas					
Back pressure steam turbine	7,740r	7,851r	6,641r	5,517r	4,166
Gas turbine	4,356r	5,006r	5,622r	5,791r	7,204
Combined cycle	6,237r	8,090r	10,200r	11,421r	18,171
Reciprocating engine	1,389r	1,520r	1,980r	2,340r	3,210
Pass out condensing steam turbine	4,515r	4,275r	5,010r	5,033r	4,380
Total natural gas	**24,237r**	**26,743r**	**29,453r**	**30,102r**	**37,130**
Renewable fuels (1)					
Back pressure steam turbine	75r	73r	62r	36r	36
Gas turbine	-	-	-	-	-
Combined cycle	-	-	-	-	-
Reciprocating engine	682r	677r	634r	635r	482
Pass out condensing steam turbine	142r	142r	193r	166r	253
Total renewable fuels	**899r**	**892r**	**889r**	**836r**	**771**
Other fuels (2)					
Back pressure steam turbine	3,619r	3,173r	3,023r	3,035r	2,562
Gas turbine	1,231r	1,109r	1,027r	1,000r	1,446
Combined cycle	4,024r	4,269r	4,082r	4,150r	4,448
Reciprocating engine	121	123	109r	93r	111
Pass out condensing steam turbine	9,891r	8,360r	8,468r	8,345r	7,881
Total other fuels	**18,886r**	**17,034r**	**16,709r**	**16,624r**	**16,449**
Total - all fuels					
Back pressure steam turbine	20,836r	17,844r	16,242r	12,818r	8,747
Gas turbine	5,670r	6,249r	6,831r	7,004r	8,941
Combined cycle	12,646r	15,327r	17,173r	18,356r	25,523
Reciprocating engine	2,345r	2,427r	2,842r	3,188r	3,866
Pass out condensing steam turbine	22,139r	19,928r	19,713r	19,838r	14,437
Total all fuels	**63,634r**	**61,775r**	**62,801r**	**61,203r**	**61,513**

(1) Renewable fuels include: sewage gas; other biogases; clinical waste; municipal waste.
(2) Other fuels include: process by-products and uranium.

6.7 CHP - heat capacity by fuel and type of installation

MWth

	1996	1997	1998	1999	2000
Coal					
Back pressure steam turbine	1,682r	1,391r	1,373r	736r	465
Gas turbine	10r	3r	3r	3r	3
Combined cycle	28r	32r	47r	25r	25
Reciprocating engine	-	-	-	-	-
Pass out condensing steam turbine	1,824r	1,822r	1,165r	1,326r	314
Total coal	**3,544r**	**3,248r**	**2,584r**	**2,090r**	**807**
Fuel oil					
Back pressure steam turbine	1,120r	699r	610r	428r	123
Gas turbine	8r	40r	73r	90r	103
Combined cycle	337r	419r	400r	389r	527
Reciprocating engine	42r	32r	34r	34r	24
Pass out condensing steam turbine	1,230r	1,420r	1,497r	1,572r	70
Total fuel oil	**2,738r**	**2,611r**	**2,614r**	**2,513r**	**847**
Natural gas					
Back pressure steam turbine	1,738r	1,756r	1,467r	1,309r	801
Gas turbine	1,035r	1,156r	1,183r	1,179r	1,270
Combined cycle	1,345r	1,617r	2,086r	2,592r	3,221
Reciprocating engine	370r	419r	519r	574r	744
Pass out condensing steam turbine	909r	968r	1,351r	1,270r	876
Total natural gas	**5,397r**	**5,916r**	**6,606r**	**6,924r**	**6,912**
Renewable fuels *(1)*					
Back pressure steam turbine	53r	54r	54r	46r	46
Gas turbine	-	-	-	-	-
Combined cycle	-	-	-	-	-
Reciprocating engine	145	149r	142	150r	138
Pass out condensing steam turbine	30r	30r	52r	57r	57
Total renewable fuels	**229r**	**233r**	**248r**	**253r**	**241**
Other fuels *(2)*					
Back pressure steam turbine	591r	461r	461r	463r	401
Gas turbine	499r	467r	416r	411r	466
Combined cycle	623r	661r	691r	643r	798
Reciprocating engine	37r	39r	34r	29r	34
Pass out condensing steam turbine	1,975r	1,658r	1,738r	1,645r	1,450
Total other fuels	**3,725r**	**3,285r**	**3,341r**	**3,192r**	**3,149**
Total - all fuels					
Back pressure steam turbine	5,184r	4,360r	3,965r	2,982r	1,836
Gas turbine	1,553r	1,666r	1,675r	1,683r	1,842
Combined cycle	2,333r	2,729r	3,224r	3,649r	4,571
Reciprocating engine	594r	640r	729r	788r	940
Pass out condensing steam turbine	5,968r	5,898r	5,803r	5,870r	2,767
Total all fuels	**15,631r**	**15,294r**	**15,397r**	**14,972r**	**11,956**

(1) Renewable fuels include: sewage gas; other biogases; clinical waste; municipal waste.
(2) Other fuels include: process by-products and uranium.

6.8 CHP capacity, output and total fuel use[1] by sector

	Unit	1996	1997	1998	1999	2000
Iron and steel and non ferrous metals						
Number of sites		7	7	6	6	6
Electrical capacity	MWe	78r	78r	74r	74r	74
Heat capacity	MWth	502r	502r	492r	491r	491
Electrical output	GWh	489r	491r	494r	492r	486
Heat output	GWh	2,371r	2,373r	2,375r	2,361r	2,377
Fuel use	GWh	3,737r	3,741r	3,748r	3,726r	3,741
of which : for electricity	GWh	576r	578r	581r	578r	571
for heat	GWh	3,161r	3,163r	3,167r	3,147r	3,169
Chemicals						
Number of sites		57r	59r	61r	60r	58
Electrical capacity	MWe	1,197r	1,296r	1,303r	1,306r	1,577
Heat capacity	MWth	7,021r	6,694r	6,688r	6,432r	4,189
Electrical output	GWh	6,266r	6,511r	7,048r	6,924r	8,688
Heat output	GWh	25,078r	25,309r	25,227r	24,625r	22,968
Fuel use	GWh	44,365r	45,627r	44,509r	42,768r	44,791
of which : for electricity	GWh	10,928r	11,881r	10,874r	9,935r	14,166
for heat	GWh	33,437r	33,745r	33,635r	32,833r	30,625
Oil refineries						
Number of sites		11r	11r	12r	13r	10
Electrical capacity	MWe	715r	715r	740r	870r	986
Heat capacity	MWth	3,330r	3,330r	3,414r	3,468r	2,995
Electrical output	GWh	3,565r	3,403r	3,712r	4,017r	4,095
Heat output	GWh	17,292r	15,077r	15,521r	15,699r	14,667
Fuel use	GWh	30,762r	27,773r	28,622r	29,495r	27,521
of which : for electricity	GWh	7,706r	7,671r	7,928r	8,563r	7,965
for heat	GWh	23,056r	20,102r	20,694r	20,931r	19,556
Paper, publishing and printing						
Number of sites		41r	41r	39r	38r	39
Electrical capacity	MWe	383r	427r	478r	485r	540
Heat capacity	MWth	1,639r	1,618r	1,518r	1,447r	1,373
Electrical output	GWh	1,966r	2,609r	2,626r	3,102r	3,376
Heat output	GWh	8,056r	7,793r	7,475r	7,245r	8,640
Fuel use	GWh	13,201r	14,362r	13,960r	14,375r	15,952
of which : for electricity	GWh	2,459r	3,971r	3,993r	4,715r	4,432
for heat	GWh	10,742r	10,391r	9,967r	9,660r	11,520
Food, beverages and tobacco						
Number of sites		42r	46r	51r	52r	56
Electrical capacity	MWe	223r	232r	336r	430r	470
Heat capacity	MWth	1,484r	1,467r	1,477r	1,402r	1,261
Electrical output	GWh	1,000r	1,093r	1,422r	2,304r	2,499
Heat output	GWh	5,228r	5,567r	5,907r	5,341r	6,064
Fuel use	GWh	8,624r	9,151r	10,218r	10,979r	11,470
of which : for electricity	GWh	1,653r	1,728r	2,342r	3,857r	3,386
for heat	GWh	6,970r	7,423r	7,876r	7,122r	8,085
Metal products, machinery and equipment						
Number of sites		8r	9r	8r	9r	14
Electrical capacity	MWe	22r	27r	25r	27r	36
Heat capacity	MWth	59r	63r	50r	59r	70
Electrical output	GWh	103r	128r	119r	135r	204
Heat output	GWh	220r	230r	169r	173r	268
Fuel use	GWh	503r	488r	436r	471r	684
of which : for electricity	GWh	210r	181r	211r	240r	327
for heat	GWh	293r	307r	226r	231r	358

6.8 CHP capacity, output and total fuel use[1] by sector (continued)

	Unit	1996	1997	1998	1999	2000
Mineral products, extraction, mining and agglomeration of solid fuels						
Number of sites		5r	5r	6r	6r	10
Electrical capacity	MWe	20r	20r	24r	24r	56
Heat capacity	MWth	126r	126r	100r	100r	88
Electrical output	GWh	111r	110r	163r	149r	313
Heat output	GWh	659r	639r	622r	573r	913
Fuel use	GWh	1,036r	971r	1,053r	989r	1,592
of which : for electricity	GWh	157r	119r	223r	225r	376
for heat	GWh	879r	852r	830r	764r	1,217
Textiles, clothing and footwear						
Number of sites		4	4	4	3	3
Electrical capacity	MWe	4	4	4r	2	2
Heat capacity	MWth	55	31	31	13	13
Electrical output	GWh	11	11	14	2	2
Heat output	GWh	111r	111r	114r	25	25
Fuel use	GWh	280r	180r	187r	34	34
of which : for electricity	GWh	132r	32	36r	4r	3
for heat	GWh	148r	148r	152r	31r	31
Sewage treatment						
Number of sites		123r	122r	122r	115r	115
Electrical capacity	MWe	93r	93r	106r	106r	101
Heat capacity	MWth	156r	161	164r	171r	159
Electrical output	GWh	437r	435r	463r	460r	423
Heat output	GWh	728r	725r	710r	706r	549
Fuel use	GWh	1,814r	1,803r	1,859r	1,829r	1,611
of which : for electricity	GWh	843r	836r	912r	888r	879
for heat	GWh	971r	967r	947r	941r	732
Electricity supply						
Number of sites		4	4	5	5	5
Electrical capacity	MWe	224r	224r	236r	236r	236
Heat capacity	MWth	271r	271r	311r	311r	301
Electrical output	GWh	642r	642r	742r	742r	737
Heat output	GWh	844r	844r	1,037r	1,037r	1,046
Fuel use	GWh	1,789r	1,789r	2,194r	2,194r	2,204
of which : for electricity	GWh	664r	664r	811r	811r	810
for heat	GWh	1,125r	1,125r	1,383r	1,383r	1,395
Other industrial branches						
Number of sites		6r	7r	12r	12r	10
Electrical capacity	MWe	22r	23r	36r	36r	27
Heat capacity	MWth	60r	72r	89r	89r	62
Electrical output	GWh	143r	118r	202r	217r	176
Heat output	GWh	296r	304r	410r	413r	328
Fuel use	GWh	664r	627r	962r	993r	768
of which : for electricity	GWh	269r	222r	416r	442r	331
for heat	GWh	395r	405r	546r	551r	437
Transport, commerce and administration						
Number of sites		667r	669r	673r	691r	721
Electrical capacity	MWe	177r	181r	189r	208r	234
Heat capacity	MWth	339r	364r	355r	379r	441
Electrical output	GWh	878r	920r	974r	1,004r	1,068
Heat output	GWh	1,294r	1,335r	1,304r	1,440r	1,675
Fuel use	GWh	3,075r	3,288r	3,397r	3,643r	4,021
of which : for electricity	GWh	1,349r	1,508r	1,659r	1,724r	1,788
for heat	GWh	1,726r	1,780r	1,739r	1,919r	2,234

6.8 CHP capacity, output and total fuel use[1] by sector (continued)

	Unit	1996	1997	1998	1999	2000
Other (2)						
Number of sites		395r	404r	436r	450r	509
Electrical capacity	MWe	144r	148r	209r	202r	294
Heat capacity	MWth	591r	596r	711r	432r	513
Electrical output	GWh	468r	478r	857r	931r	1,228
Heat output	GWh	1,459r	1,469r	1,931r	1,564r	1,994
Fuel use	GWh	2,691r	2,712r	4,067r	3,925r	4,772
of which : for electricity	GWh	747r	755r	1,492r	1,840r	2,114
for heat	GWh	1,945r	1,958r	2,574r	2,085r	2,658
Total CHP usage by all sectors						
Number of sites		1,370r	1,388r	1,435r	1,460r	1,556
Electrical capacity	MWe	3,301r	3,466r	3,759r	4,004r	4,632
Heat capacity	MWth	15,632r	15,294r	15,398r	14,972r	11,956
Electrical output	GWh	16,079r	16,949r	18,836r	20,477r	23,295
Heat output	GWh	63,635r	61,775r	62,802r	61,203r	61,513
Fuel use	GWh	112,539r	112,512r	115,212r	115,421r	119,163
of which : for electricity	GWh	27,693r	30,146r	31,477r	33,822r	37,148
for heat	GWh	84,846r	82,366r	83,735r	81,599r	82,015

(1) The allocation of fuel use between electricity and heat is largely notional and the methodology is outlined in paragraphs 6.31 and 6.32.
(2) Sectors included under Other are agriculture, community heating, leisure, landfill and incineration.

6.9 CHP - use of fuels by sector

GWh

	1996	1997	1998	1999	2000
Iron and steel and non ferrous metals					
Coal	179r	154	172	89	97
Fuel oil	438r	258r	249r	200r	206
Gas oil	-	-	-	-	-
Natural gas	196r	397r	397r	413r	427
Blast furnace gas	2,472r	2,483r	2,480r	2,436r	2,425
Coke oven gas	408r	410r	409r	546r	544
Renewable fuels (1)	-	-	-	-	-
Other fuels (2)	44r	40r	40r	42r	42
Total iron and steel and non ferrous metals	**3,737r**	**3,741r**	**3,748r**	**3,726r**	**3,741**
Chemicals					
Coal	11,472	10,198	7,876	4,826	2,416
Fuel oil	4,425r	3,702r	3,654r	3,951r	864
Gas oil	14r	7r	74r	78r	80
Natural gas	16,268r	19,129r	20,625r	22,084r	29,746
Refinery gas	347r	347r	347r	347r	393
Renewable fuels (1)	-	-	-	-	-
Other fuels (2)	11,840r	12,244r	11,932r	11,484r	11,293
Total chemical industry	**44,365r**	**45,627r**	**44,509r**	**42,768r**	**44,791**
Oil refineries					
Fuel oil	7,471r	8,382r	8,303r	8,404r	5,315
Gas oil	92r	-r	-	266r	266
Natural gas	5,444r	4,700r	5,548r	6,319r	7,257
Refinery gas	11,472r	8,409r	8,488r	8,223r	8,402
Other fuels (2)	6,283r	6,283r	6,283r	6,283r	6,282
Total oil refineries	**30,762r**	**27,773r**	**28,622r**	**29,495r**	**27,521**
Paper, publishing and printing					
Coal	2,987r	2,546r	2,130r	1,777r	731
Fuel oil	845	476r	430	474r	376
Gas oil	10	14	17	79r	21
Natural gas	9,358r	11,324r	11,381r	12,043r	14,822
Other fuels	-	2r	2	2	2
Total paper, publishing and printing	**13,201r**	**14,362r**	**13,960r**	**14,375r**	**15,952**
Food, beverages and tobacco					
Coal	2,035	2,100	1,950r	1,844	1,680
Fuel oil	1,902	977	691	585	194
Gas oil	32r	36r	50	45r	56
Natural gas	4,652r	6,036r	7,525r	8,503r	9,539
Renewable fuels (1)	2	2	2	2	2
Other fuels (2)	-	-	-	-	-
Total food, beverages and tobacco	**8,624r**	**9,151r**	**10,218r**	**10,979r**	**11,470**
Metal products, machinery and equipment					
Coal	181	136	32r	20r	32
Fuel oil	1r	1r	56r	56r	57
Natural gas	321r	352r	348r	395r	595
Other fuels (2)	-	-	-	-	-
Total metal products, machinery and equipment	**503r**	**489r**	**436r**	**471r**	**684**
Mineral products, extraction, mining and agglomeration of solid fuels					
Coal	-	-	-	-r	69
Fuel oil	13	15	-r	-r	-
Gas oil	-	-	-	-	-
Natural gas	804	737r	833r	769r	1,373
Coke oven gas	219	219r	219r	219r	150
Other fuels (2)	-	-	-	-	-
Total mineral products, extraction, mining and agglomeration of solid fuels	**1,036r**	**971r**	**1,053r**	**989r**	**1,592**

6.9 CHP - use of fuels by sector (continued)

GWh

	1996	1997	1998	1999	2000
Textiles, clothing and footwear					
Fuel oil	-	2	8	-r	-
Gas oil	-	-	-	2r	1
Natural gas	280	178r	179r	33r	33
Total textiles, clothing and footwear	**280**	**180r**	**187r**	**34r**	**34**
Sewage treatment(3)					
Fuel oil	121	125	125	115	70
Gas oil	-	-	-	-	30
Natural gas	12	12	115	116	114
Renewable fuels (1)	1,681r	1,666r	1,619r	1,599r	1,397
Other fuels (2)	-	-	-	-	-
Total sewage treatment	**1,814r**	**1,803r**	**1,859r**	**1,829r**	**1,611**
Electricity supply					
Coal	178r	178r	178r	178r	178
Natural gas	1,352r	1,352r	1,757r	1,757r	1,767
Other fuels (2)	260r	260r	260r	260r	260
Total electricity supply	**1,789r**	**1,789r**	**2,194r**	**2,194r**	**2,204**
Other industrial branches					
Coal	-	-	-	-	-
Fuel oil	-	21r	77r	108r	52
Gas oil	-	-	-	-	1
Natural gas	664r	606r	880r	879r	710
Renewable fuels (1)	-	-	5	6r	6
Other fuels (2)	-	-	-	-	-
Total other industrial branches	**664r**	**627r**	**962r**	**993**	**768**
Transport, commerce and administration					
Coal	30r	30r	30r	30r	30
Fuel oil	189	100r	110r	107r	53
Gas oil	88	58r	39r	43r	81
Natural gas	2,765	3,097r	3,209r	3,450r	3,847
Renewable fuels (1)	-	-	5	8	8
Other fuels (2)	2r	3r	5r	5r	1
Total transport, commerce and administration	**3,075r**	**3,288r**	**3,397r**	**3,643r**	**4,021**
Other (3)					
Coal	622r	596r	591r	294r	294
Fuel oil	407r	406r	414r	15r	15
Gas oil	185r	207r	208r	225r	233
Natural gas	946r	972r	2,223r	2,764r	3,620
Renewable fuels (1)	507r	507r	608r	603r	587
Other fuels (2)	23r	23r	23r	24r	24
Total other	**2,691r**	**2,711r**	**4,067r**	**3,925r**	**4,772**
Total - all sectors					
Coal	17,685r	15,937r	12,960r	9,058r	5,527
Fuel oil	15,812r	14,463r	14,117r	14,013r	7,202
Gas oil	422r	321r	388r	738r	767
Natural gas	43,061r	48,892r	55,020r	59,523r	73,850
Blast furnace gas	2,472r	2,483r	2,481r	2,436r	2,425
Coke oven gas	627r	629r	629r	766r	694
Refinery gas	11,818r	8,756r	8,835r	8,569r	8,794
Renewable fuels (1)	2,190r	2,178r	2,241r	2,219r	2,002
Other fuels (2)	18,452r	18,853r	18,543r	18,097r	17,902
Total CHP fuel use	**112,539r**	**112,512r**	**115,212r**	**115,421r**	**119,163**

(1) Renewable fuels include: sewage gas; other biogases; clinical waste; municipal waste.
(2) Other fuels include: process by-products and uranium.
(3) Sectors included under Other are agriculture, community heating, leisure, landfill and incineration.

Chapter 7
Renewable sources of energy

Introduction

7.1   This chapter provides information on the contribution of renewable energy sources to the United Kingdom's energy requirements.

7.2   The data summarise the results of an ongoing study undertaken by the ETSU (part of AEA Technology (AEAT) Environment), on behalf of the Department of Trade and Industry, to update a database containing information on all relevant renewable energy sources in the United Kingdom. This database is called RESTATS, the Renewable Energy STATisticS database. The study is partly financed by the Statistical Office of the European Communities (Eurostat).

7.3   The study started in 1989, when all relevant renewable energy sources were identified and, where possible, information was collected on the amounts of energy derived from each source. The renewable energy sources identified were the following: active solar heating; photovoltaics; onshore and offshore wind power; wave power; large and small scale hydro; biofuels; geothermal aquifers. The technical notes at the end of this chapter define each of these renewable energy sources. The database now contains 12 years of data from 1989 to 2000.

7.4   The information contained in the database is collected by a number of methods. For larger projects, an annual survey is carried out in which questionnaires are sent to project managers. For technologies in which there are large numbers of small projects, the values given in this chapter are estimates based on information collected from a sub-sample of the projects. Further details about the data collection methodologies used in RESTATS, including the quality and completeness of the information, are given in the technical notes at the end of this chapter.

7.5   Commodity balances for renewable energy sources covering each of the last three years form the first three tables (Tables 7.1 to 7.3). These are followed by the 5 year table showing capacity of and electricity generation from renewable sources (Table 7.4), a table summarising all the renewable orders (Table 7.5) and a long term trends table covering the use of renewables to generate electricity and heat (Table 7.6).

7.6   Unlike in the commodity balance tables in other chapters of the Digest, Tables 7.1 to 7.3 have zero statistical differences. This is because the data for each category of fuel are, in the main, taken from a

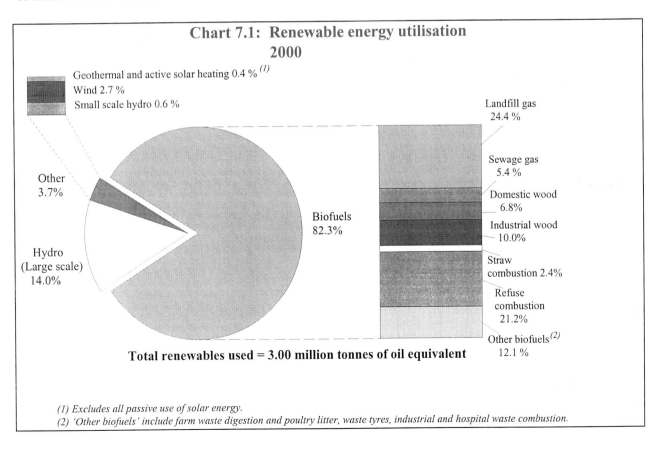

Chart 7.1: Renewable energy utilisation 2000

Geothermal and active solar heating 0.4 % *(1)*
Wind 2.7 %
Small scale hydro 0.6 %

Landfill gas 24.4 %
Sewage gas 5.4 %
Domestic wood 6.8%
Industrial wood 10.0%
Straw combustion 2.4%
Refuse combustion 21.2%
Other biofuels *(2)* 12.1 %

Other 3.7%
Hydro (Large scale) 14.0%
Biofuels 82.3%

Total renewables used = 3.00 million tonnes of oil equivalent

(1) Excludes all passive use of solar energy.
(2) 'Other biofuels' include farm waste digestion and poultry litter, waste tyres, industrial and hospital waste combustion.

single source where there is less likelihood of differences due to timing or measurement.

Renewables Orders and Obligation

7.7   In the past the main instruments for pursuing the development of renewables capacity have been the Non Fossil Fuel Obligation (NFFO) Orders for England and Wales and for Northern Ireland, and the Scottish Renewable Orders (SRO). In this chapter the term "NFFO Orders" is used is refer to these instruments collectively.   For projects contracted under NFFO Orders in England and Wales, details of capacity and generation were provided by the Non Fossil Purchasing Agency (NFPA). Information on the Scottish and Northern Ireland NFFO Orders were provided by the Scottish Executive and Northern Ireland Electricity, respectively.

7.8   Since February 2000, the United Kingdom's renewables policy has consisted of four key strands:

- a new Renewables Obligation on all electricity suppliers to supply a specific proportion of electricity from eligible renewables;
- exemption of electricity from renewables from the Climate Change Levy;
- an expanded support programme for new and renewable energy including capital grants and an expanded research and development programme;
- development of a regional strategic approach to planning and targets for renewables.

The aim is to increase the contribution of electricity from renewables in the UK to 5 per cent by the end of 2003, rising to 10 per cent in 2010, subject to the costs to consumers being acceptable.   The Renewables Obligation (and analogous Renewables (Scotland) Obligation) will be implemented by Orders under the Utilities Act 2000.   These Orders are expected to receive Parliamentary approval in autumn 2001.

Commodity balances for renewables in 2000 (Table 7.1), 1999 (Table 7.2) and 1998 (Table 7.3).

7.9   Ten different categories of renewable fuels are identified in the commodity balances. Two of these categories are themselves groups of renewables because a more detailed disaggregation could disclose data for individual companies.   The largest contribution is from biofuels, with large scale hydro electricity production contributing the majority of the remainder as Chart 7.1 shows. Only just under 4 per cent of renewable energy comes from renewable sources other than biofuels and large scale hydro. These include solar, wind, small scale hydro and geothermal aquifers.

7.10   Just under 75 per cent of the renewable energy produced in 2000 was transformed into electricity. This is an increase from 71 per cent in 1999, and 68 per cent in 1998. Whereas in 2000, municipal solid waste and landfill gas appear to dominate the picture when fuel inputs are being measured, hydro electricity dominates when the output of electricity is being measured as Table 7.4 shows. This is because on an energy supplied basis (see Chapter 5, paragraph 5.27) hydro (and wind) inputs are assumed to be equal to the electricity produced. For landfill gas, sewage sludge, municipal solid waste and other renewables a substantial proportion of the energy content of the input is lost in the process of conversion to electricity.

7.11   Overall, renewable sources, excluding passive uses of solar energy, provided 1.3 per cent of the United Kingdom's total primary energy requirements in 2000, up from 1.2 per cent in 1999 and 1.1 per cent in 1998.   If energy derived from the non-biodegradable elements of wastes are excluded (see paragraph 7.13) the figures are lower by 0.1 percentage point for each of the latest 3 years.

Capacity of, and electricity generated from renewable sources (Table 7.4)

7.12   Table 7.4 shows the capacity of, and the amounts of electricity generated from, each renewable source. Total electricity generation from renewables in 2000 amounted to 10,476 GWh, 46½ per cent of which was from large scale hydro generation. Large scale hydro generation was 5 per cent lower than in 1999 (which was the second best year for hydro generation out of the last 12). As a result renewables provided 2.8 per cent of the electricity generated in the United Kingdom in 2000 the same proportion as in 1999. Chart 7.2 shows the growth in the proportion of electricity produced from renewable sources and progress toward the objectives set in 1999 for 2003 and 2010 of 5 per cent and 10 per cent respectively. As the chart shows the variability in hydro output makes the path towards these targets a far from smooth one.

7.13   An EU Directive on the promotion of electricity from renewable energy sources is currently under negotiation in Brussels. The EU Directive proposes that Member States adopt national targets for renewables that are consistent with reaching the EU target of 12 per cent of energy (22.1 per cent of electricity) from renewables by 2010. The proposed UK "share" of this target is 10 per cent of gross electricity consumption which is comparable with our national objective for 2010.   The Directive also currently proposes that electricity from the incineration of non-biodegradable wastes is excluded

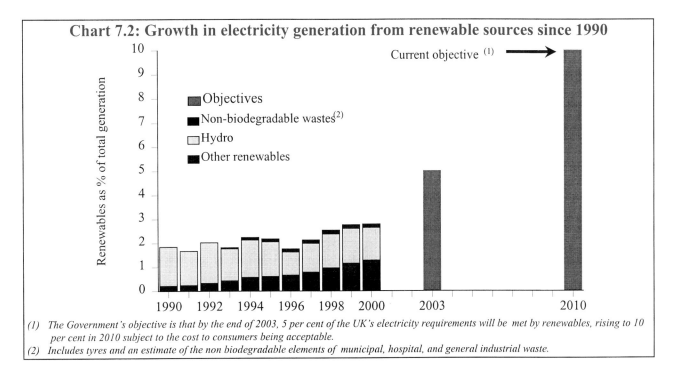

Chart 7.2: Growth in electricity generation from renewable sources since 1990

Current objective [1]

Objectives
Non-biodegradable wastes[2]
Hydro
Other renewables

Renewables as % of total generation

1990 1992 1994 1996 1998 2000 2003 2010

*(1) The Government's objective is that by the end of 2003, 5 per cent of the UK's electricity requirements will be met by renewables, rising to 10
per cent in 2010 subject to the cost to consumers being acceptable.*
(2) Includes tyres and an estimate of the non biodegradable elements of municipal, hospital, and general industrial waste.

from the calculation in the percentage contributions. If this were applied to the current UK calculation the percentage contribution to electricity generation for each of the latest three years would be around 0.2 percentage points lower (ie 2.6 per cent in 2000 in place of 2.8 per cent).

7.14   Electricity generated from renewable sources in the UK in 2000 was 2¾ per cent more than in 1999, but generation from renewables, other than hydro, in 2000 was 10½ per cent higher than in 1999 and almost double the level in 1996.

7.15   There was an increase of 28½ per cent in electricity generation from landfill gas and an increase of 11½ per cent in the total generation from onshore wind, both of which were the result of new projects being brought on-line under NFFO during the year. Output from wind farms was lower in 1999 than in

1998 because 1998 was a particularly windy year. Estimated data with the 1999 wind figure which was previously based on 1998 outputs has therefore been revised down to match the wind conditions for 1999. The largest increase in percentage terms (62 per cent) although small in volume terms was in solar photovoltaics where there was a campaign to actively encourage the take up of this technology.

7.16   There was a 10¾ per cent decrease in generation from sewage sludge digestion during 2000, and the increase in generation from municipal solid waste was only ½ per cent.

7.17   Chart 7.3 (which covers all renewables capacity except large scale hydro) shows how the electricity generation capacity from all significant renewable sources has risen steadily in the five years from 1996. The increase in 2000 in Other combustion is due to the

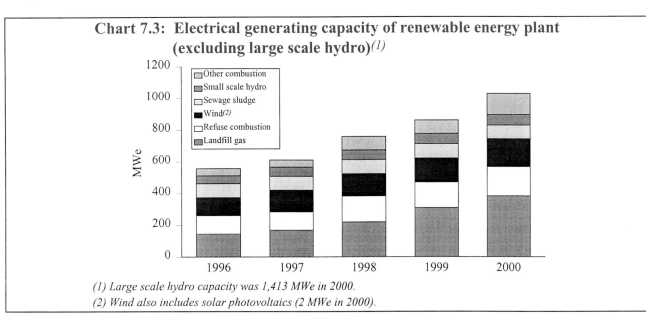

Chart 7.3: Electrical generating capacity of renewable energy plant (excluding large scale hydro)[1]

Other combustion
Small scale hydro
Sewage sludge
Wind[2]
Refuse combustion
Landfill gas

MWe

1996 1997 1998 1999 2000

(1) Large scale hydro capacity was 1,413 MWe in 2000.
(2) Wind also includes solar photovoltaics (2 MWe in 2000).

commissioning of a straw burning plant and a short rotation coppice (SRC) plant towards the end of the year. This upward trend in the capacity of new and renewable sources will continue as further projects already contracted under NFFO Orders come on line.

7.18 In 2000, 55 per cent of electricity from renewables (excluding large-scale hydro) was generated under NFFO contracts. If ex-NFFO sites (NFFO 1 and 2 in England and Wales – see paragraphs 7.20 to 7.27, below) are included the proportion increases to 89 per cent. Table 7.4, however, includes both electricity generated outside of these contracts and electricity from large-scale hydro schemes and thus reports on total electricity generation from renewables. All electricity generated from renewables is also reported within the tables of Chapter 5 of this Digest (eg Table 5.6).

7.19 Plant load factors in Table 7.4 have been calculated in terms of installed capacity and express the average hourly quantity of electricity generated as a percentage of the average capacity at the beginning and end of the year. The overall figure is heavily influenced by the availability of hydro capacity during the year which is in turn influenced by the amount of rainfall during the preceding period. Plant load factors for all generating plant in the UK are shown in Table 5.9.

Renewable orders and operational capacity (Table 7.5)

7.20 In 1990, the first year of NFFO, projects contracted within NFFO accounted for about 34 per cent of the total capacity (excluding large-scale hydro); by 1998, this figure had risen to 86 per cent, but dropped to 50 per cent in 1999 due to the expiry of NFFO 1 and 2 contracts. However, in 2000 new NFFO capacity raised the proportion back to 60 per cent. Some 907 MW of new renewables generation capacity (measured in terms of declared net capacity, DNC - see paragraph 7.71) had begun to operate by the end of 2000 as shown in Chart 7.4.

(a) Non Fossil Fuel Obligation (NFFO)
7.21 The 1989 Electricity Act empowered the Secretary of State to make orders requiring the Regional Electricity Companies in England and Wales (the RECs) to secure specified amounts of electricity from renewable energy sources.

7.22 Five NFFO Orders have been made, of which the first in 1990 was set for a total of 102 MW DNC. This first order resulted in contracts for 75 projects for 152 MW DNC and provided a premium price for the

electricity produced which was funded from a levy on electricity sales in England and Wales. (The bulk of this levy was used to support electricity from nuclear stations.)

7.23 The second Order, made in late 1991, was set for 457 MW DNC. This resulted in 122 separate contracts (for a total of 472 MW DNC) between the generators and the Non-Fossil Purchasing Agency (NFPA) which acted on behalf of the RECs. For landfill gas, sewage gas and waste-derived generation contracts were awarded at around 6p/kWh, while for wind-based generation a price of 11p/kWh was established. These prices reflected the limited period for the recovery of capital costs. The levy (which funded both nuclear and renewables until 1998) was due to be removed in 1998 but is now retained for the renewables NFFO Orders only.

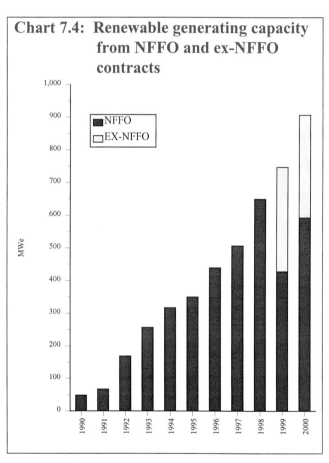

Chart 7.4: Renewable generating capacity from NFFO and ex-NFFO contracts

7.24 The third Order covers the period 1995 to 2014; this was for 627 MW DNC of contracted capacity at an average price of 4.35 p/kWh. The lower bid prices reflect the longer term contracts which are now available together with further developments which have led to improvements in the technologies. Taking into account factors such as the failure to gain planning permission it is estimated that about 300-400 MW DNC are likely to go forward for commissioning.

7.25 The fourth Order was announced in February 1997. Contracts have been let to 195 projects with a total DNC of 843 MW, at an average price of 3.46 p/kWh.

7.26 The fifth and largest Order was announced in September 1998. Contracts have been let to 261 projects with a total DNC of 1,177.1 MW, at an average price of 2.71 p/kWh.

7.27 Since the expiry of the NFFO 1 and 2 contracts on 31 December 1998, these projects are longer included in the monitoring of NFFO Orders and DTI no longer receive any status/output data on them from the NFPA. For some of these projects operational data have been obtained from other sources, while for the others estimates have been made based on output in 1997 (originally 1998 was used for these estimates but wind conditions in that year have since been found to be atypical leading to an overestimate of wind generation). Thirty four existing operational projects were contracted under the first Order and 30 under the second Order; other contracts in both Orders were for new projects.

7.28 As at the end of December 2000, 77 projects in the third Order were operational, with total capacities of 293 MW DNC. There were 62 schemes with a capacity of 157 MW DNC commissioned from the fourth Order projects and 25 schemes totalling 56 MW DNC from the fifth Order. These 164 schemes now make up a over a half of the electrical capacity from renewable sources (excluding large scale hydro capacity). Table 7.5 sets out the technologies and capacities of schemes in all five Orders.

(b)   Scottish Renewable Order (SRO)

7.29 In Scotland, the first Renewables Order was made in 1994 for approximately 76 MW DNC of new capacity and comprising 30 schemes. Four generation technology bands were covered; 12 wind, 15 hydro, 2 waste-to-energy and 1 biomass. At the end of December 2000, 16 schemes were commissioned with a capacity of 43 MW DNC.

7.30 A second SRO was launched in 1995 and was made in March 1997 for 114 MW DNC of new capacity comprising 26 schemes, nine of which were waste to energy projects, nine were hydro projects, seven were wind projects and one was a biomass project. Under this Order, at the end of 2000 there were 4 commissioned schemes with a capacity of 15 MW DNC.

7.31 A third SRO was laid before Parliament in February 1999 for 145.4 MW DNC of new capacity comprising 53 schemes. Sixteen of these are waste to

energy projects, five are hydro projects, twenty-eight are wind projects, one is a biomass project and three are wave energy projects. Under this Order, at the end of 2000 there were 4 commissioned schemes with a capacity of 14 MW DNC. Table 7.5 sets out the technologies and capacities of schemes in all three Scottish Orders.

(c)   Northern Ireland Non Fossil Fuel Obligation (NI NFFO)

7.32 In Northern Ireland a first Order was made in March 1994 for approximately 16 MW DNC comprising 20 schemes. The contracted schemes are spread throughout Northern Ireland and are divided into three technology bands. There are 6 wind schemes of around 2 MW DNC each, totalling 12.7 MW DNC; 5 sewage gas projects totalling 0.56 MW DNC; and 9 small-scale hydro schemes totalling 2.4 MW DNC. At the end of 2000, 13 schemes were commissioned with a capacity of 14.6 MW DNC.

7.33 A second NI Order was made in 1996 for 10 schemes, totalling 16 MW DNC. These comprised 2 wind schemes, 2 hydro schemes, 2 biomass, 1 biogas, 2 landfill gas and 1 municipal and industrial waste scheme, as shown in Table 7.5. At the end of 2000 five schemes were commissioned with a capacity of 3 MW DNC.

Renewable sources used to generate electricity and heat (Table 7.6).

7.34 Between 1999 and 2000 there was an increase of 13 per cent in the input of new and renewable sources into electricity generation. Nearly all of the increase is accounted for by biofuels. Fast rates of growth were recorded by solar photovoltaics (62 per cent) attributable to a vigorous promotion campaign, and landfill gas (28 per cent). Use of landfill gas for generation is now more than 3 times the level four years earlier in 1996.

7.35 Rapid growth in the use of Other biofuels in 2000 (63 per cent) was due to burning animal carcasses to produce electricity at one specialised plant and to the start up of the short rotation coppice plant.

7.36 Table 7.6 also shows the contribution from renewables to heat generation. Here only a small share comes from geothermal and active solar heating and from various wastes, while the main contribution is from wood burning, although that is declining because stringent emissions regulations affect the economics of operating older plant.

Technical notes and definitions

7.37 Energy derived from renewable sources is included in the aggregate energy tables in Chapter 1 of this Digest. The main energy tables (Tables 7.1 to 7.3) present figures in the common unit of energy, the tonne of oil equivalent, which is defined in paragraph 1.46. The gross calorific values and conversion factors used to convert the data from original units are given on page 226 of Annex A and inside the back cover flap. The statistical methodologies and conversion factors are in line with those used by the International Energy Agency and the Statistical Office of the European Communities. Primary electricity contributions from hydro and wind are expressed in terms of an electricity supplied model (see Chapter 5, paragraph 5.28) and electrical capacities are quoted as Declared Net Capacity (DNC), taking into account the intermittent nature of the power output from some renewable sources (see paragraph 7.71, below).

7.38 The various renewable energy sources are described in the following paragraphs. This section also provides details of the quality of information provided within each renewables area, and the progress made to improve the quality of this information.

Use of existing solar energy

7.39 Nearly all buildings make use of some passive solar energy because they have windows or roof lights which allow in natural light and provide a view of the surroundings. This existing use of passive solar energy is making a substantial contribution to the energy demand in the UK building stock. Passive solar design, in which buildings are designed to enhance solar energy use, results in additional savings in energy. A study in 1990, on behalf of the Department of Trade and Industry, estimated that this existing use saves 12.6 million tonnes of oil equivalent per year in the United Kingdom. This figure reflects an estimate of the net useful energy flow (heat and lighting) across windows and other glazing in the United Kingdom building stock. The figure is very approximate and, as in previous years, has therefore not been included in the tables in this chapter.

Active solar heating

7.40 Active solar heating employs solar collectors to heat water mainly for domestic hot water systems but also for swimming pools and other applications. A study for ETSU, on behalf of the Department of Trade and Industry, has provided improved estimates for this issue of the Digest. For 2000 an estimated 48.4 GWh for domestic hot water generation replaces gas heating; for swimming pools, an estimated 35.7 GWh generation for 2000 replaces gas (45 per cent), oil (45 per cent) or electricity (10 per cent).

Photovoltaics

7.41 Photovoltaics is the direct conversion of solar radiation into direct current electricity by the interaction of light with the electrons in a semiconductor device or cell. It is estimated that the electrical declared net capacity from photovoltaics is increasing at approximately 8.5 kWe per year.

Onshore wind power

7.42 A wind turbine extracts energy from the wind by means of a rotor fitted with aerodynamic-section blades using the lifting forces on the blades to turn the rotor primary shaft. This mechanical power is used to drive an electrical generator via a step-up gearbox. The figures included for generation from wind turbines are based on the installed capacities, together with an average load factor for the United Kingdom or, where figures are available, on actual generation.

7.43 There have been a total of 302 wind projects awarded contracts under NFFO. Many of these are new projects, so this has resulted in a considerable increase in electricity generation from wind since 1990. At the end of 2000, there were 73 wind generation projects operational under NFFO. More are anticipated to be commissioned over the next 3-4 years. The figures for wind in this chapter cover all known schemes in the United Kingdom. Wind capacity in 2000 was double the capacity of 5 years earlier, while electricity generated from wind is a factor of 2.4 greater over the same period. This is attributed to improvement in technologies together with the better siting of wind farms.

Offshore wind power

7.44 The UK's offshore wind resource is vast, with the potential to provide more than the UK's current demand for electricity. Offshore wind speeds are higher than those onshore (typically up to 0.5m/s higher 10 km offshore) and also less turbulent. However, elevated inland sites can have higher wind speeds.

7.45 Due to the higher costs of installing each turbine offshore it is expected that, in general, the machines will be larger than their onshore counterparts (2MW and above). This is driven by economics, with larger machine more cost effective per unit of electricity generated. The larger turbines also experience higher wind speeds, because taller towers put the rotors into the stronger winds. In addition, onshore constraints such as planning, noise effects and visual impact are likely to be reduced offshore. The

Blyth Offshore project completed its commissioning trials in December 2000. In April 2001 Crown Estates announced that 18 consortia had been successful in pre-qualifying for leases for offshore windfarms for sites of up to 30 turbines each in UK territorial waters.

Wave power

7.46 Waves in the oceans are created by the interaction of winds with the surface of the sea. Because of the direction of the prevailing winds and the size of the Atlantic Ocean, the United Kingdom has wave power levels which are amongst the highest in the world. Since 1985, the Department of Trade and Industry's shoreline programme has concentrated on an oscillating water column device on the Hebridean island of Islay. This experimental prototype came on line in late 1991 and has now been decommissioned. There are currently 3 wave schemes contracted under the third SRO for a declared net capacity of 2 MW, with one already under commission.

Large scale hydro

7.47 In hydro schemes the turbines that drive the electricity generators are powered by the direct action of water either from a reservoir or from the run of the river. Large scale hydro covers plants belonging to companies with an aggregate hydro capacity of 5 MWe and over. Most of the plants are located in Scotland and Wales and mainly draw their water from high level reservoirs with their own natural catchment areas. Figures from the schemes are provided to the Department of Trade and Industry. The data excludes pumped storage stations (see paragraph 5.60). The coverage of these large scale hydro figures is the same as that used in the tables in the Chapter 5 of this Digest. In 2000 the large scale hydro generation figure fell by 5 per cent from the 1999 figure. This was because 2000 was a relatively dry year in the catchment areas for the hydro schemes following two above average years in 1998 and 1999.

Small scale hydro

7.48 Electricity generation schemes belonging to companies with an aggregate hydro capacity below 5 MWe are classified as small scale. These are schemes being used for either domestic/farm purposes or for sale to the local regional electricity company. Data given for generation are actual figures where available, but otherwise are estimated using a typical load factor (55 per cent), or the design load factor, where known. The estimated figures for 1998 and 1997 have been calculated using a load factor of 36 per cent, while those for 1996 have been calculated using a load factor of 28 per cent to reflect the reduction of generation due to the reduced rainfall. A new survey of small scale hydro sites was carried out in 1999 giving a more detailed picture of the current situation that formed the basis for estimates in 2000; a load factor of 55 per cent was used for 1999 and 2000 data. 146 small scale hydro schemes were contracted within NFFO. Twenty two of these were existing schemes. No new schemes came on line in 2000.

Geothermal aquifers

7.49 Aquifers containing water at elevated temperatures occur in some parts of the United Kingdom at between 1,500 and 3,000 metres below the surface. This water can be pumped to the surface and used, for example, in community heating schemes. There is currently only one scheme operating in the UK at Southampton.

Biofuels

(a) Landfill gas

7.50 Landfill gas is a methane-rich biogas formed from the decomposition of organic material in landfill. The gas can be used to fuel reciprocating engines or turbines to generate electricity or used directly in kilns and boilers. In other countries, the gas has been cleaned to pipeline quality or used as a vehicle fuel. Data on landfill gas exploitation are provided from LAMMCOS, the LAndfill gas Monitoring, Modelling and COmmunication System. This is a landfill gas database maintained by ETSU and containing information on all existing landfill gas exploitation schemes. Landfill gas exploitation has benefited considerably from the NFFO and this can be seen from the large rise in the amount of electricity generated since 1992. Further commissioning of landfill gas projects under NFFO will continue to increase the amount of electricity generated from this technology. In 2000, 23 new schemes came on line under NFFO.

(b) Sewage sludge digestion

7.51 In all sewage sludge digestion projects, some of the gas produced is used to maintain the optimum temperature for digestion. In addition, many use combined heat and power (CHP) systems. The electricity generated is either used on site or sold under the NFFO. Information from these projects was provided from the CHAPSTAT Database, which is compiled and maintained by ETSU on behalf of the Department of Trade and Industry. (See Chapter 6).

(c) Domestic wood combustion

7.52 Domestic wood use includes the use of logs in open fires, "AGA"-type cooker boilers and other wood burning stoves. The figure given is an approximate estimate based on a survey carried out in 1989. A new survey to provide current information is planned for 2001.

(d) Industrial wood combustion

7.53 In 1997, the industrial wood figure (which includes sawmill residues, furniture manufacturing waste etc.) was included as a separate category for the first time. This was due to the availability of better data as a result of a survey carried out in 1996 on wood fired combustion plants above 400 kW thermal input. A follow-up survey was subsequently carried out for 2000. This survey highlighted that there were fewer sites (174) operating than in 1996 due to the imposition of more stringent emissions control.

(e) Coppice

7.54 Short rotation willow coppice development is now becoming well established with demonstration projects underway in Northern Ireland and England.

7.55 Under Northern Ireland's second Non-Fossil Fuel Renewable Energy order for electricity, two projects were live at the end of 2000. These include a 200 kW-electricity generator is installed at Blackwater Valley Museum in Co. Armagh. It is currently fuelled on wood chips produced from sawmill residues but, in the future, will make use of willow coppice. Another similar unit has been installed at Brook Hall Estate in Londonderry on a large arable farm where 100 kW of electricity can be generated through a gasifier, engine and generator fuelled off forest residues. Willow coppice is being grown on the farm and will be used as a fuel when it is ready for harvest.

7.56 In England, Project ARBRE in South Yorkshire is now under commission and will generate 8 MWe under NFFO 3. Some 500 hectares of short rotation coppiced willow have been established with a further 700 planted in spring 2000. Coppiced willow is expected to make up approximately 70 per cent of the plant's fuel requirement with the balance coming from forestry residues.

(f) Straw combustion

7.57 Straw can be burnt in high temperature boilers, designed for the efficient and controlled combustion of solid fuels and biomass to supply heat, hot water and hot air systems. There are large numbers of these small-scale batch feed whole bale boilers. The figures given are estimates based partly on 1990 information and partly on a survey of straw-fired boilers carried out in 1993-94. A 31 MW straw fired power station near Ely, Cambridgeshire has now been commissioned and has been exporting electricity since September 2000.

(g) Waste combustion

7.58 Domestic, industrial and commercial wastes represent a significant resource for materials and energy recovery. Wastes may be combusted, as received, in purpose built incinerators or processed into a range of refuse derived fuels (RDFs) for both on-site and off-site utilisation. The paragraphs below describe various categories of waste combustion in greater detail.

7.59 90 municipal solid waste (MSW) and general industrial waste (GIW) schemes, including CHP, have been contracted under the Renewables Orders. Sixteen of these are currently operational.

7.60 **Municipal solid waste combustion:** Information was provided from the refuse incinerator operators in the United Kingdom that practice energy recovery. This included both direct combustion of unprocessed MSW and the combustion of refuse derived fuel (RDF). In the latter, process waste can be partially processed to produce coarse RDF which can then be burnt in a variety of ways. By further processing the refuse, including separating off the fuel fraction, compacting, drying and densifying, it is possible to produce an RDF pellet. This pellet has around 60 per cent of the gross calorific value of British coal.

7.61 Information on projects in this area was obtained from data collected, using the RESTATS questionnaire, for 2000.

7.62 **General industrial waste combustion:** Certain wastes produced by industry and commerce can be used as a source of energy for industrial processes or space heating. These wastes include general waste from factories such as paper, cardboard, wood and plastics. Schemes burning general or industrial waste were identified through contact with equipment manufacturers. Data collected from a survey in 1994 were used to derive estimates for the overall energy contribution from the industry for subsequent years.

7.63 **Specialised waste combustion:** Specialised wastes arise as a result of a particular activity or process. Materials in this category include scrap tyres, hospital wastes, poultry litter, meal and bone and farm waste digestion. All these data are included under the 'others' category.

7.64 One tyre incinerator is known to be operating with energy recovery. This is a large plant generating electricity.

7.65 Information on hospital waste incineration is based on the 1999 RESTATS survey carried out by ETSU on behalf of the Department of Trade and Industry.

7.66 One poultry litter combustion project started generating electricity in 1992; a second began in 1993. Both of these are NFFO projects. In addition, a small-scale CHP scheme began generating towards the end of 1990 however this has now closed due to new emissions regulations. A further NFFO scheme started generating in 1998 at Thetford but during 2000 it was fuelled mainly by meat and bone.

7.67 The Agricultural Development and Advisory Service (ADAS) carried out a review of farm waste digestion in the United Kingdom for the Department of Trade and Industry during 1991-92. Included in this review was a survey that identified all the farm waste digestors in the United Kingdom and provided an estimate of the thermal energy they produced. Information was collected from these projects during the 1993 survey and this information was also used to derive estimates for 1995. In 1996 farm waste digestion was again surveyed and a new estimate derived from the information gathered. There was a farm digestion project generating electricity under the NFFO; its output was included in the 'Other' category (Table 7.6) and under 'Poultry litter, farm waste digestion, and tyres' (Tables 7.1, 7.2 and 7.3) but it has now ceased to operate. Data collected from the 1996 survey were used to derive estimates for 1997, 1998, 1999 and 2000.

Combined Heat and Power

7.68 A Combined Heat and Power (CHP) plant is an installation where there is a simultaneous generation of usable heat and power (usually electricity) in a single process. Some CHP installations are fuelled either wholly or partially by renewable sources of energy. The main renewable sources that are used for CHP are biofuels particularly sewage gas.

7.69 Chapter 6 of this Digest summarises information on the contribution made by CHP to the United Kingdom's energy requirements in 2000 using the results of a study undertaken to identify all CHP schemes. Included in Tables 6.1 to 6.9 of that chapter is information on the contribution of renewable sources to CHP generation in each year from 1996 to 2000. The information contained in those tables is therefore a subset of the data contained within the tables presented in this chapter.

Capacity and load factor

7.71 The electrical capacities are given in Table 7.5 as DNC (Declared Net Capacity), i.e. the maximum continuous rating of the generating sets in the stations, less the power consumed by the plant itself, and reduced by a specified factor to take into account the intermittent nature of the energy source e.g. 0.43 for wind. DNC represents the nominal maximum capability of a generating set to supply electricity to consumers.

7.72 Plant load factors have been calculated in terms of installed capacity (i.e. the maximum continuous rating of the generating sets in the stations) and express the average hourly quantity of electricity generated as a percentage of the average capacity at the beginning and end of the year.

Contact: *Steve Dagnall, ETSU*
steve.dagnall@aeat.co.uk
01235 433580

Mike Janes, DTI, Statistician
mike.janes@dti.gsi.gov.uk

7.1 Commodity balances 2000

Renewables and waste

	Wood waste	Wood	Poultry litter, meat and bone, farm waste digestion, straw, SRC(3) and tyres	Sewage gas	Landfill gas	Municipal solid waste
Supply						
Production	299	204	386	161	732	636
Other sources	-	-	-	-	-	-
Imports	-	-	-	-	-	-
Exports	-	-	-	-	-	-
Marine bunkers	-	-	-	-	-	-
Stock change (1)	-	-	-	-	-	-
Transfers	-	-	-	-	-	-
Total supply	299	204	386	161	732	636
Statistical difference (2)	-	-	-	-	-	-
Total demand	299	204	386	161	732	636
Transformation	-	-	314	120	717	560
Electricity generation	-	-	314	120	718	560
Major power producers	-	-	220	-	-	-
Autogenerators	-	-	94	120	718	560
Petroleum refineries	-	-	-	-	-	-
Coke manufacture	-	-	-	-	-	-
Blast furnaces	-	-	-	-	-	-
Patent fuel manufacture	-	-	-	-	-	-
Other	-	-	-	-	-	-
Energy industry use	-	-	-	-	-	-
Electricity generation	-	-	-	-	-	-
Oil and gas extraction	-	-	-	-	-	-
Petroleum refineries	-	-	-	-	-	-
Coal extraction	-	-	-	-	-	-
Coke manufacture	-	-	-	-	-	-
Blast furnaces	-	-	-	-	-	-
Patent fuel manufacture	-	-	-	-	-	-
Pumped storage	-	-	-	-	-	-
Other	-	-	-	-	-	-
Losses	-	-	-	-	-	-
Final consumption	299	204	72	41	14	76
Industry	299	-	-	-	14	41
Unclassified	299	-	-	-	14	41
Iron and steel	-	-	-	-	-	-
Non-ferrous metals	-	-	-	-	-	-
Mineral products	-	-	-	-	-	-
Chemicals	-	-	-	-	-	-
Mechanical engineering etc	-	-	-	-	-	-
Electrical engineering etc	-	-	-	-	-	-
Vehicles	-	-	-	-	-	-
Food, beverages etc	-	-	-	-	-	-
Textiles, leather, etc	-	-	-	-	-	-
Paper, printing etc	-	-	-	-	-	-
Other industries	-	-	-	-	-	-
Construction	-	-	-	-	-	-
Transport	-	-	-	-	-	-
Air	-	-	-	-	-	-
Rail	-	-	-	-	-	-
Road	-	-	-	-	-	-
National navigation	-	-	-	-	-	-
Pipelines	-	-	-	-	-	-
Other	-	204	72	41	-	35
Domestic	-	204	-	-	-	..
Public administration	-	-	-	41	-	..
Commercial	-	-	-	-	-	..
Agriculture	-	-	72	-	-	-
Miscellaneous	-	-	-	-	-	..
Non energy use	-	-	-	-	-	-

(1) Stock fall (+), stock rise (-).
(2) Total supply minus total demand.

(3) SRC is short rotation coppice.

7.1 Commodity balances 2000 (continued)

Renewables and waste

Thousand tonnes of oil equivalent

General industrial and hospital waste	Geothermal & active solar heat	Hydro	Wind	Total renewables	
					Supply
48	11	439	81	2,997	Production
-	-	-	-	-	Other sources
-	-	-	-	-	Imports
-	-	-	-	-	Exports
-	-	-	-	-	Marine bunkers
-	-	-	-	-	Stock change (1)
-	-	-	-	-	Transfers
48	11	439	81	2,997	**Total supply**
-	-	-	-	-	**Statistical difference** (2)
48	11	439	81	2,997	**Total demand**
-	-	439	81	2,232	**Transformation**
-	-	439	81	2,232	Electricity generation
-	-	372	-	592	Major power producers
-	-	67	81	1,640	Autogenerators
-	-	-	-	-	Petroleum refineries
-	-	-	-	-	Coke manufacture
-	-	-	-	-	Blast furnaces
-	-	-	-	-	Patent fuel manufacture
-	-	-	-	-	Other
-	-	-	-	-	**Energy industry use**
-	-	-	-	-	Electricity generation
-	-	-	-	-	Oil and gas extraction
-	-	-	-	-	Petroleum refineries
-	-	-	-	-	Coal extraction
-	-	-	-	-	Coke manufacture
-	-	-	-	-	Blast furnaces
-	-	-	-	-	Patent fuel manufacture
-	-	-	-	-	Pumped storage
-	-	-	-	-	Other
-	-	-	-	-	**Losses**
48	11	-	-	765	**Final consumption**
10	-	-	-	364	**Industry**
10	-	-	-	364	Unclassified
-	-	-	-	-	Iron and steel
-	-	-	-	-	Non-ferrous metals
-	-	-	-	-	Mineral products
-	-	-	-	-	Chemicals
-	-	-	-	-	Mechanical engineering etc
-	-	-	-	-	Electrical engineering etc
-	-	-	-	-	Vehicles
-	-	-	-	-	Food, beverages etc
-	-	-	-	-	Textiles, leather, etc
-	-	-	-	-	Paper, printing etc
-	-	-	-	-	Other industries
-	-	-	-	-	Construction
-	-	-	-	-	**Transport**
-	-	-	-	-	Air
-	-	-	-	-	Rail
-	-	-	-	-	Road
-	-	-	-	-	National navigation
-	-	-	-	-	Pipelines
38	11	-	-	401	**Other**
-	..	-	-	..	Domestic
38	..	-	-	..	Public administration
-	..	-	-	..	Commercial
-	-	-	-	72	Agriculture
-	..	-	-	..	Miscellaneous
-	-	-	-	-	**Non energy use**

7.2 Commodity balances 1999

Renewables and waste

	Wood waste	Wood	Poultry litter, meat and bone, farm waste digestion, straw, SRC(3) and tyres	Sewage gas	Landfill gas	Municipal solid waste
Supply						
Production	367r	204	265	189	572	580
Other sources	-	-	-	-	-	-
Imports	-	-	-	-	-	-
Exports	-	-	-	-	-	-
Marine bunkers	-	-	-	-	-	-
Stock change (1)	-	-	-	-	-	-
Transfers	-	-	-	-	-	-
Total supply	367r	204	265	189	572	580
Statistical difference (2)	-	-	-	-	-	-
Total demand	367r	204	265	189	572	580
Transformation	-	-	193	135	558	548
Electricity generation	-	-	193	135	558	548
Major power producers	-	-	193	-	-	-
Autogenerators	-	-	-	135	558	548
Petroleum refineries	-	-	-	-	-	-
Coke manufacture	-	-	-	-	-	-
Blast furnaces	-	-	-	-	-	-
Patent fuel manufacture	-	-	-	-	-	-
Other	-	-	-	-	-	-
Energy industry use	-	-	-	-	-	-
Electricity generation	-	-	-	-	-	-
Oil and gas extraction	-	-	-	-	-	-
Petroleum refineries	-	-	-	-	-	-
Coal extraction	-	-	-	-	-	-
Coke manufacture	-	-	-	-	-	-
Blast furnaces	-	-	-	-	-	-
Patent fuel manufacture	-	-	-	-	-	-
Pumped storage	-	-	-	-	-	-
Other	-	-	-	-	-	-
Losses	-	-	-	-	-	-
Final consumption	367r	204	72	54	14	32
Industry	367r	-	-	-	14	5
Unclassified	367r	-	-	-	14	5
Iron and steel	-	-	-	-	-	-
Non-ferrous metals	-	-	-	-	-	-
Mineral products	-	-	-	-	-	-
Chemicals	-	-	-	-	-	-
Mechanical engineering etc	-	-	-	-	-	-
Electrical engineering etc	-	-	-	-	-	-
Vehicles	-	-	-	-	-	-
Food, beverages etc	-	-	-	-	-	-
Textiles, leather, etc	-	-	-	-	-	-
Paper, printing etc	-	-	-	-	-	-
Other industries	-	-	-	-	-	-
Construction	-	-	-	-	-	-
Transport	-	-	-	-	-	-
Air	-	-	-	-	-	-
Rail	-	-	-	-	-	-
Road	-	-	-	-	-	-
National navigation	-	-	-	-	-	-
Pipelines	-	-	-	-	-	-
Other	-	204	72	54	-	27
Domestic	-	204	-	-	-	..
Public administration	-	-	-	54	-	..
Commercial	-	-	-	-	-	..
Agriculture	-	-	72	-	-	-
Miscellaneous	-	-	-	-	-	..
Non energy use	-	-	-	-	-	-

(1) Stock fall (+), stock rise (-).
(2) Total supply minus total demand.

(3) SRC is short rotation coppice

7.2 Commodity balances 1999 (continued)

Renewables and waste

Thousand tonnes of oil equivalent

General industrial and hospital waste	Geothermal & active solar heat	Hydro	Wind	Total renewables	
					Supply
48	11	461r	73r	2,770r	Production
-	-	-	-	-	Other sources
-	-	-	-	-	Imports
-	-	-	-	-	Exports
-	-	-	-	-	Marine bunkers
-	-	-	-	-	Stock change (1)
-	-	-	-	-	Transfers
48	11	461r	73r	2,770r	**Total supply**
-	-	-	-	-	**Statistical difference (2)**
48	11	461r	73r	2,770r	**Total demand**
-	-	461r	73r	1,968r	**Transformation**
-	-	461r	73r	1,968r	Electricity generation
-	-	381r	-	574r	Major power producers
-	-	80	73r	1,394r	Autogenerators
-	-	-	-	-	Petroleum refineries
-	-	-	-	-	Coke manufacture
-	-	-	-	-	Blast furnaces
-	-	-	-	-	Patent fuel manufacture
-	-	-	-	-	Other
-	-	-	-	-	**Energy industry use**
-	-	-	-	-	Electricity generation
-	-	-	-	-	Oil and gas extraction
-	-	-	-	-	Petroleum refineries
-	-	-	-	-	Coal extraction
-	-	-	-	-	Coke manufacture
-	-	-	-	-	Blast furnaces
-	-	-	-	-	Patent fuel manufacture
-	-	-	-	-	Pumped storage
-	-	-	-	-	Other
-	-	-	-	-	**Losses**
48	11	-	-	802r	**Final consumption**
10	-	-	-	396r	**Industry**
10	-	-	-	396r	Unclassified
-	-	-	-	-	Iron and steel
-	-	-	-	-	Non-ferrous metals
-	-	-	-	-	Mineral products
-	-	-	-	-	Chemicals
-	-	-	-	-	Mechanical engineering etc
-	-	-	-	-	Electrical engineering etc
-	-	-	-	-	Vehicles
-	-	-	-	-	Food, beverages etc
-	-	-	-	-	Textiles, leather, etc
-	-	-	-	-	Paper, printing etc
-	-	-	-	-	Other industries
-	-	-	-	-	Construction
-	-	-	-	-	**Transport**
-	-	-	-	-	Air
-	-	-	-	-	Rail
-	-	-	-	-	Road
-	-	-	-	-	National navigation
-	-	-	-	-	Pipelines
38	11	-	-	406	**Other**
-	..	-	-	..	Domestic
38	..	-	-	..	Public administration
-	..	-	-	..	Commercial
-	-	-	-	72	Agriculture
-	..	-	-	..	Miscellaneous
-	-	-	-	-	**Non energy use**

7.3 Commodity balances 1998

Renewables and waste

Thousand tonnes of oil equivalent

	Wood waste	Wood	Poultry litter, meat and bone, farm waste digestion, straw, SRC(3) and tyres	Sewage gas	Landfill gas	Municipal solid waste
Supply						
Production	437r	204	219	180	403	574
Other sources	-	-	-	-	-	-
Imports	-	-	-	-	-	-
Exports	-	-	-	-	-	-
Marine bunkers	-	-	-	-	-	-
Stock change (1)	-	-	-	-	-	-
Transfers	-	-	-	-	-	-
Total supply	437r	204	219	180	403	574
Statistical difference (2)	-	-	-	-	-	-
Total demand	437r	204	219	180	403	574
Transformation	-	-	147	126	389	550
Electricity generation	-	-	147	126	389	550
Major power producers	-	-	147	-	-	-
Autogenerators	-	-	-	126	389	550
Petroleum refineries	-	-	-	-	-	-
Coke manufacture	-	-	-	-	-	-
Blast furnaces	-	-	-	-	-	-
Patent fuel manufacture	-	-	-	-	-	-
Other	-	-	-	-	-	-
Energy industry use	-	-	-	-	-	-
Electricity generation	-	-	-	-	-	-
Oil and gas extraction	-	-	-	-	-	-
Petroleum refineries	-	-	-	-	-	-
Coal extraction	-	-	-	-	-	-
Coke manufacture	-	-	-	-	-	-
Blast furnaces	-	-	-	-	-	-
Patent fuel manufacture	-	-	-	-	-	-
Pumped storage	-	-	-	-	-	-
Other	-	-	-	-	-	-
Losses	-	-	-	-	-	-
Final consumption	437r	204	72	54	14	24
Industry	437r	-	-	-	14	-
Unclassified	437r	-	-	-	14	-
Iron and steel	-	-	-	-	-	-
Non-ferrous metals	-	-	-	-	-	-
Mineral products	-	-	-	-	-	-
Chemicals	-	-	-	-	-	-
Mechanical engineering etc	-	-	-	-	-	-
Electrical engineering etc	-	-	-	-	-	-
Vehicles	-	-	-	-	-	-
Food, beverages etc	-	-	-	-	-	-
Textiles, leather, etc	-	-	-	-	-	-
Paper, printing etc	-	-	-	-	-	-
Other industries	-	-	-	-	-	-
Construction	-	-	-	-	-	-
Transport	-	-	-	-	-	-
Air	-	-	-	-	-	-
Rail	-	-	-	-	-	-
Road	-	-	-	-	-	-
National navigation	-	-	-	-	-	-
Pipelines	-	-	-	-	-	-
Other	-	204	72	54	-	24
Domestic	-	204	-	-	-	..
Public administration	-	-	-	54	-	..
Commercial	-	-	-	-	-	..
Agriculture	-	-	72	-	-	-
Miscellaneous	-	-	-	-	-	..
Non energy use	-	-	-	-	-	-

(1) Stock fall (+), stock rise (-).
(2) Total supply minus total demand.

(3) SRC is short rotation coppice

7.3   Commodity balances 1998   (continued)

Renewables and waste

Thousand tonnes of oil equivalent

General industrial and hospital waste	Geothermal & active solar heat	Hydro	Wind	Total renewables	
					Supply
51	10	440r	75	2,593r	Production
-	-	-	-	-	Other sources
-	-	-	-	-	Imports
-	-	-	-	-	Exports
-	-	-	-	-	Marine bunkers
-	-	-	-	-	Stock change *(1)*
-	-	-	-	-	Transfers
51	10	440r	75	2,593r	**Total supply**
-	-	-	-	-	**Statistical difference** *(2)*
51	10	440r	75	2,593r	**Total demand**
-	-	440r	75	1,727r	**Transformation**
-	-	440r	75	1,727r	Electricity generation
-	-	364r	-	511r	Major power producers
-	-	76	75	1,216	Autogenerators
-	-	-	-	-	Petroleum refineries
-	-	-	-	-	Coke manufacture
-	-	-	-	-	Blast furnaces
-	-	-	-	-	Patent fuel manufacture
-	-	-	-	-	Other
-	-	-	-	-	**Energy industry use**
-	-	-	-	-	Electricity generation
-	-	-	-	-	Oil and gas extraction
-	-	-	-	-	Petroleum refineries
-	-	-	-	-	Coal extraction
-	-	-	-	-	Coke manufacture
-	-	-	-	-	Blast furnaces
-	-	-	-	-	Patent fuel manufacture
-	-	-	-	-	Pumped storage
-	-	-	-	-	Other
-	-	-	-	-	**Losses**
51	10	-	-	866r	**Final consumption**
10	-	-	-	461r	**Industry**
10	-	-	-	461r	Unclassified
-	-	-	-	-	Iron and steel
-	-	-	-	-	Non-ferrous metals
-	-	-	-	-	Mineral products
-	-	-	-	-	Chemicals
-	-	-	-	-	Mechanical engineering etc
-	-	-	-	-	Electrical engineering etc
-	-	-	-	-	Vehicles
-	-	-	-	-	Food, beverages etc
-	-	-	-	-	Textiles, leather, etc
-	-	-	-	-	Paper, printing etc
-	-	-	-	-	Other industries
-	-	-	-	-	Construction
-	-	-	-	-	**Transport**
-	-	-	-	-	Air
-	-	-	-	-	Rail
-	-	-	-	-	Road
-	-	-	-	-	National navigation
-	-	-	-	-	Pipelines
41	10	-	-	405	**Other**
-	..	-	-	..	Domestic
41	..	-	-	..	Public administration
-	..	-	-	..	Commercial
-	-	-	-	72	Agriculture
-	..	-	-	..	Miscellaneous
-	-	-	-	-	**Non energy use**

7.4 Capacity of, and electricity generated from, renewable sources[1]

	1996	1997	1998	1999	2000
Declared Net Capacity (MWe)					
Onshore wind	113.0	135.4	139.4	150.5	173.8
Solar photovoltaics	0.3	0.5	0.6	1.2	2.0
Hydro:					
Small scale	49.1	58.5	61.6	63.6	66.1
Large scale (2)	1,406.2	1,397.0	1,413.0	1,413.0	1,413.0
Biofuels:					
Landfill gas	145.7	169.4	220.6	309.0	382.6
Sewage sludge digestion	87.2	86.8	89.8	91.3	85.3
Municipal solid waste combustion (3)	115.0	115.0	162.1	160.6r	184.0
Other (4)	45.5	45.6	84.2	84.2	133.0
Total biofuels	393.4	416.8	556.7	645.1r	784.9
Total	**1,962.0**	**2,008.1**	**2,171.3**	**2,273.4r**	**2,439.7**
Generation (GWh)					
Onshore wind (5)	488	667	877	850r	946
Solar Photovoltaics	-	-	-	1	1
Hydro:					
Small scale (5)	118	164	206	232	239
Large scale (2)	3,275	4,005	4,911r	5,128r	4,869
Biofuels:					
Landfill gas	708	918	1,185	1,703	2,188
Sewage sludge digestion	410	408	386	410	366
Municipal solid waste combustion (3)	777	929	1,348	1,359	1,368
Other (4)	326	338	318	515	499
Total biofuels	2,221	2,593	3,237	3,987	4,421
Total	**6,101**	**7,428**	**9,231**	**10,199r**	**10,476**
Load factors (per cent) (6)					
Onshore wind (5)	25.4	27.2	30.7	28.2r	28.0
Hydro	25.3	30.3	37.2r	38.6r	36.7
Biofuels	61.2r	62.5r	64.7r	63.3r	58.8
Total	**32.2r**	**36.5r**	**42.7r**	**43.9r**	**42.2**

(1) Includes some waste of fossil fuel origin.
(2) Excluding pumped storage stations. Capacities are as at the end of December except for the capacities of installations of major power producing companies which for 1995 are recorded as at the end-March of the following year.
(3) Includes combustion of refuse derived fuel pellets.
(4) Includes the use of farm waste digestion, waste tyre combustion and poultry litter combustion.
(5) Actual generation figures are given where available, but otherwise are estimated using a typical load factor or the design load factor, where known.
(6) Load factors are calculated based on installed capacity rather than DNC - see paragraph 7.72.

7.5 Renewable orders and operational capacity

Technology band	Contracted projects		Live projects operational at 31 December 2000 *(1)*	
	Number	Capacity MW	Number	Capacity MW
England and Wales				
NFFO - 1 (1990)				
Hydro	26	11.85	19	8.75
Landfill gas	25	35.50	19	30.78
Municipal and industrial waste	4	40.63	3	37.08
Other	4	45.48	4	45.48
Sewage gas	7	6.45	6	5.98
Wind	9	12.21	7	11.66
Total	**75**	**152.12**	**58**	**139.73**
NFFO - 2 (late 1991)				
Hydro	12	10.86	10	10.46
Landfill gas	28	48.45	26	46.39
Municipal and industrial waste	10	271.48	2	31.50
Other	4	30.15	1	12.50
Sewage gas	19	26.86	18	19.06
Wind	49	84.43	24	52.53
Total	**122**	**472.23**	**81**	**172.44**
NFFO - 3 (1995)				
Energy crops and agricultural and forestry waste - gasification	3	19.06	1	8
Energy crops and agricultural and forestry waste - other	6	103.81	2	69.50
Hydro	15	14.48	8	11.74
Landfill gas	42	82.07	42	82.07
Municipal and industrial waste	20	241.87	6	77.42
Wind - large	31	145.92	9	36.81
Wind - small	24	19.71	9	7.93
Total	**141**	**626.92**	**77**	**293.47**
NFFO - 4 (1997)				
Hydro	31	13.22	5	1.42
Landfill gas	70	173.68	51	135.71
Municipal and industrial waste - CHP	10	115.29	2	14.98
Municipal and industrial waste - fluidised bed combustion	6	125.93		
Wind - large	48	330.36	1	2.53
Wind - small	17	10.33	3	2.03
Anaerobic digestion of agricultural waste	6	6.58		
Energy crops and forestry waste gasification	7	67.34		
Total	**195**	**842.73**	**62**	**156.67**
NFFO - 5 (1998)				
Hydro	22	8.87		
Landfill gas	141	313.73	23	53.88
Municipal and industrial waste	22	415.75		
Municipal and industrial waste - CHP	7	69.97		
Wind - large	33	340.16		
Wind - small	36	28.67	2	1.69
Total	**261**	**1,177.15**	**25**	**55.57**
NFFO Total	**794**	**3,271.15**	**303**	**817.88**
Scotland				
SRO - 1 (1994)				
Biomass	1	9.80	1	9.80
Hydro	15	17.25	6	4.04
Waste to Energy	2	3.78	2	3.78
Wind	12	45.60	7	25.13
Total	**30**	**76.43**	**16**	**42.75**
SRO - 2 (1997)				
Biomass	1	2.00		
Hydro	9	12.36		
Waste to Energy	9	56.05	4	15.00
Wind	7	43.63		
Total	**26**	**114.04**	**4**	**15.00**

7.5 Renewable orders and operational capacity (continued)

	Technology band	Contracted projects		Live projects operational at 31 December 2000 (1)	
		Number	Capacity MW	Number	Capacity MW
Scotland (continued)					
SRO - 3 (1999)	Biomass	1	12.90		
	Hydro	5	3.90		
	Waste to Energy	16	49.11	1	3.94
	Wave	3	2.00		
	Wind - large	11	63.43	1	8.29
	Wind - small	17	14.06	2	1.62
	Total	**53**	**145.40**	**4**	**13.85**
SRO Total		**109**	**335.87**	**24**	**71.60**
Northern Ireland					
NI NFFO - 1 (1994)	Hydro	9	2.37	7	1.89
	Sewage gas	5	0.56		
	Wind	6	12.66	6	12.66
	Total	**20**	**15.59**	**13**	**14.55**
NI NFFO - 2 (1996)	Biogas	1	0.25		
	Biomass	2	0.30	2	0.30
	Hydro	2	0.25	1	0.08
	Landfill gas	2	6.25		
	Municipal and industrial waste	1	6.65		
	Wind	2	2.57	2	2.57
	Total	**10**	**16.27**	**5**	**2.95**
NI NFFO Total		**30**	**31.86**	**18**	**17.50**
All Renewables Obligations		**933**	**3,638.88**	**345**	**907.00**

(1) Sites that have closed and sites that are not currently using renewables as fuel (4.8 MW) have been excluded.

7.6 Renewable sources used to generate electricity and heat[1]

Thousand tonnes of oil equivalent

	Hydro		Biofuels					Total
Onshore wind [2]	Small scale	Large scale [3]	Landfill gas	Sewage sludge digestion [4]	Municipal solid waste combustion [5]	Other [6]	Total biofuels	
Used to generate electricity								
1989	0.7	10.9	400.7	45.6	90.5	143.4	-	279.5	691.8
1990	0.8	10.9	436.8	45.6	103.6	110.7	-	260.0	708.5
1991	0.7	12.2	385.4	68.2	107.6	111.9	0.6	288.3	686.6
1992	2.8	12.8	454.1	123.6	107.6	136.3	17.5	385.1	854.8
1993	18.7	13.6	356.2	146.6	123.8	189.0	58.9	518.4	907.0
1994	29.5	13.6	424.3	169.5	118.3	304.8	114.5	707.1	1,174.6
1995	33.7	14.2	401.7	184.3	134.6	315.3	133.2	767.4	1,217.0
1996	41.9	10.1	281.6	232.1	134.6	325.9	131.3	823.9	1,157.5
1997	57.3	14.1	344.4	301.1	133.7	409.9	138.2	982.8	1,398.7
1998	75.4	17.7	422.3r	388.8	126.5	549.9	146.6	1,211.8	1,727.2r
1999	73.1r	19.9	441.0r	558.4	134.6	547.6r	192.9	1,434.2	1,967.6r
2000	81.3	20.5	418.6	717.6	120.2	559.8	313.9	1,667.7	2,232.0

		Biofuels								Geo-	Total
Active solar heating [7]	Landfill gas	Sewage sludge digestion [4]	Wood combustion - domestic [8]	Wood combustion - industrial	Straw combustion [9]	Municipal solid waste combustion [5]	Other [10]	Total biofuels		thermal aquifers [11]	
Used to generate heat											
1989	7.7	30.0	33.9	174.1	-	71.7	49.9	22.6	382.1		0.8	390.6
1990	6.4	34.2	34.6	174.1	-	71.7	49.3	23.1	387.0		0.8	394.2
1991	6.8	36.3	43.5	174.1	-	71.7	53.2	23.5	402.2		0.8	409.8
1992	7.1	31.5	43.5	204.2	-	71.7	49.0	31.3	431.1		0.8	439.0
1993	7.4	15.0	34.0	204.2	236.8	71.7	44.8	37.3	643.7		0.8	651.9
1994	7.7	18.9	52.1	204.2	455.1	71.7	46.8	43.6	892.4		0.8	901.0
1995	8.1	15.1	58.5	204.2	498.1	71.7	48.5	51.4	947.4		0.8	956.4
1996	8.5	16.6	58.5	204.2	505.5	71.7	50.6	46.2	953.2		0.8	962.6
1997	9.0	15.5	58.2	204.2	506.1	71.7	14.3	51.0	920.9		0.8	930.7
1998	9.4	13.6	54.1	204.2	436.9r	71.7	24.1	50.7	855.3		0.8	865.5r
1999	10.0	13.6	54.2	204.2	367.7r	71.7	32.0	48.0	791.4		0.8	802.1r
2000	10.5	13.6	41.1	204.2	298.6	71.7	76.4	48.0	753.5		0.8	764.8

	Active solar heating [7]	Onshore wind	Hydro	Biofuels	Geothermal aquifers [11]	Total
Total use of renewable sources						
1989	7.7	0.7	411.6	661.6	0.8	1,082.4
1990	6.4	0.8	447.7	647.0	0.8	1,102.7
1991	6.8	0.7	397.6	690.5	0.8	1,096.4
1992	7.1	2.8	466.9	816.1	0.8	1,293.9
1993	7.4	18.7	369.8	1,162.1	0.8	1,558.9
1994	7.7	29.5	437.9	1,599.5	0.8	2,075.6
1995	8.1	33.7	415.9	1,714.8	0.8	2,173.4
1996	8.5	41.9	291.7	1,777.1	0.8	2,120.0
1997	9.0	57.3	358.5	1,903.7	0.8	2,329.3
1998	9.4	75.4	440.0r	2,067.1r	0.8	2,592.7r
1999	10.0r	73.1	460.9r	2,225.0r	0.8	2,769.8r
2000	10.5	81.3	439.1	2,464.9	0.8	2,996.8

(1) Includes some waste of fossil fuel origin.
(2) For wind and hydro, the figures represent the energy content of the electricity supplied, but for biofuels the figures represent the energy content of the fuel used.
(3) Excluding pumped storage stations.
(4) No estimate is made for digestors where gas is used to heat the sludge.
(5) Includes combustion of refuse derived fuel pellets.
(6) Includes electricity from farm waste digestion , poultry litter combustion and waste tyre combustion.

(7) Based on a survey carried out in 1995 and updated using data from the Solar Trade Association.
(8) An approximate estimate of domestic combustion based on a survey carried out in 1989; a moisture content of 50% is assumed.
(9) An approximate estimate based on a limited survey carried out in 1994 and on information collected in 1990.
(10) Includes heat from waste tyre combustion, hospital waste combustion, general industrial waste combustion and farm waste digestion.
(11) Based on information collected by the 1994 RESTATS questionnaire.

Chapter 8
Foreign trade

Introduction

8.1   This section brings together detailed figures on imports and exports of fuels and related materials, generally in both quantity and value terms. Table 8.1 gives an overall view for all fuels, Tables 8.3 to 8.5 present more detailed figures for crude oil, petroleum products and coal and other solid fuels. Table 8.2 presents a long term view of the value of imports and exports of fuels from 1970 to 2000.

8.2   The information in this section is largely derived from returns made to HM Customs and Excise, and corresponds to that published in the *Overseas Trade Statistics of the United Kingdom* (O.T.S.). The figures for 2000 are provisional.

Imports and exports of fuel and related materials (Table 8.1)

8.3   This table presents import, export and net export figures in quantity and value terms broken down by the main fuel groups for the years 1996 to 2000.

8.4   To allow the values of imports and exports to be compared, additional series are included presenting import values on a "free on board" (f.o.b.) basis. Import values are normally recorded in "cost, insurance and freight" (c.i.f.) prices whereas f.o.b. prices are always used for export values. This approach is similar to that used by the Office for National Statistics in the overall trade figures when they compile the Balance of Payments. Fuller descriptions of the c.i.f. and f.o.b. methods of valuing imports and exports are given in paragraph 8.25 of the Technical Notes.

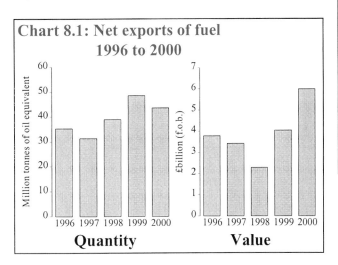

Chart 8.1: Net exports of fuel 1996 to 2000

Quantity

Value

8.5   Chart 8.1 illustrates the recent trends in the trade balance in fuels, both in terms of value and

quantity. Trends in the value of the trade balance since 1970 can be seen in Chart 8.3, whilst figures are given in Table 8.2.

8.6   In 2000 the United Kingdom was a net exporter of fuels, in financial terms, with a surplus, on a balance of payments (f.o.b.) basis, of £6.7 billion, £2.4 billion higher than the surplus in 1999. The surplus of crude oil and petroleum products in 2000 was £6.2 billion compared to £4.2 billion in 1999.   These increases reflect an increase in crude oil and petroleum product prices during 2000.

8.7   In volume terms the United Kingdom was also a net exporter of fuels in 2000, with net exports amounting to 43.5 million tonnes of oil equivalent (mtoe). This compares with surpluses of 48.5 mtoe in 1999.

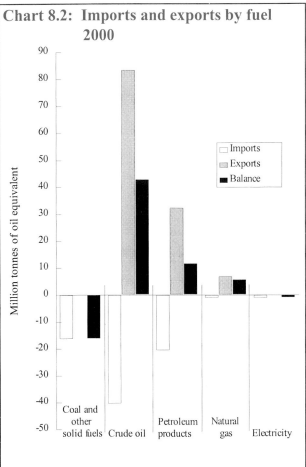

Chart 8.2: Imports and exports by fuel 2000

8.8   The figures for trade in individual fuels in 2000 are illustrated in Chart 8.2. This shows the extent to which the United Kingdom's trading position for all fuels is dominated by petroleum. The United Kingdom continues to be a net exporter of fuels largely as a result of high exports and low imports of crude oil and petroleum products.

Long term trends:
Value of imports and exports of fuels 1970 to 2000 (Table 8.2)

8.9   Values of imports (c.i.f.) and exports (f.o.b.) broken down by the main fuel groups are given in Table 8.2 which is based on Table 8.1 with the series extended back to 1970. Import values on a f.o.b. basis are also included, enabling net exports to be presented on a comparable f.o.b. basis over the same period.

8.10   Although between 1989 and 1992 the United Kingdom was a net importer of fuels in volume terms, there has been a financial surplus in fuels, on a balance of payments (f.o.b.) basis, in every year since 1981, except for 1989. This is because the unit values of our exports have tended to be higher than that of our imports.

8.11   As can be seen in Chart 8.3 the United Kingdom's trade in fuels was dominated by imports until exports started to grow substantially in the mid-1970s, when production from the North Sea started coming on line, achieving a trade surplus in 1981. This surplus has been sustained, in value terms, since 1981, except for a small deficit in 1989, and amounted to just over £63 billion over the period 1981 to 2000. However, these surpluses were reduced by the fall in oil prices in 1986, and then by the fall in North Sea production following the Piper Alpha accident in 1988 and the resulting safety work. Although the trade surplus had increased steadily from 1992 to 1996, there were falls in 1997 and 1998 due to the fall in the price of crude oil. Prices of crude oil and petroleum products increased in 1999 and again in

2000 giving it, in current price terms, the highest yet net surplus.

UK imports and exports of crude oil and petroleum products (Table 8.3)

8.12   The data in this table outline the pattern of trade in oil in the United Kingdom.   Table 8.3 shows quantities in thousands of tonnes, of crude oil and refined petroleum products, and unit values per tonne, with import values on a c.i.f. basis and export values on a f.o.b. basis. The total values of crude oil imports, on a f.o.b. basis, are shown in Table 8.1.

8.13   The United Kingdom has been a net exporter of oil since 1981. Broadly the level of crude oil exports reflects North Sea production. Exports were reduced because the Piper Alpha accident reduced production from 1988 and then production levels remained lower until 1992 as higher levels of maintenance and safety work prolonged platform shutdowns.   In 2000 production of crude oil dropped, resulting in higher imports of crude oil which are visible in the trade figures. Chart 8.4 shows the level of imports, exports and net exports in f.o.b. value terms from 1996 to 2000.

8.14   The main product imported into the United Kingdom in 2000 was aviation turbine fuel (kerosene), 667 thousand tonnes more than fuel oil which had been the main import up to 2000. The main product exported in 2000 was gas oil/diesel oil.

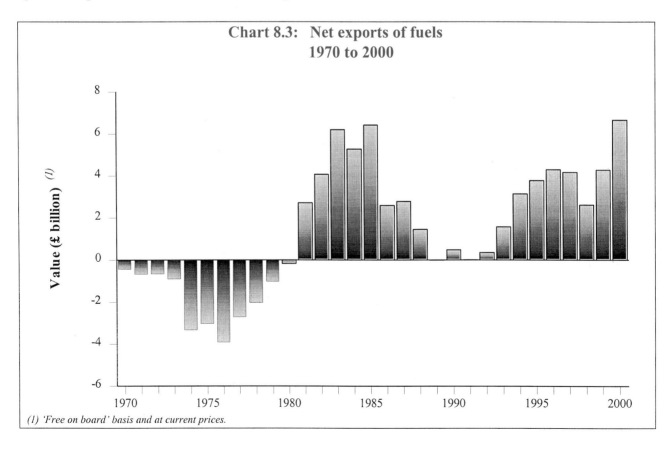

Chart 8.3:   Net exports of fuels 1970 to 2000

Value (£ billion) [1]

(1) 'Free on board' basis and at current prices.

8.15 Imports of petroleum products have grown from 18.6 million tonnes in 1999 to 19.4 in 2000, due to increased imports of aviation turbine fuel, motor spirit and aviation spirit needed to meet UK demand for these fuels that cannot be met by UK refineries. Exports of petroleum products increased in 2000 to 28.1 million tonnes from 26.3 million tonnes in 1999. This increase was mainly due to an increase in exports of gas oil and fuel oil. Exports of motor spirit have continued to decrease, falling by more than 15 per cent between 1999 and 2000 due to refinery closures and any surplus UK production previously exported now goes to meet UK demand. Just over 75 per cent of UK petroleum product exports in 2000 went to other EU countries. The largest customers are the Netherlands (although this would include oil destined for onward trade to other countries), the Irish Republic, Belgium (including Luxembourg) and France. The USA, who receive 12 per cent of petroleum products exports, are the largest non-EU customer.

UK imports and exports of crude oil by country (Table 8.4)

8.16 The data in Table 8.4 show details of trade in crude oil by country. The import data are on a 'country of origin' (or production) basis as far as possible. Since the introduction of 'Intrastat' at the start of 1993, recording of country of origin for Intra-EU trade has been optional, so a small amount may be recorded as country of consignment i.e. the country from which the goods were consigned to the United Kingdom as opposed to the true country of origin. This change has had little impact, as virtually all of the UK's imported crude oil is supplied direct from countries outside the EU, in particular Norway.

8.17 Norway supplied just under 75 per cent of the United Kingdom's imports of crude oil in 2000. The Middle East accounted for just under 5 per cent of imports, coming mainly from Saudi Arabia. Over a half of the remaining imports came from Algeria, Russia and Mexico. In 2000, over half of the United Kingdom exports of crude oil went to EU countries. Most of the non-EU export trade was with the United States of America. Whilst the bulk of the exports to Germany are for refining and consumption there, the exports to the Netherlands include oil destined for onward trade to other countries.

8.18 In most years, the average value per tonne of crude oil exported from the UK is higher than that for imported crude oil. However, there are a couple of exceptions in recent years in 1996 and 1998 when the import value per tonne was greater than the export figure. The second half of 1999 saw a significant increase in prices of crude oil on international markets due to the actions of OPEC member countries to reduce world supply, leading to the differential increasing to £5.36 per tonne in 1999. This action by OPEC countries was maintained in 2000 and is the reason why the volume of imports of crude oil into the UK in 2000 was 5 per cent higher than in 1999, while the value of imports increased by 75 per cent.

Imports and exports of solid fuels (Table 8.5)

8.19 Table 8.5 gives a breakdown of imports and exports of steam coal, coking coal, anthracite and other solid fuels by country of origin or destination. The imports and exports data are provided by HM Customs and Excise, but where there have been apparent misclassifications by the importers of the types of coal (e.g. because the country of origin does not produce that type of coal) the DTI has made adjustments.

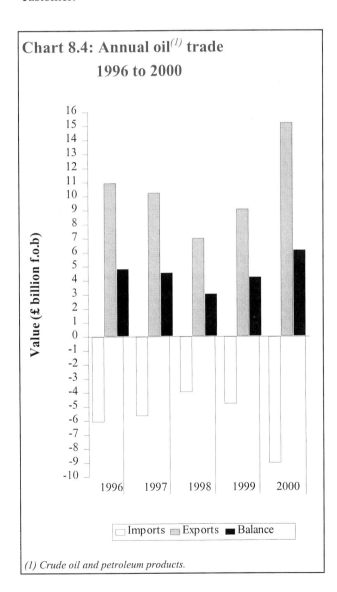

Chart 8.4: Annual oil[(1)] trade 1996 to 2000

Value (£ billion f.o.b)

Imports   Exports   Balance

(1) Crude oil and petroleum products.

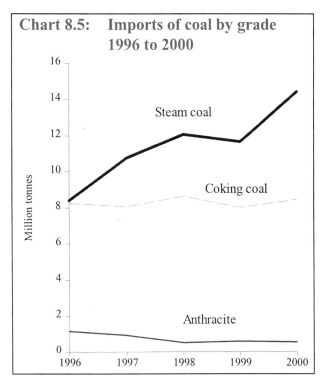

Chart 8.5: Imports of coal by grade 1996 to 2000

Steam coal

Coking coal

Anthracite

Million tonnes

8.20 In 2000, the UK imported 23½ million tonnes of coal, 15½ per cent more than in 1999. 36 per cent of coal imports were of coking coal, of which only limited amounts are produced in the United Kingdom. The figures for imports of coal by grade are illustrated in Chart 8.5.

8.21 In 2000, 70 per cent of the United Kingdom's imports of coal came from just three countries: Australia, Colombia and South Africa. A further 24 per cent of coal imports came from three additional countries, USA (mainly coking coal), Canada (coking coal) and Poland (mainly steam coal). Steam coal imports came mainly from Colombia (39 per cent), South Africa (32 per cent) and Poland (8 per cent). Imports of steam coal from the USA were still substantially lower in 2000 than two years earlier in 1998 accounting for 6 per cent of the total compared with 26 per cent in 1998, whereas imports of steam coal from South Africa in 2000 were nearly double the volumes imported in each of the last few years. All but a very small fraction of UK coking coal imports came from Australia (58 per cent), the USA (23 per cent) and Canada (19 per cent). Imports of coal by country of origin are illustrated in Chart 8.6.

8.22 Exports of coal and other solid fuel amounted to 1.1 million tonnes in 2000, an increase of 6 per cent on 1999. The UK's largest export markets in 2000 were Norway (30 per cent), the Irish Republic (25 per cent), France (11 per cent), Sweden (7 per cent) and Belgium/Luxembourg (6 per cent).

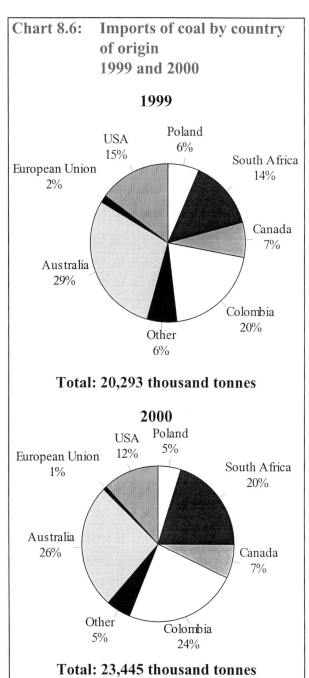

Chart 8.6: Imports of coal by country of origin 1999 and 2000

1999

European Union 2%
USA 15%
Poland 6%
South Africa 14%
Canada 7%
Colombia 20%
Other 6%
Australia 29%

Total: 20,293 thousand tonnes

2000

European Union 1%
USA 12%
Poland 5%
South Africa 20%
Canada 7%
Colombia 24%
Other 5%
Australia 26%

Total: 23,445 thousand tonnes

Technical notes and definitions

8.23 The figures of imports and exports quoted are largely derived from notifications to HM Customs and Excise, and may differ from those for actual arrivals and shipments, derived from alternative and/or additional sources, in the sections of the Digest dealing with individual fuels. Data in Table 8.1 also include unpublished revisions to Customs data which cannot be introduced into Tables 8.3 to 8.5.

8.24 All quantity figures in Table 8.1 have been converted to million tonnes of oil equivalent to allow data to be compared and combined. This unit is a measure of the energy content of the individual fuels; it is also used in the Energy section of this Digest where further explanation can be found. (See Chapter 1, paragraphs 1.46 to 1.47). The quantities of imports and exports recorded in the Overseas Trade Statistics in their original units of measurement, are converted to tonnes of oil equivalent using weighted gross calorific values and standard conversion factors appropriate to each division of the Standard International Trade Classification (SITC). The electricity figures are expressed in terms of the energy content of the electricity traded.

8.25 Except as noted in Table 8.1, values of imports are quoted "c.i.f." (cost, insurance and freight); briefly this value is the price which the goods would fetch at that time, on sale in the open market between buyer and seller independent of each other, with delivery to the buyer at the port of importation, the seller bearing freight, insurance, commission and all other costs, etc., incidental to the sale and delivery of the goods with the exception of any duty or tax chargeable in the United Kingdom. Values of exports are "f.o.b." (free on board), which is the cost of the goods to the purchaser abroad, including packing, inland and coastal transport in the United Kingdom, dock dues, loading charges and all other costs, charges and expenses accruing up to the point where the goods are deposited on board the exporting vessel or at the land boundary of Northern Ireland.

8.26 Figures of the value of net exports in Tables 8.1 and 8.2 are derived from exports and imports measured on a Balance of Payments (B.O.P) basis.

The figures have been revised back to 1970 in this edition of the Digest of UK Energy Statistics to maintain consistency with the European System of Accounts 1995, the basis on which figures are published by the Office for National Statistics. This means exports as recorded by HM Customs and Excise will differ from those recorded by the Office for National Statistics on a B.O.P basis. Table 8.1 shows figures on both basis.

8.27 Figures correspond to the following items of S.I.T.C (Rev 3).

Coal	321.1 and 321.2
Other solid fuels	322.1 and 325 (part)
Crude oil	333
Petroleum products	334, 335, 342 and 344 (plus Orimulsion reclassified to division 278 during 1994)
Natural gas	343
Electricity	351

8.28 Figures for trade within the European Union given in Tables 8.4 and 8.5 cover trade between the other 14 Member States belonging to the Union in 2000.

8.29 In 1993 the Single European Market was created. At that time a new system for recording the trade in goods between member states called INTRASTAT was introduced. As part of this system allows small traders to only have an obligation to report their annual trade and some trading supply returns late, it is necessary to include adjustments for unrecorded trade. This is particularly true of 1993, the first year of the system, and particularly true for coal imports in that year.

8.30 Quarterly data on imports and exports of fuels and related materials are published in September, December, March and June on the DTI website at www.dti.gov.uk/energy/energystats/energystats.htm under *Total Energy*.

Contact: Rachael Winther
020 7215 6178

8.1 Imports and exports of fuels [1]

Quantity					Million tonnes of oil equivalent
	1996	1997	1998	1999	2000[2]
Imports					
Coal and other solid fuel	12.7	14.2	15.1	14.6	16.5
Crude oil	44.8	45.3	39.5	32.7	40.5
Petroleum products	17.8	15.1r	17.9	20.0	20.8
Natural gas	1.4	1.3	0.4	0.3	2.0
Electricity	1.4	1.4	1.1	1.2	1.2
Total imports	78.2	77.4r	74.0	68.8	80.9
Exports					
Coal and other solid fuel	1.0	1.1	0.9	0.8	1.0
Crude oil	83.4	76.6	80.4	81.8r	82.7
Petroleum products	27.8	29.4	30.1	30.4	32.3
Natural gas	1.4	1.7	1.5	4.4r	8.3
Electricity	-	-	-	-	-
Total exports	113.5	108.7	113.0	117.4r	124.4
Net exports					
Coal and other solid fuel	-11.8	-13.2	-14.2	-13.8	-15.5
Crude oil	38.6	31.3	40.8	49.1r	42.3
Petroleum products	10.0	14.2r	12.3	10.3r	11.6
Natural gas	0.0	0.3	1.1	4.1r	6.4
Electricity	-1.4	-1.4	-1.1r	-1.2	-1.2
Total net exports	35.3	31.3r	38.9r	48.5r	43.5

Value					£ million
Imports - O.T.S basis (c.i.f.)					
Coal and other solid fuel	694	714	687	599	696
Crude oil	4,035	3,647	2,170	2,273	5,095
Petroleum products	1,821	1,433r	1,415r	1,961	3,430
Natural gas	117	103	43	27	135
Electricity	391	406	374	396	373
Total imports	7,058	6,303r	4,689r	5,256r	9,729
Exports (f.o.b.)					
Coal and other solid fuel	82	82	69	61	74
Crude oil	7,426	6,322	4,485	6,148r	10,202
Petroleum products	3,268	3,239	2,328	2,849r	4,872
Natural gas	65	80	80	230r	577
Electricity	2	1	3	8r	5
Total exports	10,843	9,724	6,965r	9,297r	15,729
Net exports - O.T.S basis					
Coal and other solid fuel	-612	-632	-619r	-537	-623
Crude oil	3,391	2,676	2,315	3,875r	5,107
Petroleum products	1,446	1,806r	913r	888r	1,442
Natural gas	-52	-23	37	203r	441
Electricity	-389	-405	-371	-387	-368
Total net exports	3,784	3,421r	2,276r	4,041r	6,000
Imports - B.O.P. basis (f.o.b.) [4]					
Oil [3]	6,120	5,680	3,975	4,839	9,050
Other fuels	1,167	1,146	915	753	959
Total imports	7,287	6,826	4,890	5,592	10,009
Net exports - B.O.P. basis [4]					
Oil [3]	4,823	4,549	3,045	4,233	6,161
Other fuels	-516	-371	-420	53	513
Total net exports	4,307	4,178	2,625	4,286	6,674

Source: H.M. Customs and Excise

(1) See Energy Trends on the internet for the latest quarterly figures (see paragraph 8.30 and Annex F).
(2) Provisional.
(3) Crude oil and petroleum products.
(4) The Balance of Payments figures have been revised to be on a ESA95 basis.

8.2 Value of imports and exports of fuels, 1970 to 2000 [1][2]

£ million

		1970	1971	1972	1973	1974	1975
Imports (c.i.f.)	Coal and other solid fuels	2	46	57	27	66	110
	Crude oil	687	930	914	1,296	3,726	3,371
	Petroleum products (3)	242	259	257	389	823	810
	Natural gas	11	10	9	9	8	14
	Electricity	2	-	2	-	-	1
Total imports		944	1,245	1,239	1,721	4,623	4,306
Exports (f.o.b.)	Coal and other solid fuels	29	22	17	27	65	84
	Crude oil	8	10	21	23	29	30
	Petroleum products (4)	170	204	201	320	681	705
Total exports		207	236	239	370	775	819
Imports (f.o.b.)	Oil (5)	816	1068	1053	1,498	4,340	4,043
	Other fuels (6)	17	48	63	34	77	122
Total imports		833	1116	1116	1,532	4,417	4,165
Net exports[8]	Oil (5)	-503	-696	-660	-948	-3,372	-3,051
(B.O.P basis)	Other fuels	14	-24	-44	-4	-6	-29
Total net exports		**-489**	**-720**	**-704**	**-952**	**-3,378**	**-3,080**

		1976	1977	1978	1979	1980	1981
Imports (c.i.f.)	Coal and other solid fuels	86	84	82	148	228	171
	Crude oil	4,445	3,971	3,506	3,678	4,292	4,112
	Petroleum products (3)	1,089	1,128	1,023	1,591	1,856	2,173
	Natural gas	21	44	188	356	521	699
	Electricity	-	-	-	-	-	-
Total imports		5,641	5,227	4,799	5,773	6,897	7,155
Exports (f.o.b.)	Coal and other solid fuels	72	80	90	100	180	372
	Crude oil	178	918	1,236	2,710	4,220	7,096
	Petroleum products (4)	1,004	1,086	1,038	1,500	2,017	2,148
Total exports		1,254	2,084	2,364	4,310	6,417	9,616
Imports (f.o.b.)	Oil (5)	5,407	5,051	4,504	5,242	6,182	6,366
	Other fuels (6)	121	154	291	517	742	883
Total imports		5,528	5,205	4,795	5,759	6,924	7,249
Net exports[8]	Oil (5)	-3,922	-2,723	-1,930	-721	280	3,092
(B.O.P basis)	Other fuels	-28	-41	-151	-351	-446	-375
Total net exports		**-3,950**	**-2,764**	**-2,081**	**-1,072**	**-166**	**2,717**

		1982	1983	1984	1985	1986	1987
Imports (c.i.f.)	Coal and other solid fuels	218	264	651	716	456	390
	Crude oil	3,951	3,308	3,993	4,341	2,440	2,703
	Petroleum products (3)	2,413	2,506	4,360	4,071	2,079	1,880
	Natural gas	815	977	1,307	1,511	1,320	878
	Electricity	-	-	-	-	80	242
Total imports		7,397	7,055	10,311	10,639	6,375	6,093
Exports (f.o.b.)	Coal and other solid fuels	330	239	88	178	190	109
	Crude oil	8,542	10,111	12,173	13,006	6,281	6,765
	Petroleum products (4)	2,365	2,776	3,047	3,611	2,200	1,893
Total exports		11,237	13,126	15,308	16,795	8,671	8,767
Imports (f.o.b.)	Oil (5)	6,390	5,879	8,274	8,385	4,547	4,751
	Other fuels (6)	1,081	1,274	2,029	2,257	1,877	1,561
Total imports		7,471	7,153	10,303	10,642	6,424	6,312
Net exports[8]	Oil (5)	4,607	6,891	6,860	8,030	4,012	4,045
(B.O.P basis)	Other fuels	-530	-672	-1,572	-1,595	-1,413	-1,258
Total net exports		**4,077**	**6,219**	**5,288**	**6,435**	**2,599**	**2,787**

(1) See Energy Trends on the internet for the latest quarterly figures (see paragraph 8.30 and Annex F).
(2) See the notes to the Foreign Trade section of this and earlier editions of the Digest.
(3) Includes petroleum products not used as fuel, eg lubricants, and liquefied petroleum gases other than natural gas.
(4) Includes petroleum products not used as fuel, eg lubricants, and liquefied petroleum gases, and small quantities of natural gas.
(5) Crude oil and petroleum products.
(6) Data prior to 1985 include small quantities of non-fuel products (eg peat). These items are excluded from the c.i.f. import data and the export data
(7) Provisional.
(8) Net exports are the difference between exports and imports on a Balance of Payments (B.O.P) basis – see Table 8.1 for figures in the period 1996 to 2000. The B.O.P. figures have been revised back to 1970 to be on a ESA95 basis.

8.2 Value of imports and exports of fuels, 1970 to 2000[1][2](continued)

£ million

		1988	1989	1990	1991	1992	1993
Imports (c.i.f.)	Coal and other solid fuels	472	513	630	734	744	731
	Crude oil	2,044	3,079	4,033	3,887	3,745	4,078
	Petroleum products (3)	1,546	1,889	2,427	2,063	1,711	1,766
	Natural gas	692	615	519	472	397	327
	Electricity	268	305	225	343	369	426
Total imports		5,022	6,401	7,834	7,499	6,966	7,328
Exports (f.o.b.)	Coal and other solid fuels	96	109	119	97	63	73
	Crude oil	4,515	4,024	5,172	4,370	4,413	5,147
	Petroleum products (4)	1,646	2,039	2,455	2,640	2,401	3,149
	Natural gas	-	-	-	-	2	28
	Electricity	-	-	25	-	-	-
Total exports		6,257	6,172	7,771	7,107	6,879	8,397
Imports (f.o.b.)	Oil (5)	3,645	5,102	6,443	6,010	5,562	6,011
	Other fuels	1,470	1,482	1,471	1,613	1,561	1,465
Total imports		5,115	6,584	7,914	7,623	7,123	7,476
Net exports[8]	Oil (5)	2,685	1,222	1,631	1,274	1,610	2,594
(B.O.P basis)	Other fuels	-1,228	-1,226	-1,147	-1,260	-1,254	-1,017
Total net exports		**1,457**	**-4**	**484**	**14**	**356**	**1,577**

		1994	1995	1996	1997	1998
Imports (c.i.f.)	Coal and other solid fuels	598	601	694	714	687
	Crude oil	3,241	3,236	4,035	3,647	2,170
	Petroleum products (3)	1,689	1,542	1,821	1,433r	1,415r
	Natural gas	231	105	117	103	43
	Electricity	388	408	391	391	374
Total imports		6,148	5,892	7,058	6,303r	4,689r
Exports (f.o.b.)	Coal and other solid fuels	75	70	82	82	69
	Crude oil	6,095	6,428	7,426	6,322	4,485
	Petroleum products (4)	2,776	2,621	3,268	3,239	2,328
	Natural gas	45	54	65	80	80
	Electricity	-	-	2	1	3
Total		8,991	9,174	10,843	9,724	6,965r
Imports (f.o.b.)	Oil (5)	5,144	5,062	6,120	5,680	3,975
	Other fuels	1,201	1,100	1,167	1,146	915
Total imports		6,345	6,162	7,287	6,826	4,890
Net exports[8]	Oil (5)	3,941	4,331	4,823	4,549	3,045
(B.O.P basis)	Other fuels	-788	-542	-516	-371	-420
Total net exports		**3,153**	**3,789**	**4,307**	**4,178**	**2,625**

		1999	2000(7)
Imports (c.i.f.)	Coal and other solid fuels	599	696
	Crude oil	2,273	5,095
	Petroleum products (3)	1,961	3,430
	Natural gas	27	135
	Electricity	396	373
Total imports		5,256	9,729
Exports (f.o.b.)	Coal and other solid fuels	61	74
	Crude oil	6,148r	10,202
	Petroleum products (4)	2,849r	4,872
	Natural gas	230r	577
	Electricity	8r	5
Total exports		9,297	15,729
Imports (f.o.b.)	Oil (5)	4,839	9,050
	Other fuels	753	959
Total imports		5,592	10,009
Net exports[8]	Oil (5)	4,233	6,161
(B.O.P basis)	Other fuels	53	513
Total net exports		**4,286**	**6,674**

8.3 Imports and exports of crude oil and petroleum products

	1996		1997		1998	
	Quantity (Thousand tonnes)	Value per tonne (£)	Quantity (Thousand tonnes)	Value per tonne (£)	Quantity (Thousand tonnes)	Value per tonne (£)
Imports (c.i.f.)						
Crude oil	**40,496**	**98.79**	**41,253r**	**87.47r**	**36,868r**	**61.83r**
Refined petroleum products *(1)*						
Petroleum gases *(2)*	633r	128.10r	519r	140.85r	507r	107.60r
Motor spirit and aviation spirit	814r	147.78r	1,850r	143.52r	1,496r	110.40r
Other light oils and spirit *(3)*	830r	135.19r	928r	130.52r	1,124r	96.59r
Aviation turbine fuel (kerosene)	1,270r	142.05r	1,666r	132.17r	2,890r	93.76r
Other kerosene	157r	146.53r	167r	141.33r	119r	110.64r
Gas oil/diesel oil	1,678r	131.49r	1,820r	127.24r	2,994r	95.25r
Fuel oil *(4)*	9,095r	76.23r	8,182r	71.74r	7,184r	53.81r
Lubricating oils	484r	179.43r	554r	167.05r	364r	165.41r
Petroleum coke	1,049r	45.46r	985r	45.31r	883r	48.09r
Other *(5)*	132r	67.92r	69r	130.46r	25r	168.01r
Total refined petroleum products	**16,142r**	**97.54r**	**16,722r**	**99.65r**	**17,584r**	**78.59r**
Exports (f.o.b)						
Crude oil	**76,475r**	**97.88r**	**65,551r**	**90.60r**	**68,745r**	**60.99r**
Refined petroleum products *(1)*						
Petroleum gases *(2)*	3,522r	140.29r	3,958r	144.35r	3,849r	87.96r
Motor spirit and aviation spirit	7,355r	130.40r	8,846r	122.40r	7,009r	93.22r
Other light oils and spirit *(3)*	1,433r	132.47r	1,712r	140.25r	1,513r	77.08r
Aviation turbine fuel (kerosene)	607r	137.06r	749r	118.86r	801r	90.39r
Other kerosene	89r	136.35r	120r	133.85r	163r	108.18r
Gas oil/Diesel oil	5,072r	121.65r	2,989r	106.82r	5,772r	76.90r
Fuel oil *(4)*	5,200r	78.81r	5,764r	66.68r	6,165r	47.55r
Lubricating oils	1,189r	166.79r	3,435r	132.26r	749r	123.57r
Petroleum coke	662r	183.19r	544r	186.52r	716r	136.58r
Other	98r	108.76r	79r	141.97r	137r	113.27r
Total refined petroleum products	**25,227r**	**122.70r**	**28,197r**	**115.97r**	**26,873r**	**79.68r**

(1) Excludes pitch, mineral tars and natural gas.
(2) Includes small quantities of unidentified non-petroleum gases.
(3) Includes wide-cut gasoline, white spirit and petroleum naphthas.
(4) Includes partly refined oil for further processing.
(5) Includes Orimulsion.

8.3 Imports and exports of crude oil and petroleum products (continued)

	1999		2000	
	Quantity (Thousand tonnes)	Value per tonne (£)	Quantity (Thousand tonnes)	Value per Tonne (£)
Imports (c.i.f.)				
Crude oil	**33,151r**	**71.46r**	**36,898**	**134.42**
Refined petroleum products *(1)*				
Petroleum gases *(2)*	845r	120.54r	1,119	131.81
Motor spirit and aviation spirit	1,547r	118.17r	2,022	155.35
Other light oils and spirit *(3)*	468r	88.67r	240	199.60
Aviation turbine fuel (kerosene)	4,163r	109.49r	5,761	192.95
Other kerosene	102r	118.62r	181	224.79
Gas oil/diesel oil	4,788r	112.94r	3,988	188.60
Fuel oil *(4)*	5,892r	60.93r	5,275	111.05
Lubricating oils	83r	179.59r	155	256.68
Petroleum coke	644r	47.43r	683	48.07
Other *(5)*	60r	138.06r	18	190.81
Total refined petroleum products	**18,591r**	**94.00r**	**19,441**	**158.20**
Exports (f.o.b)				
Crude oil	**68,114r**	**81.28r**	**71,615**	**135.56**
Refined petroleum products *(1)*				
Petroleum gases *(2)*	5,564r	100.17r	5,398	149.40
Motor spirit and aviation spirit	5,922r	108.24r	4,625	194.45
Other light oils and spirit *(3)*	2,339r	116.42r	3,551	168.84
Aviation turbine fuel (kerosene)	722r	103.08r	521	184.11
Other kerosene	143r	155.96r	185	223.99
Gas oil/Diesel oil	5,550r	98.63r	6,931	162.56
Fuel oil *(4)*	5,326r	63.97r	6,176	108.42
Lubricating oils	137r	106.11r	257	182.23
Petroleum coke	449r	153.69r	265	290.11
Other	171r	122.91r	168	170.08
Total refined petroleum products	**26,323r**	**97.25r**	**28,077**	**156.40**

Source: H.M. Customs and Excise

8.4 Imports and exports of crude oil by country

	1996			1997			1998		
	Quantity Thousand tonnes	Value (£million)	Value per tonne (£)	Quantity Thousand tonnes	Value (£million)	Value per tonne (£)	Quantity Thousand tonnes	Value (£million)	Value per tonne (£)
Imports (c.i.f.)									
Middle East									
Abu Dhabi	-	-	-	39	4.2	108.58	-	-	-
Dubai	-	-	-	-	-	-	65	4.3	65.95
Iran	937	86.3	92.03	-	-	-	38	3.0	78.05
Kuwait	1,494	132.8	88.90	1,550	124.1	80.09	1,042	51.5	49.47
Oman	-	-	-	-	-	-	-	-	-
Saudi Arabia	847	80.5	95.09	1,842	138.0	74.89	2,309r	114.8r	49.72r
Other countries	804r	66.6r	82.68r	245r	19.1r	77.91r	482r	26.6r	55.15r
Total Middle East	**4,084r**	**366.2r**	**89.68r**	**3,676r**	**285.4r**	**77.64r**	**3,935r**	**200.1r**	**50.86r**
Algeria	1,746	175.5	100.55	341	35.7	104.50	610r	40.8r	66.95r
Angola	-	-	-	80	6.8	84.68	-	-	-
Latvia	1196r	112.2r	93.83r	1,084	91.5	84.38	1,120r	67.0r	59.82r
Libya	238	21.0	88.29	-	-	-	-	-	-
Lithuania	-	-	-	-	-	-	-	-	-
Mexico	723	60.3	83.44	796	59.2	74.39	890	43.2	48.50
Netherlands	697r	62.8r	90.16r	264r	22.5r	85.16r	16r	0.9r	55.34r
Nigeria	1,568	174.5	111.29	214	20.6	96.24	560	34.8	62.14
Norway	26,515r	2,700.7	101.86r	30,699	2,771.2	90.27	24,938r	1,539.4r	61.73r
Russia	452r	40.2r	88.96r	567	49.2	86.87	812r	46.5r	57.31r
Venezuela	1,340	90.6	67.61	1,445	82.3r	56.94r	1,340	51.2	38.23
Other countries	1,938r	196.6r	101.46r	2,086r	184.2r	88.30r	2,646r	255.5r	96.55r
Total Non Middle East	**36,412r**	**3,634.5r**	**99.82r**	**37,577r**	**3,323.2r**	**88.44r**	**32,933r**	**2,079.4r**	**63.14r**
Total imports	**40,496**	**4,000.7**	**98.79**	**41,253r**	**3,608.6r**	**87.47r**	**36,868r**	**2,279.6r**	**61.83r**
Exports (f.o.b.)[1]									
European Union									
Belgium and Luxembourg	224r	22.0r	98.45r	884r	79.6r	90.01r	1,037	58.7	56.61
Denmark	70	7.1	101.00	-	-	-	-	-	-
Finland	3,688	352.3	95.51	1,211r	115.3r	95.20r	656	39.0	59.42
France	13,748r	1,374.9r	100.00	11,980r	1,089.4r	90.94r	12,147r	750.6r	61.79r
Germany	15,346r	1,497.1r	97.56r	16,299r	1,497.5r	91.88	17,258r	1,069.3r	61.96r
Greece	-	-	-	-	-	-	-	-	-
Irish Republic	303	28.8	94.97	86	7.1	82.34r	4	0.2	56.93
Italy	1,465	137.8	94.06	643r	60.4r	93.81	652	40.6	62.27r
Netherlands	13,309r	1,274.5r	95.76	12,868r	1,150.3r	89.39r	13,275r	826.0r	62.22r
Portugal	383	42.6	111.07	789r	71.9r	91.20r	1,253r	74.8r	59.66
Spain	1,680	166.8	99.27	3,437r	315.1r	91.67r	3,166r	188.3r	59.48r
Sweden	1,282	114.8	89.50r	851r	72.7r	85.48r	756	59.4r	78.63r
Total EU	**51,498r**	**5,018.5**	**97.45r**	**49,048r**	**4,459.3r**	**90.92r**	**50,206r**	**3,106.9r**	**61.88r**
Canada	1,953	184.3	94.35	1,049	95.4	90.99	719r	43.4r	60.32r
Norway	496r	51.6r	104.06r	902r	79.6r	88.21r	761r	42.0r	55.09r
U.S.A.	18,369	1,814.4	98.77	12,447r	1,115.9r	89.66r	12,645r	743.8r	58.82r
Other countries	4,158	416.7	100.22	2,105r	188.6r	89.58r	4,413r	256.9r	58.20r
Total exports	**76,475r**	**7,485.6r**	**97.88r**	**65,551r**	**5,938.8r**	**90.60r**	**68,745r**	**4,192.9r**	**60.99r**

(1) Includes re-exports.

8.4 Imports and exports of crude oil by country (continued)

	1999			2000		
	Quantity Thousand tonnes	Value (£million)	Value per tonne (£)	Quantity Thousand tonnes	Value (£million)	Value per tonne (£)
Imports (c.i.f.)						
Middle East						
Abu Dhabi	-	-	-	-	-	-
Dubai	-	-	-	-	-	-
Iran	-	-	-	-	-	-
Kuwait	-	-	-	-	-	-
Oman	-	-	-	-	-	-
Saudi Arabia	1,026r	65.1r	63.47r	1,573	220.0	139.90
Other countries	973r	62.3r	64.05r	233	25.0	107.40
Total Middle East	**1,999r**	**127.4r**	**63.76r**	**1,806**	**245.0**	**135.71**
Algeria	1,045r	95.4r	91.28r	1,992	319.8	160.56
Angola	-	-	-	-	-	-
Latvia	342r	27.7r	80.96r	27	2.9	105.49
Libya	-	-	-	155	27.8	179.19
Lithuania	26r	2.5r	93.36r	-	-	-
Mexico	875	57.7	66.02	782	95.2	121.63
Netherlands	1,159r	102.3r	88.21r	-	-	-
Nigeria	460	34.7	75.50	252	40.9	162.54
Norway	22,218r	1,791.0r	80.61r	27,523	3,809.3	138.40
Russia	584r	44.1r	75.45r	1487	186.3	125.28
Venezuela	1,071	50.2	46.86	671	58.0	86.48
Other countries	3,372r	35.9r	10.66r	2,204	174.8	79.31
Total Non Middle East	**31,152r**	**2,241.5r**	**71.95r**	**35,092**	**4,714.8**	**134.36**
Total imports	**33,151r**	**2,368.9r**	**71.46r**	**36,898**	**4,959.9**	**134.42**
Exports (f.o.b.)[1]						
European Union						
Belgium and Luxembourg	1,189	97.2	81.78	966	116.3	120.40
Denmark	-	-	-	-	-	-
Finland	701	52.7	75.19	816	105.0	128.76
France	11,326r	881.9r	77.87r	10,330	1,376.4	133.24
Germany	11,661	977.4	83.82	11,324	1,532.1	135.30
Greece	74	6.2	83.63	-	-	-
Irish Republic	70	3.6	51.00	-	-	-
Italy	1,234	92.1	74.62	471	53.1	112.83
Netherlands	11,354r	933.0r	82.18r	13,978	1,937.1	138.59
Portugal	1,403	106.5	75.90	694	87.2	125.61
Spain	3,655	286.4	78.35	2,090	277.9	132.94
Sweden	635	51.6	81.25	315	40.4	128.09
Total EU	**43,302r**	**3,488.5r**	**80.56r**	**40,984**	**5,525.6**	**134.82**
Canada	623	42.1	67.58	1,577	199.3	126.44
Norway	99	5.6	56.39	85	7.9	92.58
U.S.A.	20,259r	1,688.6r	83.35r	26,365	3,591.8	136.23
Other countries	3,832	311.7	81.36	2,604	383.1	147.15
Total exports	**68,114r**	**5,536.6r**	**81.28r**	**71,615**	**9,707.8**	**135.56**

Source: HM Customs and Excise

8.5 Imports and exports of solid fuel

Thousand tonnes

1996	Imports (1)				Exports			
	Steam coal	Coking coal	Anthracite	Other solid fuel	Steam coal	Coking coal	Anthracite	Other solid fuel
European Union								
Austria	-	-	-	-	5	-	-	-
Belgium/Luxembourg	5	-	14	4	14	-	90	2
Denmark	-	-	-	-	13	-	6	4
Finland	-	-	-	-	-	-	-	-
France	-	-	23	22	99	-	60	28
Germany	3	-	148	30	16	-	3	1
Irish Republic	16	-	24	6	324	3	153	7
Italy	-	-	-	-	-	-	-	-
Netherlands (2)	71	-	182	5	37	-	4	-
Spain	-	-	-	11	12	-	42	-
Sweden	20	-	13	7	-	-	8	47
Total European Union	**114**	**-**	**405**	**85**	**520**	**3**	**366**	**80**
Australia	-	3,748	-	2	-	-	-	-
Canada	-	1,410	-	28	-	-	-	-
Colombia	2,726	-	98	-	-	-	-	-
Indonesia	19	3	5	-	-	-	-	-
Norway	6	-	-	4	66	-	20	234
People's Republic of China	-	-	30	482	-	-	-	-
Poland	563	149	138	49	-	-	-	-
Republic of South Africa	1,323	-	236	-	-	-	-	-
Russia	-	-	75	29	-	-	-	-
United States of America	3,644	2,878	135	19	-	-	-	-
Venezuela	-	-	-	-	-	-	-	24
Vietnam	-	-	26	-	-	-	-	-
Other countries	8	58	2	104	9	-	2	1
Total all countries	**8,403**	**8,245**	**1,151**	**801**	**596**	**3**	**389**	**349**
Value of imports (cif)/export (fob) (£m) (3)	248.1	319.4	68.7	59.1	24.4	97.8	26.4	26.2
Value per tonne (£)	29.52	38.73	59.73	73.79	40.97	32.59	67.79	75.10

1997	Steam coal	Coking coal	Anthracite	Other solid fuel	Steam coal	Coking coal	Anthracite	Other solid fuel
European Union								
Austria	-	-	-	-	10	-	-	-
Belgium/Luxembourg	7	-	38	9	13	-	75	2
Denmark	-	-	-	-	-	-	2	1
Finland	-	-	-	-	-	-	-	22
France	3	-	6	14	101	-	59	30
Germany	3	-	83	16	133	-	19	-
Irish Republic	50	-	14	1	317	-	137	7
Italy	-	-	-	-	3	-	1	12
Netherlands (2)	66	-	117	15	45	-	6	2
Spain	-	-	-	6	31	-	11	-
Sweden	-	-	-	4	6	1	5	43
Total European Union	**129**	**-**	**258**	**65**	**659**	**1**	**314**	**119**
Australia	505	3,857	-	1	-	-	-	-
Canada	-	1,632	-	18	-	-	-	-
Colombia	2,763	-	47	-	-	-	-	-
Indonesia	78	-	6	-	-	-	-	-
Norway	100	-	2	1	64	-	91	221
People's Republic of China	3	-	75	616	-	-	-	-
Poland	532	51	117	24	-	-	-	-
Republic of South Africa	2,262	13	197	3	-	-	-	-
Russia	-	-	36	68	-	-	-	-
United States of America	4,281	2,519	150	-	-	-	-	1
Venezuela	97	-	-	-	-	-	-	-
Vietnam	-	-	15	-	-	-	-	-
Other countries	6	-	28	90	7	-	7	4
Total all countries	**10,756**	**8,072**	**931**	**886**	**731**	**1**	**414**	**345**
Value of imports (cif)/export (fob) (£m) (3)	289.8	298.3	80.5	55.6	31.5	0.1	25.7	26.0
Value per tonne (£)	27.85	36.95	62.93	62.79	43.0	44.33	62.03	71.82

8.5 Imports and exports of solid fuel (continued)

Thousand tonnes

1998	Imports (1)				Exports			
	Steam coal	Coking coal	Anthracite	Other solid fuel	Steam coal	Coking coal	Anthracite	Other solid fuel
European Union								
Austria	-	-	-	-	-	-	-	-
Belgium/Luxembourg	31	-	-	14	-	-	49	1
Denmark	-	-	-	-	-	-	8	-
Finland	-	-	-	-	-	-	-	16
France	-	-	-	20	78	-	23	19
Germany	19	-	6	13	141	-	2	-
Irish Republic	28	-	4	1	234	-	54	9
Italy	-	-	-	-	-	-	-	8
Netherlands (2)	150	-	19	1	41	-	11	1
Spain	3	-	-	-	78	-	21	-
Sweden	-	-	-	-	16	-	3	64
Total European Union	**231**	**-**	**29**	**49**	**588r**	**-**	**171r**	**118**
Australia	1,115	3,495	-	-	-	-	-	-
Canada	-	1,552	-	52	-	-	-	-
Colombia	3,819	-	-	-	2	-	-	-
Indonesia	24	-	-	-	-	-	-	-
Norway	117	-	3	-	94	-	107	225
People's Republic of China	-	-	132	602	-	-	-	-
Poland	875	-	75	20	-	-	1	-
Republic of South Africa	2,302	-	162	-	1	-	1	-
Russia	-	-	20	49	-	-	-	-
United States of America	3,142	3,599r	6	18	-	-	-	-
Venezuela	399	-	-	-	-	-	-	-
Vietnam	-	-	80	-	-	-	-	-
Other countries	55	-	12	51	4r	-	2r	2
Total all countries	**12,079**	**8,646**	**519**	**841**	**689**	**-**	**282**	**345**
Value of imports (cif)/export (fob) (£m) (3)	314.1	298.2	28.3	46.3	25.5	-	18.0	28.8
Value per tonne (£)	25.96	34.49	56.34	54.96	37.01	-	63.78	66.00

1999	Imports (1)				Exports			
	Steam coal	Coking coal	Anthracite	Other solid fuel	Steam coal	Coking coal	Anthracite	Other solid fuel
European Union								
Austria	-	-	-	-	-	-	-	-
Belgium/Luxembourg	59	-	11	14	-	-	69	-
Denmark	-	-	-	-	3	-	3	5
Finland	-	-	-	-	-	-	-	22
France	1	-	1	6	32	-	65	25
Germany	3	-	5	4	27	-	11	-
Irish Republic	34	-	10	8	200	-	77	8
Italy	-	-	-	-	-	-	-	-
Netherlands (2)	193	-	-	-	10	-	9	1
Portugal	-	-	-	-	3	-	-	-
Spain	-	-	-	-	25	-	43	-
Sweden	-	-	-	-	1	-	4	84
Total European Union	**290r**	**-**	**27**	**32r**	**301r**	**-**	**281r**	**145r**
Australia	1,688	4,262	-	-	-	-	-	-
Canada	-	1,427	-	18	-	-	-	-
Colombia	4,136r	-	-	-	-	-	-	-
Indonesia	82	-	-	-	-	-	-	-
Norway	43	-	-	-	113	-	42	149
People's Republic of China	81	24	144	322	-	-	-	-
Poland	1,286	-	13	14	1	-	-	-
Republic of South Africa	2,673	38	210	-	1	-	-	-
Russia	139	-	33	12	-	-	-	-
United States of America	746	2,269r	2	-	-	-	-	-
Venezuela	472	-	-	-	-	-	-	-
Vietnam	-	-	167	-	-	-	-	-
Other countries	39r	-	2r	37	18r	-	4	4r
Total all countries	**11,675r**	**8,020**	**598r**	**435r**	**434**	**-**	**327r**	**298r**
Value of imports (cif)/export (fob) (£m) (3)	302.5	244.3	30.7	19.2	19.8	-	18.2	19.0
Value per tonne (£)	24.95	30.47	51.25	43.98	45.74	-	55.49	63.97

8.5 Imports and exports of solid fuel (continued)

2000	Imports (1)				Exports			
	Steam coal	Coking coal	Anthracite	Other solid fuel	Steam coal	Coking coal	Anthracite	Other solid fuel
European Union								
Austria	-	-	-	-	-	-	-	-
Belgium/Luxembourg	7	-	4	36	-	-	71	1
Denmark	-	-	-	-	4	-	8	-
Finland	-	-	-	-	-	-	-	36
France	-	2	-	14	3	-	74	50
Germany	-	-	-	1	1	-	12	5
Irish Republic	13	-	6	7	210	4	54	17
Italy	-	-	-	-	-	-	-	-
Netherlands (2)	144	-	4	41	10	-	5	2
Portugal	-	-	-	-	-	-	-	-
Spain	-	-	-	-	-	-	31	-
Sweden	-	-	-	-	-	-	8	65
Total European Union	**164**	**2**	**14**	**99**	**228**	**4**	**263**	**176**
Australia	1,222	4,881	-	-	-	-	-	-
Canada	-	1,633	-	15	-	-	-	-
Colombia	5,649	-	-	-	-	-	-	-
Indonesia	-	-	9	-	-	-	-	-
Norway	22	-	2	2	120	-	38	182
People's Republic of China	-	-	143	263	-	-	-	-
Poland	1,083	-	24	2	-	-	-	-
Republic of South Africa	4,578	-	178	-	-	-	-	-
Russia	447	11	33	22	-	-	-	-
United States of America	811	1,935	26	26	-	-	-	-
Venezuela	208	-	-	-	-	-	-	-
Vietnam	-	-	123	-	-	-	-	-
Other countries	241	-	6	68	3	-	5	102
Total all countries	**14,425**	**8,462**	**558**	**497**	**351**	**4**	**306**	**460**
Value of imports (cif)/export (fob) (£m) (3)	367.0	262.0	39.5	26.2	24.7	0.2	16.1	29.4
Value per tonne (£)	26.36	30.96	37.40	52.74	38.97	56.77	52.71	63.87

Source : H.M. Customs and Excise

(1) *Country of origin basis.*
(2) *Includes extra-EU coal routed through the Netherlands.*
(3) *Value of imports are "cif" (cost, insurance and freight) and value of exports are "fob" (free on board). See technical note for fuller definition.*

Digest of United Kingdom Energy Statistics 2001

Annexes

Annex A: Energy and commodity balances, calorific values and conversion factors

Annex B: Energy and the environment

Annex C: UK oil and gas resources

Annex D: Glossary

Annex E: Major events in the energy industry

Annex F: Further sources

Department of Trade and Industry

Annex A
Energy and commodity balances, conversion factors and calorific values

Balance principles

A.1   This Annex outlines the principles behind the balance presentation of energy statistics. It covers these in general terms. Fuel specific details are given in the appropriate chapters of this publication.

A.2   Balances are divided into two types which perform different functions.

a) *commodity balance* - expressed for each energy commodity using the units usually associated with the commodity. By using a single column of figures, it shows the flow of the commodity from its sources of supply through to its final use. Commodity balances are presented in the individual fuel chapters of this publication.

b) *energy balance* - presents the commodity balances in a common unit and places them alongside one another in a manner which shows the dependence of the supply of one commodity on another. This is useful as some commodities are manufactured from others. The layout of the energy balance also differs slightly from the commodity balance. The energy balance format is used in Chapter 1.

A.3   Energy commodities can be either primary or secondary. Primary energy commodities are drawn (extracted or captured) from natural reserves or flows, whereas secondary commodities are produced from primary energy commodities. Crude oil or coal are examples of primary commodities whilst petrol or coke are secondary commodities manufactured from them. For balance purposes electricity may be considered to be both primary electricity (for example, hydro, wind) or secondary (produced from steam turbines using steam from the combustion of fuels).

A.4   Both commodity and energy balances show the flow of the commodity from its production, extraction or import through to its final use.

A.5   A simplified model of the commodity flow underlying the balance structure is given in Chart A.1. It illustrates how primary commodities may be used directly and/or be transformed into secondary commodities. The secondary fuels then enter final consumption or may also be transformed into another energy commodity (for example, electricity produced from fuel oil). To keep the diagram simple these "second generation" flows have not been shown.

A.6   The arrows at the top of the chart represent flows to and from the "pools" of primary and secondary commodities from imports and exports and, in the case of the primary pool, extraction from reserves (e.g. the production of coal, gas and crude oil).

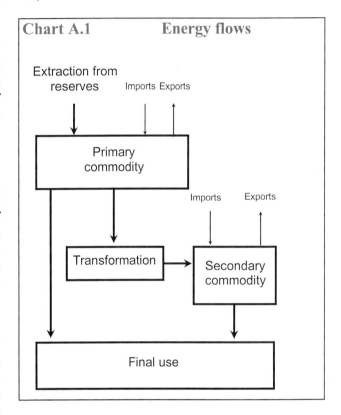

Chart A.1   Energy flows

Commodity balances (Tables 2.1 to 2.6, 3.1 to 3.6, 4.1, 5.1, and 7.1 to 7.3)

A.7   A commodity balance comprises a supply section and a demand section. The supply section gives available sources of supply (ie exports are subtracted). The demand section is divided into a transformation section, a section showing uses in the energy industries (other than for transformation) and a section covering uses by final consumers for energy or non-energy purposes. Final consumption for energy purposes is divided into use by sector of economic activity. The section breakdowns are described below.

Supply

Production

A.8   Production, within the commodity balance, covers indigenous production (extraction or capture of primary commodities) and generation or manufacture of secondary commodities. Production is always gross; that is it includes the quantities used during the extraction or manufacturing process.

Other sources

A.9   Production from other sources covers sources of supply which do not represent "new" supply. These may be recycled products, recovered fuels (slurry or waste coal), or electricity from pumped storage plants. The production of these quantities will have been reported in an earlier accounting period or have already been reported in the current period of account. Exceptionally, the *Other sources* row in the commodity balances for ethane, propane and butane is used to receive transfers of these hydrocarbons from gas stabilisation plants at North Sea terminals. In this manner the supplies of primary ethane, propane and butane from the North Sea are combined with the production of these gases in refineries so that the disposals may be presented together in the balances.

Imports and exports

A.10   The figures for imports and exports relate to energy commodities moving into or out of the United Kingdom as part of transactions involving United Kingdom companies. Exported commodities are produced in the United Kingdom and imported commodities are for use within the United Kingdom (although some may be re-exported before or after transformation). The figures thus exclude commodities either exported from or imported into HM Customs bonded areas or warehouses. These areas, although part of the United Kingdom, are regarded as being outside of the normal United Kingdom's customs boundary, and so goods entering into or leaving them are not counted as part of the statistics on trade used in the balances.

A.11   Similarly, commodities that only pass through the United Kingdom on their way to a final destination in another country are also excluded. However, for gas these transit flows are included because it is difficult to identify this quantity separately without detailed knowledge of the contract information covering the trade. This means that for gas there is some over statement of the level of imports and exports, but the net flows are correct.

A.12   The convention in these balances is that exports are shown with a negative sign.

Marine bunkers

A.13   These are deliveries of fuels (usually fuel oil or gas oil) to ships of any flag (including the United Kingdom) for consumption during the voyage to other countries. Marine bunkers are treated rather like exports and shown with a negative sign.

Stock changes

A.14   Additions to (- sign) and withdrawals from stocks (+ sign) held by producers and transformation industries correspond to withdrawals from and additions to supply, respectively.

Transfers

A.15   There are several reasons why quantities may be transferred from one commodity balance to another:

- a commodity may no longer meet the original specification and be reclassified;
- the name of the commodity may change through a change in use;
- to show quantities returned to supply from consumers. These may be by-products of the use of commodities as raw materials rather than fuels.

A.16   A quantity transferred from a balance is shown with a negative sign to represent a withdrawal from supply and with a positive sign in the receiving commodity balance representing an addition to its supply.

Total supply

A.17   The total supply available for national use is obtained by summing the flows above this entry in the balance.

Total demand

A.18   The various figures for the disposals and/or consumption of the commodities are summed to provide a measure of the demand for them. The main categories or sectors of demand are described in paragraphs A.20 to A.41.

Statistical difference

A.19   Any excess of supply over demand is shown as a statistical difference. A negative figure indicates that demand exceeds supply. Statistical differences arise when figures are gathered from a variety of independent sources and reflect differences in timing, in definition of coverage of the activity, or in commodity definition. Differences also arise for methodological reasons in the measurement of the flow of the commodity e.g. if there are differences between the volumes recorded by the gas producing companies and the gas transporting companies. A non-zero statistical difference is normal and, provided that it is not too large, is preferable to a statistical difference of zero as this suggests that a data provider has adjusted a figure to balance the account.

Transformation

A.20   The transformation sector of the balance covers those processes and activities which transform the original primary (and sometimes secondary) commodity into a form which is better suited for specific uses than the original form. Most of the transformation activities correspond to particular energy industries whose main business is to manufacture the product associated with them. Certain activities involving transformation take place to make products which are only partly used for energy needs (coke oven coke) or are by-products of other manufacturing processes (coke oven and blast furnace gases). However, as these products and by-products are then used, at least in part, for their energy content they are included in the balance system.

A.21 The figures given under the activity headings of this sector represent the quantities used for transformation. The production of the secondary commodities will be shown in the *Production* row of the corresponding commodity balances.

Electricity generation

A.22   The quantities of fuels burned for the generation of electricity are shown in their commodity balances under this heading. The activity is divided into two parts, covering the major power producers (for whom the main business is the generation of electricity for sale) and autogenerators (whose main business is not electricity generation but who produce electricity for their own needs and may also sell surplus quantities). The amounts of fuels shown in the balance represent the quantities consumed for the gross generation of electricity. Where a generator uses combined heat and power plant, the figures include only the part of the fuel use corresponding to the electricity generated.

A.23   In relation to autogenerators' data, the figures for quantities of fuel used for electricity generation appear under the appropriate fuel headings in the *Transformation* sector heading for *Autogenerators*, whilst the electricity generated, appears in the *Electricity* column under *Production*. A breakdown of the information according to the branch of industry in which the generation occurs is not shown in the balance but is given in Chapter 1, Table 1.9. The figures for energy commodities consumed by the industry branches shown under final consumption include all use of electricity, but exclude the fuels combusted by the industry branches to generate the electricity.

Petroleum refineries

A.24   Crude oil, natural gas liquids and other oils needed by refineries for the manufacture of finished petroleum products are shown under this heading.

Coke manufacture and blast furnaces

A.25   Quantities of coal for coke ovens and all fuels used within blast furnaces are shown under this heading. The consumption of fuels for heating coke ovens and the blast air for blast furnaces are shown under "Energy industry use".

Patent fuel manufacture

A.26   The coals and other solid fuels used for the manufacture of solid patent fuels are reported under this heading.

Other

A.27   Any minor transformation activities not specified elsewhere are captured under this heading.

Energy industry use

A.28   Consumption by both extraction and transformation industries to support the transformation process (but not for transformation itself) are included here according to the energy industry concerned. Typical examples are the consumption of electricity in power plants (e.g. for lighting, compressors and cooling systems) and the use of extracted gases on oil and gas platforms for compressors, pumps and other uses. The headings in this sector are identical to those used in the transformation sector with the exception of *Pumped storage*. In this case the electricity used to pump the water to the reservoir is reported.

Losses

A.29   This heading covers the intrinsic losses which occur during the transmission and distribution of electricity and gas (including manufactured gases). Other metering and accounting differences for gas and electricity are within the statistical difference, as are undeclared losses in other commodities.

Final consumption

A.30   *Final consumption* covers both final energy consumption (by different consuming sectors) and the use of energy commodities for non-energy purposes, that is *Non energy use*. Final consumption occurs when the commodities used are not for transformation into secondary commodities. The energy concerned disappears from the account after use. Any fuel use for electricity generation by final consumers is identified and reported separately within the transformation sector. When an enterprise generates electricity, the figure for final consumption of the industrial sector to which the enterprise belongs includes its use of the electricity it generates itself (as well as supplies of electricity it purchases from others) but does not include the fuel used to generate that electricity.

A.31   The classification of consumers according to their main business follows, as far as practicable, the *Standard Industrial Classification (SIC1992).* The qualifications to, and constraints on, the classification are described in the technical notes to Chapter 1, paragraphs 1.77 to 1.81. Table 1E in Chapter 1 shows the breakdown of final consumers used, and how this corresponds to the SIC1992.

Industry

A.32   Two sectors of industry (iron and steel and chemicals) require special mention because the activities they undertake fall across the transformation, final consumption and non-energy classifications used for the balances. Also, the data permitting an accurate allocation of fuel use within each of these major divisions are not readily available.

Iron and steel

A.33   The iron and steel industry is a heavy energy user for transformation and final consumption activities. Figures shown under final consumption for this industry branch reflect the amounts which remain after quantities used for transformation and energy sector own use have been subtracted from the industry's total energy requirements. Use of fuels for transformation by the industry may be identified within the transformation sector of the commodity balances.

A.34   The amounts of coal used for coke manufacture by the iron and steel industry are in the transformation sector of the coal balance. Included in this figure is the amount of coal used for coke manufacture by the companies outside of the iron and steel industry, i.e. solid fuel manufacturers. The corresponding production of coke and coke oven gas may be found in the commodity balances for these products. The use of coke in blast furnaces is shown in the commodity balance for coke, and the gases produced from blast furnaces and the associated basic oxygen steel furnaces are shown in the production row of the commodity balance for blast furnace gas.

A.35   Fuels used for electricity generation by the industry are included in the figures for electricity generation by autogenerators and are not distinguishable as being used by the iron and steel sector in the balances. Electricity generation and fuel used for this by broad industry group are given in Table 1.9.

A.36   Fuels used to support coke manufacture and blast furnace gas production are included in the quantities shown under *Energy industry use.* These gases and other fuels do not enter coke ovens or blast furnaces but are used to heat the ovens and the blast air supplied to furnaces.

Chemicals

A.37   The petro-chemical industry uses hydrocarbon fuels (mostly oil products and gases) as feedstock for the manufacture of its products. Distinguishing the energy use of delivered fuels from their non-energy use is complicated by the absence of detailed information. The procedures adopted to estimate the use are described in paragraphs A.40 and A.41 under *Non energy use.*

Transport

A.38   Figures under this heading are almost entirely quantities used strictly for transport purposes. However, the figures recorded against road transport usually include some fuel that is actually consumed in some "off-road" activities. Similarly, figures for railway fuels include some amounts of burning oil not used directly for transport purposes. Transport sector use of electricity includes all electricity used in industries classified to SIC1992 Groups 60 to 63. Fuels supplied to cargo and passenger ships undertaking international voyages are reported as *Marine bunkers* (see paragraph A.13). Supplies to fishing vessels are included under "agriculture".

Other sectors

A.39   The classification of all consumers groups under this heading, except *domestic,* follows *SIC1992* and is described in Table 1E in Chapter 1. The consistency of the classification across different commodities cannot be guaranteed because the figures reported are dependent on what the data suppliers can provide.

Non energy use

A.40   The non energy use of fuels may be divided into two types. They may be used directly for their physical properties e.g. lubricants or bitument used for road surfaces, or by the petro-chemical industry as raw materials for the manufacture of goods such as plastics. In their use by the petro-chemical industry, relatively little combustion of the fuels takes place and the carbon and/or hydrogen they contain are largely transferred into the finished product. However, in some cases heat from the manufacturing process or from combustion of by-products may be used. Data for this energy use are rarely available. Depending on the feedstock, non energy consumption is either estimated or taken to be the deliveries to the chemicals sector.

A.41 Both types of non energy use are shown under the *Non energy use* heading at the foot of the balances.

The energy balance (Tables 1.1 to 1.3)

Principles
A.42 The energy balance conveniently presents:

- an overall view of the United Kingdom's energy supplies;
- the relative importance of each energy commodity;
- dependence on imports;
- the contribution of our own fossil and renewable resources;
- the interdependence of one commodity on another.

A.43 The energy balance is constructed directly from the commodity balances by expressing the data in a common unit, placing them beside one another and adding appropriate totals. However, some rearrangement of the commodity balance format is required to show transformation of primary into secondary commodities in an easily understood manner.

A.44 Energy units are widely used as the common unit, and the current practice for the United Kingdom and the international organisations which prepare balances is to use the tonne of oil equivalent or a larger multiple of this unit, commonly thousands. One tonne of oil equivalent is defined as 10^7 kilocalories (41.868 gigajoules). The tonne of oil equivalent is another unit of energy like the gigajoule, kilocalorie or kilowatt hour, rather than a physical quantity. It has been chosen as it is easier to visualise than the other units. Due to the natural variations in heating value of primary fuels such as crude oil, it is rare that one tonne of oil has an energy content equivalent to one tonne of oil equivalent, however it is generally within a few per cent of the heating value of a tonne of oil equivalent. The energy figures are calculated from the natural units of the commodity balances by multiplying by factors representing the calorific (heating) value of the fuel. The gross calorific values of fuels are used for this purpose. When the natural unit of the commodity is already an energy unit (electricity in kilowatt hours, for example) the factors are just constants converting one energy unit to another.

A.45 Most of the underlying definitions and ideas of commodity balances can be taken directly over into the energy balance. However, production of secondary commodities and, in particular, electricity are treated differently and need some explanation. The components of the energy balance are described below, drawing out the differences of treatment compared with the commodity balances.

Primary supply
A.46 Within the energy balance, the production row covers only extraction of primary fuels and the generation of primary energy (hydro, nuclear, wind). Note the change of row heading from *Production* in the commodity balances to *Indigenous production* in the energy balance. Production of secondary fuels and secondary electricity are shown in the transformation sector and not in the indigenous production row at the top of the balance.

A.47 For fossil fuels, indigenous production represents the marketable quantity extracted from the reserves. Indigenous production of *Primary electricity* comprises hydro-electricity, wind and nuclear energy. The energy value for hydro-electricity is taken to be the energy content of the electricity produced from the hydro power plant and not the energy available in the water driving the turbines. A similar approach is adopted for electricity from wind generators. The electricity is regarded as the primary energy form because there are currently no other uses of the energy resource "upstream" of the generation. The energy value attached to nuclear electricity is discussed in paragraph A.51.

A.48 The other elements of the supply part of the balance are identical to those in the commodity balances. In particular, the sign convention is identical so that figures for exports and international marine bunkers carry negative signs. A stock build carries a negative sign to denote it as a withdrawal from supply whilst a stock draw carries a positive sign to show it as an addition to supply.

A.49 The *Primary supply* is the sum of the figures above it in the table, taking account of the signs, and expresses the national requirement for primary energy commodities from all sources and foreign supplies of secondary commodities. It is an indicator of the use of indigenous resources and external energy supplies. Both the amount and mixture of fuels in final consumption of energy commodities in the United Kingdom will differ from the primary supply. The "mix" of commodities in final consumption will be much more dependent on the manufacture of secondary commodities, in particular electricity.

Transformation
A.50 Within an energy balance the presentation of the inputs to and outputs from transformation activities requires special mention as it is carried out using a compact format. The transformation sector also plays

a key role in moving primary electricity from its own column in the balance into the electricity column so that it can be combined with electricity from fossil fuelled power stations and the total disposals shown.

A.51   Indigenous production of primary electricity comprises nuclear electricity, hydro electricity and electricity from wind generation. Nuclear electricity is obtained by passing steam from nuclear reactors through conventional steam turbine sets. The heat in the steam is considered to be the primary energy available and its value is calculated from the electricity generated using the average thermal efficiency of nuclear stations, currently 37.25 in the United Kingdom. The electrical energy from hydro and wind is transferred from the *Primary electricity* column to the *Electricity* column using the *transfers* row because electricity is the form of primary energy and no transformation takes place. However, because the form of the nuclear energy is the steam from the nuclear reactors, the energy it contains is shown entering electricity generation and the corresponding electricity produced is included with all electricity generation in the figure, in the same row, under the *Electricity* column.

A.52   Quantities of fuels entering transformation activities (fuels into electricity generation, crude oil into petroleum product manufacture (refineries), or coal into coke ovens) are shown with a negative sign to represent the input and the resulting production is shown as a positive number.

A.53   For electricity generated by Major power producers, the inputs are shown in the *Major power producers* row of the *coal, manufactured fuel, primary oils, petroleum products, gas, renewables* and *primary electricity* columns. The total energy input to electricity generation is the sum of the values in these first seven columns. The *Electricity* column shows total electricity generated from these inputs and the

transformation loss is the sum of these two figures, given in the *Total* column.

A.54   Within the transformation sector, the negative figures in the *Total* column represent the losses in the various transformation activities. This is a convenient consequence of the sign convention chosen for the inputs and outputs from transformation. Any positive figures represent a transformation gain and, as such, are an indication of incorrect data.

A.55   In the energy balance the columns containing the input commodities, for both electricity generation and oil refining, are separate from the columns for the outputs. However, for the transformation activities involving solid fuels this is only partly the case. Coal used for the manufacture of coke is shown in the coke manufacture row of the transformation section in the coal column, but the related coke and coke oven gas production are shown combined in the *Manufactured fuels* column. Similarly, the input of coke to blast furnaces and the resulting production of blast furnace gas are not identifiable and have been combined in the *Manufactured fuels* column in the *Blast furnace* row. As a result, only the net loss from blast furnace transformation activity appears in the column.

A.56   The share of each commodity or commodity group in primary supply can be calculated from the table. This table also shows the demand for primary as well as foreign supplies. Shares of primary supplies may be taken from the *Primary supply* row of the balance. Shares of fuels in final consumption may be calculated from the final consumption row.

Energy industry use and final consumption

A.57   The figures for final consumption and energy industry use follow, in general, the principles and definitions described under commodity balances in paragraphs A.28 to A.41.

Standard conversion factors

1 tonne of oil equivalent (toe)	$= 10^7$ kilocalories
	$= 396.83$ therms
	$= 41.868$ GJ
	$= 11,630$ kWh

1 therm = 100,000 British thermal units (Btu)

The following prefixes are used for multiples of joules, watts and watt hours:

kilo (k)	$= 1,000$	or 10^3
mega (M)	$= 1,000,000$	or 10^6
giga (G)	$= 1,000,000,000$	or 10^9
tera (T)	$= 1,000,000,000,000$	or 10^{12}
peta (P)	$= 1,000,000,000,000,000$	or 10^{15}

WEIGHT
1 kilogramme (kg)	$= 2.2046$ pounds (lb)
1 pound (lb)	$= 0.4536$ kg
1 tonne (t)	$= 1,000$ kg
	$= 0.9842$ long ton
	$= 1.102$ short ton (sh tn)
1 Statute or long ton	$= 2,240$ lb
	$= 1.016$ t
	$= 1.120$ sh tn

VOLUME
1 cubic metre (cu m)	$= 35.31$ cu ft
1 cubic foot (cu ft)	$= 0.02832$ cu m
1 litre	$= 0.22$ Imperial gallon (UK gal.)
1 UK gallon	$= 8$ UK pints
	$= 1.201$ U.S. gallons (US gal)
	$= 4.54609$ litres
1 barrel	$= 159.0$ litres
	$= 34.97$ UK gal
	$= 42$ US gal

LENGTH
| 1 mile | $= 1.6093$ kilometres |
| 1 kilometre (km) | $= 0.62137$ miles |

TEMPERATURE

1 scale degree Celsius (C) = 1.8 scale degrees Fahrenheit (F)

For conversion of temperatures: $°C = 5/9 \ (°F - 32)$; $°F = 9/5 \ °C + 32$

Average conversion factors for petroleum

	Imperial gallons per tonne	Litres per tonne		Imperial gallons per tonne	Litres per tonne
Crude oil:			**Gas/diesel oil:**		
Indigenous	264	1,199	Gas oil	257	1,169
Imported	260	1,181	Marine diesel oil	253	1,150
Average of refining throughput	262	1,192			
			Fuel oil:		
Ethane	601	2,730	All grades	222	1,021
Propane	433	1,974	Light fuel oil:		
Butane	381	1,746	1% or less sulphur	237	1,071
Naphtha (l.d.f.)	322	1,448	>1% sulphur	232	1,067
			Medium fuel oil:		
Aviation gasoline	308	1,395	1% or less sulphur	237	1,081
			>1% sulphur	225	1,038
Motor spirit:			Heavy fuel oil:		
All grades	299	1,349	1% or less sulphur	226	1,037
Unleaded Super	292	1,342	>1% sulphur	222	1,011
Premium	299	1,348			
Ultra low sulphur petrol	297	1,348			
Leaded Premium	300	1,361	**Lubricating oils:**		
Lead replacement petrol	300	1,342	White	249	1,131
			Greases	245	1,156
Middle distillate feedstock	286	1,116	Other	249	1,148
Kerosene:			Bitumen	214	1,021
Aviation turbine fuel	275	1,246	Petroleum coke	185	843
Burning oil	274	1,246	Petroleum waxes	261	1,187
			Industrial spirit	302	1,247
DERV fuel: all	260	1,195	White spirit	278	1,278
0.005% or less sulphur	260	1,203			
>0.005% sulphur	264	1,183			

Note: The above conversion factors, which for refined products have been compiled by the UK Petroleum Industry Association, apply to the year 2000, and are only approximate for other years.

A.1 Estimated average gross calorific values of fuels

	GJ per tonne		GJ per tonne
Coal:		Renewable sources:	
All consumers (weighted average) *(1)*	27.0	Domestic wood *(2)*	10.0
Power stations *(1)*	26.0	Industrial wood *(3)*	11.9
Coke ovens *(1)*	30.4	Straw	15.0
Low temperature carbonisation plants		Poultry litter	8.8
and manufactured fuel plants	30.3	Meat and bone	17.3
Collieries	29.6	General industrial waste	16.0
Agriculture	29.2	Hospital waste	14.0
Iron and steel	30.7	Municipal solid waste *(4)*	9.5
Other industries (weighted average)	26.8	Refuse derived waste *(4)*	18.6
Non-ferrous metals	25.1	Short rotation coppice *(5)*	10.6
Food, beverages and tobacco	29.5	Tyres	32.0
Chemicals	28.7		
Textiles, clothing, leather etc.	30.4	Petroleum:	
Paper, printing etc.	28.7	Crude oil (weighted average)	45.7
Mineral products	28.5	Petroleum products (weighted average)	45.8
Engineering (mechanical and		Ethane	50.7
electrical engineering and	29.3	Butane and propane (LPG)	49.4
vehicles)			
Other industries	30.2	Light distillate feedstock for gasworks	47.7
		Aviation spirit and wide cut gasoline	47.3
		Aviation turbine fuel	46.2
Domestic		Motor spirit	47.0
House coal	30.9	Burning oil	46.2
Anthracite and dry steam coal	33.6	Gas/diesel oil (DERV)	45.6
Other consumers	29.2	Fuel oil	43.1
Imported coal (weighted average)	28.0	Power station oil	43.1
Exports (weighted average)	31.8	Non-fuel products (notional value)	43.8

	GJ per tonne		MJ per cubic metre
Coke (including low temperature	29.8	Natural gas *(6)*	39.4
carbonisation cokes)		Coke oven gas	18.0
Coke breeze	24.8	Blast furnace gas	3.0
Other manufactured solid fuel	30.8	Landfill gas	38.6
		Sewage gas	38.6

(1) Applicable to UK consumption - based on calorific value for home produced coal plus imports and, for "All consumers" net of exports.
(2) Based on a 50 per cent moisture content.
(3) Average figure covering a range of possible feedstock.
(4) Average figure based on survey returns.
(5) On an "as received" basis. On a "dry" basis 18.6 GJ per tonne.
(6) The gross calorific value of natural gas can also be expressed as 10.936 kWh per cubic metre. This value represents the average calorific value seen for gas when extracted. At this point it contains not just methane, but also some other hydrocarbon gases (ethane, butane, propane). These gases are removed before the gas enters the National Transmission System for sale to final consumers. As such, this calorific value will differ from that readers will see quoted on their gas bills.

Note: The above estimated average gross calorific values apply only to the year 2000. For calorific values of fuels in earlier years see Table A.2 and previous issues of this Digest. See the notes in Chapter 1, paragraph 1.75 regarding net calorific values. The calorific values for coal other than imported coal are based on estimates provided by the main coal producers. The calorific values for petroleum products have been calculated using the method described in Chapter 1, paragraph 1.49. The calorific values for coke oven gas and blast furnace gas are provided by the Iron and Steel Statistics Bureau (ISSB).

Data reported in this Digest in 'thousand tonnes of oil equivalent' have been prepared on the basis of 1 tonne of oil equivalent having an energy content of 41.868 gigajoules (GJ), (1 GJ = 9.478 therms) - see notes in Chapter 1, paragraphs 1.46 to 1.49.

A.2 Estimated average gross calorific values of fuels, 1970, 1980, 1990 and 1996 to 2000

GJ per tonne (gross)

	1970	1980	1990	1996	1997	1998	1999	2000
Coal								
All consumers (1)(2)	..	25.6	25.5	25.9	26.1	26.1	26.2	26.2
All consumers - home produced plus imports minus exports (1)	..	..	..	26.9	27.2	27.2	27.0r	27.0
Power stations (2)	23.7	23.8	24.8	25.1	25.3	25.4	25.5	25.6
Power stations - home produced plus imports (1)	..	..	..	25.4	25.6	25.8	25.9r	26.0
Coke ovens (2)	29.8	30.5	30.2	31.4	31.4	31.3	31.5	31.2
Coke ovens - home produced plus imports (1)	..	..	..	32.0	32.0	32.0	30.5r	30.4
Low temperature carbonisation plants and manufactured fuel plants	29.8	19.1	29.2	30.0	30.4	30.5	30.1	30.3
Collieries	24.9	27.0	28.6	26.2	27.8	29.6	29.3	29.6
Agriculture	31.1	30.1	28.9	28.9	29.1	28.5	28.9	29.2
Iron and steel industry	29.1	29.1	28.9	31.3	31.3	31.3	30.7	30.7
Other industries (1)	27.0	27.1	27.8	27.3	27.0	26.9	26.6	26.8
Non-ferrous metals	..	..	23.1	25.4	25.1	24.5	25.1	25.1
Food, beverages and tobacco	28.4	28.6	28.1	28.1	28.7	29.7	29.4	29.5
Chemicals	25.8	25.8	27.3	27.1	27.3	28.9	29.7	28.7
Textiles, clothing, leather & footwear	27.4	27.5	27.7	30.2	30.4	30.2	30.1	30.4
Pulp, paper, printing, etc.	26.5	26.5	27.9	27.7	27.4	29.0	27.7r	28.7
Mineral products	..	..	28.2	27.4	27.0	26.6	26.7	28.5
Engineering (3)	27.7	27.7	28.3	29.3	29.6	29.4	29.3	29.3
Other industry (4)	28.4	28.4	28.5	27.0r	29.6r	30.1r	29.1r	30.2
Unclassified	..	..	27.1	..	..	..	..	..
Domestic								
House coal	29.1	30.1	30.2	30.6	30.6	30.9	30.9	30.9
Anthracite and dry steam coal	33.8	33.3	33.6	33.9	33.9	34.1	33.5	33.6
Other consumers	29.1	27.5	27.5	30.4	29.3	29.2	29.1	29.2
Imported coal (1)	..	..	28.3	29.8	29.3	29.2	28.2r	28.0
of which Steam coal				26.9	26.9	27.0	26.8r	26.6
Coking coal				32.0	32.0	32.0	30.4r	30.4
Anthracite				31.1	31.4	32.0	31.2	31.2
Exports (1)	..	..	29.0	29.5	30.7	30.8	31.7	31.8
of which Steam coal				28.5	30.4	30.1	32.1	31.0
Anthracite				31.0	30.9	31.4	31.5	32.6
Coke (5)	28.1	28.1	28.1	29.8	29.8	29.8	29.8	29.8
Coke breeze	22.9	24.4	24.8	24.8	24.8	24.8	24.8	24.8
Other manufactured solid fuels (1)	28.1	27.6	27.6	30.2	30.4	30.7	30.9	30.8
Petroleum								
Crude oil (1)	..	45.2	45.6	45.7	45.7	45.7	45.7	45.7
Liquified petroleum gas	49.6	49.6	49.4	49.4	49.4	49.4	49.4	49.4
Ethane	52.3	52.3	50.6	50.7	50.7	50.7	50.7	50.7
LDF for gasworks/Naphtha	47.8	47.8	47.9	47.7	47.7	47.7	47.7	47.7
Aviation spirit and wide-cut gasoline (AVGAS & AVTAG)	47.2	47.2	47.3	47.3	47.3	47.3	47.3	47.3
Aviation turbine fuel (AVTUR)	46.4	46.4	46.2	46.2	46.2	46.2	46.2	46.2
Motor spirit	47.0	47.0	47.0	47.0	47.0	47.0	47.1	47.0
Burning oil	46.5	46.5	46.2	46.2	46.2	46.2	46.2	46.2
Vaporising oil	46.0	45.9	45.9	..	..	..	..	..
Gas/diesel oil (including DERV)	45.5	45.5	45.4	45.4	45.4	45.5	45.6	45.6
Fuel oil	43.0	42.8	43.2	43.2	43.3	43.2	43.2	43.1
Power station oil	43.5	42.8	43.2	43.2	43.3	43.2	43.2	43.1
Non-fuel products (notional value)	..	42.2	43.2	43.3	43.4	43.3	43.4	43.8
Petroleum coke	..	..	39.5	39.5	39.5	39.5	39.5	39.5
Orimulsion (6)	..	..	29.7	29.7	29.7	..	..	..

(1) Weighted averages.
(2) Home produced coal only.
(3) Mechanical engineering and metal products, electrical and instrument engineering and vehicle manufacture.
(4) Includes construction.
(5) Since 1995 the source of these figures has been the ISSB.
(6) Orimulsion use ceased in 1997.

Annex B
Energy and the environment

Introduction

B.1 The operations of the energy sector in the UK, as elsewhere, can affect the environment in many different ways. Detrimental effects can result from exploration, production, transportation, storage, conversion and distribution. The final use of the energy and the disposal of waste products can also damage the environment.

B.2 The particular areas of potential environmental concern related to the energy sector are:- ambient air quality; acid deposition; coal mining subsidence; major environmental accidents; water pollution; maritime pollution; land use and siting impact; radiation and radioactivity; solid waste disposal; hazardous air pollutants; stratospheric ozone depletion; and climate change. Fossil fuels are responsible for the majority of emissions of greenhouse gases and other pollutants such as sulphur dioxide, black smoke, oxides of nitrogen and carbon monoxide.

B.3 While the impact of energy use on the environment is important, information on emissions and oil spills are published elsewhere. Rather than replicate information, this annex gives an overview of some of the impacts of energy use on the environment without going into the detail of the methodology or providing the background data. The data sources are listed in the section at the end of this annex.

Greenhouse gases

B.4 Naturally-occurring greenhouse gases maintain the earth's surface at a temperature 33°C warmer than it would be in their absence. Water vapour is by far the most important greenhouse gas but there are also significant natural sources of carbon dioxide, methane, ozone and nitrous oxide. At present greenhouse gas concentrations in the atmosphere are increasing as a result of human activities. There is new and stronger evidence that most of the warming observed over the last 50 years is attributable to human activities.

B.5 Targets for emission reductions cover a basket of six greenhouse gases: carbon dioxide, methane, nitrous oxide, hydrofluorocarbons, perfluorocarbons, sulphur hexafluoride. The most important of these from an energy perspective is carbon dioxide, where 95% of emissions come from fuel combustion. Carbon dioxide emissions contribute more than 80 per cent of the potential global warming effect of anthropogenic emissions of greenhouse gases. Although this gas is naturally emitted by living organisms, these emissions are balanced by the uptake of carbon dioxide by the biosphere during photosynthesis; they therefore tend to have no net effect on atmospheric concentrations. The burning of fossil fuels, however, releases carbon dioxide fixed by the biosphere over many millions of years, and thus increases its concentration in the atmosphere.

B.6 In 2000, the main sources of carbon dioxide emissions (on an Intergovernmental Panel on Climate Change basis) were power stations (28 per cent), industry (24 per cent), transport (22 per cent) and the domestic sector (15 per cent). In 2000, 152 million tonnes of carbon are estimated to have been emitted as carbon dioxide from the UK. Between 1990 and 2000, emissions fell by 7½ per cent, despite a small increase in emissions between 1999 and 2000. This increase was due to the increased levels of coal consumption by power stations to make up for a shortfall during maintenance and repair at gas and nuclear stations. Towards the end of 2000, coal prices were lower than gas prices causing coal-fired generation to be chosen over gas. Carbon dioxide emissions are directly related to the type of fuel used, gas emitting fewer emissions per unit of fuel than coal.

Air pollution

B.7 Air pollution can have a wide range of environmental impacts, with excessively high levels potentially affecting soil, water, wildlife, crops, forests and buildings as well as damaging human health. The main air pollutants associated with fossil fuel combustion are sulphur dioxide, Black Smoke and PM_{10}, nitrogen oxides and carbon monoxide.

B.8 Sulphur dioxide is a gas produced by the combustion of sulphur-containing fuels such as coal and oil. In 1999 there were 1.2 million tonnes of sulphur dioxide emitted, 68 per cent lower than 1990 and 82 per cent lower than in 1970. The decrease is a result of lower coal and fuel oil consumption over the period. In addition, since 1993, flue-gas desulphurisation has come progressively into operation on the 6 GWe of coal-fired generating capacity at the Drax and Ratcliffe-on-Soar power stations, helping to reduce emissions further.

B.9 "PM_{10}" and "Black Smoke" refer to two different measurement methods for fine, suspended particles in the air. These particles may come from a wide range of man-made and natural sources, including incomplete fuel combustion, wind-blown soil, and dust generated by activities such as quarrying. By 1999 emissions of PM_{10} are estimated to have fallen by 65 per cent since 1970, largely as a result of an 83 per cent fall in emissions from the domestic sector. In 1999, Black Smoke emissions were around 44 per cent lower than in 1990 and 75 per cent lower than in 1970.

B.10 A number of nitrogen compounds including nitrogen dioxide, nitric oxide and nitrogen oxides are formed in combustion processes when nitrogen in the air or the fuel combines with oxygen. These compounds can add to the natural acidity of rainfall. The total level of emissions in 1999 (at 1.6 million tonnes of nitrous oxide) was 42 per cent lower than in 1990, with substantial falls from both road transport and power stations, the two largest contributing sectors. Emissions from power stations have declined recently due to increased output from nuclear stations, combined cycle gas turbine stations replacing coal-fired plant, together with the effect of the installation of low NO_x burners at other coal fired power stations. The fall in emissions from road transport is mainly due to tighter emissions standards for passenger and goods vehicles, including the introduction of catalytic converters on all new cars since 1993.

B.11 Carbon monoxide is derived from the incomplete combustion of fuel. On a UNECE basis, 4.8 million tonnes of carbon monoxide were emitted, a level 33 per cent lower than 1990 and 44 per cent lower than in 1970. Two thirds of carbon monoxide emissions in the UK come from road transport, despite large reductions over the past thirty years due to tighter emission standards and the introduction of catalytic converters.

B.12 Lead emissions from petrol-engined vehicles fell from 7.5 thousand tonnes in 1980 to virtually zero in 2000 as a result of the gradual take-up of unleaded petrol followed by the ban of leaded petrol from general sale at the end of 1999.

Oil pollution, oil spills and gas flaring

B.13 The amounts of oil spilled are small around the coasts of the United Kingdom and offshore (North Sea) in relation to total oil production, with the amounts discharged on drill cuttings, and with produced water generally much larger than from offshore installation spills. The total amount of oil spilled offshore during 2000 was 78 tonnes which continues the downward trend of recent years.

B.14 The number of oil spills recorded increased from 300 in 1996 to 423 in 2000. The increase reflects the trend for reporting even the smallest of spills, 405 of those reported in 2000 were for spills of less than 1 tonne.

B.15 The discharge of oil-contaminated water from offshore installations is permitted by an exemption granted under the Prevention of Oil Pollution Act 1971, but the oil content must not exceed 40 parts per million. In 2000, of 68 installations discharging produced water, 3 exceeded this target when averaged over the whole year. These installations took steps to rectify the problem and there were significant improvements in performance by the end of 2000. The average content of oil in produced water for the year, for the UKCS as a whole, was 21.5 parts per million,

the same as in 1999, which was the lowest value yet recorded in the UKCS.

B.16 Under the terms of petroleum production licences, gas may be flared only with the consent of the Secretary of State. Flaring at onshore fields in 2000 was minimal, whilst 4.76 million cubic metres of gas a day was flared at offshore installations. Flaring at offshore installations in 2000 was 17 per cent lower than in 1999.

Data sources

B.17 Greenhouse gas emissions and air pollution statistics up to 1999 are published in the National Atmospheric Emissions Inventory which is compiled by the National Environmental Technology Centre (NETCEN) on behalf of Department for Environment, Food and Rural Affairs (DEFRA). Data and information on how the data have been compiled can be found:
- on the NETCEN website at www.aeat.co.uk/netcen/airqual/statbase/;
- on the DEFRA website, as part of the Digest of Environmental Statistics at www.defra.gov.uk;
- in a news release that was published on 28 March 2001 on the DEFRA website at www.defra.gov.uk;
- in the *Energy Sector Indicators* publication from the DTI.

B.18 The 2000 carbon dioxide figures are provisional DTI estimates. They were published in an article that formed part of the March 2001 edition of Energy Trends and can be found on the DTI website at www.dti.gov.uk/epa/et.htm.

B.19 Figures for the total number of oil spills reported are collected by the Advisory Committee on Protection of the Sea Annual Surveys of Oil Pollution around the Coasts of the United Kingdom. The *Development of the oil and gas resources of the United Kingdom 2001* publication (the *'Brown Book'*) gives more detail about oil pollution, oil spills and gas flaring.

Contacts:
Rachael Winther (Statistician, Emissions)
020 7215 6178
Kevin Williamson (Statistician, Oil pollution and gas flaring)
020 7215 5184

Annex C
United Kingdom oil and gas resources

Introduction

C.1   This section provides background information on the United Kingdom's resources of crude oil and natural gas reserves, production (including a split by field), disposal and operations. This information is intended as a supplement to that in the commodity balances included in the main part of this chapter. Most of the data (including those on gas) are obtained from the Department of Trade and Industry's Petroleum Production Reporting System. Further information can be obtained from the DTI publication *Development of UK Oil and Gas Resources 2001*, known as the *Brown Book*.

C.2   The annual statistics relate to the calendar years, or the end of calendar years, 1996 to 2000 and the data cover the United Kingdom Continental Shelf (onshore and offshore). Annual data for production, imports and exports of crude oil during the period 1970 to 2000 are given in Table 3.11.

Oil and gas reserves (Table C.1)

C.3   This table shows estimated reserves of oil and gas at the end of 2000. Estimates of initial recoverable reserves in present discoveries are given and, also, ranges of recoverable oil reserves (discovered and undiscovered) originally in place. The table also includes the range of potential additional reserves existing in discoveries that do not meet the criteria for inclusion as possible reserves defined below.

C.4   The terms **proven, probable** and **possible** are applied on a field by field basis and are given the following meanings in this context:

(i)   **Proven** - those reserves which on the available evidence are virtually certain to be technically and economically producible (i.e. those reserves which have a better than 90 per cent chance of being produced).

(ii)   **Probable** - those reserves which are not yet **proven** but which are estimated to have a better than 50 per cent chance of being technically and economically producible.

(iii)   **Possible** - those reserves which at present cannot be regarded as **probable** but are estimated to have a significant but less than 50 per cent chance of being technically and economically producible.

C.5   Chart C.1 shows the changes in discovered recoverable oil and gas reserves and cumulative production since 1980, and shows that over this period the reserves (proven, probable and possible) have increased roughly in line with cumulative production, so that remaining reserves have until recently been broadly unchanged.

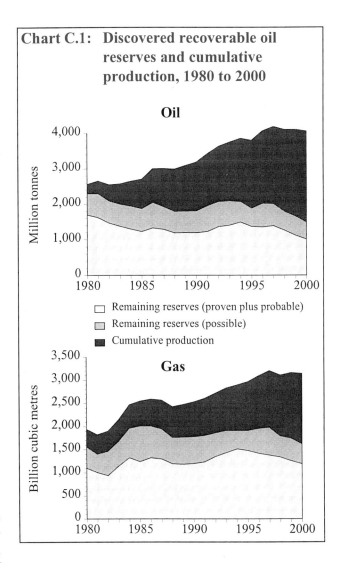

Chart C.1:   Discovered recoverable oil reserves and cumulative production, 1980 to 2000

□ Remaining reserves (proven plus probable)
▨ Remaining reserves (possible)
■ Cumulative production

C.6   Estimates for the size of reserves of oil and gas underneath the United Kingdom Continental Shelf are revised on an annual basis. This allows new discoveries of oil and gas reserves and reassessments of existing discoveries to be incorporated. These reassessments are needed so that overall estimates of reserves can take into account new information on existing fields as well as changes in the overall economic climate. Only if it is economically viable to exploit the discovery will oil and gas actually be produced from any discovered reservoir.

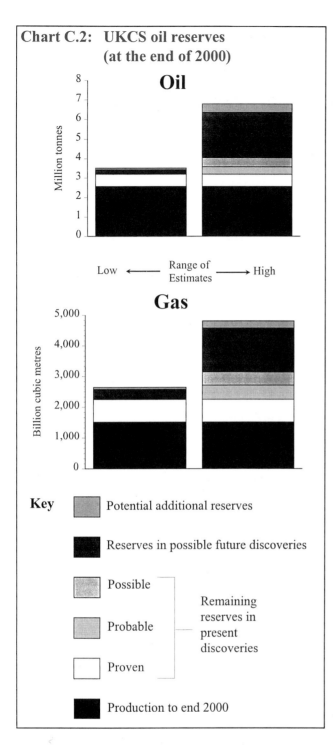

Chart C.2: UKCS oil reserves (at the end of 2000)

Oil

Million tonnes

Low ← Range of Estimates → High

Gas

Billion cubic metres

Key

- Potential additional reserves
- Reserves in possible future discoveries
- Possible ⎫
- Probable ⎬ Remaining reserves in present discoveries
- Proven ⎭
- Production to end 2000

C.8   At the end of 2000 remaining proven, probable and possible oil reserves stood at 1,490 million tonnes. This is a decrease of 180 million tonnes on the equivalent remaining proven, probable and possible reserves figure at the end of 1999. On top of actual production of 126 million tonnes in 2000, the estimates of originally recoverable reserves in present discoveries were revised downwards by 55 million tonnes. Remaining gas reserves on the same basis were 1,600 billion cubic metres at the end of 2000, 150 billion cubic metres lower than at the end of 1999. Production of gas was 115 billion cubic metres in 2000, on top of which the estimates of the size of gas reserves in current discoveries were revised downwards by 35 billion cubic metres.

C.9   These revisions to the estimates of discovered recoverable reserves are due to limited replacement of reserves from exploration successes or by fields previously held as only having potential additional reserves. This lack of replacement discoveries is due to the impact of low oil prices during 1998 and the first half of 1999 affecting the economics of field exploitation and also affecting company decisions with regards to exploration and development activities.

C.10   Table C.I contains simplified data on cumulative production of oil and gas compared to the latest estimates for the ranges of UK reserves of oil and gas, based on data for reserves in existing discoveries and adding in estimates for reserves yet to be discovered. The ranges of estimates for oil and gas reserves are illustrated in Chart C.2.

C.7   In recent years, advances in the technology used in the production of oil and gas, and economic situations, have been such that discoveries that were made sometimes several years ago have only recently become economically viable. As such, much of the increase in the estimates of the United Kingdom's discovered recoverable reserves of oil and gas over recent years is made up of reassessments of known deposits of oil and gas rather than the discovery of new deposits. This is one of the reasons why the average size of oil and gas fields that have come into production in recent years is much smaller than during the 1970s and 1980s (see paragraph C.15 and Chart C.4).

Table CI: UK reserves of oil and gas

OIL	Million tonnes	Production as percentage of original reserves
Cumulative production to end 2000	2,570	
Original size of reserves in present discoveries:		
Lower	3,200	80%
Upper	4,060	63%
Total original size of reserves (present plus future discoveries):		
Lower	3,510	73%
Upper	6,800	38%

GAS	Billion cubic metres	Production as percentage of original reserves
Cumulative production to end 2000	1,518	
Original size of reserves in present discoveries:		
Lower	2,255	67%
Upper	3,145	48%
Total original size of reserves (present plus future discoveries):		
Lower	2,650	57%
Upper	4,820	31%

C.11 Looking at the upper end of the ranges of estimates of the UK's discovered recoverable reserves of oil, cumulative production to the end of 2000 is estimated to be nearly two-thirds (63 per cent) of the total expected (proven, probable and possible) from the recoverable reserves originally present in current discoveries. Taking the lower end of the ranges of total UK estimated recoverable reserves of oil (i.e. reserves in current discoveries plus the additional reserves anticipated to exist in future discoveries), a further 3.5 billion tonnes of oil may be found in the future on top of the 4 billion tonnes of reserves originally related to present discoveries. That is 3.5 billion tonnes on top of the total of production and reserves in Chart C.1. Taking this most pessimistic view of estimates of future discoveries of oil reserves (but adding it to the top of the range of originally recoverable discovered reserves), the UK has already extracted nearly three-quarters (73 per cent) of the total reserves originally present. If the upper end of estimates of future reserves is used, the UK has extracted just over one-third (38 per cent) of the total recoverable reserves.

C.12 Similarly, looking at the upper end of the ranges of estimates of the UK's discovered recoverable reserves of gas, cumulative production to the end of 2000 is estimated to be two-thirds (67 per cent) of the recoverable reserves originally present in current discoveries. Taking the lower end of the ranges of total UK estimated recoverable reserves of gas, a further 2.7 billion cubic metres of gas may be found in the future compared with the 3.1 billion cubic metres of reserves originally related to present discoveries. Taking this most pessimistic view of estimates of future discoveries of reserves of gas (but adding it to the top of the range of originally recoverable discovered reserves), the UK has already extracted over half (57 per cent) of the total reserves present. If the upper end of estimates of future reserves is used, the UK has extracted under one-third (31 per cent) of the total recoverable reserves.

Offshore oil and gas fields and associated facilities (Table C.2)

C.13 Table C.2 and Table C.8 provide operational details for the past five years. Table C.2 shows numbers of offshore oil and gas fields and of associated production facilities, including miles of operational pipelines, at the end of each year up to 2000.

C.14 This table also shows that the number of offshore oil fields in production and under development rose from 114 at the end of 1996 to 138 at the end of 2000. For offshore gas fields the equivalent increase has been from 72 to 94. These significant increases are shown in Chart C.3 (offshore fields in production).

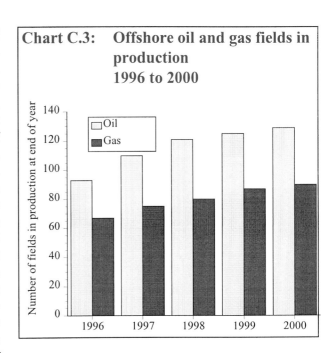

Chart C.3: Offshore oil and gas fields in production 1996 to 2000

C.15 The average size of fields commencing production has fallen during the 1990s (see Chart C.4). This reflects a decline in the size of fields discovered compared with the early development of the North Sea, and improved technology providing cost-effective means of extracting oil and gas from smaller fields and hitherto unpromising locations. The Cost Reduction in the New Era (CRINE) initiative was initiated in the mid-1990s to help reduce industry production costs. Industry co-operation can allow the joint development of smaller fields that individually would not otherwise be economic. CRINE was followed by the establishment of the Oil and Gas Industry Task Force, whose main objective was to create a climate for the UKCS to retain its position as a pre-eminent active centre for oil and gas exploration, development and production. Its aim was to keep the UK contracting and supplies industry at the leading edge in terms of overall competitiveness. In September 1999, the Task Force announced a number of targets for the UKCS in 2010 including: investment in UKCS activity sustained at £3 billion per annum; total production (of oil and gas) at 3 million barrels of oil equivalent per day; and prolonged self sufficiency in oil and gas. The job of turning these targets into reality now rests in the hands of the Task Force's successor, PILOT, whose remit is to ensure that the recommendations and initiatives established by the Task Force are brought forward and to give the industry every opportunity to address any relevant future issues. For more information visit the PILOT web-site at www.pilottaskforce.co.uk.

C.16 Table C.2 also gives the numbers of production facilities installed, and length of pipelines operational. The length of offshore oil pipelines operational has increased by 27 per cent between 1996 and 2000, while the length of offshore gas pipelines has increased by 19 per cent in the period. For further information on the length of pipelines awaiting commissioning, or under construction, refer to *The Development of UK Oil and Gas Resources 2001.*

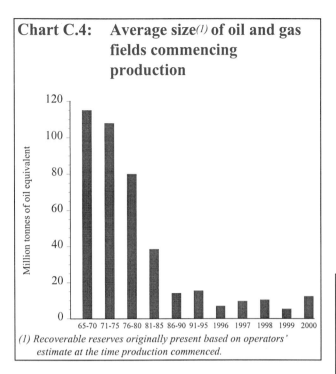

Chart C.4: Average size[(1)] of oil and gas fields commencing production

Million tonnes of oil equivalent

(1) Recoverable reserves originally present based on operators' estimate at the time production commenced.

due to the fact that when oil prices went to around $10 per barrel from late 1998 to early 1999, oil companies cut back on all but essential maintenance work (subject to safety not being compromised). The maintenance round in 2000 saw companies both catching up on previously postponed work, and also finding that the work they needed to do was more extensive than first thought. The low oil prices during 1998 and 1999 also had an effect on expenditure by oil companies on exploration for and development of new fields (see paragraphs C.37 to C.38). Methane production has grown each year over the five-year period from 90 billion cubic metres in 1996 to 115 billion cubic metres in 2000.

Production (Table C.3, C.6 and C.7)

C.17   These tables show production of crude oil and methane (effectively, natural gas) onshore and offshore. Table C.3 shows totals for production of oil and gas, including condensates from gas and oil fields, and production of ethane, propane and butane. Table C.6 gives production of crude oil broken down by field and Table C.7 shows methane production by field. In addition both tables show cumulative production to the end of 2000.

Production of oil and gas (Table C.3)

C.18   Table C.3 shows gross production of crude oil and natural gas (well extraction less gas flared, vented or re-injected) from oil fields. Methane includes associated gas from oil fields, measured after initial separation of the gas from the oil on the fields. The gas is then further processed at onshore gas separation plants to yield methane $[C_1]$, ethane $[C_2]$, propane $[C_3]$, butane $[C_4]$, and condensates $[C_{5+}]$. Production of methane $[C_1]$, and condensate $[C_{5+}]$ from gas fields is measured at the field.

C.19   The table also shows that while landward production of crude oil in 2000 was 38 per cent lower than in 1996, it still accounted for 2½ per cent of UK crude oil production in 2000, almost all from Wytch Farm.

C.20   Chart C.5 shows the recent trend in total oil production from 1996 to 2000. After increasing each year from 1996 to reach a record level of 137 million tonnes in 1999, production declined in 2000 to be 2.7 per cent lower than in 1996. The general lower level of production seen in 2000 was largely due to the summer maintenance round having a longer and greater impact than in earlier years. This was partly

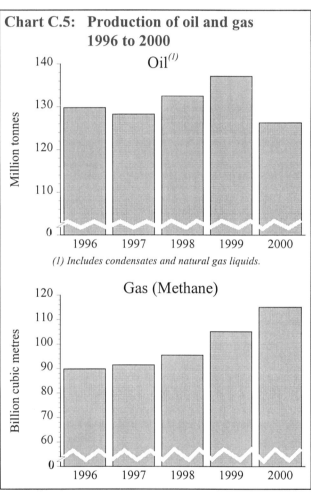

Chart C.5: Production of oil and gas 1996 to 2000

Oil[(1)]

Million tonnes

(1) Includes condensates and natural gas liquids.

Gas (Methane)

Billion cubic metres

Production of crude oil by field (Table C.6)

C.21   The figures show gross production (defined above). The first production of offshore oil from the UK sector of the Continental Shelf came in 1975, from the Argyll, Auk and Forties fields.

C.22   With the exceptions of Blenheim, Donan, Emerald, Maureen, Medwin and Moira, every field producing oil in 1996 was still producing in 2000. Production from the Cyrus field was suspended in 1992 and recommenced in 1996. Production from those fields that have been established for some time has been dropping in recent years. This is illustrated in Chart C.6 below, where oil production in each year for the years 1991 to 2000 has been broken down by the age group of the fields in production during that year. Two charts are given the first with the actual amounts of crude oil produced during the year for each age group. The second chart shows the same data transformed to show what percentage of total production each year comes from each age group of field.

C.23   It can be seen from the production chart that during the 1990s the amount of oil produced from older fields that first started production prior to 1990 has been in decline. Indeed, it is noticeable how even with those fields that started production in the period 1990 to 1994, a clear steady decline in production volumes is visible during the second half of the 1990s. As mentioned above (paragraph C.15) this is due to the nature of more recent discoveries, where smaller size fields have been discovered and developed where, with the use of new technology, the crude oil can be extracted at a much greater rate than in the past, leading to a much quicker exhaustion of the reserves in that particular field. The contribution from newer fields, i.e. those that have come into production since 1995, is also clearly a significant factor in the high level of production seen in the second half of the 1990s. In 2000, these newer fields accounted for 46 per cent of total oil production in the year. A list of the top ten oil producing fields in 2000 is given in Table C.II.

Table CII: Top ten UK crude oil producing fields in 2000

Field	2000 production (million tonnes)	Production as percentage of annual total
Schiehallion	6.26	5.3
Foinaven	4.58	3.9
Harding	4.32	3.7
Alba	4.23	3.6
Nelson	4.08	3.5
Brent	3.53	3.0
Magnus	2.92	2.5
Wytch Farm	2.92	2.5
Scott	2.77	2.3
Forties	2.72	2.3
Total top ten fields	38.32	32.5
Total crude oil production	117.88	

Production of methane by field (Table C.7)

C.24   The figures represent gross production from each field and include methane used for drilling, production and pumping operations, but excluding gas flared, vented or re-injected. The first production of offshore methane (natural gas) from the UK sector of the Continental Shelf came in 1967, from the West Sole field.

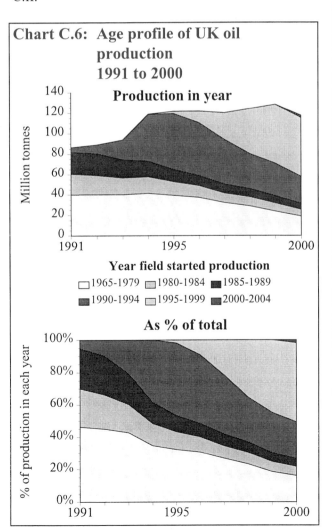

Chart C.6: Age profile of UK oil production 1991 to 2000

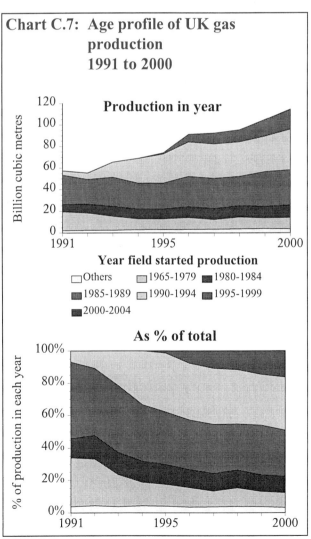

Chart C.7: Age profile of UK gas production 1991 to 2000

C.25   The table shows that methane production in 2000 was 28 per cent higher than in 1996, with production starting at 4 new gas fields during 2000.

Associated gas was also produced for the first time from 6 oil and condensate producing fields during the year. Since 1996 the amount of associated gas produced from oil fields has increased, for example, with the expansions of the CATS, FLAGS and SAGE systems that have occurred. As mentioned above for older oil fields, the older gas fields that were discovered in the Southern North Sea have reduced the level of their production in recent years as the reserves originally present in the fields become depleted, for example, the Thames complex and Leman fields. Chart C.7 below illustrates this. The extent of the decline in gas production from older fields is not as significant as seen for oil fields (Chart C.6). Two gas fields ceased production during the period in question, Camelot North-East in June 1998 and Cleeton in February 1999.

Transportation of crude oil production (Table C.4)

C.26   This table shows the mode of transportation of crude oil production, with separate figures for each main pipeline system and cumulative figures to the end of 2000.

C.27   The figures are compiled from the monthly returns sent to the Department of Trade and Industry by operators of oil fields and onshore terminals under the Petroleum Production Reporting System. Crude oil includes condensate and residual dissolved gases present in the disposals of crude oil by the industry. Heavier natural gases (ethane, propane and butane) and condensates produced in the treatment of liquid or gaseous hydrocarbons at the terminals are excluded. All pipeline systems terminate at one or other of the onshore terminals as indicated in the footnotes to the table. Crude oil is loaded directly offshore into adapted tankers by means of special facilities installed on certain fields. Until 1990 Brent and Thistle were served by both offshore loading and pipeline systems. In 1997, offshore loading from the Fulmar system ceased following the systems' connection to Teeside via the Norwegian pipeline from the Ekofisk system (Norpipe).

C.28   Between 1996 and 2000 the amount of oil loaded offshore rose by 55 per cent compared with a 19 per cent decrease in transportation by offshore pipeline systems. Transportation of crude oil produced from Joanna and Judy to Teeside via Norpipe commenced in 1995.

Disposals of crude oil (Table C.5)

C.29   Table C.5 and Chart C.6 show how crude oil is disposed of, split between amounts to UK refineries and exports (see technical notes, paragraphs C.44 to C.46) by country of destination (from which it may be transhipped elsewhere). The figures are obtained from returns made to the Department of Trade and Industry

by operators of oil fields and onshore terminals under the Petroleum Production Reporting System (see paragraphs C.39 to C.41).

C.30   The exports figures in this table may differ from those compiled by the United Kingdom Petroleum Industry Association (UKPIA) and published in the main text of this chapter. UKPIA figures also include re-exports. These are products that might originally have been imported into the UK and stored before being exported back out of the UK, as opposed to actually having been produced in the UK.

C.31   The volume of exports of crude oil in 2000 was 5 per cent higher than in 1996, with disposals to UK refineries having decreased by 17 per cent. Exports of crude oil in 2000 were 2 per cent lower than in 1999 due to the decrease in production of crude oil in the year. During 1997 the price of crude oil fell by roughly 25 per cent. This was due to several factors involving increased supply (production by several of the larger members of OPEC exceeded their agreed quotas and oil started to flow from Iraq under the "Oil for Food" arrangements) and reduced demand, particularly in Asia.

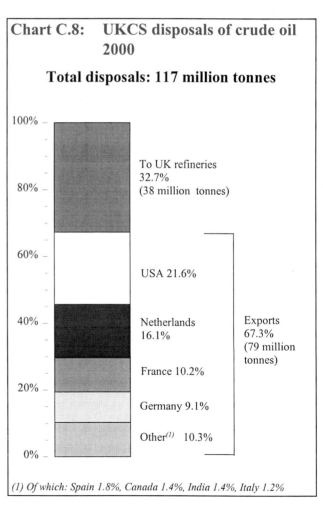

Chart C.8:   UKCS disposals of crude oil 2000

Total disposals: 117 million tonnes

To UK refineries 32.7% (38 million tonnes)

USA 21.6%

Netherlands 16.1%

France 10.2%

Germany 9.1%

Other[1] 10.3%

Exports 67.3% (79 million tonnes)

(1) Of which: Spain 1.8%, Canada 1.4%, India 1.4%, Italy 1.2%

C.32   The economic downturn in many of the countries of South East Asia in 1997 had a significant downward effect on global oil demand, since these countries had been exhibiting the strongest growth in demand in recent years. These factors led to a surplus of oil being available, thus reducing the price for crude oil on international markets. This had the effect of reducing the profit margins for exporting UK produced crude oil, given the extra transport costs involved in moving the oil from the UK to other areas in the world. Thus an increasing proportion of the crude oil extracted from the North Sea went for consumption in the UK, and the exports of the UK to more distant destinations such as the USA and Canada reduced while exports to European destinations increased.

C.33 However, with the agreement of OPEC member countries to impose production cuts, and delays in the availability of oil from Iraq back onto international markets, price rises were seen during the latter part of 1998 and through 1999. During 2000 OPEC continued to operate production quotas to help maintain the price for crude oil on international markets within their target price band. In addition, the introduction of tighter specifications for motor spirit in the US in the middle of 2000 led to an increased demand for both higher quality crude oil and products. As such, the situation whereby it is more profitable for oil companies to export oil from the North Sea rather than use it in UK refineries has returned, and companies have continued to export similar quantities of crude oil in 2000 as in 1999 despite the lower level of production.

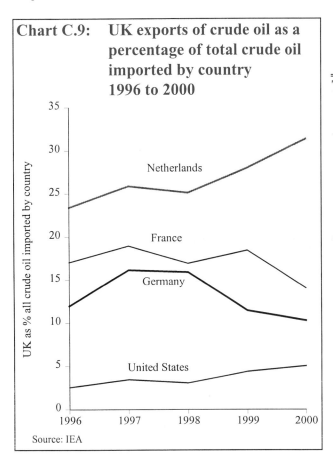

Chart C.9: UK exports of crude oil as a percentage of total crude oil imported by country 1996 to 2000

Source: IEA

C.34 Chart C.9 illustrates this point by showing what proportion of the total amount of crude oil imported by the USA, France, the Netherlands and Germany is supplied by the UK. Whilst the USA represents a significant market for UK exports of

crude oil, 5 per cent of total crude oil imports into the USA in 2000 were from the UK, an increase on the level in 1999. The UK is a significant contributor to other European countries, as shown by the data for trade with France, Germany and the Netherlands given in the chart. The growth in 2000 in exports to the Netherlands is related to the presence of the Rotterdam spot market. As such much of the oil exported to the Netherlands is not actually consumed there, but is sold on to other countries.

Gas flaring at oil fields and terminals

C.35 Previous editions of this Digest have included tables showing the volumes of gas flared at each oil field and terminal. One of the changes that has been made to the format and content of the Digest is that these data no longer appear as a separate table. Detailed information by field can still be found in the *Development of UK Oil and Gas Resources 2001,* known as the *Brown Book.* Details are given in Table C.III of the total amounts of gas flared in recent years. The amounts of gas flared shown in this table are not included in Tables C.3 and C.7. Flaring at gas fields is minimal due to the fact that facilities exist for the gas to be put into the field transportation pipelines rather than being flared.

C.36 The amount of gas flared in 2000 was 1.8 billion cubic metres, 19 per cent lower than in 1999 and 29 per cent lower than in 1996. This level of discharge is equivalent to 1½ per cent of the production of gas from offshore gas fields.

Table CIII: Gas flaring at oil fields and terminals, 1996 to 2000

			Million cubic metres
	Onshore	Offshore	Total
1996	110	2,429	2,539
1997	100	2,022	2,122
1998	106	2,004	2,110
1999	99	2,102	2,201
2000	51	1,742	1,793

Sales and expenditure by operators and other production licensees (Table C.8)

C.37 Table C.8 shows the value of sales, operating and exploration expenditure, gross trading profits and development expenditure, by operators and other production licensees.

C.38 Total receipts increased by 45 per cent in 2000, compared with 1999, with the recovery of oil prices from the low levels seen in 1998 increasing the value of sales. While operating costs fell slightly by 2 per cent, exploration expenditure fell by 17 per cent. As a result gross trading profits rose by 62 per cent in 2000. Total development expenditure was down 10 per cent on the level in 1999, reflecting the decrease in drilling of development wells in 2000 (216 compared with 234 in 1999 and 261 in 1996).

Technical notes and definitions

Petroleum Products Reporting System

C.39   Licensees operating on the UK Continental Shelf are required to make monthly returns on their production of hydrocarbons to the Department of Trade and Industry. The DTI stores this information in the Petroleum Production Reporting System (PPRS). The PPRS is used to report flows, stocks and uses of hydrocarbon from the well-head through to final disposals from a pipeline or terminal and is the major source of the information presented in this chapter.

C.40   Returns are collected covering field, pipeline and terminal data compiled by relevant reporting units. Each type of return is provided by a single operator, but usually covers the production of a number of companies, since frequently operations carried out on the Continental Shelf involve several companies working together.

C.41   Every production system has one or more sets of certified meters to measure oil and gas or condensate production. The flows measured by the meters are used to check the consistency of returns, and are therefore used to assure the accuracy of the PPRS.

Sales and expenditure by operators and other production licensees

C.42   The data given in Table C.8 are compiled from the Quarterly Inquiry into Oil and Natural Gas carried out by the DTI.   This inquiry collects information from operators and other production licence holders. The information collected covers all income and expenditure directly related to the production of oil and natural gas, including exploration, development and other capital expenditures together with operating costs and the value of sales.   It covers all companies normally classified under Division 11 Group 1 of the Standard Industrial Classification 1992.

C.43   Information on the industry is published quarterly in *Energy Trends*, and in *The Development of UK Oil and Gas Resources 2001*.   Annual information on the industry as a whole, which includes the expenditures and sales of non-exclusive exploration licence holders, drilling and other contractors, is available from the Office for National Statistics (ONS), published up to 1993 in the *Annual Census of Production* and in the *Annual Inquiries into Production* from 1994 onwards. For more details on the information available, contact the ONS library in Newport, Gwent on 01633-812399.

Exports

C.44   As stated in paragraph C.30 above, the term exports used in Table C.5 refers to figures recorded by producers of oil and gas for their exports.   These figures may differ from the figures for exports compiled by HM Customs and Excise (HMCE) and given in Chapter 8.   In addition HMCE now differentiate between EU and non-EU trade by using the term dispatches for trade going to other EU countries, with exports retained for trade going to non-EU countries.   The differences can occur between results from the two sources of information because whilst the trader's figures are a record of actual shipments in the period, for non-EU trade HMCE figures show the trade as declared by exporters on documents received during the period stated.

C.45   In addition, trade in oil frequently involves a "string" of transactions, which can result in the actual destination of the exports changing several times even after the goods have been dispatched.   As such, differences can arise between the final country of destination of the exports as recorded by the producers themselves and in the HMCE figures.   The HMCE figures also include re-exports.   These are products that might originally have been imported into the UK and stored before being exported back out of the UK, as opposed to actually having been produced in the UK.

C.46   In versions of the Digest before 1997, these exports were called "shipments" in an attempt to highlight their difference from the other sources of trade data.   However, their name has now been changed to more clearly represent that the movements actually are movements out of the United Kingdom.

Units of measurement for gas

C.47   The basic unit of measurement for quantities of flows and stocks is volume in cubic metres at $15°C$ temperature and 1.01325 bars pressure.

Monthly and Quarterly data

C.48   Monthly and quarterly data on the production of crude oil and natural gas from the UKCS, along with details of imports and exports of oil, oil products and gas are available. This information can be obtained free of charge by following the links given at the Energy Statistics section of the DTI web-site, at: www.dti.gov.uk/energy/energystats/energystats.htm

Contact: Kevin Williamson (Statistician)
        020 7215 5184
        Clive Evans
        020 7215 5189
        Ian Montague
        020 7215 2711

C.1 Estimated oil and gas reserves on United Kingdom Continental Shelf [1]

(As at 31 December 2000)

Million tonnes

Oil reserves [2]

	Proven [3]	Probable [3]	Proven plus Probable	Possible [3]
Initial recoverable oil reserves in present discoveries				
Fields in production or under development	3,145	245	3,390	300
Other significant discoveries not yet fully appraised	-	140	140	180
Decommissioned fields	55	-	55	-
Total initial reserves in present discoveries	**3,200**	**380**	**3,580**	**480**

Range of recoverable oil reserves (discovered and undiscovered) originally in place	Range of oil reserves
Cumulative production to end of 2000	2,570
Remaining reserves in present discoveries	630-1,490
Reserves in potential future discoveries	
North and Central North Sea 56°N - 62°N	190-1,130
West of Shetlands	30-470
West of Scotland	0-520
Remainder of UK continental shelf	5-180
Total recoverable oil reserves originally in place on the UK continental shelf [4]	**3,425-6,360**
Potential additional reserves [5]	85-440

Billion cubic metres

Gas reserves [6]

	Proven [3]	Probable [3]	Proven plus Probable	Possible [3]
Initial recoverable gas reserves in present discoveries				
Fields in production or under development				
Dry gas fields	1,480	90	1,570	70
Associated gas from oil fields	340	55	395	55
Gas from condensate fields	405	90	495	85
Other significant discoveries not yet fully appraised				
Dry gas fields	-	100	100	75
Associated gas from oil fields	-	20	20	25
Gas from condensate fields	-	110	110	120
Total initial reserves in present discoveries	**2,255**	**460**	**2,715**	**430**

Range of recoverable gas reserves (discovered and undiscovered) originally in place	Range of gas reserves
Cumulative production to end of 2000 [7]	
Dry gas fields	1,166
Associated gas from oil fields	352
Remaining reserves in present discoveries	
Dry gas fields	315-650
Associated gas from gas condensate fields and oil fields	395-950
Gas reserves in potential future discoveries [8]	325-1,440
Total recoverable gas reserves originally in place on the UK continental shelf [4]	**2,585-4,585**
Potential additional reserves [5]	65-235

(1) Includes onshore and offshore.
(2) With the exception of the production figures, entries are rounded to the nearest 5 million tonnes, and include gas liquids and liquefied products.
(3) The terms "proven", "probable" and "possible" are applied on a field by field basis and are given the internationally accepted meanings in this context. See Annex C, paragraph C.4.
(4) Rounded aggregate of the component ranges; the likelihood of the true figure lying outside this range is much smaller than for the individual component ranges.
(5) The potential additional reserves exist in discoveries that do not meet the criteria for inclusion as possible reserves.
(6) With the exception of the production figures, entries are rounded to the nearest 5 billion cubic metres.
(7) Excludes gas flared and gas used on platforms.
(8) Certain areas including the West of Scotland not assessed.

C.2 Offshore oil and gas fields and associated facilities

At end of year

	Unit	1996	1997	1998	1999	2000
Offshore oil fields						
Fields in production *(1)*	Number	93	110	121	125	129
Fields under development	"	21	19	17	13	9
Production facilities (installed):						
fixed production platforms *(2)*	"	68	68	70	70	71
floating production platforms	"	12	10	15	17	17
offshore loading systems *(2)*	"	15	15	15	15	15
flare towers	"	3	3	3	3	3
oil pipelines (operational) *(3)*	Kilometres	2,773	2,863	3,183	3,515	3,534
condensate pipelines (operational)	"	184	239	306	306	337
associated gas pipelines (operational)	"	3,290	3,299	3,343	3,413r	3,413
onshore terminals oil (operational) *(3)*	Number	5	5	5	5	5
onshore terminals associated gas (operational)	"	4	4	4	4	5
Offshore gas fields						
Fields in production *(4)*	Number	67	75	80	87	90
Fields under development	"	5	5	8	3	4
Production facilities (installed):						
fixed production platforms *(5)*	"	149	152	154	158	160
flare towers *(5)*	"	1	1	1	1	1
dry gas pipelines (operational)*(6)*	Kilometres	2,275	2,320	2,603	3,211	3,231
onshore terminals (operational)	Number	9	9	9	9	9

(1) Includes Statfjord, Murchison fields and condensate fields.
(2) Fields connected to an offshore loading system. Excludes Statfjord 'A' 'B' and 'C' platforms and their offshore loading systems and the 2 pumping platforms on the Norwegian Ekofisk - Teeside oil pipeline.
(3) Excludes the 350 kilometre Ekofisk - Teeside oil pipeline and the 39 kilometre Heimdal-Brae Condensate pipeline.
(4) Includes Frigg field and Rough field (which was granted approval in principle in 1982 for use as gas storage).
(5) Includes the 4 platforms and flare tower in the UK sector of Frigg field but excludes the 2 platforms in the Norwegian sector, platforms are counted if landed or operational.
(6) Includes the UK No.1 pipeline Frigg field to St. Fergus but excludes the parallel 350 kilometre Norwegian No.2 pipeline.

C.3 Production of oil and gas[1]

		Unit	1996	1997	1998	1999	2000
Crude oil	Land	Thousand tonnes	5,251	4,981	5,161	4,285	3,247
	Offshore	"	116,679	115,340	118,919r	124,001r	114,635
Condensates:	Land	"	-	-	-	-	-
	Offshore gas fields *(2)*	"	637	620	587	584r	508
	Offshore oil fields *(3)*	"	913	925	1,147	1,375r	1,463
Ethane *(3) (4)*		"	1,814	1,752	1,646	2,022	1,884
Propane *(3)*	Land	"	107	116	124	104	76
	Offshore	"	2,619	2,724	2,908	2,749	2,648
Butane *(3)*	Land	"	99	108	115	96	70
	Offshore	"	1,621	1,667	1,885	1,909	1,713
Total oil production		"	**129,742**	**128,234**	**132,491r**	**137,125r**	**126,245**
Methane *(5)*	Land *(6)*	Million cubic metres	382	388	335	310	675
	Offshore *(7)*	"	89,514	91,170	95,171	104,761r	114,358

(1) Monthly data on overall production of methane and crude oil are available - See paragraph C.48 and Annex F.
(2) Includes condensate from the United Kingdom share of the Frigg field.
(3) Gaseous hydrocarbons associated with crude oil production.
(4) Excludes that part of the ethane from the Far- north Liquids and Associated Gas System (FLAGS) which is supplied to BG Trading Ltd as part of a predominantly methane mixture.
(5) Excludes gas flared, vented or re-injected.
(6) Excludes colliery methane.
(7) Includes the UK share of the Frigg field associated gas (notionaly methane) produced and used on oil production platforms, and associated gas (notionaly methane) delivered to St Fergus via the CATS, FLAGS, Frigg, Fulmar and SAGE pipeline systems. May include small quantities of other gases.

C.4 Transportation of crude oil production

Thousand tonnes

		1996	1997	1998	1999	2000	Total to end 2000
Offshore production:	Offshore loaded (1)	27,050	29,374	33,957r	38,400	41,894	493,739
Pipeline systems:	Brent system (2)	23,094	19,575	17,394	16,240	12,862	581,126
	Ninian system (3)	14,026	11,900	11,308	10,340r	9,245	318,087
	Flotta system (4)	10,653	9,575	10,061	9,564r	8,251	286,253
	Forties system (5)	40,229	37,932	38,215r	41,444	35,177	666,731
	Teeside system (6)	1,088	6,435	7,619	7,819	6,867	30,439
	Beatrice field	437	449	365	194	137	20,525
Total pipelines		89,527	85,866	84,962r	85,601r	72,539	1,903,161
Onshore production:	Rail, road and pipeline (7)	5,251	4,981	5,161	4,285	3,247	50,683

(1) Production from Alba, Angus, Argyll, Auk (to 1996), Banff, Beryl, Bittern, Bladon, Blenheim, Buckland, Captain, Clyde (to 1995), Cook, Crawford, Curlew, Cyrus (to 1993), Dauntless, Donan, Douglas, Duncan, Durward, Emerald, Fergus, Fife, Flora, Foinaven, Fulmar (to 1996), Gannet A, B, C, D (to 1996), Gryphon, Guillemot A, NW and W, Harding, Hudson (to 1994), Innes, Kittiwake, Lennox, Leven (to 1996), Linnhe, Machar (to 1996), Mallard, Maureen, Medwin, Moira, Ness, Nevis, Pierce, Ross, Schiehallion, Statfjord (UK), Teal and Teal South.

(2) Brent, North Cormorant, South Cormorant, Deveron, Don, Dunlin, Dunlin SW, Eider, Hudson, Hutton, Hutton NW, Merlin, Murchison(UK), Osprey, Pelican, Tern and Thistle.

(3) Alwyn North, Columba BD, E, Dunbar, Ellon, Grant, Heather,

Lyell, Magnus, Magnus South, Ninian, Staffa and Strathspey.

(4) Chanter, Claymore, Galley, Hamish, Highlander, Iona, Ivanhoe, MacCulloch, Petronella, Piper, Renee, Rob Roy, Rubie, Saltire, Scapa, and Tartan.

(5) Andrew, Arbroath, Arkwright, Balmoral, Beinn, Birch, Blair, Brae C, E, N, S, W, Brimmond, Britannia, Bruce, Buchan, Cyrus, Drake, Egret, Erskine, Everest, Fleming, Forties, Glamis, Heron, Keith, Kingfisher, Larch, Lomond, Machar, Marnock, Miller, Monan, Montrose, Mungo, Nelson, Scott, Sedgwick, Shearwater, Stirling, Telford, Thelma, Tiffany and Toni.

(6) Auk, Clyde, Fulmar, Gannet A, B, C, D, E, F and G, Janice, Joanne, Judy, Leven, Medwin and Orion.

(7) Wytch Farm including Kimmeridge, Stowborough, Wareham; and the West Midlands fields.

C.5 Disposals of crude oil[(1)]

Thousand tonnes

	1996	1997	1998	1999	2000
UK refineries	46,403	48,961	46,887	47,170	38,335
Exports:	75,462	71,933	77,322	80,613	79,061
Albania	-	-	-	-	84
Bahamas (2)	-	-	257	143	65
Belgium	218	820	1,035	1,193	1,038
Canada	1,815	999	808	625	1,667
China	-	-	-	1,588	519
Croatia	428	-	-	-	-
Denmark	145	69	-	-	-
Finland	3,579	1,253	788	929	690
France	14,312	15,168	15,261	15,177	11,975
Germany	12,546	15,692	17,406	11,879	10,732
Gibraltar	-	-	-	-	77
India	-	-	-	277	1,638
Italy	1,513	931	1,219	1,819	1,459
Japan	-	-	-	256	-
Lithuania	-	-	-	-	251
Madagascar	-	-	81	-	-
Martinique (2)	80	84	87	-	84
Morocco	-	-	-	-	163
Netherlands (3)	13,727	14,933	15,591	16,540	18,912
Norway	593	814	1,087	1,297	542
Poland	2,404	1,608	1,494	682	368
Portugal	379	867	1,157	1,394	714
Puerto Rico (2)	560	-	-	-	-
Republic of Ireland	302	-	82	69	-
Singapore	-	-	255	278	-
South Africa	271	-	1,028	-	-
South Korea	-	-	-	260	-
Spain	1,560	3,762	3,403	4,040	2,107
Sweden	1,380	1,025	1,266	1,024	636
Turkey	-	69	-	-	-
USA	19,650	13,478	15,017	21,142	25,340
Unknown	-	360	-	-	-
Total disposals (4)	**121,865**	**120,893**	**124,209**	**127,783**	**117,395**

(1) Monthly data for aggregate disposals to refineries and exports are available - See paragraph C.48 and Annex F.

(2) Some of the exports to the Caribbean area may have been for transhipment to the USA.

(3) Exports to the Netherlands include oil for transhipment or in transit to other destinations (e.g. Belgium and Germany).

(4) Includes disposals of onshore production. The difference between disposals and production as shown in Table C.3 is accounted for by losses, platform and other field stock changes and by terminal and transit stock changes.

C.6 Production of crude oil by field

Thousand tonnes

	1996	1997	1998	1999	2000	Total to end 2000
Offshore						
Alba	3,804	4,844	4,376	3,989	4,227	27,307
Alwyn North	982	886	1,071	1,092r	886	29,997
Andrew	855	2,794	3,239	3,293	2,537	12,718
Arbroath	1,450	1,108	1,113	1,099	930	14,772
Arkwright	65	462	299	185	260	1,271
Auk	458	646	783	621	557	16,804
Balmoral	410	467	391	354	275	13,799
Banff	380	278	-	1,110	786	2,554
Beatrice	437	449	365	194	137	20,525
Beinn	388	286	214	116	30	1,748
Beryl	4,229	3,744	2,957	2,293	1,618	99,079
Birch	1,024	767	499	226	94	2,895
Bittern	-	-	-	-	1,149	1,149
Brae Central	405	383	474	288	242	5,568
Brae East	2,735	2,071	1,457	1,190	836	14,261
Brae North	468	361	412	334	279	16,374
Brae South	522	442	411	268	250	31,933
Brae West	-	107	1,128	1,546	1,632	4,413
Brent	9,077	6,255	6,046	4,530	3,533	250,053
Brimmond	20	60	80	48	48	256
Britannia	-	-	555	1,846	1,616	4,017
Bruce	1,703	1,287	897	1,842	1,645	12,027
Buchan	535	444	401	344	350	15,664
Buckland	-	-	-	474	1,599	2,073
Captain	-	1,451	2,833	2,522	2,456	9,262
Chanter	102	49	15	7	8	531
Claymore	2,151	2,094	1,816	1,656	1,562	67,963
Clyde	666	697	638	586	449	16,191
Columba B	146	177	150	154	537	1,164
Columba D (1)	667	332	169	88	-	1,692
Columba E	-	-	217	170	153	540
Cook	-	-	-	-	406	406
Cormorant North	1,468	1,475	1,636	1,539	1,416	48,339
Cormorant South	967	1,011	807	858	914	24,775
Curlew	-	86	1,436	1,506	816	3,844
Cyrus	202	603	540	402	253	2,610
Deveron	58	26	52	40	10	2,137
Don	169	108	100	89	69	1,998
Douglas	747	1,587	1,339	948	835	5,456
Drake	-	79	281	316	260	936
Dunbar	2,372	2,418	2,067	1,883r	1,631	12,166
Dunlin	753	806	634	626	525	48,755
Dunlin South West	258	197	231	231	109	1,026
Egret	-	-	-	383	214	597
Eider	814	653	616	600	355	13,965
Ellon	138	395	281	128r	152	1,189
Erskine	-	35	1,141	881	82	1,788
Everest	276	312	285	235	202	1,942
Fergus	249	561	276	161	81	1,328
Fife	1,622	1,076	819	361	585	5,209
Fleming	-	93	506	476	423	1,498
Flora	-	-	152	505	495	1,152
Foinaven	-	221	3,753r	4,330	4,577	12,881
Forties	5,141	4,104	3,993	3,491	2,718	326,714
Fulmar	1,039	546	468	373	228	71,130
Galley	-	-	945	1,358	1,600	3,903
Gannet A	1,313	1,191	1,013	865	710	6,695
Gannet B	97	58	35	29	29	620
Gannet C	1,638	1,150	918	687	390	9,121
Gannet D	408	436	466	359	477	3,159

C.6   Production of crude oil by field   (continued)

Thousand tonnes

	1996	1997	1998	1999	2000	Total to end 2000
Offshore continued						
Gannet E	-	-	644	366	362	1,372
Gannet F	-	326	463	327	208	1,324
Gannet G	-	-	-	268	696	964
Glamis	72	50	47	36	21	2,429
Grant	-	-	134	257r	215	606
Gryphon	1,877	1,540	1,347	1,093	903	10,885
Guillemot A	249	1,025	687	419	283	2,663
Guillemot North West	-	-	-	-	37	37
Guillemot West	-	-	-	-	441	441
Hamish	4	17	10	8	6	444
Harding	1,928	3,855	4,650	4,276	4,324	19,033
Heather	285	251	225	204	191	15,111
Heron	-	-	382	2,366	2,465	5,213
Highlander	272	149	188	102	159	9,553
Hudson	1,515	1,593	400	1,243	1,225	10,024
Hutton	900	786	581	557	414	26,189
Hutton North West	296	307	262	294	83	16,566
Iona	-	28	13	77	53	171
Ivanhoe	519	400	282	239r	365	8,748
Janice	-	-	-	1,710	1,349	3,059
Joanne	323	1,198	1,383	923	537	4,403
Judy	99	650	766	531	428	2,500
Keith	-	-	-	-	59	59
Kingfisher	-	211	914	675	468	2,268
Kittiwake	1,055	629	443	228	157	9,624
Larch	-	-	168	15	72	255
Lennox	105	453	886	855	1,336	3,635
Leven	59	83	42	37	125	878
Lomond	181	197	206	182	186	1,365
Lyell	432	278	215	146	116	2,881
MacCulloch	-	583	1,998	1,752	1,352	5,685
Machar	443	-	396	1,730	1,496	5,527
Magnus	4,540	3,087	3,144	3,042	2,920	93,763
Magnus South	235	383	435	482	310	1,845
Mallard	-	-	148	700	459	1,307
Marnock	-	-	13	746	982	1,741
Medwin	7	-	-	-	-	144
Merlin	-	64	581	858	606	2,109
Miller	6,458	5,188	3,437	2,729	2,054	41,183
Monan	-	-	75	341	163	579
Montrose	90	64	64	56	38	11,453
Mungo	-	-	706	1,873	2,442	5,021
Murchison (UK) (2)	680	805	791	743	501	37,284
Nelson	7,072	5,595	4,689	4,509	4,084	37,711
Ness	80	171	104	123	41	4,076
Nevis	184	744	1,082	1,593	1,446	5,049
Ninian	2,419	2,364	2,195	2,051	1,721	148,328
Orion	-	-	-	137	322	459
Osprey	1,297	1,202	754	530	295	10,703
Pelican	1,530	1,268	1,257	1,075	519	5,849
Petronella	137	119	123	52	61	4,530
Pierce	-	-	-	1,414	2,505	3,919
Piper	3,144	2,413	1,949	1,488	1,154	131,757
Renee	-	-	-	706	237	943
Rob Roy	1,075	570	289	271r	191	13,460
Ross	-	-	-	720	1,233	1,953
Rubie	-	-	-	182	341	523

Thousand tonnes

	1996	1997	1998	1999	2000	Total to end 2000
Offshore continued						
Saltire	1,829	1,906	1,333	756	478	10,582
Scapa	946	914	769	638	444	13,964
Schiehallion *(3)*	-	-	1,196	5,107	6,255	12,558
Scott	7,028	5,562	4,525	4,012	2,767	42,246
Sedgwick *(4)*	-	52	496	-	-	548
Shearwater	-	-	-	-	82	82
Statfjord (UK) *(2)*	3,394	3,576	2,342	1,766	1,186	73,652
Stirling	42	37	9	16	17	182
Strathspey	1,810	1,329	1,005	643	413	8,294
Tartan	474	333	331	272	240	13,496
Teal	-	1,090	1,121	1,215	1,509	4,935
Teal South	44	267	122	136	79	648
Telford	104	1,517	1,519	1,012	1,091	5,243
Tern	2,777	2,590	2,284	2,122	1,801	30,601
Thelma	165	1,308	1,050	904	772	4,199
Thistle	535	429	362	305	287	53,034
Tiffany	1,762	1,203	761	425	275	8,326
Toni	1,056	683	793	654	467	5,732
Other offshore *(5)*	102	100	-	-	202	895
Fields no longer in production:						
Angus	-	-	-	-	-	1,378
Argyll	-	-	-	-	-	9,878
Bladon	-	108	278	155	32	573
Blair	-	-	-	-	-	83
Blenheim	845	398	229	142	38	2,748
Crawford	-	-	-	-	-	539
Dauntless	-	197	308	38	-	543
Donan	282	193	-	-	-	2,021
Duncan	-	-	-	-	-	2,262
Durward	-	273	588	45	-	906
Emerald	41	-	-	-	-	2,365
Innes	-	-	-	-	-	755
Linnhe	-	-	-	-	-	101
Maureen	444	445	473r	173	-	29,815
Moira	29	16	12	3	-	560
Staffa	-	-	-	-	-	511
Total offshore	**116,679**	**115,340**	**118,919r**	**124,001r**	**114,635**	**2,397,795**
Wytch Farm	4,728	4,475	4,684	3,864	2,915	43,194
Other landward fields *(6)*	523	506	477	421	332	7,489
Total onshore	**5,251**	**4,981**	**5,161**	**4,285**	**3,247**	**50,683**
Total production	**121,930**	**120,321**	**124,080r**	**128,286r**	**117,882**	**2,448,478**

(1)   From 2000 Columba D is included with Columba B figures.
(2)   UK share of field.
(3)   Production figures include those for the 'Loyal' accumulation.
(4)   From 1999 Sedgwick is included with Brae West figures.
(5)   Production from extended well tests other than those within established fields.
(6)   Includes production from mining licence areas and extended well tests.

C.7 Production of methane by field

Million cubic metres

	1996	1997	1998	1999	2000	Total to end 2000
Alison	128	91	97	18	53	418
Alwyn North *(1)*	1,829	2,039	1,730	1,608	1,288	30,818
Amethyst East	1,416	848	870	724	612	11,640
Amethyst West	421	515	423	262	471	3,377
Anglia	439	284	391	296	383	4,076
Ann	428	270	140	166	160	2,204
Audrey	1,197	1,171	729	531	624	17,819
Baird	459	435	374	311	138	2,153
Barque	1,829	2,244	1,503	1,327	2,190	12,796
Barque South	-	8	2	-	-	16
Bessemer	777	812	735	692	1,204	4,359
Boulton	-	-	925	459	587	1,971
Bruce *(1)*	6,577	5,613	4,959	5,164	5,678	39,367
Bure	55	42	64	12	18	1,907
Bure West	-	-	22	124	169	315
Caister Bunter	295	343	235	315	306	2,167
Caister Carboniferous	649	642	364	390	257	3,872
Callisto *(2)*	254	254	199	45	-	854
Camelot Central and South	403	846	563	187	206	5,606
Camelot North	84	49	30	1	-	890
CATS *(3)*	2,334	4,429	10,126	13,605	13,618	48,979
Clipper	1,190	1,152	669	598	1,101	9,275
Corvette	-	-	-	1,782	1,048	2,830
Dalton	-	-	-	267	471	738
Davy *(4)*	930	806	719	908	881	4,441
Dawn	170	92	94	102r	29	488
Deben	-	-	66	240	93	399
Delilah	-	-	42	103	100	245
Dunbar *(1)*	1,371	1,359	1,121	1,133	1,216	7,177
Ellon *(1)*	521	791	448	162	129	2,414
Excalibur	876	599	681	552	453	4,204
FLAGS *(5)*	6,459	6,948	7,417	7,596	10,307	114,174
Frigg *(6)*	466	191	511	253	367	72,823
Fulmar *(7)*	1,716	1,505	1,890	2,104	-	14,654
Galahad	456	707	509	431	344	2,553
Galleon	1,398	1,501	1,493	1,168	1,677	8,025
Galley *(1)*	-	-	257	410	460	1,127
Ganymede *(2)*	1,708	1,655	947	1,148	1,773	7,763
Gawain	929	820	798	666	694	3,999
Grant *(1)*	-	-	322	672	675	1,669
Guinevere	243	271	227	232	222	2,008
Hamilton	-	1,176	1,752	1,416	1,685	6,029
Hamilton North	625	667	546	454	543	2,835
Hewett and Della	2,188	1,301	1,324	1,133r	1,484	116,907
Hyde	357	284	291	259	219	2,342
Indefatigable *(8)*	2,139	1,507	2,055	1,345	1,197	126,882
Indefatigable South West *(8)*	242	210	179	198	126	1,018
Ivanhoe and Rob Roy *(1)*	152	79	38	48	15	1,769
Johnston	585	469	327	540	667	3,267
Keith *(1)*	-	-	-	-	12	12
Ketch	-	-	-	297	1,233	1,530
KX	81	60	62	52	46	328
Lancelot	685	621	557	761	696	5,571
Leman	3,468	3,013	4,740	3,060	3,957	298,032

Million cubic metres

	1996	1997	1998	1999	2000	Total to end 2000
Malory	-	-	126	668	571	1,365
Markham *(9)*	807	663	514	485	463	5,408
Mercury	-	-	-	5r	402	407
Miller *(10)*	2,534	2,028	1,254	1,109	624	15,364
Millom	-	-	-	29	144	173
Mordred	26	82	17	39	43	207
Morecambe North	2,626	2,930	1,294	848	3,872	14,524
Morecambe South	7,099	6,170	7,993	9,971	8,436	86,342
Murdoch	1,127	1,150	1,376	836	1,197	8,147
Neptune	-	-	-	17r	1,466	1,483
Newsham	68	127	94	71	60	420
Orwell	789	720	832	667	716	6,554
Pickerill	1,345	1,288	879	626	366	10,418
Piper/Tartan Area *(1)*	950	633	452	421	396	13,239
Ravenspurn North	2,942	2,968	1,580	1,319	1,294	23,337
Ravenspurn South	1,253	1,433	1,186	1,006	871	12,688
Renee/Rubie *(1)(11)*	-	-	-	1	-10	-9
Ross *(1)*	-	-	-	28	89	117
Rough *(12)*	-	-	-	-	204	4,574
SAGE *(13)*	7,321	8,035	10,398	15,459r	16,802	72,412
Schooner	243	1,245	1,088	1,237	882	4,695
Sean East	512	301	227	253	148	2,007
Sean North and South	942	639	50	312	581	6,219
Shearwater *(14)*	-	-	-	-	93	93
Skiff	-	-	-	-	94	94
Thames	157	119	60	92	107	6,494
Trent	80	279	347	521	341	1,568
Tristan	27	18	7	90	35	1,004
Tyne North	-	76	130	255	222	683
Tyne South	109	539	435	479	360	1,922
Valiant North	277	295	334	172	274	4,380
Valiant South	349	391	397	298	538	6,838
Vampire	-	-	-	367	727	1,094
Vanguard	109	120	132	78	166	2,491
Victor	1,657	1,724	1,064	949	970	22,915
Viking B *(15)*	628	687	629	2,465	2,034	83,351
Vulcan	656	827	816	584	952	13,685
Waveney	-	-	137	741	594	1,472
Welland North West	358	386	629	326	212	5,242
Welland South	117	173	210	155	76	2,159
Wensum	3	3	-	2	-	52
West Sole	857	1,224	1,218	1,170	1,050	49,995
Windermere *(16)*	-	279	438	320	273	1,310
Yare	51	14	72	21	7	1,721
Others *(17)*	3,175	3,361	3,719	3,937	3,734	53,477
Fields no longer in production:						
Camelot North East	204	58	2	-	-	890
Cleeton	1,587	1,466	472	5	-	10,268
Esmond	-	-	-	-	-	8,866
Forbes	-	-	-	-	-	1,473
Gordon	-	-	-	-	-	3,994
Total offshore	**89,514**	**91,170**	**95,171**	**104,761r**	**114,358**	**1,600,362**

C.7 Production of methane by field (continued)

Million cubic metres

	1996	1997	1998	1999	2000	Total to end 2000
Wytch Farm	245	242	156	149	111	1,722
Other landward fields	137	146	179	161	564	1,736
Total onshore (18)	**382**	**388**	**335**	**310**	**675**	**3,458**
Total production (19)	**89,896**	**91,558**	**95,506r**	**105,071r**	**115,033**	**1,603,820**

(1) Associated gas used offshore or delivered to land via the Frigg pipeline system.
(2) With effect from August 1999 production from fields in the Jupiter area (Callisto, Europa, Ganymede and Sinope) and Bell (Conoco) have been reported with Ganymede.
(3) Gas delivered to land via the Central Area Transmission System (CATS) from Andrew, Drake, Egret, Erskine, Everest, Fleming, Heron, Janice, Joanne, Judy, Lomond, Machar, Marnock, Monan and Mungo.
(4) With effect from December 1998 Davy includes the Brown field for which separate data are unavailable.
(5) Gas delivered to land via the Far-north Liquids and Associated Gas System (FLAGS) from, Brent, North and South Cormorant, Magnus, Magnus South, Murchison (UK), Pelican, Statfjord (UK), Strathspey and Thistle. With effect from 2,000 gas previously shown separately as Fulmar is included in the FLAGS figure. Gas used offshore is included in Others (see (16)).
(6) UK share only.
(7) Gas delivered to land via the Fulmar pipeline from Bittern, Clyde, Cook, Curlew, Fulmar, Gannet A – G, Guillemot A, NW and W, Kittiwake, Leven, Mallard, Medwin, Nelson, Orion, Teal and Teal South. See footnote (5) regarding 2,000 figures. Gas used offshore is included in Others (see (16)).
(8) Separate data for Indefatigable South West is only available from October 1995.
(9) UK share only. Exported to Netherlands.
(10) Gas delivered direct to Boddam (Peterhead) power station by dedicated pipeline.
(11) Renee and Rubie fields are linked in to the Frigg pipeline system. This system incorporates pipelines linked to production fields that span the UK and Norwegian Continental Shelf boundary. As such, production data is derived from a system of back-allocation of gas from the totals received at the mainland terminals to individual production systems, rather than from production returns for the fields themselves. This allocation system, which is operated by the licence holders, is run like a bank account, with negative "production" allowed as part of the system in a similar way to an overdraft. The operators of Renee and Rubie will thus be expected to make put more gas into the system in future years to make up this negative amount.
(12) Converted for use as an off-peak storage unit with effect from 1985.
(13) Gas delivered to land via the Scottish Area Gas Evacuation (SAGE) system from the Beryl, Brae and Scott areas and from Britannia.
(14) Shearwater – Elgin Area Line (SEAL).
(15) Includes production for Vixen.
(16) Exported to Netherlands via Markham.
(17) Associated gas, mainly methane, produced and used mainly on Northern Basin oil production platforms including those in the FLAGS and Fulmar systems.
(18) Excludes colliery methane.
(19) Gross production, i.e. includes own use for drilling purposes, production and pumping operations, but excludes gas flared and vented.

C.8 Sales and expenditure by operators and other production licensees[1]

					£ million
	1996	1997	1998	1999	2000
Sales *(2)*					
Crude oil	11,849	10,327	7,487	10,257	16,129
Natural gas liquids	748	700	551	727r	1,111
Natural gas	5,295	5,254	5,313	5,031r	6,611
Revenues from pipelines and terminals and other operators' revenues	1,243	1,279	1,453	1,435r	1,525
Total receipts	**19,135**	**17,560**	**14,805r**	**17,450r**	**25,376**
Operating expenditure					
Oil fields	3,100	3,122	3,067	2,955r	3,117
Gas fields	878	1,023r	1,122r	1,294r	1,171
Total operating expenditure *(3)*	4,009	4,184	4,301r	4,531r	4,425
Gross trading profits *(4)*	**15,126**	**13,376**	**10,504r**	**12,919r**	**20,951**
Development expenditure					
Platforms and modules	2,049	1,715	2,064	1,022r	1,119
Offshore loading systems	247	316	154	74r	46
Pipelines	171	133	268	99	84
Terminals	157	167	85	76	91
Production and appraisal wells	1,635	1,841	2,327	1,642r	1,266
Other items	68	65	155	200	180
Total development expenditure	4,326	4,228	5,053	3,102r	2786
Exploration expenditure *(5)*	1,097	1,194	762	457	377
Other capital expenditure *(6)*	38	35	-58	-39	-38

(1) Quarterly data on the value of production and investment in the UKCS are available - See paragraph C.48 and Annex F.
(2) Deliveries on sale to third parties valued at the amount charged or appropriations by associated companies and other disposals at the landed c.i.f. value or post initial treatment valuation used for Petroleum Revenue Tax.
(3) Includes other costs not attributable to oil or gas fields.
(4) Gross trading profits are given as total receipts less total operating expenditure.
(5) Includes the cost of appraisal wells drilled prior to development approval.
(6) Other capital investment of operators and production licensees not classified to fields. This, together with development and exploration expenditure equals capital expenditure.

Annex D
Glossary

Advanced gas-cooled reactor (AGR)

A type of nuclear reactor cooled by carbon dioxide gas.

Anthracite

Within this publication, anthracite is coal classified as such by UK coal producers and importers of coal. Typically it has a high heat content making it particularly suitable for certain industrial processes and for use as a domestic fuel.

Anthropogenic

Produced by human activities.

Associated Gas

Natural gas found in association with crude oil in a reservoir, either dissolved in the oil or as a cap above the oil.

Autogeneration

Generation of electricity by companies whose main business is not electricity generation, the electricity being produced mainly for that company's own use.

Aviation spirit

A light hydrocarbon oil product used to power piston-engined aircraft power units.

Aviation turbine fuel

The main aviation fuel used for powering aviation gas-turbine power units (jet aircraft engine.

Benzole

A colourless liquid, flammable, aromatic hydrocarbon by-product of the iron and steel making process. It is used as a solvent in the manufacture of styrenes and phenols but is also used as a motor fuel.

Biogas

Energy produced from the anaerobic digestion of sewage and industrial waste.

Bitumen

The residue left after the production of lubricating oil distillates and vacuum gas oil for upgrading plant feedstock. Used mainly for road making and construction purposes.

Blast furnace gas

Mainly produced and consumed within the iron and steel industry. Obtained as a by-product of iron making in a blast furnace, it is recovered on leaving the furnace and used partly within the plant and partly in other steel industry processes or in power plants equipped to burn it. A similar gas is obtained when steel is made in basic oxygen steel converters, this gas is recovered and used in the same way.

Breeze

Breeze can generally be described as coke screened below 19 mm (¾ inch) with no fines removed, but the screen size may vary in different areas and to meet the requirements of particular markets.

BNFL

British Nuclear Fuels plc.

Burning oil

A refined petroleum product, with a volatility in between that of motor spirit and gas diesel oil primarily used for heating and lighting.

Butane

Hydrocarbon (C_4H_{10}), gaseous at normal temperature, but generally stored and transported as a liquid. Used as a component in Motor Spirit to improve combustion, and for cooking and heating (see LPG).

Calorific values (CVs)

The energy content of a fuel can be measured as the heat released on complete combustion. The SI (Système International - see note below) derived unit of energy and heat is the Joule. This is the energy per unit volume of the fuel and is often measured in GJ per tonne. The energy content can be expressed as an upper (or gross) value and a lower (or net) value. The difference between the two values is due to the release of energy from the condensation of water in the products of combustion. Gross calorific values are used throughout this publication.

CO_2

Carbon dioxide. Carbon dioxide contributes about 60 per cent of the potential global warming effect of man-made emissions of greenhouse gases. Although this gas is naturally emitted by living organisms, these emissions are offset by the uptake of carbon dioxide by plants during photosynthesis; they therefore tend to have no net effect on atmospheric concentrations. The burning of fossil fuels, however, releases carbon dioxide fixed by plants many millions of years ago, and thus increases its concentration in the atmosphere.

Coke oven coke

The solid product obtained from carbonisation of coal, principally coking coal, at high temperature, it is low in moisture and volatile matter. Used mainly in iron and steel industry.

Coke oven gas

Gas produced as a by-product of solid fuel carbonisation and gasification at coke ovens, but not from low temperature carbonisation plants. Synthetic coke oven gas is mainly natural gas which is mixed with smaller amounts of blast furnace and basic oxygen steel furnace gas to produce a gas with almost the same quantities as coke oven gas.

Coking coal

Within this publication, coking coal is coal sold by producers for use in coke ovens and similar carbonising processes. The definition is not therefore determined by the calorific value or caking qualities of each batch of coal sold, although calorific values tend to be higher than for steam coal.

Colliery methane

Methane released from coal seams in deep mines which is piped to the surface and consumed at the colliery or transmitted by pipeline to consumers.

Combined cycle gas Turbine (CCGT)

Combined cycle gas turbine power stations combine gas turbines and steam turbines which are connected to one or more electrical generators in the same plant. The gas turbine (usually fuelled by natural gas or oil) produces mechanical power (to drive the generator) and heat in the form of hot exhaust gases. These gases are fed to a boiler, where steam is raised at pressure to drive a conventional steam turbine, which is also connected, to an electrical generator.

Combined Heat and Power (CHP)

CHP is the simultaneous generation of usable heat and power (usually electricity) in a single process. The term CHP is synonymous with cogeneration and total energy, which are terms often used in the United States or other Member States of the European Community. The basic elements of a CHP plant comprise one or more prime movers driving electrical generators, where the steam or hot water generated in the process is utilised via suitable heat recovery equipment for use either in industrial processes, or in community heating and space heating. For further information see paragraph 6.30.

Conventional thermal power stations

These are stations which generate electricity by burning fossil fuels to produce heat to convert water into steam, which then powers steam turbines.

Cracking/conversion

A refining process using combinations of temperature, pressure and in some cases a catalyst to produce petroleum products by changing the composition of a fraction of petroleum, either by splitting existing longer carbon chain or combining shorter carbon chain components of crude oil or other refinery feedstock's. Cracking allows refiners to selectively increase the yield of specific fractions from any given input petroleum mix depending on their requirements in terms of output products.

Crude oil

A mineral oil consisting of a mixture of hydrocarbons of natural origins, yellow to black in colour, of variable density and viscosity.

DERV	Diesel engined road vehicle fuel used in internal combustion engines that are compression-ignited (see gas diesel oil).
Distillation	A process of separation of the various components of crude oil and refinery feedstocks using the different temperatures of evaporation and condensation of the different components of the mix received at the refineries.
DNC	Declared net capacity and capability are used to measure the maximum power available from generating stations at a point in time. See paragraphs 5.63, 5.64 and 7.71 for a fuller definition.
Downstream	Used in oil and gas processes to cover the part of the industry after the production of the oil and gas. For example, it covers refining, supply and trading, marketing and exporting.
Embedded Generation	Embedded generation is electricity generation by plant which has been connected to the distribution networks of the public electricity distributors rather than directly to the National Grid Company's transmission systems. Typically they are either smaller stations located on industrial sites, or combined heat and power plant, or renewable energy plant such as wind farms, or refuse burner generators. The category also includes some domestic generators such as those with electric solar panels. For a description of the current structure of the electricity industry in the UK see paragraphs 5.3 to 5.8 of Chapter 5.
Energy use	Energy use of fuel mainly comprises use for lighting, heating or cooling, motive power and power for appliances. See also non-energy use.
ESA	European System of National and Regional Accounts. An integrated system of economic accounts which is the European version of the System of National Accounts (SNA).
EESoPs	A review of the Energy Efficiency Standards of Performance Programme which currently supports the replacing of electric heating with Community Heating based CHP.
Ethane	A light hydrocarbon gas (C_2H_6) in natural gas and refinery gas streams (see LPG).
EUROSTAT	Statistical Office of the European Communities (SOEC).
Exports	For some parts of the energy industry, statistics on trade in energy related products can be derived from two separate sources. Firstly, figures can be reported by companies as part of systems for collecting data on specific parts of the energy industry (e.g. as part of the system for recording the production and disposals of oil from the UK continental shelf). Secondly, figures are also available from the general systems that exist for monitoring trade in all types of products operated by HM Customs & Excise. Before the 1997 edition of the Digest, the term "shipment" was used to distinguish figures derived from the former source from those export figures derived from the systems operated by HM Customs & Excise. To make it clearer for users, a single term is now being used for both these sources of figures (the term exports) as this more clearly states what the figures relate to, which is goods leaving the UK.
Feedstock	In the refining industry, a product or a combination of products derived from crude oil, destined for further processing other than blending. It is distinguished from use as a chemical feedstock etc. See non-energy use.
Final energy consumption	Energy consumption by final user - i.e. which is not being used for transformation into other forms of energy.

Fossil fuels	Coal, natural gas and fuels derived from crude oil (for example petrol and diesel) are called fossil fuels because they have been formed over long periods of time from ancient organic matter.
Fuel oils	The heavy oils from the refining process; used as fuel in furnaces and boilers of power stations, industry, in domestic and industrial heating, ships, locomotives, metallurgic operations, and industrial power plants etc.
Fuel oil - Light	Fuel oil made up of heavier straight-run or cracked distillates and used in commercial or industrial burner installations not equipped with pre-heating facilities.
Fuel oil - Medium	Other fuel oils, sometimes referred to as bunker fuels, which generally require pre-heating before being burned, but in certain climatic conditions do not require pre-heating.
Fuel oil - Heavy	Other heavier grade fuel oils which in all situations require some form of pre-heating before being burned.
Gas Diesel Oil	The medium oil from the refinery process; used as a fuel in diesel engines (i.e. internal combustion engines that are compression-ignited), burned in central heating systems and used as a feedstock for the chemical industry.
GDP	Gross domestic product.
GDP deflator	An index of the ratio of GDP at current prices to GDP at constant prices. It provides a measure of general price inflation within the whole economy.
Gigajoule (GJ)	A unit of energy equal to 10^9 joules (see note on joules below).
Gigawatt (GW)	A unit of electrical power, equal to 10^9 watts.
Gigawatt hour (GWh)	Unit of electrical energy, equal to 0.0036 TJ. A 1 GW power station running for one hour produces 1 GWh of electrical energy.
HMCE	HM Customs and Excise.
Imports	See the first paragraph of the entry for exports above. Before the 1997 edition of the Digest, the term "arrivals" was used to distinguish figures derived from the former source from those import figures derived from the systems operated by HM Customs & Excise. To make it clearer for users, a single term is now being used for both these sources of figures (the term imports) as this more clearly states what the figures relate to, which is goods entering the UK.
International Energy Agency (IEA)	The IEA is an autonomous body located in Paris which was established in November 1974 within the framework of the Organisation for Economic Co-operation and Development (OECD) to implement an international energy programme.
Indigenous production	For oil this includes production from the UK Continental Shelf both onshore and offshore.
Industrial spirit	Refined petroleum fractions with boiling ranges up to 200ºC dependent on the use to which they are put – e.g. seed extraction, rubber solvents, perfume etc.
Joules	A joule is a generic unit of energy in the conventional SI system (see note on SI below). It is equal to the energy dissipated by an electrical current of 1 ampere driven by 1 volt for 1 second; it is also equal to twice the energy of motion in a mass of 1 kilogram moving at 1 metre per second.

Landfill gas	The methane-rich biogas formed from the decomposition of organic material in landfill.
LDF	Light distillate feedstock.
Liquefied petroleum gas (LPG)	Gas usually propane or butane, derived from oil and put under pressure so that it is in liquid form. Often used to power portable cooking stoves or heaters and to fuel some types of vehicle, e.g. some specially adapted road vehicles, fork-lift trucks.
Lead Replacement Petrol (LRP)	An alternative to Leaded Petrol containing a different additive to lead (in the UK usually Potassium based) to perform the lubrication functions of lead additives in reducing engine wear.
Lubricating oils	Refined heavy distillates obtained from the vacuum distillation of petroleum residues. Includes liquid and solid hydrocarbons sold by the lubricating oil trade, either alone or blended with fixed oils, metallic soaps and other organic and/or inorganic bodies.
Magnox	A type of gas-cooled nuclear fission reactor developed in the UK, so called because of the magnesium alloy used to clad the uranium fuel.
Major power producers	Companies whose prime purpose is the generation of electricity (paragraph 5.59 of Chapter 5 gives a full list of major power producers).
Motor spirit	Blended light petroleum product used as a fuel in spark-ignition internal combustion engines (other than aircraft engines).
Natural gas	Natural gas is a mixture of naturally occurring gases found either in isolation, or associated with crude oil, in underground reservoirs. The main component is methane; ethane, propane, butane, hydrogen sulphide and carbon dioxide may also be present, but these are mostly removed at or near the well head in gas processing plants.
Naphtha	(Light distillate feedstock) – Petroleum distillate boiling predominantly below 200°C.
Natural gas - compressed	Natural gas that has been compressed to reduce the volume it occupies to make it easier to transport other than in pipelines. Whilst other petroleum gases can be compressed such that they move into liquid form, the volatility of natural gas is such that liquefaction cannot be achieved without very high pressures and low temperatures being used. As such, the compressed form is more usually used as a "half-way house".
Natural gas liquids (NGL's)	A mixture of liquids derived from natural gas and crude oil during the production process, including propane, butane, ethane and gasoline components (pentanes plus).
NETA	New Electricity Trading Arrangements - In England and Wales these arrangements replaced the "the pool" from 27 March 2001. The arrangements are based on bi-lateral trading between generators, suppliers, traders and customers and are designed to be more efficient, and provide more market choice.
Non-energy use	Includes fuel used for chemical feedstock, solvents, lubricants, and road making material.
NFFO	Non Fossil Fuel Obligation. The 1989 Electricity Act empowers the Secretary of State to make orders requiring the Regional Electricity Companies in England and Wales to secure specified amounts of electricity from renewable sources.

NO_X	Nitrogen oxides. A number of nitrogen compounds including nitrogen dioxide are formed in combustion processes when nitrogen in the air or the fuel combines with oxygen. These compounds can add to the natural acidity of rainfall.
OFGEM	The regulatory office for gas and electricity markets.
Orimulsion	An emulsion of bitumen in water that can be used as a fuel in some power stations.
ONS	Office for National Statistics. Formerly the Central Statistical Office (CSO).
OTS	Overseas Trade Statistics of the United Kingdom.
Patent fuel	A composition fuel manufactured from coal fines by shaping with the addition of a binding agent (typically pitch). The term manufactured solid fuel is also used.
Petrochemical feedstock	All petroleum products intended for use in the manufacture of petroleum chemicals. This includes middle distillate feedstock of which there are several grades depending on viscosity. The boiling point ranges between $200^{\circ}C$ and $400^{\circ}C$.
Petroleum cokes	Carbonaceous material derived from hydrocarbon oils, uses for which include metallurgical electrode manufacture and in the manufacture of cement.
Petroleum wax	Includes paraffin wax, which is a white crystalline hydrocarbon material of low oil content normally obtained during the refining of lubricating oil distillate, paraffin scale, slack wax, microcrystalline wax and wax emulsions.
Photovoltaics	The direct conversion of solar radiation into electricity by the interaction of light with the electrons in a semiconductor device or cell.
Plant capacity	The maximum power available from a power station at a point in time (see also paragraph 5.63 of Chapter 5).
Plant loads, demands and efficiency	Measures of how intensively and efficiently power stations are being used. These terms are defined in paragraphs 5.65 and 5.66 of Chapter 5.
PPRS	Petroleum production reporting system. Licensees operating in the UK Continental Shelf are required to make monthly returns on their production of hydrocarbons (oil and gas) to the DTI. This information is recorded in the PPRS, which is used to report flows, stocks and uses of hydrocarbon from the well-head through to final disposal from a pipeline or terminal (see paragraphs C.39 to C.41 of Annex C).
Process oils	Partially processed feedstocks which require further processing before being classified as a finished product suitable for sale. They can also be used as a reaction medium in the production process.
Primary fuels	Fuels obtained directly from natural sources, e.g. coal, oil and natural gas.
Primary electricity	Electricity obtained other than from fossil fuel sources, e.g. nuclear, hydro and other non-thermal renewables. Imports of electricity are also included.
Propane	Hydrocarbon containing three carbon atoms (C_3H_8), gaseous at normal temperature, but generally stored and transported under pressure as a liquid.
PWR	Pressurised water reactor. A nuclear fission reactor cooled by ordinary water kept from boiling by containment under high pressure.
Reforming	Processes by which the molecular structure of different fractions of petroleum can be modified. It usually involves some form of catalyst, most often platinum, and

allows the conversion of lower grades of petroleum product into higher grades, improving their octane rating. It is a generic term for processes such as cracking, cyclization, dehydrogenation and isomerisation. These process generally led to the production of hydrogen as a by-product which can be used in the refineries in some desulphurization procedures.

Refinery fuel

Petroleum products produced by the refining process that are used as fuel at refineries.

Renewable energy sources

Renewable energy includes solar power, wind, wave and tide, and hydroelectricity. Solid renewable energy sources consist of wood, straw and waste, whilst gaseous renewable consist of landfill gas and sewage gas.

Reserves

With oil and gas these relate to the quantities identified as being present in underground cavities. The actual amounts that can be recovered depend on the level of technology available and existing economic situations. These continually change, hence the level of the UK's reserves can change quite independently of whether or not new reserves have been identified.

RPI

Retail Price Index (RPI) is published by the Office for National Statistics. RPI is calculated using prices collected on a day near the middle of the month.

SI (Système International)

Refers to the agreed conventions for the measurement of physical quantities.

SIC

Standard Industrial Classification in the UK. Last revised in 1992 and known as SIC92, replaced previous classifications SIC80 and SIC68. Now compatible with European Union classification NACE Rev1 (Nomenclature générale des activités économiques dans les Communautés européennes as revised in October 1990).

Secondary fuels

Fuels derived from natural primary sources of energy. For example electricity generated from burning coal, gas or oil is a secondary fuel, as are coke and coke oven gas.

Steam coal

Within this publication, steam coal is coal classified as such by UK coal producers and by importers of coal. It tends to be coal having lower calorific values; the type of coal that is typically used for steam raising.

SO_2

Sulphur Dioxide. Sulphur dioxide is a gas produced by the combustion of sulphur-containing fuels such as coal and oil.

Synthetic coke oven gas

Mainly a natural gas, which is mixed with smaller amounts of blast furnace, and BOS (basic oxygen steel furnace) gas to produce a gas with almost the same quantities as coke oven gas.

Temperature correction

The temperature corrected series of total inland fuel consumption indicates what annual consumption might have been if the average temperature during the year had been the same as the average for the years 1961 to 1990.

Tonne of oil equivalent (toe)

A common unit of measurement which enables different fuels to be compared and aggregated. (See paragraphs 1.46 to 1.47 of Chapter 1 for further information).

Tars

Viscous materials usually derived from the destructive distillation of coal which are by-products of the coke and iron making processes.

Therm

A common unit of measurement similar to a tonne of oil equivalent which enables different fuels to be compared and aggregated. (refer to Annex A).

Thermal efficiency

The thermal efficiency of a power station is the efficiency with which heat energy contained in fuel is converted into electrical energy. It is calculated for fossil fuel burning stations by expressing electricity supplied as a percentage of the total energy content of the fuel consumed (based on average gross calorific values). For nuclear stations it is calculated using the quantity of heat released as a result of fission of the nuclear fuel inside the reactor.

UKCS	United Kingdom Continental Shelf.
UKPIA	UK Petroleum Industry Association. The trade association for the UK petroleum industry.
Ultra low sulphur Diesel (ULSD)	A grade of diesel fuel which has a much lower sulphur content (less than 0.005 per cent or 50 parts per million) and of a slightly higher volatility than ordinary diesel fuels. As a result it produces fewer emissions when burned. As such it enjoys a lower rate of excise duty in the UK than ordinary diesel (by 3 pence per litre) to promote its use. Virtually 100 per cent of sales of DERV fuel in the UK are ULSD.
Ultra low sulphur Petrol (ULSP)	A grade of motor spirit with a similar level of sulphur to ULSD. (less than 0.005 per cent or 50 parts per million). In the March 2000 Budget it was announced that a lower rate of excise duty than ordinary petrol for this fuel would be introduced during 2000, which was increased to 3 pence per litre in the March 2001 Budget. It has quickly replaced ordinary premium grade unleaded petrol in the UK market place.
Upstream	A term to cover the activities related to the exploration, production and delivery to a terminal or other facility of oil or gas for export or onward shipment within the UK.
VAT	Value added tax.
Watt (W)	The conventional unit to measure a rate of flow of energy. One watt amounts to 1 joule per second.
White spirit	A highly refined distillate with a boiling range of about 150ºC to 200ºC used as a paint solvent and for dry cleaning purposes etc.

Annex E
Major events in the Energy Industry since 1990

1990 **Electricity**

The new licensing regime for electricity companies was established along with the post of Director General of Electricity Supply (DGES) by the 1989 Electricity Act. The Act also gave powers to the Secretary of State for Trade and Industry to replace existing public electricity boards by Plc's. The Office of Electricity Regulation (Offer now merged with OFGAS to form OFGEM) set up in shadow form.

Provisions of the Act came into force in March. The Central Electricity Generating Board (CEGB) was split into four companies, National Power and PowerGen (fossil fuel generation), Nuclear Electric (nuclear generation) and the National Grid Company (NGC) (transmission). Twelve Regional Electricity Companies replaced the Area Electricity Boards. At the same time, the South of Scotland Electricity Board and North of Scotland Hydro-Electric Board were replaced by Scottish Power and Scottish Hydro-Electric (generation, transmission, supply and distribution) and Scottish Nuclear (nuclear generation). The ordinary shares in the National Grid were transferred to the 12 Regional Electricity Companies (RECs).

At vesting, (31 March) price controls, put in place by the Government, came into being for the transmission business of NGC and the supply and distribution businesses of the RECs. There was not a generation price control as this sector was open to competition from the start.

The 12 Regional Electricity Companies in England and Wales were floated on the London Stock Exchange in December. The Government retained a special share in each of the privatised companies, known as the 'Special Share', which prevented any other investor from buying more than 15 per cent of the shares for a period of five years.

At the same time the market for customers with demand exceeding 1 MW was opened up to competition.

During 1990 the Electricity Pool was established. This was a trading mechanism (now superseded) which called generators online to provide a "pool" of electricity for suppliers to purchase. Other than for a few very large contracts, there were no direct contracts between generators and suppliers/users.

New and Renewable Energy

The first Non Fossil Fuel Obligation (NFFO-1) Renewable Order for England and Wales made for 102 MW Declared Net Capacity (DNC).

1991 **Electricity**

60 per cent of the shares in National Power and PowerGen were floated on the London Stock Exchange in March. The Government retained the remaining 40 per cent of shares. Scottish Power and Scottish Hydro Electric were floated in June. The Government retained ownership of Nuclear Electric. In England and Wales the long-term costs of generation from nuclear sources were funded from the proceeds of the "Fossil Fuel Levy" on supplies of certain electricity. In Scotland contracts were established with the Scottish PESs for the output of the Scottish nuclear generating stations.

New and Renewable Energy

The second Non Fossil Fuel Obligation (NFFO-2) Renewables Order for England and Wales was made for 457 MW Declared Net Capacity.

Oil

The Gulf War began in mid-January and ended in late February, following the occupation of Kuwait by Iraq in August 1990. This provoked worldwide concern about the availability of oil. The annual average price of crude oil rose sharply, and took two years to settle back to its pre-war level.

One hundred oil and gas fields were in production in the UK.

1992   **Electricity**

In March, generation in Northern Ireland was transferred from Northern Ireland Electricity to four independent generation companies. Northern Ireland Electricity plc became responsible for transmission and distribution and supply. A special share was retained in Northern Ireland Electricity.

Gas

Following the withdrawal of BG's legal monopoly relating to the non-tariff or contract market for customers with demand greater than 25,000 therms per annum, British Gas was prompted in March by the Director General of Fair Trading to create the conditions whereby competing suppliers should be able to supply at least 60 per cent of the market for customers whose demand exceeded 25,000 therms. In August, the market sector open to competition was extended to include customers with an annual demand of between 2,500 and 25,000 therms. The agreement between British Gas and the Director General of Fair Trading was then redefined as 45 per cent of the market for demand greater than 2,500 therms per annum.

1993   **Coal**

Coal Review White Paper, "The Prospects for Coal", published on 23rd March. Main conclusions were:

- subsidy to be offered to bring extra tonnage down to world market prices,

- no pit to be closed without being offered to the private sector,

- no changes to the gas and nuclear sectors,

- increased investment in clean coal technology,

- regeneration package for mining areas increased to £200 million.

On 2nd December the Coal Industry Bill was published. Its main features were:

- to enable privatisation,

- to establish the Coal Authority,

- to protect the rights of third parties,

- to safeguard pension and concessionary fuel entitlements

- to retain HSE and HM Mines Inspectorate as bodies responsible for mine safety & inspection.

Electricity

In June, Northern Ireland Electricity plc was floated on the London Stock Exchange.

Gas

The Monopolies and Mergers Commission published a report on competition in gas supply.

Oil

Unleaded petrol sales accounted for 50 per cent of the total UK market for motor spirits.

1994

Coal

Coal Authority brought into legal existence under Section 1 of the Coal Industry Act 1994 on 19th September.

The 31st October was the Coal Authority "Restructuring Date". Ownership of Britain's coal reserves was transferred to the Authority and it assumed its full range of functions including powers to license coal operations.

In December, British Coal Corporation's mining activities were sold to the private sector.

Electricity

In April, competition in the electricity market was extended to include all customers whose demand exceeded 100 kW.

From 1 April the revised (tightened) supply price control took effect.

OFFER imposed the first Energy Efficiency Standards of Performance (EESOPs) on electricity companies, requiring them to promote and carry out energy efficiency measures for their customers. At the same time OFFER included within the price controls a charge of £1 per customer per year to pay for the measures. This first EESOP covered the period 1994-1998, but was subsequently extended, at the same level, until March 2000.

New and Renewable Energy

The third Non Fossil Fuel Obligation (NFFO-3) Renewables Order for England and Wales was made for 627 MW Declared Net Capacity (DNC).

The first Scottish Renewables Order (SRO-1) for Scotland was made for 76 MW Declared Net Capacity (DNC).

The first Northern Ireland NFFO (NI-NFFO-1) Renewables Order was made for 16 MW Declared Net Capacity (DNC).

VAT

In April the Government introduced VAT on domestic fuel at a rate of 8 per cent.

1995

Coal

The Domestic Coal Consumers Council was abolished.

Electricity

In March the Government's 'Special Share' in each of the Regional Electricity Companies expired. The companies were then exposed to the full disciplines and opportunities of the market, including acquisitions and mergers. In 1995 there were four bids involving Regional Electricity Companies, followed by a further seven successful bids in 1996 and two more in the first half of 1997.

In March, the Government also floated its remaining 40 per cent share in National Power and PowerGen on the London Stock Exchange. It did, however, retain its 'special share' in these companies.

Following a review, the distribution price control was revised from 1st April.

The DGES decided to review again the Distribution Price Control following Northern Electric's defence against a take-over bid from Trafalgar House.

The National Grid Company was floated on the London Stock Exchange in December. As a result, customers of the Regional Electricity Companies received a discount of £50 on their electricity bills in early 1996 as their share of the benefit from the sale. Before the company was floated, its Pumped Storage Business was transferred to a new company, First Hydro, which was then sold to a US generator, Mission Energy. The Government still holds a special share in the National Grid Company which is not time limited.

Gas

The Gas Act 1995 set out the Government's plans for the liberalisation of all gas markets, including the domestic sector. The Government and the industry put into place the licensing framework and the administrative/computer framework required to support the forthcoming gas pilot trials.

By the end of 1995, there were 40 independent gas marketing companies selling gas to UK end-users. They had captured 80 per cent of the firm industrial and commercial market, and 70 per cent of the market for "interruptible" sales.

The development of a "gas bubble" (an excess of supply over demand) in 1995 and into 1996 led to a sharp fall in the spot price of gas from 0.7p/KWh to around 0.4p/KWh (10p per therm). The main beneficiaries of this were customers on short term gas contracts.

Oil

Production from the UK sector of the North Sea and onshore sites reached a new record level of output at 130.3 million tonnes per annum.

Nuclear

In February, electricity generation began at Sizewell B, the UK's only pressurised Water Reactor, whose construction had been completed the previous year.

In May the Government published a White Paper on the prospects for nuclear power in the UK. It concluded that nuclear power should continue to contribute to the mix of fuels used in electricity generation, provided it maintained its current high standards of safety and environmental protection; that building new nuclear power stations was not commercially attractive; and that there was no justification for any government intervention to support the construction of new nuclear stations.

Energy Conservation

The Home Energy Efficiency Act 1995 (HECA) requires all UK local authorities, with housing responsibilities, to prepare an energy conservation report, identifying practicable and cost-effective measures to significantly improve the energy efficiency of all residential accommodation in their area; and to report on progress in implementing the measures.

1996

Coal

In January the company Coal Investments ceased trading, closing four pits and selling two to Midlands Mining Ltd.

In May the National Audit Office published its report into the privatisation of British Coal's mining activities.

Electricity

The revised Distribution Price control (further tightened as a result of the second review in 1995) took effect from 1st April.

In July 1996 Eastern Group leased a total of 6 GW of coal-fired electricity generation capacity from National Power (4 GW) and PowerGen (2 GW). As a result, the pool price cap was lifted.

Bids made by National Power and Powergen for Southern Electric and Midlands Electricity respectively in 1995, which would have allowed significant vertical integration between generation and supply in the industry, were prohibited by the President of the Board of Trade in April following an investigation by the Monopolies and Mergers Commission.

Gas

On 6 February in response to the separation of licensing for gas distribution and supply in the Gas Act 1995, British Gas Plc announced it was demerging into two companies, one responsible for the transmission of gas (BG Transco) and one for the supply of gas (Centrica).

On 1st April, the first stage of the introduction of competition in the domestic market began - around 540,000 customers in South West England were enabled to purchase their gas from a variety of suppliers. By the end of the year just under 20 per cent of households switched to a new supplier, whose prices were on average 10-20 per cent less than those charged by British Gas.

Nuclear

The nuclear generating industry was formally restructured on 31 March 1996 in preparation for privatisation. A holding company, British Energy plc (BE) was created, together with two subsidiary companies - Nuclear Electric Ltd, which now operates the PWR and five AGR stations in England and Wales, and Scottish Nuclear Ltd, which operates two AGR stations in Scotland. In July 1996 British Energy, which operates the AGR/PWR nuclear electricity power stations in the UK was floated on the London Stock Exchange by the Government. Magnox stations remained in the public sector under the ownership of Magnox Electric plc. Magnox Electric and BNFL merged early in 2000.

Because of the privatisation of British Energy, on 1st November, the Fossil Fuel Levy in England and Wales was reduced from 10 per cent to 3.7 per cent (on 1st April 1997 it was reduced further to 2.2 per cent).

The premium element of prices payable in Scotland under the Nuclear Energy agreement ended in July 1996. A new Fossil Fuel Levy was introduced at a rate of 0.5 per cent to support renewable energy.

In September, AEA Technology, the commercial arm of the UK Atomic Energy Authority, was privatised.

Regulation

On 10th June, the Office for the Regulation of Electricity and Gas (OFREG) was formed to perform a similar role in Northern Ireland to that of OFFER and OFGAS in England and Wales. It was unique in that it was the only combined utility regulatory office in the UK.

1997

Regulation

In June, the Government announced a review of utility regulation, to cover in particular electricity, gas, telecommunications, and water. It was aimed at ensuring that consumers get a fair deal from regulation, and at making regulation more consistent, transparent and accountable.

Electricity

Revised Transmission Price control took affect from 1st April reducing prices further over four years.

In October, the Government announced a review of the electricity trading arrangements including the Electricity Pool. OFFER were asked to report by July 1998.

In December, the Government announced a review of fuel sources for power stations. A consultation paper was issued in June 1998.

The Regulator announced a proposed timetable starting in April 1998 for the rollout of the final stage of supply competition using customer postcodes. The Regulator subsequently modified the timetable and put in place arrangements for the extensive testing of the systems necessary to make competition work.

Gas

Following the increased expenditure on exploration and development of gas fields in the North Sea in the early 1990s, gas production increased to the point where the UK became a net exporter of gas for the first time.

By March competition in the domestic market was extended to include another 0.5 million households in Avon and Dorset and 1.1 million households in the South East of England, bringing the total to two million customers. Over 20 per cent of these households switched to a new supplier by the end of 1997

In November 1997, as part of the next stage in the liberalisation of the gas industry, competition was extended to another 2.5 million domestic customers in Scotland and North East England.

Nuclear

On 1 April 1997 the Fossil Fuel Levy in England and Wales was reduced to 2.2 per cent (from 3.7 per cent in November 1996).

New and Renewable Energy

The fourth Non Fossil Fuel Obligation (NFFO-4) Renewables Order for England and Wales made for 873 MW Declared Net Capacity (DNC).

The second Scottish Renewables Order (SRO-1) was made for 112 MW of capacity.

John Battle, Minister for Science, Energy and Industry, announced a review of renewables energy policy on 6 June 1997.

VAT

On 1 September, VAT on domestic gas and electricity supplies was reduced to 5 per cent.

Windfall tax

In the July Budget, the Government announced that the privatised utilities would have to pay a one-off windfall tax on the excessive profits they had made, payable in two instalments - one in 1997 and the other in 1998. Altogether this was expected to raise £5.2 billion.

Winter Fuel Payments

Winter Fuel Payments were introduced in the winter of 1997 for Great Britain (a similar scheme existed in Northern Ireland). Everyone over the age of 60 received the payment, regardless of whether they are getting a state Pension or any other social security benefits.

1998

Coal

The 5-year contracts with the electricity generators ended in March 1998.

Silverdale Colliery closed in December 1998.

Electricity

The final stage of opening electricity supply markets began in September and was completed in May 1999.

The Government published a White Paper (CM 4071) on energy sources for power generation, and adopted a more restrictive policy towards consents for new power stations, but with special provisions for CHP.

The Monopolies and Mergers Commission recommendation on revised transmission and distribution price control on Northern Ireland Electricity, which was subject to judicial review, was upheld by the Northern Ireland Court of Appeal.

Gas

Introduction of supply competition in Great Britain was completed in May 1998.

In April the gas levy was reduced to zero.

The European Union Gas Liberalisation Directive entered into force in August 1998.

In October the UK - Belgium interconnector became operational, providing a path for UK gas exports to markets in Europe as well as another route for imports of gas into the UK.

Revision of Frigg Treaty with Norway was signed in August 1998.

New and Renewable Energy

The fifth Non-fossil fuel obligation (NFFO) Order was laid in September 1998 for 1,177 MW of capacity.

Oil

International agreement reached on decommissioning and disposal of offshore structures.

New Regulations required Environmental Impact Assessments for offshore projects.

200 oil and gas fields in production in the UK.

Nuclear

In January, the Government transferred its shareholding in Magnox Electric to BNFL as the first stage of a merger of the two companies. Full integration of the combined business of the two companies was completed early in 2000.

The Health and Safety Executive and the Scottish Environment Protection Agency completed a full audit of safety at UKAEA Dounreay.

The acceptance of a small consignment of uranium from Georgia for non-proliferation reasons was subject to scrutiny by the Trade and Industry Committee, who approved of the Government's decision.

Utility Regulation

In March, following an inter-departmental review, the Government published a Green Paper entitled 'A fair deal for consumers' on utility regulation aimed at ensuring that consumers got a fair deal from regulation, and at making regulation more consistent, transparent, and accountable. The Government's conclusions, in the light of consultation, were published in July, including confirmation that the regulators for gas and electricity should be merged and that the Electricity Act 1989 should be amended to require the distribution businesses of the PESs to be licensed separately from their supply businesses. Detailed proposals on energy and the creation of independent consumer councils were published in November.

In October, the Government published its consultation document on "Possible Provisions for Energy Efficiency Standards of Performance in the New Framework of Utility Regulation".

A new gas regulator was appointed in November 1998, he also took over as electricity regulator in January 1999.

1999   Nuclear

The Government announced that it was looking to introduce a Public Private Partnership (PPP) into BNFL, subject to the company's overall progress towards achieving targets on safety, health, environmental and business performance as well as further work undertaken by the DTI and its advisers. The Government's working assumption was that PPP would involve BNFL as a whole. Existing legislation provided for the sale of up to 49 per cent of the company.

BNFL, in partnership with US engineering group Morris Knudsen, acquired the global nuclear business of the US company Westinghouse.

Following Government approval, BNFL commenced uranium commissioning of its Sellafield mixed oxide (MOX) fuel plant.

Electricity

Opening of supply market to full competition was completed in May.

At the end of June, Ferrybridge and Fiddlers Ferry power stations were sold by Powergen to Edison Mission Energy, and at the end of November National Power sold DRAX to AES.

The implementation date for the EU Electricity Liberalisation Directive was February 1999, which required an initial 25 per cent market opening to be implemented, with nearly all the Member States adhering to the timetable.

In October 1999 the Director General of Gas and Electricity supply (DGGES), published a report on Pool Prices. This concluded that the trading arrangements facilitated the exercise of market power. He proposed the introduction of a good market behaviour condition in the licences of the main generators.

New and Renewable Energy

In March 1999, a third Scottish Renewables Order (SRO) was made for 150 MW (DNC) of capacity.

In March 1999 the Government published a consultation paper "New and Renewable Energy - Prospects for the 21st Century". The legal provision for a new renewables mechanism was the Utilities Bill announced in the Queen's speech in November 1999.

Coal

In March 1999, the Government issued mineral planning guidance with respect to opencast mining.

In April 1999, the Department published its policy paper Energy Paper 67 on research and development into cleaner coal technologies.

In July 1999 Calverton Colliery closed.

In October 1999, the Government's Coal Field Task Force published a progress report relating to the problem of those communities affected by pit closures.

Utility Regulation

New name for the combined OFFER and Ofgas electricity and gas market regulator announced as Office of Gas and Electricity Markets - OFGEM.

In April, in its response to consultation, the Government confirmed its plans to establish independent consumer councils.

In July, the Government issued a discussion note on "The Government's Provisional Conclusions on how Energy Efficiency Standards of Performance under the proposed legislation for utility regulation could work".

In November 1999 the Government announced a Utilities Reform Bill to provide a new framework for the regulation of the gas and electricity markets so as to provide a fair deal to consumers.

Fuel Poverty

The Electricity Association Fuel Poverty Task Force was set up in May 1999 to bring forward energy related proposals to help alleviate fuel poverty. The task force comprises representatives form both gas and electricity customers.

In November 1999, an Inter-Ministerial Group on Fuel Poverty was set up to take a strategic overview of the relevant policies and initiatives with a bearing on fuel poverty, and to develop and publish a UK Strategy setting out fuel poverty objectives, targets and the policies to deliver those objectives.

Gas

In June, BG announced its restructuring to separate Transco, the regulated pipeline company, from the rest of the business.

A consultation exercise into the Fundamental Review of Gas Safety was launched by the Health and Safety Executive.

In September 1999 the HSE issued a consultation document outlining the proposed amendments to "The Gas Safety (Management) Regulations (GS(M)R)", with a closing date for December 1999.

Environment

In the March 1999 Budget, the Government announced its intention to introduce a climate change levy on the supply of energy to business, following up recommendations of the Marshall Report.

The Government also followed up Lord Marshall's recommendations on emissions trading, by encouraging the launch of an industry-led project to design a pilot scheme for the UK.

Oil

16th February 1999, the key Brent crude oil benchmark price touched $9 per barrel, a record low level. However, by December 1999 the oil price had recovered to over $25 a barrel.

Production from the UKCS reached a record level of 137 million tonnes of oil.

Drilling at BP Amoco's Wytch Farm onshore field achieved two world records - longest production well drilled and greatest horizontal drilling distance achieved.

Oil & Gas industry Task-Force report published in September 1999 set a vision for the UKCS in 2010, aimed at increasing investment in UKCS activity, increasing employment in directly linked and related industries, and prolonging UK self-sufficiency in oil and gas.

2000

Fuel Poverty

In the March 2000 Budget the Government announced a change in tax rules to facilitate BG Transco's Affordable Warmth Programme which uses an innovative application of lease finance, to encourage the installation of installation of insulation and gas central heating. This programme aimed to install central heating in 850,000 local authority/registered social landlord homes and 150,000 pensioners private sector homes over the subsequent seven years.

After extensive consultation Ofgem published its Social Action Plan in March 2000. It is a framework for action across a wide range of activities to ensure that the economic benefits of liberalisation re spread fully among vulnerable and disadvantaged customers.

The new Home Energy Efficiency Scheme (HEES) was launched in June 2000 to provide a package of insulation and/or heating improvement measures for households in receipt of an income or disability benefit. The scheme will have a total budget of nearly £300 million in the first two years.

The Fuel Poverty Monitoring and Technical Group, which includes representatives from across Government as well as external organisations, was set up in June 2000. It is responsible for the development of a suite of indictors for monitoring progress on tackling fuel poverty.

The Warm Homes and Energy Conservation Act, introduced by David Amess with Government and cross party support, became law in November 2000. The Act requires the Secretary of State for England and the National Assembly for Wales 'to publish and implement a strategy for reducing fuel poverty and set targets for its implementation'.

Utility Reform
Utilities Act 2000 enacted in June.

Gas
In October, BG plc de-merged into two separate listed companies, of which Lattice Group plc is the holding company for Transco and BG Group plc includes the international and gas storage businesses.

Electricity
In March National Power sold Eggborough power station to British Energy and Killiongholme CCGT station to NRG. London Electricity purchased the Sutton Bridge CCGT station.

In April, the Secretary of State for Trade and Industry announced that he anticipated lifting the restrictions on the building of new gas-fired power stations, once new electricity arrangements were in place. This moratorium was lifted on 15 November.

In August, AES' new coal fired station at Fifoots Point began to generate.

In September, Powergen sold its Cottam powerstation to Edf.

Energy Efficiency
In July 1999 the Regulator announced his intention to raise the level of Energy Efficiency Standards of Performance (EESOP), which obliges electricity supply companies to improve energy efficiency amongst their domestic consumers, from £1.00 to £1.20 per customer with effect from April 2000. He also announced his intention to extend EESOP obligations to gas supply companies, also at a rate of £1.20 per customer.

The Utilities Act received royal assent and enabled future EESOP obligations to be set by the Government. The Government had previously indicated such an intention explaining that it was appropriate for the Government rather than the Regulator to decide social and environmental obligations that had significant financial cost. In March 2000, the Government published a consultation document, "Energy Efficiency Standards of Performance 2002-2005" seeking views on the format and level of a new EESOP, and in November, published its provisional conclusions and announced the re-naming of the obligation as the Energy Efficiency Commitment (EEC).

In November 1999 the Government launched its Good Quality CHP Standard and confirmed its target of achieving at least 10,000 MWe of CHP capacity by 2010: more than double current capacity. In December, the Government confirmed that electricity from CHP plants would be exempt from the Climate Change Levy where the electricity was used on site or sold direct to the consumers.

Coal
At the end of January 2000 Midlands Mining ceased to produce coal from its only remaining colliery, Annesley-Bentinck. It ceased to sell coal in June.

On 17 April 2000, the Secretary of State announced a coal subsidy scheme designed to assist UK coal producers through a difficult transitional period arising from adverse market conditions and the imminent relaxation of the stricter gas consents policy. The Government's objective was to enable those elements of the industry with a viable future without aid to overcome short term market problems. The subsidy scheme had to be approved by the European Commission, which was obtained in November 2000. Under the scheme, producers of qualifying coal are reimbursed for losses they incur on coal produced between April 2000 and July 2002, provided they can demonstrate long term viability and meet other conditions designed to avoid market distortions.

Oil

January 2000: establishment of PILOT, to take over the work of the Oil and Gas Industry Task Force and give effect to the Task Force's recommendations.

September 2000: signature and publication of Memorandum of Understanding between Government, oil industry, hauliers, trade unions and police to ensure continued supply of fuel in the event of any further disruption by fuel protestors.

New and Renewable Energy

In February the Government published *Conclusions in Response to the Public Consultation* ("New and Renewable Energy: Prospects for the 21st Century"). The document summarised the Government's strategy to make progress to a target of 10% of UK electricity from renewables sources by 2010, subject to the cost to consumers being acceptable.

In May the European Commission adopted a proposal for a Directive on the promotion of electricity from renewable energy sources in the internal electricity market. The Directive itself is to be agreed during 2001.

Nuclear

In February HSE published three reports into BNFL, covering

- The Storage of Liquid High Level Waste at Sellafield.
- Falsification of Data at the Mox Demonstration Facility.
- Team inspection of the Control and Supervision of Operations at Sellafield.

In March the Government announced that it considered that the earliest date possible for the introduction of any PPP into BNFL could not be before the latter part of 2002.

In April BNFL published its response to two of the HSE reports, with the third response to follow in the summer as agreed with HSE.

In May BNFL acquired the nuclear business of ABB. BNFL also announced a strategy for managing lifetimes of its Magnox stations. BNFL also closed its Hinkley Point Magnox station.

In June BNFL's Wyfla station went offline for extended repairs and maintenance that was to last for over 12 months.

On 1 September 2000, the UKAEA's Directorate of Civil Nuclear Security was transferred to the DTI as the Office for Civil Nuclear Security (OCNS), to regulate security within the civil nuclear industry. It will have operational and regulatory autonomy within DTI.

Environment

Royal Commission on Environmental Pollution report on climate change and energy

In June, the Royal Commission on Environmental Pollution published its major report "Energy - the changing climate". It referred to the need for much greater international action if concentrations of greenhouse gases were to be stabilised. It emphasised the need for a long term vision of how large scale reductions in greenhouse gas emissions, of the order of 60% of carbon dioxide emissions by 2050, might be achieved.

Climate Change Programme

The Government published in November its national Climate Change Programme. The Programme aimed to provide a strategic framework for the Government to deliver the UK's target under the Kyoto Protocol of reducing emissions of a basket of six greenhouse gases by 12.5% from 1990 levels n the period 2008-12; and also to move towards its own domestic policy goal of reducing carbon dioxide emissions by 20% from 1990 levels by 2010. The Programme drew together a wide range of existing and planned policies and measures, to engage all sectors of the economy and society in efforts to reduce greenhouse emissions. Many of these had implications for the energy sector.

2001

Fuel Poverty

In March, the Government published The UK Fuel Poverty Strategy – consultation draft. The document sets out the Government's objectives, policies and targets for alleviating fuel poverty in the UK over the next 10 years.

Environment

Climate change levy

The Government introduced the climate change levy in April 2001. The levy had been proposed in the 1999 Budget, and its design elaborated in subsequent announcements.

The levy applies to energy (coal, gas and electricity) supplied to business and the public sector. It does not apply to energy used in the domestic sector; for motive power in transport or to produce another energy product. There are exemptions for electricity generated from renewable sources and energy from quality-assured Combined Heat and Power (CHP) plants.

Levy revenues are recycled to business through an accompanying cut in employers' National Insurance contributions and a package of energy support to business which will fund energy efficiency advice to business and investment in low carbon technologies research and development, to be managed under the new Carbon Trust; as well as a new scheme of enhanced capital allowances for businesses investing in energy saving technologies.

Energy intensive sectors, as defined under certain eligibility criteria, receive an 80% levy discount in return for delivery of energy saving targets in negotiated agreements with the Government.

Emissions Trading

The Government worked closely with the business-led Emissions Trading Group to design a UK Emissions Trading Scheme. The Government published a draft Framework on 3 May 2001, providing guidance for business on how the scheme will work and how companies can join in. Final publication of the Framework is expected in July 2001, with the scheme starting in April 2002. The Government had previously confirmed it would make £30 million (net of tax) available to encourage companies to bid into the scheme and take the risks associated with taking on a binding emissions cap.

Coal

Quinquennial Review of the Coal Authority completed. RJB Mining became UK Coal in May.

Electricity

On 27 March new electricity trading arrangements (NETA) replaced the electricity pool. NETA is a screen-based trading arrangement similar to that for general commodity trading – see paragraph 5.3.

Annex F
Further sources of United Kingdom energy publications

Some of the publications listed below give shorter term statistics, some provide further information about energy production and consumption in the United Kingdom and in other countries, and others provide more detail on a country or fuel industry basis. The list also covers recent publications on energy issues and policy, including statistical information, produced or commissioned by the DTI. The list is not exhaustive and the titles of publications and publishers may alter. Unless otherwise stated, all titles are available from The Stationery Office and can be ordered through Government Bookshops and can be found on the DTI Web site at www.dti.gov.uk/energy/index.htm

Department of Trade & Industry publications on energy

Energy Statistics
Monthly, quarterly and annual statistics on production and consumption of overall energy and individual fuels in the United Kingdom together with energy prices is available in MS Excel format on the internet at: www.dti.gov.uk/energy/energystats/energystats.htm

Energy Trends
Quarterly publication. First edition June 2001. Replaces monthly Energy Trends publication. Covers all major aspects of energy. Provides a comprehensive picture of energy production and use. Contains analysis of data and articles covering energy issues. Available on subscription, with Quarterly Energy Prices publication, from ENP4f, Department of Trade and Industry, Bay 1108, 1 Victoria Street, London, SW1H 0ET, tel. 020-7215 2697/2698.

Quarterly Energy Prices
Quarterly publication. First edition June 2001. Replaced energy prices information formerly available in the monthly publication Energy Trends and the annual Digest of UK Energy Statistics. Contains tables, charts and commentary covering energy prices to domestic and industrial consumers for all the major fuels as well as presenting comparisons of fuel prices in the European Union and G7 countries. Available on subscription, with Energy Trends publication, from ENP4f, Department of Trade and Industry, Bay 1108, 1 Victoria Street, London, SW1H 0ET, tel. 020-7215 2697/2698.

Energy Sector Indicators 2000
This is a set of indicators grouped into 12 sections covering different aspects of the energy sector. The content is designed to show the extent to which secure, diverse and sustainable supplies of energy to UK Businesses and consumers at competitive prices are ensured. Available free from ENP4f, Department of Trade and Industry, Bay 1108, 1 Victoria Street, London, SW1H 0ET, tel. 020-7215 2697/2698

Development of the Oil and Gas Resources of the United Kingdom 2001
This is an annual report to parliament by Secretary of State for Trade and Industry on the activities to search for and exploit oil and gas in the UK sector of the Continental Shelf. Contains information about the upstream industry including information on the licensing and fiscal regimes governing it, production and remaining reserve levels. Available from The Stationery Office, tel 0870 600 5522.

Industrial Energy Markets: Energy markets in UK manufacturing industry 1973 to 1993 - Energy Paper 64
Using tables of data drawn from the 1989 Purchases Inquiry conducted by the Office for National Statistics, the report, which updates one produced in 1989, sets out the implications for the trends in industrial energy consumption over the period from 1973 to 1993. Available from The Stationery Office, tel 0870 600 5522. Not available on the Internet

Energy Consumption in the UK:- Energy Paper 66
A statistical review of delivered and primary energy consumption by sub-sector, end use and the factors effecting change. Available from The Stationery Office, tel 0870 600 5522. Not available on the internet.

Energy Projections for the UK:- Energy Paper 68
This paper presents the results of an exercise to update the Government's projections of future UK energy demand and related emissions of carbon and sulphur dioxides to 2020. It builds on work issued as a working paper in March 2000 and its projections underpin the Climate Change Programme launched by the DETR in November 2000. The paper contributes to policy development and assessment of the UK's efforts to meet its national and international greenhouse gases targets. Available from The Stationery Office, tel 0870 600 5522.

Energy Report 2000

> This is the seventh annual Energy Report, the purpose of which is to help competitive markets develop by setting out the key elements of energy policy and the main driving forces, both internal and external. Available from The Stationery Office, tel 0870 600 5522

Social Effects of Energy Liberalisation: The UK Experience

> This paper reviews the impact of liberalisation of the energy markets, and the effects on the fuel industries, the consumer and the environment . Available free from ENP4f, Department of Trade and Industry, Bay 1108, 1 Victoria Street, London, SW1H 0ET, tel. 020-7215 2697/2698

Energy Liberalisation Indicators in Europe: A preliminary report of a study carried out by OXERA for the Governments of the UK and the Netherlands.

> This paper presents preliminary results from a study carried out by OXERA on behalf of the Governments of the UK and the Netherlands. The study develops a set of indicators, within a hierarchical structure, for monitoring the development of competition in gas and electricity markets across Europe. The study mainly concentrates on the electricity market and presents some preliminary results for a subset of European countries including the UK and Netherlands. Available free from ENP4f, Department of Trade and Industry, Bay 1108, 1 Victoria Street, London, SW1H 0ET, tel. 020-7215 2697/2698

Energy Liberalisation Indicators in Europe: A consultation paper based on a study carried out by OXERA for the Governments of the UK and the Netherlands.

> This consultation paper sets out the methodology used and presents results for a subset of European countries including the UK and the Netherlands. Available free from ENP4f, Department of Trade and Industry, Bay 1108, 1 Victoria Street, London SW1H 0ET, tel. 020-7215 2697/2698

Social, Environmental and Security of Supply Policies in a Competitive Energy Market: A Review of Delivery Mechanisms in the United Kingdom, Summary Paper

> This paper outlines the UK experience so far in using competitive energy markets to deliver social, environmental and security of supply policies. It highlights the benefits that have emerged from this approach and sets out the instruments the Government has used to enhance policy delivery. Available free from ENP4f, Department of Trade and Industry, Bay 1108, 1 Victoria Street, London, SW1H 0ET, tel. 020-7215 2697/2698

Other publications including energy information

General

Basic Statistics of the Community (annual); *Statistical Office of the European Communities*

Digest of Environmental Statistics (annual); *Department of the Environment, Food and Rural Affairs (DEFRA)*
> *(Formerly Department of the Environment, Transport and the Regions)*

Digest of Welsh Statistics (annual); Welsh *Office* (available from ESS Division, Welsh Office, Cathays Park, Cardiff)

Eurostatistics - Data for Short Term Analysis; *Statistical Office of the European Communities*

Monthly Digest of Statistics; *Office for National Statistics*

Northern Ireland Annual Abstract of Statistics (annual); *Department of Finance and Personnel,* (available from the Policy & Planning Unit, Department of Finance & Personnel, Stormont, Belfast BT4 3SW)

Overseas Trade Statistics of the United Kingdom; *H.M. Customs & Excise*

> - Business Monitor MM20 (monthly) (extra-EU trade only)
> - Business Monitor MM20A (monthly) (intra and extra EU trade data, relatively limited level of production detail)
> - Business Monitor MQ20 (quarterly) (intra-EU trade only)
> - Business Monitor MA20 (annual) (intra- and extra-EU trade);

Purchases Inquiry 1989, 1994-1998; Office *for National Statistics*

Rapid Reports - energy and industry (ad hoc); *Statistical Office of the European Communities*

Regional Trends (annual); *Office for National Statistics*

Scottish Abstract of Statistics (annual); *Scottish Office*

United Kingdom Minerals Yearbook (annual); *British Geological Survey* (available from the British Geological Survey, Keyworth, Nottingham, NG12 5GG)

Yearbook of Regional Statistics (annual); *Statistical Office of the European Communities*

Energy

Annual Bulletin of General Energy Statistics for Europe;   *United Nations Economic Commission for Europe*

BP Statistical Review of World Energy (annual) ; (available from The Editor, BP Statistical Review, The British Petroleum Company plc, Corporate Communications Services, Britannic House, 1 Finsbury Circus, London EC2M 7BA)

Energy - Monthly Statistics;   *Statistical Office of the European Communities*

Energy Balances of OECD Countries (annual);   *OECD International Energy Agency*

Energy Statistics and Balances of OECD Countries (annual);   *OECD International Energy Agency*

Energy Statistics and Balances of Non-OECD Countries (annual);   *OECD International Energy Agency*

Energy - Yearly Statistics;   *Statistical Office of the European Communities*

UN Energy Statistics Yearbook (annual);   *United Nations Statistical Office*

Projections

Energy Projections for the UK, working paper (March 2000), ENP Directorate, DTI. Reports work in progress to update projections of the future UK energy demand and energy-related CO_2 emissions, last published in Energy Paper 65.

Coal

Annual Bulletin of Coal Statistics for Europe;   *United Nations Economic Commission for Europe*

Annual Reports and Accounts of The Coal Authority and the private coal companies - *apply to the Headquarters of the company concerned.*

Business Monitor PA 130 Coal extraction and manufacture of solid fuels (annual, ceased publication in 1994);   *Office for National Statistics*

Coal Information (annual);   *OECD International Energy Agency*

Oil and gas

Annual Bulletin of Gas Statistics for Europe;   *United Nations Economic Commission for Europe*

Annual Report of the Office of Gas Supply - OFGAS

BP Review of World Gas (annual);   (available from British Petroleum Company plc, Corporate Communications Services, Britannic House, 1 Finsbury Circus, London EC2M 7BA)

Annual Reports and Accounts of British Gas Transco, Centrica and other independent gas supply companies - *apply to the Headquarters of the company concerned.*

Business Monitor   PA 162 - Public gas supply (ceased publication in 1994); *Office for National Statistics*

Oil and Gas Information (annual); *OECD International Energy Agency*

Quarterly Oil Statistics and Energy Balances; *OECD International Energy Agency*

UK Petroleum Industry Statistics Consumption and Refinery Production (annual and quarterly);   *Institute of Petroleum* (available from IP, 61 New Cavendish Street, London W1M 8AR).

Electricity

Annual Bulletin of Electric Energy Statistics for Europe; *United Nations Economic Commission for Europe*

Annual Reports and Accounts of the Electricity Companies and Generators - *apply to the Headquarters of the company concerned.*

Annual Report of the Office of Electricity Regulation - OFGEM

Business Monitor PA 161 Production and distribution of electricity (annual, ceased publication in 1994);   *Office for National Statistics*

Electricity Supply in OECD Countries ;   *OECD International Energy Agency*

National Grid Company - Seven Year Statement - (annual)   *National Grid Company - For further details telephone 01203 423065*

Operation of Nuclear Power Stations (annual);   *Statistical Office of the European Communities*

UK Electricity (annual); *Electricity Association plc* (available from the Electricity Association plc, 30 Millbank, London SW1P 4RD)

Electricity Information (Annual); *OECD International Energy Agency*

Prices

Energy Prices (annual); *Statistical Office of the European Communities* (summarises price information published in the European Commissions *Weekly Oil Price,* and half-yearly *Statistics in Focus* on *Gas Prices* and *Electricity Prices)*

Energy Prices and Taxes (quarterly); *OECD International Energy Agency*

Electricity prices; *Eurostat* (annual)

Gas prices; *Eurostat,* (annual)

Environment

Digest of Environmental Statistics (Annual); *Department of the Environment, Food and Rural Affairs (DEFRA) (Formerly Department of the Environment, Transport and the Regions).* Available via Internet at: www.environment.detr.gov.uk/des.

Indicators of Sustainable Development for the United Kingdom; *Department of the Environment, Food and Rural Affairs (DEFRA) (Formerly Department of the Environment, Transport and the Regions).*

Quality of life counts, *Indicators for a strategy for sustainable development for the United Kingdom: a baseline assessment.*

Environment Statistics; EUROSTAT (Annual).

UK Environment; DEFRA adhoc/one-off release.

Renewables

New and Renewable Energy, *Prospects for the 21st Century. This consultation paper reports on the outcome of the review conducted by the Government and the possible ways forward in implementing the Government's new drive for renewables.*

Fuel Poverty

The UK Fuel Poverty Strategy – consultation draft:- Produced by the The Department of Trade and Industry and Department of the Environment, Food and Rural Affairs *(DEFRA)* (Formerly Department of the Environment, Transport and the Regions). The strategy sets out the Government's objectives, policies and targets for a lleviating fuel poverty in the UK over the next 10 years.

English House Condition Survey – 1996 Energy Report:- *Produced by the Department of the Environment, Food and Rural Affairs (DEFRA) (Formerly Department of the Environment, Transport and the Regions). This report presents the detailed findings of the 1996 English House Condition Survey (EHCS) on the energy efficiency and thermal performance of the stock, energy action by occupants and landlords and the potential for future energy and carbon savings.*

Useful energy related websites

The DTI website can be found at http://www.dti.gov.uk, the energy information and statistics website is at http://www.dti.gov.uk/epa

Other Government websites

Ofgem (at COI site)	www.ofgem.gov.uk
Department for Environment, Food and Rural Affairs (formerly DETR)	www.defra.gov.uk
Department for Transport, Local Government and the Regions (formerly DETR)	www.dtlr.gov.uk
Customs and Excise	www.hmce.gov.uk
ONS	www.statistics.gov.uk
COI	www.nds.coi.gov.uk
UK Parliament	www.parliament.uk
Scottish Parliament	www.scottish.parliament.uk
The National Assembly for Wales	www.wales.org.uk/
Transport Statistics	www.transtat.dtlr.gov.uk

Other useful energy related websites

International Energy Agency	www.iea.org
Eurostat	www.europa.eu.int/comm/eurostat/
UK Petroleum Industry Association	www.ukpia.com
Institute of Petroleum	www.petroleum.co.uk
US Energy Information Administration	www.eia.doe.gov/
ETSU	www.etsu.com
Electricity Association	www.electricity.org.uk
BP	www.bp.com/index.asp
UK Offshore Operators Association	www.ukooa.co.uk
NETCEN (Air quality estimates)	www.aeat.co.uk/netcen/airqual/welcome.html.
BRE	www.bre.co.uk
Coal Authority	www.coal.gov.uk/
Iron and Steel Statistics Bureau	www.issb.co.uk/
Europa	www.europa.eu.int/
UK Offshore Operators Association (UKOOA)	www.ukooa.co.uk/
HM Government Online	www.open.gov.uk/
energywatch	www.energywatch.org.uk/

The Stationery Office	www.the-stationery-office.co.uk/

NOTES

NOTES

NOTES